Penny Yee

ATTENTION and PERFORMANCE XI

Proceedings of the Eleventh International Symposium on Attention and Performance
Eugene, Oregon, July 1–8, 1984

DEDICATION

*To our colleague Jeff Holtzman,
May his spirit be reflected
in our collective efforts*

The goal of Attention and Performance XI was the integration of the concept of attention across disciplines. Jeff Holtzman's research, a sample of which is reported in this volume, exemplifies this approach. It was with profound regret that we learned of his untimely death just as this volume went to press.

ATTENTION and PERFORMANCE XI

Edited by
Michael I. Posner
University of Oregon, Eugene, Oregon
Oscar S. M. Marin
*Good Samaritan Hospital,
Portland, Oregon*

LEA LAWRENCE ERLBAUM ASSOCIATES, PUBLISHERS
1985   Hillsdale, New Jersey   London

Copyright © 1985 by the International Association for the Study of Attention and Performance
All rights reserved. No part of this book may be reproduced in
any form, by photostat, microform, retrieval system, or any other
means, without the prior written permission of the publisher.

Lawrence Erlbaum Associates, Inc., Publishers
365 Broadway
Hillsdale, New Jersey 07642

Library of Congress Cataloging in Publication Data

Main entry under title:

Attention and performance XI.

"Proceedings of the Eleventh International Symposium on Attention and Performance, Eugene, Oregon, July 1–8, 1984"—P.
Includes bibliographies and indexes.
1. Attention—Congresses. 2. Performance—Congresses. 3. Selectivity (Psychology)—Congresses.
4. Orientation (Psychology)—Congresses. I. Posner, Michael I. II. Marin, Oscar. III. International Symposium on Attention and Performance (11th : 1984 : Eugene, Or.) IV. Title: Attention and performance 11.
V. Title: Attention and performance eleven.
BF321.A82 1985   153.7'33   85-10269
ISBN 0-89859-639-4

Printed in the United States of America
10 9 8 7 6 5 4 3 2 1

Contents

List of Contributors and Participants   xvii

Preface   xxi

Group Photo   xxiv

PART I: ASSOCIATION LECTURE

1. **Cognitive Neuropsychology and the Study of Reading**
   Max Coltheart   3
   Abstract   3
   Introduction   4
   Dual-Route Models of Reading Aloud   8
   The Nature of the Nonlexical Procedure   14
   The Nature of the Lexical Procedure   19
   The Architecture of the Reading System   21
   Morphological Processing   24
   Syntax and Sentence Comprehension During
     Reading   29
   Conclusions   33
   References   34

PART II: TUTORIAL REVIEWS

2. **Aspects of Cortical Organization Related to Selective Attention and Selective Impairments of Visual Perception: A Tutorial Review**
   A. Cowey   41
   Abstract   41
   Introduction   41
   Parallel Pathways in Vision From Eye to
     Brain   42

vi CONTENTS

       Visual Disorders Following Cortical Damage   51
       Advantages of Multiple Sensory
          Representations   55
       Conclusions   57
       References   58

3. **Visual–Spatial Attention, Orienting, and Brain Physiology**
   Steven A. Hillyard, Thomas F. Munte, and Helen J. Neville **63**
   Abstract   63
   Introduction   63
   Behavioral Studies   64
   Electrophysiological Indices of Spatial
      Attention   65
   Attention to Central and Peripheral Visual
      Locations   68
   Attention to Features and Locations   72
   Phasic Orienting and Sustained Attention   74
   References   82

4. **Visual Search and Visual Attention**
   John Duncan **85**
   Abstract   85
   Introduction   86
   Terminology   86
   "Nonsearch" Tasks   87
   The Number of Targets   88
   The Number of Nontargets   94
   Identification and Use of Stimulus
      Information   100
   Conclusions   102
   References   103
   Addendum   105

5. **Perceptual Integration and Postcategorical Filtering**
   D. A. Allport, S. P. Tipper, and N. R. J. Chmiel **107**
   Abstract   107
   Introduction   108
   Experiments   111
   General Discussion: Negative Priming and Perceptual
      Integration   128
   References   130

CONTENTS vii

6. **Attention Division or Attention Sharing?**
   David Navon **133**
   Abstract   133
   Introduction   133
   A Mind Without Resources   134
   Alternative Explanations for Task
      Interference   137
   References   145

7. **Looking Forward to Moving Soon: Ante Factum Selective Processes in Motor Control**
   Jean Requin **147**
   Abstract   147
   Introduction   147
   Stage Versus Modulation Conceptions of
      Preparation   149
   Selective Preparation and Motor
      Programming   152
   Permissive Versus Executive Brain
      Processes   157
   Conclusions   164
   References   165

PART III: ORIENTING OF ATTENTION

8. **The Spatial Structure of Visual Attention**
   Cathryn J. Downing and Steven Pinker **171**
   Abstract   171
   Introduction   171
   Experiment 1   173
   Experiment 2   179
   General Discussion   185
   References   186

9. **Facilitatory and Inhibitory Components of Orienting in Visual Space**
   Elizabeth Ann Maylor **189**
   Abstract   189
   Introduction   190
   Experiment 1   191
   Experiment 2   194

Experiment 3   197
Experiment 4   199
General Conclusions   201
References   203

10. **Accessing Features and Objects: Is Location Special?**
    Mary Jo Nissen **205**
    Abstract   205
    Introduction   205
    Experiment 1   208
    Experiment 2   211
    Discussion   217
    References   218

11. **Vibrotactile Reaction Times in Left and Right Hemispace: Stimulus and Response Uncertainty and Gravitational and Corporeal Coordinates**
    John L. Bradshaw and Jane M. Pierson **221**
    Abstract   221
    Introduction   221
    Experiment 1   223
    Experiment 2   228
    Experiment 3   230
    Experiment 4   232
    General Discussion   234
    References   236

12. **Analogical and Logical Disorders Underlying Unilateral Neglect of Space**
    Edoardo Bisiach, Anna Berti, and Guiseppe Vallar ... **239**
    Abstract   239
    Introduction   239
    The Experiment   240
    Discussion   243
    References   248

13. **Selective Spatial Attention: One Center, One Circuit, Or Many Circuits?**
    Giacomo Rizzolatti, Maurizio Gentilucci, and Massimo Matelli **251**
    Abstract   251
    Introduction   251

Methods 253
Results 255
Discussion 261
References 264

PART IV: SENSORY SYSTEMS AND SELECTION: VISION

14. Attending to the Spatial Frequency and Spatial Position of Near-Threshold Visual Patterns
Norma Graham, Patricia Kramer, and Nancy Haber .. **269**
Abstract 269
Introduction 269
Extrinsic-Uncertainty Effects 270
Concurrent Experiments 273
Hearsay Evidence 277
Primary-Plus-Probe Experiments 278
Perception of Complex Visual Stimuli 279
Appendix: Concurrent Experiments 282
References 283

15. Smooth Eye Movements as Indicators of Selective Attention
Eileen Kowler and Carolina Zingale **285**
Abstract 285
Introduction 286
The Effect of Selective Attention on Smooth Eye Movements 287
The Effect of Selection of the Target for Smooth Eye Movements on Visual Processing 290
Conclusions 296
References 298

16. Interactive Processes in Perceptual Organization: Evidence from Visual Agnosia
Glyn W. Humphreys, M. Jane Riddoch, and Philip T. Quinlan **301**
Abstract 301
Introduction 301
Experiment 1: Processing Compound Letters 305

CONTENTS

Experiment 2: Visual Search Against Homogeneous
  Distractors   307
Experiment 3: Subitization   313
General Discussion   316
References   317

17. Imagery and Language Processing: A Neurophysiological Approach
Stephen M. Kosslyn, Rita S. Berndt, and Timothy J. Doyle 319

Abstract   319
Introduction   319
The Imagery Task Battery   321
Image Generation   323
Image Maintenance   327
Image Scanning   329
Image Rotation   330
References   334

PART V: SENSORY SYSTEMS AND SELECTION: AUDITION

18. The Importance of Transients for Maintaining the Separation of Signals in Auditory Space
Ervin R. Hafter and Thomas N. Buell 337

Abstract   337
Introduction   337
Sound Localization   338
Trains of High-Frequency Clicks   339
Interaural Variability   341
Post Onset Effects: A Form of Saturation   343
Post Onset Saturation as the Primary Limiting Factor
  in Localization   345
Interaction with Other Parameters   345
The Neural Site of Saturation   346
Some Consequences of a Binaural System that
  Receives only Transients   348
Attempts to Discover What Constitutes an
  Onset   349
Summary   352
References   353

CONTENTS

19. **Stimulus Processing: Reflections in Event-Related Potentials, Magnetoencephalogram, and Regional Cerebral Blood Flow**
    R. Näätänen 355
    Abstract   355
    Introduction   355
    Processing of Unattended Stimuli and ERPs   356
    Mismatch Negativity   358
    Mechanisms of Selective Attention   365
    Overview   368
    References   371

20. **Comparisons Across Paradigms: An ERP Study**
    Anthony W. K. Gaillard and Cornelis J. Verduin 375
    Abstract   375
    Introduction   375
    Method   379
    Results   380
    Discussion   383
    References   387

PART VI: ATTENTION AND MOTOR CONTROL

21. **Information Encapsulation and Automaticity: Evidence from the Visual Control of Finely Timed Actions**
    Peter McLeod, Carmel McLaughlin, and Ian Nimmo-Smith 391
    Abstract   391
    Introduction   391
    Experiment 1A   394
    Experiment 1B   397
    Experiment 2   398
    Discussion   402
    Appendix   405
    References   405

22. **The Role of Position of Gaze in Movement Accuracy**
    B. Biguer, M. Jeannerod, and C. Prablanc 407
    Abstract   407
    Introduction   407

xii CONTENTS

      The Temporal Pattern of Eye, Head, and Arm
         Movements During Pointing at a Visual
         Target   408
      The Contribution of Coordinated Eye and Head
         Movements in Hand-Pointing Accuracy   415
      References   423

23. **Eye Movement Control Following Corpus Commissurotomy in Humans**
      Jeffrey D. Holtzman **425**
      Abstract   425
      Introduction   425
      General Methods   427
      Experiment 1   428
      Experiment 2   433
      Experiment 3   436
      General Discussion   437
      References   439

24. **Stimulus Selection and Conditional Response Mechanisms in the Basal Ganglia of the Monkey**
      Robert H. Wurtz **441**
      Abstract   441
      Introduction   441
      Stimulus-Selection Mechanisms   442
      Conditional Response Mechanisms   449
      Conclusion   453
      References   454

25. **Attention and Coding Effects in S–R Compatibility Due to Irrelevant Spatial Cues**
      Carlo Umilta and Roberto Nicoletti **457**
      Abstract   457
      Introduction   458
      Experiment 1   460
      Experiment 2   462
      Experiment 3   463
      Experiment 4   466
      General Discussion   468
      References   470

PART VII: DIVIDING AND SUSTAINING ATTENTION

26. Toward a Model of Attention and the Development of Automatic Processing
Walter Schneider **475**
    Abstract   475
    Introduction   475
    Model Overview   476
    Structure of the Model   478
    Category-Search Procedure   479
    Summary   490
    References   491

27. Sustained Attention: A Multifactorial Approach
Raja Parasuraman **493**
    Abstract   493
    Introduction   493
    Taxonomy of Vigilance   494
    Experiment 1: Habituation of ERPs and Vigilance Decrement   496
    Experiment 2: Tonic Arousal, Time of Day, and Vigilance: The Effects of Memory Load   500
    Experiment 3: Probing Sustained Attention Capacity   502
    A Multifactor Model of Sustained Attention   505
    References   508

28. Discrete and Continuous Models of Divided Attention
Jeff Miller **513**
    Abstract   513
    Introduction   513
    Experiment 1   515
    Experiment 2   522
    General Discussion   525
    References   527

29. Word Load and Visual Hemifield Shape Recognition: Priming and Interference Effects
Marcel Kinsbourne and Mark Byrd **529**
    Abstract   529
    Introduction   529

xiv CONTENTS

    Method   533
    Results   534
    Discussion   537
    References   542

PART VIII: ATTENTION TO SYMBOLS AND WORDS

30. The Perceptual Record: A Common Factor in Repetition Priming and Attribute Retention?
Kim Kirsner and John Dunn 547
    Abstract   547
    Introduction   547
    A Model of Perceptual Analysis   550
    Attribute Retention   552
    Two Forms of Memory   554
    Experiment   554
    Discussion   559
    Appendix   562
    References   563

31. Dissociable Domains of Selective Processing
William A. Johnston and Veronica J. Dark 567
    Abstract   567
    Introduction   567
    Method   572
    Results   576
    Discussion   579
    References   582

32. Is Semantic Priming Automatic?
James E. Hoffman and Frank W. MacMillan 585
    Abstract   585
    Introduction   585
    Experiment 1   587
    Experiment 2   590
    Experiment 3   594
    Final Discussion   596
    References   598

33. Necessary Conditions for Repeated-Letter Inferiority: The Role of Positional Uncertainty
Gideon Keren and Louis C. Boer 601
    Abstract   601

Introduction 601
Experiment 1 606
Experiment 2 609
General Discussion 610
References 612

34. Precueing of Alternatives on the Identification of Letters in Masked Words: An Attentional-Explanatory Hypothesis
Daniel Holender **613**

Abstract 613
Introduction 613
Experiments 1, 2, and 3 618
Discussion 624
References 628

35. Visual Selection from Multielement Displays: A Model for Partial Report
Claus Bundesen, Hitomi Shibuya, and Axel Larsen .. **631**

Abstract 631
Introduction 631
Model 633
Experiment 635
Discussion 643
Appendix 646
References 648

Author Index 651

Subject Index 667

Contributors and Participants

Dr. Alan Allport, University of Oxford, Department of Experimental Psychology, South Parks Road, Oxford OX1 3UD, England

Dr. Fred Attneave, University of Oregon, Department of Psychology, Eugene, Oregon 97403, USA

Dr. Rita S. Berndt, University of Maryland Medical School, Department of Neurology, Baltimore, Maryland 21201, USA

Dr. Anna Berti, Istituto di Clin. Neurologica, Via Francesco Sforza 35, 20122, Milano, Italy

Dr. B. Biguer, Laboratory of Experimental Psychology, Inserm u 94, 16 Avenue du Doyen Lepine, 69500 Bron, France

Dr. Chen Bing, University of California, San Diego, Department of Psychology, La Jolla, California 92093, USA

Dr. Edoardo Bisiach, Istituto di Clin. Neurologica, Via Francesco Sforza 35, 20122 Milano, Italy

Dr. Louis C. Boer, Inst. for Perception TNO, Kampweg 5, Postbus 23, Soesterberg, The Netherlands

Dr. Herman Bouma, P.O. Box 513, 5600 MB, Eindhoven, The Netherlands

Dr. John Bradshaw, Monash University, Department of Psychology, Clayton, Victoria 3168, Australia

Dr. Thomas N. Buell, University of California, Department of Psychology, Berkeley, California 94720, USA

Dr. Claus Bundesen, Copenhagen University, Psychology Laboratory, Njalsgade 90, DK-2300 Copenhagen S. Denmark

Dr. Mark Byrd, Shriver Center, 200 Trapelo Road, Waltham, Massachusetts 02254, USA

Dr. N. R. J. Chmiel, University of Oxford, Department of Experimental Psychology, South Parks Road, Oxford OX1 3UD, England

Dr. Neal Cohen, Johns Hopkins University, Department of Psychology, Baltimore, Maryland 21218, USA

Dr. Max Coltheart, Birbeck College, University of London, Department of Psychology, Malet Street, London, WC1E 7HX England

Dr. Alan Cowey, University of Oxford, Department of Psychology, South Parks Road, Oxford OX1 3UD, England

Dr. Veronica Dark, University of Utah, Department of Psychology, Salt Lake City, Utah 84112, USA

Dr. Cathryn Downing, Stanford University, Department of Psychology, Jordon Hall, Building 420, Stanford, California 94305, USA

Dr. Timothy J. Doyle, Harvard University, Department of Psychology and Social Relations, 33 Kirkland Street, Cambridge, Massachusetts 02138, USA

Dr. John Duncan, MRC Applied Psychology Unit, 15 Chaucer Road, Cambridge CB2 2EF, England

CONTRIBUTORS AND PARTICIPANTS

Dr. John Dunn, University of Western Australia, Department of Psychiatry and Behavioural Science, Nedlands WA 6009, Australia

Dr. Tony Gaillard, Institute of Perception TNO, P. O. Box 23, 37bg ZG Soesterberg, The Netherlands

Dr. Maurizio Gentilucci, University of Parma-Via Gramsci, Inst. of Human Physiology, 14-43100 Parma, Italy

Dr. Norma Graham, Columbia University, Department of Psychology, New York, New York 10027, USA

Dr. Nancy Haber, Columbia University, Department of Psychology, New York, New York 10027, USA

Dr. Ervin Hafter, University of California, Department of Psychology, Berkeley, California 94720, USA

Dr. Steven Hillyard, University of California, Department of Neuroscience M008, School of Medicine, La Jolla, California 92093, USA

Dr. James Hoffman, University of Delaware, Department of Psychology, Newark, Delaware 19711, USA

Dr. Daniel Holender, Lab. de Psych. Exper., 117 av, Adolph Buyl, B 1050 Brussels, Belgium

Dr. Jeff Holtzman, Cornell University Medical College, Division of Cognitive Neuroscience, Department of Neurology, 515 East 71st, New York, New York 10021, USA

Dr. Glyn Humphreys, Birbeck College, University of London, Department of Psychology, Malet Street, London WC1E 7HX, England

Dr. Earl Hunt, University of Washington, Department of Psychology, NI-25, Seattle, Washington 98195, USA

Dr. Marc Jeannerod, Laboratory of Experimental Psychology, Inserm u 94, 16 Avenue du Doyen Lepine, 69500 Bron, France

Dr. William Johnston, University of Utah, Department of Psychology, Salt Lake City, Utah 84112, USA

Dr. Daniel Kahneman, University of British Columbia, Department of Psychology, Vancouver, British Columbia V5T 1W5, Canada

Dr. Steven Keele, University of Oregon, Department of Psychology, Eugene, Oregon 97403, USA

Dr. Gideon Keren, Institute for Perception TNO, Kampweg 5, Postbus 23, Soesterberg, The Netherlands

Dr. Marcel Kinsbourne, Shriver Center, 200 Trapelo Road, Waltham, Massachusetts 02254, USA

Dr. Kim Kirsner, University of Western Australia, Department of Psychology, Nedlands, Perth 6009, Australia

Dr. Sylvan Kornblum, University of Michigan, Mental Health Research Institute, 205 Washtenaw Place, Ann Arbor, MI 48109, USA

Dr. Steven Kosslyn, Harvard University, Department of Psychology and Social Relations, 33 Kirkland Street, Cambridge, Massachusetts 02138, USA

Dr. Eileen Kowler, Rutgers University, Department of Psychology, New Brunswick, New Jersey 08903, USA

Dr. Patricia Kramer, Columbia University, Department of Psychology, New York, New York 10027, USA

CONTRIBUTORS AND PARTICIPANTS

Dr. **Axel Larsen,** Copenhagen University, Institute of Clinical Psychology, Njalsgade 94 DK-2300, Copenhagen S. Denmark

Dr. **Carmel McLaughlin,** University of Oxford, Department of Experimental Psychology, South Parks Road, Oxford OX1 3UD, England

Dr. **Peter McLeod,** University of Oxford, Department of Experimental Psychology, South Parks Road, Oxford OX1 3UD, England

Dr. **Frank W. MacMillan,** University of Delaware, Department of Psychology, Newark, Delaware 19711, USA

Dr. **Oscar Marin,** Good Samaritan Hospital, Department of Neurology, P.O. Box 280, NW 1022 NW 22nd. & Lovejoy, Portland, Oregon 97210, USA

Dr. **Massimo Matelli,** University of Parma-Via Gramsci, Inst. of Human Physiology, 14-43100 Parma, Italy

Dr. **Elizabeth Maylor,** University of Manchester, Center for Research into Aging, Department of Psychology, Manchester, England

Dr. **Jeff Miller,** University of California, San Diego, Department of Psychology C-009, La Jolla, California 92093, USA

Dr. **Thomas Munte,** University of California, Department of Neuroscience M008, School of Medicine, La Jolla, California 92093, USA

Dr. **Risto Näätänen,** University of Helsinki, Department of Psychology, Ritarik 5, 00170, Helsinki 17, Finland

Dr. **Helen J. Neville,** Salk Institute Neuropsychology Department, La Jolla, California 92037, USA

Dr. **David Navon,** University of Haifa, Department of Psychology, Haifa 31949, Israel

Dr. **Roberto Nicoletti,** Instituto di Psicologia, Piazza Capitaniato 5, Padova, Italy

Dr. **Ian Nimmo-Smith,** University of Oxford, Department of Experimental Psychology, South Parks Road, Oxford OX1 3UD, England

Dr. **Mary Jo Nissen,** University of Minnesota, Psychology Department, N218 Elliott Hall, Minneapolis, Minnesota 55455, USA

Dr. **Raja Parasuraman,** Catholic University of America, Department of Psychology, 620 Michigan Avenue, N.E., Washington, DC 20008, USA

Dr. **Jane Pierson,** Monash University, Department of Psychology, Clayton 3168, Victoria, Australia

Dr. **Steven Pinker,** Massachusetts Institute of Technology, Department of Psychology E10-018, Cambridge, Massachusetts 02139, USA

Dr. **Michael Posner,** University of Oregon, Department of Psychology, Eugene, Oregon 97403, USA

Dr. **C. Prablanc,** Laboratory of Experimental Psychology, Inserm u 94, 16 Avenue du Doyen Lepine, 69500 Bron, France

Dr. **Philip Quinlan,** Birbeck College, University of London, Department of Psychology, Malet Street, London WC1E 7HX, England

Dr. **Bob Rafal,** Roger Williams General Hospital, Department of Medicine, 825 Chalkstone Avenue, Providence, Rhode Island 02908, USA

Dr. **Jean Requin,** C.N.R.S. I.N.P. 03, 31, Chemin Joseph-Aiguier, 13402 Marseille, France

Dr. **Jane Riddoch,** Birbeck College, University of London, Department of Psychology, Malet Street, London WC1E 7HX, England

CONTRIBUTORS AND PARTICIPANTS

Dr. Giacomo Rizzolatti, University of Parma-Via Gramsci, Inst. of Human Physiology, 14-43100 Parma, Italy

Dr. Walter Schneider, University of Illinois, Department of Psychology, Urbana, Illinois 61801, USA

Dr. Hitomi Shibuya, University of Tsukuba, Department of Psychology, Tsukuba, Japan

Dr. Arnold Starr, University of California—Irvine, Neurology, Irvine, California 92717, USA

Dr. Saul Sternberg, Bell Laboratories, Room 2D 446, Murray Hill, New Jersey 07974, USA

Dr. S. P. Tipper, University of Oxford, Department of Experimental Psychology, South Parks Road, Oxford OX1 3UD, England

Dr. Anne Treisman, University of British Columbia, Department of Psychology, Vancouver, British Columbia V5T 1W5, Canada

Dr. Carlo Umilta, University di Parma, Istituto di Fisiologia Umana, Via Gramsci 14, 43100 Parma, Italy

Dr. Guiseppe Vallar, Clinica Neurologica II, Via F. Sforza 35, 20122 Milano, Italy

Dr. Cornelis J. Verduin, Institute of Perception TNO, P.O. Box 23, 37 bg ZG Soesterberg, The Netherlands

Dr. Eric Wanner, Alfred P. Sloan Foundation, 630 Fifth Avenue, New York, New York 10111, USA

Dr. Robert Wurtz, N.I.H., Building 10-6C420, Bethesda, MD 20205, USA

Preface

Attention and Performance XI was held in Eugene, Oregon, on July 1 to 8, 1984. The meeting's topic was a quest for the mechanisms of attention. With few exceptions, the central emphasis in previous meetings of the Attention and Performance Association was on the information-processing approach to normal human cognition. This emphasis has been supplemented, on occasion, by studies employing EEG methods, but there have not been systematic attempts to relate the information-processing approach to work in the neurosciences. In this volume we seek to emphasize the search for mechanism with such methods of approach as the following: anatomical, physiological, neuropsychological, behavioral, and computational. We believe this to be in accord with recent developing trends in cognition and particularly with developments in the study of attention.

The Association lecture and the six tutorial reviews, which form Chapters 1 to 7, provide a basic introduction to each of these methods. In his Association lecture, Coltheart lays out the logic of using neurological patients to dissociate the components of performance in reading. The Association lecturer is chosen for distinguished contributions to the entire field without regard to the specific theme of the meeting. However, the neuropsychological method of analysis that Coltheart describes so beautifully is applied by Bisiach, Berti, and Vallar; Humphreys, Riddoch, and Quinlan; Holtzman and Biguer, Jeannerod and Prablanc to issues central to attention.

Cowey's tutorial describes anatomical studies of the visual system. These studies provide the rationale for the importance of stimulus location in guiding visual selection. Selection by location is emphasized in all the chapters included in the section on orienting, which follows the tutorials.

Hillyard, Munte, and Neville show how electrical recording can be used to separate two forms of selectivity based upon stimulus location. One form is quite early in processing and occurs under high load conditions. A second form is later in processing and appears to occur even under conditions of minimal load. This second form of selection is also discussed in the section on orienting. The use of changes in electrical activity to index selectivity is used by Näätänen; Gaillard and Verduin; and Wurtz in later sections of the book.

Reaction time and errors are the methods most frequently used to infer internal mechanisms from studies of human performance. Duncan reviews studies using these methods to discriminate targets from nontargets. He argues that many nontargets can be monitored in parallel but only one target can be attended to at a time. Allport, Tipper, and Chmiel present performance studies that require subjects to select a target event from a simultaneous nontarget. They observe the detailed affects of the selected item upon performance of the following trial. Their results suggest that forms of selection that stress physical features (e.g., by color or cued location) do not exclude the unselected stimuli from having important consequences in later processing.

The tutorials by Navon and Requin stress examination of the logic of computations performed in selection. Navon discusses the role resource limits, cross talk, and other mechanisms could have in producing evidence of interference between tasks. Requin discusses how performance and physiological constraints may influence our definition of a motor program.

The shorter chapters that follow the tutorial reviews are divided into five sections by their content. These are: orienting of attention (selection by location), sensory systems and selection, attention and motor control, dividing and sustaining attention, and attention to symbols and words. The tutorials can also be considered as introductions to these sections: Hillyard et al.'s to Section III, Cowey's to the visual chapters of Section IV, Requin's to Section V, Navon's to Section VII, and Duncan's and Allport et al.'s to Section VIII.

The meeting was marked by an intense discussion that was surprisingly free of separation by discipline (psychology, neurophysiology, neurology), method (electrical recording, anatomy, lesion, performance measures), or geographical location. Rather, there was a strong sense of common progress. It was clear that studies at the anatomical and physiological levels were capable of providing important constraints to the computations that guide selection in skilled normal performance. There were efforts to use clinical data to supplement studies of normal persons and also efforts to use studies of normal humans to interpret clinical syndromes. We hope the spirit of common adventure evident at the meeting will at least be partly conveyed to the reader in this volume.

The meeting itself was made possible through a generous grant from the Sloan Foundation, to which we are most grateful. The organization of the meeting was greatly aided by the executive committee of the Association—in particular, Saul Sternberg, the president. We also are grateful to the many local people who aided with arrangements. The authors themselves, several participants, and other reviewers provided help in editing the volume in a timely manner. We are particularly grateful to Steven W. Keele, who assisted throughout, and to Judy Trexel, who handled many local arrangements and coordinated the editing of the volume.

Michael I. Posner
Oscar S. M. Marin

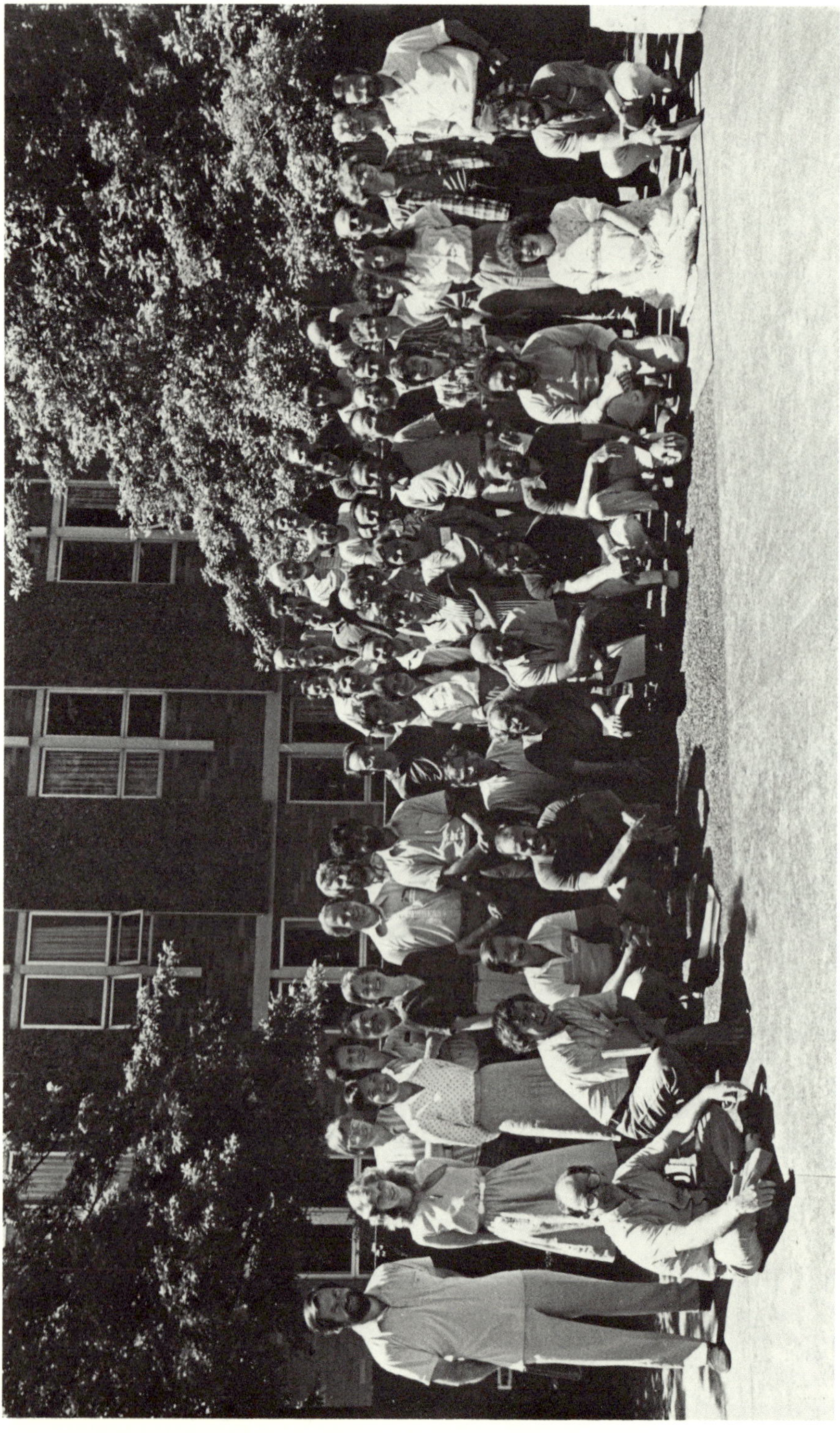

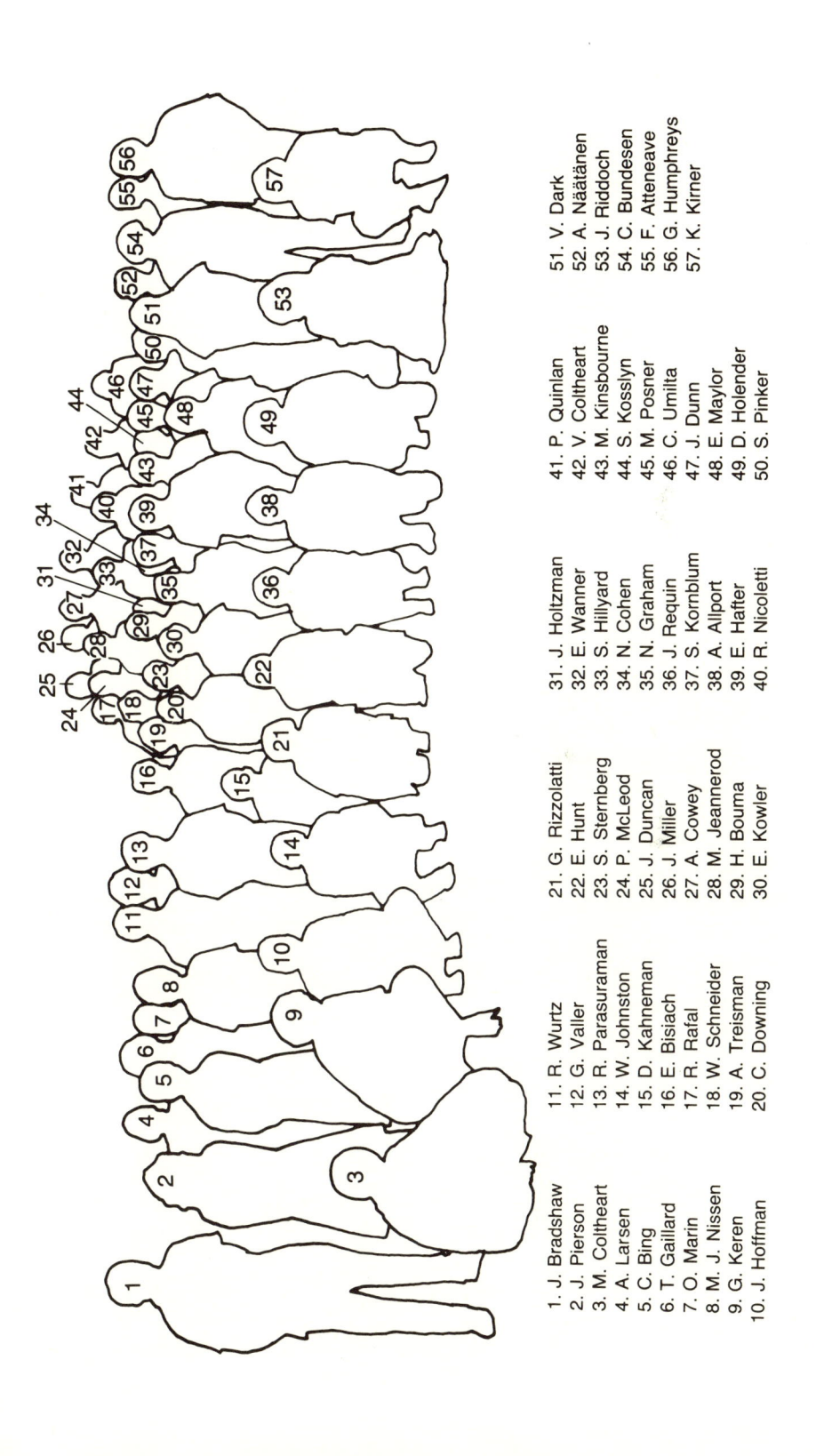

1. J. Bradshaw
2. J. Pierson
3. M. Coltheart
4. A. Larsen
5. C. Bing
6. T. Gaillard
7. O. Marin
8. M. J. Nissen
9. G. Keren
10. J. Hoffman
11. R. Wurtz
12. G. Valler
13. R. Parasuraman
14. W. Johnston
15. D. Kahneman
16. E. Bisiach
17. R. Rafal
18. W. Schneider
19. A. Treisman
20. C. Downing
21. G. Rizzolatti
22. E. Hunt
23. S. Sternberg
24. P. McLeod
25. J. Duncan
26. J. Miller
27. A. Cowey
28. M. Jeannerod
29. H. Bouma
30. E. Kowler
31. J. Holtzman
32. E. Wanner
33. S. Hillyard
34. N. Cohen
35. N. Graham
36. J. Requin
37. S. Kornblum
38. A. Allport
39. E. Hafter
40. R. Nicoletti
41. P. Quinlan
42. V. Coltheart
43. M. Kinsbourne
44. S. Kosslyn
45. M. Posner
46. C. Umiltà
47. J. Dunn
48. E. Maylor
49. D. Holender
50. S. Pinker
51. V. Dark
52. A. Näätänen
53. J. Riddoch
54. C. Bundesen
55. F. Atteneave
56. G. Humphreys
57. K. Kirner

ASSOCIATION LECTURE

1 Cognitive Neuropsychology and the Study of Reading

Max Coltheart
Birkbeck College

ABSTRACT

The basic aim of cognitive neuropsychology is to demonstrate relationships between, on the one hand, explicit theories of normal cognitive processes and, on the other hand, the patterns of behavior exhibited by people in whom brain damage has caused impairments of cognitive processes. Generally, an information-processing system consisting of a number of modular information-processing components is postulated as underlying the normal performance of some specific mental activity. Disorders in the performance of that activity are successfully interpreted when one can show that the pattern of impairments and preservations exhibited by an individual patient is precisely that pattern which would be yielded if, within the relevant information-processing system, certain of the system's components are damaged or abolished, whereas the remainder continue to function normally.

When such attempts at theoretical interpretation succeed, at least two things have been accomplished. The success of the interpretation provides evidence in favor of the theory of normal processing that led to the interpretation; and the interpretation provides an economical explanation of the pattern of behavior exhibited by the patient.

Work of this sort has proliferated in the past decade. This proliferation was first evident in the study of reading. More recently, cognitive neuropsychology has spread first to the study of aspects of language other than reading, and then to aspects of cognition other than language. At present, virtually all major aspects of cognition are being studied from the perspective of cognitive neuropsychology.

This chapter concentrates on what is at present the best-developed sphere of cognitive neuropsychology: the analysis of acquired disorders of reading in terms of models of normal skilled reading. Basic data from patients with acquired dyslexia has provided evidence in favor of the view that the normal reading system comprises two basic processing procedures, the *lexical* and the *non-lexical* procedures. More detailed studies of such patients have provided evidence concerning detailed properties of each of these procedures. Recent work has moved on from studying the reading of single words to investigations of morphological and syntactic processing in reading and to investigations of sentence comprehension. Examples of such work are discussed.

INTRODUCTION

The aim of cognitive psychology is to learn more about how the mind works—to formulate descriptions of the processes that occur during the execution of any mental activity such as perception, attention, object recognition, planning, the production or comprehension of spoken or written language, thinking, remembering, or controlling actions. A predominant approach to the formulation of descriptions of this sort has been to conceive of the execution of different mental activities as requiring the use of different dedicated information-processing systems. In such a view, attempting to understand how people perform a particular mental activity means attempting to describe the information-processing system dedicated to this particular activity. Furthermore, to describe such a system is to specify its internal structure—to indicate what are the information-processing components within the system and the routes of intercommunication between them.

It is clear that this approach to cognitive psychology has, as one of its foundations, a thoroughgoing *modularity*. Not only is each of the various mental activities considered to be associated with its own information-processing module, but also each of these modules may itself be considered to be composed of a collection of smaller, more specialized, component modules.[1] For example, in their chapter in this book, Allport, Tipper, and Chmiel refer to "a perspective that views the brain as an assembly of specialized subsystems," and Kosslyn, Berndt, and Doyle assert that visual imagery is not a single, unitary ability, but can be analyzed into a set of abilities, each of which in turn can be analyzed into a set of "processing modules."

It is also clear that this approach to cognitive psychology has its critics, not the least of whom is Neisser (1976; see also Neisser, 1983). Figure 1.1, taken from Neisser (1976), eloquently expresses his view concerning the intellectual worth of the componential approach to the study of mental activities. I hope to

---

[1] I am not using the term *module* in the sense adopted by Fodor (1983) in his treatise on the modularity of the mind. Fodor's sense of the term does not capture the concept of modularity as it applies to the kinds of information-processing models I discuss in this chapter. For example, the model I describe on page 21 would be regarded as modular in character by information-processing theorists, but its components are not modules in Fodor's sense—for example, they are not innate, not informationally encapsulated, and not hard-wired.

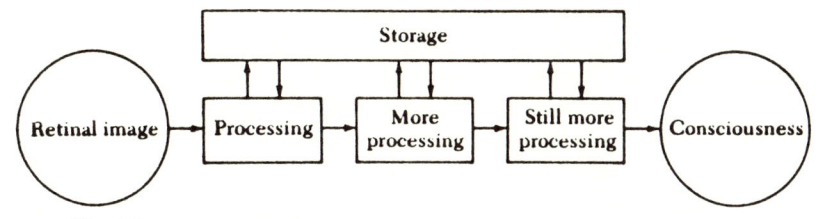

Fig. 1.1. Modular modelling of cognition as viewed by Neisser (1976).

persuade the reader, by the examples I discuss in this chapter, that Neisser's evaluation of this way of doing cognitive psychology is unduly pessimistic, that in fact in the past quarter of a century a great deal has been learned from work that has adopted this approach, and that its usefulness has by no means been exhausted. I hope to achieve these aims by persuading the reader that the application of componential analyses of cognition in a particular sphere—the study of people with disorders of cognition—is in fact opening up new avenues for discovering more, not only about disordered cognition, but also about normal cognitive processes.[2]

Componential models of mental activities abound in all branches of cognitive psychology. Those who pursue this paradigm usually proceed by deducing, from the postulated properties of the components of such a model, how subjects ought to behave in laboratory studies of relevant tasks, and then carry out experimental investigations to assess the correctness or otherwise of such predictions.

In recent years, however, an alternative way of developing and testing these kinds of theories has been growing in popularity. Instead of studying the performance of subjects with *normal* cognitive skills, one selects for study people with specific *defects* in the ability to execute the mental activity in which one is interested. It might have turned out, of course, that sufficiently specific defects of cognition would not be observed, or that it would not be possible to establish clear links between models of normal cognitive processing and the behavior of those with disorders of cognition. My aim is to demonstrate that this is not in fact how matters have turned out. Instead, I argue, the past decade has seen the rapid expansion of a discipline that has come to be called *cognitive neuropsychology*.

I use this term to refer to any work in cognitive psychology that exhibits either or both of the following two properties:

1. An attempt is made to evaluate some model of a particular cognitive process by exploring the extent to which that model can be used to explain the

---

[2]I do not mean to imply here that the componential analysis of disordered cognition is a relatively new endeavor, because, of course, Lichtheim and Wernicke were analyzing disorders of language in this way a century ago. But they were using this approach to try to learn more about the localization of cognitive functions in the brain, not to learn more about the structure of the information-processing system subserving linguistic performance, an entirely different matter (Mehler, Morton, & Jusczyk, 1984).

various different patterns of impairments and perservations of abilities evident in people suffering from various different disorders of that cognitive process. Whenever a pattern of impairments and preservations is observed that, according to the model, could not arise, this counts as evidence against the model.

2. An attempt is made to explain people's cognitive disorders in a theoretically motivated way: One seeks to show that the constellation of symptoms exhibited by a person is precisely that constellation that would be expected if, within the multicomponent information-processing system postulated as responsible for the cognitive process in question, a certain subset of the components had been damaged or abolished while the remaining components were continuing to function normally.

This way of attempting to bring about a *rapprochement* between cognitive psychology and clinical neuropsychology makes, of course, a number of assumptions. I mention what are perhaps the two most important. First, it is assumed that brain damage does not create new processing modules for performing any cognitive task, so that abnormal functioning will take the form of using a subset of the modules normally available. Second, it is assumed that the basic architecture of the normal processing system is the same from person to person within a given environment, so that one expects to be able to use evidence from a variety of different patients to make statements about a single basic architecture, even though each patient may have a different and unique pattern of impairments of that architecture.

One can identify various isolated examples of work that represent early instances of cognitive neuropsychology. In the 1960s studies of memory disorders sometimes were specifically concerned with using data from patients with memory disorders to evaluate models of normal memory, for example. It was then often argued that two of the components of the normal memory system were short-term memory and long-term memory, and that these were serially arranged so that all access to long-term memory occurred via short-term memory. This model was challenged by Shallice and Warrington (1970) because, they argued, the patient they had investigated had deficient short-term memory but spared access to long-term memory. Another early example of cognitive neuropsychology as I have defined it is represented by the work of Marshall and Newcombe (1966). The patient they studied made semantic errors in reading aloud single words—reading, for example, *antique* as "vase" or *gnome* as "pixie." Marshall and Newcombe used information about the particular forms of semantic relationships evident in such errors to make suggestions about how semantic representations are normally structured in the lexicon.

Various other isolated examples of this kind of work emerged in the 1960s and early 1970s. In the past decade, however, and particularly in the past 5 years, there has been a remarkable proliferation of cognitive-neuropsychological work.

This proliferation was first evident in the study of reading (see, e.g., Beauvois & Derouesne, 1979; Coltheart, 1978; Coltheart, Patterson, & Marshall, 1980; Patterson & Marcel, 1977; Saffran, Schwartz, & Marin, 1976; and Shallice & Warrington, 1975). More recently, cognitive neuropsychology has spread first to the study of aspects of language other than reading, and then to the study of aspects of cognition other than language, so that it is now difficult to think of any major aspect of cognition that is not currently being studied from the perspective of cognitive neuropsychology. One finds cognitive-neuropsychological investigations of visual object recognition (Humphreys, Riddoch, & Quinlan, this volume), the planning of action (Shallice, 1982), spelling (Ellis, 1982), sentence comprehension (Caramazza & Berndt, in press), sentence production (Saffran Schwartz, & Marin, 1980), mental arithmetic (Warrington, 1982), attention (Posner, Cohen, & Rafal, 1982), and short-term memory (Caramazza, Basili, Koller, & Berndt, 1981), as well as a continuation of studies of amnesia.

This puts me in something of a quandary. It would be an enjoyable task to attempt to put together an evaluation of current work in cognitive neuropsychology as it relates to all aspects of cognition, and this might be of interest to those cognitive psychologists who are mainly familiar only with studies of normal subjects. To do this in any detail, however, would require a book, not a chapter. My alternatives are, therefore, either to deal briefly with each of a wide range of aspects of cognition, or to consider in much more depth only some aspects of cognition.

I have chosen the latter course of action, and thus concentrate in the rest of this chapter on the cognitive neuropsychology of language, particularly that of reading. This is not only because of my own interests but also because it is clear that this is by far the most developed aspect of cognitive neuropsychology, and so offers the best opportunity for surveying a frontier of the subject.

As mentioned previously, early work in cognitive neuropsychology included studies of memory and studies of reading. If my assessment concerning the current status of these two lines of work is correct, it is worth considering how the difference has come about. An answer is suggested by Baddeley (1982): "It is less clear that we have made progress in studying the amnesic syndrome . . . we have been able to test some input and storage theories, but at present we simply do not have adequately developed theories of normal retrieval" [p. 70]. In contrast, over the past 10 years models of normal reading (at least at the single-word level) have been developed that have been sufficiently explicit and sufficiently comprehensive to make their application to the interpretation of reading disorders reasonably straightforward.

An excellent way of learning that a model is less detailed or less explicit than one had thought is to attempt to apply it to the explanation of patients' performances in cognitive domains to which the model is intended to apply. Another way in which models can be immensely useful is in providing a vocabulary to describe the various types of *representations* relevant to any complex information-processing operation, such as reading aloud. As a general principle, it would seem that cognitive neuropsychology can only really flourish when both adequate studies of disordered cognition *and* sufficiently explicit models of normal processing within the relevant cognitive domain are available. So, if I am to use the cognitive neuropsychology of reading as my principal example, then, it is appropriate to begin by saying something about models of normal reading.

DUAL-ROUTE MODELS OF READING ALOUD

Reading aloud consists of transforming an orthographic representation into a phonological one. Any model meant to describe the mental system we use when we read must include machinery for performing such transformations. Most—though certainly not all—such models incorporate two different procedures for these transformations, each capable of carrying out certain types of orthographic-to-phonological conversion. These models form the class of dual-route models of reading aloud. Early examples of this approach to explaining oral reading include Laberge (1972), Baron (1973), Marshall and Newcombe (1973), Meyer, Schvaneveldt, and Ruddy (1974), Baron and Strawson (1976), and Coltheart (1978). A contemporary version of this type of model is described by Patterson and Morton (1985).

To a very considerable degree, the development of such models was initially motivated by reflecting upon the properties of the English writing system rather than in response to evidence from experimental studies of reading. The existence of two different procedures for reading aloud was considered to be a consequence of the existence of two different types of letter string, both of which the normal reader of English can read aloud: the pronounceable nonword and the exception word.

The fact that never-before-seen letter strings like *kweab* or *jyd* can be appropriately converted from orthographic to phonological form was taken as a demonstration that reading aloud cannot depend entirely on the use of previously learned associations between whole orthographic forms and their associated phonological representations. Instead, it is argued, the procedure used to read nonwords aloud depends on general knowledge of the rules specifying the correspondences, in English, between orthographic *segments* and their phonological counterparts: rules such as that the segment *ea* is to be recoded as the phoneme /i/ (as in *bead, meat, seam,* and many other English words).

But it follows that, if this or anything like this is a correct account of how we read nonwords aloud, then a second procedure for reading aloud must exist, because the normal reader can correctly read aloud letter strings that the rule-based procedure would *wrongly recode*—namely, exception words. For example, application of the rule *ea* → /i/, needed to read a letter string like *kweab*, would cause errors in reading exception words like *steak* or *bread*. Under normal circumstances such errors are not made by normal readers, not even with extreme cases such as *yacht* or *sew,* which contain correspondences that exist in no other word of English. To read *sew* aloud correctly must require access to information specific to that word, rather than general information about spelling–sound correspondences. It follows that if reading aloud ever depends on access to previously learned information in this way, then at least two procedures for reading aloud must exist, because the normal reader also can correctly read aloud letter strings for which such access is not possible—namely, nonwords.

If we refer to the system that contains the information we have acquired about each of the words of our language as a mental lexicon, then it is natural to refer to the reading procedure that depends on access to this store as the *lexical* procedure for reading aloud, and hence also natural to use the term *nonlexical* to refer to the procedure that makes no use of word-specific lexical information.

In summation, then, the basic idea of dual-route models is that the reading aloud of nonwords can only be achieved by using the nonlexical procedure, whereas the correct reading aloud of exception words requires the use of the lexical procedure. The third type of letter string—the regularly spelled word— can be read aloud by the lexical procedure (because such items are present in the lexicon) and also by the nonlexical procedure (because such items conform to the standard spelling–sound correspondences of English).

In recent years, the view that there are dual procedures underlying normal oral reading has not gone without challenge. Specifically, the concept of a purely nonlexical route has come under attack, with assertions that even the reading of nonwords depends on access to lexical information (Glushko, 1979a, 1979b, 1981; Henderson, 1982; Kay & Marcel, 1981; Marcel, 1980). This controversy is currently being pursued in investigations of reading performance in normal readers; see, for example, Parkin (1982, 1984), Seidenberg, Waters, Barnes, and Tanenhaus (1984), and, for reviews, Henderson (1985a), Kay (1985), and Patterson and Morton (1985). In my view, the claim that nonwords are read by normal readers without recourse to word-specific lexical information continues to be tenable. But this is a chapter about cognitive neuropsychology, and so it must be concerned with the use of data from disordered reading to illuminate the controversy about what procedures are used to read aloud.

If two separate procedures exist for reading aloud, then (for this is what separate *means* to the cognitive neuropsychologist) one would expect to find patients in whom one of the procedures is impaired while the other is intact. Of course, there are uninteresting reasons why one might fail to discover such patients (uninteresting to cognitive psychology, that is, but of course meaningful to the neurologist concerned with the neural basis of function). It could be that the two procedures, although functionally and anatomically distinct, are localized in the brain so adjacently that it is unlikely that any form of brain damage could affect one procedure while sparing the other. Or, the two procedures, though functionally distinct, may not be sharply localized in the brain at all, in which case again it might not be possible for brain damage to affect one system and spare the other. It is because of these possibilities that *associations* of deficits observed in neuropsychological research are often considered to be of much less value as evidence than *dissociations*.

What is more, it is generally considered that the double dissociation is of more value than the single dissociation. If one finds a patient, for example, with a deficit of the nonlexical procedure and sparing of the lexical procedure, but not the reverse, the claim that this indicates the existence of two separate procedures could be disputed by the counterclaim that reading nonwords is simply more difficult or less familiar a task than reading words, even if the two tasks use a common procedure, and neurological damage may compromise difficult tasks more than easier ones. This counterclaim is not applicable to inferences based on a double dissociation—that is, the observation in some patients of selective sparing of the lexical procedure and in others of selective sparing of the nonlexical procedure.[3]

Thus we arrive at the following question: Does one see patients with a disorder of reading in which the nonlexical procedure (as it is described in dual-route models of reading) is impaired or abolished while the lexical route is spared, and does one also observe the opposite pattern in other patients?

Phonological Dyslexia: Impairment of the Nonlexical Procedure

This pattern of reading disorder was first described by Beauvois and Derouesne (1979) and subsequently by Shallice and Warrington (1980) and Patterson (1982). All of the patients they described exhibited, as a consequence of cerebral injury, a selective impairment in the ability to read pronounceable nonwords relative to the ability to read words.

In none of these patients was nonword reading completely abolished, nor did any of them approach complete intactness in the ability to read words (although it was perfectly clear for all the cases that nonword reading had been affected far more strongly than word reading). The most recently described case of phonological dyslexia, however, does closely approach these extremes. It is the case of W. B. (Funnell, 1983), who was employed as transport manager to a food-processing company, and who suffered a major cerebrovascular accident to the left hemisphere in 1978, when he was 68 years old. This patient was *entirely* unable to read nonwords aloud; he scored 0/20 correct with a list of four- or five-

---

[3]Although this assessment of the comparative methodological value of associations, single dissociations, and double dissociations is fairly standard in cognitive neuropsychology, I believe that the cases against the usefulness of associations and of single dissociations have been much overstated, and that there ways of making perfectly legitimate inferences from both of these patterns. However, nothing in this chapter depends on accepting this viewpoint.

letter nonwords (he made no response to 11 of these, and produced visually similar words as responses to 8 others). In contrast, his ability to read aloud single words presented without context was nearly intact: With a variety of word lists incorporating abstract words, words of various syntactic classes, irregularly spelled words, and affixed words, percent correct averaged 85, and none of the aforementioned variables affected reading accuracy. Here, then, is a particularly marked example of the kind of reading performance that one would expect to see if the dual-route account of reading were correct and if, in this patient, one of the routes, the nonlexical route, had been abolished.

Although Funnell's data obviously are completely compatible with a dual-route model, it also might be the case that they are just as compatible with other types of model, in which case the importance of W. B. vis-à-vis models of reading would be lessened. But it is not easy to discover models of oral reading that conflict with the dual-route model and that are explicit enough to allow predictions to be made concerning patterns of disordered reading. It seems to me that the only potential example of an alternative and conflicting approach is to be derived from suggestions by Marcel (1980; see also Kay & Marcel, 1981).

Marcel proposed that it is not true that nonwords are read aloud without reference to lexical information about the spellings and pronunciations of real words—that is, he rejected the concept of a nonlexical procedure for nonword reading. Instead, he suggested that the operation of three processes—*orthographic segmentation, phonological segmentation,* and *phonological assembly*—allow the reader to read nonlexical stimuli (nonwords) by lexical means. Orthographic segmentation of a nonword like *slint*, for example, into segments such as *sl-* and *-int* permits access to the orthographic lexical representations of words appropriate to these segments: *slow, slate, mint, sprint,* and so on. Lexical mappings between orthography and phonology in turn allow access to the phonological forms of these words. If the appropriate phonological segments (that is, /sl/- and -/Int/) can be extracted from these lexical phonological forms, then assembly of these phonological segments would yield the desired pronunciation of the nonword.

Now any model in which the procedure for reading words is entirely separate from the procedure for reading nonwords obviously can provide a simple explanation of phonological dyslexia. If, however, one wants to deny that these two procedures are completely separate, how is phonological dyslexia to be explained? Marcel's answer to this question was to point out that in his model the processes of orthographic segmentation, phonological segmentation, and phonological assembly are necessary for nonword reading but not for word reading (because if the input is a word, its unanalyzed form will contact a representation in an orthographic input system and via this the word's phonological form can be retrieved without any need for phonological segmentation or phonological assembly). Therefore, a deficit in any one of these processes will create difficulties in reading nonwords but not in reading words.

In Marcel's account, then, because W. B. could not read nonwords at all, he should be seriously deficient in at least one of these three processes; to find out, Funnell (1983) investigated these processes. She tested orthographic segmentation by presenting W. B. with items like *alforsut*—that is, nonwords in which words were orthographically embedded. W. B. was not, of course, able to read these nonwords, but he was not asked to: His task was to read the embedded words, and he did so without error. This would seem to demonstrate that he had no deficit at all in his ability to perform orthographic segmentation.

It might be argued here that this result is not in conflict with Marcel's model because the representation of the word *for* will still be available in W. B.'s word-recognition system and access to this representation from the stimulus *alforsut* would permit the response "for." But this will not do, because in Marcel's account of orthographic segmentation and access to orthographic representations, the word *for* is *not* accessed from the nonword *alforsut*, as this quotation from Kay and Marcel (1981) makes clear:

> A printed letter string is segmented in all possible ways. . . . Each segment automatically accesses matching segments in the orthographic lexical input addresses of all words which contain those segments *in equivalent positions* (italics added) [p. 401].

W. B.'s competence at phonological segmentation was tested by speaking single words to him and asking him to respond with the first phoneme of each word—for example, to respond /kə/ to "cat." He scored 14/15 correct on this test. Therefore, unless performance with noninitial phonemes would have been worse, phonological segmentation was virtually intact in this patient.

W. B.'s ability to perform phonological assembly was tested by speaking the individual phonemes of a word to him separately ("/də/" .. "/ɒ/" .. "/gə/") and asking him to repeat the whole word. He was clearly impaired at this, scoring 6/10, but his ability was sufficiently preserved to make it impossible to ascribe the complete abolition of nonword reading to a complete inability to perform phonological assembly.

Hence, the only attempt to account for phonological dyslexia by a theoretical framework other than the dual-route model makes predictions that are falsified by these studies of W. B., which leaves the dual-route model without competitors at present as a source for explanations of phonological dyslexia. To put this another way: The existence of phonological dyslexia is strong evidence in favor of the dual-route model. As already noted, however, for the evidence to be really strong one needs a double dissociation between the two reading procedures postulated by the model. Hence, we turn to a consideration of a second form of reading disorder.

Surface Dyslexia: Impairment of the Lexical Procedure

This pattern of reading disorder was first described by Marshall and Newcombe (1973) and subsequently by Shallice and Warrington (1980), Shallice, Warrington, and McCarthy (1983), and Coltheart, Masterson, Byng, Prior, and Riddoch (1983). A volume edited by Patterson, Marshall, and Coltheart (1985) is devoted to a review of current knowledge about the syndrome. These sources describe a number of patients who exhibited, as a consequence of cerebral injury, a selective difficulty in reading aloud exception words relative to their ability to read matched, regularly spelled words.

In the early descriptions of surface dyslexia, the reading of regular words was never completely intact, so it could not be claimed that the nonlexical procedure was completely spared. However, in the case described by Bub, Canceliere, and Kertesz (1985), precisely this claim can be made. Their case, M. P., who was employed as the bookkeeper and general manager of an apartment building, suffered a severe head injury in 1979 at the age of 59, after being knocked down by a motor vehicle. A consequence of this injury was that M. P.'s ability to read exception words aloud correctly was severely impaired, whereas her ability to read regular words and nonwords was unaffected. Furthermore, almost all of the wrong responses she made when reading exception words were "regularizations"—that is, responses arising from correct application of English spelling–sound rules to words that violate these rules. Examples from M. P.'s responses to exception words are:

have → /heIv/ (as in cave)
lose → /ləʊz/ (as in hose)
own → /aʊn/ (as in down)
steak → /stik/ (as in beak)

No case of surface dyslexia has yet been reported in which no exception words at all could be read correctly. Thus, in all cases it has remained possible for *some* words to be read by the lexical procedure. For M. P., whether a word could be read correctly by the lexical procedure depended heavily on word frequency, as shown in Fig. 1.2. It would seem, then, that the appropriate interpretation of this patient's disorder is that the nonlexical procedure remains entirely intact whereas the lexical procedure has been damaged in such a way that it only can deal fully successfully with very high-frequency words: The number of words whose lexical representations remain accessible is very small, and the probability of any word's being in this retained set depends on its frequency.

The two patients just described demonstrate a double dissociation between reading via the lexical procedure and reading via the nonlexical procedure that is extremely clear. It would seem, then, that the two patients in particular, and the forms of acquired dyslexia known as phonological and surface dyslexia in general, provide strong evidence in support of the view that the information-processing system we use for reading aloud—for transforming orthography into phonology—ought to be thought of as comprising two separate components.

However, the relationship between the dual-route model and current knowledge about acquired dyslexia is in fact much more intimate than I so far have

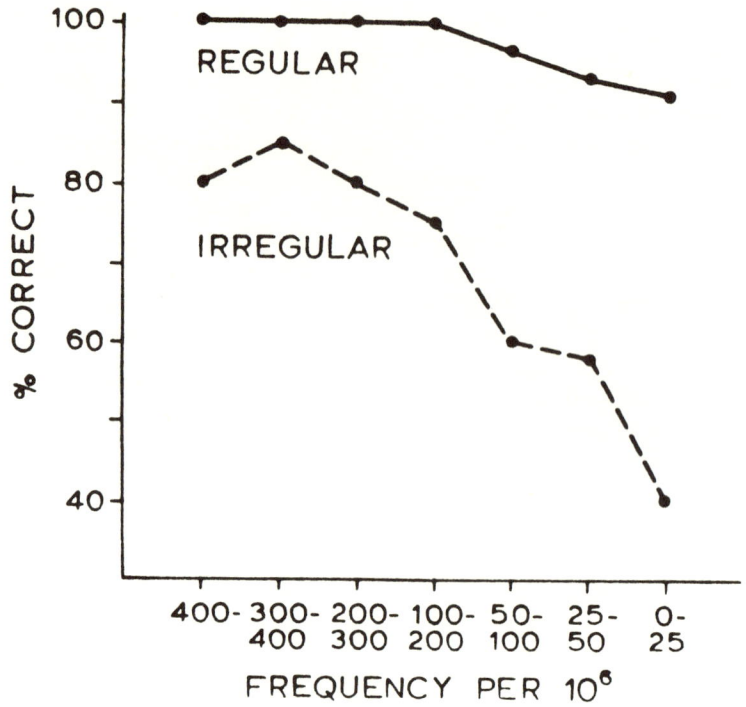

FIG. 1.2. Accuracy of reading aloud regular and irregular words as a function of word frequency (Patient M.P. — see Bub et al., 1985).

described. Data from studies of acquired dyslexia have not only provided evidence of the existence of a lexical and a nonlexical procedure but also have provided quite detailed information about the properties of each of these two procedures.

THE NATURE OF THE NONLEXICAL PROCEDURE

It was argued previously that the way the nonlexical procedure converts orthography to phonology is by using a system of spelling-to-sound correspondences. I now attempt to clarify what this system might be like, by considering just what kinds of orthographic units and phonological units might be used by such a system.

One proposal (Coltheart, 1978) is that the phonological unit is the phoneme, and that larger phonological segments such as the consonant cluster or the syllable do not act as units onto which orthographic segments are directly mapped by the nonlexical procedure. It follows from this proposal that the orthographic unit is the written equivalent of the phoneme. In English, individual phonemes are often represented by letter sequences rather than by single letters, so the orthographic unit we are considering here is not the letter. The term *grapheme* often refers to the written representation of a phoneme, and I follow this terminology. In this view spelling–sound correspondences consist of rules relating *individual graphemes* to *individual phoneme*, that is, grapheme-phoneme correspondences (GPCs). The alternative proposal (e.g., Shallice & McCarthy, 1985; Shallice et al., 1983) is that orthographic units larger than the grapheme and phonological units larger than the phoneme also are represented in the spelling–sound correspondence system.

These two views differ in relation to words like *book* or *find*. Although the standard pronunciation of the grapheme *oo* is /u:/, when it is followed by a *k* it is usually pronounced /ʊ/. A system that uses orthographic units like *ook*—that is, units larger than the grapheme—could take advantage of such regularities. For such a system words like *book* or *find* would be regular, whereas a system that operated solely at the graphemic level would wrongly translate them.

The account of the nonlexical procedure originally offered by Coltheart (1978) possessed at least two extreme properties: (a) it postulated that, in the system of GPCs, each grapheme was associated with *only one* phoneme; and (b) it postulated that the *only* orthographic unit used was the grapheme. Neither of these postulates has survived the past 7 years' research. Evidence against the first is provided by Campbell and Besner (1981), who showed that whether normal subjects assigned the phoneme /θ/ or the phoneme /ð/ to the grapheme *th* in initial position in a nonword embedded in a printed sentence was influenced by whether the nonword occupied a function-word or a content-word position in the sentence.[4] This could not occur if GPCs were solely one-to-one mappings.

Evidence against the second postulate is provided by Kay and Lesser (1985). They used three types of nonword: An example matched trio is *gean, geak,* and *gead*. In words ending *-ean*, the *ea* is always /i/; in words ending *-eak*, the *ea* is usually /i/, but not invariably (e.g., *steak, break*); in words ending *-ead*, the *ea* is usually *not* /i/. In a pure GPC view, the final consonant will be irrelevant as far as the pronunciation assigned by the subject is concerned. In contrast, if orthographic units larger than the grapheme are used (units such as *-ean* or *-eak* or *-ead*), then the assignment /i/ should be less common for *eak* and still less common for *ead;* this is what Kay and Lesser found with their normal subjects.

Thus both postulate (a) and postulate (b) must be relinquished: GPC mappings are not one to one, and the nonlexical procedure does not operate solely at the graphemic level. Nevertheless, it does seem to be the case that one-to-one assignment at solely the graphemic level is very much the *predominant* process in nonword reading. For example, Kay and Lesser (1985) found that about 80% of their subjects gave the vowel assignment specified by GPC correspondences

---

[4]The point here is, of course, that in English initial *th-* is voiced in function words and unvoiced in content words.

even with nonwords of the *-ead* variety, where this assignment occurs in few words. Hence I proceed with some further discussion of what the GPC system might be like and how it might be related to various aspects of acquired dyslexia, while pointing out that issues of the kind I have just been considering are the subject for much dispute at present (see, for example, Bub, Canceliere, & Kertesz, 1985; Coltheart et al., 1983; Henderson, 1985a; Kay, 1985; Kay & Lesser, 1985; Patterson & Morton, 1985; Shallice et al., 1983).

Take as an example the nonword *chooth*. The correct pronunciation of this nonword consists of three phonemes. Therefore, if GPCs are to be used in reading this nonword aloud the three orthographic segments corresponding to these phonemes must be identified—that is, the letter string must be parsed into its constituent *graphemes*, with, as mentioned earlier, the term grapheme meaning the written representation of a phoneme. The result of applying this process to the letter string *chooth* is to yield the three graphemes ⟨ch⟩, ⟨oo⟩, and ⟨th⟩. The next step is to determine, from the set of grapheme–phoneme correspondences, what phoneme should be assigned to each of these three graphemes: The correct assignments are the phonemes /tʃ/, /u:/, and /θ/. Finally, these three separate phonemes must be blended into a single, unified phonological form.

Here we have fractionated the nonlexical procedure into a sequence of three components: first graphemic parsing, then phoneme assignment, then blending. This theory of the nature of the nonlexical procedure is illustrated in Fig. 1.3. Are there any data from studies of acquired dyslexia that may be used to assess

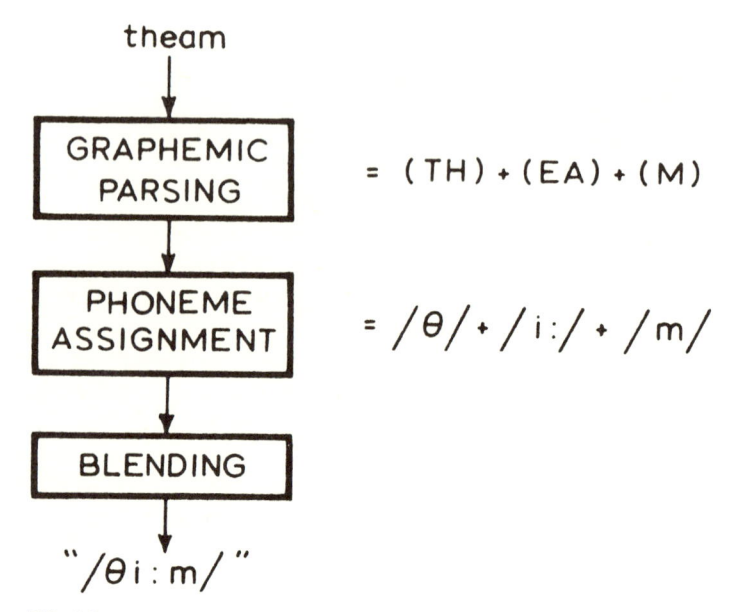

FIG. 1.3. A model of the non-lexical procedure for reading aloud.

the plausibility of the model set out in Fig. 1.3? We already have seen that patients exist in whom the nonlexical procedure is severely impaired or even abolished whereas the lexical procedure remains relatively or virtually intact: This is phonological dyslexia. According to the model of the nonlexical procedure we now are considering, however, there are several different ways in which the nonlexical procedure can be disrupted, because this procedure consists of several different components. Remorselessly pursuing the logic of cognitive neuropsychology, we now ask: Among those patients with an acquired dyslexia in which the nonlexical procedure is impaired, can one distinguish those with an impairment of graphemic parsing, those with an impairment of phoneme assignment, and those with an impairment of blending? Any one of these impairments would, of course, produce poor performance in nonword reading, but for different reasons.

It appears as if it may be possible to observe such distinctions. The existence of a selective disruption of the graphemic parsing stage of the nonlexical procedure was first discussed by Beauvois and Derouesne (1979). In a group of acquired dyslexics, all of whom showed impaired use of the nonlexical procedure, some patients were worse at reading nonwords that required graphemic parsing (e.g., *cau*) than at reading nonwords for which graphemic parsing was not essential because a one-to-one mapping of *letters* to phonemes existed (e.g., *iko* or *ko*). Other patients did not perform differently with these two types of nonword.[5]

More recently, an extremely clear case of impaired graphemic parsing has been described by Newcombe and Marshall (1985). In 1978 their case, M. S., sustained a severe closed head injury, at the age of 18, that left him with very impaired reading and spelling. The first point to note about this case was that the patient's ability to read by the *lexical* procedure was greatly reduced. He is a devotee of rock music and was able to read some words from this semantic sphere, such as *purple* (from *Deep Purple*) and *angel* (from *Angelwitch*), as well as *police* (possibly from the band Police), *pint,* and *beer,* but apart from an extremely small sight vocabulary of such words his reading aloud was accomplished by using the nonlexical procedure. Thus, we can observe in this patient the operation of the nonlexical procedure virtually in isolation. The patient's *nonlexical* procedure also was impaired, in a way that the following examples make very clear:

fight → /fIghʌt/
phrase → /pəhəræsi/

---

[5]In my sense of "grapheme," graphemic parsing is converting letters to graphemes, to each of which a phoneme can then be assigned. If graphemic parsing is not carried out, phonemes can still be assigned to *letters,* and for letter strings in which there is one-to-one mapping of letters to phonemes, the omission of graphemic parsing will be irrelevant.

match → /mætkəhə/
cheap → /kəhæp/
advice → /ædvIki/

Surely it is obvious what is going on here: The patient is using *letter*–phoneme correspondences, not grapheme–phoneme correspondences—that is, he is not parsing the letter string into graphemes before the phoneme assignment stage. He is, however, correctly assigning phonemes to the orthographic elements he uses (namely, single letters), and correctly blending these phonemes. If this is so, he should be competent at reading words that do not need graphemic parsing—that is, words in which there is a one-to-one relationship of letters to phonemes—and indeed this was so: He correctly read such words as *snob, soft, hand,* and *blast.* It therefore seems entirely justified to propose that in this patient the disorder of the nonlexical procedure takes the form of a gross impairment of the graphemic parsing stage with relative preservation of the phoneme assignment and blending stages.

I have already discussed case W. B. (Funnell, 1983) as an example of a patient who, like M. S., showed an impairment of the nonlexical procedure. But W. B.'s impairment was different from that of M. S. As we have seen, M. S. was competent at the phoneme-assignment stage, because he could read reasonably well nonlexically as long as graphemic parsing was not called for. In contrast, W. B. was entirely unable to assign phonemes to their written representations: When presented with single letters and asked to give their *sounds* (e.g., to respond /kə/ to *k*), he could not do so at all, even though he could *name* letters (e.g., could respond /keI/ to *k*) quite well (83% correct) and could write letters to dictation when given their sounds (91% correct). As already pointed out, W. B. was moderately good at identifying a word when he heard its constituent phonemes, so his blending ability was at least partially preserved. We do not have unambiguous information about his graphemic parsing ability.[6]

These two patients, then, provide support for the particular characterization of the nonlexical procedure under discussion: M. S. reads in the way one would expect if the graphemic parsing stage is selectively impaired, whereas the phonemic assignment stage is the critical source of W. B.'s inability to read nonwords. Some fragments of evidence that the blending stage may also sometimes be compromised in patients with a disorder of the nonlexical procedure is provided when one examines the kinds of responses made to nonwords by a patient, C. B., briefly investigated in collaboration with S. Byng.

---

[6]Funnell (1983) briefly describes a second patient, F. L., who could read nonwords but could not give the letter sounds of single printed letters, so that she could respond /kə/ to *kuh* but not to *k*. Unless one wants to propose that the nonlexical procedure includes syllabic-level correspondences even for letter sequences that do not occur in any English word (such as *kuh*), it is not clear how any model of reading aloud could explain this result.

When tested, this patient made almost no errors in reading single words, scoring 75/81, but was correct with only 1/18 three-letter nonwords when asked to read them aloud. Many of her responses took the form of uttering the individual phonemes corresponding to the letters of the nonword as an unblended sequence; for example:

uze → /ʌ/../s/../e/../z/
sem → /əm/../e/../s/../em/
owt → /əʊ/../uː/../wə/../we/../ti/../tə/../uːwətə/
vot → /və/../əʊ/../vəʊ/../vəʊt/../və/../əʊ/.. /tə/
hab → /hə/.../bə/.../hæd /.../hæb /
mab → /mə/../mæn/../mə/../mæn/../mə/../bə/../mæ/..bə/

It is evident from these responses that the phoneme-assignment stage of the nonlexical procedure was functioning well in this patient; this is clearly shown by her very good performance in giving the syllabic sounds of single printed letters: 22/26 correct. The contrast with the patient W. B., who was described earlier, is particularly interesting: Both patients essentially were unable to read even the simplest nonwords aloud, but clearly for quite different reasons.

THE NATURE OF THE LEXICAL PROCEDURE

I have argued not only that evidence from acquired dyslexia supports the view that the reading system involves two different procedures for reading aloud—a lexical and a nonlexical procedure—but also that such evidence can tell us something about the characteristics of the two procedures. In the case of the nonlexical procedure, what is suggested is that this procedure consists of a sequence of three processing stages, as illustrated in Fig. 1.3. What can we learn about the characteristics of the other procedure, the lexical procedure, from studies of acquired dyslexia?

So far in this chapter, the lexical procedure has been characterized as an undifferentiated process that accepts orthographic representations as inputs and, when these inputs are words, can produce appropriate phonological representations as outputs. I have neglected reading *comprehension,* but obviously the lexical processing of words must include a procedure for accessing semantics. The simplest way to adapt to this requirement is to propose that, when the lexical procedure is used to read aloud, a printed word contacts its semantic representation (allowing comprehension), and in turn this semantic representation is used to access the word's phonological representation (allowing reading aloud). If the task is only to understand the word, the second step is not needed.

Evidence from acquired dyslexia rules out this particular view of the lexical procedure. For example, Schwartz, Saffran, and Marin (1980) described a patient who could correctly read aloud many exception words even though her ability to comprehend single printed words had been almost completely abolished by a progressive dementing illness. The point about this patient is that she could not have been reading these exception words by the nonlexical procedure (because such words are incorrectly encoded by this procedure), nor could she have been reading via semantics (because she could not access semantics from print). So a third route for reading aloud must exist—a lexical but not semantic route, involving direct mappings from visual word-recognition units to phonological representations. The patient M. P. (Bub, Canceliere, & Kertesz, 1985) discussed earlier provides the same sort of evidence because she could read aloud a substantial number of high-frequency exception words but could not access semantics from print.

An independent line of evidence has been provided (Coltheart et al., 1983) for the view that the lexical procedure for reading aloud does not depend on passing through semantics to reach phonology. The dyslexic they studied was asked to give definitions of single printed words. A number of cases were noted in which (a) the stimulus was an exception word; (b) the stimulus also was a homophone; and (c) the patient defined the stimulus as its homophone—for example, *bury* was defined as "a fruit on a tree." The occurrence of this type of error is evidence that lexical access to phonology can be achieved without lexical access to semantics. The argument here is as follows: *Bury* must have been given a correct phonological code (otherwise it would not have been confused with another word with the same phonological code). This code must have been obtained lexically (because the nonlexical procedure gives *wrong* phonological codes to exception words). But correct access from orthography to *semantics* did not occur (otherwise the word would have been correctly defined). Therefore, models of the lexical procedure must be formulated in such a way that they allow access to lexical phonology to occur when access to semantics has not occurred.

Yet another piece of evidence for the independence of lexical phonology from semantic access comes from a patient already discussed in this chapter: W. B. (Funnell, 1983). W. B. read words aloud well, averaging about 85% correct. Because his nonlexical system for reading was nonexistent, his reading must have been entirely lexical. Funnell was able to show that access from a word (whether spoken or written) to its semantics was rather poor in this patient: Specifically, the patient often could only determine the general semantic category of the word. For example, when he saw the word *orange,* he would know that it was a kind of fruit but not which kind, and hence was unsure whether the word he was seeing was *orange* or *lemon,* though he would know it was not *glove.* Given this patient's inexactness of semantic access from print, he could not possibly have achieved his high accuracy level in reading aloud by proceeding to phonology via semantics, and he could not possibly have been reading nonlexically; so once again we are forced to adopt the view that there is a direct lexical pathway from orthography to phonology.

THE ARCHITECTURE OF THE READING SYSTEM

I began this chapter by pointing out that, if one adopts an information-processing approach to theorizing about reading, then attempting to understand what goes on when we read amounts to attempting to gain insights into the nature of the information-processing system that processes printed input. Consideration of various kinds of data from patients exhibiting various patterns of acquired dyslexia leads to the view that the reading system consists of two major components, a lexical processing procedure and a nonlexical processing procedure. More detailed scrutiny of data from acquired dyslexia provides suggestions about the structure of each procedure. Specifically, each procedure is itself composed of a particular set of component procedures in a particular configuration. Thus, we arrive at a certain conception of the architecture of the reading system, illustrated in Fig. 1.4.

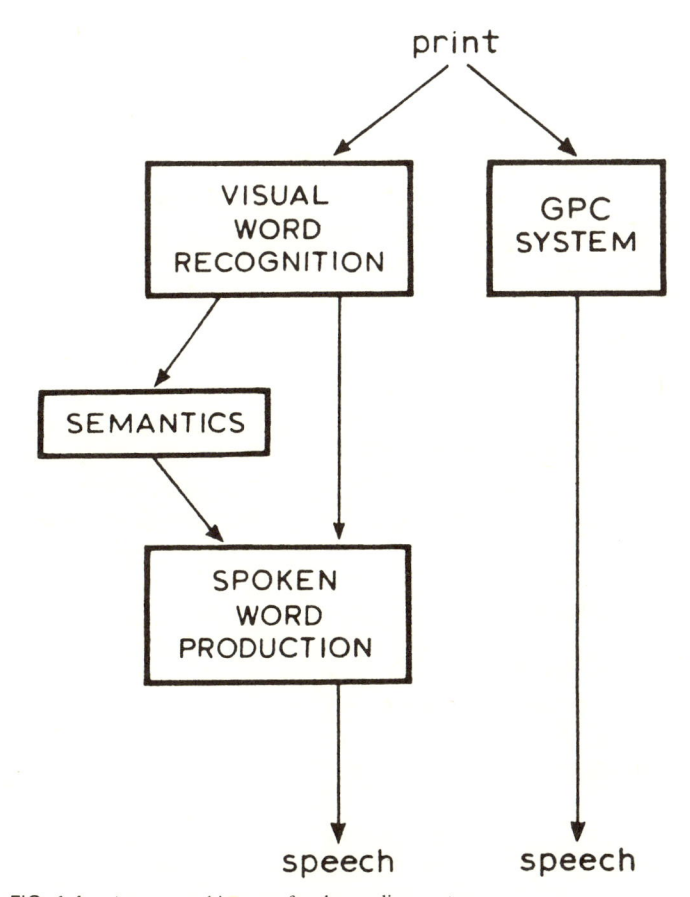

FIG. 1.4. A gross architecture for the reading system.

It would, of course, be entirely contrary to the spirit of cognitive neuropsychology to advance a view of the reading system derived from investigations of acquired reading disorders that was inconsistent with data from studies of normal reading. The system illustrated in Fig. 1.4 is, in fact, adequately compatible with what we know at present about processes involved in normal reading. More importantly, however, there are aspects of this proposed reading system that are meant to characterize normal reading but that have been discovered solely from studying disordered reading.

Consider, for example, the semantic priming effect observed in experiments on naming latency with normal subjects. Why is it that a normal subject is faster at naming the printed word *doctor* when the word *nurse* has just been seen than when the prior word is semantically unrelated to the word *doctor?* Two possibilities that have been considered as explanations for this effect are:

1. Within the visual word-recognition system, there is an associative network such that when a particular word is recognized, the detectors for semantically related words are primed.
2. There is a feedback loop from the semantic system to the visual word-recognition system; once a word contacts its representation in the semantic system, the representations of semantically related words in that system are activated, and these feed back onto their representations in the visual word-recognition system, thus facilitating subsequent recognition.

The patient M. P. (Bub, Canceliere & Kertesz, 1985), referred to earlier, allows us to adjudicate between these competing explanations of the semantic priming effect on naming latency. Even though she had almost entirely lost the capacity to comprehend single printed words, her mean naming latencies for such words were in the normal range and, furthermore, as is shown in Table 1.1, her naming latency showed an effect of word frequency. As already mentioned, access to the semantic system from print was almost entirely abolished for this patient. Therefore, if the semantic priming effect depends on access to the semantic system and subsequent feedback to the visual word-recognition system, M. P. should not show such priming in her naming performance. If, instead, the priming effect is produced by an associative network that is intrinsic to the visual word-recognition system, M. P. should show an effect of priming, at least for high-frequency words, because such words were still accessible in the visual word-recognition system (as shown by her ability to read most high-frequency exception words). Table 1.2 gives the results of an experiment on semantic priming of naming latency. Obviously, there is no priming effect, even though words are named very promptly. So we conclude that the semantic priming of word reading depends on accessing the meanings of words, rather than on being produced by some property of the visual word-recognition system. In contrast,

TABLE 1.1
Naming Latencies for Regular Words
in Patient M. P.[a]

	High Frequency	Low Frequency
Mean	619	671
SD	96	119

[a]From Bub, Canceliere, and Kertesz, 1985.

the word-frequency effect in naming cannot solely depend on the actions of the semantic system, because M. P., who names words without using the semantic system, showed a word-frequency effect in her naming latencies.[7]

It is not easy to think of any straightforward ways in which one might have investigated *normal* readers so as to reach these conclusions concerning the loci of the semantic priming and frequency effects. Hence, I offer this as an example where the study of acquired dyslexia has been superior to the study of normal reading *as a source of information about the normal reading system.*

The postulation of a lexical but nonsemantic pathway between visual word recognition and word phonology constitutes another example. We have seen that there are three quite different patterns of acquired dyslexia, all implying that a word can be read aloud lexically yet without semantic mediation. I know of no data from studies of intact readers that require one to propose that this lexical/nonsemantic route exists.

The time has now come to acknowledge that there is a little more to reading than the naming and comprehension of single words. To put this another way: I have discussed three linguistic domains relevant to reading (orthography, semantics, and phonology), but have not mentioned two other domains: morphology

TABLE 1.2
Naming Latencies for Primed and Unprimed
Words in Patient M. P.[a]

	Primed	Unprimed
Mean	588	594
SD	71	79

[a]From Bub, Canceliere, and Kertesz, 1985.

---

[7]The interpretation of these fascinating results is perhaps a little clouded by the possibility that naming latency in normal subjects is reduced by associative priming but not by semantic priming (Lupker, 1984). Because we do not know what forms of prime-target relationship existed in Bub's stimuli, we cannot be certain that *normal* subjects would have shown a priming effect with them.

and syntax. As soon as one considers reading beyond the single-word level, one can no longer continue to ignore morphological and syntactic processing. Fortunately, recent work on the cognitive neuropsychology of reading has dealt with both of these domains.

MORPHOLOGICAL PROCESSING

Among the problems evident in some patients with acquired dyslexia are specific difficulties in processing morphological structure during reading. The most obvious indication of such difficulties is the so-called *derivational error* (more properly, morphological error): The patient correctly processes the root morpheme of the word he or she is trying to read, but makes addition, deletion, or substitution errors in processing inflectional or derivational affixes. Such a patient might, for example, read *walked* as "walk," "walks," "walker," or "walking." Such errors are a prominent feature of, but are not confined to, the reading disorder known as deep dyslexia (Coltheart et al., 1980: see especially Chapter 14).

There are a number of different loci within the reading system at which processing difficulties might cause morphological errors in reading aloud. At least the following three possibilities are worth considering:[8]

1. *Input errors.* If there is a component within the visual word-recognition system that has the task of analyzing the morphological structure of printed words, damage to this component might be responsible for morphological errors in reading.

2. *Central errors.* A second possibility is that some aspect of a general morphological processing system concerned with the processing of affixes is damaged, and when morphologically complex words are presented to the morphological system by the visual word-recognition system, this damage causes morphological errors. This hypothetical central system would be one that is responsible for applying morphological knowledge to the processing of affixes irrespective of whether the input is spoken or printed.

---

[8] An error such as reading *walked* as "walk" could also, of course, be a visual error, like reading *wallet* as "wall". The possibility that morphological errors are really visual, not morphological, has not yet been conclusively refuted. It would be refuted if one could show that patients exist who make errors like *walked* → "walk" but not errors like *wallet* → "wall". This demonstration would be conclusive, however, only if there is control of both the imageability and the frequency of the whole words (walked vs. wallet) and also of their segments (walk vs. wall). I thank E. Funnell for pointing this out to me.

3. *Output errors.* Finally, it may be that the patient has difficulties in uttering the affix portions of affixed words (perhaps, for example, because they are usually unstressed).

Once one identifies the locus of morphological errors in any patient, then further studies of that patient can provide evidence concerning how morphological processing is normally carried out at the input or central or output stage.

Currently, my collaborators and I are investigating these possibilities by administering syntactic acceptability tests: Patients are presented single printed sentences and must judge whether they are grammatically correct or not. If the nongrammatical sentences in such tests are nongrammatical only because inappropriate affixes are used, then one can distinguish between various loci for morphological errors by giving the tests twice, once with written presentation and once with spoken presentation. A patient whose morphological processing deficit lies within the visual word-recognition system (or its communication to subsequent systems) will be able to tell that *he painter* is ungrammatical when he or she hears it but not when he or she sees it. A patient whose deficit is central, affecting the general ability to process morphology, will be equally impaired whether input is auditory or visual. Finally, a patient whose morphological errors in reading are only *output* errors will succeed with the syntactic acceptability task regardless of modality of input.[9]

Moody (1984) has used this approach with four acquired dyslexics: D. C., N. H., B. P., and B. S. All four of these patients exhibited the characteristics of phonological dyslexia (single-morpheme words were read well and nonwords read very badly) and all made frequent morphological errors in reading aloud inflected verbs presented as single words. As a first step toward identifying the locus of their morphological processing deficits, the patients were given the task of deciding whether sentences were syntactically acceptable or not; unacceptable sentences were unacceptable only because the verb inflection was incorrect. For example, sentences like *Tomorrow he will cooked the dinner* or *At this moment he is kicks the ball.* were used. The task was administered twice on separate occasions, once with the sentences spoken and once with them printed. The results, shown in Table 1.3, are clear. All patients are almost perfect with auditory presentation and almost at chance with visual presentation. The ungrammaticality of these sentences is solely morphological, so it is unlikely that the poor performance with visual presentation is due to a syntactic rather than a morphological deficit (especially because the same pattern of results was observed with two-word phrases as stimuli). It would seem, therefore, that these

---

[9]As Linebarger, Schwartz, and Saffran (1983) discuss, one needs to consider the possibility here of intonational cues to grammaticality in the auditory condition.

TABLE 1.3
Sentence Acceptability Judgments by Four Patients
with Acquired Dyslexia[a]

	Visual Presentation	Auditory Presentation
D. C.	.51[b]	1.00
N. H.	.66	1.00
B. P.	.55	.98
B. S.	.61	.98

[a]From Moody, 1984.
[b]Chance level is 0.50.

patients do not have a general problem at a central locus affecting all morphological processing, nor can their morphological errors in reading aloud just be output errors. All of them must have some problem involving a morphological processing procedure that is part of the visual word-recognition system. Hence, by studying these patients further we may learn more about this procedure.

In fact, there is a substantial body of literature, from studies of *normal* subjects, that concerns different theories about morphological processing during visual word recognition; see, for example, Henderson (1985b), Murrell and Morton (1974), Taft and Forster (1975) and Stanners, Neiser, and Painton (1979). It would thus seem appropriate, now that it is clear that these patients have difficulty at this stage of reading, to consider briefly such theories.

Because the number of English morphemes is far smaller than the number of English words, considerable economies of storage could be achieved if the units in the visual word-recognition system corresponded to individual morphemes rather than to individual words. A common way of putting this point is to argue that, because the words *look, looked, looks,* and *looking* share a common root morpheme with a fixed semantic representation, one might as well access this semantic representation via a single unit, *look,* in the visual recognition system, a unit used to recognize all the inflectional and derivational forms of this root morpheme. This storage economy would entail a considerable additional complexity of processing mechanisms. First, there must be some system of analysis of the printed input that allows a variety of printed forms to access the same recognition unit. Second, there would have to be some system that retained for subsequent use information about which particular affix had been present; otherwise the reader could not distinguish between various affixed forms of a particular root morpheme.

This view about word recognition appears to rest on the assumption that the meaning of a morphologically complex word is a direct function of the meanings of its constituent morphemes. This assumption is scarcely tenable (see, for example, Henderson, 1985b; Jackendoff, 1975), at least for derivational forms.

Take the three *-ion* nominalizations *action* (the result of acting), *ingestion* (the act of ingesting), and *congregation* (those who are congregating). The effect of the suffix on the meaning of the root is quite different in these three cases. Therefore, one cannot think of the suffix as having a constant meaning regardless of the root to which it is applied. Similar but much less severe difficulties exist for the assumption that the meaning of an *inflected* word corresponds to the meanings of its individual morphemes.

Disregarding these points, let us suppose that the members of any set of words having a common root morpheme (*find, finds, finding, finder*) are recognized via the same unit in the visual word-recognition system. How is this accomplished? One possibility is that all word beginnings or word endings that might be affixes are stripped from a printed word before access to the visual word-recognition system. There must be a system, in normal readers, that retains information about what affix was removed. If this system is damaged, morphological errors in reading aloud would occur.

This can be tested by using pseudoaffixed words such as *corner* or *master*. If the ending *-er* is removed from all words with that ending (regardless of whether the ending is a morpheme or not), and if patients make morphological errors in reading because they cannot retain these stripped segments, then pseudomorphological errors (reading *corner* as "corn") should be as common as true morphological errors (reading *caller* as "call"). Moody (1984), therefore, presented 10 words ending with *-er* as a true suffix and 10 words ending with an *-er* that was not a suffix to the four patients for reading aloud. Each item was presented twice on separate occasions. The results are shown in Table 1.4. Notice that pseudomorphological errors did not occur at all, which is evidence against the view that all potential affixes are stripped from words prior to access to the visual word-recognition system.[10]

A second theory that has been proposed concerning morphological processing in normal reading is that there is a first pass through the visual word-recognition system before any affix stripping is attempted. Monomorphemic words like *corner* will be found in this first pass because they exist as entries in this lexicon. Multimorphemic words will not be found: *Caller* does not exist in the lexicon because it is recognized via *call*, and so affix stripping is then attempted. In this view, if affix retention is impaired, morphological errors will occur in reading truly affixed words but not in reading pseudoaffixed words.

A technique used by Patterson (1980) allows one to test this theory. The patient is asked to judge whether letter strings are words or not. All the strings consist of a genuine root plus a genuine affix, but some are words (*calling*) and

---

[10] Because there were, for all the pseudoaffixed words, several different ways of adding letters at the end of the pseudostems of these stimuli to make real words, it does not seem likely that this result can be explained in terms of differential opportunity to guess correctly the word endings given only the stems or pseudostems.

TABLE 1.4
Reading Aloud of Genuinely Suffixed Words
and Matched Pseudosuffixed Words
in Four Cases of Acquired Dyslexia[a]

	Genuinely Suffixed Words	Pseudosuffixed Words
D. C.	.90	1.00
N. H.	.45	1.00
B. P.	.35	1.00
B. S.	.55	1.00

[a]From Moody, 1984.

others are not (*callest*). On the stripping-second view, none of these strings will be accessed in the first pass through the lexicon. The affixes will then be stripped, and, on the second pass, the roots will be found. But if patients who make morphological errors in reading aloud lose the affixes, they will be unable to judge whether the letter string is a word or not.

This is not how Moody's patients behaved, however. Their scores in a lexical decision task using such stimuli ranged from 56/60 correct to 59/60 correct. Hence, although when presented with a letter string such as *calling* they might read it as *calling, calls,* or *called,* this is not simply because they have lost information about the suffix prior to the word-recognition stage, because such loss would prevent them from being able to judge that the suffix in *calling* is appropriate whereas the suffix in *callest* is not.

Let us, therefore, entertain a third theory about morphological processing during reading. Let us suppose that *called* and *calling* have separate entries in the visual word-recognition system, but that the code that is transmitted from this system to higher stages of the reading system specifies the root morpheme and the form of inflection—*call* + ⟨past tense⟩ or *call* + ⟨present continuous⟩, for

TABLE 1.5
Reading Aloud of Morphologically Regular
Past Tenses and Morphologically Irregular
Past Tenses in Four Patients
with Acquired Dyslexia[a]

	Regular Past Tenses	Irregular Past Tenses
D. C.	.45	1.00
N. H.	.35	.95
B. P.	.25	.90
B. S.	.45	.90

[a]From Moody, 1984.

example. If this were so, one would expect it also to be true for morphologically irregular words like *bought*. Just as *called* = *call* + ⟨past tense⟩, so *bought* = *buy* + ⟨past tense⟩. In this view, morphological errors arise because the inflectional marker is lost. It follows that morphological errors should be observed even with morphologically irregular words like *buy;* a patient who sometimes reads *called* as "call" should sometimes read *bought* as "buy." So Moody (1984) selected a set of 20 past tenses of morphologically regular verbs and 20 past tenses of morphologically irregular verbs—past tenses such as *dug, shook,* and *bought*—matched with the regular verbs on word frequency. Percent correct oral reading for these items is shown in Table 1.5. Morphological errors in reading the irregular past tenses are almost entirely absent.[11,12]

I have proposed three accounts of how morphological processing might occur during reading, and have described evidence conflicting with all three accounts. This is the place to propose a fourth account, a theory of morphological decomposition during reading that can accommodate all this evidence. Unfortunately, I have been unable to think of one.

SYNTAX AND SENTENCE COMPREHENSION DURING READING

A number of authors have proposed that a sentence, once it has been seen (or heard), must be held in some form of buffer memory that serves as a source of data for the syntactic-analysis system; the buffer memory is considered to be crucial for preserving information about the *order* of the words in the sentence. This general view can be made more specific: It can be claimed that words accumulate in this buffer memory until the end of a sentence constituent (say, a clause) is reached, at which point syntactic analysis of the contents of the buffer is carried out, so that an abstract representation of the constituent's syntactic structure is produced. At this point, the contents of the buffer are no longer needed and so the buffer may be purged; this is the interpretation of his results offered by Jarvella (1970, 1971). A second way of being more specific about the nature of this buffer memory is to claim that words are represented in it in a phonological code, even when the sentence is presented visually (Baddeley, 1979; Baddeley & Lewis, 1981; Kleiman, 1975).

---

[11]Henderson (1985b) points out that errors of the kind *bought* → "buy" *can* be found in the responses of deep dyslexics (Coltheart, Patterson, & Marshall, 1980, Appendix 1). These may well be semantic errors, which are common in the reading of deep-dyslexic patients. Alternatively, morphological errors may arise at one stage in phonological dyslexia and at a different stage in deep dyslexia.

[12]As pointed out to me by A. Caramazza, it would be particularly interesting to have information about these patients' *comprehension* of these irregularly inflected forms.

There is good evidence that phonological coding is not needed for comprehension of single printed words. Such evidence is provided both by studies of normal readers (see, for example, Coltheart, 1980) and by data from acquired dyslexia. In the form of reading disorder known as deep dyslexia, the ability to recode a printed letter string into phonological form prior to accessing its lexical entry is completely abolished and the ability to retrieve the phonological forms of words from the lexicon is severely impaired, yet there can be substantial sparing of the ability to understand single printed words: Saffran and Marin (1977) estimated that a deep-dyslexic reader they studied had a reading comprehension vocabulary of 16,500 words.

If these views about normal reading are correct, then one ought to see a dramatic dissociation between single-word comprehension and sentence comprehension in patients with phonological impairments. Such impairments should result in a pattern of reading performance in which comprehension of single words is intact while comprehension of clauses and sentences is impaired. What is more, a specific prediction can be made about the form of this impairment: The patients will err precisely when they need adequate syntactic analyses to understand the clauses or sentences. I discuss four relevant studies.

The first is that of Caramazza et al. (1981). Their patient, M. C., had a severe repetition deficit (digit span of only one item with auditory presentation, two items with visual presentation), coupled with good comprehension of single printed or spoken words. The short-term memory impairment existed even when there was no requirement to repeat the items (in probed recognition memory of four-word lists), so the deficit was of storage, not of output. Assuming that the buffer memory used in repetition and probed recognition is the buffer store needed for sentence comprehension, M. C. should be impaired at comprehending sentences.

This was tested using sentence–picture matching: M. C. saw or heard a sentence and then had to choose the matching picture from a set of four. Two types of sentences were used. Some were semantically nonreversible sentences such as *The dog is eating the bone* and here the three distractor pictures consisted of one with the nouns altered and two with both nouns and the verb altered, syntactic structure remaining unaltered. The remaining sentences were semantically reversible, such as *The dog is chasing the cat,* and here there was there was one distractor picture with nouns changed, one with nouns and verb changed, and one with the nouns reversed, i.e., "a syntactic distractor", here a picture in which it is the cat which is doing the chasing. The results are shown in Table 1.6.

M. C. did make some lexical errors, but the main effect here is that he was far worse at understanding the reversible than the nonreversible sentences, and frequently chose the syntactic distractors when sentences were reversible. Perfect performance with the nonreversible sentences could be achieved without any appreciation of the syntactic structure of the sentence: All that is needed is to

TABLE 1.6
Sentence–Picture Matching by Patient M. C.[a]

Sentence Type	Presentation Mode	Total Correct	Error Type Lexical	Error Type Syntactic
Nonreversible	Auditory	32	4	—
	Visual	29	7	—
Reversible	Auditory	21	2	13
	Visual	16	9	11

[a]From Caramazza, Basili, Koller, and Berndt, 1981.

comprehend the two nouns and the verb. With the reversible sentences, however, to distinguish between the correct picture and the syntactic distractor it is essential to determine syntactic structure and assign thematic roles to the nouns of the sentence. M. C.'s difficulties with such sentences are what we would expect to see if the buffer memory whose severe impairment is revealed by his repetition performance is also used to hold the words of a printed (or heard) sentence while syntactic analyses are carried out. Alternatively, M. C.'s difficulties might be due to impaired syntactic processing: He may be imperfect at assigning thematic roles correctly to nouns in sentences he hears or sees.

Similar results were obtained in studies of a rather different kind of patient, J. S. (Caramazza, Berndt, & Basili, 1983). This patient performed extremely poorly on a very wide range of tasks involving phonological processing, even comprehension or repetition of single spoken words. His comprehension of single *printed* words, on the other hand, was excellent. His comprehension of printed sentences was tested by sentence–picture matching. With sentences like *The block is under the pyramid,* he made virtually no errors when the distractor involved a different spatial preposition (a picture of a block beside a pyramid) or a different noun (a picture of a block under a ball). However, when the distractor picture was the reversal of the correct one (a picture of a pyramid under a block), performance was not much above chance (16/24 correct, chance 12/24). Thus, when J. S. reads a sentence such as the example just given, he knows that it describes a vertical alignment and that it is about a block and a pyramid, but is very poor at the syntactic analysis required for the determination of the relationship of the two nouns to the spatial preposition.

As mentioned previously, this result could be due either to a defect of an input buffer needed to hold sentences while they are being processed syntactically and morphologically *or* to a defect of the syntactic or morphological processing systems. However, the latter form of defect appears to be indicated by results obtained with a different task: sentence acceptability judgment. This patient correctly rejected every anomalous sentence he was shown when the anomaly was semantic (e.g., *The barber captured the razor.*) but when anomalies were only syntactic/morphological (e.g., *The girl will dressing the doll.*), he detected the anomaly in only one out of 10 instances.

The patient described by Vallar and Baddeley (1984) had a less severe impairment of the buffer memory, as her digit span was three (auditory presentation), and she did not make errors in comprehending reversible sentences up to eight words long (such as *The boy shows the cat to the dog.*) even when the distractor picture was the reversal of the correct one. Because the capacity of her buffer memory was merely somewhat reduced (rather than being close to zero, as was the case with M. C. and J. S.), Vallar and Baddeley reasoned that syntactic processing deficits in reading comprehension might show up if longer sentences were used. They thus devised a sentence-acceptability test using sentences averaging about 16 words in length. When anomalies were semantic (e.g., the acceptable sentence *There is no doubt that champagne is something that can be bought in shops.* versus the anomalous sentence *It is true that physicians comprise a profession that is manufactured in factories, from time to time.*), the patient's performance was almost flawless, both with auditory presentation (26/28 correct) and with visual (26/28 correct). However, when the anomalies were produced by interchanging two words but leaving the sentence still grammatically correct (e.g., *One could reasonably claim that sailors are often lived in by ships of various kinds.*), the patient did not perform significantly above chance with either modality of presentation—that is, she could not detect anomalies when these were produced solely by altering the order of words in sentences.

The final case I wish to mention is described by Bub, Black, Howell, and Kertesz (1985). This patient differed from the other three cases in that her syntactic processing deficit was confined to reading and did not appear for sentences she heard. She was good at detecting semantic anomalies, such as in *The bird flew up the book.*, with either spoken or printed sentences. When the anomaly was produced by altering word order to make a sentence ungrammatical (e.g., *They gave me ride a home.*), her performance was good for spoken sentences (87% correct) but exactly at chance for printed sentences. The modality specificity of this deficit is particularly interesting, though one would need to find a way of ruling out an explanation in terms of intonational cues (see footnote 9). Furthermore, this task involved sentence-grammaticality judgments, not sentence comprehension, and the relationship between these two sentence-processing tasks is not yet clear.

There is no doubt that these studies of sentence comprehension in patients with phonological impairments and/or defective short-term auditory/verbal memory are particularly interesting. There is also no doubt that much more remains to be done before we can be sure exactly what the studies are telling us about sentence comprehension. A number of points need to be made here. First, all of this work depends on arguments by association, and so is vulnerable to the possibility that a patient might turn up tomorrow in whom a sentence-comprehension defect dissociates from a phonological or short-term memory defect.

Second, we have not yet learned very much from this work about the nature of the syntactic and morphological processing needed for sentence comprehension; it is important to show that this processing uses some kind of phonologically coded input buffer, but that does not tell us very much about the nature of the processing itself. Third, the sentence-processing tasks used so far are a somewhat heterogeneous collection, and we need explicit theories about how each one (sentence-grammaticality judgment, semantic-anomaly judgment, and sentence–picture matching) is normally performed if we are to learn anything detailed from abnormalities of performance (or we need to use such abnormalities to develop the theories). Last, it is essential to be able to distinguish abnormalities of sentence processing due to impaired memory for input (especially input order) from abnormalities due to impaired syntactic or morphological processing of that input, even though both forms of abnormality are interesting and important for the understanding of sentence comprehension.

CONCLUSIONS

Although I have chosen in this chapter to focus largely on reading, because in my view it is there that cognitive neuropsychology is at present most advanced, I nevertheless argue that important insights into the normal functioning of other cognitive processes, particularly visual-object recognition, spoken-sentence comprehension, and working memory, have certainly been achieved by studies of people with impaired abilities in these spheres. Simply to show that a particular model of normal functioning is consistent with a variety of patterns of abnormal functioning constitutes a contribution to cognitive psychology as well as to neuropsychology, but, I have argued, cognitive neuropsychology already does more than this. I have given examples in which adjudications between competing theories of normal processing have been achieved by appropriate studies of abnormal processing; I have given examples in which aspects of existing models that would have been difficult to elucidate by studying normal subjects have been clarified by studying people with cognitive disorders; and I have given examples indicating how, in cases in which a satisfactory theory of normal processing has not yet been achieved, studies of abnormal processing can be used to constrain future theorizing about normal processing.

ACKNOWLEDGMENTS

I am extremely grateful to the following for criticisms of an earlier draft of this chapter: A. D. Baddeley, R. Berndt, D. Besner, M. Black, D. E. Broadbent, S. Byng, R. Campbell, D. Caplan, A. Caramazza, M. Davies, A. W. Ellis, E. Funnell, L. Henderson, D.

Howard, R. Job, R. Lesser, A. J. Marcel, G. Miceli, S. Moody, J. Morton, F. Newcombe, K. E. Patterson, J. Riddoch, E. Saffran, G. Sartori, and G. Vallar.

REFERENCES

Baddeley, A. D. (1979). Working memory and reading. In P. A. Kolers, M. E. Wrolstad, & H. Bouma (Eds.), *The processing of visible language* (pp. 355–370). New York: Plenum.

Baddeley, A. D. (1982). Implications of neuropsychological evidence for theories of normal memory. In D. E. Broadbent, & L. Weiskrantz, (Eds.), *The neuropsychology of cognitive function* (pp. 59–72). London: The Royal Society.

Baddeley, A. D., & Lewis, M. (1981). Inner active processes in reading. In A. M. Lesgold & C. A. Perfetti, (Eds.), *Interactive processes in reading* (pp. 107–129). Hillsdale, NJ: Lawrence Erlbaum Associates.

Baron, J. (1973). Phonemic stage not necessary for reading. *Quarterly Journal of Experimental Psychology, 25,* 241–246.

Baron, J., & Strawson, C. (1976). Use of orthographic and word-specific knowledge in reading words aloud. *Journal of Experimental Psychology: Human Perception and Performance, 2,* 386–393.

Beauvois, M.-F., & Derouesne, J. (1979). Phonological alexia: Three dissociations. *Journal of Neurology, Neurosurgery and Psychiatry, 42,* 1115–1124.

Bub, D., Black, S., Howell, J., & Kertesz, A. (1985). Speech output processes and reading. In M. Coltheart, R. Job, & G. Sartori (Eds.), *The cognitive neuropsychology of language.* London: Lawrence Erlbaum Associates Limited.

Bub, D., Canceliere, A., & Kertesz, A. (1985). Whole-word and analytic translation of spelling to sound in a non-semantic reader. In K. E. Patterson, J. C. Marshall, & M. Coltheart (Eds.), *Surface dylexia: Cognitive and neuropsychological studies of phonological reading.* London: Lawrence Erlbaum Associates Limited.

Campbell, R., & Besner, D. (1981). This and thap: Constraints on the production of new, written words. *Quarterly Journal of Experimental Psychology, 33A,* 375–396.

Caramazza, A., Basili, A. G., Koller, J., & Berndt, R. S. (1981). An investigation of repetition and language processing in a case of conduction aphasia. *Brain and Language, 14,* 235–271.

Caramazza, A., & Berndt, R. (in press). A multi-component deficit view of agrammatic Broca's aphasia. In M.-L. Kean, (Ed.), *Agrammatism.* New York: Academic.

Caramazza, A., Berndt, R., & Basili, A. M. (1983). The selective impairment of phonological processing. *Brain and Language, 18,* 128–174.

Coltheart, M. (1978). Lexical access in simple reading tasks. In G. Underwood (Ed.), *Strategies of information-processing* (pp. 151–216). London: Academic.

Coltheart, M. (1980). Reading, phonological coding and deep dyslexia. In M. Coltheart, K. E. Patterson, & J. C. Marshall (Eds.), *Deep dyslexia* (pp. 197–226). London: Routledge & Kegan Paul.

Coltheart, M., Masterson, J., Byng, S., Prior, M., & Riddoch, J. (1983). Surface dyslexia. *Quarterly Journal of Experimental Psychology, 35A,* 469–496.

Coltheart, M., Patterson, K. E., & Marshall, J. C. (Eds.) (1980). *Deep dyslexia.* London: Routledge & Kegan Paul.

Ellis, A. W. (1982). Spelling and writing (and reading and speaking). In A. W. Ellis (Ed.), *Normality and pathology in cognitive function* (pp. 113–146). London: Academic.

Fodor, J. A. (1983). *The modularity of mind.* Cambridge, MA: MIT Press.

Funnell, E. (1983). Phonological processes in reading: New evidence from acquired dyslexia. *British Journal of Psychology, 74,* 159–180.

Glushko, R. J. (1979a). The organization and activation of orthographic knowledge in reading aloud. *Journal of Experimental Psychology: Human Perception and Performance, 5,* 674–691.

Glushko, R. J. (1979b). *The psychology of phonography: Reading aloud by orthographic activation and phonological synthesis.* Ph.D. dissertation, University of California, San Diego.

Glushko, R. J. (1981). Principles for pronouncing print: The psychology of phonography. In A. M. Lesgold & C. A. Perfetti (Eds.), *Interactive processes in reading* (pp. 61–84). Hillsdale, NJ: Lawrence Erlbaum Associates.

Henderson, L. (1982).*Orthography and word recognition in reading.* London: Academic.

Henderson, L. (1985a). Issues in the modelling of pronunciation assembly in normal reading. In K. E. Patterson, J. C. Marshall, & M. Coltheart (Eds.), *Surface dyslexia: Cognitive and neuropsychological studies of phonological reading.* London: Lawrence Erlbaum Associates Limited.

Henderson, L. (1985b). Toward a psychology of morphemes. In A. W. Ellis (Ed.), *Progress in the psychology of language* (Vol. 1). London: Lawrence Erlbaum Associates Limited.

Jackendoff, R. S. (1975). Morphological and semantic regularities in the lexicon. *Language, 51,* 639–671.

Jarvella, R. J. (1970). Effects of syntax on running memory span for connected discourse. *Psychonomic Science, 19,* 235–236.

Jarvella, R. J. (1971). Syntactic processing of connected discourse. *Journal of Verbal Learning and Verbal Behavior, 10,* 409–416.

Kay, J. (1985). Mechanisms of oral reading: A critical appraisal of cognitive models. In A. W. Ellis (Ed.), *Progress in the psychology of language* (Vol. 1). London: Lawrence Erlbaum Associates Limited.

Kay, J., & Lesser, R. (1985). The nature of phonological processing in oral reading: Evidence from surface dyslexia. *Quarterly Journal of Experimental Psychology, 37A,* 39–82.

Kay, J., & Marcel, A. J. (1981). One process, not two, in reading aloud: Lexical analogies do the work of non-lexical rules. *Quarterly Journal of Experimental Psychology, 33A,* 397–414.

Kleiman, G. (1975). Speech recoding in reading. *Journal of Verbal Learning and Verbal Behavior, 24,* 323–339.

LaBerge, D. (1972). Beyond auditory coding. In J. F. Kavanagh, & I. G. Mattingly, (Eds.), *Language by eye and by ear* (pp. 241–248). Cambridge, MA: MIT Press.

Linebarger, M., Schwartz, M., & Saffran, E. (1983). Sensitivity to grammatical structure in so-called agrammatic aphasics. *Cognition, 13,* 361–392.

Lupker, S. J. (1984). Semantic priming without association: a second look. *Journal of Verbal Learning, 23,* 709–733.

Marcel, A. J. (1980). Surface dyslexia and beginning reading: A revised hypothesis of the pronunciation of print and its impairments. In M. Coltheart, K. E. Patterson, & J. C. Marshall (Eds.), *Deep dyslexia* (pp. 227–258). London: Routledge & Kegan Paul.

Marshall, J. C., & Newcombe, F. (1966). Syntactic and semantic errors in paralexia. *Neuropsychologia, 4,* 169–176.

Marshall, J. C., & Newcombe, F. (1973). Patterns of paralexia. *Journal of Psycholinguistic Research, 4,* 169–176.

Mehler, J., Morton, J., & Jusczyk, A. W. (1984). On reducing language to biology. *Cognitive Neuropsychology, 1,* 83–116.

Meyer, D., Schvaneveldt, R., & Ruddy, M., (1974). Functions of graphemic and phonemic codes in visual word recognition. *Memory and Cognition, 2,* 309–321.

Moody, S. (1984). *Agrammatic reading in phonological dyslexia.* Ph.D. thesis, University of London.

Murrell, G., & Morton, J. (1974). Word recognition and morphemic structure. *Journal of Experimental Psychology, 102,* 963–968.

Neisser, U. (1976). *Cognition and reality.* San Francisco: Freeman.

Neisser, U. (1983). Components of intelligence or steps in routine procedures? *Cognition, 15,* 189–197.
Newcombe, F., & Marshall, J. C. (1985). Reading and writing by letter-sounds. In K. E. Patterson, J. C. Marshall, & M. Coltheart (Eds.), *Surface dyslexia: Cognitive and neuropsychological studies of phonological reading.* London: Lawrence Erlbaum Associates Limited.
Parkin, A. J. (1982). Phonological recoding in lexical decision: Effects of spelling-to-sound regularity depend on how regularity is defined. *Memory and Cognition, 10,* 43–53.
Parkin, A. J. (1984). Redefining the regularity effect. *Memory and Cognition, 12,* 287–292.
Patterson, K. E. (1980). Derivational errors. In M. Coltheart, K. E. Patterson, & J. C. Marshall (Eds.), *Deep dyslexia* (pp. 286–306). London: Routledge & Kegan Paul.
Patterson, K. E. (1982). The relation between reading and phonological coding: Further neuropsychological observations. In A. W. Ellis (Ed.), *Normality and pathology in cognitive functions* (pp. 77–112). London: Academic.
Patterson, K. E., & Marcel, A. J. (1977). Aphasia, dyslexia and the phonological coding of written words. *Quarterly Journal of Experimental Psychology, 29,* 307–318.
Patterson, K. E., Marshall, J. C., & Coltheart, M. (1985). *Surface dyslexia: Cognitive and neuropsychological studies of phonological reading.* London: Lawrence Erlbaum Associates Limited.
Patterson, K. E., & Morton, J. (1985). From orthography to phonology: An attempt at an old interpretation. In K. E. Patterson, J. C. Marshall, & M. Coltheart (Eds.), *Surface dyslexia: Cognitive and neuropsychological studies of phonological reading.* London: Lawrence Erlbaum Associates Limited.
Posner, M. I., Cohen, Y., & Rafal, R. D. (1982). Neural systems control of spatial orienting. In D. E. Broadbent & L. Weiskrantz, (Eds.), *The neuropsychology of cognitive function* (pp. 187–198). London: The Royal Society.
Saffran, E., & Marin, O. S. M. (1977). Reading without phonology: Evidence from aphasia. *Quarterly Journal of Experimental Psychology, 29,* 515–525.
Saffran, E., Schwartz, M., & Marin, O. S. M. (1976). Semantic mechanisms in paralexia. *Brain and Language, 3,* 255–265.
Saffran, E., Schwartz, M., & Marin, O. S. M. (1980). The word order problem in agrammatism: II. Production. *Brain and Language, 10,* 263–280.
Schwartz, M., Saffran, E., & Marin, O. S. M. (1980). Fractionating the reading process in dementia: Evidence for word-specific print-to-sound associations. In M. Coltheart, K. E. Patterson, & J. C. Marshall, (Eds.), *Deep dyslexia* (pp. 259–269). London: Routledge & Kegan Paul.
Seidenberg, M. S., Waters, G., Barnes, M. A., & Tanenhaus, M. K. (1984). When does irregular spelling and pronunciation affect word recognition? *Journal of Verbal Learning and Verbal Behaviour, 23,* 383–404.
Shallice, T. (1982). Specific impairments of planning. In D. E. Broadbent & L. Weiskrantz (eds.), *The neuropsychology of cognitive function* (pp. 199–210). London: The Royal Society.
Shallice, T., & McCarthy, R. (1985). Phonological reading: From patterns of impairments to possible procedures. In K. E. Patterson, J. C. Marshall, & M. Coltheart (Eds.), *Surface dyslexia: Cognitive and neuropsychological studies of phonological reading.* London: Lawrence Erlbaum Associates Limited.
Shallice, T., & Warrington, E. K. (1970). Independent functioning of verbal memory stores: A neuropsychological study. *Quarterly Journal of Experimental Psychology, 22,* 261–273.
Shallice, T., & Warrington, E. K. (1975). Word recognition in a phonemic dyslexic patient. *Quarterly Journal of Experimental Psychology, 27,* 187–199.
Shallice, T., & Warrington, E. K., (1980). Single and multiple component central dyslexic syndromes. In M. Coltheart, K. E. Patterson, & J. C. Marshall (Eds.), *Deep dyslexia* (pp. 119–145). London: Routledge & Kegan Paul.

Shallice, T., Warrington, E. K., & McCarthy, R. (1983). Reading without semantics. *Quarterly Journal of Experimental Psychology, 35A,* 111–138.

Stanners, R. F., Neiser, J. J., & Painton, S. (1979). Memory representation of prefixed words. *Journal of Verbal Learning and Verbal Behaviour, 18,* 733–743.

Taft, M., & Forster, K. I. (1975). Lexical storage and retrieval of prefixed words. *Journal of Verbal Learning and Verbal Behaviour, 14,* 638–647.

Vallar, G., & Baddeley, A. D. (1984). Phonological short-term store, phonological processing, and sentence comprehension: A neuropsychological study. *Cognitive Neuropsychology, 1,* 121–142.

Warrington, E. K. (1982). The fractionation of arithmetic skills: A single case study. *Quarterly Journal of Experimental Psychology, 34A,* 31–52.

TUTORIAL REVIEWS

2
Aspects of Cortical Organization Related to Selective Attention and Selective Impairments of Visual Perception: A Tutorial Review

A. Cowey
Oxford University

ABSTRACT

There are several projection pathways from the eye to the brain. Their cells are physiologically as well as morphologically different. Although the projection from the lateral geniculate nucleus is directed almost exclusively to the primary visual cortex (V1) in primates, there is extensive segregation even within this pathway. From V1 information is distributed to additional visual areas along pathways with characteristic contrasting properties. There are at least 12 different visual areas and collectively they cover more than a third of the entire neocortex in monkeys. Although they are extensively interconnected there is good evidence that the resulting "cross-talk" does not eradicate the parallel processing. Perceptual signs of the latter can be seen in monkeys and patients with focal brain damage. The main advantage of multiple visual maps may be economy of connections, ease of specifying them and minimizing errors during development, and permitting ontogenetic or evolutionary changes in one process without necessarily affecting others. They may also make it easier to inhibit particular groups of cells in connection with selective attention; evidence is presented for the existence of several types of cortical inhibitory neurons that may have this role.

INTRODUCTION

No experimental psychologist, especially one concerned with information processing, can fail to be aware of the pervasive influence of ideas about serial and parallel processing on our ideas about how the brain works. What I try to do in this chapter, if possible without getting bogged down in a detailed consideration of the extent to which processing is serial or parallel, is describe anatomical and physiological evidence for parallel processing within the visual pathways, attempt to relate this evidence to selective disorders of visual perception in neurological patients and in experimental animals, and consider the possible advantages of parallelism, including the idea that it assists selective attention.

PARALLEL PATHWAYS IN VISION FROM EYE TO BRAIN

Anatomical Studies

It has been known for many years that there are several different morphological types of retinal ganglion cells in primates (see Boycott & Dowling, 1969, for a review). They were revealed by the Golgi method, which, apparently at random, impregnates a small proportion of neurones and, if one is lucky, displays the entire cell body, axon, and dendritic array. No one has yet found a better method of displaying small numbers of neurones, but the Golgi method reveals nothing about the destination of the axons of impregnated retinal ganglion cells nor does it reveal the total number of different cell types. Moreover, because small numbers are involved, the relative proportions of different cell types may be unrepresentative. These problems have recently been overcome by injecting the retrogradely transported enzyme horseradish peroxidase (HRP) into the optic nerve, from which it back fills all types of retinal ganglion cells, or into discrete parts of the brain, from which it back fills only ganglion cells projecting to those regions. By appropriate histochemical methods the labeled ganglion cells can be displayed in flat mounts of the entire retina.

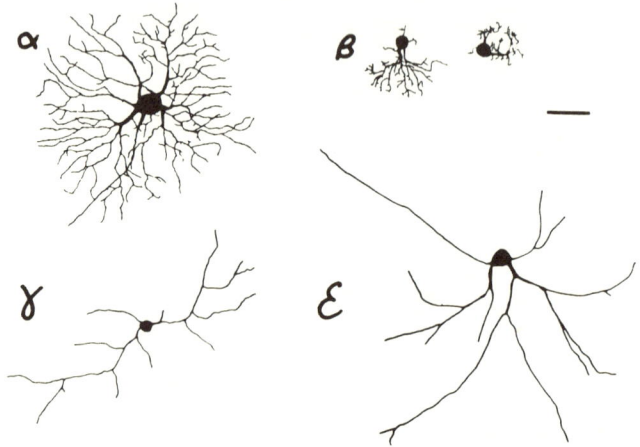

FIG. 2.1. Drawings of HRP-filled retinal ganglion cells from the rhesus monkey to show the four main types. All four lay about 7 mm from the fovea—that is, at an eccentricity of roughly 30 degrees. Scale bar = 50 μm. (From Perry & Cowey, 1984; Perry et al., 1984).

When deposited in the optic nerve, HRP reveals four classes of ganglion cells in macaque monkeys (see Fig. 2.1; see also Perry & Cowey, 1981, 1984; Perry, Oehler, & Cowey, 1984). At any given eccentricity from the fovea, α cells have larger cell bodies and dendritic fields than β cells, but in both the dendritic tree is profusely branched, even when it is very small, as in foveal β cells. γ cells have small cell bodies, like β cells, but a large and sparsely branched dendritic tree. ε cells are similar but the cell body is larger and the sparse dendrites are stouter. α cells almost certainly correspond to the parasol cells of Polyak (1941) and diffuse stratified cells of Boycott and Dowling (1969) as described in Golgi material; β cells correspond to Polyak's midget ganglion cells; γ and ε cells correspond to the small-diffuse and garland cells of Polyak and the unstratified cells of Boycott and Dowling. This simple quadripartite classification into α, β, γ, and ε ignores finer distinctions based on the level or levels at which the dendrites branch in the inner plexiform layer.

When HRP is injected into different visual nuclei of the thalamus or midbrain, a very different pattern of results is found (Leventhal, Rodieck, & Dreher, 1981; Perry et al., 1984). First, only β cells project to the four parvocellular layers of the dorsal lateral geniculate nucleus. Second, when the magnocellular layers are injected, α cells are labeled, plus a few small cells too poorly filled to be certain whether they are β or γ. They could even be β cells spuriously labeled as a result of their fibers' traversing the magnocellular layers en route to the parvocellular layers. Third, injections in the midbrain label predominantly γ and ε cells; only a few α cells and no β cells are labeled. In other words, the different cell types show conspicuous segregation with respect to their targets in the brain.

How many of each type are there? By labeling all ganglion cells that project to the midbrain it can be shown that there are about 110,000 γ and ε cells. Injections of HRP into magnocellular dLGN back fill about 10% of the ganglion cells in the center of the labeled area of the retina at all retinal positions. As there are about 1.4×10^6 retinal ganglion cells in each eye, the number of α cells is about 140,000. The remaining majority—that is, about 1,150,000—must therefore be β cells, a conclusion supported by the observation that HRP deposited in the optic nerve labels predominantly β cells.

Although the cell types projecting to other, and much smaller, nuclei have not been studied (perigeniculate, accessory, suprachiasmatic), the overall pattern of segregation could hardly be abolished whatever the retinal innervation of these nuclei.

Turning to the routes by which visual information first reaches the cortex, it is now clear that the segregation persists. The methods of uncovering it are to study patterns of degenerating terminals following very small lesions in the thalamus or midbrain, or by injecting transportable substances into cell groups in the thalamus. The results of several experiments are shown schematically in Fig. 2.2, in which the principal lamination of the striate cortex is shown according to Brodmann's (1909) scheme. The most striking features are that the parvocellular

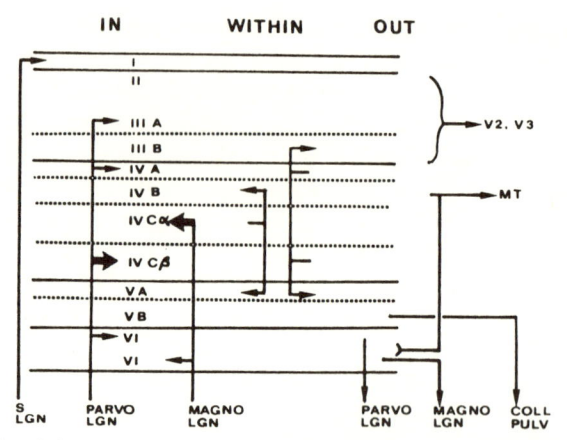

FIG. 2.2. Schematic diagram of the laminae of the striate cortex (V1) in the monkey to show: (1) the main projections from the lateral geniculate nucleus; (2) connections within V1; (3) cortical and subcortical projections from V1. The two most conspicuous input pathways are shown by heavy arrows. According to Ungerleider (personal communication), V3 receives its input from layer IVB of V1—that is, the projection does not even overlap that to V2. Abbreviations: S, superficial; parvo, parvocellular; magno, magnocellular; coll, superior colliculus; pulv, inferior pulvinar.

LGN, representing perhaps the entire population of β cells, projects heavily to layers IVA and IVCβ, and sparsely to the upper part of VI. In addition, there is an input from parvocellular layers to isolated groups of cells in layers II and III (the so-called cytochrome oxidase puffs). The magnocellular layers, representing α cells, project to IVCα and sparsely to lower VI. Moreover, there is evidence that the spiny stellate cells in the various subdivisions of layer IV have their dendrites confined to a particular sublamina—that is, the clear laminar separation of different geniculate imputs is not simply anulled by recipient cells whose dendrites span all layers (Lund, Henry, MacQueen, & Harvey, 1979). The parvocellular recipient zones of layer IV project in turn to layers IIIB and VA, whereas the magnocellular recipient layer IVCα projects to IVB and VA (Lund & Boothe, 1975). Even further translaminar connections have been described in cats (Gilbert & Wiesel, 1979) but there is still no accepted general scheme for primates.

There may be two further parallel geniculocortical pathways. Beneath the magnocellular dLGN layers are two thin and previously overlooked S laminae. They receive a sparse retinal input (Compos-Ortega & Hayhow, 1972; Kaas, Huerta, Weber, & Harting, 1978), and in the bush baby (Carey, Fitzpatrick, & Diamond, 1979) the cells project to layer I of the striate cortex. A similar projection from the ventral C layers of LGN in the cat is known to be physiologically different (W type) from the two other main geniculostriate pathways (X and

Y), leading to the interesting suggestion that in primates too there is a physiologically W-like pathway that innervates layer I of the striate cortex.

The final pathway from LGN to cortex was uncovered even more recently. HRP injections in the prestriate cortex label a population of cells throughout all layers of dLGN (Benevento & Yoshida, 1981; Bullier & Kennedy, 1983; Fries, 1981; Yukie & Iwai, 1981). In size they are intermediate between parvo- and magnocellular neurones, they survive removal of the striate cortex, and at a rough estimate they form less than 1% of geniculate neurones. Their physiological properties and laminar termination outside the striate cortex are unknown. Anatomically they are in a position to contribute to the residual visual sensitivity that survives removal of the striate cortex and which, in man, is not accompanied by any acknowledgment of visual experience—that is, "blindsight" (Weiskrantz, 1980; Weiskrantz, Warrington, Sanders, & Marshall, 1974).

Physiological Studies

The results of recording from single retinal ganglion cells have been reviewed by de Monasterio (1981). There are three main types. Ganglion cells of the first type are spectrally opponent, they form about 85% of ganglion cells representing the fovea, they are X-like in showing linear spatial summation within the receptive field and having slow conduction velocities, they have the smallest receptive fields, and they can be antidromically activated from dLGN but not from midbrain. Cells with these physiological properties are found in parvocellular LGN. There is, therefore, overwhelming evidence that retinal β cells are the substrate of the X-like high-resolution color-opponent system projecting to layers IVa and IVCB of the striate cortex.

The second physiological type of ganglion cell is spatially but not spectrally opponent, has receptive field centers up to four times as large as those of the first type, has faster conduction velocities, and has Y-type nonlinear spatial summation in the receptive field surround. These cells project to the LGN, where cells with similar properties occur in magnocellular layers, and in small numbers to the superior colliculus. Thus, there is equally strong evidence that retinal α cells are the substrate of the spectrally broad-band, highly contrast-sensitive, Y-like input to layer IVCα of striate cortex.

The third and last group is physiologically heterogeneous, and represents about 10% of ganglion cells. The most common have large receptive fields, poorly defined spatial opponency, nonlinear spatial summation, the lowest conduction velocities, and no color opponency. They project to tectum and pretectum and rarely to LGN. It would be surprising if they did not represent the output of retinal γ and ϵ cells. Physiologically, there are grounds for likening them to W cells as described in the cat, but there is as yet no evidence that they innervate the S laminae of LGN and hence layer I of the striate cortex.

CORTICAL VISUAL AREAS

Gross Organization

In 1881 there occurred a famous encounter between Goltz and Ferrier on the notion of Localization of Function in the Cerebral Cortex, which Goltz opposed. In 1981, at a meeting in Oxford to celebrate the centenary of that influential debate, no one questioned the idea that different parts of the cortex did different things (see Phillips, Zeki, & Barlow, 1984, for an account of the meeting). But it proved surprisingly difficult to decide how to characterize a cortical area—for example, a visual area. One way is to insist that there is a topographic map of all or part of the retina. Another is to include a region in which there may be no visuospatial map but in which some other set of visual qualities is represented— for example, a cortical representation in which something like color or faces (sic) are coded irrespective of their position on the retina. A third is to say that a region *within* which there are intercalated groups of neurones each concerned with separate visual qualities (e.g., color and orientation) is one visual area not two, especially if there is an abrupt change in the properties of cells in every layer at the borders with other areas. Finally, it might be said of a visual area that the vast majority of cells should respond selectively in association with visual stimuli and not with nonvisual stimuli or with eye movements in darkness. The last requirement would exclude polysensory areas and areas like frontal eye fields. Some of the discussion in 1981 perhaps reflected the hair splitting beloved of academics, but it has an underlying seriousness. In what follows a visual area is loosely defined as a region where there is a visuotopic representation or, failing that, where some other set of visual characteristics is represented.

Even as recently as 1960, in a discussion of evidence for two secondary visual areas in rabbits, it was possible (Brindley, 1960) to write: "There is not yet any evidence for the existence of such widely diffused visual afferent fibres to the cortex in primates; but it would not be surprising if some were discovered" [p. 116]. Since then additional visual areas have been discovered in the cortex of monkeys at a rate of about one every 2 years, and the posterior third of the entire cerebral cortex is now a patchwork quilt of visual areas. Almost every review of their properties is incomplete when it appears, but those by Cowey (1981), Zeki (1978, 1982), Allman, Baker, Newsome, and Peterson (1981), Van Essen and Maunsell (1983), Gattass, Sousa, and Covey (1985), are reasonably comprehensive. Fig. 2.3 shows the position in the brain of the rhesus monkey of the dozen or so visual areas. Their extent and precise positions almost certainly vary between animals (Van Essen, Newsome, & Maunsell, 1984), so the maps are far from being an atlas. In Fig. 2.3 the intraparietal, lunate, superior temporal, and inferior occipital sulci have been opened to reveal their depths, which are often more complicated than portrayed here. V1 is the striate cortex. V1 and V2 are by far the largest areas. Area MT is also known as STS or ST1 or V5 or the motion

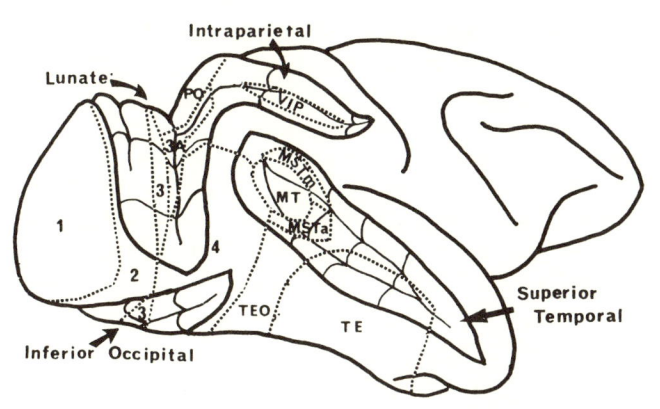

FIG. 2.3. Diagram of a dorsolateral view of the right hemisphere of a rhesus monkey showing the position of various visual areas. Anterior is to the right. Four of the major sulci have been opened to reveal their recesses, but the interior folds are often more complex than portrayed here. Several of the visual areas continue on the medial and ventral aspects. As described in the text several of these areas are known under different names or numbers.

area. Several of the areas are split around the representation of the horizontal retinal meredian. The lower portion of V3 is also known as VP. V4 is sometimes called the color area. Area TE is also known as IT. V3a and V1P have also been called $1P_1$ and $1P_2$ respectively.

The major forward projections from these areas are shown in Fig. 2.4, which is modified from Ungerleider (1985) and chosen because it emphasizes the two

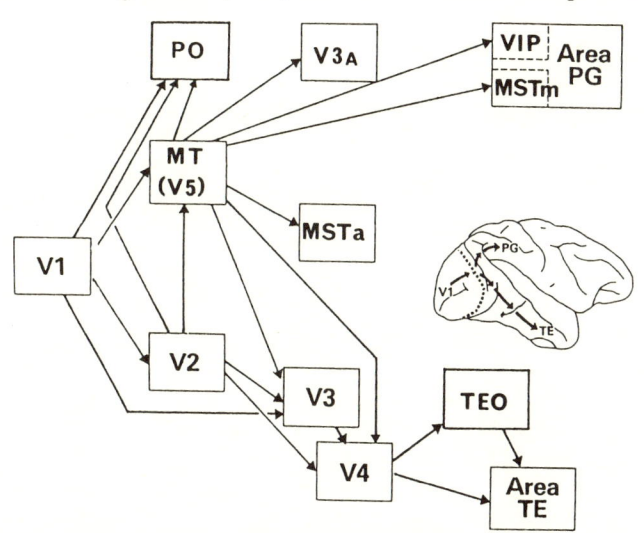

FIG. 2.4. Major forward connections from visual areas shown in Fig. 2.3. The diagram is modified from Ungerleider (1985), in which two major "streams" from V1 are emphasized, reaching parietal and temporal lobes respectively.

major streams from V1 to the temporal and parietal lobes respectively. Shuffling the arrows in a quest to understand how the brain works may smack of stirring chicken entrails in a quest for the truth, but one thing is obvious: There is ample opportunity for both serial and parallel processing within the visual cortex, so much so that different authors have used the same data to promote one or the other. Because the purpose of this chapter is to consider evidence that parallel processing occurs, serial hierarchical models are not pursued further; they have been advanced by Cowey (1979, 1981) and by Van Essen and Maunsell (1983).

If the parallel pathways from eye to V1 are continued in some way, their signs should appear in at least four ways—namely: (a) pattern of outputs from V1, and from other areas; (b) differences in topography in separate areas; (c) different physiological properties in different visual areas that are not easily explicable by a serial hierarchical model; model; (d) radically different effects on vision of removing different areas. These are now considered in turn, the last at somewhat greater length in a separate section.

Origin of the Outputs from V1

The right side of Fig. 2.2 shows the positions of cells bodies whose axons leave the striate cortex for other parts of the brain (see Lund, Lund, Hendrickson, Bunt, & Fuchs, 1975; Lund et al., 1979; Stone, 1983; Weller & Kaas, 1981, for reviews). The most striking feature is the parcellation. V2 and V3 receive their input from supragranular layers of V1, MT from layer IVB and the giant pyramidal cells in layer VI, parvo- and magnocellular LGN from smaller pyramids in the upper and lower portions of layer VI respectively, and the midbrain and pulvinar from layer V. The laminar source of projections to PO is unknown. Even where the projection to two separate areas comes from the same laminae, there is now good evidence that different cell groups are involved. For instance, in both cat and monkey it can be shown by injecting two different retrogradely transported flourescent dyes into retinotopically corresponding regions of V2 and V3 that only 3% of labeled cells in V1 are double labeled—that is, the other 97% project either to V2 *or* V3. Moreover, they occupy slightly different horizontal positions within layers II and III (Bullier, 1984). Even more striking is the recent demonstration by retrograde axonal transport of HRP microinjected into V2 (Livingstone & Hubel, 1984) that the cytochrome oxidase blobs of VI project selectively to the narrow cytochrome oxidase stripes in V2, whereas the interblob regions in V1 project to the interstripe regions in V2—that is, there is a lateral as well as a horizontal separation of parallel outputs from V1.

The laminar differences in receptive field properties of cells in V1 is well known (see Dow, 1974, for example). Cells with nonoriented receptive fields are most common in the ventral part of layer IV, direction-selective cells in the upper part of layer IV, orientation-selective cells in layers II, IIIA, and VI, Y-like cells in layers IV to VI. There is also a horizontal segregation, with wavelength selective cells predominant in the cytochrome oxidase blobs, and orientation-selective cells between the blobs (Livingstone & Hubel, 1984). If the narrow cytochrome oxidase stripes and interstripe regions in V2 prove to have the same emphasis on wavelength and orientation, respectively, the evidence for parallel processing will be stronger than anyone imagined when first considering the projections from V1 to V2.

Information about the cells of origin of forward projections from other visual areas—for example, V2 to V4, V4 to TE—is scant, but there is evidence in the cat of a continuation of the principle that different cells, sometimes but not necessarily in the same laminae, are responsible for parallel outputs (Bullier, 1984).

Differences in Topography

There is evidence that not all portions of the contralateral visual field are represented in each visual area. V2 lacks a representation beyond 80°, V3 represents only the central 40°, and V4 the central 50° (Gattass et al., 1985). But MT follows V1 in providing a representation out to 90° (Gattass & Gross, 1981).

Receptive field size also varies substantially. Whatever field size indicates, and that is far from clear, it is apparent that at any given eccentricity receptive fields are largest in MT and smallest in V1. Area PO is unusual in having foveal receptive fields that are much larger than in any other region, but peripheral fields that resemble those of V4 at 30° and are much smaller than those of MT at extreme eccentricities. Another way of describing this is to say that in area PO, receptive field size shows little variation with eccentricity. The largest fields of all are found in inferotemporal cortex (area TE), where the mean size is 25 deg^2. Although there is no visuotopic representation here—that is, all fields include the fovea and their peripheral boundaries are uncorrelated with position within area TE—there is a strong foveal emphasis in that the responses to a stimulus diminish with eccentricity (Gross, Desimone, Albright, & Schwartz, 1984). It is interesting that the opposite arrangement is found in many cells in the inferior parietal cortex (Motter & Mountcastle, 1981).

Another gross feature of the topography of visual areas that has sometimes been used to contrast them is the coarseness or crudeness of the map. Unfortunately, coarseness is one of those misleading terms that everyone understands until it is explained! For example, in some accounts coarseness seems to mean large receptive fields and it is implied that large fields *necessarily* indicate an imprecise map. But it is theoretically possible to have large receptive fields and an exquisitely precise map as long as field centers are retinotopically arranged. Scatter of receptive field centers—that is, the extent to which neighboring cells in a visual area have receptive fields that are close or distant—is a much better measure, but magnification factor (see next paragraph) must also be taken into account. Scatter was estimated in area MT by Gattass and Gross (1981), who plotted observed eccentricity of receptive field centers against the value expected from the map, where isoeccentricity contours are, of course, mean values. Although scatter increases with eccentricity, so does receptive field size, and the ratio of scatter and RF size does not vary with eccentricity. In other words, scatter is closely correlated with the size of the receptive fields. I know of no other evidence that the same relationship would not be found in other visual areas—that is, there is no evidence that *coarseness* varies in any way that is not already described by variations in receptive field size and magnification factor.

Magnification factor (MF) refers to the extent of cortex representing each degree of visual field. The cortical measurement is often linear but an area measurement is better if MF is not identical in different radial directions, as some recent investigations indicate (Van Essen et al., 1984). There is some inconsistency in the published comparisons of MF in different cortical areas. It is often stated that MF for central as opposed to peripheral retina is relatively higher in some visual areas than others. For example, Allman et al. (1981) report that in the owl monkey the proportion of each of four visual areas devoted to the central 10° of vision varies from 4% to 73%. Similar gross relative differences have been reported in macaque monkeys. However, Gattass and Gross (1981) and Gattass et al. (1985) found no significant differences among the power functions for MF and eccentricity in V1, V2, V3, V4, and MT in macaque monkeys—that is, each area is no more than an expanded or compressed version of the others, something that is easily obscured by the very large absolute differences in MF at any given eccentricity. The exception is area PO (and its presumed homolog area M in the owl monkey) where MF increases with eccentricity.

Variations in Physiological Properties

When comparing the receptive field properties of cells in different visual areas it is important to consider variation *within* an area. For example, the proportion of cells that are selective or biased for wavelength in V1 falls with eccentricity, whereas the proportion tuned to orientation rises (Zeki, 1983c). In contrast, the proportion of orientation-selective cells in V4 falls with eccentricity, whereas wavelength selective cells are independent of eccentricity. Ideally, therefore, one ought to know something about variation within all areas being compared in order to avoid unrepresentative differences (or similarities!) that can arise from comparing properties at different eccentricities in different areas. Bearing this in mind it is evident that genuine differences are present. In the four most extensively explored extrastriate visual areas of the owl monkey, tuning to orientation, size, direction, and velocity of movement, and background versus "object" movement are so unequally represented that it is not misleading to say that each area is specialized. Similar differences are present in macaque monkeys. For example, the retinal disparities coded in retinotopically equivalent regions of V1 and V2 are smaller in V1, but a higher proportion of cells code disparity in V2

(Fischer & Poggio, 1979; Poggio & Fischer, 1977). Recordings at matching eccentricities in V1 and V2 and within 5° of the foveal representation show that the mean optimal spatial frequency in V1 is two octaves above that in V2, although spatial-frequency bandwidths are much the same, whereas temporal-frequency bandwidths are much narrower in V2 than V1, although the range of cut-off temporal frequencies is much the same (Foster, Gaska, Nagler, & Pollen, 1983). An even more striking difference was reported in cats, where cells in V2 but not in V1 responded to illusory contours across the receptive field (Van der Heydt, Peterhans, & Baumgartner, 1984). The absence of "color"-coded cells from V3, V3a, and MT is particularly striking (Andersen, Guld, & Sjo, 1983; Baizer, 1982; Gattass & Gross, 1981; Van Essen, Maunsell, & Bixby, 1981; Zeki, 1978), as is the additional indifferences of cells in MT to shape, size, and orientation (see Van Essen & Maunsell, 1983, for a review). Just as each hypercolumn in V1 contains all the machinery for analyzing, in one part of the visual field, stimulus orientation (Hubel & Wiesel, 1977) and wavelength (Horton, 1984; Livingstone & Hubel, 1984), so too in area MT each 500μm slab of cortex contains systematically arranged columns coding direction and axis of motion for a particular part of the visual field (Albright, Desimone, & Gross, 1984). Regional specialization for "color" coding is more controversial (e.g., Anderson et al., 1983; Schein, Marroco, & de Monasterio, 1982; Zeki, 1983a, 1983b), but if we ignore for the moment the question of wavelength coding as opposed to "color" coding, and the precise bandwidth of the cells, and if we recognize that patches of color-coded cells undoubtedly lie alongside patches where orientation is more important (which can lead to sampling artefacts), then it is clear that the proportion of cells concerned with color is much higher in V2 and V4 than in V3, V3a, and MT.

Somewhat surprisingly, less is known about the physiological properties of cells in other visuotopic areas (e.g., PO, V3a) than in area TE. There have been several reports from separate laboratories that cells in this region may respond to "complex and meaningful" stimuli such as hands, faces, and objects. The earliest reports were understandably viewed with caution given that a large range of simpler stimuli (e.g., gratings) were not also presented. However, it is now clear that although many such cells will indeed respond selectively to simple ingredients of a complex object like its color, outline, or texture, a subset buried deep in the superior temporal sulcus is stubbornly selective for faces (Desimone, Albright, Gross, & Bruce, 1984). They have not been reported in any other visual area.

VISUAL DISORDERS FOLLOWING CORTICAL DAMAGE

If the pathways and areas just described really do reflect extensive parallel processing and what is processed is not identical or even similar in separate pathways, then damage in different pathways ought to produce dissimilar visual disorders. Simply to predict differences without specifying them is obviously a weak tactic, but it sums up our woeful ignorance about the exact relation between the properties of cortical neurones and the behavior of the organism. There is evidence from experimental studies of monkeys and from neurological patients.

Monkeys

The obvious advantage of studying monkeys is that a particular visual area can be removed with minimal damage to others. Unfortunately, maps of the type shown in Fig. 2.2 are so recent that few investigations have been made with their guidance, and many older investigations clearly removed or damaged several areas. Removing the representation of the central retina in V2 strikingly elevates stereoacuity thresholds without affecting global stereopsis, whereas larger but more anterior lesions in area TE have relatively slight effects on stereoacuity but clear effects on global stereopsis (Cowey, 1985). Although other discriminations remain to be tested, the result does support the physiological evidence of disparity coding in V2. Lesions in cytoarchetectonic area 7, which involve visual areas 3A and VIP (see Figs. 2.3 and 2.4), disrupt the monkey's ability to discern the spatial relations among objects without in the slightest disrupting the ability to discriminate between the objects themselves (see Ungerleider & Mishkin, 1982, for review). Removing area TE in monkeys severely impairs visual-discrimination learning, but the character of the defect is still elusive. It is not a memory disorder and sensory thresholds are not disturbed, with the possible exception of stereoptic thresholds, which presumably do not contribute to discriminations for which stereopsis is irrelevant because they can be made with one eye. However, it has recently been shown by Weiskrantz and Saunders (1984) that the animals, like some neurological patients, have trouble recognizing objects that are changed in some way (orientation, shading, size) from the familiar view. In other words, area TE may be involved in visual categorization and shape constancy. Given the conspicuous presence of so-called face cells in area TE, it is unfortunate that facial recognition, so dramatically impaired in prosopagnosic patients, has not been tested in monkeys with ablation of area TE.

There is widespread agreement that the physiological properties of cells in visual area MT indicate its involvement in the perception of movement. This role has not yet been thoroughly assessed. Removing or extensively damaging area MT does not affect the displacement threshold for detecting sudden movement of a small luminous spot (Collin & Cowey, 1980), but the mere fact that something has moved is probably registered by several systems. Discrimination of velocity and direction have not been examined, although Newsome, Wurtz, Dursteler, & Mikami (1983) have demonstrated that a small lesion to part of area MT impairs eye movements to a target that appears in the corresponding part of the visual field and then moves laterally.

According to Zeki (e.g. 1983a, 1983b, 1983c), area V4 is especially concerned with color in that, in addition to having cells tuned to wavelength, it possesses a population that responds to what a human observer would describe as a particular color despite large variations in the spectral composition of the light reflected from it—that is, they display color constancy. There are no published accounts of the consequences of selectively removing V4, but Cowey and Heywood (unpublished) have found a substantial increase in the threshold for discriminating between "Munsell" colors, which is consistent with a defect in wavelength discrimination. However, the animals are also impaired at pattern and orientation discriminations and the combined impairment is not surprising given the intercalation in V4 of regions in which wavelength or orientation are coded. Color constancy has been examined in only one experiment (Wild, Butler, Carden, & Kulikowski, 1984), in which it was found that removing V4 impaired the ability of rhesus monkeys to select from two milticolored plaques the one containing a desaturated green patch when the ratio of red to green monochromatic incident light was varied. I am not aware of any examination of color constancy in neurological patients, but the hue-discrimination impairment in monkeys clearly resembles cerebral achromatopsia in patients, to which we now turn.

Neurological Patients

Cerebral achromatopsia is associated with bilateral damage to the ventral prestriate cortex (Meadows, 1974). The patient reports that the world looks grey or washed out and performance on naming, sorting, matching, and discriminating hues is poor. There is invariably some associated object agnosia. Yet, the trichromatic mechanism of the retinostriate pathways is intact, as judged by increment threshold measures for monochromatic targets on different monochromatic backgrounds (Mollon Newcombe, Polden, & Ratcliff, 1980). It is as if wavelength were still coded but had become inaccessible to cortical channels concerned with the perception of color.

Specific disorders of the perception of movement are equally rare, but just as illuminating. In the clearest example, reported by Zihl, von Cramon, and Mai (1983), the patient had no impression of movement in depth and could reliably discriminate between stationary and moving targets only in the peripheral field. In central vision, movement was only experienced when it was slower than 10 degrees/sec. When objects moved, their change of position was well detected but not their trajectory. Continuous movement was not registered, so that waterfalls resembled glaciers. The cerebral lesion was bilateral and centered on the lateral occipitotemporal junction, and the authors not surprisingly suggest that it involved a visual area with properties like that of area MT in monkeys.

Reports of disorders of stereoscopic depth perception following cortical damage are more common (see Danta, Hilton, & O'Boyle [1978] for review), even though they may often remain undetected because the patient has excellent monocular cues to depth. Again, the lesion is in the prestriate cortex and, although field defects are a common concomitant symptom, there is no necessary association.

As is well known, large parietal lesions, especially in the right hemisphere, lead to contralateral visual neglect. But smaller lesions, probably centered on Brodmann's area 7, produce a curious mislocation of simple, readily detected visual targets (Cole, Schutta, & Warrington, 1962; Holmes, 1918; Ratcliff & Davies-Jones, 1972). The parallel with the misreaching and impaired perception of spatial relationships evident in monkeys with parietal ablations that include visual areas in the intraparietal sulcus (see Fig. 2.3) is compelling.

Finally, there are a variety of more complex visual disorders that are collectively referred to as visual agnosia. Two that have aroused great interest because of their apparent relative specificity are prosopagnosia and faulty visual categorization. Prosopagnosia is a defect in recognizing faces (for review, see Damasio, Damasio, & van Hoesen, 1982). The damage is usually, perhaps always, bilateral in the ventromedial occipitotemporal cortex. The patient is bad at recognizing faces by sight, even his or her own in the mirror. But naming, drawing, and describing the components of faces may be normal. It is tempting to attribute the disorder to the destruction of an area such as that within the central third of the superior temporal sulcus in monkeys and within which cells responding selectively to faces have been described. But there are problems that must not be concealed. The vast majority of so-called face cells show poor discrimination among different faces and their removal might be expected to impair the discrimination of faces from nonfaces rather than make it difficult to identify particular faces. Perhaps face cells collectively signal facial identity in a manner that the recorded activity of individual cells can never reveal. A further problem is that there is no good evidence that a prosopagnosic patient is not also impaired at recognizing other individual members of a class containing many examples—for example, flowers, dogs, motor cars. Of course, such a generalized shape-recognition defect would not be surprising after damage to a region in which a large proportion of the cells could be said to be concerned with shape rather than with the particular shape that makes up a face.

Warrington (1982) has described and reviewed the visual-categorization defect in which the patient has difficulty in recognizing familiar objects from unusual views. The patient responds as if lacking any object-centered representation of the visual scene, a conclusion reached by Weiskrantz and Saunders in characterizing the visual defect caused by anterior inferotemporal lesions in monkeys.

If the posterior cortex of the human brain is anything like that shown in Fig. 2.2, the rarity of the selective defects just described should not surprise or dismay us. Only very rarely will accidental brain damage neatly destroy one visual area. For this reason dissociation of symptoms in a handful of patients is more informative than their association in the majority. Precise verification of the locus of the damage is also much more difficult to establish in patients, notwithstanding PET and NMR scans, and at present it is frankly foolhardy to attempt to relate any precise region of the human brain to any one of the secondary visual areas shown in Fig. 2.2, apart from the striate cortex V1.

ADVANTAGES OF MULTIPLE SENSORY REPRESENTATIONS

According to the principle of modularity (e.g., Marr, 1976, 1982) any large computation should be divided into small, nearly independent, and specialized subprocesses. This principle of modular design ensures that a small change in one part of a system does not inevitably affect other parts. When applied to organisms it allows evolutionary improvements to occur in some processing system without requiring extensive compensatory adjustments in others. The same applies to ontogenetic changes that occur during development or in association with learning. A module in Marr's sense is a separate part of a *process;* it is not necessarily a spatially isolated area of tissue like a visual area. In theory, separate processing modules could be spatially interlocked and all the computations performed by the visual cortex could go on within one area. So, do the multiple visual areas correspond to processing modules? I think they do, and not only for the reasons already advanced. There are good reasons why local interactions in the retina are much more important than distant ones—for example, lateral inhibition between elements concerned with adjacent contours is almost a prerequisite for efficiently coding information about contours. Lateral excitatory and inhibitory interactions are just as prominent in the cortex, where again they contribute to the precise tuning of individual cells and where once again the interactions occur between cells representing the same or adjacent parts of the retina. A topographic map of the retina in the cortex is therefore useful because interconnections can be kept short. Presumably they are also easier to specify than in an area where the appropriate target cells are randomly dispersed. However, if all the processing modules lie within a single visual area, even one that is topographically arranged, the problem of connecting the right parts and of keeping connections short reappear, as does the problem of altering a module, either in ontogeny or evolution, without perturbing others. A solution to these problems is to segregate the processing modules so that they are not physically intermeshed—that is, to have multiple sensory representations of the kind described here for vision but now equally clear in the somatosensory and auditory systems (Woolsey, 1981a, 1981b).

There is yet another advantage of the modular arrangement. It would be surprising in any complex process like vision if it were not an advantage to be able to ignore or suppress the activity or output of some modules, for example in attending selectively to some part of the visual field or to some feature within it, like color or orientation. By segregating modules it is, in theory, easier to suppress or enhance them simply by exposing the target and making it easier to hit. Unfortunately, our knowledge about the anatomical and physiological basis of any selective inhibition of modules is patchy and the gaps are yawning. Nevertheless, some things are established. The first is that all long connections between thalamus and cortex and between different cortical areas—that is, those that are not entirely confined to grey matter—are excitatory in the sense that (a) their first effect on target neurones is an excitatory postsynaptic potential; and (b) their synaptic terminals are morphologically asymmetrical and filled with spherical vescicles, as in terminals where excitation has been demonstrated. It is therefore doubtful whether any long projection pathway directly produces inhibition at its target. The second is that several different types of cortical interneurone are inhibitory in the sense that (a) their synaptic terminals are morphologically symmetrical and filled with flattened or pleomorphic vescicles, as in terminals where inhibition has been demonstrated in the postsynaptic target; and (b) they synthesize and release γ-aminobutyric acid (GABA), which is known to inhibit postsynaptic targets.

What types of neurones produce these presumed excitatory and inhibitory connections and how are they arranged? Throughout the cortex pyramidal cells occur predominantly above and below layer IV. With few exceptions their axons enter the white matter and project to another cortical area or to subcortex, and these terminals are always of the presumed excitatory type (see Feldman [1984] for review). Some varieties of nonpyramidal cell—for example, some bipolar and spiny stellate cells—also give rise to asymmetric synapses locally—that is, these cells are thought to lead to excitation of neighboring neurones above and below them in a small region of cortex entirely within a single area. In other words, pyramidal cells excite other cells in distant areas, bipolar and spiny stellate cells excite their neighbors.

The best-known presumed inhibitory interneurons are the chandelier (or axoaxonic) cell, the double-bouquet cell, and the basket cell (see Jones & Hendry [1984], Peters]1984], and Somogyi & Cowey [1981, 1984] for reviews). Each double-bouquet cell has its cell body in layers II to III and an unmistakable multibranched, vertically oriented axon traversing layers II to V and providing symmetrical (inhibitory?) synapses chiefly on the dendritic shafts of other nonpyramidal cells. They are, therefore, in an excellent position to inhibit neighbors above and below them, just as bipolar and spiny stellate cells excite them. Of course, if they were to inhibit other inhibitory interneurones the net effect would be disinhibition. Inhibition applied to one dendrite has no effect on the remaining dendrites of a cell, suggesting that the double-bouquet cell contributes to the selective tuning of neurones by opposing a subset of the excitatory inputs to the dendrites.

The cortical basket cell (see Jones & Hendry [1984] and Martin [1985] for reviews) has its cell body in layers III to V and its axon divides into numerous horizontally disposed collaterals that extend for a mm or so. Although some of the terminals end on dendritic shafts, the greatest proportion contribute to pericellular baskets that encapsulate the soma of a pyramidal cell. Basket cells are therefore in a position to exert an even greater inhibitory effect on pyramidal cells and there is both anatomical and pharmacological evidence that they are inihibitory. Each basket cell may contact more than 300 pyramidal cells, so the opportunity for conspicuous inhibition is great. But there is still no good evidence about the precise role of the inhibition. It is undoubtedly more laterally dispersed than in double-bouquet cells and the nonuniform lateral distribution of the axons have suggested to many that in the visual cortex it could mediate inhibition between slabs representing different eyes.

The chandelier or axoaxonic cell (see Peters [1984] and Somogyi, Freund, & Cowey [1982] for reviews) has the unique feature of confining its presumed inhibitory terminals exclusively to the axon hillock of pyramidal cells, where action potentials are generated and propagated. The chandelier cell can therefore throttle the output of pyramidal cells no matter what the excitatory input to the dendrites of the pyramidal cells. It is chiefly pyramidal cells in layers II to III that are inhibited, including those projecting across the corpus callosum to the other hemisphere. Because these cells form the major projection to other cortical areas and to layers V and VI immediately below them, Martin (1985) has proposed that the chandelier cell plays a central role in arousal and sleep. This is consistent with increased metabolic activity in the upper layers during slow-wave sleep (i.e., the chandelier cells are active) compared with layers V to VI (i.e., the excitatory projection from upper to lower layers has been silenced). It is also known that the release of GABA, the presumed neurotransmitter of chandelier cells, increases during slow-wave sleep.

If only we know more about the inputs and outputs of these different cells! There is no doubt that the machinery exists to produce profound inhibition in the cerebral cortex and that in theory specific parts of the visuotopic representation together with specific processing modules (e.g., for movement or color) could be silenced or muffled, like briefly sending a small region to sleep. Whether the information leading to regional inhibition associated with voluntary selective attention traverses the pathways shown in Fig. 2.4 or whether it arrives from the extrinsic thalamic nuclei and so-called nonspecific projections from the brain stem to cortex—that is, that it acts on but is additional to everything described in Fig. 2.3 and 2.4, is unknown. The first neuronal events in that volition are even more mysterious.

CONCLUSIONS

This review has emphasized the evidence for parallel processing of information from the eye to cortical visual areas. This is not meant to imply that serial hierarchical processing is absent or insignificant. It certainly pervades individual pathways—for example, in the convergence that leads to the center-surround arrangements of retinal ganglion cells or the huge receptive fields in visual areas MT and TE—and it would be surprising if some cells in an area like V4 did not receive converging information from several different visual areas. Serial and parallel processing are not mutually exclusive means of processing information any more than Anglicanism and Catholicism are incompatible forms of Christian belief.

Perhaps the weakest feature of the review is the absence, freely acknowledged, of any good evidence that identified separate pathways at one stage of processing match-up with those at a subsequent stage. For example, although the outputs from the two major morphologically and physiologically distinct divisions of dLGN innervate different laminae of V1, there is little *detailed* information about the intracortical events that then occur and lead to the parallel outputs from V1 to other visual areas. Just what is kept separate? It is certainly not a marked separation of X and Y systems, at least in the cat, but wavelength and movement do seem to be emphasized in separate channels. Information about the details of connections between areas beyond V1 is even less satisfactory.

In discussing the advantages of multiple sensory representations the review mentions inhibitory processes that could underlie selective attention. The appropriate local intracortical circuits exist; indeed, one of the most exciting developments in the past few years has been the mounting evidence for the distribution, structure, physiological properties, and putative neurotransmitters of cortical inhibitory interneurons. But their effects are confined to their immediate neighbors. The long pathways by which they are instructed to exert their inhibition are obscure.

ACKNOWLEDGMENT

I take pleasure in thanking the Master and Fellows of St. Johns College, Cambridge, for the Kenneth Craik Award for 1984, and for inviting me to spend some time at the College, where I was able to prepare part of this review.

REFERENCES

Albright, T. D., Desimone, R., & Gross, C. G. (1984). Columnar organization of directionally sensitive cells in visual area MT of the macaque. *Journal of Neurophysiology, 51,* 16–31.

Allman, J. M., Baker, J. F., Newsome, W. T., & Peterson, S. E, (1981). Visual topography and function: Cortical visual areas in the owl monkey. In C. N. Woolsey (Ed.), *Cortical sensory organization Vol. 2 Multiple visual areas* (pp. 171–185). Clifton, N.J.: Humana Press.

Andersen, V. O., Guld, C., & Sjo, O. (1983). Color processing in prestriate cortex of vervet monkey. In J. D. Mollon & L. T. Sharpe (Eds.), *Colour vision* (pp. 297–301). London: Academic Press.

Baizer, J. S. (1982). Receptive field properties of V3 neurons in monkey. *Investigative Ophthalmology and Visual Science, 23,* 87–95.

Benevento, L. A., & Yoshida, K. (1981). The afferent and efferent organization of the lateral geniculo-prestriate pathway in the macaque monkey. *Journal of Comparative Neurology, 203*, 455–474.

Boycott, B. B., & Dowling, J. E. (1969). Organization of the primate retina: Light microscopy. *Philosophical Transactions of the Royal Society*, B255, 109–184.

Brindley, G. S. (1960). *Physiology of the retina and visual pathway* (1st ed.). London: Edward Arnold.

Brodmann, K. (1909). *Vergleichende Lokalisationslehre der Grosshirnrinde in ihren Prinzipien dargestellt auf Grund des Zellenbaues.* Leipzig: J. A. Barth.

Bullier, J. (1984). Input and output streams in visual cortex. *Abstract, Primate Society of Great Britain.* Perceptual and Learning Abilities of Primates, Easter Conference, p. 11.

Bullier, J., & Kennedy, H. (1983). Projection of the lateral geniculate nucleus onto cortical area V2 in the macaque monkey. *Experimental Brain Research, 53,* 168–172.

Carey, R. G., Fitzpatrick, P., & Diamond, I. T. (1979). Layer I of striate cortex of Tupaia glis and Galago senegalensis: Projections from the thalamus and claustrum revealed by retrograde transport of horseradish peroxidase. *Journal of Comparative Neurology, 186,* 393–438.

Cole, M., Schutta, H. S., & Warrington, E. K. (1962). Visual disorientation in homogeneous halffields. *Neurology, 12,* 257–263.

Collin, N. G., & Cowey, A. (1980). The effect of ablation of frontal eye fields and superior colliculi on visual stability and movement discrimination in rhesus monkeys. *Experimental Brain Research, 40,* 251–260.

Compos-Ortega, J. A., & Hayhow, W. R. (1972). On the organization of the visual cortical projection to the pulvinar in Macaca mulatta. *Brain Behavior and Evolution, 6,* 394–443.

Cowey, A. (1979). Cortical maps and visual perception. *Quarterly Journal of Experimental Psychology, 31,* 1–17.

Cowey, A. (1981). Why are there so many visual areas? In F. O. Schmitt, F. G. Worden, G. Adelman, & S. G. Dennis (Eds.), *The organization of the cerebral cortex* (pp. 395–413). Cambridge, Mass.: MIT Press.

Cowey, A. (1985). Disturbances of stereopsis by brain damage. In D. Ingle (Ed.), *Brain mechanisms and spatial vision.* NATO Advanced Study Institute Series). The Hague: Martinas Nijhoff.

Cowey, A. & Heywood, C. H. (Unpublished ms.) Hue and pattern discrimination impairments following removal of visual area 4 in monkeys.

Damasio, A. R., Damasio, H., & van Hoesen, G. W. (1982). Prosopagnosia: Anatomic basis and behavioral mechanisms. *Neurology, 32,* 331–341.

Danta, G., Hilton, R. C., & O'Boyle, D. J. (1978). Hemisphere function and binocular depth perception. *Brain, 101,* 569–589.

de Monasterio, F. M. (1981). Functional properties and presumed roles of retinal ganglion cells of the monkey. In J. Szentagothai, J. Hamori, & M. Palkovits (Eds.), *Advances in physiological sciences Vol. 2 Regulatory functions of the CNS subsystems* (pp. 261–270). Oxford: Pergamon Press.

Desimone, R., Albright, T. D., Gross, C. G., & Bruce, C. (1984). Stimulus selective properties of inferior temporal neurons in the macaque. *Journal of Neuroscience, 4,* 2051–2062.

Dow, B. M. (1974). Functional classes of cells and their laminar distribution in monkey visual cortex. *Journal of Neurophysiology, 37,* 927–946.

Feldman, M. L. (1984). Morphology of the neocortical pyramidal neuron. In A. Peters & E. G. Jones (Eds.), *Cerebral cortex Vol. 1 Cellular components of the cerebral cortex* (pp. 123–200). New York: Plenum Press.

Fischer, B., & Poggio, G. F. (1979). Depth sensitivity of binocular cortical neurons of behaving monkeys. *Proceedings of the Royal Society, London, B204,* 409–414.

Foster, K. H., Gaska, J. P., Nagler, M., & Pollen, D. A. (1983). Spatial and temporal frequency selectivity of neurons in V1 and V2 of the macaque monkey. *Society for Neuroscience, Abstracts, 9,* 618.

Fries, W. (1981). The projection from the lateral geniculate nucleus to the prestriate cortex in the macaque monkey. *Proceedings of the Royal Society, London, B213*, 73–80.

Gattass, R., & Gross, C. G. (1981). Visual topography of straite projection zone (MT) in posterior superior temporal sulcus of the macaque. *Journal of Neurophysiology, 46*, 621–638.

Gattass, R., Sousa, A. P. B., & Covey, E. (1985). Cortical visual areas of the macaque: Possible substrates for pattern recognition mechanisms. In C. Chagas (Ed.), *Pattern recognition mechanisms*. Vatican City: Pontificiae Academiae Scientiarum Scripta Varia. in press.

Gilbert, C. D., & Wiesel, T. N. (1979). Morphology and intracortical projections of functionally characterised neurones in the cat visual cortex. *Nature, 280*, 120–125.

Gross, C. G., Desimone, R., Albright, T. D., & Schwartz, E. L. (1985). Inferior temporal cortex and pattern recognition. In C. Chagas (Ed.), *Pattern recognition mechanisms*. Vatican City: Pontificiae Academiae Scientiarum Scripta Varia, in press.

Holmes, G. (1918). Disturbances of visual orientation. *British Journal of Ophthalmology, 2*, 449–468.

Horton, J. C. (1984). Cytochrome oxidase patches: a new cytoarchitectonic feature of monkey visual cortex. *Philosophical Transactions of the Royal Society, London. B304*, 199–253.

Hubel, D. H., & Wiesel, T. N. (1977). Functional architecture of macaque monkey visual cortex. *Proceedings of the Royal Society, London, B198*, 1–59.

Jones, E. G., & Hendry, S. H. C. (1984). Basket cells. In A. Peters & E. G. Jones (Eds.), *Cerebral cortex Vol. 1 Cellular components of the cerebral cortex* (pp. 309–336). New York: Plenum Press.

Kaas, J. H., Huerta, M. F., Weber, J. T., & Harting, J. K. (1978). Patterns of retinal terminations and laminar organization of the lateral geniculate nucleus of primates. *Journal of Comparative Neurology, 182*, 517–554.

Leventhal, A. G., Rodieck, R. W., & Dreher, B. (1981). Retinal ganglion cell classes in old-world monkey: Morphology and central connections. *Science, 213*, 1139–1142.

Livingstone, M. S., & Hubel, D. H. (1984). Anatomy and physiology of a color system in the primate visual cortex. *Journal of Neuroscience, 4*, 309–356.

Lund, J. S., & Boothe, R. G. (1975). Interlaminar connections and pyramidal neuron organization in the visual cortex, area 17, of the macaque monkey. *Journal of Comparative Neurology, 159*, 305–334.

Lund, J. S., Henry, G. H., MacQueen, C. L., & Harvey, A. R. (1979). Anatomical organization of the primary visual cortex (area 17) of the cat: A comparison with area 17 of the macaque monkey. *Journal of Comparative Neurology, 184*, 599–618.

Lund, J. S., Lund, R. D., Hendrickson, A. E., Bunt, A. H., & Fuchs, A. F. (1975). The origin of efferent pathways from the primary visual cortex, area 17, of the macaque monkey as shown by retrograde transport of horseradish peroxidase. *Journal of Comparative Neurology, 164*, 287–304.

Marr, D. (1976). Early processing of visual information. *Philosophical Transactions of the Royal Society, London, 275*, 483–524.

Marr, D. (1982). *Vision*. San Francisco: Freeman.

Martin, K. A. C. (1985). Neuronal circuits in cat striate cortex. In A. Peters & E. G. Jones (Eds.), *Cerebral cortex Vol. 2* New York: Plenum Press. (in press).

Meadows, J. C. (1974). Disturbed perception of colours associated with localized cerebral lesions. *Brain, 87*, 615–632.

Mollon, J. D., Newcombe, F., Polden, P. G., & Ratcliff, G. (1980). On the presence of three cone mechanisms in a case of total achromatopsia. In G. Verriest (Ed.), *Colour vision deficiencies* (Vol. 5, pp. 130–135). Bristol: Hilger.

Motter, B. C., & Mountcastle, V. B. (1981). The functional properties of the light-sensitive neurons of the posterior parietal cortex studied in waking monkeys: Foveal sparing and opponent vector organization. *Journal of Neuroscience, 1*, 3–26.

Newsome, W. T., Wurtz, R. H., Dursteler, M. R., & Mikami, A. (1983). Deficits in pursuit eye movements after chemical lesions of the motion-related visual areas in the superior temporae sulcus of the macaque monkey. *Society for Neuroscience, Abstracts, 9*, 154.

Perry, V. H., & Cowey, A. (1981). The morphological correlates of X- and Y-like retinal ganglion cells in the retina of monkeys. *Experimental Brain Research, 43*, 226–228.

Perry, V. H., & Cowey, A. (1984). Retinal ganglion cells that project to the superior colliculus and pretectum in the macaque monkey. *Neuroscience, 12*, 1125–1137.

Perry, V. H., Oehler, R., & Cowey, A. (1984). Retinal ganglion cells that project to the dorsal lateral geniculate nucleus in the macaque monkey. *Neuroscience, 12*, 1101–1123.

Peters, A. (1984). Chandelier cells. In A. Peters & E. G. Jones (Eds.), *Cerebral cortex Vol. 1 Cellular components of the cerebral cortex*, (pp. 361–380) New York: Plenum Press.

Phillips, C. G., Zeki, S., & Barlow, H. B. (1984). Localization of function in the cerebral cortex. Past, present and future. *Brain, 107*, 327–361.

Poggio, G. F., & Fischer, B. (1977). Binocular interaction and depth sensitivity in striate and prestriate cortex of behaving rhesus monkeys. *Journal of Neurophysiology, 40*, 1392–1405.

Polyak, S. L. (1941). *The retina*. Chicago: University of Chicago.

Ratcliff, G., & Davies-Jones, G. A. B. (1972). Defective visual localization in focal brain wounds. *Brain, 95*, 49–60.

Schein, S. J., Marroco, R. T., & de Monasterio, F. M. (1982). Is there a high concentration of color-selective cells in areas V4 of the monkey visual cortex? *Journal of Neurophysiology, 47*, 193–213.

Somogyi, P., & Cowey, A. (1981). Combined Golgi and electron microscopic study on the synapses formed by double-bouquet cells in the visual cortex of cat and monkey. *Journal of Comparative Neurology, 195*, 547–566.

Somogyi, P., & Cowey, A. (1984). Double-bouquet cells. In A. Peters & E. G. Jones (Eds.), *Cerebral cortex Vol. 1 Cellular components of the cerebral cortex* (pp. 337–360). New York: Plenum Press.

Somogyi, P., Freund, T. F., & Cowey, A. (1982). The axo-axonic interneuron in the cerebral cortex of the rat, cat and monkey. *Neuroscience, 7*, 2577–2607.

Stone, J. (1983). *Parallel processing in the visual system*. New York: Plenum Press.

Ungerleider, L. G. (1985). The corticocortical pathways for object recognition and spatial perception. In C. Chagas (Ed.), *Pattern recognition mechanisms* Pontificiae Academiae Scientiarum Scripta Varia.

Ungerleider, L. G., & Mishkin, M. (1982). Two cortical visual systems. In D. J. Ingle, M. A. Goodale, & R. J. W. Mansfield (Eds.), *Analysis of visual behaviur* (pp. 549–586). Cambridge, MA: MIT Press.

van der Heydt, R., Peterhans, E., & Baumgartner, G. (1984). Illusory contours and cortical neuron responses. *Investigative Ophthalmology and Visual Sciences, 25* (Abstract Supplement), 278.

Van Essen, D. C., & Maunsell, J. H. R. (1983). Hierarchical organization and functional streams in the visual cortex. *Trends in Neuroscience, 6*, 370–375.

Van Essen, D. C., Maunsell, J. H. R., & Bixby, J. L. (1981). The middle temporal visual area in the macaque: Myeloachitecture, connections, functional properties and topographic organization. *Journal of Comparative Neurology, 199*, 293–326.

Van Essen, D. C., Newsome, W. T., & Maunsell, J. H. R. (1984). The visual field representation in striate cortex of the macaque monkey: Asymmetries, anisotropies, and individual variability. *Vision Research, 24*, 429–448.

Warrington, E. K. (1982). Neuropsychological studies of object recognition. *Philosophical Transactions of the Royal Society, London, B298*, 15–33.

Weiskrantz, L. (1980). Varieties of residual experience. *Quarterly Journal of Experimental Psychology, 32*, 315–386.

Weiskrantz, L., & Saunders, R. C. (1984). Impairments of visual object transforms in monkeys. *Brain, 107*, 1033–1072.

Weiskrantz, L., Warrington, E. K., Sanders, M. D., & Marshall, J. (1974). Visual capacity in the hemianopic field following a restricted occipital ablation. *Brain, 97,* 709–728.

Weller, R. E., & Kaas, J. H. (1981). Cortical and subcortical connections of visual cortex in primates. In C. N. Woolsey (Ed.), *Cortical sensory organization Vol. 2 Multiple visual areas* (pp. 121–155). Clifton, NJ: Humana Press.

Woolsey, C. N. (Ed.). (1981a). *Cortical sensory organization Vol. 1 Multiple somatic areas.* Clifton, NJ: Humana Press.

Woolsey, C. N. (Ed.). (1981b). *Cortical sensory organization Vol. 3 Multiple auditory areas.* Clifton, NJ: Humana Press.

Wild, H., Butler, S., Carden, D., & Kulikowski, J. J. (1984). The effects of bilateral removals of cortical area V4 on colour constancy in the rhesus monkey. *Abstracts, Primate Society of Great Britain.* Perceptual and Learning Abilities of Primates, Easter Conference, p. 6.

Yukie, M., & Iwai, E. (1981). Direct projection from dorsal lateral geniculate nucleus to the prestriate cortex in macaque monkey. *Journal of Comparative Neurology, 201,* 81–98.

Zeki, S. (1978). Functional specialization in the visual cortex of the rhesus monkey. *Nature, 274,* 423–428.

Zeki, S. (1983a). Colour coding in the cerebral cortex: The reaction of cells in monkey visual cortex to wavelength and colours. *Neuroscience, 9,* 741–765.

Zeki, S. (1983b). Colour coding in the cerebral cortex: The responses of wavelength-selective and colour-coded cells in monkey visual cortex to changes in wavelength composition. *Neuroscience, 9,* 767–781.

Zeki, S. (1983c). The distribution of wavelength and orientation selective cells in different areas of monkey visual cortex. *Proceedings of the Royal Society, London, B217,* 449–470.

Zeki, S. M. (1982). The mapping of visual functions in the cerebral cortex. In Y. Katsuki, R. Norgren, & M. Sato (eds.), *Brain mechanisms of sensation* (pp. 105–128). New York: Wiley.

Zihl, J., von Cramon, D., & Mai, N. (1983). Selective disturbance of movement vision after bilateral brain damage. *Brain, 106,* 313–340.

3 Visual–Spatial Attention, Orienting, and Brain Physiology

Steven A. Hillyard
Thomas F. Munte
University of California, San Diego

Helen J. Neville
The Salk Institute

ABSTRACT

This chapter deals with electrophysiological techniques for evaluating mechanisms of visual-spatial attention, with particular emphasis on recordings of event-related brain potentials (ERPs) from human subjects. Experiments are reviewed suggesting that attention to spatial location involves an early, "intraperceptual" selection of visual information, which takes place for both foveal and peripheral inputs. When stimuli are selected on the basis of multiple stimulus features such as color and location, the ERP latencies provide evidence for a hierarchical ordering of cue selections. Selection by location is usually the earliest to occur and produces a distinct physiological signature that includes modulation of short-latency ERP components. A stimulus-by-stimulus analysis of the time course of spatial attention showed that ERP selectivity is small for the first stimulus following an attention-directing cue, but builds up rapidly thereafter. These results suggest a basic difference in the attentional mechanisms that come into play during the sustained evaluation of a relevant spatial location and those that produce immediate costs and benefits to single events that follow a priming cue.

INTRODUCTION

Everyday experience suggests that we can voluntarily direct our attention to different objects and locations in the visual surroundings independently of our eye movements. Observers of no less stature than Helmholtz have remarked upon the subjective impression of improved clarity of those portions of the visual field that lie within the focus of attention (Jonides, 1980). The nature of this apparent facilitation of visual processing for stimuli at attended spatial positions has been vigorously investigated and debated over the past several decades (for reviews, see Jonides, 1980; Posner, 1980). One basic issue concerns the locus of selectivity—whether spatial attention influences the quality of perceptual information that is received or whether it only impacts subsequent decision processes. In other words, is sensory transmission modulated at an early, "intraperceptual" level (Johnston & Dark, 1982), or does sensory information build up automatically, outside of attentional control? This chapter considers this question of early versus late selection from the perspective of electrophysiological studies of visual event-related potentials (ERPs) in human subjects. In addition, evidence from ERP studies is presented that suggests separate mechanisms for the phasic orienting and the sustained focusing of spatial attention.

BEHAVIORAL STUDIES

Numerous studies have demonstrated improved processing of inputs to spatial locations that are cued or primed on a trial-by-trial basis. In one type of design, in which attention is directed to a particular location in a "cluttered" field of stimuli, subjects can generally identify the cued item more rapidly and/or accurately than items at noncued locations (e.g., Beck & Ambler, 1973; Colegate, Hoffman, & Eriksen, 1973; Eriksen & Hoffman, 1973; Jonides, 1980; Sperling & Melchner, 1978). This form of spatial cueing has often been described in terms of an attentional "spotlight" metaphor, whereby stimuli falling within a zone having a diameter of about 1° surrounding an attended locus receive improved perceptual processing (Eriksen & Hoffman, 1973; Hoffman, 1975; Hoffman & Nelson, 1981).

There is also considerable evidence for facilitated processing of spatially cued targets that appear alone in an otherwise empty visual field. This occurs when a prior cue indicates the most likely location for a subsequent target to appear. Experiments by Posner and associates (Posner, Cohen, & Rafal, 1982; Posner, Nissen, & Ogden, 1978; Posner, Snyder, & Davidson, 1980) used a simple RT task to show both a speeding of responses (benefits) to stimuli in the cued location and a slowing of RT (costs) to targets at unprimed locations, both in relation to a "neutral" cue condition. The benefits of spatial cueing are also manifest in improved stimulus detectability (Bashinski & Bacharach, 1980; Remington, 1980; Van der Heijden & Eerland, 1973) and in speeded choice RTs between alternative forms (Posner et al., 1980). This spatial facilitation has been interpreted as a consequence of the orienting or alignment of attention to an expected location, leading to a more efficient detection of items so situated (Posner, 1980).

When an attention-directing cue occurs at the same peripheral location as the subsequent target, an inhibitory process appears to be superimposed on the spatial facilitation effect. Following an initial period of response facilitation, the RT to a spatially coincident target was found to be retarded in relation to a target presented at an uncued location (Posner & Cohen, 1984; Posner, Cohen, Choate, Hockey, & Maylor, 1984; Posner et al., 1982). This inhibitory effect was shown to depend on a physical energy change at the target location and was interpreted as a basic sensory mechanism for suppressing inputs to recently stimulated locations; such a mechanism would favor shifts of attention to novel events occurring in previously quiet locations.

Posner et al. (1984) suggested that the inhibitory influence of stimulus repetition would tend to counteract attentional selectivity when stimuli are presented in continuous "streams" rather than on a trial-by-trial basis. Indeed, paradigms which required sustained attention to repetitive stimulus sequences produced much smaller attentional costs and benefits than when trials were discretely cued (Posner et al., 1980, 1984). Posner and colleagues considered these findings to favor the view that spatial attention involves an active and effortful orienting of attention rather than a sustained "passive filtering" of inputs. They suggested that subjects find it difficult to maintain their set or differential preparation for a particular location during periods of sustained attention. Hence, trial-by-trial cueing generally induces the stronger attention effects.

ELECTROPHYSIOLOGICAL INDICES OF SPATIAL ATTENTION

Interestingly, the conditions that tended to diminish behavioral selectivity in the studies of Posner and colleagues (rapidly presented streams of repetitive stimuli) are precisely those that favor electrophysiological indicators of spatial attention. In a typical ERP experiment, stimuli are flashed equiprobably to right and left locations in random order at a fairly rapid rate (2 to 3/sec). Subjects are given verbal instructions to focus attention on the flashes in one field and to ignore events in the opposite field while fixating a central point. Their task usually is to discriminate occasional "targets" that are interspersed at random among the more frequent "standard" flashes on the attended side. Runs of attend-left and attend-right conditions are given in counterbalanced order, each lasting from one to several minutes and presenting up to several hundreds of stimuli. The ERPs triggered by the flashes are then recorded from different scalp regions and computer averaged separately for each class of stimulus and condition of attention. ERPs to each type of stimulus are generally averaged across an entire run without regard to the sequential position of the stimulus.

Typical ERP changes produced in such an experiment are illustrated in Fig. 3.1 (Hillyard, Simpson, Woods, Van Voorhis, & Munte, 1984). The basic effect, discovered by Eason, Harter, and White (1969), is an enlargement of a series of positive and negative peaks in the ERP waveform during the interval

ERPs to Left Flashes

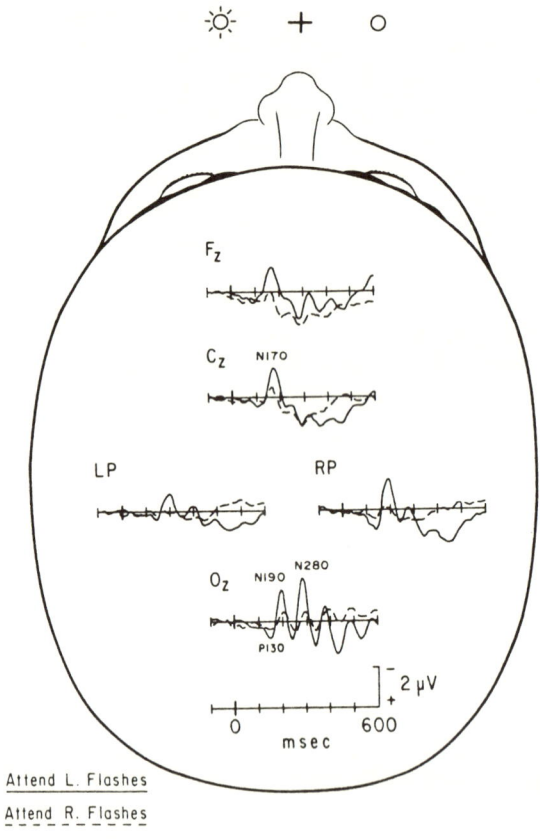

FIG. 3.1. Grand average ERPs over 12 subjects in response to standard (nontarget) flashes in the left visual field. The subject's task was to report occurrences of the slightly brighter targets in the sequence of flashes in one visual field at a time. Solid tracings show ERPs elicited by the left flashes during the attend-left condition; dashed tracings show recordings during the attend-right condition. ERPs are shown for different scalp sites located over frontal (Fz), central (Cz), occipital (Oz), and left (LP) and right (RP) parietal areas. The ERPs to right field flashes (not shown) have a mirror-image pattern of enhanced N1 amplitude over the LP recording site. (Based on Hillyard et al., 1984.)

100 to 300 msec poststimulus in response to attended-field flashes. At the posterior (occipital) recording sites the earliest enhanced peak is the positive "P1" wave (also designated by its peak latency in msec, which ranges from "P100" through "P150"). The P1 wave onsets between 70 and 100 msec poststimulus according to the brightness and retinal location of the stimulus. The P1 is followed by succession of negative (N) and positive (P) components labeled N1

(N150 to N190), P2 (P200 to P250), and N2 (N260 to N290). The P1 wave tends to be bilaterally symmetrical whereas the later waves are usually larger over the scalp contralateral to the stimulus. Over the parietal and anterior scalp the N1 component shows very large attention-related modulations and is strongly lateralized to the contralateral side. This general ERP pattern has been reproduced under a variety of stimulus parameters and task assignments (Eason, 1981; Harter, Aine, & Schroeder, 1982; Hillyard et al., 1984; Hillyard & Munte, 1984; Van Voorhis & Hillyard, 1977), with the P1 and N1 modulations being the most consistently observed.

The fact that attention-related changes are seen in the earliest observable component of the occipital ERP (the P1) suggests that information is being gated or filtered at a fairly early stage of visual processing. Because the neural generators of these attention-sensitive ERP components are not known at present, however, the anatomical locus of this selectivity cannot be specified with certainty. Eason and associates have suggested that early attentional gating may take place subcortically, at the level of the lateral geniculate (Eason, 1981) or even in the retina itself (Eason, Oakley, & Flowers, 1983). The lateral geniculate nucleus is indeed well supplied with inputs from the reticular system that would be capable of modulating sensory transmission through this relay in such a fashion (Singer, 1977; Skinner & Yingling, 1977).

Further support for the early gating hypothesis comes from the high degree of similarity of the waveforms of the ERPs elicited by attended and unattended flashes; the components elicited by attended flashes are simply enlarged and show little or no alteration in morphology. This would be expected if spatial attention acts by modulating (either through inhibition or facilitation) the sensory inputs that give rise to the entire evoked P1-N1-P2-N2 sequence. However, given that single unit activity can be evoked in parietal and frontal association cortices at latencies as early as 70 to 80 msec in monkeys (Bushnell, Goldberg, & Robinson, 1981; Wurtz, Goldberg, & Robinson, 1980), which corresponds roughly to the onset latency of the human P1 wave, it is possible that the spatial attention effect may be imposed on the ERP at higher cortical levels. Indeed, the earliest level of the visual cortical pathways where spatial-selective unit activity has been consistently recorded in monkeys is in the prelunate visual association area (Boch & Fischer, 1983; Fischer & Boch, 1981), and these units also have a mean latency of some 80 msec. Units in striate (area 17) and prestriate (area 18) cortical regions reportedly show little evidence of attentional enhancement or spatial selectivity in relation to targeted saccadic eye movements (Wurtz et al., 1980). However, the procedures used to induce selective attention differ considerably between the human and monkey experiments, so the possibility of early cortical or subcortical gating still remains viable in both species.

When attention is directed to the lateral visual fields, the N1 component has a maximum amplitude over the contralateral parietal scalp and occurs some 20 to 30 msec earlier than the occipital N1 peak (Fig. 3.1). The waveform of the parietal N1 bears a strong resemblance to that of the evoked discharge of attention-sensitive units in the posterior parietal lobe of monkeys that have been recorded under comparable conditions of spatial attention (Mountcastle, Andersen, & Motter, 1981; Wurtz et al., 1980). Although the latencies are 30 to 50 msec longer in humans, the similarity in response morphology and attentional sensitivity suggests that the parietal ERP may reflect the averaged neuronal population activity profile in those parietal lobe areas concerned with the control of attention to extrapersonal space. The fact that the parietal ERP is sensitive to both visual and auditory attention (Hillyard et al., 1984) suggests that the registration of inputs in parietal cortex is controlled by an attentional process that selects both for modality and spatial location. Further work is needed, however, to determine whether the parietal N1 enhancement involves an additional level of selectivity beyond that reflected in the occipital P1–N1 sequence.

ATTENTION TO CENTRAL AND PERIPHERAL VISUAL LOCATIONS

Most studies of ERPs and visual–spatial attention have been limited to stimuli in the peripheral visual fields. Considerable evidence exists, however, that information presented to the fovea is attended and processed in a different way from more lateralized inputs (Breitmeyer & Ganz, 1976; Trevarthen, 1968; Ungerleider & Mishkin, 1982). This raises the possibility that the spatial focusing of attention may operate in different fashion for stimuli presented to the central and peripheral retina. As described below, Neville and Lawson (in preparation) have examined this question in a study that delivered sequences of visual stimuli to foveal as well as peripheral locations in an unpredictable order.

Methods

Subjects fixated a point in the center of a video monitor and in separate blocks of trials focused their attention on one of three locations, situated 18° to the left or right of fixation or at the fovea, respectively. Sequences of white squares (.5° wide, 33 msec in duration) were presented in random order at all three locations at ISIs ranging between 200 and 400 msec. The task was to detect the direction of apparent motion of infrequent (20%) "target" stimuli occurring at the attended location. Subjects pressed one of eight response buttons to indicate the direction of the movement along vertical, horizontal, or diagonal axes. The target stimuli consisted of the illumination of one .5° square for 33 msec followed immediately by the illumination of one of eight adjacent squares for an additional 33 msec, which produced a clear illusory movement in the direction of the second stimulus. ERPs were recorded from several positions over homologous regions of the left and right hemispheres referred to the linked mastoids (recording bandpass .01 to 100 Hz).

Results

Focused attention, both to the peripheral and to the foveal flashes, produced marked enhancements of the early positive (P1, 130 msec) and negative (N1, 160 msec) components; a repeated-measures analysis of variance showed the effect of attended/unattended location to be significant at the .001 level for base-to-peak measures of both components. For both peripheral and foveal stimuli, the increase in P1 was largest over the occipital region and was bilaterally symmetrical. However, the increase in N1 had a markedly different scalp distribution for peripheral and foveal stimuli. As shown in Fig. 3.2, the major attention-related increase in N1 amplitude to the peripheral stimuli occurred over the parietal region of the hemisphere contralateral to the attended visual field. By contrast, the largest effects of foveally directed attention on N1 occurred over the occipital regions, where the increase was bilaterally symmetrical (see Table 3.1). This distributional difference was reflected in a significant interaction ($p < .001$) for stimulus location × direction of attention × recording site. Superimposed on the contralateral parietal distribution of the N1 enhancement for peripheral stimuli was a tendency for its enhancement to be larger from over the right than the left hemisphere ($p < .05$).

A right hemispheric predominance was also evident in later ERP components. Between 300 and 600 msec poststimulus, the ERP to the attended standards was slightly positive, but the unattended standards elicited a broad negativity (Fig. 3.2). Thus, the effect of attention in this latency zone was the emergence of a positive difference (PD) component that was evident in the "difference waveform" formed by subtracting the unattended from the attended ERPs. The amplitude of PD was larger over the right than the left hemisphere for both left and right visual field stimuli (main effect of hemisphere, $p < .01$). The PD associated with attention to the fovea, however, was bilaterally symmetrical.

Discussion

It appears that early attentional selection can operate on information presented to the fovea as well as to the periphery of the visual fields. In both cases, the mechanisms underlying spatial attention include an early modulation of the sensory response (reflected in amplitude increases in the P1 and N1 components) and the activation of subsequent processes (the PD) that provide evidence for hemispheric specialization. The attention-related changes in the N1 component were greater over occipital regions bilaterally for the foveal stimuli, in contrast with the contralateral–parietal distribution of N1 to peripheral events. This suggests that different pathways are being modulated for deployment of attention to different regions of the visual fields. This distributional difference could arise in part from inputs being gated preferentially into the more posterior portions of the striate cortex that contain the representation of the central visual fields during foveally directed attention. The enlarged parietal response for laterally directed

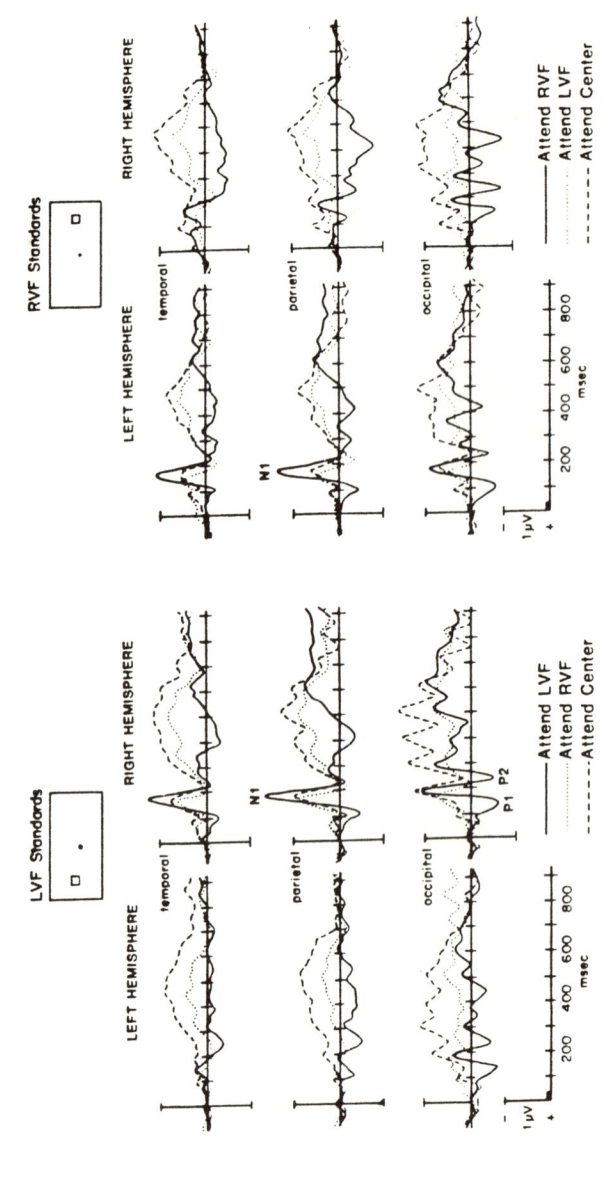

FIG. 3.2. Grand average ERPs over 12 subjects to peripheral standard stimuli located in the right (RVF) and left (LVF) visual fields. The superimposed tracings show ERPs recorded from homologous pairs of electrodes over the right and left cerebral hemispheres under three conditions of attention (to the RVF, the LVF, and the central stimuli). Note the contralateral distribution of the N1 component, followed by late slow waves that vary in distribution according to attentional condition.

TABLE 3.1
Mean Baseline Peak Amplitudes (μV) of P1 and N1 Components
to Flashes at Different Locations
and under Different Attention Conditions

P1 Amplitude

Parietal Sites

Location	LVF		RVF		CENTER	
Attend	L. Hem.	R. Hem.	L. Hem.	R. Hem.	L. Hem.	R. Hem.
LVF	.46	.58	.29	.25	.46	.73
RVF	.28	.29	.57	.48	.40	.71
CENTER	.32	.18	.21	.05	.72	.89

Occipital Sites

Location	LVF		RVF		CENTER	
Attend	L. Hem.	R. Hem.	L. Hem.	R. Hem.	L. Hem.	R. Hem.
LVF	.88	1.06	.40	.42	1.56	1.71
RVF	.18	.42	1.10	.88	1.32	1.45
CENTER	.51	.53	.46	.33	2.30	2.48

N1 Amplitude

Parietal Sites

Location	LVF		RVF		CENTER	
Attend	L. Hem.	R. Hem.	L. Hem.	R. Hem.	L. Hem.	R. Hem.
LVF	−.30	−1.90	−.74	−.55	−1.11	−1.10
RVF	−.38	−1.10	−1.47	−.76	−.91	−1.45
CENTER	−.59	−1.24	−.90	−.90	−1.36	−1.94

Occipital Sites

Location	LVF		RVF		CENTER	
Attend	L. Hem.	R. Hem.	L. Hem.	R. Hem.	L. Hem.	R. Hem.
LVF	−.73	−1.42	−.82	−.76	−1.12	−1.27
RVF	−.92	−1.24	−1.22	−.89	−.86	−1.40
CENTER	−1.11	−1.48	−1.13	−1.30	−2.02	−2.40

attention is also consistent with the evidence that parietal areas are concerned more with the processing of peripheral than central events (e.g., Ungerleider & Mishkin, 1982).

Observations of larger attention effects over the right hemisphere are in agreement with the large clinical literature describing a greater role for the right hemisphere in visuospatial functions (e.g., Heilman & Valenstein, 1979). However, the fact that these asymmetries were not evident for foveal attention suggests that the special role of the right hemisphere in spatial orientation may be limited to analysis of the peripheral visual fields.

ATTENTION TO FEATURES AND LOCATIONS

When visual stimuli are selected on the basis of sensory features such as color, brightness, orientation, size, or shape, a distinctive ERP signature is produced that differs markedly from the P1–N1–P2–N2 sequence enhanced with spatial selection. For example, when subjects discriminate sequences of colored flashes and react selectively to flashes of one color, the attended stimuli elicit a broad negative ERP in the 150 to 350 msec range that appears to be largely endogenous. If the stimuli have two or more sensory dimensions that vary orthogonally, and the target stimulus is defined by a specific combination of these features, the associated ERP latencies provide evidence for a regular ordering of feature selections (Harter et al., 1982; Hillyard & Kutas, 1983; Previc & Harter, 1982).

The interaction between attention to location and to color has been studied by Harter et al. (1982) and by Hillyard and Munte (1984). The design of the latter study is shown in Fig. 3.3. Vertical bars colored either red (R) or blue (B) were flashed to right or left locations situated 5° lateral to a fixation point. During each experimental run these four stimuli were presented in random order at ISIs of 350 to 500 msec while subjects attended to one color–location combination at a time (e.g., "attend to blue bars on the left"). Their task was to detect and react to occasional (20%) "target" bars, having the designated color–location, that were slightly shorter than the more frequent "standard" bars.

The ERPs were averaged across the different color–location stimulus classes according to whether the stimulus had the attended or unattended color (C+ or C−) or location (L+ or L−). As shown in Fig. 3.3, all stimuli at the attended location (L+) elicited an enlarged occipital P1–N1–N2 sequence (labeled P122–N168–N264), regardless of whether their color was attended (C+/L+) or unattended (C−/L+). Thus, the early selection on the basis of location proceeded independently of selection by color. The converse was not true, however; the selection for color, indexed by a broad N150–350 component, was strictly dependent on stimulus location. The N150–350 was elicited only by bars of the attended color at the attended location, and there was little evidence for any color selection at the unattended location. This ERP pattern indicates that the process-

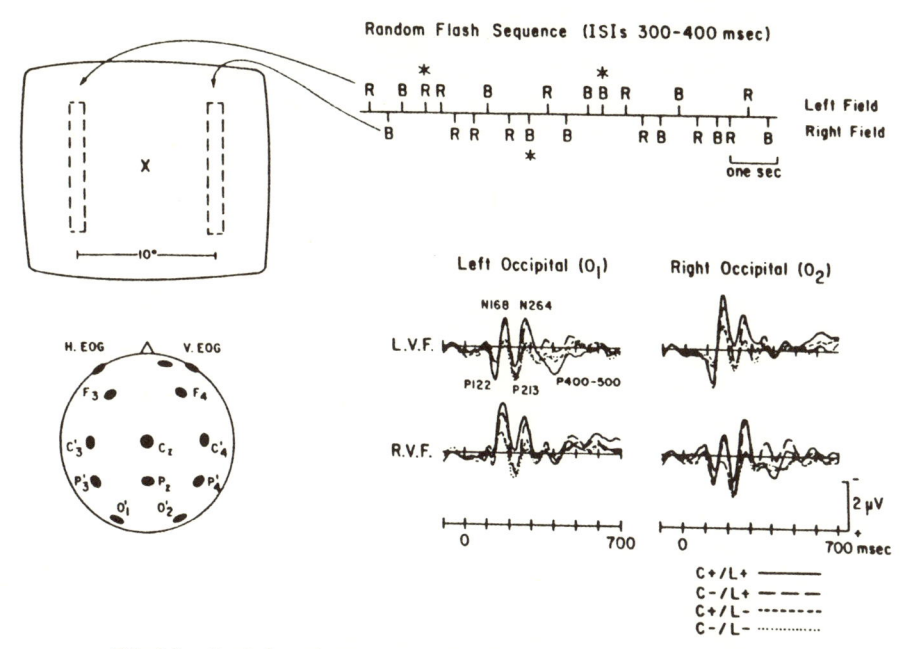

FIG. 3.3. Depiction of stimulus sequences in the color–location selection experiment. The ordering of red (R) and blue (B) bars in the right and left visual fields was randomized. Asterisks represent occasional "targets" that were slightly shorter in height than the more frequent "standard" stimuli. The ERPs shown are grand average waveforms over 14 subjects, averaged according to attended stimulus class: The bars were either attended (C+/L+), had the attended color but not location (C+/L−), had the attended location but not color (C−/L+), or had neither attribute (C−/L−). (Based on Hillyard & Munte, 1984.)

ing of stimulus color is hierarchically dependent on the prior selection for location. When the stimulus locations were brought closer together in a separate condition, however, so that the spatial discrimination was more difficult and time consuming than the color discrimination, this hierarchical pattern was lost, and color selection occurred without regard to stimulus location.

This ERP evidence that stimuli are selected for different features at specific latencies and with hierarchical contingencies that depend on cue discriminability provides strong support for "early selection" or intraperceptual theories of attention. If stimuli presented to unattended locations were processed fully, as specified by late selection theories, this processing seems to take place with little or no ERP signature.

These ERP results and those of Harter and associates also provide support for the position taken by Treisman and Gelade (1980) that "features come first in perception" [p. 98], in contrast with the Gestaltist hypothesis that the perception of feature conjunctions or wholistic "objects" is primary. The ERP signs of simple feature selection generally precede the signs of object or conjunction selection, particularly when one attribute is more rapidly discriminable than the other(s) (Hansen & Hillyard, 1983; Harter et al., 1982; Previc & Harter, 1982). Moreover, the finding that conjunction-specific components were restricted to stimuli at attended locations is consistent with Treisman and Gelade's view that spatially focused attention is a prerequisite for the combining of feature information into a unified percept. Focal attention, then, seems to enable a further processing of events falling within its spotlight, which includes a more detailed examination of the relevant features and their integration into perceptual objects.

However, the suggestion from the ERP findings that spatial attention involves an early gating of inputs to unattended locations may be at odds with Treisman and Gelade's proposal that separable features such as color are registered automatically and in parallel across the visual field. If unattended inputs are gated precortically, this would presumably reduce the influx of information about all the features of those stimuli. Hence, the phenomenon of preattentive feature registration and grouping that has been demonstrated in the studies of Treisman and collaborators may take place only when attention is distributed across the visual fields rather than being focused on one location.

PHASIC ORIENTING AND SUSTAINED ATTENTION

The contrast between the robust spatial-attention effects manifested in the ERPs during sustained attention tasks and the diminished behavioral selectivity reported by Posner et al, (1980, 1984) remains puzzling. One way to reconcile these findings would be if attentional selectivity were only present for the first few stimuli of each block. In this case, the practice of averaging ERPs over an entire block would yield a misleading picture, because the overall attention effect would result from the averaging together of ERPs from early and late trials having very different characteristics.

The time course of attentional selectivity has been studied on a stimulus-by-stimulus basis by Donald and Young (1982) in the auditory modality. Tone sequences were presented to the right and left ears while subjects listened for target tones selectively in one ear at a time. The tones were presented in blocks separated by intervals of 6 seconds. ERPs were averaged separately for each sequential tone position within a block in both attended and unattended channels. By averaging across a sufficiently large number of blocks, it was found that the differential enhancement of the early negativity (N1 at 100 msec) to attended-channel tones was present for the very first tone in each block and did not decrement over the succeeding tones.

As described later, we have employed a similar design to study the stimulus-by-stimulus time course of sustained visual–spatial attention. Subjects were cued before each block of stimuli as to which visual field was to be attended throughout that block. The stimuli were sequences of "bars" flashed to right or left field locations in random order, and each subject's task was to detect slightly shorter "target" bars in the cued field while ignoring those in the opposite field. By examining ERPs to stimuli at each successive position within a block and averaging across blocks, it could be determined whether the ERP attention effect decays with stimulus repetition, as suggested by the data of Posner et al., or is sustained throughout the block, like the auditory attention effect studied by Donald and Young. A third possibility, of course, is that attentional selectivity would actually build up over successive stimuli, as Treisman, Squire, and Green (1974) observed in a dichotic listening task.

Methods

Each trial began with a warning tone pip followed after 300 msec by a left or right pointing arrow that cued the direction of attention for the succeeding block of bar stimuli. The first bar occurred 1900 msec after the directional cue, and each block contained 15 to 20 white vertical bars flashed in random order to the left or right visual field at intervals of 350 to 600 msec (rectangular distribution). The bars were flashed for 32 msec each at locations 7° lateral to a central fixation point. The majority (90%) of the bars were taller (3° in height) and were designated as "standards," whereas the less frequent "targets" (10%) subtended 2.5° in height. Each new trial began 6 seconds after the conclusion of the previous block of bars.

The assigned task on each trial was to focus attention exclusively on the sequence of bars on the side cued by the arrow and to respond with a button press to the randomly occurring targets at that location. Each experimental run consisted of 14 such trials, and the entire experiment consisted of 32 runs administered over two recording sessions on separate days. The direction of the cue was unpredictable on each trial, as was the right–left ordering of the bars within blocks. However, over the course of the experiment each randomized sequence of bars was presented twice, preceded once by a left arrow and once by a right arrow. This ensured that the comparisons of ERPs to stimuli at attended and unattended locations would not be confounded with physical stimulus differences.

ERPs were recorded to each flashed bar from homologous pairs to left and right scalp electrodes, referred to linked mastoids. Reported here are data from left to right occipital sites (01 and 02, International 10–20 system) and left and right parietal sites (LP and RP, located halfway along the line between the Pz site and the ear canal). Scalp recordings were taken with a bandpass of 0.01 to 60 Hz (half amplitude cut-offs), and eye position was monitored via D.C. recordings of the vertical and horizontal electrooculogram.

ERPs were averaged using a general purpose computer according to the serial position of the bars within the left and right sequences and according to whether attention was directed left or right. Because the attention effects were similar for left and right stimulus sequences, the ERPs to attended left bars and attended right bars were averaged together for recording sites contralateral and ipsilateral to the stimulus. The ERPs to unattended left and right sequences were similarly averaged together.

Results

The waveform of the posterior ERPs to the bar stimuli included the following major components: a bilaterally symmetrical P1 (P140) peak that was largest over occipital sites, an N1 (N190) peak that was largest over the contralateral scalp and had a similar amplitude parietally and occipitally, and an extended negativity that followed the N1 and lasted until around 400 msec (the N250–400). Each of these components showed a distinct time course for its attention effect.

Figure 3.4 shows the contralateral ERPs to bars at the first through sixth serial positions. (Note that the stimulus number here refers to sequential position *within* a left or right field sequence, not *across* the two sequences.) Visual inspection of the waveforms indicates a sizable N1 amplitude differential between flashes at attended versus unattended locations that is present for the first stimulus in each sequence and continues unabated through at least the sixth stimulus. (Some blocks only had six bars on one side due to the vagaries of the stimulus randomization.)

Repeated-measures analyses of variance were performed on the ERP component amplitudes referred to a 200 msec prestimulus baseline, with factors of attended/unattended location, serial position, and hemisphere of recording (contra/ipsi to stimulus). The main effect of attended versus unattended location on the N1 peak amplitude was highly significant ($p < .001$) at both occipital and parietal sites, and the attention effects evaluated at each serial position also reached significance (Fig. 3.5). There was no significant tendency for this attention effect to increase or decrease across stimuli (interaction of attended/unattended location × stimulus position, n.s.). However, there was an overall decline in N1 amplitudes across stimulus position for both attended and unattended ERPs ($p < .001$).

In contrast with the behavior of the N1 peak, the posterior P1 (P140) wave did not show strong attention effects in this task, and the attended/unattended differential did not become significant until the fourth stimulus (parietal sites) or sixth stimulus (occipital sites) had been presented. The slow, late occipital negativity (N250–400) showed a different pattern, with significant attention effects emerging on the second stimulus and persisting through the fifth stimulus.

To increase the comparability of these ERP data with the primed-RT task of Posner et al., a further analysis was done with the ERPs to the very first stimuli in the sequences. In the previously described analyses, ERPs were averaged

3. VISUAL-SPATIAL ATTENTION   77

SEQUENTIAL POSITION EFFECT

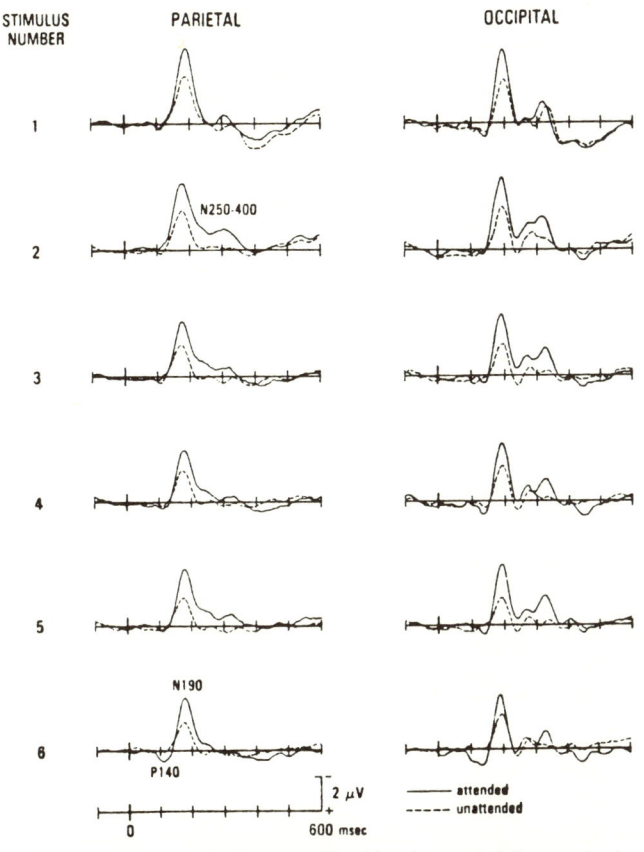

FIG. 3.4. Grand average ERPs (over 12 subjects) recorded from parietal and occipital scalp sites in response to visual bars flashed at each position within the sequence. ERPs to attended-side bars were collapsed across right and left field presentations, and the same was done for unattended-side bars. ERPs shown are from scalp sites contralateral to the visual field of the stimulus. Each pair of overlapped tracings compares the ERPs averaged across attended bar sequences (solid lines) with those to unattended bar sequences (dotted lines).

separately for stimulus positions 1, 2, ..6 within a particular visual field without regard to what had been presented in the opposite field. However, the first bar in a given field in a block may or may not have been preceded by a bar in the opposite field (on a 50/50 basis), due to the random nature of the right/left stimulus ordering. Hence, ERPs can be examined separately for those bars that were the very first to follow the arrow cue and those bars that were the first to occur on their side but were preceded by one or more bars on the opposite side. This comparison is shown for the parietal recording sites in Fig. 3.6.

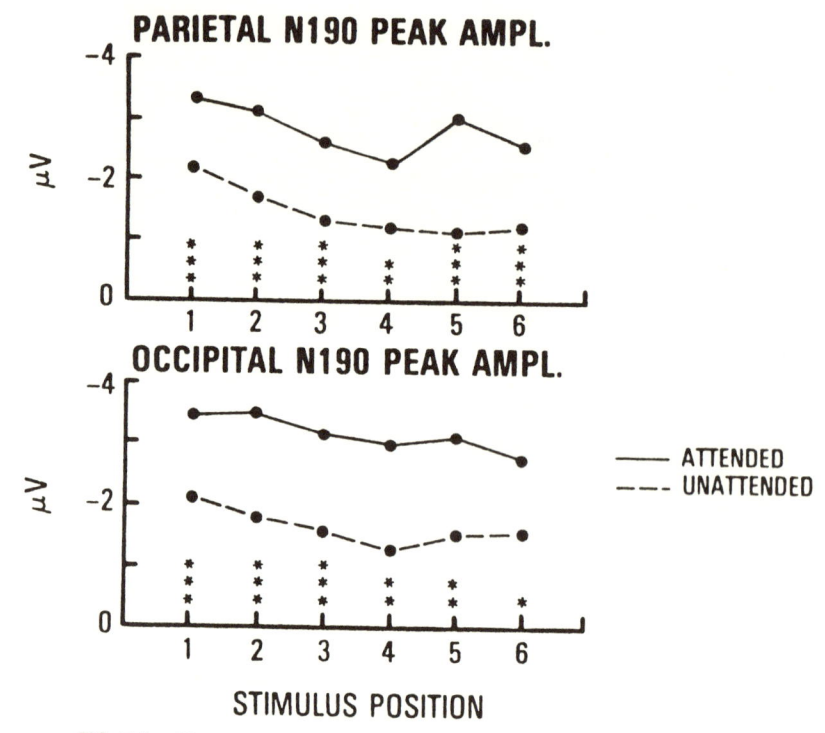

FIG. 3.5. Mean amplitude across 12 subjects of baseline-peak N1 (N190) amplitudes, shown separately for each serial stimulus position. Asterisks indicate statistical significance (ANOVA) of the attended versus unattended amplitude comparison at each position (***: $p < .001$; **: $p < .01$; *: $p < .05$).

The attention-related modulation of the N1 peak was considerably smaller for the unpreceded first bars than for the preceded first bars. This preceded/unpreceded difference in the N1 attention effect was significant at both parietal (-2.27 versus -1.43 μV, $p < .05$) and occipital (-2.32 versus -1.55 μV, $p < .01$) sites. As shown in Fig. 3.6, this difference was due primarily to a reduction in N1 amplitude to bars on the unattended side when preceded by bars in the opposite field. When unpreceded, both attended and unattended bars elicit large N1 amplitudes. The preceded/unpreceded comparison did not reach significance for any other components.

Discussion

On the basis of this stimulus-by-stimulus ERP analysis, it appears that selection by location is small for the very first stimulus that follows an attention-directing cue but develops rapidly thereafter. The principal N1 measure showed an enhanced spatial selectivity to the stimulus that followed the very first one, and this high level of selectivity was maintained throughout the block. The occipital N250–400 showed a similar pattern, but with a tendency toward smaller attention effects for the latter stimuli in the sequence. The short-latency P1 wave took longer to develop spatial selectivity and did not differentiate between attended and unattended locations until after several stimuli had been presented.

A strong tendency was also observed for ERP amplitudes to decline over stimulus repetitions for both attended and unattended fields (Fig. 3.5). This overall decline in N1 is most likely attributable to neuronal refractory period effects, which typically occur when successive stimuli are delivered at intervals too short to allow full recovery of the neural generator processes for the ERP (Picton, Hillyard, & Galambos, 1976). These ERP refractory effects can be quite stimulus specific and may well be linked with the inhibitory influences on RT observed by Posner et al. (1982, 1984) when targets occur at recently stimulated locations. However, in the present experiment, stimuli occurred with equal probability in cued and uncued locations, such that inhibitory sensory mechanisms could not in themselves account for the selective attention effects on the ERPs.

The observed pattern of incrementing ERP selectivity over the first few stimuli contrasts with the time course of the attentional costs and benefits produced

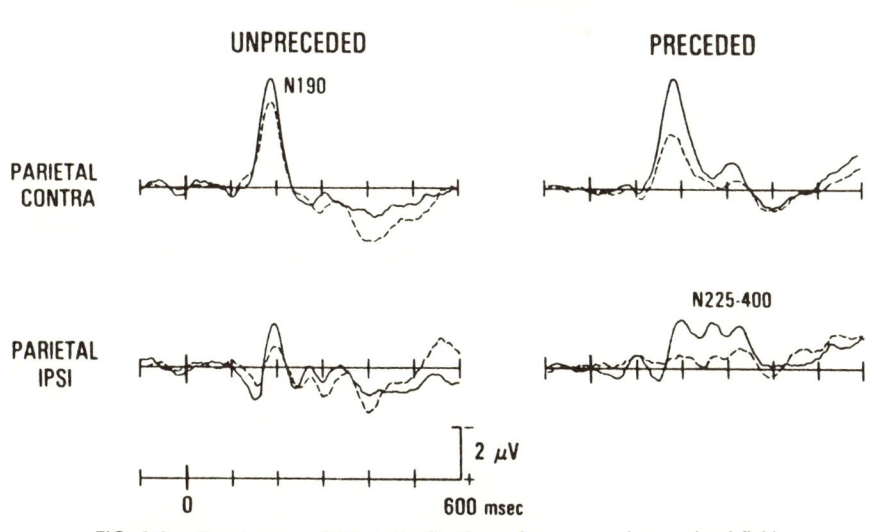

FIG. 3.6. Grand average ERPs to the first bars of a sequence in one visual field averaged separately according to whether those bars were or were not preceded by one or more bars in the opposite field. Superimposed tracings show ERPs to bars on attended (solid tracings) and unattended (dashed tracing) sides. ERPs from recording sites contralateral and ipsilateral to the stimulus were averaged separately.

by a spatial priming cue in the RT experiments of Posner et al. (1980, 1984). These behavioral priming effects were small when target stimuli were presented in blocks and showed a decrementing pattern with stimulus repetition. In fact, the RT costs and benefits were largest under conditions where a single target stimulus followed each attention-directing prime, which would correspond to the unpreceded stimulus in the present ERP experiments. Because the ERP and RT indices showed nearly inverse changes with stimulus repetition, it seems reasonable to suppose that they reflect fundamentally different mechanisms of spatial selective attention.

For reasons discussed previously, we have considered the attention-related modulation of the P1–N1 components to be an index of early perceptual selection by spatial location. If this form of selection is indeed poorly developed for the first stimulus after an attention-directing cue, how can we account for the RT costs and benefits obtained by Posner and his colleagues? One possibility is that these small ERP modulations do reflect an early selection mechanism that is responsible for a portion of the spatial priming effects upon RT and upon signal detectability (e.g., Bashinski & Bacharach, 1980). It seems necessary, however, to postulate an additional level of selectivity that is not reflected in the P1–N1 changes and perhaps acts at a later stage of processing to influence RT measures in the trial-by-trial cueing paradigms. This second level evidently becomes less selective with stimulus repetition, whereas the early selectivity associated with the P1–N1 enhancement is maximized during sustained attention to repetitive stimulation. Whether this inferred second level of selection operates at a perceptual or postperceptual stage of processing remains to be determined.

In this connection, it seems likely that postperceptual factors of expectancy and surprise would play a significant role in producing spatial cueing effects on RT. For example, the priming cue may induce an expectation for an event at the cued location together with a preparatory set to respond to that specific stimulus upon its detection. If an "invalid" stimulus should occur instead, the disconfirmation of the subject's expectancy may provoke a general surprise or arousal reaction that could interfere with rapid responding. Further work is needed to disentangle the relative contributions of expectancy/set factors from those of early perceptual selection in producing RT costs and benefits in these priming tasks.

The finding of large N1 components to unpreceded stimuli at both attended and unattended locations indicates that it may be difficult to suppress processing of phasic inputs that are presented in an otherwise empty field. When no reference stimuli are present to hold attention, there may be an automatic orienting toward any new stimulus. Indeed, the ERP data suggest that only after a stimulus has been presented at the attended location does it become possible to suppress inputs to the unattended location effectively. The occurrence of a relevant event may provide a spatial cue for focusing the subject's attention to that location, thereby allowing rejection of subsequent events on the irrelevant side. This corresponds to Naatanen's (this volume) proposal that stimuli are selected or rejected by virtue of the degree to which they match the cue characteristics of the "attentional trace" held in memory of the attended event class. A further implication of the present data is that rejection of inputs to irrelevant locations does not require the building up of a sensory image of the to-be-ignored stimulus. In other words, a stimulus may be rejected without having been seen immediately beforehand.

From these considerations, it seems likely that the early selection indexed by these ERP changes may be even more effective during attention to natural scenes that contain stable objects to capture and hold a person's attention. This "focal attention" (Treisman & Gelade, 1980) would then enable a more detailed evaluation of events within its spotlight and a relative suppression of events at other locations. The dependency of the ERP effect on cueing the attended location is in line with Posner's (1980) view that spatial attention involves "an active process of maintaining the orientation" rather than a "passive filter that can easily be set in place and left" [p. 8].

There is still considerable uncertainty about the functional significance of the different attention-sensitive ERP components. The posterior P1 and N1 waves seem to be consistently enlarged during sustained spatial attention, whereas subsequent components including P2, N2, N250–450, and PD seem to be more task specific and probably reflect the particular processing demands of the situation. The dissociations observed between the occipital P1 and the parieto-occipital N1 components, moreover, suggest that they may reflect different aspects of early selection. Based on the greater attentional lability of the N1 component and its more parietal distribution with peripherally directed attention, we would speculate that the N1 enhancement is a sign of parietal-lobe activity associated with the orienting of attention. In this interpretation, stimuli that trigger attentional orienting or fall within the attentional spotlight would elicit an enlarged N1 response, which represents activity in a topographically ordered cortical representation of visual space and designates a specific region thereof to receive further processing. This neural activity could represent a spatial "tagging" of the potentially relevant event, rather than the actual information about its properties. Such an orienting of attention could be mediated by inputs to the parietal lobes from the superior colliculus-pulvinar (Breitmeyer & Ganz, 1976) or the geniculo-striate system (Ungerleider & Mishkin, 1982). Modulations of the occipital P1 wave (and possibly other occipital components as well), on the other hand, may represent the actual gating of stimulus information in the primary visual pathway. This early selectivity evidently takes longer to develop and may depend on an accurate localization of the attended stimulus by the orienting system. Combined research efforts in both humans and animals (Galambos & Hillyard, 1981) should help to clarify the anatomical and neurophysiological bases of these different components of visual–spatial attention.

ACKNOWLEDGMENTS

This work was supported in part by grants from N.I.M.H. (MH-25594), N.I.H. (NS-14365), the Alfred P. Sloan Foundation, the John D. and Catherine T. MacArthur Foundation, and the Axe-Houghton Foundation.

REFERENCES

Bashinski, H. S., & Bacharach, V. R. (1980). Enhancement of perceptual sensitivity as the result of selectively attending to spatial locations. *Perception and Psychophysics, 28,* 241-248.

Beck, J., & Ambler, B. (1973). The effects of concentrated and distributed attention on peripheral acuity. *Perception and Psychophysics, 14,* 225-230.

Boch, R., & Fischer, B. (1983). Saccadic reaction times and activation of the prelunate cortex: parallel observations in trained Rhesus Monkeys. *Experimental Brain Research, 50,* 201-210.

Breitmeyer, B. G., & Ganz, L. (1976). Implications of sustained and transient channels for theories of visual pattern masking, saccadic suppression, and information processing. *Psychological Review, 83,* 1-36.

Bushnell, M. C., Goldberg, M. E., & Robinson, D. L. (1981). Behavioral enhancement of visual responses in monkey cerebral cortex: I. Modulation in posterior parietal cortex related to selective visual attention. *Journal of Neurophysiology, 46,* 755-772.

Colegate, R. L., Hoffman, J. E., & Eriksen, C. W. (1973). Selective encoding from multielement visual displays. *Perception and Psychophysics, 14,* 217-224.

Donald, M. W., & Young, M. J. (1982). A time-course analysis of attentional tuning of the auditory evoked response. *Experimental Brain Research, 46,* 357-367.

Eason, R. G. (1981). Visual evoked potential correlates of early neural filtering during selective attention. *Bulletin of the Psychonomic Society, 18,* 203-206.

Eason, R., Harter, M., & White, C. (1969). Effects of attention and arousal on visually evoked cortical potentials and reaction time in man. *Physiology and Behavior, 4,* 283-289.

Eason, R. G., Oakley, M., & Flowers, L. (1983). Central neural influences on the human retina during selective attention. *Physiological Psychology, 11,* 18-28.

Eriksen, C. W., & Hoffman, J. E. (1973). The extent of processing of noise elements during selective encoding from visual displays. *Perception and Psychophysics, 14,* 155-160.

Fischer, B., & Boch, R. (1981). Enhanced activation of neurons in prelunate cortex before visually guided saccades of trained Rhesus monkeys. *Experimental Brain Research, 44,* 129-137.

Galambos, R., & Hillyard, S. (1981). Electrophysiological approaches to human cognitive processing. *Neurosciences Research Program Bulletin, 20,* 141-265.

Hansen, J. C., & Hillyard, S. A. (1983). Selective attention to multidimensional auditory stimuli in man. *Journal of Experimental Psychology: Human Perceptual Performance, 9,* 1-19.

Harter, M. R., Aine, C., & Schroeder, C. (1982). Hemispheric differences in the neural processing of stimulus location and type: Effects of selective attention on visual evoked potentials. *Neuropsychologia, 20,* 421-438.

Heilman, K. M., & Valenstein, E. (Eds.). (1979). *Clinical neuropsychology.* New York: Oxford University.

Hillyard, S. A., & Kutas, M. (1983). Electrophysiology of cognitive processing. *Annual Review of Psychology, 34,* 33-61.

Hillyard, S. A., & Munte, T. F. (1984). Selective attention to color and locational cues: An analysis with event-related brain potentials. *Perception and Psychophysics, 36,* 185-198.

Hillyard, S. A., Simpson, G. V., Woods, D. L., Van Voorhis, S., & Munte, T. (1984). Event-related brain potentials and selective attention to different modalities. In F. Reinoso-Suarez & C. Ajmone-Marsan (Eds.), *Cortical integration* (pp. 395–414). New York: Raven Press.

Hoffman, J. E. (1975). Hierarchical stages in the processing of visual information. *Perception and Psychophysics, 18,* 348–354.

Hoffman, J. E., & Nelson, B. (1981). Spatial selectivity in visual search. *Perception and Psychophysics, 30,* 283–290.

Johnston, W. A., & Dark, V. J. (1982). In defense of intraperceptual theories of attention. *Journal of Experimental Psychology: Human Perception and Performance, 8,* 407–421.

Jonides, J. (1980). Towards a model of the mind's eye's movement. *Canadian Journal of Psychology, 34,* 103–112.

Mountcastle, V. B., Andersen, R. A., & Motter, B. C. (1981). The influence of attentive fixation upon the excitability of the light-sensitive neurons of the posterior parietal cortex. *Journal of Neuroscience, 1,* 1218–1235.

Neville, H. J., & Lawson, D. (In preparation). *Attention to central and peripheral visual space in a movement detection task: An event-related potential and behavioral study.*

Picton, T. W., Hillyard, S. A., & Galambos, R. (1976). Habituation and attention in the auditory system. In W. Keidel & W. Neff (Eds.), *Handbook of sensory physiology Vol. 5 The auditory system.* (Part 3: Clinical and Special Topics, pp. 345–389). Berlin: Springer Verlag.

Posner, M. I. (1980). Orienting of attention. *Quarterly Journal of Experimental Psychology, 32,* 3–25.

Posner, M. I., & Cohen, Y. (1984). Components of visual orienting. In H. Bouma & D. Bouwhuis (Eds.), *Attention and performance X* (pp. 531–556). Hillsdale, NJ: Lawrence Erlbaum Associates.

Posner, M. I., Cohen, Y., Choate, L., Hockey, R., & Maylor, E. (1984). Sustained concentration: Passive filtering or active orienting? In S. Kornblum & J. Requin (Eds.), *Preparatory states and processes* (pp. 49–68). Hillsdale,NJ: Lawrence Erlbaum Associates.

Posner, M. I., Cohen, Y., & Rafal, R. D. (1982). Neural systems control of spatial orienting. *Philosophical Transactions of the Royal Society of London, B298,* 187–198.

Posner, M. I., Nissen, M. J., & Ogden, W. C. (1978). Attended and unattended processing modes: The role of set for spatial location. In H. L. Pick & E. Saltzman (Eds.), *Modes of perceiving and processing information* (pp. 137–157). Hillsdale, NJ: Lawrence Erlbaum Associates.

Posner, M. I., Snyder, C. R. R., & Davidson, B. J. (1980). Attention and the detection of signals. *Journal of Experimental Psychology: General, 109,* 160–174.

Previc, F. H., & Harter, M. F. (1982). Electrophysiological and behavioral indicants of selective attention to multifeature gratings. *Perception and Psychophysics, 32,* 465–472.

Remington, R. W. (1980). Attention and saccadic eye movements. *Journal of Experimental Psychology: Human Perception and Performance, 6,* 726–744.

Singer, W. (1977). Control of thalamic transmission by corticofugal and ascending reticular pathways in the visual system. *Physiological Review, 57,* 386–420.

Skinner, J. E., & Yingling, C. D. (1977). Central gating mechanisms that regulate event-related potentials and behavior. In J. E. Desmedt (Ed.), *Attention, voluntary contraction and event-related cerebral potentials. Progress in clinical neurophysiology.* (Vol. 1, pp. 30–69). Karger: Basel.

Sperling, G., & Melchner, M. J. (1978). The attention operating characteristics: Examples from visual search. *Science, 202,* 315–318.

Treisman, A. M., & Gelade, G. (1980). A feature-integration theory of attention. *Cognition and Psychology, 12,* 97–136.

Treisman, A., Squire, R., & Green, J. (1974). Semantic processing in dichotic listening? *Memory and Cognition, 2,* 641–646.

Trevarthen, C. B. (1968). Two mechanisms of vision in primates. *Psychologische Forschung, 31,* 299–337.

Ungerleider, L. G., & Mishkin, M. (1982). Two cortical visual systems. In D. J. Ingle, R. J. W. Mansfield, & M. A. Goodale (Eds.), *The analysis of visual behavior* (pp. 549–586). Cambridge, Mass.: MIT Press.

Van der Heijden, A. H. C., & Eerland, E. (1973). The effect of cueing in a visual signal detection task. *Quarterly Journal of Experimental Psychology, 25*, 496–503.

Van Voorhis, S. T., & Hillyard, S. A. (1977). Visual evoked potentials and selective attention to points in space. *Perception and Psychophysics, 1*, 54–62.

Wurtz, R. H., Goldberg, M. E., & Robinson, D. L. (1980). Behavioral modulation of visual responses in the monkey. In J. M. Sprague & A. N. Epstein, *Progress in Psychobiology and Physiological Psychology* (Vol. 9, pp. 43–83). New York: Academic Press.

4 Visual Search and Visual Attention

John Duncan
MRC Applied Psychology Unit England

ABSTRACT

Research on visual attention deals with the limit on our ability to identify several stimuli at once. In visual search, this leads to concern with both the number of targets and the number of nontargets in a display. Although research usually concentrates on the number of nontargets, I suggest that it is useful to consider targets and nontargets together. Effects of multiple targets motivate the distinction between a first, parallel stage of perceptual processing, and a second, limited-capacity stage (Broadbent, 1958). They show that even when a target attribute can be used at the first stage to guide access to the second, the attribute cannot be reported until such access has occurred. This holds even for simple attributes such as tilt and closure. When an experiment manipulating the number of nontargets suggests parallel search, this does not show that the task can be performed without involving the limited-capacity stage. Rather, it shows the efficiency of selective access to that stage, and as such cannot be clearly interpreted without knowing the effect of multiple targets. One way to put the conclusions might be that many stimulus attributes are "identified" at the first stage but cannot yet be reported. I suggest, however, that it is misleading to talk of a stage at which information is "identified" or "analyzed." The enterprise instead is to understand the different processes of information *use*.

A lively discussion following this chapter involved the author and professors Kahneman and Treisman. This resulted in discussion of specific experiments related to the issues raised following page 105. Following a trip by the author of this chapter to the University of British Columbia, some experiments were designed that relate to the issues raised in this chapter. Duncan has kindly permitted the inclusion of these experiments as an addendum to his paper in the spirit of giving the reader as complete a picture of the issue as possible.

INTRODUCTION

One problem addressed in research on visual attention is the limit on our ability to identify several stimuli at once. In visual search there are potentially two aspects to this. A display might contain multiple *targets*—that is, stimuli whose presence or attributes are to be reported—or multiple *nontargets*—that is, stimuli to be rejected or ignored.

The number of nontargets has been the focus of interest in the great majority of research. Functions of reaction time (RT) or accuracy against this number have been used to support distinctions between automatic and controlled processing (Schneider & Shiffrin, 1977), processing of single features versus conjunctions (Treisman & Gelade, 1980), and so on. In this chapter I try to show that exclusive emphasis on the number of nontargets is unfortunate. A great deal can be learned about the nature of ''attention'' in vision by considering the joint effects of targets and nontargets.

I deal mainly with experiments trying to eliminate eye movements by using small displays and/or brief exposures. Where limits emerge in identifying several stimuli at once, they should not be produced by the need to scan large displays.

The first two sections of the chapter lay out the field by introducing some terminology and by suggesting that some tasks often considered nonsearch can be considered special cases of search.

TERMINOLOGY

Throughout this discussion I speak of a target's *defining attribute*—that is, the attribute by which it is distinguished from nontargets—and its *reported attribute*—that is, the attribute described in the response. For example, if the task were to name the red letter in a display containing five green letters and one red, the defining attribute would be color and the reported attribute would be shape. Experiments manipulating the number of nontargets obviously concern the processing of defining attributes—that is, the separation of targets and nontargets—whereas experiments manipulating the number of targets mainly concern the processing of reported attributes.

I also draw a distinction between *compound* and *simple* search. In compound search, the stimulus information separating targets from nontargets in itself tells nothing about which of the possible responses to choose: that is, defining and reported attributes are different. One example, as just described, would be naming the red letter in a display of one red and five green letters (defining attribute = color; reported attribute = shape). Another would be naming the color of the digit in a display containing one digit and five letters, all in different colors (defining attribute = alphanumeric class; reported attribute = color). In simple search the stimulus information that separates targets from nontargets is also sufficient to determine the correct response. In the clearest case, this means that the task is simply to decide whether a target is present or not. Examples would include deciding whether an array of colored characters contains one in red (defining and reported attribute = color), or whether an array of nontarget letters contains a target digit (defining and reported attribute = alphanumeric class).

Of course, there are tasks that are hard to classify. Suppose, for example, that the subject is to name the digit in a display of one digit and five letters. One plausible assumption is that information sufficient to determine whether each character is a digit is also sufficient to determine its identity, if it is a digit. If this is so, then the task is simple search, because information separating targets from nontargets is also sufficient to determine the response. An alternative possibility, however, is that one or a few stimulus features might sometimes be sufficient to classify a character as digit or letter, although further information is needed to determine exactly which digit or letter it is (Broadbent, 1971). In this case we should be dealing with compound search.

The distinction between compound and simple search is very similar to Broadbent's (1970, 1971) distinction between stimulus set and response set. As used by Broadbent, stimulus set covered tasks in which defining and reported attributes were different; an additional implication, however, has sometimes been that the defining attribute is relatively simple (e.g., color) and the reported attribute relatively complex (e.g., shape), which is not relevant to the definition of compound search. Response set was intended mainly to cover tasks such as naming the digit in a display of one digit and five letters, whereas here, simply deciding whether a target is present is taken to be the clearest case of simple search.

"NONSEARCH" TASKS

It may be useful to point out that two tasks often called *nonsearch* are, within the just-described framework, better seen as special cases of search—special only in their particular defining attributes. This helps establish the range of tasks to which the arguments of the present chapter should apply.

In one nonsearch task the defining attribute is location. For example, Eriksen and Eriksen (1974) asked subjects to identify a letter at fixation, ignoring flanking letters to either side. Banks, Larson, and Prinzmetal (1979) flashed a pair of letters to one side of fixation, cueing the subject in advance to report either the more peripheral or the more central letter. Such tasks are called nonsearch because the subject knows target position in advance and so, apparently, need not search through nontargets. Consider, however, the following two tasks. The first is typical search: The subject names the letter in red, with a display size of one (single red letter in one of three possible locations) or three (three letters, two white and one red, in the same three locations). The second is typical nonsearch: The subject names the letter at fixation, with a display size of one (single letter at fixation) or three (three letters, one at fixation flanked by two to either side). Except that in the first task the defining attribute is color whereas in the second it is location, the two tasks are very similar.

It is worth pointing out that results in the two tasks would be similar, too: Performance would be worse with display size three than one, unless the difference between target and nontargets, on the defining attribute, was substantial (in the first case, a large difference in color [Carter, 1982]; in the second, a large spatial separation [e.g., Bouma, 1978]). Typically, however, the results would be explained quite differently: In the first task the drop in performance would be ascribed to limits in the ability to process the color of three characters simultaneously, hence determining which is the target; in the second, it might be ascribed to peripheral contour interaction or *lateral masking*. An exception is the work of Wolford and Chambers (1983), whose approach to nonsearch in part reflects its similarity to search. They suggest that the interfering effect of nontargets adjacent to the target may be a mixed phenomenon, reflecting peripheral contour interaction in part, but in part also limits on the use of location information to distinguish between target and nontargets.

The second nonsearch task is defined by the absence of explicit nontargets. As an example, the subject might be asked to detect a flash of light occurring at one of two possible locations, in an otherwise "empty" field (Posner, Nissen, & Ogden, 1978; see also Bashinski & Bacharach, 1980). Here both defining attribute (i.e., the difference between target and nontarget locations) and reported attribute are luminance. The task might be thought not to involve search, because only one explicit stimulus is presented. This amounts, however, to the assumption that nontargets that are areas of "empty" field are in some way not equivalent to nontargets that differ from targets on the basis of other defining attributes—an assumption there is reason to doubt (Duncan, 1981).

The general point is that, although it might be surprising to discover that all stimulus attributes are processed similarly, it should not simply be assumed that some attributes are special. This is especially true when similar phenomena occur in nonsearch and search tasks.

THE NUMBER OF TARGETS

Compound Search

Suppose that, in compound search, a display of N characters is made up of T targets and $N-T$ nontargets. For example, a display of eight digits might contain a variable T digits colored red (to be reported) and $N-T$ colored green (to be ignored). Obviously enough, the probability of reporting any given target in the display goes down as the number of targets goes up. Sample data of my own for this task are shown in Fig. 4.1 (Duncan, 1979). Digit displays contained either

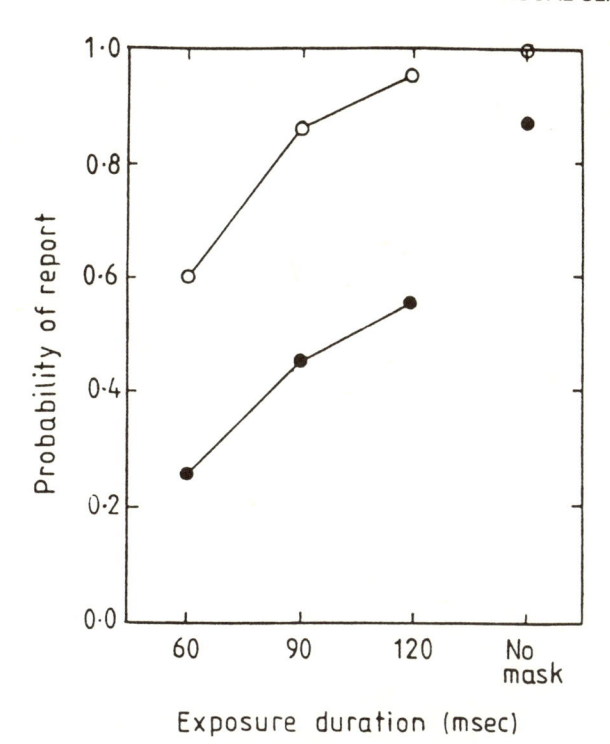

FIG. 4.1. Report of red target digits among green nontargets. ○— = one-target displays; ●— = four-target displays.

one (red) target and seven (green) nontargets, or four of each color. Displays were shown for 60, 90, or 120 msec and were followed at once by a mask of random red and green line segments, or for 120 msec with no mask. The task was to report verbally as many red digits as possible. The graph shows the probability of target report as a function of exposure duration. Evidently, this probability is much higher for single-target displays, even with exposures so brief that very little is reported and output interference seems correspondingly unlikely.

These results are very similar to those that, in Broadbent's (1958) filter theory, first inspired the idea that the perceptual system has two stages: a first, parallel stage followed by a second stage of limited capacity. The experiments of the 1950s established that, although it is hard to identify the content of two speech messages simultaneously (e.g., one to either ear, or one in a male and one in a female voice), it is quite easy to pick one message on the basis of a simple physical characteristic such as location or voice and to identify the content only of that one. Broadbent proposed that a first, parallel stage of perceptual analysis serves to determine simple stimulus characteristics like location and voice. A second stage, of limited capacity in that it cannot easily deal with two messages at once, serves to identify the more complex characteristics of message content. The data are explained as follows: If two messages must both be identified, there will be difficulties at the second stage. But if target and nontarget messages can be separated at the first stage, only the target message need pass on to the second, and performance will be correspondingly improved. The results in Fig. 4.1 suggest the same theoretical approach. Red and green digits are separated at the first stage. Only red digits pass on to the second stage, whose limited capacity causes difficulty as the number of targets is increased. Here, I call the first stage the *preselective system,* and the second the *limited-capacity system.*

It is often assumed that the preselective system is entirely without capacity limitation, in that multiple stimuli can be processed without any mutual interference. Difficulties in dealing with several stimuli at once are ascribed entirely to the second stage. In fact, this conclusion is not entirely justified. While still proposing that there is a first stage of analyzing defining attributes (location, voice, color, etc.) and a second stage of analyzing reported attributes, one might suggest that capacity limits occur in both stages, though perhaps much less severely in the (rather simple) analyses of the first (cf. Johnston & Heinz, 1978). Data of the above sort really only show that, in these compound search tasks, one *major* limit on our ability to identify several stimuli at once occurs *after* nontargets have been rejected.

I return later to the question of whether the preselective stage is entirely without capacity limitation, which empirically depends on the effects of the number of *nontargets.* Here, it is sufficient to conclude that, for compound search, it might make sense to propose that the defining attribute is analyzed first with little or no capacity limitation, the reported attribute is analyzed second with substantial capacity limitation, and because the reported attribute is analyzed only for targets, performance declines as the number of targets increases.

Simple Search

A major part of my argument rests on the finding that, in simple search as in compound search, there are large effects of the number of targets. It is useful to begin with an experiment by Duncan (1980b), though the task had elements of both simple and compound search. Subjects were shown brief displays made up of four alphanumeric characters arranged to form a plus sign centered on fixation. The task was to detect digit targets among letter nontargets. One response was made for targets detected in the horizontal limb of the plus (9 and 3 o'clock positions), another for targets detected in the vertical limb (12 and 6 o'clock). In a single display, targets could occur in either, neither, or both limbs, and correspondingly the subject could make either, neither, or both responses. For each limb, accuracy was much lower when the *other* limb contained a correctly detected target (a ''hit'') than when it contained correctly rejected nontargets (a "correct rejection"). Indeed, performance on one limb A, when the *other* limb B had a correct rejection, was almost as good as in a control condition requiring that only A be attended. As before, the results showed that the accuracy of detecting a given target goes down when other targets are detected in the display, whereas simultaneous nontargets have little effect.

In this task, although alphanumeric class was the defining attribute, both alphanumeric class and location were reported attributes (both target presence and location were reported). Was the requirement to report location important, or would similar results be obtained in a straightforward case of simple search? In a further experiment (Duncan, 1980b, Experiment 2) subjects reported only whether the display contained one or two digit targets, ignoring location altogether. Still, there was evidence of substantial interference between simultaneous targets. Another approach is to have subjects report target names rather than locations (Duncan, 1983). As discussed before, this is simple search if stimulus information sufficient to categorize a character as digit or letter is also sufficient to identify it. Again it was found that the probability of reporting a particular target went down when there were other targets in the display.

Although more data are needed, the results do suggest that, in simple as in compound search, increasing the number of targets in the display can produce a substantial decrease in performance. Again this suggests two successive perceptual stages. Nontargets can be rejected in parallel after preselective processing; hence the number of nontargets in the display has little effect. Targets, however, must pass on to the limited-capacity system. The important new point is that, because defining and reported attributes are the same, it makes no sense to propose that the former are analyzed at the first stage and the latter at the second. The conclusion instead is that preselective processing of the defining/reported attribute, even though producing information that can be used to direct a target to the limited-capacity system, does not provide information that can yet be used for report. The experience is that the target is only "seen" when it "draws attention" to itself.

An important question is whether results depend on the use of a complex defining/reported attribute like alphanumeric class. Many authors have proposed that access to the limited-capacity stage is unnecessary for the report of simple stimulus features such as tilt, size, or closure (e.g., Kahneman, Treisman, & Burkell, 1983; Treisman & Gelade, 1980; Treisman & Paterson, 1984). I describe two experiments casting light on this. The first was like the experiment of Duncan (1980b), except that subjects detected tilted target lines among vertical nontargets. Again, displays were in the form of a plus sign centered on fixation. Each of the four stimuli was a line 1/4° in length, centered 1 3/4° from fixation. Nontargets were vertical, whereas targets were tilted 45° either clockwise or counterclockwise, with the direction of tilt determined randomly. Targets appeared independently in horizontal and vertical limbs, with probability one-third for each limb. Subjects were provided with one key to press for targets detected in the horizontal limb and another for targets in the vertical, so they could press zero, one, or two keys on each trial.

The trial began when the subject pressed a footswitch. In the "simultaneous" condition, a fixation point was shown for 500 msec, followed by the display for T msec (set individually for each subject, range 45 to 80 msec), and a backward mask for 500 msec (four identical masking "characters" in the four positions of the display, each made up of horizontal and vertical line segments and covering an area of $1/3°$ square). A blank interval of $2000 + T$ msec preceded a marked interval of 2000 msec during which responses could be made. The "successive" condition was similar except that only one limb was presented at a time. The 500 msec fixation point was followed by presentation of the first limb for T msec and its mask for 500 msec; a further 500 msec fixation interval was followed by presentation of the second limb for T msec and its mask for 500 msec. A blank interval of 1000 msec preceded the marked interval of 2000 msec during which responses for both limbs could be made. For a given subject the order of presenting horizontal and vertical limbs was fixed, though counterbalanced across subjects.

Each of four subjects served in five sessions, the first for practice. There were two blocks of trials per condition per day, with condition alternating between blocks. Each block had 12 warm-up and 108 scored trials. Data from the last four sessions were pooled for each subject, and mean scores (transformed to the d' and β parameters of signal-detection theory) are shown in Table 4.1.

In the simultaneous condition, performance on each limb was much worse when the concurrent event (i.e., the event of the *other* limb) was a hit than when it was a correct rejection. In the successive condition, as expected, accuracy was independent on the two limbs. The interaction of condition and concurrent event was significant—$F(1,3) = 40.6$, $p < .01$; planned comparisons showed that performance in the simultaneous condition with a concurrent hit was significantly worse than both performance in the simultaneous condition with a concurrent correct rejection—$F(1,3) = 69.2$, $p < .01$—and performance in the successive condition with a concurrent hit—$F(1,3) = 23.2$, $p < .02$. Note that,

TABLE 4.1
Detecting Tilted Target Lines among Vertical Nontargets

		Simultaneous		*Successive*	
		Horizontal Limb	Vertical Limb	Horizontal Limb	Vertical Limb
Concurrent hit	d'	2.12	1.72	3.18	2.52
	β	1.89	2.98	1.43	2.91
Concurrent correct rejection	d'	3.12	2.63	3.03	2.26
	β	6.34	1.56	1.39	4.05

with a concurrent correct rejection, performance was no worse in the simultaneous than in the successive condition.

Again, it must be asked whether results depended on the need to report target location as well as presence. The second experiment was designed to avoid location reports. Display dimensions were as before. Nontargets were horizontal and vertical lines 1/4° in length (orientation determined randomly and separately for each nontarget). There were two types of target, 45°-tilted lines as before, and boxes measuring 1/4° × 1/8°, oriented at random either horizontally or vertically. Targets of the two types appeared anywhere in the display, independently and with probability one-third each. Subjects were provided with one key for tilted targets, another for boxes. Only the "simultaneous" condition was used. This time the 500-msec fixation interval was followed by the display for T msec (range 100 to 150 msec) and a backward mask for 2 sec. Responses could be made as soon as the mask appeared. Each of four subjects served in a practice session (12 blocks of 54 trials each) and two experimental sessions (each having one warm-up block followed by 16 scored blocks). Mean scores, based on pooled data from the two experimental sessions, are shown in Table 4.2. Again, performance was worse with a concurrent hit than with a concurrent correct rejection—$F(1,3) = 93.0$, $p < .005$.

Several points may be made about these experiments. First, in each case results were the same, though weaker, contrasting simply trials with and without a concurrent target on the other limb (first experiment) or of the other type (second experiment), ignoring the concurrent response. This eliminates several possible alternative explanations of the data. Second, several details of procedure may be important. Simultaneous targets were not all identical, reducing the likelihood of perceptual grouping. Masking was used to encourage resource-limited rather than data-limited performance (Norman & Bobrow, 1975). Target probability was low, encouraging the strategy of passing only targets to the limited-capacity stage (Duncan, 1980b; Moray, Fitter, Ostry, Favreau, & Nagy, 1976). Although further work is needed to establish the influence of these factors, it should be noted that experiments with identical or grouped targets, performance limited by low luminance rather than masking, and high target

TABLE 4.2
Detecting Tilted Lines and Boxes among Horizontal and Vertical Lines

		Tilted Lines	Boxes
Concurrent hit	d'	2.88	1.71
	β	3.19	2.45
Concurrent correct rejection	d'	3.57	2.17
	β	3.19	1.24

probability may not show the same pattern of results (Townsend, Hu, & Ashby, 1981; Wickelgren, 1967).

At least provisionally, the results suggest that the distinction between a preselective stage, at which nontargets are rejected, and a limited-capacity stage, to which targets must gain access if they are to be reported, is as important for the detection of simple feature targets as for detection of digits and letters. Even when the defining/reported attribute is a simple feature, simultaneous targets cannot be detected without substantial interference. Even for these attributes, the conclusion is that information used preselectively to guide access to the limited-capacity stage cannot yet be reported.

One suggestion (Hoffman, 1978) is that preselective processing of the defining/reported attribute is inaccurate. Crude analysis of each stimulus at this stage serves to direct the best target candidates to the second stage, where a final, more accurate decision is made. This model may be assessed by considering the effects of nontargets, because in essence it proposes that access to the second stage is probabilistic: Access probability is greater for targets than for nontargets, but nonzero for both. Consider the data shown in Table 4.1. If it sometimes happened, in the simultaneous condition, that nontargets from one limb B gained access to the limited-capacity system but were then (on more careful analysis) correctly rejected, performance on limb A, for all trials with a concurrent correct rejection, could not be as good as performance in the successive condition, in which the limited-capacity system was never occupied by material from limb B during the time that limb A was presented. These data suggest that, *whenever* a stimulus from limb B entered the limited-capacity system, it was *always* reported as a target—that is, the preselective decision that a stimulus was a target was never overturned. When the defining/reported attribute is more complex, however, there is a slight loss of performance in the simultaneous condition, even with a concurrent correct rejection (Duncan, 1980b). This indeed suggests that the process of keeping nontargets out of the limited-capacity system is a little inaccurate. The next section takes up this point in more detail.

THE NUMBER OF NONTARGETS

Interpreting Functions of RT or Accuracy against the Number of Nontargets

A great deal of visual search work deals with effects of the number of nontargets, usually in simple search. The task might be to decide whether a particular letter is present in a display of other letters (Atkinson, Holmgren, & Juola, 1969), whether a display of Ts contains one that is tilted (Beck & Ambler, 1973), whether a display of colored stimuli contains one that is blue (Treisman & Gelade, 1980), and so on. Capacity limitation—that is, some limit on the ability to process several stimuli at once (with respect to the defining attribute)—is inferred from decreases in speed or accuracy with increases in the number of stimuli N in the display.

One difficulty with this type of experiment is that several factors other than capacity limitation can contribute to performance decrements accompanying an increase in N. These range from the effects of contour interaction and retinal eccentricity to the increase in total finishing time for a set of N parallel stochastic processes, and the increased chance that one will yield an erroneous positive outcome (Duncan, 1980a; Eriksen & Spencer, 1969). Various solutions have been attempted, including (a) modeling of particular effects other than capacity limitation, and ascribing to capacity limitation only decrements in excess of predictions (Shaw, 1984); (b) the assumption that those functions of reaction time against N that suggest parallel search are produced preselectively, whereas those that suggest serial search are produced by passing stimuli one at a time to the limited-capacity system (Treisman & Gelade, 1980); (c) attempts to circumvent known effects other than capacity limitation experimentally—for example, by manipulating not the total size of the display, but the number of items shown at one time (Duncan, 1980b; Eriksen & Spencer, 1969; Shiffrin & Gardner, 1972). Here I deal not with the problem of showing that a particular result is due to capacity limitation, but with the problem of how, given that this can be done, the limitation should be interpreted.

In fact results from this sort of experiment provide the major motivation for the idea, already discussed, that access to the limited-capacity system is not required for the report of some stimulus attributes. For example, Schneider and Shiffrin (1977) found that, after extensive training on a particular set of targets and nontargets, neither the accuracy nor the speed of target detection was much influenced by the number of displayed nontargets. They suggested that well-learned classifications can be performed without the involvement of any limited-capacity process. Treisman and Gelade (1980) found that reaction-time functions suggest parallel search when the defining attribute is a single perceptual feature (e.g., color), but serial search when it is a conjunction of features (e.g., a particular color paired with a particular shape). They concluded that preselective processes deal with an object's different features separately; the limited-capacity system is needed to determine how features go together. Shaw (1984) found that the loss of performance with increasing N was explicable without postulating capacity limitation when the defining attribute was luminance, but not when it was shape. She suggested that only the shape discrimination involved a limited-capacity system.

It is interesting to contrast these results, concerning effects of multiple nontargets, with those already described for multiple targets. For example, Beck and Ambler (1973) found that performance was independent of the number of nontargets in search for tilted Ts among upright Ts. In line with the proposal of Treisman and Gelade (1980), this might suggest analysis and report of a single feature (tilt) without the involvement of a limited-capacity system. The data in Tables 4.1 and 4.2 confirm that detecting a tilted target is not influenced by the presence of simultaneous upright nontargets, but the data also show substantial interference from a simultaneous target. Treisman and Gelade (1980) found little effect of nontargets when subjects searched for either one of two possible targets, each defined by possession of a single feature ("blue" or "curved"). The data in Table 4.2, from a similar task, again show substantial interference between simultaneous targets.

The interpretation in terms of the previous distinction between preselective and limited-capacity stages is straightforward. Parallel processing of many stimulus attributes at the preselective stage can serve to reject nontargets, and to direct only targets to the limited-capacity system. If nontargets are rejected efficiently at the first stage, their number will have no effect. It may be postulated, however, that *no* stimulus attribute can be overtly reported unless the target itself gains access to the limited-capacity system. Thus, for no stimulus attribute will it be possible to deal in parallel with simultaneous targets. In this respect it is wrong to conclude that any attribute can be perceived "without attention." Experiments dealing with multiple nontargets may suggest this, but experiments dealing with multiple targets show it to be false.

What conclusions follow, given such a model, from experiments contrasting performance with different defining attributes—for example, single features versus conjunctions? Various patterns of results might emerge in an experiment assessing effects of both the number of targets and the number of nontargets:

1. At one extreme, the number of nontargets might have no effect, whereas simultaneous targets cause difficulty. This apparently is the case when the defining attribute is tilt (Beck & Ambler, 1973; see also Table 4.1). The conclusion is (a) that the preselective processing of the defining attribute is entirely parallel—that is, there is no interference between simultaneous stimuli; (b) the rejection of nontargets at this stage is perfect. Note that if (b) did not hold, occasional nontargets would gain access to the limited-capacity stage, causing performance decrements as the number of nontargets increased.

2. At the opposite extreme, targets and nontargets might be exactly equal in their effects—that is, adding a target to the display would have exactly the same effect as adding a nontarget. This has been shown for unfamiliar target–nontarget categorizations (Duncan, 1980b, Experiment 3). Speculatively, it might also hold when the defining attribute is a conjunction of features, where effects of the number of nontargets clearly imply serial search (Treisman & Gelade, 1980). Note, though, that at present this is no more than a speculation, because experiments of this sort with simultaneous targets have not been done. Here the conclusion is that there is no rejection of nontargets after preselective processing—that is, access to the limited-capacity system is equal for targets and nontargets.

3. One suspects that results with most defining attributes will occupy the middle ground. Thus, there will be some effect of the number of nontargets, but

a much larger effect of targets (Duncan, 1980b). Two possibilities are that (a) even the first, preselective stage is not entirely without capacity limitation, though less severe than the limitation of the second stage (cf. the model of Johnston & Heinz [1978], discussed earlier); (b) the rejection of nontargets following preselective analysis is imperfect (cf. the model of Hoffman [1978], also discussed earlier)—that is, nontargets sometimes gain access to the second stage.

What I have tried to show is that experiments contrasting performance with different defining attributes really are not dealing with the question of which attributes can be responded to without involvement of any limited-capacity system. Instead they concern the efficiency of selection—that is, the extent to which, with a given defining attribute, nontargets can be excluded from access to limited-capacity mechanisms. In all probability, efficiency forms a continuum at the ends of which lie extreme "parallel" and extreme "serial" search. It follows that experiments dealing only with the number of nontargets are not highly informative. Even if performance declines with increasing N, and if effects unrelated to capacity limitation can be shown not to be responsible (which usually they cannot), one knows only that one is not dealing with extreme case (1) just described, in which the exclusion of nontargets is perfect. To obtain more complete information on the efficiency of selection, one needs experiments dealing with both multiple nontargets and multiple targets.

The recent work of Bundesen and colleagues is noteworthy here (Bundesen, Pedersen, & Larsen, 1984; Bundesen, Shibuya, & Larsen, this volume). Subjects reported as many targets as possible from brief displays in which numbers of targets and nontargets varied separately. The probability of reporting a given target decreased as the number of either targets or nontargets increased, but much faster for the number of targets. A mathematical model with one parameter reflecting the efficiency of selective access to a limited-capacity stage gave a good account of the data, and variations in this one parameter accounted for changes in performance with different defining attributes. Extensions to this work, and in particular the use of "pure" cases of simple search, should prove very rewarding.

The Experiment of Kahneman et al. (1983)[1]

I have proposed that no attribute of a target can be reported (in the sense that a detection response is made) without access to the limited-capacity stage. A recent experiment by Kahneman et al. (1983) apparently suggests the opposite. The target was a white, three-letter word, and each nontarget was a string of three, colored, filled nonsense shapes. The important contrast was between an

---

[1]See page 105 for further discussion of this point.

identification task, in which the subject read the target word aloud, and a detection task, in which the subject simply pressed a key if there was a target present. The function of RT against the number of nontargets was much steeper in identification than in detection. Kahneman et al. (1983) suggested that identifying a word requires access to the limited-capacity stage, and that the time for selective access depends on the number of nontargets. If all that is required is detection of the target color, however, a response can be initiated directly at the preselective stage (see also Treisman, Kahneman, & Burkell, 1983).

At first sight the result is puzzling, given the framework of this chapter. Assuming that the functional defining attribute is color, the influence of nontargets (reflecting the efficiency of keeping nontargets out of the limited-capacity system) should have been the same in both tasks. Note, however, that with these stimuli, targets and nontargets differed in several respects—that is, there were several defining attributes, any one or combination of which could in principle have been used to direct the target to the limited-capacity system. Performing in a similar experiment I became aware that, in the detection task, I was "thinking" only of the target's color, whereas in identification, I was "thinking" only of the fact that it was a word. If differing task demands in fact led to the adoption of different functional defining attributes, there would be no reason to expect equal effects of the number of nontargets—that is, equal efficiencies of selection.

To test this idea, subjects were practiced in each task, and the defining attribute suspected to be irrelevant was then removed. Thus, for detection, the prediction was that performance would be unaltered when nontargets were also words, because selection was based entirely on color. For identification, the prediction (counterintuitive, at least to judge from the reactions of some subjects!) was that performance would be unaltered when nontargets were made the same color as the target.

In the detection task, the target was a magenta word, either ASH or HAS, written in upper case and measuring $2° \times 3/4°$. Each nontarget was a meaningless string of three symbols (e.g., "&($") of the same size as the target, colored white, green, orange, or yellow. The number of items in the display varied from one to four, and at each display size, half the displays had one target, the others none. Items were positioned around an imaginary circle, with a diameter of about 6°, which was centered on fixation; possible positions corresponded to 2, 4, 6, 8, 10, and 12 o'clock, with actual positions chosen at random on each trial. All nontargets in a display were different in both color and shape. After a 1-sec fixation interval, displays were flashed for 180 msec. The subject pressed a key with the right hand for target-present displays, left hand for target-absents; the key press initiated a 1 sec intertrial interval. After seven blocks of 48 trials (display size, target presence randomized), the subject was transferred to a task that was identical except that each nontarget was either the word ASH or HAS, and there were five further blocks.

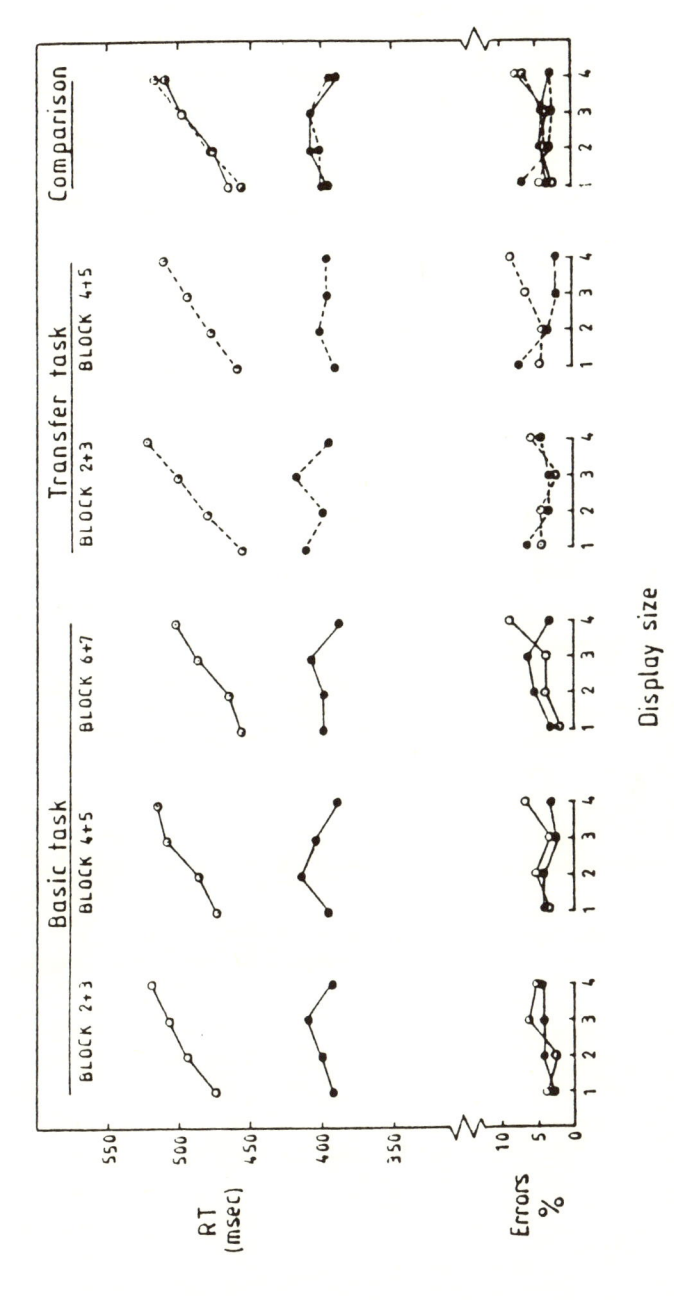

FIG. 4.2. RTs and error percentages for detection and identification of a magenta target word. ● = detection; ○ = Choice; — = basic tasks; ---- = transfer tasks.

The identification task was the same except that one target was present in every display. The subject pressed a key with the right hand for HAS, left hand for ASH. After seven blocks in which nontargets were meaningless symbol strings in white, green, orange, and yellow, subjects were transferred to a task that was identical except that each nontarget was magenta, and there were five further blocks.

Each of eight subjects served in a single session. Detection and identification were performed in counterbalanced order. Transfer tasks were not mentioned until they began. In each task, subjects were told the colors and shapes of targets and nontargets, with no attempt to emphasize one dimension or the other.

Results are shown in Fig. 4.2. The first block of each task was ignored. Fig. 4.2 shows RT and error data separately for each pair of blocks in both basic and transfer tasks. The extreme right shows the mean for blocks four to seven of the basic tasks accompanied by the mean for blocks two to five of transfer. Only data from target-present trials are shown for the detection task (only these are comparable to identification displays), though target-absent data were similar.

Results from the basic tasks replicated the findings of Kahneman et al. (1983). The effect of display size on RT was much greater in identification—$F(3,31) = 16.9$, $p < .001$. In fact, RTs did not increase at all with display size in detection, though in similar experiments I have not obtained such extreme results (see also Kahneman et al., 1983).

More importantly, transfer results in both tasks indeed suggested that shape was irrelevant in detection, whereas color was irrelevant in identification. In neither case did removal of the irrelevant defining attribute have any major effect. The last four blocks of each basic task were compared with the last four of transfer, and no main effect of basic versus transfer, or interaction with display size, approached significance (all $Fs < 1$). Figure 4.2 suggests that in identification there may have been some slope increase when transfer began, but it was neither significant nor permanent.

These results suggest caution when targets and nontargets differ in several respects—that is, when there are several defining attributes. Common sense may not be sufficient to tell which attribute is actually used, and in fact this may depend on other aspects of the task. It would be interesting to know why, in identification, subjects did not use the defining attribute that would have made nontarget rejection most effective. For present purposes, however, the puzzle of why slopes differed in (these particular) detection and identification tasks seems to have been solved: There was a difference in functional defining attribute.

IDENTIFICATION AND USE OF STIMULUS INFORMATION

I have discussed how, in the original proposals of a first, parallel perceptual stage followed by a second, limited-capacity stage, there was the underlying idea that some stimulus attributes (e.g., in hearing, location and voice) are "identified" or "analyzed" at the first stage, others (e.g., verbal content) only at the second. In this chapter I have suggested a different picture. Although, after the first stage, many different stimulus attributes can be used to guide access to the second stage, no attribute can yet be reported. Sometimes such a conclusion is said to imply that stimuli are "identified" at the first stage, but "unconsciously." I would like to suggest that this way of talking, of asking whether information has been "analyzed" or "identified" at a particular stage, is misleading.

What does it mean to ask whether information has been "analyzed" or "identified" at some stage? Naively, we might say that information initially is "not represented" in the nervous system, but then it is "analyzed" and becomes "represented." For example, we might say that the identity of a letter A is "not represented" on the retina, but after perceptual analysis is "represented" in the brain. (Sometimes we speak of the letter's "contacting its representation.") This, however, is inaccurate. The identity of an A is certainly represented on the retina in the sense that retinal states corresponding to an A are different from retinal states corresponding to a B—if the information were not represented in this sense, no amount of further work by the brain could create it. What we should say is that on the retina, identity is not represented in an especially useful form—that is, a lot of work is still needed to do anything on its basis.

This corresponds to Marr's (1982) idea of more and less explicit representation. The more explicitly information is represented, the more easily it may be used. For example, a written decimal number represents quite explicitly the fact of whether it is exactly divisible by 10, but rather less explicitly whether it is exactly divisible by two.

It should be obvious that a question of how explicitly information is represented simply cannot be asked without specification of the system that is going to use it. A decimal number may represent explicitly the fact of whether it is divisible by 10 to a system (like our brain) that can check to see whether the final digit is zero; to any other system it does not. Questions of whether information is explicit are questions not just about the representation, but about the system using it: The two must always be asked together.

In fact, when psychologists ask whether information is or is not "analyzed" preselectively, their experiments rest on showing that information can or cannot be used in a particular way. This chapter, for example, has dealt with the ability to direct access to the limited-capacity stage (cf. Treisman, 1960), whereas other work deals with semantic priming (Allport, 1977; MacKay, 1973) or the production of autonomic responses (Corteen & Dunn, 1974). Although these may be discussed as experiments on how completely preselective information is "identified," in fact it is obvious that they concern the whole process of how information is used to produce a particular effect.

Thus, we may suppose that, in the course of the perceptual process, stimulus information is transformed in various ways, or is represented in various different "codes." We may not, however, point to a particular code and ask whether at this point information has been "analyzed" or "identified"—without at the same time specifying the particular use of the information that we have in mind. Without this, there simply would be no way of settling the issue of whether information is or is not "explicit."

Note now that, in the nervous system, many different uses can be made of the same information. The information that a letter is an A rather than a B might underlie perceptual grouping (e.g., if there are several As in the visual field), directing access to the limited-capacity system, semantic priming, overt report, and so on. It follows that there might be many different senses in which information is "identified," corresponding to the many different uses of the information that may be made. For each of these uses one may ask how the information needs to be coded, at what stage of the perceptual process that use becomes possible, and so on. But, at least potentially, these are separate questions for each separate use. Relationships between uses—for example, whether they rely on the same criteria of "explicitness," whether they depend on information coded in the same way, whether they involve common processes with common errors—can only be determined empirically.

What is implied by talking of a stage at which information is "analyzed" or "identified" is that there exists a stage of the perceptual process before which no use of some particular information can be made, and after which all uses can begin, based upon its output. In other words, there is one stage of putting the information into a code suitable for the whole list of uses in which one is interested. Empirically this could be so. For example, it could be that no use of information concerning feature conjunction can be made before the limited-capacity stage (Treisman & Gelade, 1980). But this indeed is something to be discovered empirically, by looking at correlations between different uses (Treisman & Gelade, 1980; Treisman & Paterson, 1984), not an assumption to be built into our very framework for asking questions about perception.

In sum, I am arguing that questions simply about whether information has been "identified" at some perceptual stage are put mistakenly. They imply a question about the explicitness of information separate from a specification of how it is used. In the study of perception, we do not wish to know when and how information is "identified," but rather the different uses to which it is put, and the processes underlying each one.

CONCLUSIONS

I have suggested that the distinction between compound and simple search—similar to Broadbent's (1970, 1971) distinction between stimulus and response set—provides an important framework within which to interpret the phenomena of visual search. The effect of the number of targets in compound search corresponds to the findings in audition that led Broadbent (1958) originally to postulate two successive perceptual stages, parallel (preselective) followed by serial (limited capacity). Corresponding effects in simple search show that information which, at the first stage, can be used to guide selective access to the second cannot yet be used for report. Effects of the number of nontargets, within such a system, do not show that access to the limited-capacity stage is needed for the report of some attributes but not for others. Rather, they give evidence on the efficiency of selective access—that is, evidence on one particular use of stimulus information. I have suggested, though, that they are best interpreted in conjunction with effects of the number of targets.

I have also dealt with a more general principle. There is no real way to ask a question about stimulus identification separate from a specification of how information is used. The enterprise, accordingly, is not to determine how and where information is "identified," but to understand the processes of the different uses to which it is put. I would suggest that this is the correct context within which to view the conclusion that, at the preselective stage, information can be used for one purpose (guiding access to the limited-capacity system) but not another (overt report).

ACKNOWLEDGMENTS

Extremely useful comments on an earlier draft of this chapter were provided by Donald Broadbent, an anonymous referee, and Mike Posner.

REFERENCES

Allport, D. A. (1977). On knowing the meaning of words we are unable to report: The effects of visual masking. In S. Dornic (Ed.), *Attention and performance VI* (pp. 505–533). Hillsdale, NJ: Lawrence Erlbaum Associates.

Atkinson, R. C., Holmgren, J. E., & Juola, J. F. (1969). Processing time as influenced by the number of elements in a visual display. *Perception and Psychophysics, 6,* 321–326.

Banks, W. P., Larson, D. W., & Prinzmetal, W. (1979). Asymmetry of visual interference. *Perception and Psychophysics, 25,* 447–456.

Bashinski, H. S., & Bacharach, V. R. (1980). Enhancement of perceptual sensitivity as the result of selectively attending to spatial locations. *Perception and Psychophysics, 28,* 241–248.

Beck, J., & Ambler, B. (1973). The effects of concentrated and distributed attention on peripheral acuity. *Perception and Psychophysics, 14,* 225–230.

Bouma, H. (1978). Visual search and reading: Eye movements and functional visual field: A tutorial review. In J. Requin (Ed.), *Attention and performance VII* (pp. 115–147). Hillsdale, NJ: Lawrence Erlbaum Associates.

Broadbent, D. E. (1958). *Perception and communication.* London: Pergamon.

Broadbent, D. E. (1970). Stimulus set and response set: Two kinds of selective attention. In D. Mostofsky (Ed.), *Attention: Contemporary theories and analysis* (pp. 51–60). New York: Appleton-Century-Crofts.

Broadbent, D. E. (1971). *Decision and stress.* London: Academic.

Bundesen, C., Pedersen, L. F., & Larsen, A. (1984). Measuring efficiency of selection from briefly

exposed visual displays: A model for partial report. *Journal of Experimental Psychology: Human Perception and Performance, 10,* 329–339.
Carter, R. C. (1982). Visual search with color. *Journal of Experimental Psychology: Human Perception and Performance, 8,* 127–136.
Corteen, R. S., & Dunn, D. (1974). Shock-associated words in a nonattended message: A test for momentary awareness. *Journal of Experimental Psychology, 102,* 1143–1144.
Duncan, J. (1979). *Partial reports based on color and on alphanumeric class: Evidence for a late selection theory of attention.* Unpublished manuscript.
Duncan, J. (1980a). The demonstration of capacity limitation. *Cognitive Psychology, 12,* 75–96.
Duncan, J. (1980b). The locus of interference in the perception of simultaneous stimuli. *Psychological Review, 87,* 272–300.
Duncan, J. (1981). Directing attention in the visual field. *Perception and Psychophysics, 30,* 90–93.
Duncan, J. (1983). Perceptual selection based on alphanumeric class: Evidence from partial reports. *Perception and Psychophysics, 33,* 533–547.
Eriksen, B. A., & Eriksen, C. W. (1974). Effects of noise letters upon the identification of a target letter in a non-search task. *Perception and Psychophysics, 16,* 143–149.
Eriksen, C. W., & Spencer, T. (1969). Rate of information processing in visual perception: Some results and methodological considerations. *Journal of Experimental Psychology Monograph, 79*(2, Pt. 2).
Hoffman, J. E. (1978). Search through a sequentially presented visual display. *Perception and Psychophysics, 23,* 1–11.
Johnston, W. A., & Heinz, S. P. (1978). Flexibility and capacity demands of attention. *Journal of Experimental Psychology: General, 107,* 420–435.
Kahneman, D., Treisman, A., & Burkell, J. (1983). The cost of visual filtering. *Journal of Experimental Psychology: Human Perception and Performance, 9,* 510–522.
MacKay, D. (1973). Aspects of the theory of comprehension, memory, and attention. *Quarterly Journal of Experimental Psychology, 25,* 22–40.
Marr, D. (1982). *Vision.* San Francisco: Freeman.
Moray, N., Fitter, M., Ostry, D., Favreau, D., & Nagy, V. (1976). Attention to pure tones. *Quarterly Journal of Experimental Psychology, 28,* 271–283.
Norman, D. A., & Bobrow, D. G. (1975). On data-limited and resource-limited processes. *Cognitive Psychology, 7,* 44–64.
Posner, M. I., Nissen, M. J., & Ogden, W. C. (1978). Attended and unattended processing modes: The role of set for spatial location. In H. L. Pick & E. J. Saltzman (Eds.), *Modes of perceiving and processing information* (pp. 137–157). Hillsdale, NJ: Lawrence Erlbaum Associates.
Schneider, W., & Shiffrin, R. M. (1977). Controlled and automatic human information processing: I. Detection, search, and attention. *Psychological Review, 84,* 1–66.
Shaw, M. L. (1984). Division of attention among spatial locations: A fundamental difference between detection of letters and detection of luminance increments. In H. Bouma & D. G Bouwhuis (Eds.), *Attention and performance X* (pp. 109–121). Hillsdale, NJ: Lawrence Erlbaum Associates.
Shiffrin, R. M., & Gardner, G. T. (1972). Visual processing capacity and attentional control. *Journal of Experimental Psychology, 93,* 72–83.
Townsend, J. T., Hu, G. G., & Ashby, F. G. (1981). Perceptual sampling of orthogonal straight line features. *Psychological Research, 43,* 259–275.
Treisman, A. M. (1960). Contextual cues in selective listening. *Quarterly Journal of Experimental Psychology, 12,* 242–248.
Treisman, A., & Gelade, G. (1980). A feature integration theory of attention. *Cognitive Psychology, 12,* 97–136.
Treisman, A., Kahneman, D., & Burkell, J. (1983). Perceptual objects and the cost of filtering. *Perception and Psychophysics, 33,* 527–532.

Treisman, A., & Paterson, R. (1984). Emergent features, attention, and object perception. *Journal of Experimental Psychology: Human Perception and Performance, 10*, 12–31.
Wickelgren, W. A. (1967). Strength theories of disjunctive visual detection. *Perception and Psychophysics, 2*, 331–337.
Wolford, G., & Chambers, L. (1983). Lateral masking as a function of spacing. *Perception and Psychophysics, 33*, 129–138.

ADDENDUM: A REPLY TO DUNCAN

Anne Treisman
Daniel Kahneman
University of British Columbia

Duncan found our experiment sufficiently embarrassing to his position that he ran a control experiment to explain it away. Unfortunately, he ran the wrong control. The proper test, when conducted, does not confirm Duncan's prediction. At issue are two theoretical claims: (a) that attention must be focused on a target, only and always, if a response to that target is required (Duncan, this volume); (b) that some responses can be made without focusing on the target (e.g., in simple detection tasks) whereas choice responses based on further analysis of the target (e.g., reading a word selected by its color) require focused attention and induce "filtering costs" (Kahneman, Treisman, & Burkell, 1983).

Duncan's position is incompatible with a result in which the same target, selected on the same attribute, shows a different effect of distractors depending on the response required. This is precisely the result that we obtained in comparing the effect of irrelevant colored shapes on reading a white word or on detecting its presence. To dismiss this result, Duncan proposed the further hypothesis that subjects may prefer, when possible, to use the same attribute to control selection and response. This strategy might have led our subjects, in the reading condition only, to use wordness rather than color as a selection cue. The difference in selection cue could then explain the difference in slopes.

The experiments that Duncan conducted are not a proper test of his position against ours, because both analyses predict the same results—namely, a positive slope in the reading task and a flat function in detection. However, his position entails another prediction that is interesting, counterintuitive, and, as it turns out, wrong. A reading task in which the distractors are red words and the target is a white word should show no slope, because search by color, both in our original experiment and in his, shows no effect of display size. Our position, on the other hand, is that reading should still show a slope because it requires a choice response to the selected stimulus.

We conducted the critical experiment, as well as an additional detection experiment, in which the target (a word) and the distractors (nonsense shapes) were all white. Except for these changes, the conditions and procedures were the same as in Kahneman et al. (1983, Experiment 3). Table 4.1A summarizes the results of the three sets of experiments. The findings are unequivocal: There is no evidence that selection by color eliminates the slope in the reading task, or that a discrimination between words and nonsense shapes necessarily induces a slope in detection. The slope is steep and essentially identical in the three reading experiments, and substantially flatter in the three detection experiments. We conclude that the difference is not explained by a change in the functional attributes controlling selection. Rather, we argue that when a simple feature is available to define a target, detection is spatially parallel, whereas reading and other choice responses that depend on further analysis of the target require attention and show filtering costs.

Duncan was right in pointing out an ambiguity in our original experiment. When the target and the distractors differ in several attributes, it cannot be assumed that subjects will use the same selection strategy regardless of the required response. Duncan's suggestion that subjects may prefer to use the same attribute for selection and for response is intriguing, and deserves further research. Finally, if Duncan was right in his original assessment that his theoretical position cannot allow different effects of the same distractors on detection and on selective reading, then his theoretical position is in trouble.

TABLE 4.1A
Summary of Experimental Conditions and Slopes
of Display-Size Effects in Experiments by Kahneman, Treisman,
and Burkell (1983), Duncan (This Volume), and Present Study

Attributes Controlling		Task	
Selection	Response	Detection	Reading
Color or word	Color	6.6[a] (Kahneman et al., 1983)	—
Color or word	Word	—	20.4[a] (Kahneman et al., 1983)
Color	Color	0.0[b] (Duncan)	18.5 (present study)
Word	Word	1.4 (present study)	20[b] (Duncan)

[a]The mean slopes across several experiments, which varied the amount of practice, order of conditions, and response mapping.

[b]The numbers given for the Duncan studies are approximate. They were estimated from the graphs, averaging the four blocks of the transfer task.

5 Perceptual Integration and Postcategorical Filtering

D. A. Allport
S. P. Tipper
N. R. J. Chmiel
Oxford University

ABSTRACT

This chapter is concerned with the perceptual encoding of unattended visual objects. We review some aspects of the controversy regarding early versus late selection, from a perspective that views the brain as an assembly of specialized subsystems, having massively parallel computational capabilities within as well as between subsystems.

We then turn to some new experiments. Our main approach is to use indirect (priming) measures to observe the effects of unattended object encoding on the speed of response to subsequent, related stimuli. In these experiments a typical priming stimulus consists of two simultaneously presented figures, one in red, one in green. The subject attempts to identify the red figure (the *target*) and to ignore the green one. If the previously ignored *distractor* figure is presented as the next target for selective naming, RT is consistently *increased*—that is, *negative priming* effects are found.

We explore this phenomenon of negative priming through a series of experiments, including the use of visual masking to prevent the overt identification of either target or distractor objects in the priming stimulus. Under conditions of masking such that the identity of neither target nor distractor can be reported (although the *presence* of a stimulus can be detected with as much as 90% accuracy) it appears that internal representations specific to the identity and conceptual category of *both* objects are activated and can facilitate subsequent processing of related stimuli. Longer exposure of the priming stimulus enables overt reporting of the target item alone. Under these conditions, if the previous distractor figure recurs as the next target item in a probe display composed of two (e.g., red/green) figures, we find negative priming. However, when the probe consists of a single figure (i.e., when the probe task does not require a response based on selective, cross-domain cueing), the negative-priming effect disappears and, under certain conditions, becomes facilitatory.

We consider two principle classes of explanation for these effects. The first model postulates inhibitory processes associated with internal representations of the to-be-ignored object(s). The second model asserts that associative bindings between colour and form-identity codes are made pre-attentively with respect both to attended and ignored objects. According to this model, negative priming reflects the time-cost of re-establishing new attribute-bindings.

INTRODUCTION

One of the objectives of the meeting for which this chapter was prepared was to draw on contributions from the neurosciences, as well as from psychology, in our attempt to understand the mechanisms of attention. As the starting point of our chapter, therefore, we would like to point to some features of processing in the brain, as well as some more general considerations, that have influenced our thinking about selective processes in vision:

1. The first and most obvious point is the massive degree of parallelism. A network of neural elements whose basic computational speed is measured in milliseconds is evidently capable of computing entire, complex behaviors within a few hundred milliseconds—that is, in current computational terms, in extremely few time steps (Feldman & Ballard, 1982).

2. A wide range of attributes of the retinal image appears to be represented in distinct areas of the brain, frequently in the form of separate, retinotopic "maps" of their respective attribute domains (Cowey, 1979, 1981).

3. A small range of more complex figural properties has been found, to which individual neurons at a number of sites in the temporal lobe and elsewhere show strong selective response (e.g., to "face" patterns) while they are insensitive to the size or retinal location of their trigger features (e.g., Desimone, Albright, Gross, & Bruce, 1984; Perrett, Rolls, & Caan, 1982). That is, these more complex features no longer appear organized in the form of a spatial map.

4. Beyond the inferotemporal cortex, for example in substantia innominata and elsewhere, there is clear evidence of cells whose activity is related to the learned significance of complex visual stimuli for particular classes of action but that are driven only by *visual* inputs (Rolls, 1981). Again, there seems to be no suggestion of a spatiotopic map here.

5. Clearly, despite such findings, singularly little is yet known about the neurophysiological representation, or categorization, of visual objects. These findings certainly do not imply that a single cell can "recognize" any complex category of visual forms (Cowey, 1981). The tuning of individual cells, even those with the most complex trigger features, is not nearly sharp enough; unam-

biguous object recognition must presumably depend on the combined activity of large numbers of cells within one (or more) complex attribute domain (Anderson, 1977; Anderson & Hinton, 1981). If so, then we might think of the hypothetical concept nodes (logogen units, etc.) in an abstract semantic network as implemented, at the neurophysiological level, in the form of distributed patterns of activity and of computation within such a system as a process of iterative "relaxation," or settling to a particular activity pattern (Hinton, 1981; Allport, 1985). It would seem most unlikely, however, that such concept nodes, implemented in this way, are replicated for every possible location to provide, directly, a spatiotopic map of their respective object categories.

The points just listed are not new, but they hold some interesting implications for information-processing models of selective attention.

First, the massively parallel, apparently modular organization of processing in the nervous system does not suggest any compelling limitation on the concurrent analysis of multiple visual objects, up to and including their categorization in terms of known forms and of learned actions that they afford (Allport, 1980a, 1980b). Of course, there may be such limitations; we simply observe that the available neurophysiology does not appear to require them. In contrast, the demands of coherent action impose a *strong* requirement of selectivity (Keele & Neill, 1978; Posner, 1978). Visually guided actions are typically directed toward just one among the multiple objects in our environment, where "object" may be defined in terms of the possible actions that it affords. A predator, for example, encounters a pack of similar prey animals, but must direct its attack selectively toward just one of them; information about the other objects, therefore, though available to the predator's senses, must be somehow decoupled from the immediate direction of its action (Allport, 1980a). Let us call this process *selection for action*.

The end product of perceptual processing, we assume, is an internal model or description of the immediate environment, coded in terms of the spatial disposition of objects, of their forms and surfaces, and of their potential significance for action (their "semantic" attributes). Such a view, although admittedly speculative, appears to meet with a rather wide range of agreement. Certainly, if an organism's choice of action at any instant is to be efficient, that choice must be based on as rich as possible a description of its surroundings, in which multiple objects are already described in terms of "semantic" properties as well as of their locations and other sensory attributes. Undoubtedly, the identity, location, and other attributes of many different objects can be held concurrently in memory (e.g., Jones, 1976). What, then, might limit their concurrent perceptual encoding into such a representation?

One hypothesis is as follows: Sensory *and* categorical (semantic, associative) attributes of visually presented objects are encoded in respect of the entire visual input, in parallel. The result, for a number of visual attributes such as motion, color, and (stereo)depth, is represented in the form of a distinct retinotopic map of each attribute (cf., Marr, 1981). Any one of these maps could, in principle, be used to control (retinotopic) spatial orientation, and hence, *perhaps,* selection for action. Categorical/semantic attributes, on the other hand, could not at this stage direct orientation toward a particular location, because (as argued previously) their representation is not intrinsically spatiotopic. If the codes representing (nonspatial) categorical attributes are to be integrated into the spatial selection and control of action, they must first be linked to codes (*place tokens*) in *other,* spatiotopically organized, attribute domains. The suggestion has been put forward on several occasions (Allport, 1977, 1979a, 1979b; Coltheart, 1980; Marcel, 1983a; Treisman & Gelade, 1980; Treisman, Sykes, & Gelade, 1977; van der Heijden, 1981) that a process responsible for linking or integrating codes across different domains of representation may be a critical and even, according to some proposals, a rate-limiting step in the construction of an integrated perceptual description, on which selection for action (and perhaps phenomenal awareness) is based.

These various theoretical proposals differ, however, on at least two important issues: (a) the extent to which categorical (learned, associative) attributes can be encoded in parallel, "preattentively"; (b) the stage at which integration across different attribute domains is first achieved. Regarding the first of these issues, Kahneman and Treisman (1984) have recently summarized the case for a precategorical "filter" theory, according to which all but a subset of incoming sensory information is selectively excluded from categorical or semantic encoding. Central to their argument is the claim that "selection by stimulus set is easier than by response set . . . surely one of the most salient and robust observations of the filtering paradigm." Consequently, "It is a major advantage of filter theory that it can explain this fact. . . . Late selection models provide no explanation" (Kahneman and Treisman, 1984, p. 41). We have three comments to make.

1. When cross-domain selective cueing between "physical" and "categorical" attribute domains does not involve selection in terms of spatial location, but only, as for example in Lawrence's (1971) "RSVP" task, in terms of time of occurrence, selection can be about as efficient when cued by "categorical" or by "physical" attributes (McLean, Broadbent, & Broadbent, 1983).

2. When selection for action depends on orientation toward a particular (object) *location*—as it appears most commonly to do—stimulus attributes whose neural representation takes the form of a spatiotopic "map" are, of course, able to cue such orientation directly, in a way that attribute domains lacking a spatiotopic representation could not do. To cite only one example, when selection is cued by a "physical" attribute (e.g., curved versus angular letter shape) but one that would appear not to be coded *explicitly* in its own retinotopic feature map, selection is actually less efficient than by alphanumeric category (Bundesen,

Pedersen, & Larsen, 1984). Those "physical" attributes that provide effective selection cues in cross-domain cueing tasks appear to be, in every case, attribute domains that possess spatiotopic representation.

3. This being so, the superiority of stimulus set over response set in selective cueing tasks (or the finding that the efficiency of selection depends on the spatial separation of relevant and irrelevant objects) in itself provides not the slightest evidence whether categorical attributes of objects are already encoded in parallel, independently of the selective cueing process, or only contingently, after it. As regards the controversy between "early" versus "late" selection models, the efficiency of stimulus set is simply irrelevant.

In the experiments described in this chapter we have attempted both to assess the general class of theoretical proposal regarding the preselective encoding of categorical attributes, just reviewed, and, in the last part of the chapter, to adjudicate between two alternative hypotheses: (a) that cross-domain linkage, or *perceptual integration,* is achieved only in respect of those visual objects that are selected for action and whose identity and location the subject could, in principle, report; versus (b) that cross-domain links are formed *pre*selectively with respect to all visual objects, including those that are successfully "ignored" and whose categorical identities cannot be directly reported or acted on. We call these alternative hypotheses, respectively (a) *selective* and (b) *preselective integration.*

EXPERIMENTS

Two figures are presented simultaneously, one in red, one in green—for example, a red *A* and a green *B*. The subject is requested, in advance, to report the identity of (i.e., to name) the red object; the green object, the subject is told, is irrelevant and should be ignored. Now suppose, as essentially all models of "late" selection suppose, that codes representing *both* the letter identities, *A* and *B,* are activated, as are codes representing "red" and "green." Clearly, then, it is a necessary condition for successful performance of the task that the code representing the attribute red, in the color domain, be correctly bound to the code representing the letter identity *A*. The question that interests us, however, is whether the corresponding bindings between green and *B* are also formed with respect to the *to be ignored* object, as the preselective integration model would predict.

To approach this question experimentally, however, requires some careful consideration. Obviously, we cannot ask the subject to respond directly to the to-be-ignored object, since in this case the object would presumably then cease to be ignored. A method often used to investigate the encoding of irrelevant, "distractor" objects is to observe their effects on the response to a simultaneously presented target stimulus (e.g., Eriksen & Schultz, 1979; Santee & Egeth, 1982). As a measure of the efficiency of the selection process this method has much to recommend it, but as a means of establishing the nature of encoding of the distractor objects it suffers from one important limitation: Suppose that a given manipulation of the irrelevant, distractor object(s) has no measurable effect on response to the target object. How are we to tell whether this is because the distractors have not been encoded along the manipulated dimensions, or because, although they have been so encoded, the efficiency of the selection process is not affected by this fact? We give below a concrete example (Experiments 6 to 8) in which it is clear that the first interpretation would have been seriously mistaken.

The solution that we adopt is to look for effects of encoding of the to-be-ignored object on the subject's response to a *subsequent* stimulus event—that is, we use an indirect, priming paradigm, in which the relatedness of the distractor object to an immediately following "probe" stimulus is manipulated.

The paradigm is best illustrated by a simple demonstration, which the reader is invited to try for him- or herself, and which serves to introduce two interesting effects. However, *before* turning to the test-stimuli overleaf (Fig. 5.1), please read the instructions provided on this page carefully. Then try out the task, using the test stimuli in Fig. 5.1, before reading on.

Instructions for Figure 5.1.

DO NOT INSPECT THE STIMULUS LISTS IN ADVANCE
Fig. 5.1 contains three lists of letters, each list arranged in a vertical column. Each list is made up of *pairs* of superimposed letters, one letter drawn in *solid black* (—), the other letter in a *dotted line* (.......). The task is to read the *solid black* letters aloud *as fast as possible,* starting at the top of each list, and to *ignore* the dotted letters. Before commencing, cover all three lists with a sheet of cardboard. When ready, expose one list at a time, and *cover it again as soon as* you reach the bottom of the list, without glancing back at the list. Do this for each list. Try to decide which list can be read most easily.

When you have completed the test in Fig. 5.1, following these instructions, you are invited to examine the three lists. Their construction differs only in the selection of the task-irrelevant (dotted) distractors. List 1 represents a control condition, with no systematic relation between target and distractor letters. In List 2 (the suppression condition), each distractor letter is the same as the immediately next target letter. In List 3 (redundant) all the distractors throughout the list are identical.

Experiment 1: Negative Priming

An experiment was performed using stimulus lists constructed in the same way as those shown in Fig. 5.1, but with *red* and *green* target and distractor letters,

5. POSTCATEGORICAL FILTERING 113

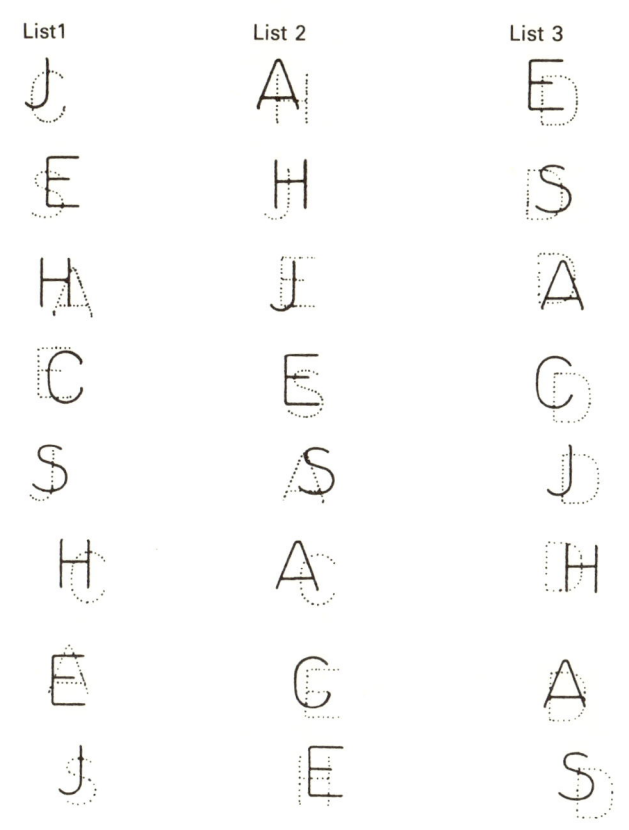

List 1	List 2	List 3
J	A	E
E	H	S
H	J	A
C	E	C
S	S	J
H	A	H
E	C	A
J	E	S

FIG. 5.1 See Instructions on preceding page.

respectively. Six letters (A, C, E, H, J, S) were used throughout. The letters were .9 cm high 1 cm apart, in columns of 26 per list. The same target letters appeared in each condition but in randomized order. Twenty subjects each read 11 lists: two practice lists and then three experimental lists in each of the three conditions outlined previously. The order of presentation was randomized differently for each subject. The instructions emphasized that the subject was to read the red letters aloud as fast as possible and to ignore the green letters.

The mean reading times for each condition (and differences from control) were as shown in Table 5.1. Analysis of variance indicated a reliable difference between conditions ($p < .01$); Newman-Keuls multiple comparison further showed each condition to be significantly different from every other ($p < .01$).

After completing the experiment, when the construction of the stimulus lists was pointed out to them, the subjects uniformly expressed surprise. (If the instructions accompanying Fig. 5.1 were followed, the reader may have been similarly surprised to discover, after reading List 3, that the same distractor letter had been repeated throughout the list.)

TABLE 5.1
Mean Reading Times

	Suppression	Control	Redundant
Time per list (sec)	16.0 (+0.7)	15.3	14.5 (−0.8)
Equivalent time per item (msec)	615 (+27)	588	558 (−30)

The results of this simple demonstration experiment illustrate three main points:

1. Even when self-paced, subjects engaged in this selective reading task show little awareness of the identity of the unattended distractors, though of course all subjects are aware that irrelevant, green letters are in fact present and overlapping the red target letters. This finding is similar to results reported by Rock and Gutman (1981) and Neisser and Becklen (1975). Both groups of authors suggest that subjects' lack of awareness of the "unattended" objects reflects simple lack of processing.

2. Counter to this view, when the letter to be named is identical to the immediately preceding distractor, there is an item-specific priming effect, as "late selection" models might predict. However, far from *facilitating* subsequent response to the repeated item, the priming effect is inhibitory. We find *negative priming* by preceding task-irrelevant distractors. (The effect is perhaps related to an analogous finding by Neill, 1977, and by Dalrymple-Alford & Budayr, 1966, using the Stroop color-naming task. See Tipper, 1984, and Experiment 9 later in this chapter.)

3. On the other hand, if the same distractor item is repeated throughout the list, the time needed for selective reading of the target items is *reduced*.

Because the negative priming is apparently specific to the repeated letter identity, it follows that subjects must have encoded information regarding the visual form or identity of the unattended items. Further, because the priming is negative or "inhibitory," the interesting possibility arises that, in the course of selecting the target and rejecting the distractor item for control of the reading-aloud response, processes mediating representation of the distractor undergo some form of suppression or inhibition; as a result, when the same item recurs and is to be responded to, there is an additional cost in processing time. Moreover, if suppression or inhibition of the distractor identity is an essential part of the process of selection, we might indeed expect that repeated suppression of the same distractor (as in the redundant condition) should reduce interference from this stimulus, and hence reduce the time needed to select and respond to the target. We attempt to evaluate this "suppression" hypothesis in a later section of the chapter.

Experiment 2: Negative Priming across Changes in Visual Form

A question immediately arises regarding the level of representation to which the negative priming by task-irrelevant distractors applies. We performed a simple variation of Experiment 1, in which, for half the subjects, the target letters were all in lower case (and red) whereas the distractors were in upper case (and green). Only the control and suppression conditions were run. There were 34 subjects, 17 in each group.

We again obtained a significant negative priming effect, for *both* groups of subjects. Indeed, when the negative priming had to operate *across* typographic case the difference between suppression and control conditions was, if anything, marginally greater (26 msec per item) than when all stimuli were in upper case (22 msec). In both groups, all but two subjects showed the negative-priming effect ($p < 0.001$ by sign test, in each case). It seems clear, therefore, that the distractor items must have been encoded at least to the level of orthographic ("abstract") letter identity.

Experiment 3: Negative Priming in Picture Naming (Tachistoscopic Presentation)

The two previous experiments relied on a measure of self-paced reading speed to reveal benefits and costs in processing time. In the experiments that follow we turn to tachistoscopic presentation using pattern masking, and we record naming latencies for each probe stimulus individually. We also turn to line drawings of familiar objects as the experimental stimuli.

In Experiment 3 (and, with variations of detail, in Experiments 4 and 5) the sequence of events on each trial was as follows: A fixation cross, visible for 900 ms, was replaced by two, spatially superimposed line drawings of objects, one drawn in red, the other in green. This compound stimulus is referred to as the *priming display*. Subjects were instructed to attend to and to remember the red object, and to ignore the green one. After a brief exposure duration, mean 35 ms in Experiment 3, adjusted individually for each subject (see below), the priming display was, in turn, replaced by a pattern mask of randomly arranged red and green line fragments, which remained on for 100 ms. (In Experiment 3 only, the priming display was delivered to the subject's left eye, the mask to his or her right eye.) The fixation cross then reappeared for a further 900 ms (ISI of 1 sec), to be followed by a second pair of superimposed red/green line figures (mean duration 40 ms), which were again followed by a pattern mask of 100 ms duration. The second pair of red/green figures is referred to as the *probe display*. Red and green drawings each subtended approximately 6° to 8°, centered on fixation.

There were 24 subjects. Their primary task, they were told, was to name the red figure in the probe display (the *probe target*) aloud, as fast as possible; the green figure was irrelevant and was to be ignored. After responding as rapidly as possible to the probe target, subjects were then to attempt to *recall* the red figure from the preceding display (the *prime target*).

Different prime and probe targets and distractors were used on each trial, without replacement. The prime targets were unrelated either to their superimposed prime distractors, or to the subsequent probe target. On one half of the trials (suppression) the prime distractor was identical in form to the subsequent probe target. On the remaining trials (control) the prime distractor and subsequent probe were unrelated. Trials were presented in mixed (randomized) sequence.

Prior to the main experimental session, each subject received practice in naming the red figure in a series of superimposed red/green line drawings under dichoptic masking. The stimulus onset asynchrony (SOA) between the test stimulus and the mask, to be used during the experimental session, was then established for each subject, using five new red/green displays, as follows: For each display, masking SOA began at 10 ms and was increased on successive trials by 5 ms steps until the subject named the red object correctly. Then 5 ms were added to the longest SOA required, and this value determined the SOA used for presentation of the prime display; a further 5 ms were added for the probe duration. None of the line drawings used in the practice or SOA-setting session recurred in the main experimental session.

Recognition of Distractors. Two methods were used to obtain an index of overt identification of the prime distractors:

1. Following Rock and Gutman (1981), on the final trial, in place of the probe display the subject was unexpectedly asked to recall the preceding *green* figure (the prime distractor). Four out of the 24 subjects were able to do so. To put it another way, at the time when the probe normally occurred, 20 subjects were unable overtly to identify the immediately preceding prime distractor. (The prime display on the catch trial was the same for all subjects.) Subsequent analysis showed that the same four subjects had also failed to report the prime target on 33% of the preceding trials, in contrast to only 13% for the remaining 20 subjects. Naming RTs recorded for these subjects were also more than 150 ms longer than the average of the remaining 20 subjects. These four subjects, it appeared, were not consistently able to follow the selection instructions with respect to the prime display; their data were therefore dropped from the main RT analysis.

2. Following the catch trial, subjects were presented with a recognition test consisting of 15 black line drawings, five chosen randomly from the prime targets, five from the prime distractors, and five previously unseen, "new" drawings. Subjects responded positively to 73% of the prime targets, 12% of the prime distractors, and 8% of the new figures. Newman-Keuls analysis confirmed

that prime targets were selected reliably more often than the other two groups ($p < .01$), but that there was no significant difference between the rate of acceptance of prime distractors and the false positive rate to new items.

Naming Latencies. Only trials on which subjects correctly reported the preceding prime targets were included (5.5% and 5.8% naming errors occurred in control and suppression conditions respectively). The mean RT to name the probe target in the control condition was 749 ms; in the suppression condition—that is, when preceded by a figurally identical prime distractor—it was 797 ms. Analysis of variance confirmed that this difference of 48 ms negative priming was reliable ($p < .01$).

The difference between RTs in suppression and control conditions was further analyzed with respect to those trials on which the preceding prime target was correctly reported ("hits") or not ("misses"). Fourteen subjects were available for this analysis, having misses in both suppression and control conditions. Hit trials showed a mean difference of 50.8 ms *negative* priming, as before; misses, however, showed the reverse facilitation—that is, when the subjects failed to report the prime target, the occurrence of an identical prior distractor resulted in RTs 52.2 ms *faster* than control.

We thus confirm the negative priming effect, under conditions in which overt identification of the distractor prime is controlled and appears to be minimal, and there is no repetition of target stimuli within the experiment. Moreover, on those occasions on which, with brief presentation, it appears that *neither* the prime target nor its accompanying distractor can be reported, the negative priming apparently reverses to become facilitatory. This latter phenomenon is investigated further in Experiments 4 and 5. A similar pattern of results was found when the experiment was repeated at a shorter ISI (Tipper, 1984).

Experiment 4: Negative Priming by Semantically Related Distractors: Dependence on Successful selection for action

Experiment 2 showed that the negative priming by ignored distractors occurred even when prime and probe stimuli differed in physical form, but shared the same name. It therefore becomes of interest to establish whether priming by task-irrelevant distractors can affect the processing of probe stimuli that were related to them in terms of neither physical stimulus characteristics, nor of the specific *response* to be made (same name), but only in terms of shared categorical or *semantic* attributes. Experiment 4 was therefore designed to examine priming by categorically related distractors. It also included a condition in which the probe target was categorically related to the previously *attended* picture (the prime target), as well as a control condition, as before, in which neither the prime target nor the prime distractor were related to the probe. A set of 10 drawings, forming five categorically related pairs—cat–dog, chair–table, hammer–spanner, trumpet–guitar, hand–foot—was used throughout the experiment. (Individual drawings subtended 4.7° to 6.4°.) Experiment 3 had also provided some evidence that, when subjects failed to select the prime target for subsequent overt recall, the "inhibitory" priming effect of the task-irrelevant distractor disappeared, and was indeed replaced by a facilitation effect. We therefore ran Experiment 4 under two different exposure conditions of the prime display, referred to as *long* and *short* SOA. For the long SOA, exposure duration of the prime display was determined as in Experiment 3. (Masking, in this and subsequent experiments, however, was monoptic. Mean long SOA was 90 ms, range 60 to 130 ms.) For the short SOA, exposure duration (and correspondingly the masking SOA) of the priming display was reduced to a level at which explicit identification of *either* of the two objects in the priming display approximated to chance levels. The short SOA was established individually for each subject as follows: Subjects were shown examples of all 10 drawings used in the experiment, both singly and in overlaid, red/green pairs as they would be presented. Their task, they were told, was to identify *either* object in the display. If unsure they were asked to guess. Masking SOA started at 100 ms, with a different picture pair on each trial. On each occasion that a subject correctly reported one of the drawings, the SOA was reduced by 5 ms. Trials were continued until the subject failed to identify either drawing on five consecutive trials. The SOA at which this occurred was then used for that subject for the remainder of the experiment. Mean SOA resulting from this procedure was 21 ms (range 15 to 35 ms).

Subjects then received a further series of trials in which, on a random 50% of occasions, a blank white field was presented in place of the red/green figure. Subjects were asked to judge the presence or absence of the latter. When a subject responded "present" he or she was also asked to guess the identity of one of the drawings. Practice proceeded until the subject was responding "present" on about 50% of the trials; he or she then received 30 further trials. Presence/absence judgments in these trials were 71.5% correct; on the same trials, even when subjects could be persuaded to identify the stimuli (on only 14% of correct "present" judgments), the accuracy of their reports was not significantly better than chance. In contrast, in the long SOA condition, after naming the probe, subjects failed to recall the prime target on only 2.07% of trials. (These trials were dropped from the RT analysis.) In the final catch trial (long SOA only) no subject correctly identified the immediately preceding distractor.

ISI between priming and probe displays was 1.2 sec. The probe display, like the priming display, was followed immediately by a pattern mask for 100 ms, Exposure duration of the probe display was adjusted, as in Experiment 3, to be just sufficient for accurate identification of the red target object (mean SOA 115 ms).

There were 20 new subjects. Four blocks of experimental trials alternated between long and short SOA, counterbalanced (20 trials per prime type in each, in randomized sequence). Each block began with six trials of practice.

Mean latencies to name the probe target in the six conditions (and differences from control) were as shown in Table 5.2. Analysis of variance indicated a significant ($p < .01$) interaction of prime type with prime-display duration (long versus short SOA), in both the subjects' and the materials' analyses. Considering the long SOA condition first, as might be expected there is facilitation due to a previously attended, categorically related prime ($p < .01$). Of much greater interest, we find a negative priming effect ($p < .05$) from preceding, category-related, successfully ignored distractors. In contrast, following the priming displays at the short SOA, where *neither* priming object could be overtly identified, RT to a probe target categorically related to *either* of these objects shows a reliable facilitation ($p < .01$ in each case). This pattern of results bears a remarkable resemblance to results reported by Marcel (1980). He found facilitation of both sets of associates of a homographic prime, when the prime word was pattern masked and could not be reported, but selective facilitation of one set and inhibitory priming of the other when the (biased) homographic prime could be explicitly reported. Facilitation by a pattern-masked prime has, of course, been reported by several other investigators (e.g., Carr, McCauley, Sperber, & Parmelee, 1982; Evett & Humphreys, 1981).

Three points seem worth making here. First, negative priming by categorically related distractors (at long SOA) supports our finding in Experiment 2 that the phenomenon of negative priming is not tied to physical similarity between prime and probe. Second, because the effects are dependent on categorical or semantic attributes of the preceding primes, it follows that—in all three cases—the distractor stimuli, whose identity the subjects are unable to report, have nevertheless been encoded in terms of such categorical attributes. Finally, the rather dramatic reversal of the effect at short SOA encourages our belief that the negative priming effect is dependent on some property of the selective process in successful selection for action.

TABLE 5.2
Mean Latencies

	Long SOA *(Prime Target* *Identified)*	*Short SOA* *(Prime Target* *Not Identified)*
Attended categorical	658 ms (−27)	658 ms (−30)
Control	685 ms	688 ms
Distractor categorical	705 ms (+20)	664 ms (−24)

Experiment 5: Replication and Extension of Experiment 4

The procedures described in Experiment 4 were repeated with 20 new subjects, treating exposure duration of the priming display as a between-subject variable. In addition to the priming conditions investigated in Experiment 4, Experiment 5 included two other priming relationships between the probe target and the objects in the priming display: (a) distractor repetition, in which the prime distractor is structurally identical to the subsequent probe (equivalent to the condition labeled suppression in Experiment 3); (b) attended repetition, in which the prime *target* is identical to the subsequent probe. In other respects the procedure was identical to that in Experiment 4.

Exposure durations of the priming displays in short and long SOA conditions were established individually as in Experiment 4 (mean short SOA 23 ms, range 15 to 45 ms; mean long SOA 112 ms, range 70 to 140 ms). Subsequent presence/absence judgments under the short SOA condition yielded 90% accuracy. However, following correct "present" judgments subjects overtly identified only 16.5% of objects correctly—that is, a little below the chance expectation of 20% for an ensemble of 10 possible (paired) objects.

In the long SOA condition, subjects failed to report the prime target, after naming the probe, on only 2.1% of trials. In the catch trial at the end of the experiment none of these 10 subjects was able to report the preceding distractor object. Mean correct naming latencies in the five priming conditions (and differences from control), for both long and short SOA, were as shown in Table 5.3. Separate analyses of variance were made at long and at short SOA. For long SOA priming there was a significant main effect of prime type ($p < .01$, both by materials and by subjects). Attended repetition resulted in significantly faster naming times than control and than attended categorical ($p < .01$). Both these effects are expected, though the nonsignificant effect of semantic priming is not (cf. Dannebring & Briand, 1982). Of principal interest, the results confirm the finding of significant ($p < .05$) negative priming by categorically related distrac-

TABLE 5.3
Mean Correct Naming Latencies

	Long SOA (Prime Target Identified)	Short SOA (Prime Target Not Identified)
Attended repetition	615 ms (−80)	661 ms (−32)
Attended categorical	677 ms (−18)	651 ms (−42)
Control	695 ms	693 ms
Distractor categorical	726 ms (+31)	671 ms (−22)
Distractor repetition	746 ms (+51)	660 ms (−33)

tors obtained in Experiment 4, as well as by distractor repetition ($p < .01$).

In marked contrast, with short SOA priming, all four priming conditions, taken as a group, are now significantly *faster* than control (again, both in the materials' and in the subjects' analysis) though the priming conditions do not differ significantly among themselves. Indeed, the overall mean RT for repetition priming (660 ms) is identical to that for categorical priming (661 ms); both are reliably faster than control. These results, again, appear to provide evidence of high-level encoding of stimuli whose identity is not available for explicit report.

The complete pattern of results adds to our confidence that the phenemena already observed in Experiment 3 and 4 are robust. Again, we find negative priming, by semantically related (as well as by figurally identical) distractors, only when the prime *target* can be correctly reported—that is, when the to-be-ignored distractor responsible for the priming effect has been successfully *selected against*.

Experiments 6, 7, and 8: Selection for Action among Spatially Nonoverlapping Objects, and the Encoding of Distractors

The preceding five experiments have all required the subject to select for naming one of two spatially superimposed visual forms; in every experiment we have made use of a priming paradigm to study properties of the subjects' encoding of the to-be-ignored distractor object. In the following two experiments (6 and 7) we depart temporarily from both these procedures.

It may be that selection for action among spatially overlapping objects is a rather special case, and that the conclusions that we have arrived at about the encoding of task-irrelevant distractor objects do not apply to selection among spatially separated visual forms. A number of authors who have maintained a belief in the compulsory nature of "early" selection among incoming sensory messages—that is, prior to the stage at which they can be encoded in terms of categorical or action-related attributes—also maintain that the efficiency of such a process of selection will vary inversely with the spatial separation of the wanted from the unwanted stimuli or, more subtly, with their configural, Gestalt, relations (e.g., Broadbent, 1982; Kahneman & Henik, 1981; LaBerge, 1983).

An analogy is sometimes invoked with the adjustable beam of a spotlight. According to Broadbent (1982), whatever is within the beam "obtains access to a further processing system" [p. 271]; information falling outside the beam, by implication, does not. For some, this "further processing" is thought of as a process of construction, or verification, by which the unattended information is simply "not picked up" (e.g., Hochberg, 1970; Neisser, 1976). For others, the "early" selection process simply prevents incoming information from *activating* categorical/semantic representational codes ("dictionary units," etc.). Francolini and Egeth (1980) offer a representative (if rather cautious) statement of such a view:

> The mandatory activation of the meaning of an item may . . . be *restricted* to just those items that are deemed relevant. . . . Since activation depends on relevance, it is not totally automatic. We believe our findings contradict theories that propose that well-learned stimuli will be processed regardless of where attention is directed . . . [p. 339–340, italics added].

Selection, in Francolini and Egeth's experiments, is between spatially separated figures, and relevance is cued by color. In a rather similar statement, based on similar results, Kahneman and Chajzyk (1983) conclude that ". . . the involuntary reading of a distant colour word can be *prevented* by focusing attention on the relevant visual object" [p. 498, italics added]. The evidence invoked by all these authors, to the effect that stimuli that are "not selected"—that fall outside the spotlight beam—are not in fact "processed" in terms of their semantic or categorical attributes, takes one of two main forms. First, such categorical information cannot be reported, or otherwise directly acted upon; second, and most importantly, the categorical nature of the *unselected,* ignored objects does not affect the amount of interference (or facilitation) that they exercise on the speed or accuracy of response to a simultaneously presented target object. Moreover, such interference (or facilitation) has been repeatedly found to diminish with spatial separation (or with configural separation) of the relevant and irrelevant sensory information.

However, as we pointed out earlier, the fact that selection for action is strongly affected by spatial variables, and may be most effectively cued by stimulus attributes that possess spatiotopic representation in the nervous system, does not itself provide evidence that other (nonspatial, "nonsensory") attributes are not also encoded, independently of that selection. The absence of interference (or facilitation) by "unattended" sensory objects would justify claims that "activation . . . (is) restricted," "reading . . . (is) prevented," and so on, *only* if we can assume that absence of interference or facilitation implies absence of activation (or of "further processing"); equivalently, only if we can assume that "activation of meaning" *always* produces interference.

We do not know whether this assumption is true. In the following three experiments we set out to test it.

In one set of conditions we arrange that the target for selection and naming is always at the same location—namely at the center of fixation—and in a known color, whereas the distractor is at a different, noncentral location, and in a different color. Under these conditions, we suppose, the attentional spotlight can be sharply focused, and therefore selection of the target should be maximally efficient and there should be minimal interference (or facilitation) caused by the distractor. In another set of conditions, neither the location of the target nor the distractor is precisely known in advance of presentation, but can be at any one of four positions spaced around the fixation point; selection is cued by color (red versus green). Under these second conditions, we expect a diffused attentional spotlight, inefficient selection enabling substantial "further processing" of the distractor, and hence substantial interference by it. (Let us call these two types of selection conditions "easy" and "difficult" selection, respectively.)

In Experiments 6 and 7 we confirm that these expectations, as regards interference or facilitation effects, are indeed correct. However, for those who argue from the diminution or absence of *interference* (cost or benefit) by unattended objects to the diminution or absence of *encoding* of these same objects, there is presumably a further, rather strong prediction. Suppose that, immediately following target selection under each of these conditions, a further probe stimulus is presented, categorically related to the immediately preceding distractor. In this case, according to the assumption that we wish to test, we might expect some *semantic priming* by the distractor object under the difficult selection conditions, where categorical encoding of the distractor cannot be prevented, but a diminution or complete absence of such priming under the easy selection conditions in the prime display, where categorical encoding of the distractor ex hypothesi can be efficiently prevented. Experiment 8 is designed to test this prediction.

In all three experiments we used the same set of line drawings as in Experiment 5. The target object in these experiments, however, was always *green,* the distractor always red. Each drawing subtended a visual angle of approximately 3.2°. In Experiments 6 and 7 the subjects' task was simply to name the target object aloud as fast as possible, and to ignore the distractor. In the easy selection condition the target object appeared centered on the fixation point, and the distractor appeared randomly 5° right or left of fixation. In the difficult selection condition, target and distractor both appeared equidistant from fixation at the diagonally opposite corners of an imaginary square, and separated approximately 5° center to center.

Experiment 6: Categorically Related versus Unrelated Distractors. In Experiment 6, the distractor was either categorically related, or unrelated, to the simultaneously presented target. There were 16 subjects. Easy and difficult selection trials occurred in separate blocks and were each preceded by a session of practice. There were 20 trials in each condition. Stimulus exposure, prior to the pattern mask, was 130 ms.

Mean latencies to name the target object, and error percentages, were as shown in Table 5.4. Errors in naming occurred significantly more frequently ($p < .01$) when the distractor was categorically related to the target, but *only* in the difficult selection condition; error rate did not differ significantly in the other three conditions. Subjects also named the target significantly (84 ms) faster in the easy than in the difficult conditions ($p < .01$). In the easy condition, the pres-

TABLE 5.4
Mean Latencies and Error Rates

	Easy Selection	Difficult Selection
Related distractor	617 ms (3.4%)	684 ms (8.1%)
Unrelated distractor	612 ms (2.5%)	711 ms (4.4%)
Difference	− 5 ms	27 ms

ence of a categorically related distractor clearly had no significant effect on naming latency. Under the difficult selection condition, related distractors had a small but significant ($p < .05$) facilitation effect (cf. Schaffer & LaBerge, 1979; Underwood, 1977).

Evidently the categorical identity of the distractor affects both the time needed to name the target and the accuracy of doing so, but *only* in the difficult selection condition. (The apparent trade-off in speed and accuracy occurs only *within* the difficult selection condition; it could therefore only result from subjects' encoding of the categorical identity of the distractor object.) As was anticipated, the categorical relatedness of the distractor had no discernible effect on target selection when that selection was made sufficiently easy.

Experiment 7: Distractor Present or Absent. The design of this experiment was identical to that of Experiment 6, except that there was now either a categorically unrelated distractor or no distractor in the display. There were 16 subjects, none of whom served in Experiment 6. Mean naming latencies (and error rates) were as shown in Table 5.5. There were no significant differences in errors between any of the conditions. Naming times were significantly (57 ms) shorter in easy than in difficult selection ($p < .01$). Moreover, the presence of a distractor significantly increased (54 ms) the time to select and name the target in the difficult selection condition ($p < .01$); it had no significant effect in the easy condition.

Experiment 8: Categorical Priming by Task-Irrelevant Distractors, under Conditions of Easy and Difficult Selection/Rejection of the Priming Stimulus.
In this experiment we return again to the paradigm of priming by a preceding, task-irrelevant distractor that we studied in Experiments 3 to 5. The probe dis-

TABLE 5.5
Mean Naming Latencies and Error Rates

	Easy Selection	Difficult Selection
Distractor present	610 ms (3.2%)	679 ms (5.3%)
Distractor absent	598 ms (2.5%)	625 ms (4.2%)
Difference	12 ms	54 ms

play containing the target and superimposed distractor, and the relations between the probe and the preceding priming display, were the same as those in Experiment 4: attended categorical, distractor categorical, and control (unrelated). As in all our previous priming experiments, the priming display always contained a target object and a categorically unrelated distractor. The physical arrangement of the priming stimuli was identical to the displays (with unrelated distractors) presented for naming in Experiments 6 and 7, in both easy and difficult selection conditions.

There were 16 subjects. The instructions and procedure were essentially the same as in Experiments 3 to 5. Subjects were instructed to attend to, and to remember, the *green* object in the priming display, and to ignore the red figure, which was irrelevant. When the subsequent probe display appeared, subjects were to name the green object (the probe target) as fast as possible, and to ignore the superimposed red figure. As in previous experiments, it was emphasized that rapid naming of the probe target was the primary task. After doing so, subjects were to attempt to recall the green object from the preceding display (the prime target).

Both the priming display and the probe display were presented for 130 ms and were immediately followed by a pattern mask composed of red and green line fragments. ISI between priming and probe display was 1.2 sec. Easy and difficult selection conditions within the priming display were run separately, each preceded by a practice session.

Subjects failed to recall the preceding prime target on less than 1% of all trials, and no more frequently in difficult than in easy prime displays. Errors in naming the probe target occurred on 3.05% of trials. The proportion of errors did not differ significantly between priming conditions. Mean correct naming latencies (and differences from control) were as follows:

TABLE 5.6
Mean Correct Naming Latencies

	Easy Selection	*Difficult Selection*
Attended categorical	678 ms (−26)	690 ms (−37)
Control	704 ms	727 ms
Distractor categorical	726 ms (+22)	741 ms (+14)

Not surprisingly, priming by the previously identified *target* object (attended categorical) significantly facilitated naming of a related probe, when the prime target was easy or difficult to select. Of much greater interest, when the probe was semantically related to the preceding, to-be-ignored distractor object, we again find a negative priming effect, as in our earlier experiments. The effect was significant following easy selection but just failed to reach significance in the difficult selection condition. (However, in the overall analysis, we find no hint of an interaction between the type of prime and selection difficulty.)

Three simple points can be made: First, negative priming by semantically ✓ related distractors is not confined to spatially superimposed priming displays. Indeed, when the to-be-attended prime target appears always centered on fixation, and the distractor responsible for the priming effect occurs (as in the easy selection condition), 5° away to right or left, negative priming of a categorically related probe appears to be no less effective than when the priming distractor was spatially superimposed on the target. (Experiments 4 and 5 showed an equivalent negative priming effect, with categorical primes, of 20 and 31 ms, respectively.) Second, semantic priming is produced by distractors, in easy selection conditions, that had no detectable effect on the *efficiency of selection* of their accompanying targets. Third, the results offer no support whatever for the prediction, outlined earlier, of a diminution in semantic priming by distractors that are easy to select out, relative to distractors that are difficult to select out.

Clearly, our findings require corroboration and extension to other selective-attention situations. In the meantime, we take leave to doubt that the absence of Stroop-like interference or facilitation effects produced by concurrently presented distractors can provide secure evidence for the *absence* of higher-level processing of those distractors.

Experiment 9: Simplex versus Duplex Probes

One feature of our experimental paradigm that we have held constant throughout the series of experiments described so far is that the probe display, like the priming display, consisted of *two* figures (in the probe display, physically superimposed); and that the naming response required of the subjects was therefore, necessarily, a *selective* response (cued by color). There were several reasons for this choice, but none of any weight: One was with a view to continuity with our preliminary, list-reading experiments; a second was that degrading a probe stimulus by superimposing irrelevant contours has been shown in some cases to produce enhanced priming effects (e.g., Meyer, Schvaneveldt, & Ruddy, 1975); finally, similar selection criteria in both displays, we supposed, might enhance the efficiency of selection of the target prime.

Several considerations, however, prompted us to investigate what would happen to priming by a successfully ignored distractor, when the response to the probe stimulus no longer depended on (color-cued) *selection* among different objects or different elements of that display. One such consideration arose from an intriguing result reported by Lowe (1979). Following Neill (1977) and others, Lowe confirmed that subjects take longer to name the color of an incongruent color word, in the Stroop task, when the color to be named matches the to-be-ignored *word* of the immediately preceding trial. This so-called *suppress–say* effect appears clearly analogous to the negative priming effects that we have described. Lowe also showed, however, that the RT cost incurred in a suppress–say sequence was found only if the second (probe) stimulus was also an incongruent *Stroop* word. When the second stimulus for naming was a simple color patch, the effect of the previously ignored base word became facilitatory. As Lowe (1979) argues, this result is difficult to reconcile with the view that the suppress–say effect depends on direct suppression, or inhibition, of internal codes representing the identity of the previously ignored base word.

In view of Lowe's finding, it seemed important to discover whether the negative priming effects that we have observed are similarly dependent on probing with a compound display, also requiring selective cueing of the relevant component in that display. Other considerations that motivate this experiment become clear in the *General Discussion* later.

The experimental paradigm was essentially the same as in Experiment 3, except that, for one group of subjects, the *probe* display, as in all the preceding experiments, consisted of a physically superimposed pair of red and green figures (*duplex* probe), whereas for a second group of subjects it consisted of a single, black figure (*simplex* probe). The stimuli in all cases were letters. In the duplex probe both red and green letters were in upper case; in the simplex probe the single letter was in lower case. We reasoned that a simplex probe might be less likely to trigger any of the selective, *cross-domain cueing* processes that must be applied to the priming display, if the probe target also differed from the priming display (as in Lowe's experiments) in physical format. In Experiment 2 we obtained equivalent priming both within and across letter case. For both groups the *priming* displays consisted of red and green superimposed, upper-case letters, and subjects were instructed to attend to and later recall the red letter. In control trials, the letters in the priming display were unrelated to those in the subsequent probe display. In the experimental trials (distractor prime) the green distractor letter was the same (same name) as the subsequent probe target letter.

There were 20 subjects, 10 in each group. After naming the probe, subjects failed to report the preceding prime on only 1.9% of all trials. In the catch trial four out of 20 subjects correctly identified the preceding distractor. Errors in naming the probe occurred on 2.1% and 2.8% of trials with simplex and duplex probes, respectively. Mean naming latencies (and differences from control) were as follows:

TABLE 5.7
Mean Naming Latencies

	Duplex Probe	*Simplex Probe*
Control	572 ms	547 ms
Distractor prime	590 ms (+18)	534 ms (−13)

There was a significant interaction between prime type and probe type ($p < .01$). With the duplex probe, as before, there was a significant negative priming effect of repetition of the previously ignored distractor ($p < .01$). With the simplex probe, however, the negative priming effect disappears and is replaced by a small facilitatory effect. The pattern of results thus appears to follow closely that reported earlier by Lowe (1979).

GENERAL DISCUSSION: NEGATIVE PRIMING AND PERCEPTUAL INTEGRATION

In this series of experiments we have repeatedly observed the phenomenon of negative priming: An immediately preceding, "successfully rejected" distractor, which the subject cannot explicitly report or recognize, increases the time needed for selective response to a nominally or conceptually related probe stimulus. One apparently critical condition for the negative priming effect is that the stimulus responsible for priming should have been successfully "selected against"—that is, that *another,* simultaneously presented target object has won the selection for action, and can be reported. In our experiments, when *neither* the prime target nor the prime distractor are available for overt report, priming by the to-be-ignored object reverses and become facilitatory. A second condition for the occurrence of negative priming appears to be that the subsequent probe stimulus—the latency of response to which provides our measure of priming effects—also requires a process of selective cueing of response-relevant and -irrelevant components. (The available results do not yet tell us whether the type of selective cueing—by color, by location, and so on—has to be the same for both prime and probe displays, or not.)

We now consider two possible interpretations of these results. Lowe (1979) has argued that the elimination or indeed reversal of what we have called the negative priming effect, by means of a simplex probe, is inconsistent with any simple model of distractor inhibition as the mechanism of negative priming. We agree with this. However, the data may still be compatible with a slightly more complex inhibitory scheme. Tipper (1984) has proposed a model in which an inhibitory process selectively isolates representations of the ignored objects from the control of action, without thereby inhibiting the activated representations themselves. He further suggested that, when the probe task does not demand selective processing, the inhibitory process, affecting only the outputs of the ignored representations, may be released, thus revealing a persisting facilitation. Although this proposal evidently makes certain, rather ad hoc assumptions, it also yields some straightforward predictions, which we are currently testing. Consideration of some of the issues discussed at the beginning of this chapter, on the other hand, suggests a different interpretation.

In the introduction to this chapter, we contrasted two alternative hypotheses regarding the perceptual integration of categorical and noncategorical stimulus attributes. Both these hypotheses assumed that categorical as well as noncategorical (sensory) attributes of unattended visual objects are encoded in parallel. Our repeated finding of categorical priming by unattended (and unreportable) distractors, we believe, provides compelling evidence for this assumption. According to *one* proposal (e.g., Allport, 1977), which we called the *selective-integration hypothesis,* cross-domain linkage (integration, verification) of categorical and noncategorical attributes of the same object occurs *selectively* with respect to those objects, and only those objects, that are successfully selected for action, including, of course, deferred action or *report* (cf Treisman & Schmidt, 1982). Indeed, in its strongest form the proposal was that the process of perceptual integration was itself constitutive of such selection. An alternative hypothesis maintains that cross-domain linkages (most importantly, linkages between spatiotopic and nonspatiotopic, categorical domains) are formed *preselectively*. This is the hypothesis put forward, in slightly differing forms, by Coltheart (1980) and van der Heijden (1981); we called it the *preselective integration hypothesis*.

Imagine that the "priming" display in one of our experiments consisted of a red *A* and a green *B*, followed by a "probe" display made up of a red *B* and a green *C;* and that the subject is instructed to attend to the *red* items. As already pointed out, if codes representing the orthographic identities of *both* the objects, *A* and *B*, are activated (as our results appear to show), then correct selection of the target letter identity must depend on the correct linkage or association between the color attribute "red" and the letter identity *A*. Suppose also, however, *as the preselective integration hypothesis asserts*, that the attribute "green" has *also* been bound to the letter identity *B*. When the probe display arrives, the subject must again form associative bindings between color and letter-identity domains, in order to cue the selection of the new target letter, *B*, as the red item. But, ex hypothesi, *B* is already linked to a different color; green. Hence, additional time is needed to undo the interfering effect of the earlier association. Hence, there is an item-specific time cost or negative priming.

The same hypothesis accounts very naturally for the reversal to purely facilitatory priming effects from short SOA pattern-masked priming displays (Experiments 4 and 5), in the following way. Under these conditions categorical and noncategorical attribute codes are activated, but the object-specific linking or integration of these attributes remains uncompleted either for the target or the distractor objects. Because ex hypothesi such integration is a necessary condition of selection for action (hence, of object *report*), the subject remains "unaware" of either object's identity. Second, because such integration in the priming display is *also* the source of interference with the *new* cross-domain bindings appropriate to the probe display, if these bindings have not been formed it follows that they cannot interfere. Hence only (category-specific) *facilitation*.

Finally, the hypothesis that the negative priming effect depends on *interference* between cross-domain bindings already formed with respect to the *ignored* distractor object and the formation of *new* (identity-color, etc.) bindings with respect to the probe clearly predicts that the appearance of negative priming will depend on the particular task demands imposed by the probe. Quite specifically, negative priming should be found if the formation of new, cross-domain bindings is needed for selection of the probe response—for example (as already argued), in any cross-domain selective cueing (or "filtering") task. With a simplex probe, on the other hand, selection of a response is no longer logically dependent on the formation of new, cross-domain associations. Hence, the effect of prior encoding of the same object category can be simply facilitatory.

The preceding argument, we believe, strongly favors the preselective integration hypothesis. On the other hand, even if our interpretation of these distractor priming effects is broadly on the right lines, we are well aware of many questions that remain to be answered. To mention only two: Are many *different* attributes encoded and linked together with respect to the ignored object, or only those attributes (in our experiments, name identity and color) specifically involved in selection of the target object? In the experiments we have described, the priming displays contained no more than two objects, in just two possible colors. Granted that some bindings are formed between distractor attributes, might they be made in this case merely by default, like the "illusory conjunctions" reported by Treisman and Schmidt (1982)? Answers to these questions, we hope, should not be too difficult to obtain.

ACKNOWLEDGMENTS

This chapter has benefited from comments on an earlier version by Geoffrey Hinton, Anne Treisman, Lex van der Heijden, and an anonymous reviewer, which we very gratefully acknowledge. We also acknowledge the assistance of Emma Nieve and Margaret Cranston who carried out experiments 2 and 10, respectively. Finally, we wish to thank Donald Broadbent for many useful discussions.

REFERENCES

Allport, D. A. (1977). On knowing the meaning of words we are unable to report: The effects of visual masking. In S. Dornic (Ed.), *Attention and performance VI* (pp. 505–533). Hillsdale, NJ: Lawrence Erlbaum Associates.

Allport, D. A. (1979a). Conscious and unconscious cognition: A computational metaphor for the mechanism of attention and integration. In L. G. Nilsson (Ed.), *Perspectives on memory research* (pp. 61–89). Hillsdale, NJ: Lawrence Erlbaum Associates.

Allport, D. A. (1979b). Word recognition in reading. In P. A. Kolers, M. E. Wrolstad, & H. Bouma (Eds.), *Processing of visible language* (Vol. 1, pp. 227–257). New York: Plenum.

Allport, D. A. (1980a). Attention and performance. In G. Claxton (Ed.), *Cognitive psychology, new directions* (pp. 112–153). London: Routledge & Kegan Paul.

Allport, D. A. (1980b). Patterns and actions: Cognitive mechanisms are content-specific. In G. Claxton (ed.), *Cognitive psychology, new directions* (pp. 26–64). London: Routledge & Kegan Paul.

Allport, D. A. (1985). Distributed memory, modular subsystems and dysphasia. In S. Newman & R. Epstein (Eds.), *Dysphasia*. Edinburgh: Churchill Livingstone.

Anderson, J. A. (1977). Neural models with cognitive implications. In D. LaBerge & S. J. Samuels (Eds.), *Basic processes in reading* (pp. 27–90). Hillsdale, NJ: Lawrence Erlbaum Associates.

Anderson, J. A., & Hinton, G. E. (1981). Models of information processing in the brain. In G. E. Hinton & J. A. Anderson (Eds.), *Parallel models of associative memory* (pp. 9–48). Hillsdale, NJ: Lawrence Erlbaum Associates.

Broadbent, D. E. (1982). Task combination and selective intake of information. *Acta Psychologica, 50,* 253-290.

Bundesen, C., Pedersen, L. F., & Larsen, A. (1984). Measuring efficiency of selection from briefly exposed visual displays: A model for partial report. *Journal of Experimental Psychology: Human Perception and Performance, 10,* 329-339.

Carr, T. H., McCauley, C., Sperber, R. D., & Parmelee, C. M. (1982). Words, pictures and priming: On semantic activation, conscious identification and automaticity of information processing. *Journal of Experimental Psychology: Human Perception and Performance, 8,* 757-777.

Coltheart, M. (1980). Iconic memory and visible persistence. *Perception and Psychophysics, 27,* 183-228.

Cowey, A. (1979). Cortical maps and visual perception. *Quarterly Journal of Experimental Psychology, 31,* 1-17.

Cowey, A. (1981). Why are there so many visual areas? In F. O. Schmitt, F. G. Worden, G. Adelman, & S. G. Dennis (Eds.), *The organization of the cerebral cortex* (pp. 395-413). Cambridge, MA: MIT Press.

Dalrymple-Alford, E. C., & Budayr, B. (1966). Examination of some aspects of the Stroop colour-word test. *Perception and Motor Skills, 23,* 1211-1214.

Dannebring, G. L., & Briand, K. (1982). Semantic priming and the word repetition effect in a lexical decision task. *Canadian Journal of Psychology, 36,* 435-444.

Desimone, R., Albright, T. D., Gross, C. G., & Bruce, C. (1984). Stimulus selective properties of inferior temporal neurones in the macaque. *Journal of Neuroscience, 4,* 2051-2062.

Eriksen, C. W., & Schultz, I. (1979). Information processing in visual search: A continuous flow conception of experimental results. *Perception and Psychophysics, 25,* 249-263.

Evett, L., & Humphreys, G. (1981). The use of abstract graphemic information in lexical access. *Quarterly Journal of Experimental Psychology, 33A,* 325-250.

Feldman, J. A., & Ballard, D. H. (1982). Connectionist models and their properties. *Cognitive Science, 6,* 205-254.

Francolini, C. N., & Egeth, H. (1980). On the nonautomaticity of automatic activation: Evidence of selective seeing. *Perception and Psychophysics, 27,* 331-342.

Hinton, G. E. (1981). Implementing semantic networks in parallel hardware. In G. E. Hinton & J. A. Anderson (Eds.), *Parallel models of associative memory* (pp. 161-187). Hillsdale, NJ: Lawrence Erlbaum Associates.

Hochberg, J. (1970). Attention, organization and consciousness. In D. I. Mostofsky (Ed.), *Attention: Contemporary theory and analysis* (pp. 99-124). New York: Appleton-Century-Crofts.

Jones, G. V. (1976). A fragmentation hypothesis of memory: Cued recall of pictures and of sequential position. *Journal of Experimental Psychology: General, 105,* 277-293.

Kahneman, D., & Chajzyk, D. (1983). Tests of the automaticity of reading: Dilution of the Stroop effect by colour-irrelevant stimuli. *Journal of Experimental Psychology: Human Perception and Performance, 9,* 497-509.

Kahneman, D., & Henik, A. M. (1981). Perceptual organization and attention. In M. Kubovy & J. R. Pomerantz (Eds.), *Perceptual organization.* Hillsdale, NJ: Lawrence Erlbaum Associates.

Kahneman, D., & Treisman, A. M. (1984). Changing views of attention and automaticity. In R. Parasuraman & R. Davies (Eds.), *Varieties of attention.* New York: Academic.

Keele, S. W., & Neill, W. T. (1978). Mechanisms of attention. In E. C. Carterette (Ed.), *Handbook of perception* (Vol. 9; pp. 3-47). New York: Academic.

LaBerge, D. (1983). Spatial extent of attention to letters and words. *Journal of Experimental Psychology: Human Perception and Performance, 9,* 371-379.

Lawrence, D. H. (1971). Two studies of visual search for word targets with controlled rates of presentation. *Perception and Psychophysics, 10,* 85-89.

Lowe, D. G. (1979). Strategies, context, and the mechanism of response inhibition. *Memory and Cognition, 7,* 382-389.

Marcel, A. J. (1980). Conscious and preconscious recognition of polysemous words: Locating the selective effects of prior verbal context. In R. S. Nickerson (Ed.), *Attention and performance, VIII* (pp. 435–457). Hillsdale, NJ: Lawrence Erlbaum Associates.

Marcel, A. J. (1983). Conscious and unconscious perception: Experiments on visual masking and word recognition. *Cognitive Psychology, 15,* 197–237.

Marr, D. (1981). *Vision.* San Francisco: Freeman.

McLean, J. P., Broadbent, D. E., & Broadbent, M. H. P. (1983). Combining attributes in rapid serial visual presentation tasks. *Quarterly Journal of Experimental Psychology, 35A,* 171–186.

Meyer, D. E., Schvaneveldt, R. W., & Ruddy, M. G. (1975). Loci of contextual effects on visual word recognition. In P. M. A. Rabbitt & S. Dornic (Eds.), *Attention and performance, V* (pp. 98–118). London: Academic.

Neill, W. T. (1977). Inhibitory and facilitatory processes in selective attention. *Journal of Experimental Psychology: Human Perception and Performance, 3,* 444–450.

Neisser, U. (1976). *Cognition and reality.* New York: Appleton-Century-Crofts.

Neisser, U., & Becklen, P. (1975). Selective looking: Attending to visually superimposed events. *Cognitive Psychology, 7,* 480–494.

Posner, M. I. (1978). *Chronometric explorations of mind.* Hillsdale, NJ: Lawrence Erlbaum Associates.

Perrett, D. I., Rolls, E. T., & Caan, W. (1982). Visual neurones responsive to faces in the monkey temporal cortex. *Experimental Brain Research, 47,* 329–342.

Rock, I., & Gutman, D. (1981). Effect of inattention on form perception. *Journal of Experimental Psychology: Human Perception and Performance, 7,* 275–285.

Rolls, E. T. (1981). Processing beyond the inferior temporal visual cortex related to feeding, memory and striatal function. In Y. Katsuki, R. Norgren, & M. Sato (Eds.), *Brain mechanisms of sensation.* New York: Wiley.

Santee, J. L., & Egeth, H. E. (1982). Do reaction time and accuracy measure the same aspects of letter recognition? *Journal of Experimental Psychology: Human Perception and Performance, 8,* 489–501.

Schaffer, W. V., & LaBerge, D. (1979). Automatic semantic processing of unattended words. *Journal of Verbal Learning and Verbal Behavior, 18,* 413–426.

Tipper, S. P. (1984). *Negative priming and visual selective attention.* Unpublished D. Phil. thesis, Oxford University.

Treisman, A. M., & Gelade, G. (1980). A feature integration theory of attention. *Cognitive Psychology, 12,* 97–136.

Treisman, A. M., & Schmidt, H. (1982). Illusory conjunctions in the perception of objects. *Cognitive Psychology, 14,* 107–141.

Treisman, A., Sykes, M., & Gelade, G. (1977). Selective attention and stimulus integration. In S. Dornic (Ed.), *Attention and performance VI* (pp. 333–361). Hillsdale, NJ: Lawrence Erlbaum Associates.

Underwood, G. (1977). Attention, awareness and hemispheric differences in word recognition. *Neuropsychologia, 15,* 61–67.

van der Heijden, A. H. C. (1981). *Short term visual information forgetting.* London: Routledge & Kegan Paul.

6 Attention Division or Attention Sharing?

David Navon
University of Haifa

ABSTRACT

Multiple-task situations are often conceived of as requiring attention to be split among the tasks. A formalization of this preconception is incorporated in resource theory, which is often taken for granted for the want of better alternatives. An attempt is made to describe a processing system that is not limited by processing resources. In such a system, task interference arises mostly because of conflicts between outcomes of processes rather than because of scarcity of internal input to processes. This chapter examines experimental evidence for performance trade-off critically, and presents a novel finding suggesting that observed performance trade-off may result from demand characteristics and may vanish when instructions do not give rise to such characteristics.

INTRODUCTION

Names sometimes connote more than they should. I think this is the case with the term *attention division*. It reflects the idea that multiple processes that are to be activated at the same time have to split the usage of some mental entity among them. However deeply rooted this idea is, it is, as I show in this chapter and elsewhere (Navon, 1984), far from being adequately supported by empirical data, much less so beyond the need for such support. One step toward conceptual neutrality is to substitute a name that prejudges the issue with one that would represent the phenomena being dealt with rather than a view that might account for them. I, therefore, use the term *attention sharing*. It implies only that multiple processes are attempted at about the same time by the processing system, without making any commitment about the consequences of, or the preconditions for, such joint processing.

This might seem like terminological pedantry, but actually it is just a precursor of an attempt to reexamine in toto the conceptual framework dominating the field. I try to show here that this conceptual framework is not necessary. For that matter, I argue first that the theoretical domain being captured by that framework can be described even without reference to it, and then that the empirical effects typically accounted for by models formulated within this conceptual framework can be explained in some other ways. Then I briefly refer to some methodological difficulties in deciding between the theoretical alternatives empirically. Finally, I present some evidence that data gathering in the field may have been biased by the prevalent conceptualization of the domain.

A MIND WITHOUT RESOURCES

To attend is to select for processing. This must be the broadest possible definition within an information-processing view of the mind. It seems to capture the essence of the definition phrased by James (1890), which he believed was so obvious that "everyone knows . . ." it.

However, many students of attention (e.g., Kahneman, 1973; Kerr, 1973; Moray, 1967; Navon & Gopher, 1979; Norman & Bobrow, 1975) postulate that to attend is to commit some scarce mental entity to enable processing. That entity, most typically called resources, can be broadly defined as any internal input essential for processing (e.g., locations in storage, communication channels) that is available in quantities that are limited at any point in time. Variability in performance of a task is ascribed to the amount of that input dedicated to the task.

This sense of attention, being more restricted than the first one, must therefore be hypothetical. However, people seldom realize this. The notion of resources has become so identified with attention that the conceptual inevitability of the latter has propagated to the former by way of association. Phenomena of selection, motivation, and task interference are interpreted in terms of resources as a matter of course. And worse yet, the very same facts that the notion of resources comes to explain are considered as arguments for its indispensability. It seems, thus, that the notion has acquired a status of a paradigm in the Kuhnian sense (see Kuhn, 1962). The typical response of paradigm followers to skepticism is "But how else?" The paradigm cannot be renounced, of course, before an alternate conceptual framework is put forward and turns out to be more attractive. But first it has to be shown that the conceptual space outside the framework is not void—namely, that there might exist alternatives that are not absurd.

The notion of a processing environment in which processing does not depend on resources might seem at first blush to be as unrealistic as fantasies of an economic system that defies the law of scarcity or of a physical system that does not abide by the first law of thermodynamics (conservation of energy). If processing is the work done by our mental apparatus, how can it be accomplished without resorting to any input that is conceived of as mental energy?

However, doubting the notion of mental resources does in no way amount to denying the dependence of processing on any internal input whatsoever. Of course, some mental machinery must exist and must be necessary for the occurrence of mental activities. Furthermore, that machinery perhaps requires some additional provisions to operate. Thus, it must be false that mental work is achieved with no investment. However, that investment is not necessarily a resource in the sense focused on by recent formulations of the notion of resources (e.g., Navon, 1984; Navon & Gopher, 1979, 1980; Norman & Bobrow, 1975) and that I believe is the only sense with which a fruitful *theory* of resources can be constructed. In such a theory resources would be defined by five properties:

1. *Aggregate nature*. Resources come in units, any number of which can be invested in a certain process.
2. *Exclusive usage of units*. Resources are private commodities in the sense that each unit can be used or consumed by only one process at a time.
3. *Distributability*. Resources can be invested in more than one process at a time, in that different units are allotted to different processes.
4. *Effectiveness*. The amount of resources invested in a *single* process affects the quality of its output.
5. *Scarcity*. The amount of resources available at any point in time is limited.

I claim that the existence of mental resources of the sort just defined is hypothetical, and that however credible this notion is, it is quite possible to conceive of its logical complement—namely, that the human information-processing system does not resort to any scarce resources of that sort—and to imagine how it might be realized.

My first argument is a déjà vu type of argument; It is just an appeal to an already-existing construct. The concept of automatic processes has recently gained much popularity (see, e.g., LaBerge, 1973; Logan, 1981; Posner, 1978; Shiffrin & Schneider, 1977). One of the conventional criteria for automaticity of a process is that it does not demand resources. Thus, the idea of the existence of resource-free processing is there. Whoever has accepted this idea in the first place must be conceptually primed for the hypothesis, plausible or implausible as it may seem, that *all* processing is resource free. Whether or not empirical effects usually attributed to competition for resources can be accommodated within this hypothesis is a separate issue that is discussed later. For the moment, the point I wish to emphasize is that because it is seldom wondered what kind of processing structure could give rise to automatic processing, then there is no particular reason to reject outright, by appealing to structural arguments, the conjecture that no processing requires limited resources. On these grounds, it seems to be at least a legitimate hypothesis that is refutable only by empirical evidence.

One might contend that what is reasonable for preprogrammed, event-driven processing might not be reasonable for flexible, spontaneous processing: The latter calls for central control, hence must tax some limited mechanisms. In truth, the association between spontaneous, self-programmed, dynamically evolving processing on the one hand and central control on the other hand is not a logical necessity, as the argument presupposes, but rather a theoretical premise. As such, it might rightfully be held by the contenders, but is unconvincing when employed to argue with proponents of alternative views.

Yet, theory aside, it is a fact that people have considerable voluntary control over quality of performance, let alone over its very occurrence. Does that not suggest supply of resources as the agent by which such control is exerted? Not necessarily. Performance might be controlled by regulating the accessibility of some enabling mental entity that is *unlimited,* in which case it does not constitute a resource in the strict sense posited in resource theory.

Indeed, it is somewhat strange that motivation effects have been thought to be perfectly congruent with resource theory, let alone to be accounted for by it. Actually, such effects should have been quite annoying for a theory that posits that resources are limited. The theory could be stretched to accommodate the effects by assuming either that the fixed limit is approached only when motivation is maximal (is it ever?) or that the limit is not rigid but rather depends on motivation. Either way, the explanation does not naturally follow from the five basic premises of resource theory. Motivation effects are more readily explained when performance is assumed to depend on the amount of a mental commodity that is *not* scarce in any usual circumstances. The apparent performance limit manifested at any given level of motivation may be due to some cost associated with that commodity—for example, to the aversion induced by expending it. As the value of improving performance is presumably diminishing, performance will asymptote and at the level at which the marginal value does not exceed the cost (see formal analysis in Navon & Gopher, 1979, p. 229).

Furthermore, it is not necessary that processes are controlled by adjusting the supply of *any* mental commodity. It is conceivable that amount of processing, or its output, are controlled directly. But how can such direct controls be implemented? Several conjectures can be raised. I focus on one that seems to be the most prominent.

First, let it be postulated that processing can be done to a variable degree, for example by activating a process for a variable duration. Amount of voluntary processing is conceivably affected by the demand for such processing, and the demand is, in turn, determined by the amount of processing output required to satisfy some criterion on accuracy and speed. The more stringent the criterion, the more processing output is required, hence the more processing is called for, and the more will presumably be done. Thus, amount of processing a certain task may be directly controlled by the interest in its outcomes, regardless of whether or not resources are involved.

I hope that now the notion of a processing system that does not depend on scarce resources is more clearly envisaged. I think that the intellectual exercise of imagining such a system is important regardless of its plausibility as a hypothesis about the human mind. Resource scarcity may indeed be causal in the phenomena often attributed to it. Yet its role may be limited relative to other factors.

It is easiest to understand those factors in the context of the discussion of a system with unlimited resources. The next section concerns what those factors might be.

ALTERNATIVE EXPLANATIONS FOR TASK INTERFERENCE

The main motive behind the postulation of mental resources has been the observation that attention sharing is usually associated with some cost, be it single- to dual-task deficit or dual-task performance trade-off. How else can those effects be interpreted?

Researchers in the field have learned to discount or to control for obvious causes of interference that are considered to be peripheral, either on the sensory or on the motor sides. Kahneman (1973) expanded this category of interference effects, which he labeled "structural interference," to include all cases of competition for a single processing mechanism.

However, note that interference does not necessarily result from having to compete for scarce commodities. Recall what the everyday sense of the word *interference* is: Conversations interfere; telephone calls interfere, broadcasts interfere. Proceed to some scientific usages: Waves interfere; memory traces interfere. None of these instances of interference is usually thought to be due to competition for some scarce input. They can be rather construed as the negative effects that events *taking place* at about the same time have on each other. The effects have typically to do with some outcome, output, or side effect, occasioned by the interfering event. This sort of conflict, which I call *outcome conflict*, is qualitatively different from a case of *competition for resources* in which the events are unlikely to cooccur, or properly proceed, because they rely on the same enabling commodity and compete for it. In the case of outcome conflict, an event harms the concurrent one by *generating* something, whereas when resources are competed for, the undesirable consequences are due to what an event *withholds* from the concurrent one. Note that in both cases the conflicts arise because events occur in parallel, and they can be prevented if the events are made sequential (and spaced enough in time). The following examples make it clear that outcome conflict cannot be reduced to competition for any resources.

Suppose the production of a certain pharmaceutical product requires low air humidity for best results. The quality of that product will be degraded if manufactured in proximity to another production process (of a different product) that generates vapor. Such a degradation is due to the harmful consequences of a side effect of one production process on another rather than to any limit on the input to those processes. Thus, it is an instance of outcome conflict. It is possible to contend that a vapor-proof partition might help, hence the conflict could be eliminated if more resources, specifically such a partition, were invested. Arguments of this sort serve to perpetuate the conception that every problem in production can be blamed on resource scarcity. Therefore, it is vital to realize the fallacy in them. Granted, everything in a production environment can be said to be a resource, if increasing its amount would improve production. This is trivially true yet vacuous. For example, the partition in our story is not an input competed for by the two production processes. It is not a resource needed by any of the processes in itself. Its only function is to forestall a specific interference; it would have been useless had the factory manufactured only one of those products (or a different pair of products). Thus, installing a partition can be regarded as a change in the environment, in this case a beneficial one, rather than as an investment of a production factor.

The point is perhaps made clearer when we consider a practically immutable environment such as a jungle. Notwithstanding the hard competition for resources among neighboring plants, plants also interact in ways that have nothing to do with resource scarcity: Some photophilic plants may not flourish if shaded by leafy trees, whereas photophobic plants having similar demands for water and minerals will do quite well. Sunlight is, of course, vital for the growth of the low photophilic plants as it is for the soundness of the large trees. However, the trees do not withhold sunlight from the lower plants for the sake of having more of it. They most often *happen* to cast shade just as rocks do.

Now imagine a room in which one boy is practicing violin while his sister is practicing piano. Presumably, both will not do very well. The cause is an outcome conflict that is due to the limited efficiency of human attentional selectivity. Would it make sense to argue that the siblings are *splitting* the room space? Of course, they could have queued for the usage of the room. But once they decided to use it simultaneously, room space is *shared* by them rather than *divided* between them.[1] Thus, the room is what economists call the *fixed input*—that is, the resource that constitutes the environment in which the more flexible resources might be input in variable quantities into production. Ear-plugs could reduce the interference, but, like the partition in the first example, they represent an improvement in the environment rather than a resource that is competed for by the two siblings.

Another example is that of a staff of a newspaper. Suppose three teams of 10 persons each are working each on one story. Their common resources are three telephones, one teleprinter, and one message board. They *queue* for the teleprinter, *split* the telephones between them, and *share* the message board. Any retardation in the progress of work that is due to the limited availability of the telephones or of the teleprinter is undisputably attributed to resource scarcity. However, is the same true of errors or delays resulting from the difficulty of a user of the message board to select the message addressed to him or her? After all, message boards, unlike some other means of communication, are designed for multiple access. It makes more sense to regard confusion errors and increase in search latency as outcome conflicts that result from the fact that the message board is shared by multiple users.

Finally, consider cross-talk interference among telephone lines that is due to

---

[1]For example, can the boy use, say, two-thirds of the room space leaving the rest for his sister?

electrical induction. Such cross-talk could obviously be eliminated if the ratio of lines per cables was one. Yet, however critical this ratio is for the ability to resolve simultaneous calls, it is not a resource that is competed for by the calls, for the same reason that the partition and the earplugs in the preceding examples are not resources in this sense: It is totally irrelevant for the quality of communication when only a single call is attempted.

In summary, then, every sort of interference can be traced back to some constraint or absence. Whatever is constrained or absent might be called a resource, in the sense that had it not been so, interference would not have existed. The issue is whether we want to accept this general truism as a sufficient explanation in any specific case of interference. I believe that we would not, any more than we would blame any certain crime on the general distress of the society or on the ill nature of human beings. Interference is usefully imputed to resource scarcity only in case the resource in question satisfies the five properties listed in the previous section—namely, aggregate nature, exclusive usage of units, distributability, effectiveness, and scarcity. If it is not so, then the interference may be due to outcome conflict.

Now, what sorts of outcome conflict can be conjectured to exist in the human information-processing system?

Suppose the processing system comprises a set of potentially parallel processes. They can be parallel either because they have access to a virtually unlimited machinery required to execute them, or because each is coupled with its own machinery. However, it is quite possible that despite the abundance of machinery, cross-talk among simultaneously activated parts of it exists in much the same way that it exists in electronic systems. Thus, one possible source of outcome conflict is *cross-talk* among parallel, independent processes. Such conflict may be defined as any disruptive effect that results from imperfect separation of processes that are designed to operate in parallel without resorting to any common structure or consuming any common limited resource.

Now suppose that any single assignment our processing system is confronted with, rather than being accomplished by a single, rigid procedure, comprises a set of processes that exchange control. The advantage of such an architecture is evident: It allows for much flexibility in processing; many assignments can be met using a relatively small arsenal of processing modules. As an analogy, consider an airline that serves n cities. Instead of operating $\frac{n(n-1)}{2}$ direct flights, it would rather operate $n - 1$ flights connecting one hub airport with any other airport, and have passengers transfer at the hub airport if needed.

But modular systems have an inherent problem, which can be readily seen within the context of the airline analogy: Even supposing that the company was affluent enough to render all services at the hub airport to any number of airplanes and passengers in parallel, it would probably still face the problem of channeling transit passengers to their connecting flights. That problem would be aggravated the larger the number of incoming and departing flights and the larger the number of passengers who have to simultaneously reboard at the hub airport, so it might strike us as a problem of resource scarcity, which it is *not*. It is rather due to the simple fact that making the connection requires searching unfamiliar sets for unfamiliar targets: A passenger has to identity an unfamiliar gate, or a ground steward has to identify passengers having a certain destination. Such a problem is inherent in every case in which pairing is made between counterparts that are not habitually associated. Imagine, for instance, what would happen if several blind dates were set for the same time at the same café. Or, think of the previously mentioned problem of using a public message board. Now consider the case of a "blackboard area" in working memory onto which messages from a number of ongoing processes are written (e.g., Newell, 1973; Rumelhart, 1977), and the relevance for psychology will become clearer.

Thus, within a modular information-processing system a likely outcome conflict is the *difficulty in making nonhabitual transitions*—that is, in transferring control and throughput between processes in a manner that is determined on the fly. It is not due to resource scarcity, and it cannot be resolved by any increase in the supply of resources. Rather, it exists as long as the knowledge of a process does not include the address of its antecedent or its successor—in other words as long as throughputs are not addressed directly between successive processes, so that the input for a process is not readily available but has to be searched for.

Another possible problem in parallel processing is what might be called *matching indeterminacy*. The condition for efficient parallel modular computation is that there is a way to properly match modules subordinated to the same process. That may be implemented, for example, by tagging the modules in a way that distinguishes among different processes—for example, by the ultimate goal, by their content, or by the source of the information. In the cases considered so far such matching is possible, albeit limited or costly. In a more extreme case there is no basis at all for matching. The reason may be, for example, that while the information is being processed, its source is not retained.

An excellent example is the task of searching for conjunctive targets (see Treisman & Gelade, 1980; Treisman, Sykes, & Gelade, 1977). Simple features probably can be extracted in parallel across the entire search set. If information about their spatial origin had been preserved along with them, it would have been possible to conjoin them properly, so that parallel search for conjunctive targets would have been feasible. However, because features are detected but poorly localized (Treisman & Gelade, 1980, Experiments VIII and IX), such an attempt results in illusory conjunctions. Thus, rather than being dictated by scarcity of processing resources, the serial scan strategy that subjects adopt for conjunctive search is called for to sidestep the unwelcome product of parallel search under those conditions—namely, illusory conjunctions.

Thus far I have discussed the feasibility or the cost of routing throughputs to their potential users in case multiple processes operate in parallel. The assumption was that the processes do not require the usage of any common structure. But now suppose they do. Even then, the execution of one of the processes may impair the coincident ones not by denying or limiting their access to the structure but rather by making the structure temporarily less apt to accomplish its function.

For example, suppose word recognition is achieved via interplay of mutual facilitation and inhibition among many LTM nodes (see McClelland & Rumelhart, 1981). The pattern of activations driven by a task, reading a printed word for example, may inhibit nodes whose activation is essential for the accomplishment of the concurrent task, such as recognizing an auditorily presented word. Another example is a case in which the concurrent processes can be time-shared quite effectively, because each engages the common structures for a very brief period (say, cell x is activated by process A from t_1 to t_2 and by process B from t_{14} to t_{15}, whereas cell y is activated by process B from t_2 to t_4 and by process A from t_9 to t_{11}). Still, the structure might not serve each of the processes with the same efficiency because of problems of adaptation, satiation, and so on.

Can it be reasonably argued that such *temporary disablement* type of interference is attributable to resource scarcity? Obviously, two processing systems might do better than one, in much the same way that the musical siblings discussed earlier would have had a chance to play better had their parents owned two houses. However, given the constraints of the system, the processes in this example interfere not because they *split* the amount of some commodity, but rather because they suffer the consequences of *sharing* the same processing structure.

In summation, four types of possible outcome conflicts in human information processing have been suggested: cross-talk, difficulty in making nonhabitual transitions, matching indeterminacy, and temporary disablement. Interference cannot be ascribed to competition in any of the four for some scarce, distributable commodity of an aggregate nature, the amount of which determines the performance on a single task. Hence, all of them can be considered as theoretical possibilities that compete with resource theory in explaining task interference.

Empirical data are often quite naturally explained by resorting to outcome conflict, whereas resource-theory interpretations seem strained. One example may serve to illustrate this. Tasks usually interfere more when they are more similar or when their processing loci are closer in cerebral space (Kinsbourne, 1981, 1982). The proposal to regard the two hemispheres as two separate resource pools (e.g., Friedman & Polson, 1981; Friedman, Polson, Dafoe, & Gaskill, 1982) does not seem convincing, mainly in view of the fact that between-hemisphere interference does exist and that task interference seems to be a continuous function of cerebral distance between presumed processing loci (see Kinsbourne & Hicks, this volume). It is more plausible that the decrease in interference with greater cerebral distance is due to the smaller chances of outcome conflict between distant processing loci (cf. Kinsbourne & Hicks, this volume).

An interesting corollary of this view of task interference is that it bridges the gap between the domains of selective attention and so-called divided attention. The sorts of outcome conflict considered here have much in common with factors that are often thought to induce failures of selective attention. Whatever impedes selection of one out of many processes must hamper as well the separation among multiple ongoing processes. It falls beyond the scope of this chapter to discuss the implications of this conclusion to the field of attention, but evidently they are important.

I hope now it is clearer that resource theory does have theoretical alternatives. Are there valid tests that can help to decide empirically between the conceptually distinct alternatives? Elsewhere (Navon, 1984) it has been shown that most existing tests for ascertaining whether a certain task does or does not require resources are undiagnostic or subject to severe methodological limits. Specifically, this is true of the effects of motivation level, task difficulty, task complexity, dual-task deficit, task priority, and difficulty of concurrent task as well as of the interactive effects of task difficulty × dual-task requirement, task difficult × task priority, and task difficulty × difficulty of concurrent task. This list seems to exhaust the set of potential tests presently known.

A tempting response in view of such empirical undecidability is greater conservatism: I will keep using the terminology with which I feel comfortable—one might maintain—until it is shown to be definitely wrong. This approach would be sensible, if the terminology in question was sufficient to impose conceptual organization on phenomena in the field. Specifically, resource theory would be valuable if it *generally* afforded reasonably precise predictions, for example, about the amount of dual-task decrement in the performance of any task, x, when conjoined with any other task, y (or at least within some well-defined and relatively large subset of tasks). If it did not, then it would not only be unsubstantiated, but undesirable as well. First, using the resource terminology may mislead us to believe that the phenomena are reasonably explained, thereby inhibiting creativity in other veins. Second, when resource terminology is regarded as a sine qua non, researchers may be led to uncritically accept as facts about behavior experimental results that might be methodological artifacts. If so, then the notion of resources may sometimes generate what it then comes to explain. In the following section I present experimental data to illustrate that the danger of putting the cart before the horses in that way may be real.

PERFORMANCE TRADE-OFF—A FACT OR AN ARTIFACT?

Dual-task deficit—that is the deterioration in the performance of a task when conjoined with another one—is a prevalent finding. It is often considered as evidence that the tasks depend on resources from a pool common to both of them. However, it was argued in several places (e.g., Gopher & Navon, 1980; Kahneman, 1973; Navon, 1984; Navon & Gopher, 1979) that dual-task deficits very likely are to be partly caused by structural conflicts.

Hence, evidence of a performance trade-off—that is, evidence that performance of a task can improve only at the expense of the performance of the other one—seems a little more convincing of the economic interpretation of task interference than is dual-task deficit. The reason is that many conceivable structural conflicts between tasks (e.g., a shift of fixation that reduces the quality of sensory data for both tasks) seem to exist to the same extent in all levels of task emphasis; hence, they are ruled out as explanations for the trade-off.

Although performance trade-offs can also be explained in terms of outcome conflicts (see Navon, 1984, p. 220), they served as demonstrations par excellence of resource allocation (e.g., Gopher & Navon, 1980; Kinchla, 1980; Sperling & Melchner, 1978). Therefore, it is important to inquire how real performance trade-offs are.

One procedure for obtaining performance trade-off results is to ask subjects to divide their attention in various proportions between the tasks (e.g., Kinchla, 1980; Kinchla, Solis-Macias, & Hoffman, 1983; Regan, 1982; Sperling & Melchner, 1978). Another procedure is to vary the ratio of the levels of minimal performance requirements for the two tasks (e.g., Gopher & Navon, 1980; Wickens & Gopher, 1977). But note that both methods must convey the message to the subjects—explicitly by the former method and tacitly by the latter—that the tasks probably trade-off and/or that the cause of such a trade-off is the scarcity of a mental commodity called *attention*. It should not be surprising that subjects respond to this demand characteristic, even when its presupposition is empirically false. In other words, the observed relative levels of performance might conceivably conform to the ratio of requirements (or prescribed allocation ratio), even when the tasks do not interfere with each other. In analogy, suppose that at a certain European airport, tobacco can be purchased only in U.S. dollars and liquor can be paid for only in local currency. In addition, suppose that in the evenings the banks are closed so that currencies cannot be exchanged. In that environment, these two commodities are not competitive. Still, designated minimal-purchase quantities in a shopping list (or a suggested allocation rule) create anchor points that are likely to have an impact on actual purchases. In that case we might observe a trade-off between amounts of tobacco and liquor bought that is induced by psychological factors rather than enforced by an economic constraint. For example, a passenger who had been advised to buy much tobacco would probably buy more tobacco and less liquor than one who had been suggested to buy more liquor. Yet both passengers actually *could* buy much of *both* products.

Thus, a bias toward performance-ratio matching and against maximization of joint performance is built into both methods. It is evident that subjects' behavior actually show a disposition toward such matching from findings of square Performance Operating Characteristics[2] (e.g., Gopher & Navon, 1980; Navon, Gopher, Chillag, & Spitz, 1984). If there were no interference between tasks, and if subjects really had regarded minimal performance requirements as merely indicating the recommended minimum, they would have performed the low-

---

[2]*Performance Operating Characteristics* (POC) is the technical term coined by Norman and Bobrow (1975) to denote a graph that plots performance on one task as a function of the performance on the concurrent task in a dual-task situation.

priority task as well as they could, thereby shrinking the obtained Performance Operating Characteristic to a single point. The general problem with that matching is that it may yield results that underestimate the real limits of joint performance.

A possible remedy might be to use what may be called *the method of optimum-maximum*. With this method, performance levels are designated only for one task, and the performance on the second one is to be maximized. Then, performance on the first task is to be maximized while the performance levels on the second one are specified. In this way two curves are obtained, the combination of which might give us an idea of the full potential of the subject.

Recently, I have experimentally explored the relative merits of the method of optimum-maximum and the more conventional method of minimal performance requirements (see Navon, in press). Subjects were asked to perform concurrently two tasks, a digit-classification task in which the subject had to tell whether a visually presented digit was odd or even, and a letter-classification task in which the subject had to tell whether a visually presented Hebrew letter belonged to the first or to the second half of the alphabet. An average latency feedback indicator was displayed on the screen as a vertical arrow with variable length. The experimental trials were divided in two different conditions, a *minimal-requirements* condition and an *optimum-maximum* condition. In the minimal-requirements condition the subject was presented with two horizontal bars crossing the path of the two arrows and was told to operate so that the arrows would be at the height of the bars or higher—that is, *at least* as fast as indicated by the arrows. The requirements were set at either of five different percentiles of the subject's own latency distribution. In the minimal-requirements condition the requirements on each task were inversely related to the requirements on the other task—that is, they could be interpreted as relative priorities on the two tasks. In the optimum-maximum condition one of the same five requirements as for the minimal-requirements condition was set in turn for one of the tasks, and the subject was to try to operate as much as possible *at* the level of performance required. There was no requirement on the other task, and the instruction was to maximize the speed on that task.

I found that under the minimal-requirements condition, performance levels on the two tasks correlated negatively, but there was no trade-off in either part of the optimum-maximum condition, and performance on the to-be-maximized task was at least as high as the highest level under the minimal-requirements condition. The conclusion following quite readily from the data is that although subjects tend to adjust their performance of a task to the level being required, there is no evidence of a necessary concomitant effect on the concurrent task: If the performance of the concurrent task is to be maximized, it will be kept high regardless of how well the other task is performed. The performance trade-off that is exhibited when minimal-performance requirements are set by the experimenter seems to be due not to any limit on joint performance, but rather to some sort of compliance of the subject with what he or she figures the objectives of the experimental situation are. Subjects perform better than they are required to (and also better than under the corresponding requirement in the optimum-maximum condition), but not as well as they could were they to maximize their performance on both tasks.

Thus, the method of minimal requirements, and presumably also the method of verbal instructions to allocate attention, may give us a poor idea of the limits of joint performance. If so, conclusions that have been drawn from demonstrations of performance trade-off (e.g., Gopher, Brickner, & Navon, 1982; Navon & Gopher, 1979; Regan, 1982; Sperling & Melchner, 1978), about dependence of the tasks on some limited pool of resources, were premature.

Note that these data do not indicate that the tasks do not interfere with each other. It was quite evident that any of the tasks could be done much better in isolation. Yet, performance decrements of this sort could be due to many sorts of conflict between tasks other than having to split the same pool of resources. For example, it is intuitively reasonable that the source of conflict in this experiment was the queuing of the tasks for some single-channel processing device; but once order of processing was determined, there was no further decision that could be made about processing priorities.

What I meant to illustrate by these results is not that performance trade-off data may be spurious at times. Granted, in case they *are* valid, we still will have to face the problem of explaining them one way or another. The point is rather, that, armed with the resource nomenclature, we sometimes may hunt down what turn out to be artifacts, and then we may be too much prepossessed by it to tell them from real facts.

A Brief Summary

A critical scrutiny of the notion of mental resources indicates (a) that it is not indispensable; (b) that it is not entailed by empirical observations; (c) that it may sometimes force the observations that are meant to confirm it.

REFERENCES

Friedman, A., & Polson, M. C. (1981). The hemispheres as independent resource systems: Limited capacity processing and cerebral specialization. *Journal of Experimental Psychology: Human Perception and Performance, 7,* 1031–1058.

Friedman, A., Polson, M. C., Dafoe, C. G., & Gaskill, S. J. (1982). Dividing attention within and between hemispheres: Testing a multiple resources approach to limited-capacity information processing. *Journal of Experimental Psychology: Human Perception and Performance, 8,* 625–650.

Gopher, D., Brickner, M., & Navon, D. (1982). Different difficulty manipulations interact differently with task emphasis: Evidence for multiple resources. *Journal of Experimental Psychology: Human Perception and Performance, 8,* 146–157.

Gopher, D., & Navon, D. (1980). How is performance limited: Testing the notion of central capacity. *Acta Psychologica, 46,* 161–180.

James, W. (1890). *The principles of psychology* (Vol. 1). New York: Holt.

Kahneman, D. (1973). *Attention and effort.* Englewood Cliffs, NJ: Prentice-Hall.

Kerr, B. (1973). Processing demands during mental operations. *Memory and Cognition, 1*, 401–412.

Kinchla, R. A. (1980). The measurement of attention. In R. S. Nickerson (Ed.), *Attention and performance VIII* (pp. 213–238). Hillsdale, NJ: Lawrence Erlbaum Associates.

Kinchla, R. A., Solis-Macias, V., & Hoffman, J. (1983). Attending to different levels of structure in a visual image. *Perception and Psychophysics, 33*, 1–10.

Kinsbourne, M. (1981). Single channel theory. In D. H. Holding (Ed.), *Human skills* (pp. 65–89). Chichester, Sussex, England: Wiley.

Kinsbourne, M. (1982). Hemispheric specialization and the growth of human understanding. *American Psychologist, 37*, 411–420.

Kuhn, T. S. (1962). *The structure of scientific revolutions*. Chicago: The University of Chicago.

LaBerge, D. (1973). Attention and the measurement of perceptual learning. *Memory and Cognition, 1*, 268–276.

Logan, G. D. (1981). Attention, automaticity, and the ability to stop a speeded choice response. In J. Long and A. Baddeley (Eds.), *Attention and performance IX* (pp. 205–222). Hillsdale, NJ: Lawrence Erlbaum Associates.

McClelland, J. L., & Rumelhart, D. E. (1981). An interactive activation model of context effects in letter perception: Part 1. An account of basic finding. *Psychological Review, 88*, 375–407.

Moray, N. (1967). Where is capacity limited? A survey and a model. *Acta Psychologica, 27*, 84–92.

Navon, D. (1984). Resources—a theoretical soup-stone? *Psychological Review, 91*, 216–234.

Navon, D. (in press). Do people allocate processing resources among concurrent activities? In H. Rachlin & L. Green (Eds.), *Advances in behavioral economics* (Vol. 2). Norwood, NJ: Ablex.

Navon, D., & Gopher, D. (1979). On the economy of the human processing system. *Psychological Review, 86*, 214–255.

Navon, D., & Gopher, D. (1980). Task difficulty, resources, and dual-task performance. In R. S. Nickerson (Ed.), *Attention and performance VIII* (pp. 297–315). Hillsdale, NJ: Lawrence Erlbaum Associates.

Navon, D., Gopher, D., Chillag, N., & Spitz, G. (1984). On separability of and interference between tracking dimensions in dual-axis tracking. *Journal of Motor Behavior, 16*, 364–391.

Newell, A. (1973). Production systems: Models of control structures. In W. G. Chase (Ed.), *Visual information processing*. (pp. 463–526). New York: Academic.

Norman, D. A., & Bobrow, D. J. (1975). On data-limited and resource-limited processes. *Cognitive Psychology, 7*, 44–64.

Posner, M. I. (1978). *Chronometric explorations of mind*. Hillsdale, NJ: Lawrence Erlbaum Associates.

Regan, J. (October 1982). Short-term memory and dual-task performance. *Proceedings of the Human Factors Society 26th Annual Meeting*, Seattle.

Rumelhart, D. E. (1977). Toward an interactive model of reading. In S. Dornic (Ed.), *Attention and performance VI* (pp. 573–606). Hillsdale, NJ: Lawrence Erlbaum Associates.

Shiffrin, R. M., & Schneider, W. (1977). Controlled and automatic human information processing: II. Perceptual learning, automatic attention and a general theory. *Psychological Review, 84*, 127–190.

Sperling, G., & Melchner, M. J. (1978). The attention operating characteristic: Examples from visual search. *Science, 202*, 315–318.

Treisman, A. M., & Gelade, G. (1980). A feature-integration theory of attention. *Cognitive Psychology, 12*, 97–136.

Treisman, A., Sykes, M., & Gelade, G. (1977). Selective attention and stimulus integration. In S. Dornic (Ed.), *Attention and performance VI* (pp. 333–361). Hillsdale, NJ: Lawrence Erlbaum Associates.

Wickens, D. C., & Gopher, D. (1977). Control theory measures of tracking as indices of attention allocation strategies. *Human Factors, 19*, 349–365.

7 Looking Forward to Moving Soon: Ante Factum Selective Processes in Motor Control

Jean Requin
National Center for Scientific Research, Marseille, France

ABSTRACT

Studies conducted under the rubric of attention have, for the most part, been concerned with selective processes up to the stage of selection of action. However, beyond the broad selection of action, a specific movement must be programmed and then executed. Studies concerned with these later stages have been conducted under the preparation rubric, which is emphasized in this chapter. Because attention and motor control are concerned with the same issues of selective facilitation and inhibition, a unified conception thus should be developed. To do so would involve specifying the ambiguous meaning of preparation, which currently is used in two different ways. In the first conception, preparation has the status of a processing stage. In the second conception, preparation is viewed as a modulatory process that changes in advance the functional state of processing systems. This chapter deals with the implications of these two conceptions in interpreting experimental data about preparatory processes related to motor programming and collected by using movement-precueing and movement-priming techniques. The main help for resolving this issue probably will be in the deciphering of the neuronal organization that underlies preparatory processes. Data collected in the motor system with single-cell recording techniques supports a tentative model that stresses how selective motor set and late output stages can be conceived as separated, although more or less functionally related processes.

INTRODUCTION

Attention, as a concept covering selective activity, is responsible for the modulation of information processing and has generally been considered, until recently, as mainly acting upon sensory input. This has most often been explicitly stated in the definitions proposed for attentional processes, which emphasize the role of attention in the selection of stimuli. Furthermore, at the end of the 1970s, although several studies addressed the question of the attentional demand of movement in the frame of the dual-task paradigm, no more than half a dozen papers were written under titles associating attention with movement (as, for instance, Klein, 1976; McLeod, 1980; Posner & Cohen, 1980; Stelmach & Hughes, 1983).

It would be of interest to analyze the reasons that justified the long-lasting separation between these concepts. Several like reasons come to mind. The first has to do with processing economy, which, in the frame of a single, central bottleneck model, made an early selection stage more parsimonious than a late selection stage, because the former avoided the processing of useless information, whereas the latter did not. Another explanation lies in some of the methodological constraints that introduce a necessary difference between the experimental strategies used for analyzing selective processes acting on the input and on the output sides of behavior. McLeod (1980) has recently stressed this problem, by showing how output rather than attention interference can explain delays in probe RT.

Of importance is the role played by the linkage of attention and consciousness. For motor events it is doubtful that internal signals that determine the biomechanial features of a movement have any "direct" access to consciousness. What is most conscious is the stored representation or online perception of the changes that a movement introduces in the outside world: what it looks like for the actor observing him- or herself and, perhaps, what it feels like during its execution. Little has been added to what James (1890) claimed when he identified the stimulus for a voluntary act as an image of its consequences, built with information provided by "resident" or proprioceptive feedback and "remote" or visual feedback. The consequence of this view is that, within the framework in which attention and consciousness were inseparable concepts, movement remained indirectly concerned with attention and then only under the somewhat restricted topic of "attention and perception of sensory feedback." A large number of questions related to the role played by selective processes, such as in programming or in producing movements, were therefore outside this topic.

When selective aspects of information processing are viewed as the only consistent feature of attention research (Kinchla, 1980), it can be seen that the pendulum has swung from attention as an early-selective process to a later-selective process. Kahneman and Treisman (1984) have recently pointed out that the interest in the behavioral adaptive function of selective attention has progressively shifted, during the last 10 years, from perceptual processing to motor processing. They especially stress that this shift is closely related to a crucial paradigmatic change. Initially, in the framework of a limited-capacity model of attention, what they called the "filtering paradigm" appeared increasingly unsuccessful in localizing a privileged site for selection in the information-processing sequence. In the framework of a central or modular attentional processor's flexibly allocating processing resources to different processing stages, what they called the "selective-set paradigm" emphasized the functional role played in goal-directed behavior by controlled and automatic processing, respectively (cf. Allport, 1980; Allport, Tipper, & Chmiel, this volume).

In this context, not only does the interest in selective processes deal with all the information-processing operation, but it also acknowledges that action is the main determinant of selection and thus leads one to emphasize the role played by late-selection processes. Because the concepts both of selective attention and of specific preparation can be viewed as covering internally triggered selective sets, they are closely related and possibly not separable. However, their status in information-processing models remains loosely defined. The first part of this chapter discusses selective set, as a processing stage or as a presetting of systems. The second section deals with the implications of adopting one or the other conception in interpreting experimental data on motor programs.

A major recent change in attention and motor control is the increased interaction between cognitive psychology and behavioral neurosciences. This was realized at first by recording event-related potentials in humans during movement, and, later, by analyzing single-cell activity in behaving animals. The field of cognitive neuroscience has progressively emerged. Thus, it is useful to consider the help that data concerning neural processes underlying selective set can provide. The last part of this chapter tries to summarize some recent experimental findings about the changes that occur in neuronal activity of motor cortical areas before performing an intended movement.

STAGE VERSUS MODULATION CONCEPTIONS OF PREPARATION

One of the major changes that has occurred in attention research in the last few years is the increasing interest in selective set in motor control. This emphasis makes the division between sensory and motor processes confusing. For instance, the distinction between passive and active selective attention should be replaced by emphasis on ensuring the adequate execution of an intended action by an appropriate motor set, which results in an appropriate sensory set. The enhancement effect described by Wurtz, Goldberg, and Robinson (1980) provides an excellent example of such backward-cascade effects of goal-directed behavior. Their basic finding is that visual-related neurons of the superficial layers of the superior colliculus respond to a visual stimulus in their receptive field more strongly when the stimulus is a target for a saccadic eye movement than when the monkey maintains its gaze on the fixation point.

Wurtz and his colleagues have shown that the enhancement effect is directly associated with an anticipatory activity of the eye-movement–related neurons of the deeper layers of the superior colliculus. As these authors claimed (Wurtz et al., 1980), the enhancement effect can be considered as "clearly associated with preparation to make eye movements" [p. 61], in the sense that the preparatory activity of eye-movement–related neurons monitors the enhanced activity of the visual-related neurons.

The fact that this example is drawn from the field of behavioral neurosciences is not without significance. Because the selective aspects of information processing often are explained in terms of either controlled or automatized set, it is useful to link these concepts with those developed in the study of functional brain mechanisms underlying goal-directed behavior. Preparation is one of these concepts. However, its relations with selective attention, as well as the status of both attentional processes and preparatory processes in information-processing models underlying motor behavior, have yet to be specified.

In its most common usage (cf., for instance, Kerr, 1978; Meyer, Yantis, Osman, & Smith, 1984; Miller, 1982; Rosenbaum, 1983), the notion of preparation is mainly associated with motor activity, and covers the set of processing operations that intervene before movement execution—that is, response selection or determination, and movement planning or programming. In this sense, motor preparation is viewed as a stage, or a set of stages, in current models of information processing. It is thus different from attention. Attention is never considered as a processing stage, but as a process, outside of the information-processing sequence, that changes the functional features of one or more stages, giving priority to a specific input or output. In this context, however, the fact that one specifies preparation as "motor" implies, of course, that it also can be specified in other ways—for instance, as sensory or perceptual (see, for instance, Luce & Nosofsky, 1984; Posner, Cohen, Choate, Hockey, & Maylor, 1984). However, when preparation is specified in this manner there is an obvious shift in its meaning. Perceptual preparation is never used as an equivalent of one or several input-processing stages, but clearly covers other kinds of processes, mainly selective set.

In the different and much more restrictive meaning that we have proposed (Requin, 1980; Requin, Lecas, & Bonnet, 1984), preparation covers the processes that improve efficiency of the systems responsible for operations that take place during processing. In this way, preparation is not itself a stage, but the process that mediates the effect of an experimental "factor" (as this term was used, for instance, by Sternberg in his 1969 paper and by Garner [1980] when distinguishing between "state" factors and "process" factors, according to the level of specificity of their effects on processing stages). Preparation thus can be adequately specified as either perceptual or motor, according to the location of its effects in the structure of information processing.

It must be stressed that adopting one of the alternatives—that is, preparation either as a stage or as a change in the functional state of processing system—has some serious implications in interpreting experimental data. In serial models of information processing a stage is a functional unit that has two major characteristics. First, it cannot be subdivided and, thus, when started, is necessarily implemented. Second, its output immediately becomes the input of a subsequent stage. Both of these features can be summarized in the notion of the *irrepressibility* or the *ballistic* nature of the processing stage. The irrepressibility feature of the entire processing-stage sequence remains questionable, however, because a change in the action goal is still possible before some "point of no return" (cf. Logan, 1982; Osman, Kornblum, & Mayer, 1984). It is of interest to specify the precise location of the point of no return in order to separate the controlled part from the ballistic part of the processing stage.

Is there a difference between the processes in a RT task that occur before and those that take place after the imperative signal? Within the framework of preparation as a stage, the shortening of RT with advance information is interpreted as displacement, before the imperative signal, of some of the processing stages usually operating after it. This structural interpretation often appears in the field of motor control, for instance through the concept of *preprogramming* or *preprocessing*. According to the strict conception of a processing stage used here, one must expect that the response would be performed even on a catch trial in which there is no imperative signal. The timing of this preprocessed stage when the interstimulus interval is varied is also a problem. It appears that maintaining a preprocessing conception of preparation implies renouncing at least the *irrepressible* feature of processing stages.

In contrast, when preparation is viewed as a change in the functional state of processing systems processing stages would remain triggered by the imperative signal and the theoretical constraint that each stage is implemented and immediately followed by another stage is respected. The shortening of RT would result from a process that is different from the operations that occur following the imperative signal. For instance, preparation could be the activation or selection of subroutines that form the motor program. The selection of subroutines can be viewed as having a sufficiently flexible time course and as being more or less efficient when there is some uncertainty about the timing of the imperative signal, but without any unavoidable consequence if this signal does not occur. In contrast, the program itself, once loaded and ready to be used, will necessarily be executed. Sternberg, Monsell, Knoll, and Wright (1978) suggested a rather similar hypothesis by distinguishing the activation of the whole motor program for a speech sequence, which would occur before the imperative signal, from the retrieval of the subprogram controlling the first element of the sequence, which would be loaded after the imperative signal and would immediately trigger the execution of this element. In this conception, which can be called a *presetting* conception of preparation, preparatory processes would be *optional* processes and therefore different from the irrepressible processes that take place during processing stages. In this functional conception, preparation appears as very similar to active attention or selective set: Both processes are optional and flexible, either governed by some central processor or automatized. Note that it thus would be legitimate to utilize the notion of perceptual preparation to define selective set acting on input processing, as well as that of motor attention to define selective set acting on output processing.

SELECTIVE PREPARATION AND MOTOR PROGRAMMING

These alternative views of selective processes in motor control can determine the inferences legitimately drawn from data. An increasing amount of experimental data show that providing advance information to an individual about the biomechanical characteristics of a movement that he or she must subsequently perform—like movement, direction, or extent—reduces the time necessary to initiate this movement. Such a finding is truly at the heart of the attention and movement story. It raises as an issue the mechanism by which an individual benefits from attending to a feature of a movement that he or she will have to perform. Recall that what is manipulated in these studies is not the information about the response to be performed, but information about one or several features of the motor activity that this response involves.

According to current information-processing models, the explanation of such RT improvements due to advance information is a preparation of a motor program. It is not possible to discuss here the problem raised by the motor-program concept itself (cf., for instance, Requin, Semjen, & Bonnet, 1984). One must recall, however, that the research field being considered is closely related to a paradigm that implies a parametric conception of the programming process. In short, in this conception, the movement would result from a set of decisions or instructions specifying movement parameters that would be translated into commands given to the motor system, which determine the biomechanical features of the movement. Within this framework, a second assumption is that the analytic description, or the factoring of a movement into its spatial and dynamic dimensions, bears some isomorphic relationship to the structure of the motor program. The first step in the study of preparation for movement programming was closely related to the choice–RT paradigm. Advance information was provided about the biomechanical parameters of the movement (cf. Kerr, 1978; Semjen, 1984). For example, Fiori, Semjen, and Requin (1974) had subjects lift their fingers from a common home position to point at targets located equidistantly on a hemicircle in the horizontal plane (cf. Fig. 7.1). Across blocks of trials, the location of the targets defining the two response alternatives was varied, in order to produce movement trajectories from 0° to 180°. Changes in RT to the fixated target were considered as a function of the angle between targets, to thus control for visual eccentricity.

RT increased as the angle between trajectories increased. Two alternative explanations were suggested. The first was that the subjects attempted to prepare

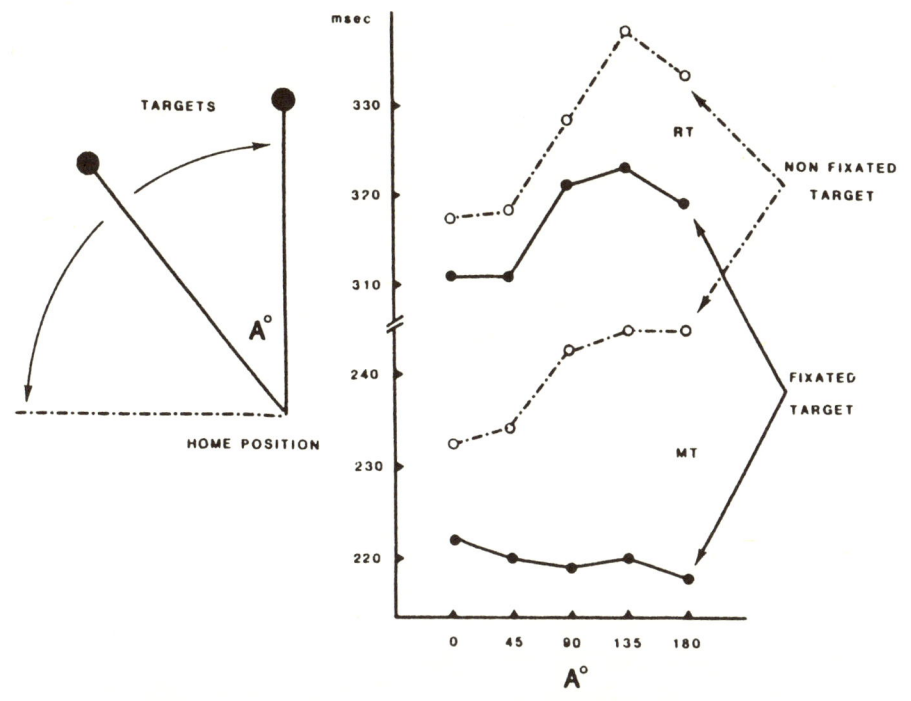

FIG. 7.1. Effect of the angle between the trajectories of pointing movements performed in a two-choice RT experiment. The relative positions (in terms of angular distance from a common starting point for movements) of the two targets corresponding to the two response alternatives were systematically varied across blocks of trials. Both targets alternately served as fixation points during the two half-blocks of trials (left panel of the figure). Mean RT and MT as a function of the angle between movement trajectories, when either the fixated target or the nonfixated target was pointed at, are shown in the right panel of the figure (modified from Fiori et al., 1974).

for both movements. This would only be possible for the common programs specifying the movement. The specificity of this preparatory process (regarding the movement that the subject actually performed) was thus supposed to decrease as the part of programming processes common to both movements decreased—that is, when trajectory angle increased. The second explanation was that the subject fully prepared for one movement, resulting in fast RT when this movement had to be performed. If the other movement had to be performed, not only would preparation for the common part of both movements be the only useful preparation, as in the previous explanation, but in addition a wrong preparation would have to be canceled, even destroyed, a process whose cost is supposed to be related to the degree to which programming processes for the two movements differ. Whatever the correct interpretation, one must stress that the first explanation bears upon the hypothesis of a facilitatory effect, whose size is related to the amount of similarity between what the subject prepares for and what he or she actually has to perform, whereas the second explanation adds to the first the hypothesis of some inhibitory effect, whose size is related to the difference between what the subject was fully prepared for and the part of preparation that remained useful for performing the actual movement.

These two ways of reasoning about preparation are precisely those underlying the two procedures that are mainly used to study motor preparation: the partial-advance information technique (or "movement-dimension precueing technique" as proposed by Rosenbaum, 1983) on one hand, and the movement-priming technique on the other. In short, in a choice–RT procedure with the precueing technique, subjects have to perform movements that can be factored in some of their possible spatial, dynamic, or anatomical features, or dimensions. Before the performance of the task, a warning signal supplies the subject with information about the dimensions of the forthcoming movements. RTs are analyzed according to the amount of information provided by the cue—that is, according to the number and the nature of the movement dimensions that have been precued. In the priming technique, the prime indicates the movement to be performed. It is followed with a high probability by the corresponding imperative signal and with a low probability by an imperative signal calling for a movement different from the primed one. RTs are analyzed according to the number and nature of the dimensions that the primed and required movements have in common.

An example of the results observed in a set of experiments (Lépine, Glencross, & Requin, unpublished results) using both of these techniques is presented in Fig. 7.2. Subjects had to control the position of two pointers in front of a vertical display panel on which eight targets were located by moving independently two handles in the vertical plane. The movement had the combination of three binary-spatial dimensions: side or arm (left vs. right), direction (upward vs. downward), and extent (short vs. large). The subject's task was to displace one of the pointers from a common home position centrally located on the display panel to the target when illuminated. A LED was located adjacent to each target. In the precueing technique, the illumination of one or two LEDs started a foreperiod, which preceded the pointing task. Illuminating the LED adjacent to the target enabled complete advance information to be given to the subject; illuminating two LEDs made it possible to give advance information about either two, one, or no dimensions of the forthcoming movement, and to systematically change the precued dimensions. For instance, when considering target 5, two dimensions (arm and direction) were precued by illuminating LEDs 5 and 7, and no dimension was precued by illuminating LEDs 5 and 3. In the priming technique, only one LED was illuminated, thus priming the adjacent target. This prime was valid for 65% of the trials, and it was "invalid" for 35% of the trials, in which each of the seven other targets were equiprobable. According to the locations of the illuminated LED and target, either two (for instance, LED 5 and

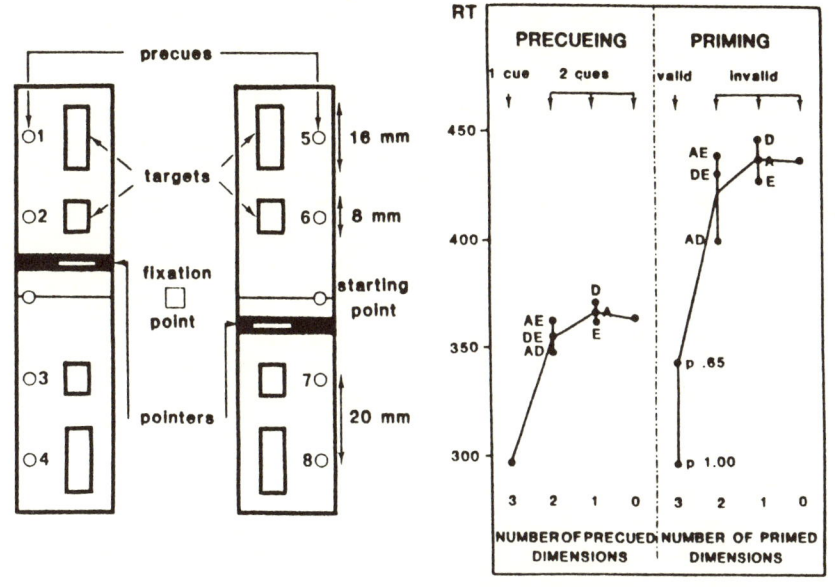

FIG. 7.2. Comparison of the results observed in a movement-precueing and a movement-priming experiment. The left part of the figure shows the display panel on which were located: (1) targets at which subjects had to point, when they were illuminated, by displacing from the starting point either a left or a right pointer that was moved by rotating either a left or a right handle; (2) LEDs, adjacent to the targets, that served as either precues or primes. Mean RTs as a function of the number and nature of the movement dimensions precued or primed are shown in the right panel of the figure (A = arm; D = direction; E = extent). See details of both procedures in the text (from Lépine et al., unpublished results).

target 6), one (for instance, LED 5 and target 7), or no (for instance, LED 5 and target 3) movement dimensions were primed.

Results showed that RT in the precueing technique decreased as a function of the number of movement dimensions that were precued. These RT changes were considerably amplified in the priming technique. Moreover, RTs differed according to the movement dimensions specified in advance. Note that the interpretation of these is complex because the benefits in RT according to whether direction (D), arm (A), or extent (E) was precued or primed differed in conditions when one of these dimensions was precued or primed to conditions when two of these dimensions were simultaneously precued or primed.

Data collected with different versions of these precueing and priming techniques is available, following Rosenbaum's (1980) initial study (Bonnet, Requin, & Stelmach, 1982; Goodman & Kelso, 1980; Lépine & Requin, 1983; Miller, 1982; Rosenbaum & Kornblum, 1982; Zelaznik, 1981). The main findings of these studies is that effects on RT of precueing or priming several movement dimensions are more or less additive or slightly underadditive. Another finding is that consistent differences are found in the extent of reduction in RT for the different dimensions. However, this is uninterpretable because there is no way to scale the differences across dimensions.

What are the implications of these results for preparation as either a processing stage or presetting process? The stage view leads one to make inferences about the structure of the motor program—for example, that programming is a serial, nonordered process. Such a conclusion appears to be puzzling in light of the usual conceptions of a hierarchical organization of the motor system. A hierarchy is hardly compatible with the possibility of programming extent before knowing movement direction, or responding limb. The results can be viewed as fitting a conception of the motor program as an "abstract representation" of movement dimensions. In this formula, "abstract" seems to mean that no relationship between this dimensional representation and a level of neural motor organization is to be sought. This view leaves us with the problem of translating the program instructions (supposed to be written in this abstract language) into commands to the executive motor system (supposed to be written in the neural terms). Whatever the likelihood of this conception, it implies a violation of the concept of processing stage. If the cue is fully informative, it would render full advance programming possible. This means that programming would not necessarily be followed by execution. In other words, that no longer could be considered as a stage within a ballistic sequence of stages, but as having the status of an optional process. The same thing can be said for priming, with the additional problem that programming in advance would be useless when the imperative signal calls for a different movement, and would thus have to be suppressed in order not to disturb the building of a new program and to avoid an erroneous response. This raises the strange question of what to "deprogram" or more generally to "deprocess." What was called a violation of the concept of processing stage is even more obvious when interpreting the effect of a cue providing partial information. The programming process would be partially displaced backward. This would imply that the programming stage is subdivided into substages, thus raising not only the same problem that was just discussed but, moreover, the question of the location of the unitary process underlying the loading of the entire program. It would alternately imply that the programming stage, as a unitary process, would not necessarily be implemented when started. At this point, one can admit that this discussion is probably based upon a much too rigid conception of processing stages. Note, however, that too loose a conception would in turn render illegitimate some of the other inferences currently drawn from data, as, for instance, that drawn from the additivity of precueing or priming effects.

Consider the alternative conception of preparation as a presetting process. The same experimental results also lead one to make inferences about the structure of the motor program but only those that the logic of the additive-factor method permits. For instance, from either the additive or underadditive effects of cueing or priming several movement dimensions, it can be concluded that programming is either a serially organized or a partially overlapping set of stages or substages, but no inference can be made about their order. In short, the fact that the efficiency of precueing or priming movement dimensions is independent of the order in which these dimensions are precued or primed does not provide any information about the order in which the stages or substages responsible for programming are processed. Presetting a stage as a functional unit would not depend on the location of this stage in the sequence of stages. The implication is that one could expect the same pattern of results in the case in which it was demonstrated that programming involves a fixed-ordered series of processing units, each devoted to specify one movement dimension. Calling for an "abstract representation" of the motor program thus does not appear to be an unavoidable implication of the data collected in this field. Continuing with the metaphor of the computer program, preselecting subroutines does not involve loading the program, but readies the program to be loaded. Thus, one can admit that the time saved by this preselection does not depend on what subroutine is preselected first, but only on the duration of this preselection operation and/or on the time needed to incorporate its output in the program when loaded.

PERMISSIVE VERSUS EXECUTIVE BRAIN PROCESSES

At this point it is justifiable to question whether the attempt to distinguish between presetting and processing is completely unwarranted and speculative or whether such a distinction can be solved empirically. One way to solve it empirically, of course, would be to define and follow an experimental strategy that could either validate or invalidate the predictions derived from one model or another. It appears difficult to conceive what this strategy could be. Another way is to draw some help for solving the problem from experimental findings that have been collected by looking at brain activity. Of course, one must first accept the basic assumption, which does not seem overly reductionist, that there is some structural isomorphism between the hypothetical construct of processing stage, as an irrepressible functional unit, and the concept of an anatomically defined neuronal system specialized in performing a functional operation in the brain. As suggested elsewhere (Requin, 1980; Requin, Lecas, & Bonnet, 1984) an increasing number of arguments render likely a direct correspondence between a three-stage serial model of motor control and a three-pathway serial organization of the motor system. Is it possible, from observing the activity of the involved brain structures before and during movements, to determine the functional differences between presetting and processing?

This question is not a new one and the neurophysiological mechanisms that may be responsible for executive versus permissive functions have often been discussed (see, for instance, Bernstein, 1967). In terms of modern neurophysiology, the mechanism by which neuronal pathways can be gated or closed is generally related either to local synaptic potentials remaining below the threshold for conveying neural impulses, or in a modular conception of brain organization (cf. Mountcastle, 1979) to the activation of local neural circuits characterized by high intraconnectivity. The pattern of these local activations within functionally specialized neuronal networks can be viewed as the mechanism underlying pre-setting processes. The amount of similarity between the pattern of local activations and the pattern of activations between modules would determine the level of specificity that permissive processes have. In short, when permissive processes result from a "process" factor they could look like an embryo of the executive processes upon which they intervene. When they result from a "state" factor, as in the case of arousal, they would have no specific functional relationship with any executive process.

Permissive processes in general and selective set in particular have been mainly studied by means of two different methodologies. The first is the analysis in human subjects of the event-related potentials that develop during preparatory periods or foreperiods preceding intended action. These include the contingent negative variation and the readiness potential. The second is the use of single-cell recording techniques for investigating neuronal activity in awake and behaving animals, after being trained in sensorimotor tasks. Because a number of review papers already have been devoted to the first field of research (see, for instance, Donchin, Coles, & Gratton, 1984), some of the experimental data that have been collected in the frame of the second approach only are briefly commented upon here. Following the studies initiated by Evarts (see Evarts & Tanji, 1974), one of the main findings of single-cell recording is that the activity of neuronal networks, involved in different ways in motor control, are modulated by what the animal knows in advance about what it has to do. This is especially true for neural structures that are presumed to be involved in motor programming, such as the cerebellum (Strick, 1983) and the motor cortex (see Evarts, 1981). This has begun to be precisely analyzed for the set of cortical areas that likely forms the terminal of this functional pathway—that is, the precentral motor cortex (see Evarts, 1984), the premotor cortex (see Weinrich & Wise, 1982), and the supplementary motor area (see Tanji, Taniguchi, & Saga, 1980).

Summarizing the data collected in this set of structures reveals that three kinds of neurons have been identified. The first and best known is what are labeled true motor units. Their activity is unaffected by set and is movement-related only. The activation of these units starts as long as 200 msec before any peripheral EMG activation. Fig. 7.3 shows an example of such a unit, which was recorded in the left precentral cortex of a monkey when performing in a between-hands choice–RT paradigm (see Lecas, Requin, & Vitton, 1982). The animal was required to press two left- and right-hand levers simultaneously. After a waiting period, a warning tone started a 1-sec foreperiod that ended with the illumination of either a left- or a right-hand visual target. The monkey was required to release the lever on the same side as the illuminated target and to point at the target as

7. LOOKING FORWARD TO MOVING SOON   159

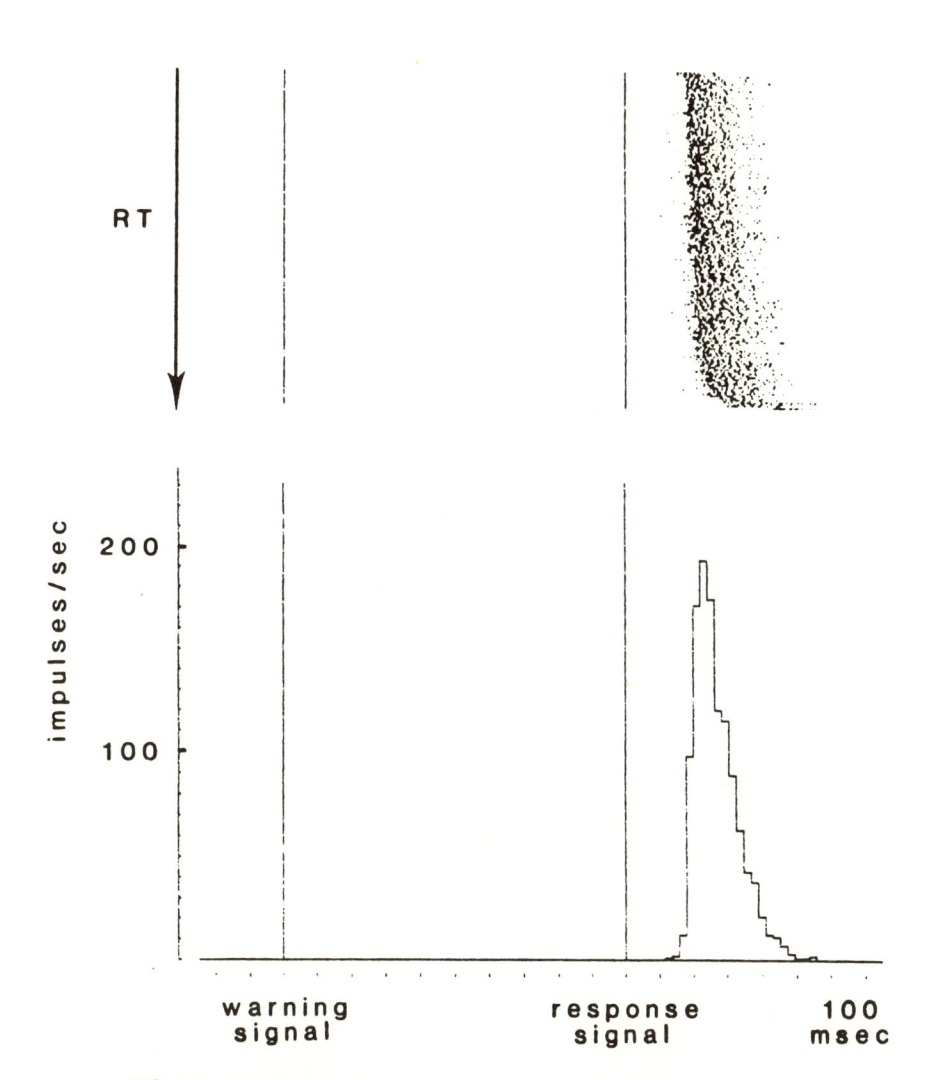

FIG. 7.3. Activity of a unit recorded in the left precentral cortex (area 4) of a monkey when performing a pointing task with its right arm. The duration of the preparatory period from the warning tone to the illumination of the target as a response signal was 1 sec. On the top of the figure, raster presentation is ordered from top to bottom according to increasing RTs. It shows, as well as the histogram of the average unit activity, that this unit was completely silent until 120 msec after the response signal, then exhibited a movement-related discharge that peaked at about 240 msec after the response signal—that is, at about the time when the monkey released a lever, which it had previously pressed to initiate the trial, before pointing at the target.

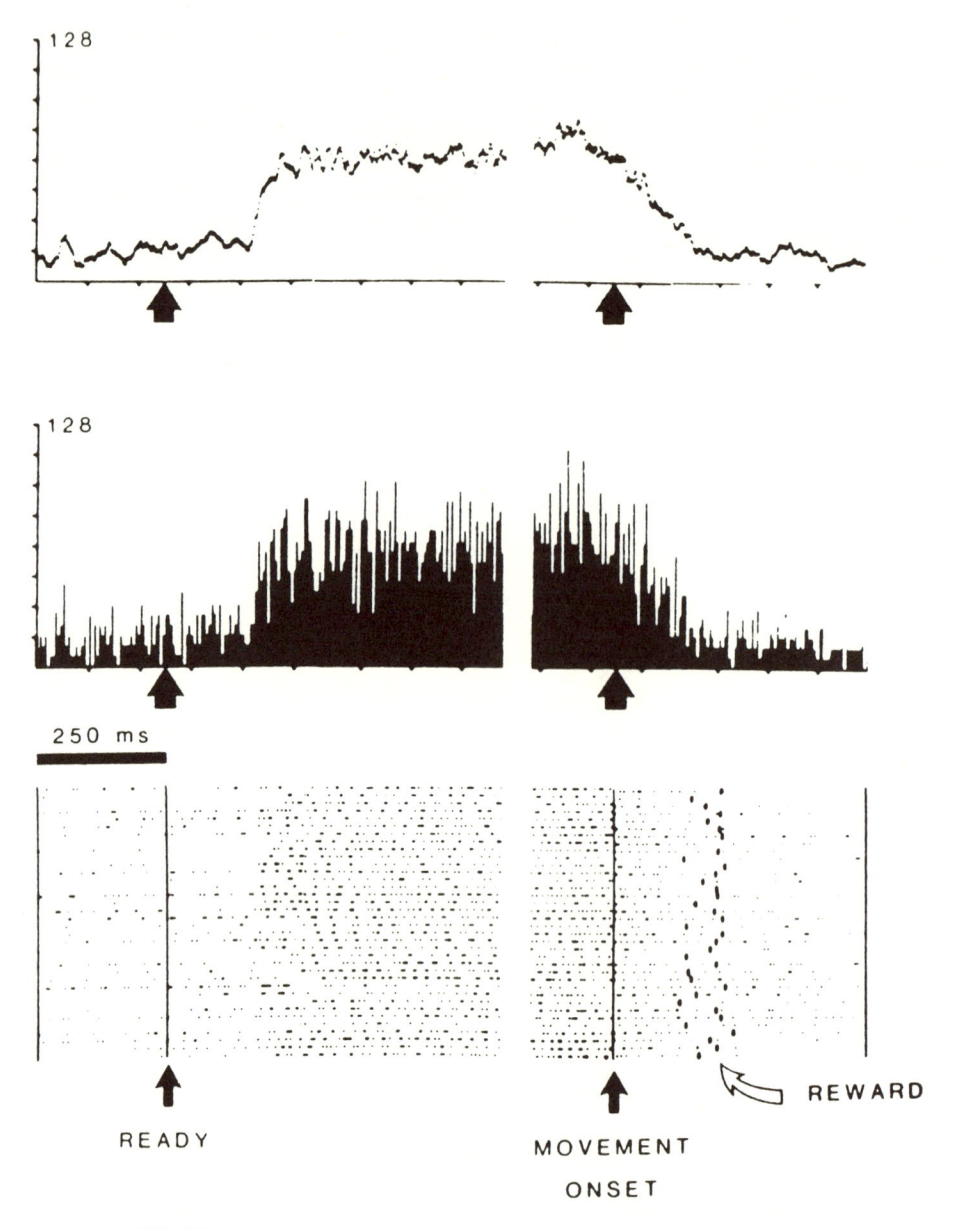

FIG. 7.4. Activity of a unit recorded in the premotor cortex (area 6) of a monkey when performing a visuospatial pointing task from one target to another among a set of four targets located in front of the animal on the horizontal plane. This unit exhibited a sustained activity from the ready signal, constituted by the illumination of the next target, to the pointing movement, triggered from 0.8 to 2.4 sec later by a go signal constituted by the illumination of a LED adjacent to the target to be pointed at. Raster presentation (bottom part) as well as average unit activity (medium and top parts) are time locked to the ready signal on the left and to the movement onset on the right (from Weinrich & Wise, 1982).

quickly as possible. The cell shown in Fig. 7.3 was completely inactive until about 180 msec before the monkey released the right lever. It then exhibited, for 250 msec, a strong movement-related activity in relation to the movement. In short, this kind of unit can be viewed as the terminal point of the programming process. Its main function is conveying the commands derived from program instructions to the peripheral effectors.

The second class of neurons can be called true presetting units. Their activity is not movement related, but rather is changed only by a cue providing the animal information about some biomechanical feature of its intended movement. Figure 7.4 shows an example of such a unit, which was recorded in the premotor cortex of a monkey when performing a visuomanual pointing task (see Weinrich & Wise, 1982). When the monkey pressed a target the next target was illuminated. That started a foreperiod of variable duration ending with the illumination of a LED adjacent to the target, which triggered the pointing movement. The resting discharge frequency of the cell shown in Fig. 7.4 increased about 150 msec after the ready signal. This sustained activation lasted during the whole foreperiod until the onset of the pointing movement, and then declined. It was specifically related to a peculiar type of intended movement. It was observed only when the ready signal informed the monkey to point at the leftmost target. Note that this presetting neuronal activity was not associated with any peripheral change in EMG. In short, this kind of neuron can be viewed as being a specific target for presetting processes.

The third kind of unit shares both of the just-described properties, in that its activity is successfully set related and then movement related. Figure 7.5 shows an example of such a unit, which was recorded at the boundary of areas 4 and 6, during the same RT task as that in which the unit shown in Fig. 7.3 was recorded. The resting discharge frequency of this cell changed about 300 to 400 msec after the warning, increasing progressively until the time when the movement-related activity occurred. The amount of this set-related activity was found to be negatively correlated with RT (see Requin, Lecas, & Bonnet, 1984). The relationship between the changes in the set-related activity and those in the movement-related activity can be examined by comparing cell discharge frequency during two subsets of trials, one corresponding to the first quartile of the RT distribution (the shortest RTs), the other corresponding to the fourth quartile of the RT distribution (the longest RTs). One can see that the largest set-related activity, which was associated with the shortest RTs, did not make the onset of the movement-related activity earlier, nor the size of this activity greater. Its main effect was to render the time of the maximum rate of the movement-related activity earlier, in proportion to the shortening of RT. This suggests that the time to reach a same rate of discharge frequency was reduced when a greater set-related activity was already present at the start of the movement-related activity, and/or that the slope of this movement-related activity change was made steeper by the presetting activity of the cell. In any case, what must be stressed is that the

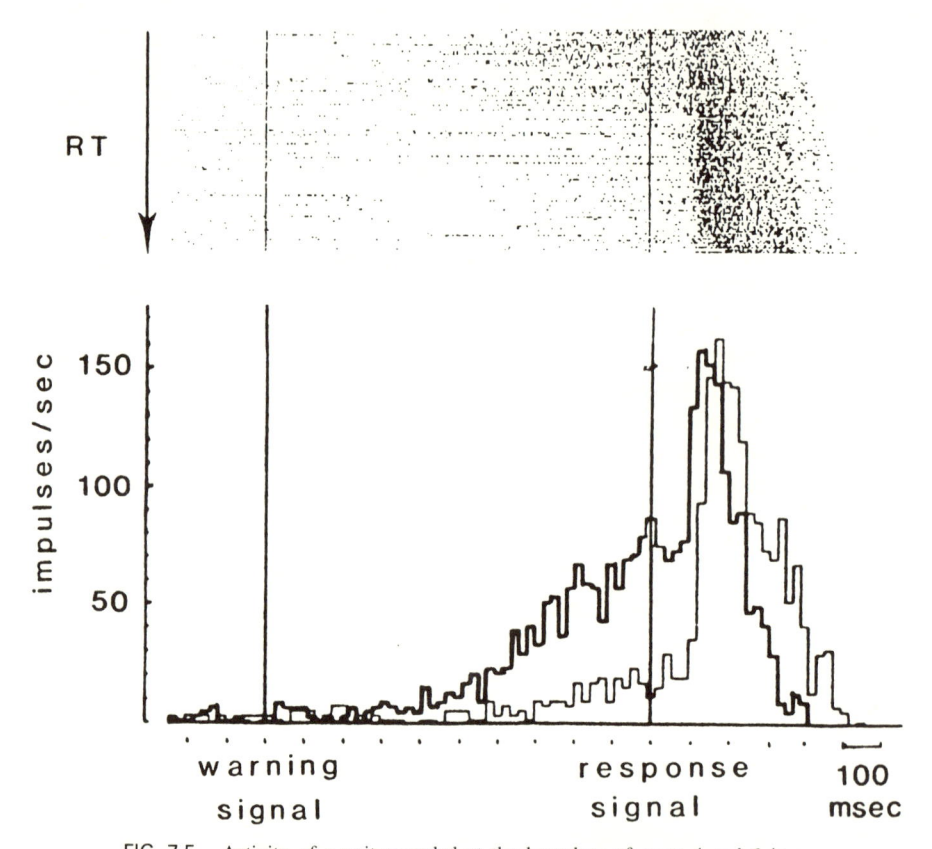

FIG. 7.5. Activity of a unit recorded at the boundary of areas 4 and 6 in a monkey when performing the same pointing task as presented in Fig. 7.3. This unit exhibited an increase of its resting discharge frequency about 250 msec after the warning signal, which progressively develops until about 100 msec after the response signal—that is, at the time when the movement-related discharge started. Histograms of average unit activity were separately computed for trials coresponding to the first (thick-line) and the fourth (fine-line) quartiles of the RT distribution. Note on the raster presentation, as well as on histograms, the negative correlation between RT and unit discharge frequency during the preparatory period.

time when the set-related activity ended and when the movement-related activity started appeared to be unchanged. What the presetting activity seems to modify is, therefore, some of the intrinsic functional properties of the subsequent neuronal processes.

To summarize (see Fig. 7.6), two kinds of neurons exist in the motor cortical areas that can be labeled permissive, because they are targets for presetting processes. An additional two kinds of neurons exist that can be labeled executive, because they receive program instructions and convey orders to the peripheral structures responsible for movement execution. One kind of neuron shares both properties and would play the role of interfacing permissive and executive processes. Given the hypothesis that these three classes of neurons constitute the elements of a basic modular organization of the premotor and motor cortical areas, one can suggest that this organization forms a possible model of the way in which presetting and processing are separable but functionally related. With few assumptions about the intraconnectivity within this module, one can speculate that the neuron specialized as being a target for presetting influences would activate the common, or interface, neuron, thus modifying the timing of its movement-related activity after it has received the program instructions. The commands sent to the peripheral motor structures would thus take into account the effect of the presetting process, because they

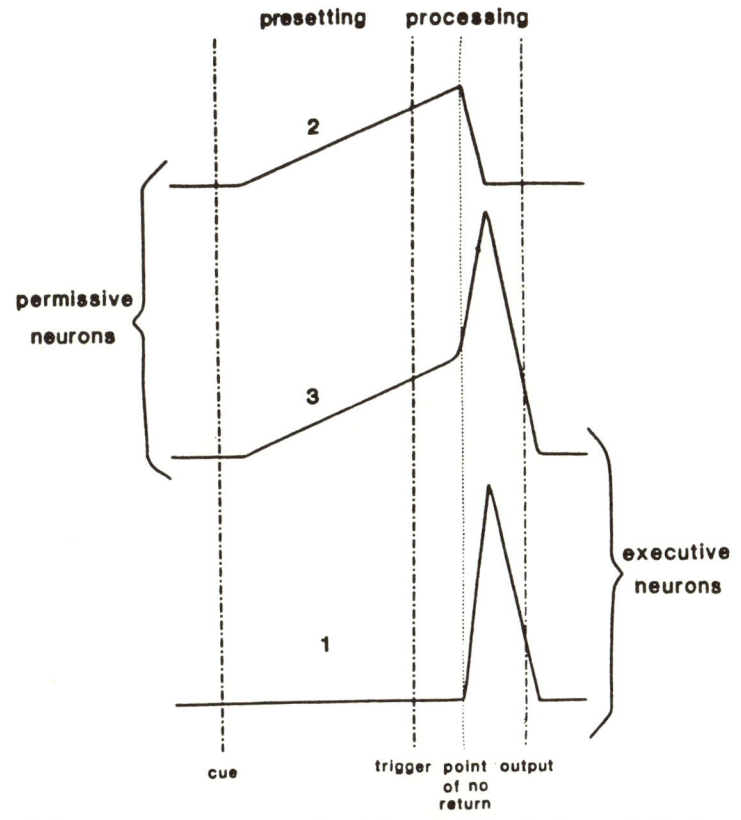

FIG. 7.6. Schematic representation of the main kinds of units recorded in the motor cortex, whose activity is related to movement performance. Two kinds of units are labeled permissive neurons, because their activity is preparation related, and two kinds of units are labeled executive neurons, because their activity is movement related. One kind of unit shares both properties. See explanations in the text.

result from a combination of the movement-related activities of the interfacing neuron and of the truly motor neuron, the former possibly enhancing the effect of the latter by gating slightly in advance the peripheral motor structures. This model does *not* imply any online consequence of the cortical presetting at the level of the spinal motor structures that control muscle activation, in agreement with the experimental findings collected in human subjects by using reflex techniques. In short, these studies have shown that manipulating experimental factors known to act on the early stages of motor organization did not result in functional changes that could explain the changes in the timing of motor performance at the level of the motor spinal structures responsible for movement execution (cf. Bonnet, Requin, & Semjen, 1981; Requin, Bonnet, & Semjen, 1977; Requin, Lecas, & Bonnet, 1984). The precise mechanism by which the presetting of motor cortical units would change the timing of the motor output would thus intervene on the final step of loading program instructions at a central level only.

CONCLUSIONS

The role that presetting processes in motor cortex possibly play in modulating the structure of the motor program stresses the features by which brain processes underlying selective motor set differ from brain processes underlying motor-control processes. An exhaustive review, extending outside the field of motor-programming operations (see also Bonnet, 1983, and Bonnet & Requin, 1982), would equally show that the presetting of the processing systems responsible for the retrieval of a response stored in memory is likely separable from the selection of the response as a processing stage. As well, the presetting of the processing systems responsible for executing the motor output should prove distinguishable from the performance of a movement as an executive operation (cf., for instance, Bonnet, 1983; Requin, Lecas, and Bonnet, 1984; Woollacott, Bonnet, & Yabe, 1984). Taken together with comparable data that have been accumulated on neural processes responsible for selective set that modulates sensory and perceptual visual processing, especially in the colliculus, the frontal eye field, and the posterior parietal cortex, it is not overly optimistic to believe that it will soon be possible to decipher the properties that separate the class of permissive processes from the class of executive processes. At the same time, we may obtain a taxonomy on the strength of the relationship between a permissive process and the executive process that it modulates. It would, of course, be even better if the use of common concepts and indeed common paradigms in the field of cognitive psychology and behavioral neurosciences could result in an increasingly common definition and taxonomy in information-processing and functional neural models.

ACKNOWLEDGMENTS

We thank Dr. Sylvan Kornblum for helpful suggestions and criticisms during preparation of this chapter. This work was supported by a grant from CNRS (ATP, number 221) and a grant from INSERM (contract number 826016).

REFERENCES

Allport, D. A. (1980). Attention and performance. In D. G. Claxton (Ed.), *Cognitive psychology: New directions* (pp. 112–153). London: Routledge & Kegan Paul.

Bernstein, N. (1967). *The coordination and regulation of movements.* London: Pergamon.

Bonnet, M. (1983). Anticipatory changes of long-latency stretch responses during preparation for directionnal hand movements. *Brain Research, 280,* 51–62.

Bonnet, M., & Requin, J. (1982). Long-loop and spinal reflexes in man during preparation for intended directional hand movements. *The Journal of Neuroscience, 2,* 90–96.

Bonnet, M., Requin, J., & Semjen, A. (1981). Human reflexology and motor preparation. In D. J. Miller (Ed.), *Exercise and sports sciences reviews* (Vol. 9, pp. 119–157). Philadelphia: Franklin Institute.

Bonnet, M., Requin, J., Stelmach, G. E. (1982). Specification of direction and extent in motor programming. *Bulletin of the Psychonomic Society, 19,* 31–34.

Donchin, E., Coles, M. G., & Gratton, G. (1984). Cognitive psychophysiology and preparatory processes: A case study. In S. Kornblum & J. Requin (Eds.), *Preparatory states and processes* (pp. 155–178). Hillsdale, NJ: Lawrence Erlbaum Associates.

Evarts, E. V. (1981). Role of motor cortex in voluntary movements in primates. In V. B. Brooks (Ed.), *Handbook of physiology: The nervous system* Vol. 2: *Motor control* (pp. 1083–1120). Baltimore: Williams and Wilkins.

Evarts, E. V, (1984). Neurophysiological approaches to brain mechanisms for preparatory set. In S. Kornblum & J. Requin (eds.), *Preparatory states and processes* (pp. 137–153). Hillsdale, NJ: Lawrence Erlbaum Associates.

Evarts, E. V., & Tanji, J. (1974). Gating of motor cortex reflexes by prior instruction. *Brain Research, 71,* 479–494.

Fiori, N., Semjen, A., Requin, J. (1974). Analyse chronométrique du pattern préparatoire à un mouvement spatialement orienté; résultats préliminaires. *Le Travail Humain, 37,* 229–248.

Garner, W. R. (1980). Association lecture: Functional aspects of information processing. In R. Nickerson (Ed.), *Attention and performance VIII* (pp. 1–26). Hillsdale, NJ: Lawrence Erlbaum Associates.

Goodman, D., & Kelso, J. A. S. (1980). Are movements prepared in parts? Not under compatible (naturalized) conditions. *Journal of Experimental Psychology: General, 109,* 475–495.

James, W. (1890). *Principles of psychology.* New York: Holt.

Kahneman, D., & Treisman, A. (1984). Changing views of attention and automaticity. In R. Parasuraman & D. R. Davies (Eds.), *Varieties of attention* (pp. 29–61). New York: Academic.

Kerr, B. (1978). Task factors that influence selection and preparation for voluntary movements. In G. E. Stelmach (Ed.), *Information Processing in motor control and learning* (pp. 55–69). New York: Academic.

Kinchla, R. A. (1980). The measurement of attention. In R. S. Nickerson (ed.), *Attention and performance VIII* (pp. 213–238). Hillsdale, NJ: Lawrence Erlbaum Associates.

Klein, R. M. (1976). Attention and movement. In G. E. Stelmach (Ed.), *Motor control: Issues and trends* (pp. 143–173). New York: Academic.

Lecas, J. C., Requin, J., & Vitton, N. (1982). Anticipatory neuronal activity in the monkey precentral cortex during reaction time foreperiod: Preliminary results. In J. Massion, J. Paillard, W. Schultz, & M. Wiesendanger (Eds.), *Neural coding of motor performance, experimental brain research* (suppl. 7. pp. 120–129). Berlin: Springer.

Lépine, D., & Requin, J. (1983). Specification of spatial dimensions in movement programming. *Society for Neuroscience Abstracts, 9,* 297–17.

Logan, G. D. (1982). On the ability to inhibit complex movements: A stop-signal study of type writing. *Journal of Experimental Psychology: Human Perception and Performance, 8,* 778–792.

Luce, R. D., & Nosofsky, R. M. (1984). Attention, stimulus range, and identification of loudness. In S. Kornblum & J. Requin (Eds.), *Preparatory states and processes* (pp. 3–25). Hillsdale, NJ: Lawrence Erlbaum Associates.

McLeod, P. (1980). What can RT tell us about the attentional demands of movement? In G. E. Stelmach & J. Requin (Eds.), *Tutorials in motor behavior* (pp. 579–589). Amsterdam: North-Holand.

Meyer, D. E., Yantis, S., Osman, A., & Smith, J. E. K. (1984). Discrete versus continuous models of response preparation: A reaction-time analysis. In S. Kornblum & J. Requin (Eds.), *Preparatory states and processes* (pp. 69–94). Hillsdale, NJ: Lawrence Erlbaum Associates.

Miller, J. (1982). Discrete versus continuous stages models of human information processing: In search of partial output. *Journal of Experimental Psychology: Human Perception and Performance, 8,* 279–296.

Mountcastle, V. B. (1979). An organizing principle for cerebral function: The unit module and the distributed system. In G. M. Edelman & V. B. Mountcastle (Eds.), *The Mindful brain* (pp. 21–42). Cambridge, MA: MIT Press.

Osman, A., Kornblum, S., & Mayer, D. E. (1984). *The point of no return in choice reaction time: A model and paradigm.* Paper read at the Eastern Psychological Association, Baltimore.

Posner, M. I., & Cohen, Y. (1980). Attention and the control of movements. In G. E. Stelmach & J. Requin (Eds.), *Tutorials in motor behavior* (pp. 243–258). Amsterdam: North-Holland.

Posner, M. I., Cohen, Y., Choate, L. S., Hockey, R., & Maylor, E. (1984). Sustained concentration: Passive filtering or active orienting? In S. Kornblum & J. Requin (Eds.), *Preparatory states and processes* (pp. 49–65). Hillsdale, NJ: Lawrence Erlbaum Associates.

Requin, J. (1980). Toward a psychobiology of preparation for action. In G. E. Stelmach & J. Requin (Eds.), *Tutorials in motor behavior* (pp. 373–398). Amsterdam: North Holland.

Requin, J., Bonnet, M., & Semjen, A. (1977). Is there a specificity in the supraspinal control of motor structures during preparation? In S. Dornic (Ed.), *Attention and performance VI* (pp. 139–174). Hillsdale, NJ: Lawrence Erlbaum Associates.

Requin, J., Lecas, J. C., & Bonnet, M. (1984). Some experimental evidence for a three-step model of motor preparation. In S. Kornblum & J. Requin (Eds.), *Preparatory states and processes* (pp. 259–284). Hillsdale, NJ: Lawrence Erlbaum Associates.

Requin, J., Semjen, A., & Bonnet, M. (1984). Bernstein's purposeful brain. In H. T. A. Whiting (Ed.), *Human motor actions: Bernstein reassessed* (pp. 467–504). Amsterdam: North-Holland.

Rosenbaum, D. A. (1980). Human movement initiation: Specification of arm, direction and extent. *Journal of Experimental Psychology: General, 109,* 444–474.

Rosenbaum, D. A. (1983). The movement precueing technique: Assumptions, applications and extensions. In R. A. Magill (Ed.), *Memory and control of action* (pp. 231–274). Amsterdam: North Holland.

Rosenbaum, D. A., & Kornblum, S. (1982). A priming method for investigating the selection of motor responses. *Acta Psychologica, 50,* 223–224.

Semjen, A. (1984). Rapid hand movement in step-tracking: Reprogramming of direction and extent. In S. Kornblum & J. Requin (Eds.), *Preparatory states and processes* (pp. 95–118). Hillsdale, NJ: Lawrence Erlbaum Associates.

Stelmach, G. E., & Hughes, B. G. (1983). Does motor skill automation require a theory of attention? In R. A. Magill (Ed.), *Memory and control of action* (pp. 275–296). Amsterdam: North Holland.

Sternberg, S. (1969). The discovery of processing stages: Extension of Donder's method. In W. G. Koster (Ed.), *Attention and performance II* (pp. 276–315). Amsterdam: North Holland.

Sternberg, S., Monsell, S., Knoll, R. J., & Wright, C. E. (1978). The latency and duration of rapid movement sequences: Comparisons of speech and typewriting. In G. E. Stelmach (Ed.), *Information processing in motor control and learning* (pp. 117–152). New York: Academic.

Strick, P. L. (1983). The influence of motor preparation on the response of cerebellar neurons to limb displacements. *Journal of Neurophysiology, 10,* 2007–2020.

Tanji, J., Taniguchi, K., & Saga, T. (1980). Supplementary motor area: Neural response to motor instructions. *Journal of Neurophysiology, 44,* 60–68.

Weinrich, M., & Wise, S. P. (1982). The premotor cortex of the monkey. *Journal of Neurosciences, 2,* 1329–1345.

Woollacott, M., Bonnet, M., & Yabe, K. (1984). Preparatory process for anticipatory postural adjustments: Modulation of leg muscles reflex pathways during preparation for arm movements in a standing man. *Experimental Brain Research, 55,* 263–271.

Wurtz, R. H., Goldberg, M. E., Robinson, D. L. (1980). Behavioral modulation of visual responses in the monkey: Stimulus selection for attention and movement. In J. M. Sprague & A. N. Epstein (Eds.), *Progress in psychobiology and physiological psychology* (Vol. 9) New York: Academic.

Zelaznik, H. (1981). The effects of force and direction uncertainty on choice reaction time in an isometric force production task. *Journal of Motor Behavior, 13,* 18–32.

III ORIENTING OF ATTENTION

8 The Spatial Structure of Visual Attention

Cathryn J. Downing
Stanford University

Steven Pinker
Massachusetts Institute of Technology

ABSTRACT

In two experiments we examined the distribution of attention across visual space and the properties of the mental representation of space underlying visual attention. In Experiment 1, subjects focused their attention on various locations in a three-dimensional display, and we measured the "costs" in detection time for stimuli at unattended locations varying in horizontal distance and in depth from the attended location. Results suggest that attention falls off with depth from the focus of attention, and more steeply for stimuli that are farther than the focus of attention than for those nearer. Furthermore, attention falls off with lateral distance from the focus of attention according to a negatively accelerating gradient defined over visual-angle separation, not real-world distance. Control conditions confirm that these effects are not artifacts of ocular accommodation.

In Experiment 2, subjects attended to one of a set of 10 locations on a CRT. Detection times for stimuli at unattended locations reveal a gradient of two-dimensional attention whose slope is related to differences in receptive field size or cortical magnification at different retinal eccentricities. We suggest that visual attention is defined in a three-dimensional representational medium whose dimensions are horizontal and vertical visual angle, scaled by a cortical magnification factor, and depth.

INTRODUCTION

In this chapter we report an experimental investigation of the way that cognitive processes can access portions of the visual world by virtue of their locations. In particular, we attempt to assess the dimensionality and metric of the internal representation of visual space that underlies visual attention.

In our studies we exploit the fact that although humans usually focus their eyes and their attention on the same location in visual space, movements of attention can occur independently of eye movements (Eriksen & Hoffman, 1972; Posner, 1978, 1980; Sperling, 1960; Sperling & Reeves, 1980). A simple demonstration of this phenomenon can be found in a set of studies by Posner and his colleagues. They have shown that when subjects expect an event such as the illumination of a light to occur in a particular location, subjects can detect the light more quickly when it does occur in that location than when they have no prior expectation about its position. On the other hand, when the light occurs at a location other than the expected location, the subjects are slower to detect it than they are when they have no prior expectation about its location. The facilitation observed for stimuli at expected locations is often referred to as an attentional *benefit;* the inhibition observed for stimuli at unexpected locations is referred to as an attentional *cost* (Posner, 1978).[1] These attentional effects occur even when a person's eyes are fixated somewhere other than the expected location (Posner, 1978; see also Remington, 1980). Further support for the separability of the eye movement and attentional systems can be found from studies of primate electrophysiology (e.g., Wurtz, Goldberg, & Robinson, 1982) and human neuropsychology (Heilman, 1979).

Investigations of the organization of cortical visual processing have revealed a number of retinotopically organized areas whose parts represent specific aspects of the visual world at particular locations (see Cowey, 1982). It seems reasonable to postulate that visual attention can operate by activating, priming, or selecting parts of these structures. If visual attention does work in this way, several questions arise. First, do the structures subserving attention represent three-dimensional space or two-dimensional retinal projections? Second, do the structures subserving visual attention represent the position of stimuli along the horizontal and vertical axes of visual space in terms of visual-angle separation or in terms of real-world distance? Third, when a particular location is attended to, what shape does the attentional "spotlight" take? Posner, Snyder, and Davidson (1980) and Hoffman and Nelson (1981) have shown that regions adjacent to attended locations can share some of the facilitation allocated to the attended location. However, we do not know whether the level of attentional facilitation for unattended locations declines as a function of their distance from the attended location, nor the shape of such a decline, nor whether such a decline is homoge-

---

[1]There is disagreement over the extent to which attentional effects in the detection of luminance increments reflect differences in the quality of the internal representation of the stimulus, differences in the amount of information about the visual world that the visual system loses, or differences in the amount of information about the stimulus the observer accumulates before deciding that the event has occurred (see Bashinski & Bacharach, 1980; Posner, 1978; Shaw, 1984; and Sperling, 1984). However, the questions addressed in this chapter, concerning the metrics according to which visual locations are selected, are largely independent of the question of exactly what is done with the selected information.

neous over the entire retina or changes shape depending on where attention is centered.

EXPERIMENT 1

In this experiment, we use a modification of the attention task used by Posner et al. (1980) in conjunction with a three-dimensional display in order to address the first two questions raised in the preceding paragraph.

Method

Subjects. Sixteen subjects participated in the experiment either for course credit or for pay. An additional subject was eliminated because he did not show simple attentional costs and benefits. All subjects were members of the Stanford University community, and had either normal or corrected-to-normal vision.

Apparatus. Each subject placed his or her chin and forehead in a restraint and with the left eye covered by an eyepatch, viewed a 102 cm × 91 cm rectangular platform lying horizontally on a table. Four small lights, .7 × 1.0 cm, were mounted on vertical stalks on the platform. There were eight possible positions for the lights, forming two parallel, curved rows of four positions each, one row behind the other. The near row was 101 cm from the subject; the far row was 171 cm. During each of the four sessions of the experiment, the subject saw four lights: Half of the subjects saw the lights at 10° left, 5° left, 5° right, and 6° right of fixation, and the other half saw them at 6° left, 5° left, 5° right, and 10° right. This yielded retinal separations of 1°, 5°, 10°, 11°, 15°, and 16° of visual angle between pairs of lights. Although the retinal position of the lights remained fixed across sessions, the lights' distance in depth along the subject's line of sight was varied from session to session. In the four configuration conditions that we used, the positions of the four lights (listed from left to right) in depth were as follows: (1) near, far, near, far; (2) far, near, near, far; (3) far, far, near, near; and (4) near, near, near, near. These particular configurations were chosen because they satisfied two constraints: that each pair of lights be seen equally often with the two lights at the same depth and with one of the lights at the near depth and one at the far depth; and that the positioning of the lights would not encourage subjects to favor one depth over the other, as might have been the case if three lights had been positioned at one depth and the fourth had been positioned at another.

A 1 × 2 cm LED chip that could display a digit was mounted on the center of the platform at a depth of 127 cm. The positions of the near lights, digit display, and far lights in depth were chosen so that the near and far lights were equally in focus when the digit display was fixated. The lights and the digit display were positioned vertically so that their projections would all lie along the same horizontal line when viewed by the subject. Because the lights fell outside Panum's area, binocular viewing would lead to double images, so subjects viewed the display monocularly. The platform was covered with wide-wale corduroy and illuminated with spotlights so that linear perspective and a texture gradient could serve as depth cues. The apparatus was controlled in real time by a microcomputer.

Procedure. On each trial, subjects fixed their eyes on the central chip, which displayed a digit from 0 to 4 indicating either that a certain light (1, 2, 3, or 4) would subsequently be illuminated with high probability, or that the illumination of any of the four lights was equiprobable (0). The subjects' task was to attend to the light indicated, or to none of the lights if they were equiprobable, without moving their eyes from the central chip, and then to press a response key whenever *any* of the four lights was lit. On most of the trials, the light to which subjects were attending was the light illuminated, but on a small percentage of the trials, one of the three unattended lights was illuminated instead.

Four blocks of 185 trials were run with each of the four configurations of the lights. Sessions using a given configuration lasted 1 hour; subjects were run in either 1- or 2-hour sessions. Within each block, 80% of the trials cued the subject to attend to one of the lights and 20% cued him or her not to attend to any particular light. A light was turned on following the cue on only 76% of the trials (the remaining trials were catch trials). When a light was turned on, 79% of the time it was the cued light, and 21% of the time it was one of the other three lights, each of the three occurring with equal likelihood. Thus, for each subject, there were 32 trials for each of the 12 combinations of retinal separation and depth separation between cue and stimulus. Each light was cued equally often, and catch trials were evenly distributed across cue types. Each subject received a different random ordering of the trials for each block of trials.

An "error" tone informed the subjects when they made either anticipatory responses or eye movements (discussed later), and the digit display flickered to reward quick responses (i.e., responses that were as fast or faster than the mean reaction times of trials in which the stimulus had occurred at the expected location and trials in which no expectancy had been set up). Trials on which errors were made were rerun at a randomly selected time later in the block.

Half the subjects wore skin electrodes that detected lateral eye movements in either direction of 5° or more. The order of configuration conditions, type of retinal projection (whether the 10° light was to the left or right of fixation), and monitoring of eye movements were counterbalanced across subjects.

Each trial began with a 1000 msec intertrial interval, followed by presentation of the cue on the central chip. The interval between the presentation of the cue and the illumination of a light varied randomly (according to a rectangular distribution) across trials, with cue lengths ranging from 400 to 800 msec in noncatch trials, and lasting a fixed length of time beyond that in catch trials. (For each subject, the additional fixed length of time on catch trials was equal to the subject's mean reaction time on the practice trials plus two standard deviations). A response or an eye movement ended both the display of the cue and the illumination of the light, and was followed by the feedback period, lasting 500 msec.

Subjects initiated each block of trials by pressing a separate "start" key. Within each block of trials the subject was given an opportunity to take a short break from the task after every tenth trial. Trials resumed after these breaks when the subject pressed the "start" key again. Otherwise, trials were initiated automatically.

Results and Discussion

Attentional costs were calculated as the amount of time that subjects required to detect a light in a particular position when they had been attending to some other location (the "unexpected" reaction time), minus the time required to detect that light when attention was not directed to any particular location (the "neutral" reaction time). These costs were computed separately for cue-stimulus pairs corresponding to different retinal separations and different separations in depth. Because retinal separations of 10° and 11° and those of 15° and 16° were so close, we averaged their costs, so that our analyses were of costs for separations of 1°, 5°, 10.5°, and 15.5°. Reaction times longer than 1000 msec or shorter than 100 msec were discarded.

By analyzing costs rather than detection times per se, we removed the component of the detection times attributable to perceptual properties of the stimulus, such as those related to the retinal eccentricity or distance in depth of the particular light illuminated. This assumes that effects of attentional activation and intrinsic properties of the stimulus are additive, an assumption that Posner's (1978) findings suggest is true, and that we examine later in this section and in Experiment 2.

We expected costs to increase as the retinal separation between cued and illuminated lights increased, reflecting the shape of the fall-off of attentional facilitation with increasing horizontal distance in the mental representation of space subserving visual attention. More importantly, we expected that if the structure or structures subserving attention represent depth, costs would be greater when the two lights were separated in depth than when they were at the same depth; conversely, if depth is not represented, costs would vary only with retinal separation, and not with separation in depth. Finally, by comparing the increase in costs with lateral distance between illuminated and attended lights at near and far positions in depth, we hoped to determine whether distance along the horizontal axis of visual space is represented in units of retinal or real-world distance.

Figure 8.1a shows that attentional costs increase according to a negatively accelerating function as the retinal separation between cued and illuminated lights increases. Furthermore, costs are greater when the lights are at different distances in depth than when they are at the same distance; this effect, however, is pronounced only at the two largest retinal separations. An analysis of variance shows that the effects of retinal separation—$F(3, 45) = 89.16, p < .001$—

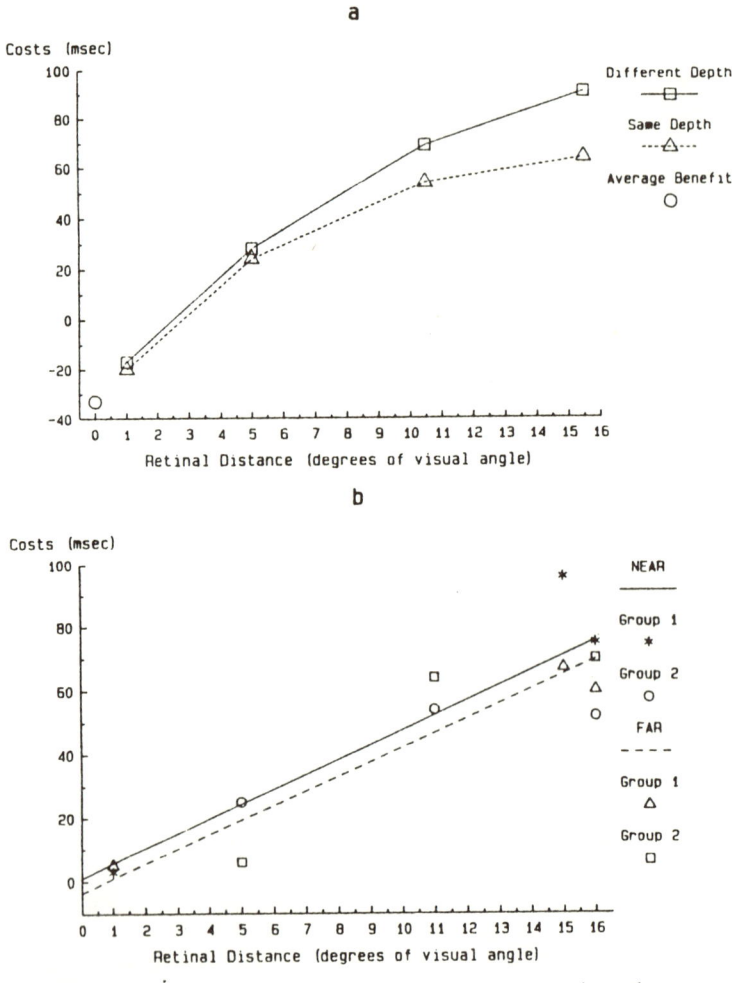

FIG. 8.1. (a) Attentional costs as a function of the retinal separation and separation in depth of the attended and illuminated lights. The average benefit is plotted as the cost for lights separated by 0°. (b) Same-depth costs as a function of the retinal separation and position in depth of the attended and illuminated lights. Group 1 and 2 saw the lights at different absolute retinal positions (see text for description of these two retinal configurations).

8. SPATIAL STRUCTURE OF ATTENTION 177

separation in depth—$F(1, 15) = 7.28, p < .05$—and the interaction of these two effects—$F(3, 45) = 3.22, p < .05$—are significant; a trend analysis shows significant linear and quadratic trends for retinal separation—$F(1, 15) = 132.86, p < .001$ and $F(1, 15) = 12.04, p < .01$, respectively—and a significant interaction between depth separation and the linear component of retinal separation—$F(1, 15) = 7.38, p < .05$. In addition, costs were significantly greater when the cued light was near and the illuminated light far (mean cost = 48 msec) than vice versa (mean cost = 37 msec)—$F(1, 15) = 6.89, p < .05$.

Figure 8.1b breaks the "same-depth" data from Fig. 8.1a into two parts, corresponding to whether the attended and illuminated lights were both near or both far.[2] With fewer data, the cost function is not as smooth, but there are no apparent differences between near–near and far–far costs. One way to assess possible differences statistically is to perform a trend analysis. When this is done, the linear component of the increase in attentional cost over visual angle is the same for near and far depths (for near depths: slope = 4.67 msec/deg, r = .88; for far depths: slope = 4.58 msec/deg, r = .94), as can be seen from the parallel regression lines plotted in Fig. 8.1b. The difference in slopes is not significant. Furthermore, there is no significant interaction between position in depth and the quadratic component of retinal separation. Thus, although we found that *separation* in depth had a significant effect on attentional costs, we found no effect of the *absolute position* in depth: Attentional costs increased at a greater rate for different-depth cue-stimulus pairs than for same-depth cue-stimulus pairs, but they increased at the same rate for all same-depth cue-stimulus pairs, regardless of whether the cued location and stimulus were both near or both far.

The results of this experiment suggest two conclusions. First, the representation of space underlying visual attention contains depth information.[3] Second, it appears that in this representation, the depth information is not used to convert the retinal metric of visual angle into a metric preserving size constancy.

There were no significant differences between the results with and without eye-movement equipment. Although costs were greater for subjects who saw the

---

[2]Note that not all of the same-depth data from Fig. 8.1a were used in this comparison, because same-depth retinal separations involving the position 5° to the right of fixation were always near. For this comparison, we had to include only same-depth retinal separations that appeared at both the near and far depths. Note also that before plotting Fig. 8.1b, we regressed the costs against visual angle separately for the two groups of subjects who viewed different configurations of lights, and subtracted the intercept for each group from each data point for that group, so as to equate for intergroup differences in gross overall costs. This subtraction does not affect our conclusions: The slopes for the near and far regression lines did not differ from one another either before or after equating group means. Tests of the interaction between the polynomial trends and position in depth were performed separately for the two groups.

[3]In an unpublished experiment with nine subjects we have replicated the finding that there are significantly greater costs when a stimulus appears at an unattended depth than when it appears at an attended depth.

most peripheral light in the left visual field than for those who saw it in the right visual field—$F(1, 14) = 5.30, p < .05$—this effect did not interact with any of the other effects in the study. The finding that costs are greater when peripheral stimuli are presented in the left visual field may be a reflection of hemispheric asymmetries in visual attention (see Heilman, 1979, p. 298), but because all subjects viewed the display with the right eye only, the difference could be attributable to temporal–nasal differences in attention instead.

One concern over the results we report is that they may in part reflect a nonadditive combination of attentional facilitation and differences in intrinsic detectability due to retinal eccentricity. This concern arises because the degree of retinal separation between cue-stimulus pairs was not completely orthogonal to the retinal position of the stimulus in this experiment. However, we can rule out the effects of such interactions in producing our results in several analyses.

First, in the condition in which attention was not directed to any particular location prior to the onset of the light, we found no significant differences in the detection times for lights at different eccentricities and distances in depth (all p's $> .10$). Second, when we examined the effect of depth separation separately for each of the four absolute retinal positions (10°, 5° on the side containing the light at 10°, 5° on the side containing the light at 6°, and 6°), collapsing across the two groups of subjects, we found: (a) greater costs for different-depth trials than for same-depth trials in all four cases (this difference was significant in three out of four cases—$p < .05$); (b) significantly greater costs for greater retinal separations in all four cases ($p < .05$); and (c) an interaction between retinal separation and depth similar to that found in the mean data in three cases (this was significant in two of those cases—$p < .05$). Third, we conducted an analysis using absolute retinal position (5°, 6°, or 10° eccentricity) and depth separation as factors (holding retinal separation between cued position and stimulus position constant at 15° or 16°), and found a significant effect of depth separation—$F(1, 14) = 10.44, p < .01$—but not an effect of absolute retinal position, nor an interaction between depth separation and retinal position (all p's $> .10$).

It is also worth noting that the overall interaction whereby depth separation affected costs for the large but not the small retinal separations (see Fig. 8.1a) cannot be attributed to differences in absolute eccentricity of the stimuli. For 5° and 15°/16° retinal separations there were both relatively central and relatively peripheral stimuli; for 1° and 10°/11° retinal separations there were only relatively central stimuli. Thus, the eccentricity of the stimulus does not predict whether or not a depth effect will be found; of the retinal separations involving relatively central stimuli, one showed a depth effect (10°/11°) and the other did not (1°), and of the retinal separations involving both relatively central and relatively peripheral stimuli, one showed a depth effect (15°/16°) and the other did not (5°).

Two other alternative explanations for the depth selectivity that we have found arise from the possibility that when a subject attends to a particular depth in response to the digit cue, he or she also accomodates the lens of the eye to that depth. However, these explanations can be shown to be highly unlikely.

One of these explanations is that when the stimulus is presented at a depth other than the attended/accommodated depth, subjects reaccommodate to the depth of the stimulus, and that the reaccommodation process interferes with the response process, thereby slowing responses to stimuli at the unattended depth. This alternative is unlikely because we found significant depth effects for stimuli too peripheral to elicit accommodative responses. In particular, we found a significant depth effect for cue-stimulus pairs separated by 15° and 16° when the stimulus was presented at 10° eccentricity—$F(1, 7) = 6.09$, $p < .05$—even though no accommodative response occurs to stimuli at 10° in situations, such as our experiment, in which the only accommodative stimulus is blur (see Ciuffreda & Kenyon, 1983, pp. 112–114).

The second alternative explanation is that responses to stimuli at the unattended depth are slower because subjects accommodate to the attended depth, thereby making stimuli at the unattended depth more blurred than those at the attended/accommodated depth. Because blurring can decrease contrast, the greater costs at unattended depths could be attributed to slower detection of low-contrast or poorly resolved stimuli. This possibility was ruled out by a control experiment in which we told people to accommodate to a particular depth (either 101 cm or 171 cm away) and then to detect stimuli either at the same depth or at a different depth; no attentional instructions were involved. We found that the blur produced at the unaccommodated depth had no effect on reaction times (mean for same depth = 331 msec, mean for different depth = 333 msec, $F(1,7) = 1.29$, $p > .10$). Thus, it appears that even if subjects did accommodate the lens of the eye to the depth where they expected a light to occur in Experiment 1, the blur that this produced at the unaccommodated depth would not have been sufficient to account for the depth effect that we found. Presumably, this is because the poor resolution in peripheral regions of the retina makes the increase in sharpness of the retinal image brought about by accommodation negligible.

EXPERIMENT 2

In Experiment 1, we assumed that the retinal position of a stimulus would not have any effect on the magnitude of attentional costs or benefits for that stimulus (see Posner, 1978). Although the analyses we performed on the data from Experiment 1 did confirm this assumption, we wanted to test it more explicitly. In particular, we wanted to determine whether the two-dimensional gradient of visual attention is identical regardless of the retinal position where it is centered; in other words, whether the visual field is homogeneous with respect to attentional selection of information by location.

There are several ways this null hypothesis of visual field homogeneity could be false. Costs and benefits could be multiplicative with differences in intrinsic detectability arising from eccentricity. In addition, overall costs and benefits could change depending on where on the retina the gradient is centered: Some parts of the retina might be intrinsically more "attendable" than others. Changes in resolution with retinal eccentricity (arising from the change in receptive field size and the related change in cortical magnification with eccentricity) could also make the gradient appear more or less sharply peaked depending on whether it lay in highly resolved or poorly resolved regions. Finally, the gradient of attention could be defined smoothly over both visual fields, or it could have different properties in the visual field where attention is focused and in the opposite field.

The only data we know of relevant to these issues come from three standard cost-benefit attention experiments conducted by Posner and his colleagues (see Posner, 1978, pp. 198–202). In these experiments, the researchers manipulated the eccentricity of two possible stimulus locations, and found that costs and benefits were the same whether stimuli were at 0.5°, 6.9°, or 25° from fixation. The similarity of costs and benefits for foveal and peripheral stimuli allowed them to conclude that (Posner, 1978) "costs and benefits from a voluntary shift of visual attention are the same, regardless of the eccentricity of the events" [p. 202].

In this experiment, we address this issue in more detail by comparing costs and benefits for various retinal separations across a wide range of positions of the cued location and stimulus. The method is similar to that of Experiment 1, except that our display was two-dimensional rather than three-dimensional (i.e., all stimulus locations were at the same depth), and contained 10 equally spaced stimulus locations rather than four unequally spaced locations.

Method

Subjects. Twelve Stanford University students participated in this experiment for either course credit or pay. As in the previous experiment, all subjects had either normal or corrected-to-normal vision. An additional four subjects did not complete the experiment because of problems in calibrating the eye-movement equipment or in the subjects' ability to follow the task instructions.

Apparatus. Subjects viewed a CRT monitor screen that measured approximately 37 cm horizontally. We again used a chin rest with a forehead restraint to position subjects' heads properly, and an eyepatch to cover each subject's left eye. Subjects fixated a cue location at the center of the screen that was positioned directly in front of the right eye. Ten unfilled boxes measuring about 1° × 1° were displayed in a horizontal row on the screen, located at 1.25°, 3.75°, 6.25°, 8.75°, and 11.25° from fixation in both directions. Each box was thus 2.5° from its neighbor. Above each box, a number from 1 to 10 was displayed, corresponding to the position of the box along the horizontal axis; the leftmost box was labeled "1" and the rightmost box "10." This display was present at all times during the experiment. As before, a microcomputer controlled the experiment.

8. SPATIAL STRUCTURE OF ATTENTION 181

Procedure. The procedure for this experiment was similar to that for Experiment 1. Subjects maintained eye fixation on the central cue location, where they saw a digit from 0 to 10 that indicated to which box, if any, they should attend. Their task was simply to press a response key as quickly as possible, without making an eye movement or an anticipation, whenever any one of the boxes was filled in.

Subjects participated in four experimental sessions of 1 to 1½ hours each. In each session, there were two blocks of 440 trials. In 86% of the trials in each block, the subject was cued to attend to one of the 10 boxes; in the remaining 14% the subject was cued to attend to none of the boxes. A stimulus was actually presented following the cue on 82% of the trials. The remaining trials were catch trials. The stimulus was presented in the attended box on approximately 71% of the noncatch trials, and was presented in one of the other nine boxes on the remainder of the noncatch trials. Each of the 90 possible cue-stimulus mismatches occurred only once in each block of trials. Over the course of the experiment, however, each mismatched cue-stimulus pair occurred eight times for each subject.

We monitored eye movements of 3.75° or more on two of the four experimental sessions for each subject. Each of the 12 subjects was randomly assigned to one of the six possible combinations of two sessions with eye-movement equipment and two sessions without. Eye movements and anticipations were handled just as in Experiment 1: Error feedback was given and the trial was rerun at a randomly selected time later in the block. If the subject's reaction time was as fast as or faster than the mean reaction time for the previous 40 trials in which the stimulus had occurred in the attended box, the subject was presented with a flickering asterisk at the center cue location.

The sequence of events within a trial was identical to that in Experiment 1, with the exception that the cue interval ranged from 600 to 1000 msec on noncatch trials, and lasted a fixed 1000 msec beyond that on catch trials. Subjects were paid 50 cents for each block on which they had "attended closely," and were informed after each block whether they had earned the bonus. The criterion for earning a bonus, which was not revealed to the subjects, was that both the mean cost and the mean benefit for the block be 5 msec or greater.

Results and Discussion

We calculated the attentional costs for all trials in which the subject had been attending to one location and the stimulus had occurred at another, as well as the benefits for all trials in which the stimulus had occurred at the attended location.[4]

---

[4]As in Experiment 1, there were practically no effects of absolute stimulus position on the detection times for the neutral trials (the slowest mean detection time was only 14 msec slower than the fastest). This makes the additivity issue nearly moot in interpreting attentional effects in this experiment.

Before calculating costs and benefits, we removed all reaction times that were at least two standard deviations above or below each subject's mean reaction time for that particular cue and stimulus combination.

The mean costs and benefits are presented in Fig. 8.2, in which stimulus position is shown along the abscissa and cued position is the parameter distinguishing the curves. One way of interpreting the graph is to think of each curve as an approximation to the shape of the attentional gradient when it is centered on different retinal locations.

As in Experiment 1, attentional facilitation falls off (i.e., costs increase) with increasing distance from the cued location. However, the shape of this fall-off is not homogeneous across the retina. The gradient is most sharply peaked, with a steeper slope, when it is centered on a cued position near the fovea than when it is centered on one of the next three positions moving toward the periphery; however, it is again more sharply peaked at the most peripheral position on each side. The benefit for expected locations (i.e., the negative peak of the gradient) changes in a similar way, with greatest benefits at the most foveal and the most peripheral cued locations. The gradient becomes very steep as it passes over near-foveal locations, regardless of where it is centered. All the gradients flatten

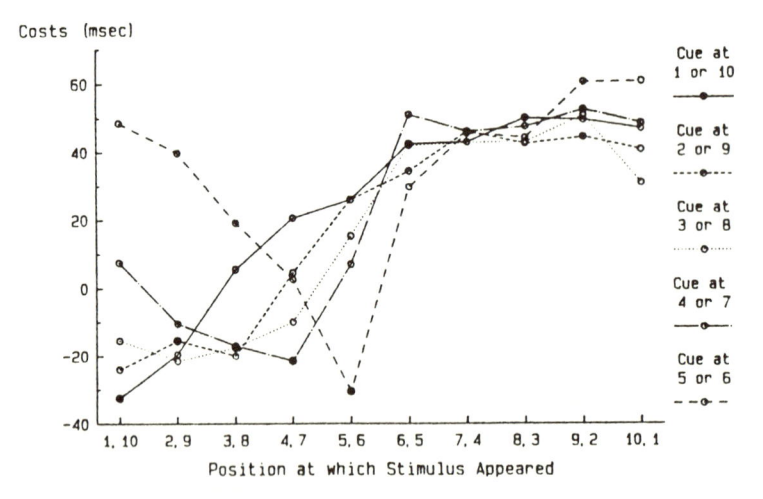

FIG. 8.2. Costs and benefits from Experiment 2. Stimulus position is shown along the abscissa and cued position is the parameter distinguishing the curves. Costs and benefits from cue-stimulus pairs in corresponding positions on either side of the midline were averaged before these data were plotted; thus, the abscissa does not represent stimulus position in left to right order but in an order from the most peripheral stimuli on the same side as the cued location (1 and 10) to the most peripheral stimuli on the side opposite to the cued location (10 and 1). The point on each curve corresponding to the benefit for the cued location is filled in (costs and benefits are plotted on the same scale).

out at a constant cost level at stimulus locations across the midline from the cued location.

We conducted two tests of the null hypothesis that the gradient is identical regardless of where it is centered: one for benefits, one for costs. Although there are benefits for stimuli at all cued locations, the amount varies significantly across different locations—$F(9, 99) = 3.60$, $p < .001$. To test the effect of retinal position on the overall costs and on the increase in costs with increasing cue-stimulus separation, we examined data from trials with separations of 12.5° or less; only within this range were the two factors of retinal separation and stimulus position orthogonal. A repeated-measures analysis of variance with factors for retinal separation (2.5°, 5°, 7.5°, 10°, and 12.5°), stimulus eccentricity (1.25°, 3.75°, 6.25°, 8.75°, or 11.25° from fixation), and stimulus field (left visual field or right visual field) showed that costs increased with increasing retinal separation—$F(4, 44) = 58.51$, $p < .0001$. This increase included a significant linear trend—$F(1, 11) = 99.39$, $p < .0001$—and a significant quadratic trend—$F(1, 11) = 14.54$, $p < .005$—but no significant higher-order trends. There was also a significant effect of stimulus eccentricity—$F(4, 44) = 2.65$, $p < .05$—and a significant interaction between stimulus eccentricity and retinal separation—$F(16, 176) = 9.13$, $p < .0001$. Thus, contrary to the null-hypothesis assumption, costs for a given retinal separation appear to depend on the retinal eccentricity of the stimulus. Costs are greater on the whole for stimuli closer to the fovea, and this effect is found mainly with smaller retinal separations (2.5°, 5°, and 7.5°). The main effect of stimulus position and its interaction with retinal separation remain significant even when the linear and quadratic components of cued location are partialled out—$F(4, 44) = 7.96$, $p < .0001$ and $F(16, 176) = 2.67$, $p < .001$, respectively.

A large part of the interaction in Fig. 8.2 may be accounted for with a single assumption: that the shape of the gradient is invariant, but that the distance metric it is defined over is not invariant across the visual field. The gradient could be defined over visual-angle units scaled by receptive field size, or, equivalently, it could be defined over the cortical representation of the visual input, where a given range of visual angle maps onto a greater extent of cortex the closer it is to the fovea. This would result in attention falling off more rapidly for retinal regions where resolution is fine than for regions where it is coarse.[5] This, in turn, could account both for the asymmetry in each of the gradients in Fig. 8.2 and for their increasing bluntness from the fovea to the periphery. It could also account for the flattening of the gradients as they cross the midline: In crossing the midline the gradient would pass through the densest region of the retina, and so the portion lying in the contralateral visual field would tend to be the

---

[5]Because all the boxes on the screen were clearly resolvable, this effect is not reducible to subjects' being unable to discriminate differences among stimulus positions in eccentric regions due to the physiological resolution of the retina.

asymptotic tail. In this simple model, there would be no factor specific to stimulus position on the retina per se, and no factor specific to crossing versus not crossing the midline.

To test this possibility, we ran several hierarchical regression analyses (see Cohen & Cohen, 1975) on the costs and benefits. A model with the linear and quadratic components of retinal separation (a crude approximation to the assumed shape of the moveable gradient), stimulus eccentricity, and the interactions of the linear and quadratic components of retinal separation with stimulus eccentricity accounted for 76.6% of the variance among the 100 means that went into Fig. 8.2. All of these regressors, except the interaction between stimulus position and the quadratic component of retinal separation, accounted for significantly more of the variance when included in the regression than when excluded, and accounted for enough additional variance to justify inclusion in the model according to the criteria suggested by Cohen and Cohen (1975). However, a simpler model, including *only* the linear and quadratic effects of retinal separation, but expressing retinal separation in terms of millimeters of cortex according to the magnification formula of Rovamo and Virsu (1979), accounts for more variance (86.4%) with three fewer free parameters. Adding the following regressors did not increase the amount of variance accounted for by an amount that would justify their inclusion in the model (see Cohen & Cohen, 1975): stimulus eccentricity; cue eccentricity; the interactions of these effects with the trend components of cortically magnified retinal separation; a variable representing whether the stimulus projected to the same hemisphere as the cued location or to the opposite hemisphere; or the interaction of this variable with scaled retinal separation. Thus, much of the interaction in Fig. 8.2 appears to be explicable in terms of the simple assumption that attention makes sharper distinctions for retinal regions with finer resolution.

In addition to effects of retinal resolution or cortical magnification, our data may show an endpoint anchoring effect. Benefits are greater and the gradient is steeper for cued locations at both ends of the series of possible stimulus locations and for locations adjacent to the fixation point. Hierarchical regression analyses testing the contribution of a variable representing the proximity of the cued location to these "landmarks" (and its interactions) revealed that this effect was significant and larger than that of the other additional regressors we had tested, although not large enough to justify inclusion in the model (see Cohen & Cohen, 1975).

It is not completely clear why we observed effects of stimulus position and Posner (1978) did not. Our data would lead one to predict that costs would be smaller for the retinal separation of 1° than for the retinal separation of 50°, even though the cued and stimulus positions were more central for the small separation. Perhaps a key difference is that in Posner's experiments, subjects in any one experiment had to detect stimuli at one of two positions, whereas in ours, 10 positions were possible. Posner's subjects may have narrowed their gradients to a very thin peak at the cued location, such that noncued positions would all fall on the tail of the gradient. Another possibility stems from the fact that the possible stimulus locations in Posner's experiments were on either side of the midline. Costs in Experiment 2 appeared to asymptote for all positions across the midline from the attended locus (see Fig. 8.2). Although our analyses did not discern a contribution of this midline-crossing factor beyond the contribution of scaled retinal separation, this question deserves further investigation.

GENERAL DISCUSSION

The results reported in this chapter suggest that the mental representation underlying visual attention has as its dimensions a visual-angle scale (presumably, both horizontal and vertical), distorted by something similar to cortical magnification or change in receptive field size, and a scale representing distance in depth. Such a representation of space is similar to the *2½-D sketch* or depth map proposed by researchers in computer vision as an intermediate stage of visual representation in the shape-recognition process (Marr, 1982; Marr and Nishihara, 1978). According to Marr, the 2½-D sketch is the first representation of the visual world from which cognitive processes can read information (see also Pinker, 1984); its dimensions are visual angle and depth, and its resolution is nonhomogeneous and proportional to the resolution of the corresponding areas of the retina. Though we would not claim that visual attention selects information directly from the 2½-D sketch, our results do suggest that the representation underlying attentional selection is organized similarly to the 2½-D sketch.

Our findings also bear out Ullman's (1984) conjecture that the "visual routine" corresponding to shifting the locus of visual processing should be applicable to specific three-dimensional regions of the visual world and not just to retinally defined regions.

In addition to suggesting the dimensions of the space represented in the areas in which visual attention exerts its effects, these data suggest what the shape of the gradient operating on these areas might be, on the assumption that attentional costs are linearly related to the amount of activation defined by the gradient.[6] Specifically, attention falls off with retinal separation according to a gradient that decreases with a negative acceleration and that can appear sharply peaked (as in Experiment 1) or relatively blunt (as for the middle locations of Experiment 2). These differences in bluntness appear to depend on the eccentricity of the attended location, and possibly on its proximity to a perceptual landmark and on the number of potential targets as well. For small retinal distances from the

---

[6]Of course, it is difficult to discriminate experimentally between a gradient of simultaneous attention applied in parallel over the entire visual field and a probability distribution governing where a circumscribed attentional "peephole" is centered.

attended locus, the height of the central peak and its immediately surrounding region changes relatively little with increasing depth from the attended region. However, at retinal distances greater than 5°, the gradient falls off more steeply with increasing depth from the attended locus. Furthermore, the fall-off of attentional activation with separation in depth may be asymmetric along the depth dimension, being steeper on the far side of the plane of maximum activation than on its near side.

Although the gradient model we have proposed seems the simplest way to explain our data, other models could be devised by trading off properties of the representation subserving attention and the shape of the gradient defined over that representation, by positing the involvement of multiple representations instead of a single one, or by assuming a nonlinear relation between measured costs and the underlying gradient of attention. For example, one might account for the data in Fig. 8.1a by positing separate structures representing two-dimensional space and depth, each with a different gradient of attention, and a nonlinear combination function that determines the detectability of an event as a joint function of its activation in the two structures. However, our data do strongly suggest that visual attention is sensitive to depth, visual angle, and retinal or cortical resolution, and these are findings that any model of visual attention must account for.

ACKNOWLEDGMENTS

This research was supported by National Science Foundation grants BNS81–14916 and 82–16546 and NIH grant RO1 HD 18381 to the second author and by the MIT Center for Cognitive Science under a grant from the Sloan Foundation, and was conducted during the first author's tenure as an NSF fellow. Portions were presented at the meeting of the Psychonomic Society in 1982. We wish to thank Larry Maloney, Misha Pavel, Molly Potter, Whitman Richards, Roger Shepard, Ewart Thomas, Barbara Tversky, Brian Wandell, and Jeremy Wolfe for helpful comments on earlier versions of this manuscript, and Roger Shepard for use of his laboratory facilities for Experiment 2.

REFERENCES

Bashinski, H. S., & Bacharach, V. R. (1980). Enhancement of perceptual sensitivity as the result of selectively attending to spatial locations. *Perception and Psychophysics, 28,* 241–280.

Ciuffreda, K. J., & Kenyon, R. V. (1983). Interactions between accommodation and vergence. In C. M. Schor & K. J. Ciuffreda (Eds.), *Vergence eye movements* (pp. 99–174). Woburn, MA: Butterworth.

Cohen, J., & Cohen, P. (1975). *Applied multiple regression/correlation analysis for the behavioral sciences.* Hillsdale, NJ: Lawrence Erlbaum Associates.

Cowey, A. (1982). Sensory and non-sensory visual disorders in man and monkey. *Philosophical Transactions of the Royal Society of London, B298,* 3–13.

Eriksen, C. W., & Hoffman, J. E. (1972). Some characteristics of selective attention in visual perception determined by vocal reaction time. *Perception and Psychophysics, 11,* 169–171.

Heilman, K. M. (1979). Neglect and related disorders. In K. M. Heilman & E. Valenstein (Eds.), *Clinical neuropsychology* (pp. 268–307). New York: Oxford University.

Hoffman, J. E., & Nelson, B. (1981). Spatial selectivity in visual search. *Perception and Psychophysics, 30,* 283–290.

Marr, D. (1982). *Vision.* San Francisco: W. H. Freeman.

Marr, D., & Nishihara, H. K. (1978). Representation and recognition of the spatial organization of three-dimensional shapes. *Proceedings of the Royal Society, 200,* 269–294.

Pinker, S. (1984). Visual cognition: An introduction. *Cognition, 18,* 1–63.

Posner, M. I. (1978). *Chronometric explorations of mind.* Hillsdale, NJ: Lawrence Erlbaum Associates.

Posner, M. I. (1980). Orienting of attention. *Quarterly Journal of Experimental Psychology, 32,* 3–25.

Posner, M. I., Snyder, C. R. R., & Davidson, B. J. (1980). Attention and the detection of signals. *Journal of Experimental Psychology: General, 109,* 160–174.

Remington, R. W. (1980). Attention and saccadic eye movements. *Journal of Experimental Psychology: Human Perception and Performance, 6,* 726–744.

Rovamo, J., & Virsu, V. (1979). An estimation and application of the human cortical magnification factor. *Experimental Brain Research, 37,* 495–510.

Shaw, M. L. (1984). Division of attention among spatial locations: A fundamental difference between detection of letters and detection of luminance increments. In H. Bouma & D. G. Bouwhuis (Eds.), *Attention and performance X* (pp. 109–120). Hillsdale, NJ: Lawrence Erlbaum Associates.

Sperling, G. (1960). Information available in brief visual presentation. *Psychological Monographs, 74*(11, whole number 498).

Sperling, G. (1984). A unified theory of attention and signal detection. In R. Parasuraman & D. R. Davies (Eds.), *Varieties of attention* (pp. 103–181). New York: Academic.

Sperling, G., & Reeves, A. (1980). Measuring the reaction time of a shift of visual attention. In R. W. Nickerson (Ed.), *Attention and performance VIII* (pp. 347–360). Hillsdale, NJ: Lawrence Erlbaum Associates.

Ullman, S. (1984). Visual routines. *Cognition, 18,* 96–159.

Wurtz, R. H., Goldberg, M. E., & Robinson, D. L. (1982). Brain mechanisms of visual attention. *Scientific American, 246,* 124–135.

9 Facilitatory and Inhibitory Components of Orienting in Visual Space

Elizabeth Ann Maylor
University of Nottingham, England

ABSTRACT

Posner and Cohen (1980) demonstrated that a brief noninformative visual cue presented in the periphery speeds the simple detection response to a target if it appears within 100 msec of the cue and in the same location, compared to a target in a different location. This *facilitation* was attributed to externally controlled covert orienting, that is, the alignment of attention with a location in visual space as the result of an external stimulus event. However, if the target appears more than 300 msec after the cue, the response is slower to a target in the same location (*inhibition*). Experiments designed to investigate further both the facilitatory and inhibitory components of visual orienting are reported in this chapter. In addition to the facilitation of both simple and choice manual responses, a target from the same location in the periphery as the cue appears to occur earlier than one from a different location, for intervals between the cue and the target of up to 500 msec. Although temporal judgments are unaffected at longer cue–target intervals, both manual and ocular responses are slower to a target appearing between 300 and 1300 msec after a cue in the periphery and in the same location than to one appearing elsewhere. It is argued here that externally controlled orienting is a necessary condition to produce inhibition. However, not every event in the visual periphery results automatically in externally controlled covert orienting. Indeed, such orienting can be reduced or even prevented by additional information present in the visual field, or by the requirements of secondary tasks. The facilitatory and inhibitory components of externally controlled orienting appear to act together to direct the eye-movement system and to maintain selectivity in visual space.

INTRODUCTION

Visual orienting has been described as the aligning of peripheral or central mechanisms with a source of sensory input (Posner, 1980). Overt orienting refers to a change in the alignment of sensory receptors (that is, eye and head movements), whereas covert orienting refers to a change in the alignment of the central processing system. A further distinction has been drawn between internally and externally controlled orienting. For example, eye movements can result from an internal search plan or be driven by an external stimulus event (Kahneman, 1973).

The consequences of internally controlled covert orienting have recently been well documented (Bashinski & Bacharach, 1980; Posner, Nissen, & Ogden, 1978; Posner, Snyder, & Davidson, 1980). The first experiments on externally controlled covert orienting, conducted by Jonides (1976), demonstrated that a peripheral stimulus can "involuntarily capture" a subject's attention. Target presentation was preceded by a cue that was a brief visual stimulus that could occur to the left or right of a central fixation point. Simple reaction time was faster when the target occurred on the same side of the visual field as the cue than when it appeared on the opposite side. Further work by Jonides (1981) attempted to compare internally and externally controlled covert orienting. Subjects were induced to shift their attention (but not their eyes) through the use of two types of visual cue, both indicating the possible stimulus locations in the visual field. Thus, either an arrow pointing to the left (presented at fixation) or a brief stimulus in the left visual field were used to inform the subject that a target stimulus could occur to the left of fixation. The arrow represents *symbolic* cueing, as the subject must interpret the cue in order to know the cued location. The second type of cue provides a more *direct* indication of stimulus location without requiring the subject to know and act upon the meaning of arbitrary symbols such as arrows. Direct cueing was shown to produce shifts of attention that were more consistent with a number of criteria for automaticity than shifts produced by symbolic cueing.

An important issue concerning externally controlled orienting is the question of *automaticity*. Several investigators (for example, Posner & Snyder, 1975; Schneider & Shiffrin, 1977) have distinguished between processes that are under conscious or strategic control and those that are automatic. Remington (1980) concluded that relevant stimuli in the peripheral visual field trigger both a saccade and a shift of attention, and that "to some degree" the attentional movement automatically follows the presentation of a significant peripheral stimulus. Considering also the evidence from the work of Jonides (1976, 1981), it does appear that externally controlled orienting occurs automatically.

A second major issue concerns the *consequences* of externally controlled orienting. Posner and Cohen (1980, 1984) demonstrated that a brief peripheral cue speeds the simple detection response to a target if it appears within 100 msec of the cue and in the same location, compared to a target in a different location. This effect was termed *facilitation*. However, the early advantage to the cued location is replaced by a subsequent *inhibition*, the slowing of the response to a target in the same location. Because facilitation occurs in response to symbolic as well as direct cues, Posner and Cohen regarded it as attentional and the result of orienting to a visual location. The inhibitory effect, however, seems to depend on the presentation of sensory information in the periphery, because it does not occur when attention is directed by a symbolic cue presented to fixation.

The experiments to be described were designed to investigate further the facilitatory and inhibitory components of externally controlled orienting by addressing the two issues just outlined. First, an experiment based on Posner and Cohen's (1980) original study is presented. This is extended to compare the effects of brief noninformative direct cueing on simple and choice manual reaction time and saccade latency. Experiment 2 is a divided attention study in which the effects of a demanding secondary task on externally controlled orienting are assessed in order to investigate the attentional nature of the facilitatory component. Finally, a double-cueing paradigm and a nonspeeded response are employed in Experiments 3 and 4, respectively, to explore the relationship between facilitation and inhibition.

EXPERIMENT 1

A replication of Posner and Cohen's general result from a simple manual reaction time task was considered important for two reasons: first, to demonstrate the reliability of the effects, and second, to provide baseline data for comparison with Experiments 2 to 4. In addition, the procedure was adapted to investigate manual and ocular choice responses to peripheral stimuli. In view of the work of Remington (1980), which demonstrated that overt and covert orienting are most closely coupled in response to an important event in the visual periphery, similar results were expected in the three cases.

Subjects. The subjects in Experiments 1 to 4, all unpaid volunteers, were undergraduates, postgraduates, and staff at the University of Durham (including the author). All reported normal or corrected-to-normal vision. Fourteen, six, and six subjects participated in Experiments 1a, 1b, and 1c, respectively.

Method

Experiment 1a: Simple Manual Reaction Time. The stimuli for this experiment, which was entirely computer controlled, were displayed on an oscilloscope. Three boxes were presented on the screen, one on the left, one in the center, and one on the right. Each box measured $1.2° \times 1.2°$ visual angle, and the distance between the central box and the peripheral boxes was 4.2°. Each subject was required to keep his or her eyes on a fixation point inside the central box throughout the experiment. A trial began with the cueing (that is, the brightening) of one of the peripheral boxes for 100 msec (the "cue"). This was followed after another 100 msec by a similar brightening of the central box. (Posner and Cohen [1980] included this in order to "summon attention back to the center" [p. 4]. In fact, identical results are obtained without this central cueing; see Maylor, 1983.) The target, a small stimulus appearing well above threshold inside one of the peripheral boxes, could occur at three different times following the onset of the cue: 100, 300, or 500 msec stimulus onset asynchrony (SOA). This disappeared when a detection response of a single key press had been made. The interval between the offset of the target and the onset of the next trial was randomly chosen from the range 200 to 700 msec. Trials when a response was made before or during the first 100 msec of target presentation were recorded as anticipation errors and were deleted from the analysis. The trials were divided so that there were equal numbers of each left–right/cue–target combination. The order of presentation of trials was randomized. In this way, the cue was noninformative because a cue on the left was equally likely to be followed by a target on the left as by one on the right.

Experiment 1b: Saccade Latency. Each subject was required to fixate on the central fixation point only until a target appeared in one of the peripheral boxes. A saccade then had to be made as quickly and as accurately as possible to the target that remained on the screen for between 500 and 900 msec. Following the offset of the target, the subject returned to the central fixation point in preparation for the next trial. Horizontal eye movements were recorded by a bifurcated fiber optic device (Findlay, 1974).

Experiment 1c: Choice Manual Reaction Time. The subject was required to fixate on the central fixation point throughout the experiment but, unlike the requirements for experiment 1a, he or she was asked to press a button under the left forefinger when a target occurred inside the left box, and a button under the right forefinger when a target occurred inside the right box.

Results

Experiment 1a. Subjects reported that they were unaware of the cueing procedure although they did notice that the three boxes, particularly the central one, tended to flicker throughout the experiment. The means of the median reaction times from each subject are presented in Fig. 9.1a. The term *valid* refers to a target following a cue in the same location, whereas *invalid* refers to a target appearing in the opposite location to the cue. The results are very similar in form to those of Posner and Cohen (1980). An ANOVA revealed a highly significant effect of SOA—$F(2,26) = 23.01$, $p < .0001$—but not of invalid–valid trial

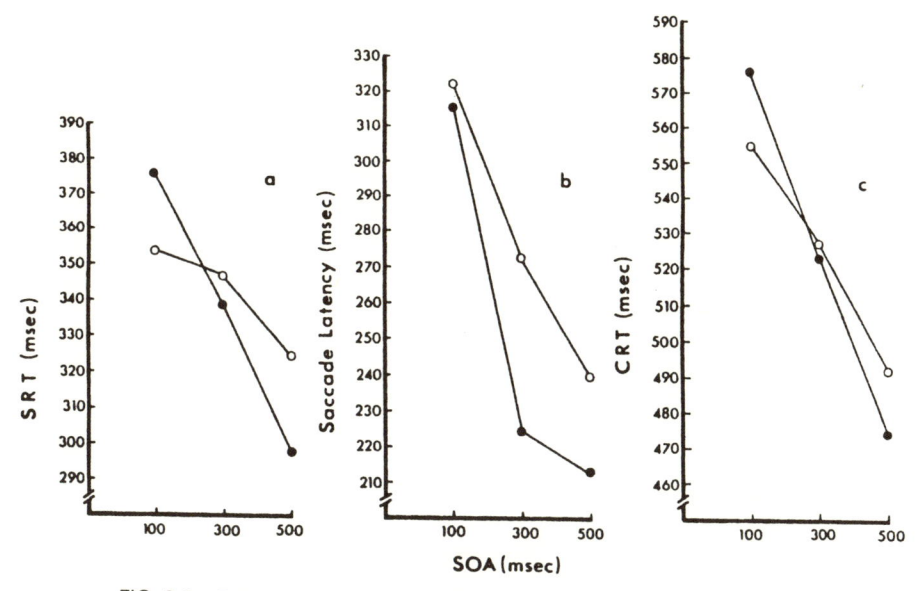

FIG. 9.1. Results of Experiment 1. Simple manual reaction time (a), saccade latency (b), and choice manual reaction time (c) as a function of SOA for valid (unfilled circles) and invalid (filled circles) trials.

type—$F(1,13) = 1.40, p > .1$. The interaction between SOA and trial type was highly significant—$F(2,26) = 63.70, p < .00001$. Thus, at the SOA of 100 msec, there is what Posner has referred to as facilitation, such that valid trials are responded to more rapidly than invalid trials. However, at the longer SOAs valid trials are actually slower, demonstrating the second effect, that of inhibition.

Experiment 1b. The median saccade latencies were analyzed with target location (left and right), SOA, and trial type as fixed-effects factors. This revealed that there was no significant effect of target location—$F(1,5) = 1.39, p > .1$—and that it did not interact with any other factor. The means of the left and right targets for the six subjects are presented in Fig. 9.1b. Again, there was a highly significant effect of SOA—$F(2,10) = 37.27, p < .001$—but also of trial type—$F(1,5) = 13.15, p < .05$. The interaction between SOA and trial type was significant—$F(2,10) = 4.81, p < .05$. Thus, the pattern for saccade latency is rather different from that for simple manual reaction time. No facilitatory component is present at an SOA of 100 msec and there is increased inhibition at 300 msec.

Experiment 1c. Experiments 1a and 1b differ in two fundamental ways and it is possible that the different results could be due to either or both of the following factors: The first is the *mode* of response (manual or ocular) and the second is the *type* of response (simple or choice). The results of the choice manual reaction time task shown in Fig. 9.1c demonstrate that the results from Experiment 1b are due to the requirement to *saccade* to the target rather than to the introduction of the *choice* decision. Again, the median reaction times were analyzed with target location (left and right), SOA, and trial type as fixed-effects factors. There were no overall effects of target location—$F(1,5) = 1.43$, $p > .1$—and trial type—$F(1,5) = .00$, $p > 0.1$—but there was a significant effect of SOA—$F(2,10) = 17.39$, $p < .001$—and an interaction between SOA and trial type—$F(2,10) = 2.26$, $p < .02$.

Discussion

Experiment 1 has demonstrated the effects of brief noninformative direct cueing on simple and choice manual reaction time and saccade latency to subsequent targets. For manual responses, detection of targets from a cued location is faster than from an uncued location 100 msec following the onset of the cue. This facilitation is interpreted as being due to externally controlled covert orienting—that is, the aligning of attention (but not the eyes) with the cued location. For SOAs of 300 and 500 msec, facilitation is replaced by inhibition such that detection of targets from the cued location is now slower than from the uncued location. The pattern for saccade latency is different in that the facilitatory component is absent (or at least not present at the three SOAs used) and inhibition is increased at 300 msec. Because the early anticipations made (a total of 18) were saccades in the direction of the cue, the lack of facilitation possibly reflects the need to suppress the relatively automatic eye-movement response to the peripheral cue, which then delays the saccade to a subsequent target at the same location. The similarity between the choice and simple manual reaction time results and the fact that anticipations were rarely made in the choice reaction time experiment support the view that the saccade latency result is due to the similarity at some level in the eye-movement generation system between the effect of the cue and the response required, rather than to the introduction of the element of choice.

EXPERIMENT 2

Posner and Cohen (1984) concluded that the facilitatory component is attentional. A direct cue in the periphery initially summons attention so that targets appearing in that location have an advantage (in terms of reaction time) over those in uncued locations. They noted that the inhibitory component occurs "without the need for any deliberate strategy on the part of the subject" [p. 537] and regarded it as sensory rather than attentional in origin. Their conclusion was that "some part of the pathway from the cued location is reduced in efficiency by the cueing" [p. 537], and that inhibition is the inevitable consequence of the presentation of any visual stimulus in the periphery. On the basis of this model

Posner, Cohen, Choate, Hockey, and Maylor (1984) predicted that the addition of a demanding secondary task would disrupt the facilitatory (attentional) component but would not affect the inhibitory (sensory) component of externally controlled orienting. In Experiment 2 subjects were required to carry out one of four secondary tasks in addition to the primary task of target detection. These involved predictable and unpredictable pursuit eye tracking of a slowly moving spot inside the central box. In the predictable conditions, the spot moved smoothly throughout the experiment. In the unpredictable conditions, at the moment when the peripheral box brightened, the fixation spot jumped to a different position within the central box and the subject was required to follow the movement with a small saccade. If overt orienting is required to the central fixation spot at the same time as a direct cue is presented in the periphery, this may affect facilitation because the orienting system will be dominated by the fixation requirements. If this is the case, it is important to know whether or not inhibition is also affected in order to test the model of Posner and Cohen described previously.

Subjects. Forty subjects were divided equally between the four conditions of this experiment.

Method

The primary task was as described for Experiment 1a. There were four secondary tasks in which each subject was required to track the movements of the fixation spot inside the central box. In the two smooth-pursuit conditions the spot moved sinusoidally either horizontally (H) or vertically (V) within the central box at a rate of approximately .5 Hz. For the remaining two conditions the spot moved in one dimension (horizontal or vertical) until the presentation of the direct cue in the periphery. It then jumped to moving in the other dimension until a detection response to the target appearing in the peripheral box had been made. At this point the spot returned to its original tracking dimension. Consequently, for one condition the intertrial tracking dimension was horizontal and the within-trial dimension was vertical (H→V), and for the other condition these were reversed (V→H). In this way a small saccade was required both at the trial onset and offset. These conditions are illustrated in the upper panel of Fig. 9.2.

Results

The results of the primary task are presented in Fig. 9.2. The patterns of results from the two smooth-pursuit eye-tracking tasks (H and V) are very similar. Two ANOVAs revealed significant effects of SOA—$F(2,18) = 22.63$ and 24.29 for the H and V conditions, respectively—trial type—$F(1,9) = 6.18$ and 16.26—and interactions between them—$F(2,18) = 29.42$ and 35.33, all $ps < .05$. Both significant facilitation at 100 msec and significant inhibition at 500 msec are

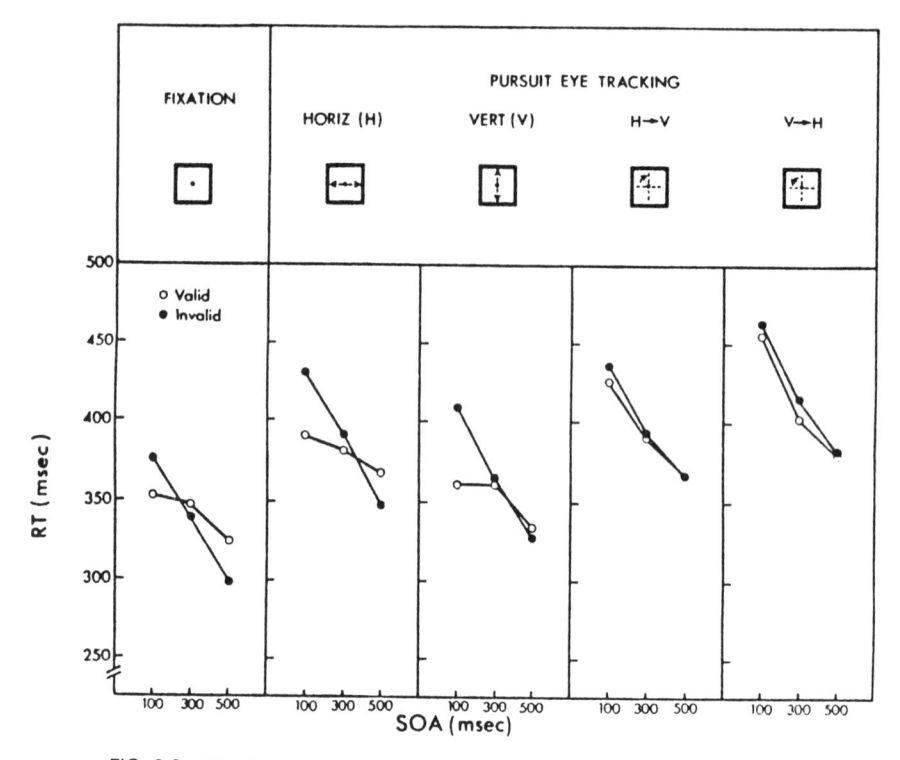

FIG. 9.2. Results of Experiment 2. The secondary tasks are illustrated in the upper panel (see text for details). The results of Experiment 1a (fixation) are included for comparison.

observed when the eyes move smoothly within the central box (H and V), although it is not clear why the former is significantly increased (H and V) and the latter decreased (V only) compared to the fixation condition.

In contrast, the requirement to prepare a small saccade at the moment when the direct cue occurs in the periphery either delays externally controlled orienting until after 500 msec or abolishes it altogether. Although it appears that there may be evidence of a small amount of facilitation at the early SOAs, this was not confirmed by the ANOVAs. There were significant effects of SOA—$F(2,18) = 29.75$ and 31.84 for the H→V and V→H conditions, respectively, $p < .0001$—but no effects of trial type—$F(1,9) = 1.69$ and 1.88, $p > .1$—nor any interactions between them—$F(2,18) = .24$ and $.84$, $p > .1$.

Discussion

It appears that facilitation can be abolished if the direct cue in the periphery occurs at the same time as a discontinuity in a central tracking task that requires the programming and execution of a small saccadic eye movement (that is, externally controlled overt orienting). In addition, there is no later inhibitory component which provides support for the view that inhibition is *dependent* on prior orienting. Thus, the results of Experiment 2 argue against Cohen's (1981) suggestion that only the facilitatory component is an active one and that under dual task conditions facilitation is attenuated, while the inhibitory component continues to exert its full influence.

EXPERIMENT 3

In addition to single direct cues in the periphery (similar to those used in Experiment 1), Posner and Cohen (1980, 1984) included trials in which both the left and right peripheral boxes brightened simultaneously. Their results demonstrated reduced facilitation at an SOA of 80 msec but as much inhibition at an SOA of 500 msec for double-cued as compared to single-cued trials. They suggested that the reduced facilitation was consistent with their earlier conclusion that attention under internal control cannot be divided effectively between two locations either side of fixation (Posner et al., 1980). However, because inhibition was not similarly reduced by double cueing, Posner and Cohen concluded that the inhibitory component is due to the sensory stimulation in the periphery and not to the externally controlled orienting produced by the cue. Contrary to this conclusion, the results from the unpredictable eye-tracking conditions of Experiment 2 suggest that inhibition does not occur if facilitation is abolished. A pilot study reported by Maylor (1983) confirmed that the facilitatory component is approximately halved by double cueing. Because of the theoretical significance of Posner and Cohen's study, Experiment 3 was designed to investigate double cueing further—in particular, its effect on the inhibitory component at longer SOAs.

Subjects. Four subjects participated in this experiment.

Method

The stimuli were two red light emitting diodes (LEDs) placed 12° to the left and 12° to the right of a central fixation point (a yellow LED). Each subject was required to fixate on the central LED throughout the experiment. Each trial began with the 300-msec presentation of the left, right, or both LEDs (the "cue"), with equal probability. After an SOA of 700, 900, or 1300 msec, the target appeared which was the LED on the left of fixation for half of the trials and the LED on the right for the remaining half. The subject was instructed to respond to the onset of the target by pressing a single key but to use the brief cue as a warning signal that a target was about to appear. The target was switched off following the detection response. The intertrial interval (the time between the offset of the target and the onset of the next trial) was randomly chosen from the range 1500 to 2500 msec.

Results

An ANOVA was conducted on the median reaction times with SOA (700, 900, and 1300 msec) and trial type (same, double, and opposite) as fixed-effects factors. The three trial types correspond to a target in the same location as a cue, a target following a double cue, and a target in the opposite location to a cue. Thus, same and opposite are equivalent to valid and invalid trial types, respectively. The overall means are presented in Fig. 9.3, and the ANOVA revealed significant effects of SOA—$F(2,6) = 9.72, p < .02$—and trial type—$F(2,6) = 21.41, p < .005$—but no interaction—$F(4,12) = 1.52, p > .1$. The inhibitory effect is shown by the same–opposite difference and can be seen to last some considerable time. The double cue, however, produces less inhibition than a single cue (same trials) but more than no cue (opposite trials); this was the case for all of the subjects. The conclusion from this experiment is that, contrary to the results of Posner and Cohen (1984), the simultaneous stimulation of more than one location does result in reduced inhibition. This is an important result, as the inhibitory component appears to be reduced by about the same amount as the facilitatory component—that is, both are approximately halved by double cueing compared to single cueing. This provides further support for the suggestion made earlier that inhibition occurs as a direct consequence of externally controlled

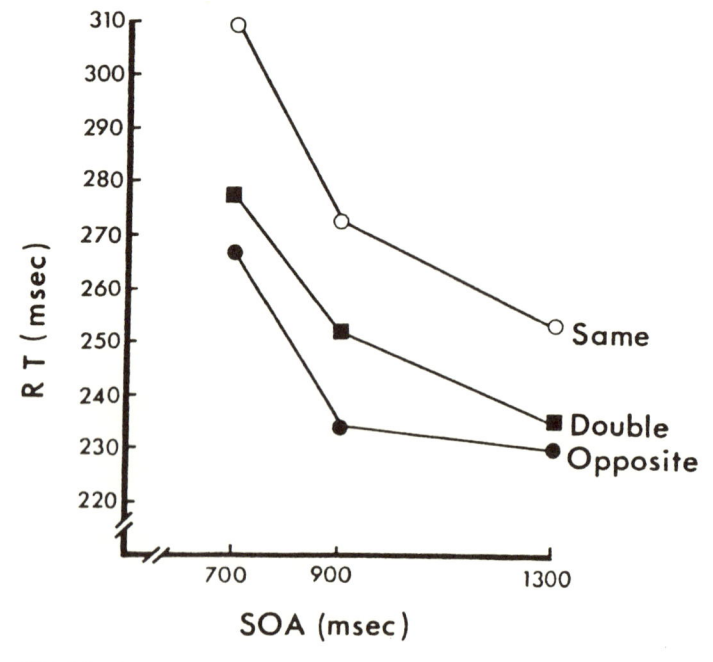

FIG. 9.3. Results of Experiment 3. Reaction time as a function of SOA for same, double, and opposite trials (see text for details).

orienting rather than as the inevitable result of sensory stimulation in the periphery.[1]

The reduced facilitation for double-cued compared to valid trials at an SOA of 80 msec in Posner and Cohen's study could be attributed to maximal facilitation at one peripheral location on half of the trials. If this were the case, the reaction time distributions for double-cued trials would be bimodal and therefore would have larger variances than single-cued trials. The pilot study mentioned previously, which was based more directly on that of Posner and Cohen, enabled a comparison to be made between the semiinterquartile ranges (SIQRs) of valid, invalid, and double-cued trials at an SOA of 100 msec. There was no significant difference between the SIQRs (52, 47, and 45 msec, respectively). Thus, it can be concluded that on double-cued trials, orienting does not occur to one peripheral box only, as though the other box had not been cued. It would, therefore, be predicted that the SIQRs of the reaction times for the three trial types of the present experiment would also be similar. This was tested by an ANOVA on the SIQRs with SOA and trial type as fixed-effects factors, which revealed no effect of SOA or trial type and no interaction between them—all $Fs < 1$.

EXPERIMENT 4

Posner and Cohen (1984) argued that the reduced facilitation at short SOAs following double cueing, combined with the evidence from Posner et al. (1980) that attention (under internal control) cannot be divided effectively between two locations either side of fixation, provides support for the view that the facilitatory component is attentional. The "prior-entry" hypothesis (see, for example, Sternberg & Knoll, 1973) states that given two simultaneous events, the attended event will be reported as occurring earlier in time than the unattended one. Experiment 4, therefore, employed a temporal order judgment paradigm in an attempt to provide converging evidence for the attentional nature of the facilitatory component.

Subjects. Two subjects participated in this experiment.

Method

Two boxes were displayed on the screen, 4.2° to the left and 4.2° to the right of a central point. The subject was required to fixate on this point throughout each of four experimental sessions. On a third of the trials no cue was presented. The

---

[1]Note that if two locations either side of fixation are stimulated *successively*, each will exhibit inhibition comparable with single cueing (Maylor, 1983). For example, a response to a target from one location may be inhibited by the cue of the current trial, while one to a target from the other location is inhibited by the target from the previous trial, the two events being separated by the intertrial interval of between 200 and 700 msec.

remaining two-thirds of the trials were divided equally between a cue on the left (the brightening of the left box for 100 msec) and a cue on the right. The experimental sessions differed according to SOA (100, 300, 500, and 1000 msec), which was defined as the time from the onset of the cue (or the onset of the trial in the case when no cue was presented) to the onset of the *first* target. Target 1 was then presented inside either the left or the right box with approximately equal probability. This was followed after an interval by the second target, which appeared in the other box. Both targets remained on the screen until the subject made a response. Each subject was given two buttons, labeled "left" and "right", and was asked to press the button corresponding to the target that appeared *first*. Following the decision there was an intertrial interval of 1500 msec before the onset of the next trial. The subject was informed that on some trials one of the boxes would appear to flash briefly but that this was to be ignored, as it was noninformative regarding the temporal order of the targets. A psychophysical procedure known as APE (Adaptive Probit Estimation; see Watt & Andrews, 1981) was used to determine the target intervals that were tested.[2]

Results

The proportions of "right-target-first" responses were plotted as a function of the lead of the right target for the three cues (left, right, and no cue). The means of the distributions—that is, the points of subjective simultaneity or PSS—were determined by Probit Analysis (Finney, 1971). All the response distributions were normal sigmoids (tested by chi-square tests of goodness of fit). The results were further analyzed by calculating the quantity [mean(left box cued) − mean(right box cued)] ÷ 2, which is a measure of the interval required (in msec) between the valid and invalid targets (as defined in Experiment 1) for subjective simultaneity. The results are presented in Fig. 9.4. It can be seen that for both subjects the invalid target must occur *before* the valid target, particularly for the first two SOAs, in order for the two targets to appear simultaneous. The effect is large (around 70 msec) at the SOA of 100 msec and decreases to zero by 1000 msec.

Experiment 4 supports the view that the presentation of a brief peripheral stimulus produces covert orienting. This is reflected in both the facilitation of manual reaction time to a subsequent stimulus in the same location and a corresponding bias of temporal order judgments. The consequence of such orienting is a type of response inhibition that affects the speed of response (both manual and ocular) to a repeated peripheral stimulus, but not judgments about its temporal properties.

---

[2]APE, an adaptive version of the Method of Constant Stimuli, selects from a number of present magnitudes in order to obtain a psychometric function.

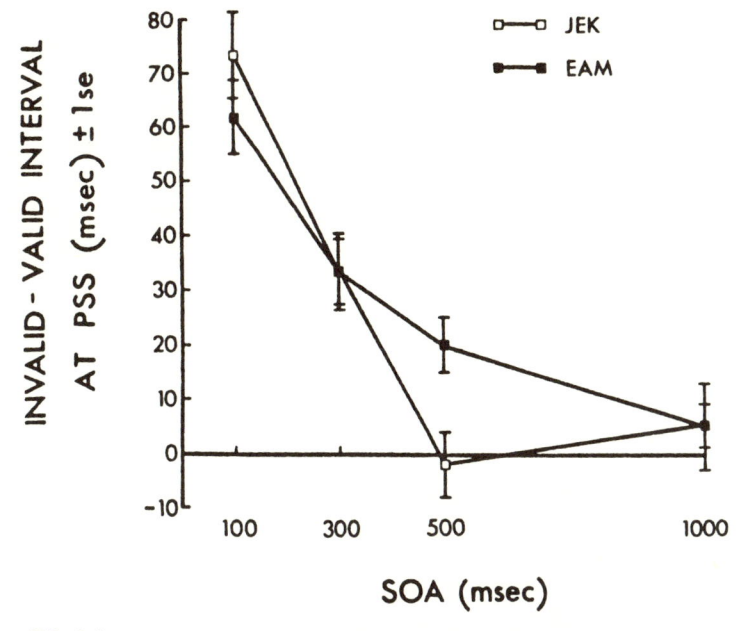

FIG. 9.4. Results of Experiment 4. The interval required between the invalid and valid targets for subjective simultaneity as a function of SOA.

GENERAL CONCLUSIONS

The Facilitatory Component

A target appearing immediately after, and in the same location as, a direct cue in the periphery is responded to more quickly (at least for manual responses) and judged to be occurring earlier than a target in a different location. Recent experiments have extended this conclusion by establishing effects of externally controlled orienting on perceptual sensitivity (Remington, 1980) and on figural and positional judgments (Krumhansl, 1982). Thus, it is suggested that after a salient event in the visual periphery (for example, a luminance change), but before overt orienting takes place, externally controlled covert orienting occurs that results in enhanced responding to and processing of further stimuli from that location for approximately 100 msec.

The Inhibitory Component

If a target appears 300 msec or more after a direct cue in the periphery and in the same location, there is an inability to respond to it as quickly, either manually or ocularly, as to a target in a different location. This inhibitory component is regarded as a consequence of externally controlled covert orienting to the cue. At least for manual responses, inhibition does not result from the need to prevent responding to the cue (Maylor, 1983). However, the complete absence of an inhibitory component using a temporal order judgment paradigm is taken as evidence that inhibition is a response-related process—that is, it reflects a reluctance to respond rapidly to a stimulus appearing in the same peripheral location as a previous one that produced orienting. It is important to note that inhibition is also observed as a result of externally controlled overt orienting, so that following an eye-movement toward and then away from an event in the periphery, both manual responses (Cohen, 1981; Posner & Cohen, 1984) and saccades (Vaughan, 1982) are slower to a target appearing in the previously fixated location than to one appearing elsewhere.

From the results of their double-cueing experiment, Posner and Cohen (1984) argued that the inhibitory component does not arise from attentional orienting but from the sensory information presented at the cued location. In their study double cueing resulted in reduced facilitation but the usual amount of inhibition, in comparison with the effects of single cueing. They concluded that externally controlled covert orienting is not a necessary condition to produce inhibition. However, the results of the double-cueing experiment reported earlier (Experiment 3), combined with the observation from Experiment 2 that inhibition does not occur if facilitation is absent, argue against this view. It appears that the inhibitory component is *dependent* on externally controlled orienting.

Finally, Posner and Cohen (1984) concluded that the facilitatory (attentional) and inhibitory components "appear to be independent and may cancel each other out. Thus if attention is not drawn away from the cued location, no net inhibition is found. Immediately after a cue there is usually a net facilitation, and no net inhibition appears to occur until attention is summoned away from the cue" [p. 541]. However, it was noted that identical results to those of Experiment 1a were obtained when central cueing (see *Method*) was omitted (Maylor, 1983). Furthermore, if the data from the SOA of 300 msec only are considered, it appears that it is possible for a subject to be slower to respond to a target from one location yet to judge it as occurring earlier than a target from another location (compare Fig. 9.1 and 9.4). Thus, the presence of attention (as inferred from temporal order judgments) is not sufficient to counteract the inhibitory effect. This is consistent with the results from an additional study, in which it was demonstrated that the inhibitory effect is as large at the fovea as it is in the periphery (Maylor & Hockey, in preparation). The complex relationship between the facilitatory and inhibitory components involved in visual orienting clearly requires further exploration. The data presented in Experiments 1 to 4, however, are consistent with Posner and Cohen's (1984) general conclusions that facilitation is associated with attention and target acquisition within a fixation and is therefore likely to be involved in the direction of the eye-movement system. Inhibition seems to operate between fixations, acting to delay orienting to a location that was sampled (either covertly or overtly) within the last second (equivalent to the time for two or three saccades).

ACKNOWLEDGMENTS

The experiments were conducted while the author was in receipt of a University of Durham Research Studentship and formed part of a doctoral thesis supervised by Dr. G. R. J. Hockey. The author is grateful to Robert Hockey, Michael Posner, and two anonymous reviewers for comments on an earlier draft of the chapter.

REFERENCES

Bashinski, H. S., & Bacharach, V. R. (1980). Enhancement of perceptual sensitivity as the result of selectively attending to spatial locations. *Perception and Psychophysics, 28,* 241–248.

Cohen, Y. A. (1981). *Internal and external control of visual orienting.* Unpublished doctoral dissertation, University of Oregon.

Findlay, J. M. (1974). A simple apparatus for recording microsaccades during visual fixation. *Quarterly Journal of Experimental Psychology, 26,* 167–170.

Finney, D. J. (1971). *Probit analysis* (3rd ed.). Cambridge, England: Cambridge University.

Jonides, J. (1976). *Voluntary vs reflexive control of the mind's eye's movement.* Paper presented to the Psychonomic Society, St. Louis.

Jonides, J. (1981). Voluntary vs automatic control over the mind's eye's movement. In J. B. Long & A. D. Baddeley (Eds.), *Attention and performance IX* (pp. 187–203). Hillsdale, NJ: Lawrence Erlbaum Associates.

Kahneman, D. (1973). *Attention and effort.* Englewood Cliffs, NJ: Prentice-Hall.

Krumhansl, C. L. (1982). Abrupt changes in visual stimulation enhance processing of form and location information. *Perception and Psychophysics, 32,* 511–523.

Maylor, E. A. (1983). *Components of orienting in visual space.* Unpublished doctoral thesis, University of Durham.

Maylor, E. A., & Hockey, G. R. J. (in prepration). *The inhibitory component of externally-controlled covert orienting in visual space.*

Posner, M. I. (1980). Orienting of attention. *Quarterly Journal of Experimental Psychology, 32,* 3–25.

Posner, M. I., & Cohen, Y. A. (1980). *Consequences of visual orienting.* Paper presented to the Psychonomic Society, St. Louis.

Posner, M. I., & Cohen, Y. A. (1984). Components of visual orienting. In H. Bouma & D. G. Bouwhuis (Eds.), *Attention and performance X* (pp. 531–556). Hillsdale, NJ: Lawrence Erlbaum Associates.

Posner, M. I., Cohen, Y. A., Choate, L., Hockey, G. R. J., & Maylor, E. A. (1984). Sustained concentration: Passive filtering or active orienting? In S. Kornblum & J. Requin (Eds.), *Preparatory states and processes.* Hillsdale, NJ: Lawrence Erlbaum Associates.

Posner, M. I., Nissen, M. J., & Ogden, W. C. (1978). Attended and unattended processing modes: The role of set for spatial location. In H. J. Pick & I. J. Saltzman (Eds.), *Modes of perceiving and processing information* (pp. 137–157). Hillsdale, NJ: Lawrence Erlbaum Associates.

Posner, M. I., & Snyder, C. R. R. (1975). Attention and cognitive control. In R. L. Solso (Ed.), *Information processing and cognition: The Loyola symposium* (pp. 55–85). Hillsdale, NJ: Lawrence Erlbaum Associates.

Posner, M. I., Snyder, C. R. R., & Davidson, B. J. (1980). Attention and the detection of signals. *Journal of Experimental Psychology: General, 109,* 160–174.

Remington, R. W. (1980). Attention and saccadic eye movements. *Journal of Experimental Psychology: Human Perception and Performance, 6,* 726–744.

Schneider, W., & Shiffrin, R. M. (1977). Controlled and automatic human information processing: I. Detection, search and attention. *Psychological Review, 84,* 1–66.

Sternberg, S., & Knoll, R. L. (1973). The perception of temporal order: Fundamental issues and a general model. In S. Kornblum (Ed.), *Attention and performance IV* (pp. 629–685). New York: Academic.

Vaughan, J. (1982). *Spatially localized inhibition: Influence on saccadic eye movements.* Paper presented to the Psychonomic Society, Minneapolis.

Watt, R. J., & Andrews, D. P. (1981). APE: Adaptive probit estimation of psychometric functions. *Current Psychological Reviews, 1,* 205–214.

10 Accessing Features and Objects: Is Location Special?

Mary Jo Nissen
University of Minnesota

ABSTRACT

This chapter proposes that the role of localization in the selection of visual information can be understood in terms of the organization of visual processing, in which each of several visual maps represents a different attribute. The experiments reported here tested the following predictions: (a) When information registered within a visual map is adequate for the task, selection by location should hold no special advantage. Results showed that selecting an item by color and reporting its location was as accurate as selecting by location and reporting color. (b) Color and shape information are registered in separate maps. The accuracies of reporting the color and shape of an item cued by its location were shown to be independent. (c) When a task requires information from corresponding locations of separate visual maps, localization is necessary for cross-referencing between maps. Results from such a task, in which subjects reported the shape and location of an item cued by its color, showed that the accuracy of shape judgments depended on and was predicted from the accuracy of locating the cued color. This set of results is consistent with findings by Treisman and Gelade (1980) that focused attention is required in searching for conjunctions but not features.

INTRODUCTION

A good deal of research on selective attention in vision and audition has involved tasks in which subjects are instructed to select information on the basis of its spatial location. We know that selection can be based on physical attributes other than location, such as the pitch or loudness of auditory stimuli or the color or brightness of visual stimuli, but selection by location has been emphasized. Current interest in visual spatial attention is strongly reflected in research on its mechanisms (Posner, 1980), consequences (Treisman & Gelade, 1980; Treisman & Schmidt, 1982), and neural basis (Mountcastle, 1978; Posner, Cohen, & Rafal, 1982; Wurtz, Goldberg, & Robinson, 1980). In view of these advances in understanding the allocation of attention to spatial locations, a relevant question is whether selecting visual information on the basis of location differs fundamentally in its role in perception from selection by other attributes.

One version of this general question is whether selection on the basis of location is uniquely efficient. Evidence from a series of studies using the partial-report technique suggests that it is. Von Wright (1968, 1970, 1972) found that although cues indicating the location, color, size, and brightness of the items to be reported all provided partial-report advantage relative to whole report, selection by location was most efficient: The difference between partial report and whole report was greatest when selection was by location. Von Wright (1968) also noted that selection by location was judged by the subjects to be particularly easy, and they tended to select by location spontaneously in the whole-report condition.

It is possible, however, that these findings resulted from the use of locations that were more discriminable from each other than the sets of colors or sizes or brightness levels that were used. As Duncan (1980) has pointed out, these differences between types of cue may reflect quantitative differences in cue discriminability rather than qualitative differences. This sort of result considered in isolation does not necessarily argue that selection by location is unique.

A second possibility concerning the role of selection by location is that it mediates selection by other visual attributes. This hypothesis is illustrated by Von Wright's (1970) suggestion that "at least when selection is easy, the initial scan of what is stored in VIS [visual information storage] serves to specify the location of the items to be further processed" (p. 285; parentheses added). Similarly, Bongartz and Scheerer (1976) argued that selection by color yields a smaller partial-report advantage than selection by location because it requires an extra processing step: localizing the target color.

Why might localization be expected to play this unique role in the selection of visual information? A view of visual processing that has emerged from work in visual psychophysics, information processing, and physiology over the last 15 years is that many properties of a visual stimulus are determined in parallel by separate mechanisms. Psychophysicists have postulated sets of filters, each sensitive to different properties of the visual image, operating in parallel and approximately independently (Regan, 1982). Within the information processing paradigm, results from matching and categorization tasks suggest parallel processing of color and shape information (Hawkins, 1969; Saraga & Shallice, 1973). Findings from visual neurophysiology indicate that there are several visual areas in the posterior cortex, each organized retinotopically but maximally sensitive to different visual properties (Cowey, 1979, 1982).

The number and degree of specificity of these visual areas is not yet known precisely, but the principle of multiple maps, each representing a different property, suggests a special role for localization in the selection of visual information. If it is supposed that the spatial layout of colors in a stimulus display is registered in a color map and the spatial layout of shapes (orientation and spatial frequency) is registered in a shape map, then localization may be necessary for cross-referencing between maps. That is, in order to report the shape of, say, the red item in the display, it would be necessary to locate the red item within the color map, select the corresponding location within the shape map, and determine the shape at that location. This unique role for localization also derives from considerations of psychophysical channels or parallel information processing mechanisms, if it is assumed that their outputs are locationally tagged. It should be noted that the proposition that location information allows cross-referencing between maps does not necessarily argue for a special role for localization in search tasks that do not require information from corresponding locations in separate maps—for example, tasks that may be supported by a single map or the activation of a higher-order category.

According to this view, the relation between the ability to identify a target item and the ability to locate it may depend on whether the search task requires corresponding information from separate maps or whether it can be supported by a single map. Results from some studies of the relation between identifying (in most instances, naming) and locating a letter have suggested that the two are independent (Krumhansl & Thomas, 1976; Logan, 1975a, 1975b). Others have shown that when subjects in a bar-probe partial-report task fail to report the correct letter, they tend to report a letter adjacent to the cued letter; this tendency increases with the delay of the cue (Eriksen & Rohrbaugh, 1970; Mewhort, Marchetti, Gurnsey, & Campbell, 1984; Townsend, 1973). If one assumes that these tasks can be supported by a single map, these results may indicate that the spatial layout of information within a map is imperfect and subject to change with time following stimulus presentation, and that such changes do not necessarily affect the information required for identification. More generally, for single-map tasks, the relative accuracies of identification and location responses, and the frequency of adjacency errors, may depend on the relative ease of discriminating the locations and the letter shapes that are used.

The crucial role of localization should be evident in tasks requiring cross-referencing between maps. Snyder (1972) asked subjects to name the one red letter that appeared in an array of 11 other black letters. His results, like those in studies using the bar-probe technique, indicated that when incorrect, subjects tended to report a letter adjacent to the cued letter. The occurrence of adjacency errors, however, does not constitute evidence against localization dependence; such errors would be expected if the spatial layout of information within either the color map or the shape map were distorted. Treisman and Gelade (1980) measured identification and localization accuracies for single-feature targets and for conjunction targets that were specified by both color and shape. They found that for single-feature targets, identification was well above chance even when the target was incorrectly localized. In contrast, when a conjunction target was mislocated, the ability to identify it was at chance. Treisman and Gelade (1980) did not formally test the localization hypothesis; there are alternative accounts of their results stemming from the greater difficulty of identifying conjunction targets. This alternative account is suggested by Baron's (1973) finding that as the relative difficulty of identification increases, the frequency of correct identification with incorrect localization decreases. Nevertheless, this and other work by Treisman and her colleagues (Treisman & Schmidt, 1982; Treisman, Sykes, & Gelade, 1977), which shows that searching for conjunctions of visual features requires serial focusing of attention, argues for a unique role for localization in perception.

The experiments reported here evaluated the role of selection by location in two types of task. Both involved the tachistoscopic presentation of an array of colored shapes, which was followed by a mask and a cue indicating the portion of the display that was to be reported. The two types of task were designed to differ in terms of whether performance could be based on information within a single map, or whether coordinated information from separate maps was required. In Experiment 1, the single-map task, subjects were cued with a color and reported the location of the cued color, or they were cued with a location and reported the color at the cued location. It was predicted that in this situation, selection by location would hold no special advantage. Performance in Experiment 2 required access to two maps: color and shape. In one condition subjects were cued with a location and reported the color and shape at that location. It was predicted that the accuracies of these two responses would be independent because they are supported by separate maps. In the other condition of Experiment 2, subjects were cued with a color and reported the location and shape of the cued color. In this situation, which is similar to the sort of task Von Wright (1970) was considering when he alluded to the special role of selection by location, the attribute on which selection is based (color) and the attribute to be reported (shape) are in separate maps. Under these circumstances, localizing the cued color should be required for selecting the corresponding shape. Thus, the accuracy of the shape response should depend on the accuracy of the location response. Further, it should be possible to predict the accuracy of the shape response given information about the ability to localize the cued color and to determine the shape at a given location.

EXPERIMENT 1

The purpose of this experiment was to compare (a) the accuracy with which subjects could report the color that appeared at a particular location with (b) the accuracy with which they could report the location at which a particular color appeared. In order to determine whether subjects would prepare differently when expecting to be cued by location versus color, both *foreknowledge* and *no-*

foreknowledge conditions were included. In the foreknowledge condition, subjects were told before each trial began whether the cue would be a location or a color cue (and thus, whether they would have to respond with a color or a location, respectively); in the no-foreknowledge condition, no advance information was given about the type of cue that would occur on each trial.

Method

Subjects. The group of 12 subjects included six women and six men ranging in age from 18 to 27 years (mean = 20.0 years). All subjects were undergraduate students at the University of Minnesota and received research credit in an introductory psychology course for participating.

Stimuli. A three-channel tachistoscope was used to present a stimulus display followed by a masking stimulus on each trial. Stimulus displays and the masking stimulus were drawn on 5 inch × 7 inch cards with colored markers. The stimulus display consisted of four colored shapes, each subtending approximately .3°, which were centered .8° above, below, left, and right of the center of the display. The shapes were a circle, a square, a triangle, and a diamond; the colors were red, green, blue, and black. Shape, color, and location were randomly combined in 64 different stimulus displays, with the following constraints: No color or shape was repeated within any display; each possible pairwise color–shape combination, color–location combination, and shape–location combination appeared in 16 displays; and each color–shape–location combination appeared in four displays. For example, a green stimulus appeared on the left in 16 displays, and in four of those 16 displays, the green stimulus was a square.

The masking stimulus, which immediately followed the offset of the stimulus display, consisted of an array of randomly oriented colored lines covering the entire 2.0° circular area of the stimulus display. A cue word was printed in black above the mask. The location-cue words were *top, bottom, left,* and *right;* the color-cue words were *red, green, blue,* and *black.*

A homogeneous white adapting field, 6.3° × 8.8°, was presented before the onset of each stimulus display. The luminance of the adapting field and the white background of the stimulus displays and mask was approximately 80 cd/m^2.

Procedure. On each trial the experimenter said "ready" and approximately 1 sec later initiated the following sequence: The adapting field appeared for 1 sec and was then replaced by the stimulus display, which was present for a duration determined separately for each subject. The offset of the stimulus display was followed immediately by the mask and cue, which appeared for 1.5 sec. Subjects were told that when the cue was the name of a location, they were to report the color that had appeared at that location, and when the cue was the name of a color, they were to report the location at which that color appeared. Subjects reported the response aloud on each trial.

Subjects performed 64 trials on each of two consecutive days. All 64 different stimulus displays were presented once within each session. Of the 64 trials within a session, 32 were location-cue trials, and 32 were color-cue trials. Each of the four location cues and each of the four color cues occurred on eight trials within a session. Cues were paired with stimulus displays such that each color and each location was cued equally often on location- and color-cue trials, respectively. The order of trials was determined randomly for each subject, with the constraint that the same type of cue (location or color) could not occur on more than eight consecutive trials.

All subjects performed in both the foreknowledge and the no-foreknowledge conditions. In the foreknowledge condition, the experimenter began each trial by saying "location word" on location-cue trials, or "color word" on color-cue trials. After a delay of about 1 sec, the experimenter said "ready" and initiated the stimulus sequence. In the no-foreknowledge condition, this advance information was not provided; trials in this condition began with the "ready" signal. Half of the subjects performed the foreknowledge condition in the first session and the no-foreknowledge condition in the second session; the remaining subjects performed the conditions in the reverse order.

At the beginning of the first session, 20 practice trials were conducted. The duration of the stimulus display was adjusted for each subject during these practice trials so that response accuracy was between 50% and 80%. Practice trials included both location- and color-cue trials. Once determined in practice trials, stimulus duration remained unchanged throughout the experimental trials of the first session. Subjects were also given 20 practice trials at the beginning of the second session. Stimulus durations during these practice trials and during the experimental trials of the second session were identical to those used in the practice and experimental trials of the first session. Stimulus durations for experimental trials varied between subjects from 90 msec to 180 msec (mean = 113.5 msec, standard deviation = 28.5 msec).

Results

Table 10.1 shows the mean accuracy of responses to location and color cues in foreknowledge and no-foreknowledge conditions. The overall accuracy on location-cue trials was 68.1%; the overall accuracy on color-cue trials was 68.2%.

The data were examined by analysis of variance, with cue (location vs. color) and condition (foreknowledge vs. no foreknowledge) as within-subject factors and order of condition (foreknowledge, no foreknowledge vs. no foreknowledge, foreknowledge) as a between-subject factor. The only significant effect was an interaction between order and condition ($F(1,10) = 8.28$, $p < .015$): Subjects

TABLE 10.1
Proportion of Correct Responses
in Experiment 1

Condition	Cue Location	Color	M
Foreknowledge	.698	.680	.689
No foreknowledge	.664	.685	.674
M	.681	.682	

were more accurate in the condition they performed second. All main effects and all other interactions failed to reach significance ($F(1,10) < 1.2$ in all cases).

Discussion

The results of Experiment 1 showed that response accuracy was equivalent on location-cue and color-cue trials. In this situation, selecting a location and reporting its color was as efficient as selecting a color and reporting its location. Furthermore, knowing the selection criterion in advance did not affect performance on this task. According to the multiple-maps framework, the information required on either location-cue or color-cue trials is available within a map representing the spatial layout of color in the display. The results suggest that under these circumstances (i.e., in "single-map" tasks), accessing information by location holds no unique advantage.

EXPERIMENT 2

Experiment 2 examined the role of selection by location in a task that presumably required access to information in separate maps—that is, a task requiring information about both the color and the shape of an item. The first condition of Experiment 2 evaluated the assumption that color and shape information are represented separately at some stage of processing, as the multiple-maps view postulates. In this condition, a location cue was used and subjects were asked to report the color and shape that appeared at the cued location. The prediction was that the accuracy of the two judgments would be independent of each other.

The second condition of Experiment 2 tested the idea that because information about the color and shape of an item are represented in separate maps, it is not possible to access one from the other directly; access between maps should require localization. This second condition used a color cue and required subjects to report the location and shape of the cued color. The hypothesis was that this task requires subjects to localize the cued color and to determine the shape at the selected location. Thus, the prediction was that the accuracy of the shape judgment should depend on the accuracy of the location judgment.

Method

Subjects. The group of subjects included five graduate students and three undergraduate students, all naive about the purpose of the experiment, and the author. The graduate students received $10 for their participation; the undergraduate students received course credit. This group of nine subjects included four women and five men ranging in age from 21 to 29 years.

Stimuli. The 64 stimulus displays and the masking stimulus with cues were the same as those used in Experiment 1. Two subjects (MK and PD) were tested on the same tachistoscope used in Experiment 1. For the other seven subjects, a two-channel tachistoscope was used. Because its viewing distance was shorter, the visual angle of the stimuli was slightly larger than in Experiment 1. Each of the four colored shapes subtended approximately .4°, and they were centered 1.1° about the center of the display. The entire display and the mask that followed it subtended 2.6°. The adapting field preceding the onset of the stimulus display was dark.

Procedure. On each trial the experimenter said "ready" and approximately 1 sec later initiated the presentation of the stimulus display, the offset of which was followed immediately by the mask and cue.

All subjects participated in a location-cue condition and a color-cue condition, which were conducted on separate days.[1] In the location-cue condition subjects were instructed to name the color and shape that had appeared at the cued location, and in the color-cue condition they were to name the location and shape of the cued color. No instructions were given regarding the order of the two responses, which subjects said aloud. The order of report adopted by each subject in each condition is shown in Table 10.2. Cues were paired with stimulus displays such that each color–shape and shape–location pair was cued equally often in the location-cue and color-cue conditions, respectively.

All subjects performed 64 trials in each cue condition. Five subjects received the location-cue condition before the color-cue condition, and four received the reverse order. Prior to each condition 20 practice trials were conducted, during which the duration of the stimulus display was adjusted for each subject so that the accuracy of both responses was between 50% and 80%. The average duration in the location-cue condition was 128 msec, and the average in the color-cue

---

[1]Subjects also performed a shape-cue condition on a separate day. Results from that condition are not reported here. They were consistent with the results from the color-cue condition.

10. ACCESSING FEATURES AND OBJECTS 213

TABLE 10.2
Stimulus Durations, Orders of Report, and χ^2 Values of Predictions for Experiment 2

	Location-Cue Condition			Color-Cue Condition			
Subject	Stimulus Duration (msec)	Order of Report[a]	Independence $\chi^2(1)$	Stimulus Duration (msec)	Order of Report[a]	Independence $\chi^2(1)$	Localization Dependence $\chi^2(2)$
RS	124	CS	0.35	163	LS	13.93[d]	4.54
CS	190	CS	12.30[d]	182	LS	16.16[d]	0.82
JG	113	CS	1.19	156	SL	9.82[c]	1.12
KK	132	CS	1.06	219	LS	3.25[b]	13.50[d]
MD	120	CS	1.52	142	SL	14.44[d]	0.91
GC	136	CS	0	92	SL	11.11[d]	4.29
MN	106	CS	0	100	LS	15.97[d]	1.89
MK	60	CS	0	110	LS	16.12[d]	1.04
PD	170	CS	1.64	151	LS	12.46[d]	0.22

[a] C = Color, S = Shape, L = Location.
[b] $p < .10$.
[c] $p < .005$.
[d] $p < .001$.

condition was 146 msec. Stimulus durations for individual subjects are shown in Table 10.2.

Results

Figure 10.1 shows the mean accuracy of the two responses in each condition. Figure 10.1A presents the results of the location-cue condition in a 2 × 2 response matrix; the cell entries correspond to the proportion of trials with correct color and correct shape responses, correct color and incorrect shape, incorrect color and correct shape, and incorrect color and incorrect shape. The marginal values are the overall probabilities of correct and incorrect color and shape responses. Results from the color-cue condition are shown similarly in Fig. 10.1B.

Tests of Independence. The data from each condition were analyzed to determine whether the two responses subjects gave on each trial were statistically independent. If independent, the accuracy of one response should not depend on whether the other was correct or incorrect. More specifically, the entries in each cell of the response matrix should equal the product of the appropriate marginal values. The values shown in parentheses in Fig. 10.1 represent the cross-products of the marginals and, thus, the results that are predicted if the two responses are independent.

A. Location – Cue Condition

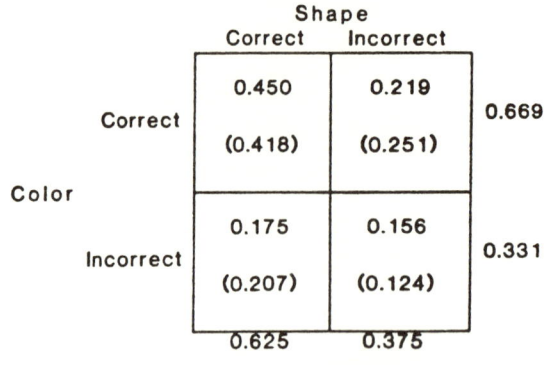

		Shape Correct	Shape Incorrect	
Color	Correct	0.450 (0.418)	0.219 (0.251)	0.669
	Incorrect	0.175 (0.207)	0.156 (0.124)	0.331
		0.625	0.375	

B. Color – Cue Condition

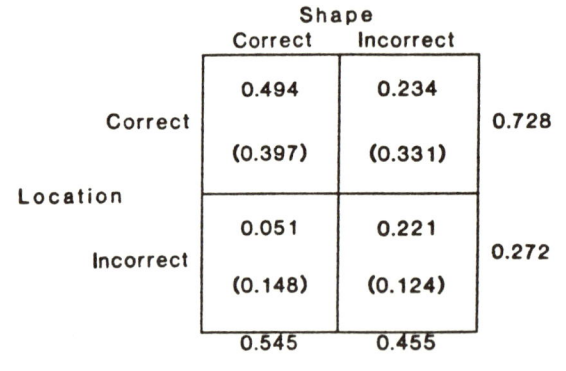

		Shape Correct	Shape Incorrect	
Location	Correct	0.494 (0.397)	0.234 (0.331)	0.728
	Incorrect	0.051 (0.148)	0.221 (0.124)	0.272
		0.545	0.455	

FIG. 10.1. Proportion of trials with correct and incorrect responses on each of two decisions in Experiment 2. Values are means of data of nine subjects. (A) Color and shape responses in the location-cue condition. (B) Shape and location responses in the color-cue condition. Values in parentheses are those predicted from independence of the two responses.

Considering first the results from the location-cue condition, the average data that are shown in Fig. 10.1A suggest independence of color and shape responses; predicted and obtained values are in good agreement. This agreement was confirmed statistically; a chi-square test indicated that the difference between predicted and obtained values was not significant ($\chi^2(1) = 1.20$, n.s.). Because evaluations of the independence of two measures that are taken from data averaged across subjects can be misleading, the results from each of the nine subjects were examined individually to determine whether, for each subject, color and shape responses were independent. These analyses showed that the accuracies of color and shape responses were independent for eight of the nine subjects. Table 10.2 includes chi-square values from these tests of independence for each subject.

10. ACCESSING FEATURES AND OBJECTS 215

In contrast to the results from the location-cue condition showing independence of color and shape judgments, the results from the color-cue condition indicated that the accuracies of location and shape judgments were not independent. The values predicted by independence for the average data are shown in parentheses in Fig. 10.1B. The predicted values differed significantly from the results ($\chi^2 (1) = 12.2, p < .005$). Similarly, analyses of the data from individual subjects showed that location and shape responses in the color-cue condition were not independent for eight of the nine subjects. The chi-square values from these individual analyses are given in Table 10.2.

Tests of Localization Dependence. The fact that accuracies of color and shape judgments were independent in the location-cue condition is consistent with the notion that those two properties of a stimulus are analyzed separately and, from the maps analogy, in separate maps. Furthermore, the finding that accuracies of location and shape judgments in the color-cue condition were not independent is consistent with the idea that integrating information from different maps requires localization. According to this notion, presentation of the color cue required subjects to determine the location of the cued color (operations within the color map), and then to determine the corresponding shape by selecting the appropriate location within the shape map.

A much stronger test of this idea goes beyond demonstrating that the location and shape judgments were not independent to predicting the response accuracies that were obtained. The average data from the color-cue condition, shown in Fig. 10.1B, are used to describe the derivation of predicted values.

It was assumed that when presented with a color cue, subjects determined the location of the cued color with probability $P(L|C)$, and they determined the shape at that location with probability $P(S|L)$. The proportion of trials on which both location and shape judgments were correct should equal the probability that the cued color was localized correctly times the probability that the shape at that location was determined correctly. That is:

$$P(L \text{ and } S|C) = P(L|C) \times P(S|L).$$

The probability of correctly localizing the cued color—$P(L|C)$—was given by the overall accuracy of location responses in the color-cue condition: $P(L|C) = .728$. Although the probability of correctly judging the shape at a given location—$P(S|L)$—was not given by results from the color-cue condition, an estimate of that value was available from the location-cue condition. The overall accuracy of judging the shape at a cued location in the location-cue condition was .625 (see Fig. 10.1A). However, that value may not indicate the effective $P(S|L)$ in the color-cue condition because it was obtained in a different block of trials with a different stimulus duration. The value of $P(S|L)$ from the location-cue condition was thus adjusted to accommodate possible differences between blocks in the following way. The location-cue condition provided a measure of

$P(C|L)$, which, according to the results of Experiment 1, is equivalent to $P(L|C)$. The proportional difference between $P(C|L)$, obtained in the location-cue condition, and $P(L|C)$, obtained in the color-cue condition, was thus taken as the correction factor for differences between blocks. That correction was applied to the measure of $P(S|L)$ from the location-cue data in order to estimate the effective $P(S|L)$ in the color-cue condition. By this procedure, the effective $P(S|L)$ in the color-cue condition was:

$$P(S|L)^* = P(S|L) \times \frac{P(L|C)}{P(C|L)} = .680.$$

As stated previously, $P(L \text{ and } S|C)$ was predicted to equal the product of $P(L|C)$, which was .728, and $P(S|L)$, which was estimated to be .680. The predicted proportion of trials with correct shape and correct location was thus .495.

On trials when the location response was incorrect, it was assumed that subjects attempted to determine the shape at that incorrectly selected location. That attempt should have succeeded on 68% of those trials, because $P(S|L)$ was estimated to be .68. It was assumed that on the remaining 32% of incorrect location trials, shape responses would be equally distributed among the remaining three alternatives, one of which was the correct shape response. Thus, the probability of correct shape given incorrect location was predicted to be .11, and the predicted joint probability of incorrect location and incorrect shape was .029.

There was good correspondence between the results obtained in the color-cue condition and these predicted results. Both are shown in Fig. 10.2. The difference between obtained and predicted values was not significant ($\chi^2 (2) = 1.25$, n.s.). Predictions were derived for the data of each of the nine subjects, using each subject's results in the location-cue condition to estimate the effective $P(S|L)$ in the color-cue condition. For each subject, the correspondence between

	Shape Correct	Shape Incorrect
Location Correct	.494 (.495)	.234 (.233)
Location Incorrect	.051 (.029)	.221 (.243)

Fig. 10.2. Results from the color-cue condition of Experiment 2, as shown in Fig. 10.1. Values in parentheses are those predicted by localization dependence.

predicted and obtained values was evaluated by a chi-square test with 2 degrees of freedom. The chi-square values, shown in Table 10.2, indicated that predicted and obtained values did not differ significantly for eight of the nine subjects.

In summary, both the average data and the individual data of all but one subject in the color-cue condition were adequately predicted from the idea that the shape of an item cannot be accessed directly from knowledge of its color; localization provides the indirect link between these separate attributes.

DISCUSSION

The results of these experiments confirm the predictions and support the idea that the selection of visual information on the basis of its location is, in certain circumstances, a uniquely important aspect of visual processing. The results suggest that the role of localization in search tasks or partial report tasks depends on whether the task requires corresponding information from separate visual maps. When it does not, as in Experiment 1, selection by location is not inevitably more efficient than selection by color. More generally, it may turn out that in single-map tasks the relative efficiency of selection by various attributes will depend on the relative ease of discriminating the values used within each attribute. For the stimuli used in Experiment 1, selection by location and selection by color produced equivalent results. Further, there was no evidence that subjects prepared differentially for the two selection criteria.

The outcome of Experiment 2, which employed a task requiring cross-referencing between maps, confirmed Von Wright's (1970) suggestion of localization dependence. The location-cue condition demonstrated, as predicted, the independence of judgments about the color and shape of an item specified by its location. Results from the color-cue condition showed that when subjects reported the shape and location of an item specified by its color, the accuracy of shape judgments depended on the accuracy of location judgments. Further, it was possible to predict the pattern of individual subjects' results in the color-cue condition from estimates of their abilities to locate a color and to judge the shape at a given location. Thus, selection by location appears to mediate selection when the selection attribute and response attribute are in separate maps. One consequence of this mediation by localization may be that in such multiple-map situations, partial report by location will necessarily be more accurate than partial report by another physical attribute, regardless of cue discriminability.

Searching for a conjunction target requires focusing attention serially on each item in a display (Treisman & Gelade, 1980), or at least on each item possessing one of the features of the conjunction target (Egeth, Virzi, & Garbart, 1984). This indicates the involvement of spatial attention in the process of accessing corresponding information in separate maps. Attending to a location may activate entries at that location in each of several maps and allow attended entries from these maps access to higher decision processes. Spatial attention can facilitate performance on single-map tasks (e.g., Butler, 1980; Posner, Nissen, & Ogden, 1978); it may allow faster or more spatially precise access to information within a map. But, as Treisman and Gelade (1980) suggested, it is possible that the selection of a spatial location is optional in such tasks, whereas it is necessary in tasks requiring cross-referencing between maps.

ACKNOWLEDGMENTS

I thank Darryl Bruce for his help in arranging for subjects and equipment. This project was supported in part by the Center for Research in Human Learning of the University of Minnesota. Portions of this work were presented at the 1979 meeting of the Psychonomic Society and the 1980 meeting of the American Psychological Association.

REFERENCES

Baron, J. (1973). Perceptual dependence: Evidence for an internal threshold. *Perception and Psychophysics, 13,* 527–533.

Bongartz, W., & Scheerer, E. (1976). Two visual stores and two processing operations in tachistoscopic partial report. *Quarterly Journal of Experimental Psychology, 28,* 203–219.

Butler, B. E. (1980). Selective attention and stimulus localization in visual perception. *Canadian Journal of Psychology, 34,* 119–133.

Cowey, A. (1979). Cortical maps and visual perception. The Grindley memorial lecture. *Quarterly Journal of Experimental Psychology, 31,* 1–17.

Cowey, A. (1982). Sensory and non-sensory visual disorders in man and monkey. *Philosophical Transactions of the Royal Society of London, B298,* 3–13.

Duncan, J. (1980). The locus of interference in the perception of simultaneous stimuli. *Psychological Review, 87,* 272–300.

Egeth, H. E., Virzi, R. A., & Garbart, H. (1984). Searching for conjunctively defined targets. *Journal of Experimental Psychology: Human Perception and Performance, 10,* 32–39.

Eriksen, C. W., & Rohrbaugh, J. (1970). Some factors determining efficiency of selective attention. *American Journal of Psychology, 83,* 330–342.

Hawkins, H. L. (1969). Parallel processing in complex visual discrimination. *Perception and Psychophysics, 5,* 56–64.

Krumhansl, C. L., & Thomas, E. A. C. (1976). Extracting identity and location information from briefly presented letter arrays. *Perception and Psychophysics, 20,* 243–258.

Logan, G. D. (1975a). On the independence of naming and locating masked targets in visual search. *Canadian Journal of Psychology, 29,* 51–58.

Logan, G. D. (1975b). On the relation between identifying and locating masked targets in visual search. *Quarterly Journal of Experimental Psychology, 27,* 451–457.

Mewhort, D. J. K., Marchetti, F. J., Gurnsey, R., & Campbell, A. J. (1984). Information persistence: A dual-buffer model for initial visual processing. In H. Bouma & D. G. Bouwhuis (Eds.), *Attention and performance X* (pp. 287–298). Hillsdale, NJ: Lawrence Erlbaum Associates.

Mountcastle, V. B. (1978). Brain mechanisms for directed attention. *Journal of the Royal Society of Medicine, 71,* 14–27.

Posner, M. I. (1980). Orienting of attention. *Quarterly Journal of Experimental Psychology, 32,* 3–25.

Posner, M. I., Cohen, Y., & Rafal, R. D. (1982). Neural systems control of spatial orienting. *Philosophical Transactions of the Royal Society of London, B298,* 187–198.

Posner, M. I., Nissen, M. J., & Ogden, W. C. (1978). Attended and unattended processing modes: The role of set for spatial location. In H. L. Pick, Jr. & E. Saltzman (Eds.), *Modes of perceiving and processing information* (pp. 137–157). Hillsdale, NJ: Lawrence Erlbaum Associates.

Regan, D. (1982). Visual information channeling in normal and disordered vision. *Psychological Review, 89,* 407–444.

Saraga, E., & Shallice, T. (1973). Parallel processing of the attributes of single stimuli. *Perception and Psychophysics, 13,* 261–270.

Snyder, C. R. R. (1972). Selection, inspection, and naming in visual search. *Journal of Experimental Psychology, 92,* 428–431.

Townsend, V. M. (1973). Loss of spatial and identity information following a tachistoscopic exposure. *Journal of Experimental Psychology, 98,* 113–118.

Treisman, A., & Gelade, G. (1980). A feature-integration theory of attention. *Cognitive Psychology, 12,* 97–136.

Treisman, A., & Schmidt, H. (1982). Illusory conjunctions in the perception of objects. *Cognitive Psychology, 14,* 107–141.

Treisman, A., Sykes, M., & Gelade, G. (1977). Selective attention and feature integration. In S. Dornic (Ed.), *Attention and performance VI* (pp. 333–361). Hillsdale, NJ: Lawrence Erlbaum Associates.

Von Wright, J. M. (1968). Selection in visual immediate memory. *Quarterly Journal of Experimental Psychology, 20,* 62–68.

Von Wright, J. M. (1970). On selection in visual immediate memory. *Acta Psychologica, 33,* 280–292.

Von Wright, J. M. (1972). On the problem of selection in iconic memory. *Scandinavian Journal of Psychology, 13,* 159–171.

Wurtz, R. H., Goldberg, M. E., & Robinson, E. L. (1980). Behavioral modulation of visual responses in the monkey: Stimulus selection for attention and movement. *Progress in Psychobiology and Physiological Psychology, 9,* 43–83.

11 Vibrotactile Reaction Times in Left and Right Hemispace: Stimulus and Response Uncertainty and Gravitational and Corporeal Coordinates

John L. Bradshaw
Jane M. Pierson
Monash University

ABSTRACT

In this chapter, we report four experiments investigating the phenomenon of right hemispace superiority in vibrotactile reaction-time tasks. In the absence of stimulus uncertainty, whether in terms of low signal intensity, or left/right predictability, there are no hand differences and either hand is faster when located in right hemispace (i.e., to the right of the midline) rather than in left hemispace. In the presence of stimulus uncertainty, hand asymmetries replace hemispace differences. Moreover, all asymmetries are eliminated when corporeal and gravitational coordinates are dissociated by requiring subjects to recline horizontally on the left or right side. Hemispace asymmetries seem to reflect a greater ability to *hold* attention to the right (as compared to the left) rather than to *shift* it to the right. Even hand asymmetries, when they occur, rather than supporting the traditional anatomical-connectivity account, may merely reflect a strategy for coping with stimulus uncertainty by directing attention to the preferred hand. However, hand rather than hemispace asymmetries prevail in the presence of stimulus uncertainty and in the absence of response uncertainty—that is, when subjects respond with the same hand to stimuli that can occur on either hand. Findings are further discussed in the context of spatial compatibility.

INTRODUCTION

Laterality effects have traditionally been ascribed to the prepotency of contralateral afferent pathways over ipsilateral routes projecting to a hemisphere specialized for a particular mode of processing (Kimura, 1961, 1967). However, receptor location and hemispace (the position in extracorporeal space to the left and right of the body midline wherein stimuli may occur and toward which responses may be initiated, as distinct from ear of entry, hand, or visual field) may be systematically confounded. In the auditory modality, loudspeakers have been substituted for earphones in a hemispace analog of dichotic listening (Bertelson, 1982; Morais, 1978) and have generated right-side advantages (RSAs) in verbal tasks. We (Pierson, Bradshaw, & Nettleton, 1983) have also obtained powerful RSAs when competing verbal stimuli are simultaneously presented from a single laterally placed loudspeaker; indeed, when such stimuli are not lateralized, but come from loudspeakers placed before and behind the subject, who believes that the signals emanate also from a laterally located dummy or inactive loudspeaker, performance is better when the dummy loudspeaker is to the right rather than to the left. Thus, it is perhaps the *perceived* location of a sound source that determines both laterality effects (though see Darwin, Howell, & Brady, 1978) and possibly the efficiency of subsequent cognitive processing: Sounds apparently coming from the right side of space may be more strongly represented in the left hemisphere than sounds seeming to come from the left. Moreover, the RSAs may disappear with head turn (Morais, 1978; Pierson et al., 1983), suggesting that head and body hemispace may somehow interact.

In a rod bisection task in the tactual modality, Bowers and Heilman (1980) found, instead of the traditional left-hand superiority, that performance was more accurate when *either* hand operated in *left* hemispace; each hemisphere is apparently concerned with the perception or mediation of activities in the contralateral spatial field, regardless of the receptor or effector used, as well as processing contralateral sensory input and mediating distal movements of the contralateral extremities. Neuroanatomical connectivity and hemispatial mechanisms may represent two semiindependent factors whose consequences are normally confounded, and may be unconfounded with an arms-across-the-midline condition. Bradshaw, Nettleton, Nathan, and Wilson (1983) confirmed and extended several of these hypotheses and observations, and found that the effects may be destroyed by 90° head turns.

With reaction-time responses to vibrotactile stimulation delivered to the forefinger of the responding hand that is placed ipsilaterally or contralaterally (across the midline), Bradshaw, Nathan, Nettleton, Pierson, and Wilson (1983) found that although the two hands did not differ in speed of response, either hand performed better when located in right hemispace. This effect was greatly reduced with 90° head turns, whose performance was better with stimulation and responding in right-of-*head* (but not right-of-*body*) hemispace. When different hands received stimulation and initiated responses, and were located in either the same or opposite hemispace, right-hemispace superiority proved to be motor rather than sensory.

Burden, Bradshaw, Nettleton, and Wilson (in press) found that children performed equally well with either hand in deciding whether or not tactual stimulus pairs had the same texture; but they also found that target stimuli presented to a hand held in left hemispace were matched significantly better than those presented to a hand held in right hemispace. When children reproduced a static holistic configuration of finger-space patterns, they demonstrated both a left-*hand* and a left-*hemispace* superiority, in both cases only at the level of presentation, not reproduction, indicating the important role of memory in these tactual effects. When children reproduced tactually perceived finger sequences, dextrals demonstrated a right-*hand* superiority, both for presentation and response, supporting the hand–hemisphere connectivity model. Sinistrals showed only a right-*hemispace* superiority (again for stimulus presentation, not reproduction), indicating that hemisphere–hemisphere relationships may dominate when processing hemisphere and preferred hand dissociate. Although so far it seems that both an anatomical connectivity account and one involving hemispheric mediation of events occurring in extracorporeal space must be reconciled, the exact structural basis of this hemiattentional mechanism remains to be identified (though see Crowne, 1983; Mesulam, 1981); nevertheless, each hemisphere presumably maps out contralateral hemispace in terms of its own spatial coordinate system (see, e.g., De Renzi, 1982).

We report four vibrotactile reaction-time studies investigating the nature of the RSA. We aimed to dissociate effects due to hand superiorities from those associated with hand placement. We investigated the effects of uncertainty in terms of stimulus intensity and of side of stimulation, and also the frame of reference for the division of hemispace, whether in terms of gravitational coordinates (around a vertical line) or of the corporeal midline of the (possibly recumbent) observer. Data were analyzed in terms of hand stimulated and/or responding (where different), and hand placement (in its own extracorporeal hemispace or crossing the midline). Findings formed the basis for a model of asymmetry based on the ability to hold, or shift, covert attention to the side of extracorporeal hemispace contralateral to the hemisphere currently processing task-related information. According to this view, the hemispheres code distal sensory–motor events occurring in contralateral hemispace, and not just the proximal receptor surfaces and effector musculature.

EXPERIMENT 1

As described earlier, reaction times to vibrotactile stimuli are performed faster by a hand held in right rather than left hemispace. Such effects may be reduced with 90° head turns, and appear to reflect response-initiation processes rather than stimulus discrimination (Bradshaw, Nathan, Nettleton, Pierson, & Wilson, 1983). We can now ask whether these motor RSAs occur only in the absence of stimulus uncertainty—that is, when the signal is sufficiently intense that the subject's processing is deployed more toward initiating a rapid response than to deciding whether or not a signal actually occurred. With near-threshold stimulation, motor RSAs may be lost and hemispace differences may instead perhaps reflect sensory determinants. The technique of Bradshaw, Nathan, Nettleton, Pierson, and Wilson (1983, Experiment 3) permits sensory and motor hand and sensory and motor hemispace effects to be separately evaluated with respect to left and right.

Method

Subjects. Twenty-four strongly dextral students at Monash University were recruited, twelve of each sex. None had a sinistral in the immediate family, and each subject's handedness was carefully ascertained by our usual pegboard task, questionnaire, and object-manipulation procedures (Bradshaw, Nettleton, & Spehr, 1982).

Apparatus. An Oticon A (47 Ohm impedance) bone-conduction vibrator was used as a transducer. Its 1.5 cm diameter vibrating surface was driven by a Wavetek Model 134 Sweep Generator oscillator, via an in-house control unit and passive attenuator (calibrated in dB) to adjust intensity. Other signal characteristics—for example, duration (80 msec) and rise-and-fall times—were controlled by an in-house electronic switch. To permit subjects to perform the task bimanually (to feel with one hand, respond with the other), the response microswitch and vibrotactile transducer were separately mounted (as in Bradshaw, Nathan, Nettleton, Pierson, & Wilson, 1983, Experiment 3), both components being individually placed on small movable baseplates. Response latencies from stimulus onset were recorded on an in-house electronic printer-timer. A signal frequency of 250 Hz was chosen: We had found earlier that this was the most easily detected frequency, and Sherrick and Craig (1982) report it as corresponding to the value for maximal sensitivity.

Procedure. Subjects were seated in front of a table, with their bodies held within a chipboard guide that extended around the sides. The transducer and response microswitch were placed in left or right hemispace, 30 cm from the midline and 14 cm to the front of the chest line. Subjects detected the signal with the index finger of one or the other hand located in one or the other hemispace, and responded immediately with the middle finger of the opposite hand (in the same or opposite hemispace as the hand receiving stimulation). White noise was played via headphones to mask any auditory cues. Subjects fixated a central eye-level fixation point 200 cm distant. The room was symmetrical around each subject, with overhead lighting, and the experimenter sat with the control apparatus directly behind the subject. Intertrial intervals varied randomly from 1.5 to 4 sec, to avoid anticipatory responses.

There were two experimental conditions—high and low intensity—each run on separate days. Half the subjects commenced with high, half with low. The high-intensity signal was clearly perceptible, and exactly corresponded to the value used in our previous study, so as to permit direct comparisons with that study. The low-intensity signal was variously set at a level just above each subject's individual detection threshold, as determined by simple psychophysical procedures. Subjects with a hand difference greater than a criterion of 4 dB were not used.

Each condition was further subdivided into two parts, *A* and *B;* half the subjects in each of the high- and low-intensity conditions commenced with Part *A,* and half with Part *B.* In Part *A* the two hands (one receiving vibrotactile stimulation, the other initiating the button-press response) occupied the same hemispace left or right—that is, there was always one arm crossing the body. Each of the following four conditions was sequentially traversed in blocks of 10 trials for a total of eight times (i.e., 320 trials overall): right hemispace, right hand stimulated, left hand responding; left hemispace, left hand stimulated, right hand responding; right hemispace, left hand stimulated, right hand responding; left hemispace, right hand stimulated, left hand responding. Half the subjects proceeded in the reverse sequence. The positions for the two hands were mutually adjacent, with the ipsilateral hand lying posterior to the contralateral one.

In Part *B* the two hands occupied opposite hemispatial positions (otherwise similar to those of Part *A*), with the two arms either extending out from the body or crossing the midline. Each of the following four conditions was sequentially traversed in blocks of 10 trials for a total of eight times (i.e., 320 trials overall): left hemispace, left hand stimulated, right hemispace, right hand responding; left hemispace, right hand stimulated, right hemispace, left hand responding; right hemispace, right hand stimulated, left hemispace, left hand responding; right hemispace, left hand stimulated, left hemispace, right hand responding. Half the subjects progressed in the reverse direction. The experimental series was preceded by a block of practice trials.

Results and Discussion

The effects of left sensory hemispace may be calculated by combining the two conditions in Part *A,* in which the two hands were in left hemispace, with the two conditions in Part *B,* in which the left (stimulated) hand was placed directly in left hemispace, and in which the right (stimulated) hand crossed the midline to left hemispace. The effects of right sensory hemispace may similarly be calculated from the combination of the remaining four conditions, two in Part *A* and two in Part *B.* Conversely, the effects of left motor hemispace may be calculated by combining the two conditions of Part A, in which the two hands were in left hemispace, with the two conditions in Part *B,* in which the left (responding) hand

TABLE 11.1
Vibrotactile RTs (msec) for 24 Subjects in Experiment 1,
for the Two Intensity Conditions (High and Low) Split by Hemispace
(Sensory, Motor) and Responding Hand, All Left and Right

	High Intensity			Low Intensity		
	Hemispace		Hand Responding	Hemispace		Hand Responding
	Motor	Sensory		Motor	Sensory	
Left	249	247	250	332	335	338
Right	245	248	245	334	331	329

was placed directly in left hemispace, and in which the right (responding) hand crossed the midline to left hemispace. The effects of right motor hemispace may similarly be calculated from the combination of the four remaining conditions, two in Part *A* and two in Part *B*. Analogous combinations between conditions in Parts *A* and *B* permit the left–right comparisons of sensory and motor hands, uncontaminated by hemispace effects (see Bradshaw, Nathan, Nettleton, Pierson, & Wilson, 1983, Experiment 3). These data are presented in Table 11.1.

In order to determine clearly the roles of sensory and motor hemispace and stimulated and responding hands (the responding hand was, of course, always opposite to the stimulated hand) under the two intensity conditions, data for these two conditions were separately analyzed, each by a four-way ANOVA. The facts were sex, sensory hemispace, motor hemispace, and hand responding, with repeated measures on the last three factors. The error terms used in this and all subsequent ANOVAs reported in this chapter were derived by summing the sum of squares for the interaction of subjects by the specific effect being examined, with the sum of squares for the nonrepeated measure (i.e., sex) by subjects by that specific effect, and dividing this by the sum of their respective degrees of freedom. We give this information in view of the significance levels obtained for what were highly consistent effects of comparatively small absolute magnitude.

For high-intensity data, the only significant effect was motor hemispace— $F(1,22) = 8.7$, $p < .01$—with performance on the right 4 msec faster than performance on the left. This replicated our previous finding of a motor RSA (Bradshaw, Nathan, Nettleton, Pierson, & Wilson, 1983, Experiment 3), our values then being remarkably similar, 249 and 255 msec, also at $p < .01$. Despite the small absolute magnitudes of these motor RSAs, the fast consistent responding of practiced subjects engaged in an easy repetitive task with a large number of trials ensured that the effects were reliable, as evidenced by the results of statistical analysis and the number of subjects (19) showing the effects. The differences between left and right sensory hemispace, and left and right responding hand were again nonsignificant, exactly as before, though it is interesting to note that in both cases there was a (nonsignificant) 5 or 6 msec right- (responding, left stimulated) hand superiority.

For low-intensity data, the previously significant motor hemispace effect now became quite nonsignificant (though it reached significance in an interaction, see the following discussion); 13 out of 24 subjects (with two ties) showed a 2 msec left-side superiority. A right sensory hemispace superiority of 4 msec over left also failed to achieve significance, although it was demonstrated by as many as 17 out of 24 subjects. Thus, there was now a trend toward a right *sensory* hemispace superiority with low-intensity signals, when stimulus rather than response uncertainty is likely to dominate decision processes. It is noteworthy that laterality effects are generally stronger at motor rather than sensory levels (see, for left-hemisphere functions, Bradshaw & Nettleton, 1981, 1983; Kimura, 1977, and, for right-hemisphere functions, LeDoux, Wilson, & Gazzaniga, 1977).

However, in the low-intensity condition two significant effects involving hand responding did emerge. The main effect proved significant—$F(1,22) = 7.4, p < .025$. Thus, the left hand stimulated/right responding was 9 msec faster than the opposite hand, with only six out of 24 subjects reversing. For high intensity, a (nonsignificant) difference of 5 msec was shown by only 14 out of 23 subjects. That the just described significant superiority of the left hand stimulated/right responding with low-intensity stimulation is likely to reflect the *motor* rather than the *sensory hand* is demonstrated by the significant interaction response hand by motor hemispace—$F(1,22) = 4.9, p < .05$. Thus, the right hand responded (with left-hand stimulation) 3 msec faster in right than in left *motor* hemispace, respectively 327 and 330 msec. Conversely, the left hand responded (with right-hand stimulation) 7 msec faster in left than in right motor hemispace, respectively 334 and 341 msec. This may reflect spatial compatibility effects between *responding* hand and *motor* hemispace; an exactly similar effect is reported in Experiment 3. On the other hand, the corresponding interaction sensory (response) hand by sensory hemispace was completely nonsignificant. In subsequent experiments we again encounter significant *hand* effects, at the motor level, when *hemispace* asymmetries, sensory or motor, are lost, and we consider possible explanations in the *General Discussion* section later in the chapter.

One further four-way ANOVA (sex, intensity, responding hand, and cross at three levels—that is, both, one, or neither arm crossed) was performed to examine the effect of crossing one or both arms. The only significant effect was intensity—$F(1,22) = 202, p < .001$; The high-intensity condition (247 msec) was, as expected, much faster than the low (333 msec). Thus, the values for both arms crossed (291 msec); one crossed, one uncrossed (295 msec); and neither arm crossed (289 msec) did not differ significantly from each other. This was, of course, a *simple* reaction-time task, in which spatial compatibility effects are unlikely to feature (Bradshaw & Umiltà, 1984). In Experiment 3, which incorporated in effect a *choice* design by randomly stimulating one or the other side, though a design of very high stimulus–response compability, the crossed-arms condition proved significantly slower than the uncrossed.

In summary, there was a right-hemispace superiority, as before, at the *motor* level, but only for *high*-intensity signals likely to be associated with response rather than stimulus uncertainty. With *low*-intensity signals there was a nonsignificant trend toward a right *sensory* hemispace superiority, when stimulus uncertainty was likely to be of paramount importance. There was also a *hand* superiority effect with low-intensity signals, probably at the *motor* level, as the *responding* hand was faster when operating in its own motor hemispace. There was no analogous effect involving stimulated hand or sensory hemispace, and, in this simple reaction-time task, crossing the arms did not increase overall RTs.

EXPERIMENT 2

We can now ask whether these RSAs relate to corporeal or gravitational coordinates of left and right. By corporeal we mean left and right as normally perceived by the upright subject, and made with reference to the midline. By gravitational, we mean left and right with respect to the *gravitational* vertical, while still facing in the direction in which a now possibly recumbent subject is looking. Thus, when a subject adopts a recumbent posture on the left side, gravitational left extends out from the top of the (recumbent) head, and gravitational right from the feet. These relationships are reversed when the subject lies on the right side. Generally, therefore, when a subject adopts a recumbent posture on one or the other side, the two coordinate systems dissociate, left–right (with respect to the body) becoming gravitationally up–down, and up–down (with respect to the body axis) becoming left–right. This Experiment repeated our earlier (Bradshaw, Nathan, Nettleton, Pierson, & Wilson, 1983, Experiment 1) unimanual vibrotactile RT task, when 22 out of 24 upright subjects demonstrated a RSA (mean of 9 msec), but now with subjects recumbent on one or the other side. Because subjects looked ahead, all sensory cues were available concerning posture.

Method

Subjects. Six male and six female dextrals were selected in accordance with the same constraints as before.

Apparatus. The apparatus was effectively the same as that used by Bradshaw, Nathan, Nettleton, Pierson, and Wilson (1983, Experiment 1), but now the same hand both received the stimulus and initiated the button-press response. Signal strength corresponded to the high-intensity levels used previously.

Procedure. Subjects lay horizontally on a couch, on their left or right sides, with their heads supported by pillows so that they were exactly in line with their body axes. As before, the room was symmetrical and had overhead lighting; an appropriately positioned fixation point was also provided.

There were two experimental conditions, *A* and *B;* half the subjects commenced with *A* and proceeded to *B,* and the remaining subjects progressed in the opposite direction. In condition *A,* the stimulated and responding arm (left or right) lay in the midline (spinal) axis of the body, either out beyond the head, or "down" the (horizontal) body between the flexed knees. Half the subjects commenced by lying on their left sides, and were turned over to their right sides for the remaining trials; with the remainder the order was reversed. There were eight blocks of 10 trials for each of the four arm-position conditions (left arm, right arm, and position beyond head, or between knees). In condition *B,* the stimulated and responding arm (left or right) either extended vertically up from the shoulder, lightly supported at the wrist, or it hung downwards (in both cases not crossing the midline), or it achieved corresponding positions while crossing the midline. As before, subjects lay on their left or right sides, with orders counterbalanced. Again there were eight blocks of 10 trials for each of the four arm-position conditions (arm left, right, out from or across the body). Thus, with 80 trials by four arm-position conditions by two experimental (*A, B*) conditions, there were 640 trials in the whole experiment.

Results and Discussion

The data were analyzed in terms of either gravitational left/right (as viewed from the recumbent subject's direction of regard, were he or she to assume a normal upright posture)—that is, condition *A*—or in terms of corporeal left/right (with respect to the spinal axis)—that is, condition *B*. In either case there was a three-way ANOVA, by sex, hand, and hemispace, with repeated measures on the last two factors.

The only effect in the gravitational data to reach significance was sex—$F(1,10) = 8.5, p < .025$; males (254 msec) proved to be 65 msec faster than females (319 msec). The right hemispace (286 msec) was only 1 msec faster than the left (287 msec)—$F(1,10) = .67$—and the left hand (286 msec) only 1 msec faster than the right (287 msec)—$F(1,10) = .09$.

Exactly the same was found with the corporeal data; males (261 msec) proved to be 53 msec faster than females (314 msec)—$F(1,10) = 9.66, p < .025$. Right (287 msec) and left (289 msec) hemispace scarcely differed—$F(1,10) = 1.73$. Although the left (285 msec) hand was 6 msec faster than the right (291 msec), this effect was again nonsignificant—$F(1,10) = 2.83$.

These corporeal data can, of course, be reanalyzed in terms of hand up/down (left or right). A three-way ANOVA was performed by sex, up/down, and hand left/right, with repeated measures on the last two factors. Even though sex was, of course, again significant, exactly as before, the other two factors and their interaction were quite nonsignificant, and hand down (287 msec) was only 3 msec faster than hand up (290 msec).

We must therefore conclude that just as 90° head turns, which dissociate head and body hemispace, destroy hemispace asymmetries in the auditory (Pierson et al., 1983), vibrotactile (Bradshaw, Nathan, Nettleton, Pierson, & Wilson, 1983), and tactual-kinesthetic (Bradshaw, Nettleton, Nathan, & Wilson, 1983) modalities, so also do dissociating corporeal and gravitational coordinates destroy the effects by requiring the subjects to adopt recumbent postures. Indeed, in an unpublished study we have recently found that the usual left-side underestimation, which occurs when subjects set a movable horizontal rod so that both extremities are judged equidistant from a central reference point, is lost when retinal and gravitational coordinates are dissociated by making the subjects lie horizontally on one or the other side, with gravitationally horizontal or vertical rod presentations. Thus, gravitational coordinates and the apparent locus of events in extracorporeal space may be determinants of perceptual asymmetries at least as important as anatomical connectivities.

EXPERIMENT 3

So far, stimuli have always been presented (and responses elicited) in *blocks* of trials to one or the other side. Do the resultant RSAs stem from subjects' developing positional sets? This is, of course, yet another aspect of stimulus and response uncertainty (cf. Experiment 1). Are RSAs lost when subjects cannot predict which side will be stimulated or from which side a response will be required—that is, are our RSAs with blocked presentations due to subjects' possessing a greater ability to *hold* attention to the right, as compared with the left? Alternatively, if RSAs are preserved when presentations (and their associated responses) alternate randomly from side to side, this might reflect a greater ability to *shift* attention to the right than to the left.

One way to present vibrotactile stimuli randomly as to side is to provide two sets of stimulus–response units, one for either hand, with the appropriate hand responding if stimulated; this is a highly compatible stimulus–response configuration in what is now otherwise essentially a *choice* reaction-time task. (Another way, which is explored in the final experiment discussed in this chapter, is to have only one hand responding for a block of trials—whichever hand is stimulated.) Under these circumstances, it might be predicted that reaction times would increase, and spatial compatibility effects (the effect of a hand's lying across the body in its "wrong" hemispace) would become manifest (Bradshaw & Umiltà, 1984), even if the task were made maximally compatible by requiring the subject to depress the vibrated finger itself. Thus, coding of spatial positions may become a relevant factor.

Method

Subjects. Eight male and eight female dextrals were drawn from the same population as before.

Apparatus and Procedure. Vibrators were taped to the forefingers of either hand, with their pads resting on the response key. As before, a high-intensity signal was used. Subjects responded immediately with the forefinger that detected stimulation. Vibrators and, separately, response keys were interchanged between hands during the experiment. There were two conditions—both arms crossed or both uncrossed—with 16 blocks each of 20 trials for each condition; stimuli were presented pseudorandomly to either side within each block, with 10 trials to either hand.

Results and Discussion

A three-way ANOVA was performed on the data, by hand, side, and sex, with repeated measures on the first two factors. Side proved nonsignificant—$F(1,14) = .62$: The left side (357 msec) was only 2 msec faster than the right (359 msec). Males were nonsignificantly faster than females, and the right hand (352 msec) was 13 msec faster than the left (365 msec)—$F(1,14) = 8.44, p < .025$. The hand by side interaction was highly significant—$F(1,14) = 64.6, p < .001$: The left hand in left hemispace (338 msec) was 54 msec faster than the left hand in right hemispace (392 msec), and the right hand in right hemispace (327 msec) was 49 msec faster than the right hand in left hemispace (376 msec). This implies that the uncrossed configuration (333 msec) was 51 msec faster than the crossed (384 msec).

The loss (indeed, nonsignificant *reversal*) of the RSA when subjects were unable to predict which side would be stimulated or would require a response suggests that these hemispace effects previously reported with blocked presentations are due to a greater ability to *hold* attention to the right (as compared to the left), rather than being due to a greater ability to *shift* attention to the right (rather than to the left).

Generally the RTs (mean of 358 msec) were considerably larger than in all our previous vibrotactile studies (245 to 290 msec), presumably as a consequence of position uncertainty, choice reaction time, or both. For almost the first time (though cf. Experiment 1, low intensity) there was now a small right *hand* superiority, perhaps due to the spatial compatibility effects evident in the hand by side interaction. Indeed, this observation of the replacement of hemispace by hand asymmetries, and the reduction in magnitude and reversal of direction of the now nonsignificant hemispace asymmetries, indicates that loss of statistical significance of hemispace asymmetries in this and the next experiment is not simply due to a more difficult task or longer RTs. Also, perhaps as a consequence of the task's being choice rather than simple reaction time, there was a deleterious effect from arms crossing the midline: In Experiment 1, *low* intensity, there had been an interaction between *response* hand and *motor* hemispace, reflecting spatial compatibility, but overall (i.e., across high and low intensity), there was no *general* effect from arms crossing the midline.

Simple effects analysis permits us to further analyze the just-described hand by side interaction, which demonstrated the superiority of the uncrossed over the crossed configuration. Thus, the 49 msec superiority of the right hand when in its own as compared to its contralateral hemispace proved no less significant, $F(1,15) = 63.8, p < .001$, than the corresponding 54 msec superiority of the left hand, $F(1,15) = 52.0, p < .001$. The cross effect was therefore similar for either hand. The fact that the right hand in right hemispace was significantly faster than the left hand in left hemispace—$F(1,15) = 6.0, p < .05$—by 11 msec, and the right hand in left hemispace was likewise significantly faster than the left hand in right hemispace—$F(1,15) = 5.8, p < .05$—by 16 msec, indicates that the overall right-hand superiority was not affected by whether or not the hands were crossed. The difference of 5 msec between the just-described two effects proved nonsignificant—$t(15) = .82$: We cannot, therefore, conclude that the right hand in left hemispace was less detrimentally affected than the left hand in right hemispace, or that hand differences in left hemispace (mediated by the right hemisphere) were less than those in right hemispace (mediated by the left hemisphere).

Spatial compatibility effects are traditionally absent from *simple* reaction-time tasks, and present in *choice* reaction-time tasks (Bradshaw & Umiltà, 1984). *Hemispace* effects may not appear in choice reaction-time tasks, in which it is necessary to encode the spatial position of the stimulated/responding limb, but may possibly appear in simple reaction-time tasks in which spatial position is unimportant. Consequently, hemispace effects might possibly reappear if the *responding* hand is held constant for a block of trials, while the *stimulated* hand continues to randomly alternate. The next experiment addressed this issue.

EXPERIMENT 4

In the previous experiment, hemispace asymmetries were replaced by hand asymmetries when the subject was unable to predict, from trial to trial, the likely locus (left, right) of the next stimulus and its associated response. The experiment aimed to develop a division of attention between the two sides; however, this unfortunately cannot be attained without the task's becoming choice, even though there is still maximal stimulus–response compatibility. However, the paradigm can be adapted so that unilateral responses are required, over blocks of trials, to stimuli that are nevertheless still divided randomly between the two sides. Thus, the subject may respond for a number of trials with a single hand in the one (same or opposite) hemispace to stimuli divided randomly between that hand and the other hand situated in the opposite hemispace. If the presence or absence of *response* uncertainty is the major determinant of whether hemispace or hand asymmetries will be manifest, then we would predict the return of hemispace effects with the proposed paradigm. If, however, any form of uncertainty, stimulus or response, is sufficient to eliminate hemispace effects, then the proposed paradigm should demonstrate hand asymmetries in the absence of hemispace effects.

Method

Subjects. Eight male and eight female dextrals were drawn from the same population as before.

Apparatus and Procedure. The only change from the previous experiment was that subjects only had a single response button for a block of trials. Thus, a vibrator was taped to both index fingers, but only one finger could respond, and did so whether that finger or its fellow on the other hand received vibrotactile stimulation. As before, there were two major conditions, both arms crossed or both uncrossed. Trials were presented in blocks of 10, and within each block, although only one hand responded for the duration of that block, left and right hands were stimulated in a pseudorandom order so that each hand received five stimulations. A different pseudorandom order was used for a total of 32 blocks, giving a total of 320 trials. The presentation order of the 32 blocks was counterbalanced between subjects. The two major conditions (arms crossed or uncrossed) were, therefore, further subdivided into a total of four response conditions, two requiring the subjects to respond with either the left or the right hand in its own hemispace, and two requiring the left or the right hand to respond in the opposite hemispace. Vibrotactile transducers and the response button were exchanged to the opposite side halfway through.

Results and Discussion

In some trials the same hand both detected and responded, and in others these responsibilities were shared between hands. In view of this, and the incomplete nature of the design, in the absence of conditions with both hands on the same side of the body, a single ANOVA encompassing all the relevant variables was impractical. Consequently, to determine the contributions of response side, response hand, stimulus side, and stimulus hand (all left and right), crossing (both arms crossed and uncrossed), and same/opposite hand stimulated and responding, six two-way ANOVAs were performed, one for each of the preceding six contrasts, with sex as the other (nonrepeated) measure.

Only two factors achieved significance, response hand—$F(1,14) = 4.56$, $p = .05$—and same/opposite hand stimulated and responding—$F(1,14) = 5.2$, $p < .05$. The right hand (396 msec) responded 8 msec faster than the left (404 msec), as in the last experiment, with only four out of 16 subjects reversing; when the same hand was stimulated and responded (391 msec), it was 18 msec faster than when opposite hands were stimulated and responded (409 msec). This 18-msec difference is almost certainly too great to reflect interhemispheric (transcallosal) transmission time (Bradshaw & Umiltà, 1984), and probably reflects attentional and/or spatial compatibility factors. Hemispace differences both at the response and at the stimulus levels were only 2 msec, and quite nonsignificant in either case. Likewise, the stimulated hand (left versus right) also differed by a nonsignificant 2 msec, as did the means of the uncrossed- (399 msec) and crossed-arm conditions. Thus, when only one hand (on a given side) responded for a block of trials, whichever hand (and side) received the stimulus, there was no advantage for the uncrossed configuration—unlike the finding of Experiment 3. The need to select a response hand seems, therefore, to determine whether the crossed configuration will be inferior to the uncrossed. The absence (in Experiment 3) of hemispace effects, and their replacement by hand effects, when both stimuli and responses occur randomly as to side, rather than in blocks, or when stimuli alone are so treated (this experiment) suggests that hemispace effects probably only occur when attention can be wholly allocated to one or the other side for a number of trials (Experiment 1, and Bradshaw, Nathan, Nettleton, Pierson, & Wilson, 1983). If so, the powerful RSAs in our verbal auditory tasks (Pierson et al., 1983) should disappear if competing unilateral stimuli are randomly alternated from side to side. Unfortunately, we cannot extend the present paradigm to investigate the possible effects of a blocked-sensory, random-response design, for obvious reasons. Nor can we easily dissociate response hemispace and hand effects, by, for example, having the same hand respond in (randomly) left and right hemispace or by having randomly left and right hands responding in the same hemispace for a block of trials, without resorting to highly artificial conditions. However, it would appear that even though RSAs in vibrotactile tasks reflect motor rather than sensory hemispace effects (Experiment 1, and Bradshaw, Nathan, Nettleton, Pierson, & Wilson, 1983, Experiment 3), and responding rather than stimulated hand (this experiment), responding with the same hand in the same hemispace for a block of trials is insufficient to overcome the effects of stimulus uncertainty (with respect to side and hand) in converting hand differences to hemispace asymmetries.

GENERAL DISCUSSION

The demonstration of hemispace effects, at least in the auditory modality (Pierson et al., 1983), with texture matching, finger spacing, and sequencing tasks (Burden, Bradshaw, Nettleton, & Wilson, in press), and with simple vibrotactile reaction times where stimulus uncertainty is low (Bradshaw, Nathan, Nettleton, Pierson, & Wilson, 1983, and Experiment 1 of this series), indicates that the position in extracorporeal space of stimuli and responding limbs is at least as important as the traditional anatomical connectivities (Kimura 1961, 1967) in determining functional asymmetries. With vibrotactile reaction-time tasks, RSAs appear, in the absence of hand asymmetries, as long as simple rather than choice reaction-time paradigms are employed, and there is no stimulus uncertainty, either in terms of low signal intensity or side of stimulation. They are robust RT differences, though of small absolute magnitude. Indeed, their value (around 5 msec) is reminiscent of behavioral (RT) estimates of interhemispheric transmission time (Bradshaw & Umiltà, 1984). The possible involvement of some such mechanism cannot, of course, be excluded, even in a task involving attentional aspects and mapping by the hemispheres of extracorporeal space, rather than conventional anatomical-pathway representation and transmission of sensory-motor information. These RSAs are reduced with 90° head turns that dissociate head and body hemispace, and are eliminated when gravitational and corporeal coordinates of hemispace are dissociated by making the subject lie horizontally on one or the other side. These RSAs, when present, are motor rather than sensory; similarly, when they give way, under certain circumstances (see the following discussion) to right *hand* superiorities, it is the *responding* rather than the *stimulated* hand that exhibits asymmetrical performance. As discussed earlier, asymmetries are often reported to be stronger at the motor than at the sensory level. However, RSAs are lost when subjects cannot predict the side of response, or of stimulation alone with side of response held constant for a block of trials. Consequently, the occurrence of RSAs with both side of stimulation and response held constant seems to reflect a greater ability to *hold* attention to the right, rather than to *shift* it to the right. Hemispace effects appear, therefore, to be *attentional* in origin, but not perhaps as envisaged by Kinsbourne (1973), who invokes an activational component, and consequently claims that laterality effects should only occur when the subject *cannot* predict the likely side of stimulation/response. If hemispace effects do stem from directional asymmetries in the ability to hold attention, with stimulus presentation directed to the same hemispace for a block of trials, we can ask how long it takes for the asymmetries to appear. Thus, in the context of the current vibrotactile reaction times, or our earlier auditory-shadowing–latency demonstrations, over a block of consecutive trials to one or the other side do we find a gradual development of a hemispace asymmetry? When does it become significant, and when does it reach asymptote? It has long been known that laterality effects increase with practice (Goldberg & Costa, 1981; Nettleton & Bradshaw, 1983); we now perhaps have a possible explanation in terms of developing asymmetries in the allocation of attention to one or the other hemispace.

A major issue is when we should expect *hand* (i.e., anatomical connectivity) effects, and when we should predict that *hemispace* effects would occur. The occurrence of hand instead of hemispace effects in a given experimental paradigm does not necessarily support the anatomical connectivity model; hand asymmetries could still be a consequence of a strategy of directing attention to a given *hand* instead of to its (normal) hemispace. Thus, a strategy for coping with stimulus uncertainty and minimizing response latencies is perhaps to direct attention to the preferred hand; in the absence of such uncertainty attention may be allocated to that region in space wherein the preferred hand would normally fall. Indeed, hand rather than hemispace effects emerged in the present series of experiments only in the presence of stimulus uncertainty—that is, with low signal intensity (Experiment 1) and with random-as-to-side stimuli (Experiment 4) or random stimuli and responses (Experiment 3). Hemispace effects again, therefore, appear to occur only if the subject can allocate attention to one side for a block of trials. Thus, hemispace effects are absent in choice and present in simple reaction-time tasks in which spatial position is unimportant in stimulus–response coding; conversely, spatial compatibility effects are present in choice and absent in simple reaction-time tasks. Similarly, it has little effect on speed whether the arms do or do not cross the midline in a simple reaction-time paradigm (Experiment 1), and when there is little stimulus uncertainty due to high signal intensity. With, however, low-intensity (and therefore uncertain) vibrotactile signals, and when both side of stimulation and response are unpredictable (Experiment 3), the crossed configuration produces longer response times than the uncrossed. Yet, when there is only one possible response (to stimuli that can occur on either side, as in Experiment 4), once again differences disappear between the crossed and the uncrossed configurations. Consequently, the need to select a *response* hand seems to determine whether the crossed configuration produces longer response times than the uncrossed.

ACKNOWLEDGMENTS

We gratefully acknowledge the assistance of Judy Bradshaw, Greg Nathan, and Lyn Wilson in collecting and analyzing data, and the many useful discussions with Norman Nettleton and Carlo Umiltà. This work was supported by a grant from the Australian Research Grants Scheme to John Bradshaw and Norman Nettleton. Please address requests for reprints to John L. Bradshaw, Department of Psychology, Monash University, Clayton, Victoria 3168, Australia.

REFERENCES

Bertelson, P. (1982). Lateral differences in normal man and lateralization of brain function. *International Journal of Psychology, 17*, 173–210.

Bowers, D., & Heilman, K. M. (1980). Pseudoneglect: Effects of hemispace on a tactile line bisection task. *Neuropsychologia, 18*, 491–498.

Bradshaw, J. L., Nathan, G., Nettleton, N. C., Pierson, J. M., & Wilson, L. E. (1983). Head and body space to left and right—III. Vibrotactile stimulation and sensory and motor components. *Perception, 12,* 651–661.

Bradshaw, J. L., & Nettleton, N. C. (1981). The nature of hemispheric specialization in man. *The Behavioural and Brain Sciences, 4,* 51–91.

Bradshaw, J. L., & Nettleton, N. C. (1983). *Human cerebral asymmetry.* Englewood Cliffs, NJ: Prentice-Hall.

Bradshaw, J. L., Nettleton, N. C., Nathan, G., & Wilson, L. (1983). Head and body space to left and right, front and rear—II. Visuotactual and kinesthetic studies and left-side underestimation. *Neuropsychologia, 21,* 475–486.

Bradshaw, J. L., Nettleton, N. C., & Spehr, K. (1982). Sinistral inverters do not possess an anomalous visuomotor organization. *Neuropsychologia, 20,* 605–609.

Bradshaw, J. L., & Umiltà, C. (1984). A reaction-time paradigm can simultaneously index spatial-compatibility and neural-pathway effects: A reply to Levy, *Neuropsychologia, 22,* 99–101.

Burden, V., Bradshaw, J. L., Nettleton, N. C., & Wilson, L. (in press). Hand and hemispace effects in tactual tasks involving interhemispheric integration in children: A maturational study. *Neuropsychologia.*

Crowne, D. P. (1983). The frontal eye field and attention. *Psychological Bulletin, 93,* 232–260.

Darwin, C. J., Howell, P., & Brady, S. A. (1978). Lateralization and localization: A "right ear advantage" for speech heard on the left. In J. Requin (Ed.), *Attention and performance VII* (pp. 261–278). Hillsdale, NJ: Lawrence Erlbaum Associates.

De Renzi, E. (1982). *Disorders of space exploration and cognition.* New York: Wiley.

Goldberg, E., & Costa, L. (1981). Hemisphere differences in the acquisition of descriptive systems. *Brain and Language, 14,* 144–173.

Kimura, D. (1961). Cerebral dominance and the perception of verbal stimuli. *Canadian Journal of Psychology, 15,* 166–171.

Kimura, D. (1967). Functional asymmetry of the brain in dichotic listening. *Cortex, 3,* 163–178.

Kimura, D. (1977). Acquisition of a motor skill after left hemisphere damage. *Brain, 100,* 527–542.

Kinsbourne, M. (1973). The control of attention by interaction between the cerebral hemispheres. In S. Kornblum (Ed.), *Attention and performance II* (pp. 239–255). New York: Academic.

LeDoux, J. E., Wilson, D. H., & Gazzaniga, M. S. (1977). Manipulospatial aspects of cerebral lateralization: Clues to the origin of lateralization. *Neuropsychologia, 15,* 743–750.

Mesulam, M.-M. (1981). A cortical network for directed attention and unilateral neglect. *Annals of Neurology, 10,* 309–325.

Morais, J. (1978). Spatial constraints on attention to speech. In J. Requin (Ed.), *Attention and performance VII* (pp. 245–260). Hillsdale, NJ: Lawrence Erlbaum Associates.

Nettleton, N. C., & Bradshaw, J. L. (1983). The effects of task, practice, and sequencing upon the lateralization of semantic decisions. *International Journal of Neuroscience, 20,* 265–282.

Pierson, J. M., Bradshaw, J. L., & Nettleton, N. C. (1983). Head and body space to left and right, front and rear—I. Unidirectional competitive auditory stimulation. *Neuropsychologia, 21,* 463–473.

Sherrick, C. E., & Craig, J. C. (1982). The psychophysics of touch. In W. Schiff & E. Foulke (eds.), *Tactual perception: A sourcebook* (pp. 55–81). Cambridge, England: Cambridge University.

12 Analogical and Logical Disorders Underlying Unilateral Neglect of Space

Edoardo Bisiach
Anna Berti
Giuseppe Vallar
Istituto di Clinica Neurologica dell'Università di Milano

ABSTRACT

A description is given, in this chapter, of an experiment in which right brain-damaged patients with unilateral neglect of egocentric space were asked to give leftward and rightward motor responses to left and right visual stimuli in crossed and uncrossed conditions. Both the side of stimulation and the side of the required response were found to affect performance. It is claimed that the behavior of patients with unilateral neglect suggests an analog structure of space representation in the brain. The cognitive status of this representation is unclear: The pattern of results in the experiment shows, however, an unmonitored failure in the execution of the algorithm governing the causal chain between initial stimulus and final response, a failure that suggests the cognitive nature of the disorder underlying unilateral neglect of space. The contribution of clinicoexperimental investigation to some critical issues in cognitive science is discussed. The inner representation of space, meant as the structure into which data from perception and active memory are organized for their spatial attributes, is seen as an analog, distributed processor. Far from being a slave device of the cognitive machinery, it appears to be closely involved not only with the control of its own activity but also with the top-level self-referential function of the nervous system.

INTRODUCTION

The basic intent of this chapter is to substantiate the claim that the disorder that underlies unilateral neglect of space is not confined to the operations of some analogical device subserving earlier stages in accessing and processing spatial information. Evidence is indeed provided that points to the concomitant, unmonitored failure of logical operations performed on a database incorporating the representation of space. This is a crucial step to be taken in order to definitely qualify unilateral neglect as a truly cognitive disorder and to pave the way for discussing some rather knotty aspects of cognition.

The experiment that is reported was originally devised to disentangle input and output aspects of unilateral neglect. Right brain-damaged patients with left neglect were asked to perform leftward and rightward movements with their right upper limbs in response to left and right visual stimuli in crossed and uncrossed conditions. We reasoned that, in this arrangement, failure to respond to left stimuli independent of the side of response would expose an input neglect once any damage involving the sensory channel could be safely ruled out. On the other hand, failure to give leftward responses independent of the side of stimulation would expose an output neglect conforming to the concept of *unilateral hypokinesia*—or defect of "intention"—of Watson, Miller, and Heilman (1978).

THE EXPERIMENT

Method

Subjects. A sample of 16 right-handed patients, eight males and eight females, aged 45 to 83 ($M = 63.19 \pm 11.14$), with clinical and instrumental (CT scan) evidence of a focal lesion confined to the right hemisphere (vascular in 16 and neoplastic in two patients) and showing left hemispace neglect, was selected. The criteria for selection were one or more left-sided omissions in a cancellation task in which the subjects had to scan an array of 13 circles (Bisiach, Luzzatti, & Perani, 1979).

Apparatus and Procedure. Each subject sat facing a frontal panel, 11 cm high and 46 cm wide, placed at a distance of about 50 cm (Fig. 12.1). The vertical midline of the panel lay in the sagittal midplane of the subject's body. Along the upper edge of the panel were eight LEDs, four in each hemifield, aligned in two rows. When activated, the LEDs in the upper row emitted a green light;

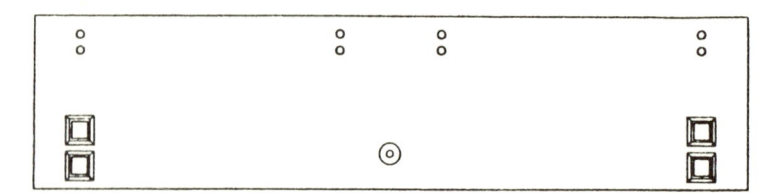

FIG. 12.1.   Front view of the panel.

those in the lower row a red light. The distance of the two medial LEDs of each row from the vertical midline was 3 cm; that of the two lateral LEDs of each row was 20 cm. In the left and in the right lower corners of the panel were four square 12 mm × 12 mm response keys: one green (above) and one red (below) on either side, at a distance of 20 cm from the vertical midline. A trigger button (3 mm in diameter) lay in central position 2.5 cm above the lower edge of the panel. The subject him- or herself started each trial of a visuomotor task by pressing the trigger button with his or her right forefinger. The size of the button was sufficiently small to require fixation, so that each half of the panel lay in the corresponding visual hemifield. The button triggered a 200-msec flash from an LED. Two keys of different color, one on either side, were lit simultaneously with the flashing of a diode. The subject was instructed to press with his or her right forefinger the lit key corresponding to the color flashed by the diode, *irrespective of the side*. The pressing of any of the four keys turned out the lit pair. There was thus a fourfold S-R contingency: left S-left R, left S-right R, right S-left R, and right S-right R. Sixteen trials for each condition were given following a fixed random schedule, with eight catch trials intermixed. After each trial the subject had to withdraw his or her hand from the panel to ensure that on the following trial central fixation was reset as the subject reached for the trigger button. It is worth reiterating that motor responses were executed by the right hand. Because this hand is unaffected by the brain lesion it is free to execute any kind of physiological movement in any direction. The visuomotor task was supplemented by two other tasks. In the first (visuoverbal), the subject was simply required to name the color of the flashing diode. In the second (verbomotor), he or she had to press a lit key according to the color named by the experimenter. In each of these tasks 16 left (stimulus or response, respectively) trials and 16 right trials were given in a fixed random order. The visuoverbal task preceded the visuomotor task; the verbomotor followed it. The verbomotor task was given to the last eight patients only.

Results

The mean scores recorded in this experiment are shown in Table 12.1. An ANOVA was carried out on correct responses, following a randomized block factorial 2 × 2 design. Significant main effects of stimulus side—$F(1,15) = 75.4, p < .000001$—and of response side—$F(1,15) = 29.4, p < .0002$—were found. Given the significant interaction between side of the stimulus and side of the response—$F(1,15) = 11.8, p < .005$—simple main effects were calculated. A significant effect of the side of stimulation was found both for trials involving left responses—$F(1,30) = 10.1, p < .005$—and for trials involving right responses—$F(1,30) = 61.2, p < .0001$; conversely, a significant effect of the side of the required response was found both for trials with left stimulation—$F(1,30) = 10.9, p < .005$—and for trials with right stimulation—$F(1,30) = 48.8, p$

TABLE 12.1
Mean Correct Responses and Mean Omission
and Commission Errors in the Four Conditions
of the Experiment (Maximum Scores: 16.00)

Condition[a]	Left S Left R	Left S Right R	Right S Left R	Right S Right R
Correct responses	2.62	5.87	6.87	14.87
Omissions	9.56	9.37	1.87	.50
Inverted responses	3.81	.75	7.25	.62

[a]Trials with stimuli of differing eccentricity are pooled for each side. S = stimulus; R = response.

< .0001. So, the significance of the main effects should not be traced back simply to the presence of a crucial condition (left stimulus and left response) but truly reflects general effects of the stimulus side and of the response side.

Table 12.1 shows that the subjects performed accurately only on the 16 trials in which both stimulus and required response were on the right. Left stimuli were seldom responded to accurately, but if the response due was to the left the performance was definitely worse. Even with right stimuli the performance deteriorated if the response due was to the left. A number of commission errors were recorded in which the response was reversed by pressing one of the keys of the wrong side: either the lit key of the wrong color, or the unlit key of the appropriate color. This happened virtually only when the response was due to the left, and it was a common feature of trials with left or right stimulation. On a little more than half of the trials with left stimuli, response was not given. Whereas virtually all right stimuli requiring right responses were responded to, a small proportion of the *same* stimuli went apparently unnoticed if the required response was to the left. It must be pointed out that this dissociation is essentially due to the performance of patient FS, examined 11 days after the onset of a cerebrovascular attack. This performance (Table 12.2) is worth separate consideration, because FS was the only patient in our series whose lesion involved the frontal lobe and spared the visual pathways. CT scan of this patient revealed a softening of the deep structures of the right frontal lobe, the head of caudate

TABLE 12.2
Scores of Patient FS

Condition	Left S Left R	Left S Right R	Right S Left R	Right S Right R
Correct responses	1	12	1	16
Omissions	9	4	8	—
Inverted responses	6	—	7	—

nucleus, the lenticular nucleus, and the capsula interna. On several unresponded trials, FS explicitly denied, as with catch trials, the occurrence of the stimulus.

On the visuoverbal task, the mean rate of response omission was 5.18 for the 16 trials with left stimulation and 1.00 for the 16 trials with right stimulation. The wrong color name was given in 1.68 trials with left stimulation and .43 trials with right stimulation. All subjects to whom the verbomotor task was administered gave an errorless performance with the exception of one patient who failed to respond to seven of the 16 trials requiring left response and gave one reversed response by pressing, on the wrong (right) side, the unlit key of the color named by the examiner.

DISCUSSION

Unilateral Neglect as a Cognitive Disorder

The results of our investigation seem to corroborate the intuition of Watson and associates about the distinctiveness of input and output stages of information processing involved in unilateral neglect. At least, output neglect, understood as a decrement in left responses irrespective of the side of stimulation, seems evident in our patients. Input neglect, understood as a decrement in detection of left stimuli irrespective of the side of response, is more resistant to discrimination from hemianopsia or hemiamblyopia. As already mentioned, it could confidently be asserted only in patients whose visual pathways were definitely spared by the lesion. In our group of patients, only FS is likely to satisfy this condition and, as shown in Table 12.2, both input and output neglect seemed to affect his behavior. These two aspects of neglect, however, can be subsumed under a more general interpretation of the syndrome.

The striking feature distinguishing unilateral neglect from other disorders of higher brain functions is the left–right anisotropy of its manifestations in the egocentric space with reference both to the sagittal midplane of the trunk and to the vertical plane where the line of sight lies (Bisiach, Capitani, & Porta, 1985). The affected hemisphere being as a rule the right (at least in clear cut, unequivocal instances of the syndrome), left stimuli may go undetected and actions toward the left side are rarely, if at all, performed. Sometimes there appears to be a definite cleavage between the affected and the unaffected side of space, though scrupulous observation may reveal a skewed sort of behavior—that is, object localization and actions performed by the patient seem to be "right justified," as it were, even within the right hemispace (Bisiach, Bulgarelli, Sterzi, & Vallar, 1983; Bisiach, Cornacchia, Sterzi, & Vallar, 1984; Kinsbourne, 1977).

As a contralateral disorder, unilateral neglect shows a misleading similarity to noncognitive disorders arising from brain damage, like hemianopia and hemiplegia. Very probably this is one reason why several attempts have been made at giving an explanation of the syndrome at an infracognitive level. However, a higher-level interpretation of unilateral neglect was already present in Zingerle's (1913) paper, in which the representational nature of the disorder was tersely argued on the grounds of mere clinical observation. More recently, though, further evidence has been given that unilateral neglect cannot be fully explained in terms of sensory or oculomotor disorders, unilateral hypokinesia, or disorders of attention to *external* objects. It has been found that patients with unilateral neglect omit details of the left side when describing actual views from a given vantage point from memory. If the opposite vantage point is subsequently prescribed, formerly unremembered left-sided details—now on the right side—are described, whereas formerly right-side details remembered previously, which would now fit in the left side of the imagined perspective, are omitted (Bisiach, Capitani, Luzzatti, & Perani, 1981; Bisiach & Luzzatti, 1978). These patients overlook the left half of visual stimuli even if, instead of being stationary and exposed to full vision, they move to and fro behind a central vertical slit so that each part of them can be equally observed and perceived but the comprehension of their shape requires a process of representational reconstruction (Bisiach et al., 1979). Furthermore, the case has recently been described (Baxter & Warrington, 1983) of a neglect patient who misspelled the left half of words, both forwards and backwards, as if reading letter after letter from words written on an imaginary display.

Once unilateral neglect has been qualified as a *representational* disorder with strict reference to this sort of evidence, should it follow that it is a *cognitive* disorder? A positive answer to this question would probably meet opposition. Indeed, if on the grounds of the just-described considerations we are to admit that the *Grundstoerung* of unilateral neglect is a breakdown of egocentric space representation, we must also admit that such a "representation" has analog properties: Damage to a spatially circumscribed area of the brain is in fact followed by a spatially circumscribed representational disorder that in many instances could be described as a representational scotoma.[1] The organization of space representation in the brain would thus conform to the principle of *first-*

---

[1] It is worth noting that the analog properties of space representation inferred from observation of brain-damaged subjects do not seem to be undermined by the argument from "tacit knowledge" advanced by Pylyshyn (1981) against the appeal to such properties in studies involving visual imagery in normal people. Pylyshyn suggests that analogies found between spatial operations performed on real objects and corresponding operations performed on mental objects (e.g., in tasks requiring mental rotation or scanning of mental images), far from disclosing the analog structure of the involved representation, betray the fact that subjects engaged in such tasks *do* imagine themselves in the act of executing such tasks in real space, and set the pace of their mental operations accordingly. It would, however, be absurd to suggest that in visual-imagery experiments, neglect patients behave as if they were not perceiving the left side of real objects on account of hemianopia: Nearly always, in fact, these patients are quite unaware of their visual field defects.

order isomorphism as defined by Shepard (1975). It would be something hardwired and therefore outside the province of cognitive science proper. This, at least, would be the conclusion of authors like Palmer (1978) and Pylyshyn (1981), if our reading of their argumentations is not inaccurate. However one chooses to settle this aspect of the matter, features in the behavior of neglect patients do seem to supply a firmer basis from which to argue the cognitive nature of their disorders.

The task in our experiment implies the execution of a very simple algorithm. If a stimulus is detected in either of his or her visual hemifields, the patient, according to instructions, must find the target key (that is, the lit key of the same color flashed by the LED). He or she must, therefore, direct his or her attention to one pair of adjoining keys. Though no constraint is imposed by instructions about the side to be explored first, and notwithstanding the lack of instrumental monitoring of ocular movements, we can safely assume from a wealth of clinical and experimental knowledge that a patient with hemineglect begins by foveating the keys on the right side. This lateralized reaction to the initial stimulus is followed by acquisition and analysis of further sensory information: a new input stage that is not critical for neglect patients because the source of information is now foveated. If, at this point, a lit key of the appropriate color is found, the operation ends by the patient's pressing this key. If the lit key of the appropriate color is not found on the right, it should be looked for and pressed on the left side. The firm establishment of this algorithm is demonstrated by the practically errorless performance on trials requiring right responses to right stimuli. There are, however, faults that reveal a principled failure in the execution of the algorithm. If a left response is required, the level of performance drops dramatically: often, indeed, either no reaction at all follows the stimulus, or the side of the response is reversed. With left stimulation, omission errors may partially be accounted for by hemiambliopia; in this case, the process simply does not start. Omission errors to such stimuli, however, might also suggest an influence exerted by the side of the required response; this seems evident in patient FS, who did not react to nine out of the 16 left stimuli requiring left response, but omitted responses only to four of the 16 (identical) left stimuli requiring right response. In this case, we may reasonably infer an internal interrupt of the process. The same is true for the lack of reaction to right stimuli requiring left responses, which was a rare event, but apparently more frequent than the lack of reaction to right stimuli requiring right responses. Commission errors are almost uniquely due to rightward derouting of responses due to the left side, independent of the side of the stimulus. The fault terminates in a wrong choice of the key color— which obviously cannot be explained in terms of sensory disorder—or in the choice of the unlit key. Such transgressions to instructions that are regularly acquired and stored in memory indicate the presence of a logical disorder affecting the very domain of the cognitive processes. Moreover, the absence of monitoring of wrong responses, as well as of those faults that—as suggested before—seem to originate from an en route blocking of the S-R chain, reveals a serious breakdown somewhere in a central processor. If this is so, little doubt should remain that the disorder manifesting itself in the clinical syndrome of unilateral neglect of space be cognitive, even if one accepts a strict definition of "cognition" as the set of syntactic operations performed on symbolic structures (Pylyshyn, 1980).

Cognitive Structures Underlying Spatial Behavior and its Control

Clinicopathological data suggest that active representation of spatial relationships among objects and parts thereof implies the processing of information, the distribution of which maps that of the external world (no matter what form of idle database organization must be addressed). This would seem to agree with a considerable amount of evidence from experimental psychology, mainly due to the work of authors like Shepard, Kosslyn, and their associates (e.g., Kosslyn, 1980; Shepard, 1975). The visuospatial "scratch-pad" envisaged by Baddeley and coworkers as a subsystem of their working memory system also seems to conform to an analog view of space representation at a certain stage of processing (Baddeley & Hitch, 1974; Baddeley & Lieberman, 1980). On the other hand, at a neurophysiological level, the distributed, topological organization of representational processes in brain structures has also been suggested (Merzenich & Kaas, 1980; Mountcastle, 1981).

A weaker meaning of "analog" might simply express the relationships among observable objects and events (e.g., the relationships between the distance that separates objects in a visual array and the reaction times obtained in experiments requiring the scanning of a mental image of that array). On this understanding, the concept seems quite neutral. A stronger meaning, however, relates to the actual structure of the inner processes underlying behavior. Palmer (1978) affirms that in this case reference to brain hardware is being made and eo ipso the question is beyond the scope of cognitive science. For the present purpose it would be too far reaching and somewhat irrelevant to engage in an argument concerning the defensibility of denying analogs the prerogative of being dealt with in the abstract—a prerogative that is granted to symbols and proposition-like representations and algorithms. Further, to avoid any possible misunderstandings, we ought to recognize that any stipulation concerning the reservation of the label "cognitive" to operations involving symbols and symbol-structures is a merely nominal transaction that may affect the directory, but not the content of our knowledge.

What matters here is that there seem to exist operations exemplifying elementary cognitive processes—however restrictive the meaning of "cognitive" may be—that might not be sensibly carved out of a supposedly independent, cognitively inert structure corresponding to Pylyshyn's (1980) concept of functional architecture. Indeed, the execution of the algorithm required to accomplish the task in our experiment, as well as the control over the said execution, seem to be *inseparable from the structure involved in the spatial layout of the task-relevant information*. Although initially created in the nervous system through verbal instructions as a linguistic structure, the algorithm at issue afterwards seems to be interwoven in the analog structure of the active database that constitutes the representation of the operational field. It is regularly performed when this representation is spared, but it becomes defective when the path of its execution leads to the area of impaired representation. There is no monitoring of the inaccessibility of a sector of the distributed database. There may be no monitoring of the internal interrupt procedure that may take place when conditions set to the required response are not favorable and that seems to delete a partially processed input. There is no monitoring of the abnormal terminations of the task by illegal default options, which occur when the configuration of the response keyboard does not provide, on the right side, a lit key whose color matches the color of the stimulus. The lack of monitoring of these faults cannot be attributed to the failure of any slave device.

Should we therefore conclude that there is no control unit separate from the structure embodying the active database and hence ascribe also to the control function the property of being distributed? Clinical neurology offers other data that might indeed corroborate the idea of a distributed, heterarchical organization of the supervisory mechanism controlling various forms of mental activity at the topmost processing level of self-analysis and monitoring. Anosognosia—that is, the absence of any indication of acknowledgment of the disorder by the patient— is not confined to the syndrome of unilateral neglect of space. It is impressively present in some types of dysphasia as well, in which—as in unilateral neglect— all forms of behavior outside the sphere of the isolated disorder may be quite normal.

The property of being distributed implies the possibility of local impairments of mechanisms of self-analysis and monitoring that, depending on the features of the disorder, might be better explained either in terms of failure within a component or disconnection between components.

Orthogonal to the distribution of the representational and self-referential functions, a further form of organization has to be considered for a full explanation of unilateral neglect, relative to the level of processing along an axis that might be roughly and provisionally identified after opposite directions of active attention and automaticity.

In spite of recurrent claims, the complex syndrome that follows damage to the right parietal lobe or to other brain structures functionally connected to this area cannot be fully explained in terms of attentional disorders only. Although neglect of the contralateral half-space constitutes the dominant symptom, there are instances in which attention may indeed be dedicated—at least temporarily—to the left, thus revealing the whimsical plexus of erroneous beliefs about objects in personal and in extrapersonal space, part of which is known under the rubric of *somato-paraphrenia*.

Attentional factors, however, closely interplay with the representational disorder. Experimentally, this has been proven beyond doubt by Posner, Cohen, and Rafal (1982). These authors found that directing covert attention ipsilaterally to a right-parietal lesion, even by means of a *central* visual cue, causes a dramatic fall in the detection of stimuli from the opposite visual hemifield. Attentional factors are apparently involved in the curious phenomenon we recently observed in a neglect patient who had been asked to read 10-letter words and nonwords obtained by substituting the first five letters of the said words with strings of readable syllables or of sole consonants. Whereas the patient often showed left-sided neglect and sometimes pathological completion of words and of readable nonwords, her reading of nonreadable nonwords was surprisingly accurate.

Although a modulation of neglect symptoms through attentional factors seem, therefore, to be undeniable, its further qualification will probably be far from easy, given the striking variability in behavior from patient to patient and even in the behavior of the same patient.

ACKNOWLEDGMENTS

This research was supported by a grant from the Ministero della Pubblica Istruzione to the first author. We gratefully acknowledge the help of Erminio Capitani, who assisted us in the statistical analysis of our data, and of Frances Anderson, who carefully reviewed the English.

REFERENCES

Baddeley, A. D., & Hitch, G. J. (1974). Working memory. In G. Bower (Ed.), *Recent advances in learning and motivation* (Vol. 8, pp. 67–89). New York: Academic.

Baddeley, A. D., & Lieberman, K. (1980). Spatial working memory. In R. S. Nickerson (Ed.), *Attention and performance VII* (pp. 521–539). Hillsdale, NJ: Lawrence Erlbaum Associates.

Baxter, D. M., & Warrington, E. K. (1983). Neglect dysgraphia. *Journal of Neurology, Neurosurgery and Psychiatry, 46,* 1073–1078.

Bisiach, E., Bulgarelli, C., Sterzi, R., & Vallar, G. (1983). Line bisection and cognitive plasticity of unilateral neglect of space. *Brain and Cognition, 2,* 32–38.

Bisiach, E., Capitani, E., Luzzatti, C., & Perani, D. (1981). Brain and conscious representation of outside reality. *Neuropsychologia, 19,* 543–551.

Bisiach, E., Capitani, E., & Porta, E. (1985). Two basic properties of space representation in the brain: Evidence from unilateral neglect. *Journal of Neurology, Neurosurgery and Psychiatry, 48,* 141–144.

Bisiach, E., Cornacchia, L., Sterzi, R., & Vallar, G. (1984). Disorders of perceived auditory lateralization after lesions of the right hemisphere. *Brain, 107,* 37–52.

Bisiach, E., & Luzzatti, C. (1978). Unilateral neglect of representational space. *Cortex, 14,* 129–133.
Bisiach, E., Luzzatti, C., & Perani, D. (1979). Unilateral neglect, representational schema and consciousness. *Brain, 102,* 609–618.
Kinsbourne, M. (1977). Hemi-neglect and hemisphere rivalry. In E. A. Weinstein & R. P. Friedland (Eds.), *Advances in neurology Vol. 18: Hemi-inattention and hemisphere specialization* (pp. 41–49). New York: Raven.
Kosslyn, S. M. (1980). *Image and mind.* Cambridge, MA: Harvard University Press.
Merzenich, M. M., & Kaas, J. H. (1980). Principles of organization of sensory-perceptual systems in mammals. *Progress in Psychobiology and Physiological Psychology, 9,* 1–41.
Mountcastle, V. B. (1981). Functional properties of the light-sensitive neurons of the posterior parietal cortex and their regulation by state controls: Influence on excitability of interested fixation and the angle of gaze. In O. Pompeiano & C. Ajmone-Marsan (Eds.), *Brain mechanisms of perceptual awareness and purposeful behavior* (pp. 67–99). New York: Raven.
Palmer, S. E. (1978). Fundamental aspects of cognitive representation. In E. H. Rosch & B. B. Lloyd (Eds.), *Cognition and categorization* (pp. 259–303). Hillsdale, NJ: Lawrence Erlbaum Associates.
Posner, M. I., Cohen, Y., & Rafal, R. D. (1982). Neural systems control of spatial orienting. *Philosophical Transactions of the Royal Society (B), 298,* 60–70.
Pylyshyn, Z. W. (1980). Computation and cognition: Issues in the foundations of cognitive science. *The Behavioral and Brain Sciences, 3,* 111–169.
Pylyshyn, Z. W. (1981). The imagery debate. Analog media versus tacit knowledge. In N. Block (Ed.), *Imagery* (pp. 151–206). Cambridge, MA: MIT Press.
Shepard, R. N. (1975). Form, formation and transformation of internal representations. In R. L. Solso (Ed.), *Information processing and cognition: The Loyola symposium* (pp. 87–122). Hillsdale, NJ: Lawrence Erlbaum Associates.
Watson, R. T., Miller, B. D., & Heilman, K. M. (1978). Nonsensory neglect. *Annals of Neurology, 3,* 505–508.
Zingerle, H. (1913). Ueber Stoerungen der Wahrnemung des eigenen Koerpers bei organischen Gehirnerkrankungen. *Monatschrift für Psichiatrie und Neurologie, 34,* 13–36.

13 Selective Spatial Attention: One Center, One Circuit, or Many Circuits?

Giacomo Rizzolatti
Maurizio Gentilucci
Massimo Matelli
Universitá di Parma

ABSTRACT

This chapter presents new evidence that in terms of attentional mechanisms the external space cannot be considered as a unitary entity. In the monkey unilateral lesions of the postarcuate cortex (area 6) or of the rostral part of the inferior parietal lobule (area 7b) produce attentional deficits that are almost exclusively restricted to the space around the body (peripersonal space). This particular type of neglect is markedly different from that following a unilateral damage to the frontal eye fields (area 8), as a result of which stimuli presented far from the animal are neglected and there is a lack of exploratory eye movements contralateral to the lesion. It is suggested that each area that organizes overt responses in space is also endowed with the capacity to produce covert attentional responses. Area 8, 7a, and superior colliculus, all centers whose neuronal activity is related to eye movements, are also the centers that control attention when the stimuli are in the far extrapersonal space. Areas 6 (postarcuate cortex) and 7b, whose neurons are related to head and arm movements, focus attention to the peripersonal space.

INTRODUCTION

The most common disorder of attention is the unilateral neglect syndrome. This syndrome is frequently found in patients with unilateral cortical, especially right parietal lesions; an essentially similar disorder is easily produced in animals after unilateral damage to various cortical areas and subcortical centers (see Benton, 1979; De Renzi, 1982; Friedland & Weinstein, 1977; Heilman, 1979; Heilman & Watson, 1979; Mesulam, 1981). The claim that the unilateral neglect syndrome is a disturbance of attention is based on the following facts: (a) stimuli presented contralateral to the lesion are often not perceived by the patients and are not responded to by the animals; (b) subjects with the hemineglect syndrome, especially in the periods immediately following the lesion, do not explore, or explore very little, the space contralateral to the lesion; (c) the hemineglect syndrome cannot be explained by elementary sensory deficits, such as contralateral hemianopia, or specific motor disturbances, like an impairment of exploratory eye movements; (d) when the acute symptomatology recedes and the responsiveness to a single stimulus recovers, a contralateral deficit can still be demonstrated with simultaneous presentation of two stimuli, one on the left and the other on the right. Patients tested in this way often report having seen only the ipsilateral stimulus.

Although an attentional interpretation of hemineglect is convincing, some difficulties nevertheless arise when the issue of the mechanisms responsible for it is addressed. There is one basic theoretical dichotomy that should be considered at the outset. Is the deficit due to an impairment of a central mechanism controlling attention and for which a specific cortical area is essential or does no such "master" center exist, many areas instead playing an equally important role in spatial attention?

According to a master center model the well-established fact that hemineglect may result after damage to various cortical areas and subcortical centers is explained by postulating that these areas (secondary attentional areas) are involved in attention because they are under the control of and may act via the central attentional mechanism. Although never formulated so explicitly, this model (or variants of it) is implicitly accepted by many neurologists when they maintain that the (right) parietal lobe plays a central role in hemineglect. According to them the parietal lobe is the attention master center (De Renzi, 1982; Mesulam, 1981).

An alternative way to explain the multiplicity of areas whose damage produces neglect is to reject the idea of a master center and to admit: (a) that all areas whose damage produces neglect are endowed with the property of giving salience to stimuli they receive, provided that these stimuli have those properties that Titchener (1966) described as "attentional"; (b) that these areas are able to modify their responsiveness according to previous events, such as a high probability that a stimulus will occur in a certain part of the visual space; (c) that each area controls the shift of attention toward different parts of the visual space related to the type of motor behavior that is organized by that area. According to this multicentric model (see Rizzolatti, 1983) no lesion will produce a complete incapacity to shift attention, except, maybe, when diaschisis is present.

In previous experiments we have shown that lesions of the frontal cortex in macaque monkeys produce two distinct neglect syndromes (Rizzolatti, Matelli, & Pavesi, 1983). The first, caused by a lesion of the postarcuate cortex (area 6), is characterized by a unilateral neglect for the contralateral half of the body, especially the contralateral face, and for the contralateral space located immediately around the body. This space surrounding the animal has been called by us peripersonal space (Rizzolatti et al., 1983; Rizzolatti, Scandolara, Matelli, & Gentilucci, 1981b). The second syndrome, caused by a damage of area 8, concerns the visual modality but not the somatosensory one. The contralateral space far from the animal is mostly affected and the attention deficit is accompanied by a deficit in the exploratory eye movements toward the contralateral hemispace.

The dicotomy between peripersonal and far space found after frontal lesions is suggestive of independent circuits controlling the attention toward objects within and outside the animal's reach, especially if one considers that anatomically area 8 and area 6 are targets of different pathways from posterior associative areas. In the first part of the present study data are presented on the effects of lesions of that part of parietal lobe (area 7b) that projects to the postarcuate cortex. The data showed that a damage to this area produces attentional deficits that are not global but are related to the peripersonal space. In the second part of the study some new quantitative data are presented on the attention deficits following damage to the postarcuate cortex. These data confirm the dicotomy between the peripersonal and far space and give indications that the mechanisms underlying the peripersonal neglect in the monkeys are similar to those found in humans after parietal damage.

METHODS

Subjects and Operation

The experiments were carried out on six monkeys (three Macaca irus and three Macaca nemestrina). In four animals (three Macaca irus and one Macaca nemestrina) a lesion was placed in the rostral part of the inferior parietal lobule (area 7), and in two in the postarcuate premotor cortex (area 6). All lesions were unilateral. The ablations were made by subpial aspiration under microscope control using a narrow gauge sucker. At the end of the operation the dura was sewn, the bone replaced, the muscle planes reconstructed, and the skin sutured. All animals recovered within a few hours after the operation and were tested on the following day. The monkeys with parietal lesions were neurologically examined and tested for responsiveness to visual stimuli (food, menace) in the peripersonal and extrapersonal far space (see the following section); the animals with the frontal lesions were, in addition, tested on a behavioral saccade test.

Visual Neurological Testing

We studied with particular care each animal's responses to visual stimuli located around its mouth (peripersonal buccal space), within the reach of its arm (distant peripersonal space), and outside it (extrapersonal far space). The testing was performed with the animal sitting in a primate chair. Because the testing procedure has been described in detail elsewhere (Rizzolatti et al., 1983) here it is only briefly summarized. The peribuccal space was tested as follows:

1. A piece of food held by forceps was moved first in front of the mouth, then on the right and on the left of it.
2. Two pieces of food, kept initially close to one another in front of the mouth, were moved—one toward the right, the other toward the left.
3. Two pieces of food, kept close to one another, were centrally presented; then one was moved laterally while the other remained in front of the animal.
4. The blink response to menace was tested.

The distant peripersonal space was studied by observing the orienting reaction of the monkey to food moved at about 30 cm from it and by examining its capacity to reach for it. As in the peribuccal space testing, single and double stimuli were used. Hand preference and accuracy of reaching were also studied by placing pieces of food on a horizontal plane located in front of the animal and observing how the food was grasped. The far space was examined in the same way as the distant peripersonal space, but the stimuli were moved 60 cm from the animal. The various trials of each test were repeated many times on different days. The last preoperative session and the most significant parts of postoperative sessions were recorded on videotape.

Fixation and Saccade Tasks

The two animals with frontal lesions (VRD1 and ROS4) were conditioned to perform two tasks: a fixation task and a saccade task (Goldberg & Wurtz, 1972; Wurtz, 1969). During the initial training the animal learned the two tasks with its head free. It sat in a primate chair and by depressing a bar turned on a fixation light (generated by a LED) that stayed on for a variable length of time between .5 sec and 2 sec. The fixation light then dimmed for .6 or .7 sec according to the monkey and, if the monkey released the bar during that time, it was rewarded with a drop of fruit juice (fixation task). The animal faced either a small cylindric screen (the radius of the horizontal circumference was 10 cm) located at a distance of 10 cm (perimeter 1) or a cylindric screen (the radius of the horizontal circumference was 30 cm) located at 30 cm (perimeter 2), or, finally, a tangent screen located at 1.5 m (perimeter 3). When the animal learned the fixation task using the three perimeters, the saccade task was started. In this task the fixation light appeared as in the fixation task, but, after .4 sec, it was turned off and a peripheral light was turned on at one of various possible locations on the screen. The peripheral light dimmed after a variable delay (.7 to 2 sec) for .6 to .7 sec and the monkey had to release the bar during that time to be rewarded. Typically the monkey oriented toward the peripheral light and maintained fixation there until the bar was released. Animals were tested using all three perimeters. Each of the three perimeters carried, during a routine testing, 19 LEDs: one at the centers, nine on its right half, nine on its left half. They were located symmetrically at the following locations: elevation 10°, 0°, −30°, azimuth for each elevation 10°, 20°, 25°. When the animals learned the fixation and the saccade task (more than 70% of correct responses) they were anesthetized with ketamine hydrochloride, and four hollow stainless steel cylinders (two on each side) were cemented to the skull. These served as anchors for metal rods attached to the primate chair and allowed, during the experiments, a rigid fixation of the head. Further, a search coil was implanted under the conjunctiva of one eye according to the method of Judge, Richmond, and Chu (1980). After the implantation of these devices, the animals were again tested on the two tasks, but this time with their heads rigidly fixed. Eye movements were recorded using the magnetic search-coil technique (Fuchs & Robinson, 1966; Robinson, 1963). A typical session was subdivided in blocks. In each block four peripheral points were tested, two on the right, two on the left of the fixation LED. A block consisted of 30 trials; in 10 of them, only the central light was shown, in the others the peripheral lights were presented. Each peripheral point on a perimeter was tested 10 times. Then the perimeter was changed and the same testing was repeated with the second and the third perimeter. The experiments were controlled by a PDP 11-23 computer. The number of correct responses (bar releasing) and the time for releasing the bar were analyzed on line. The pretraining was considered finished when the animals maintained for at least 5 days a performance higher than 70%. The last two sessions were used for data collection. The position of the eyes at the beginning and at the end of the sessions were controlled; those trials in which the eyes fixated correctly the initial and final target were considered correct trials. In several sessions two stimuli were simultaneously presented. The description of this experimental procedure is given with the results.

RESULTS

Parietal Monkeys

In one monkey (P1) we destroyed only the region of area 7b where, according to Hyvarinen and his coworkers (Hyvarinen, 1982; Leinonen & Nyman, 1979), the mouth is represented; in the other three (P3, P4, and P5) the lesion extended more caudally. Area 7a was spared in all animals. The extent of the lesions is shown in Fig. 13.1.

All monkeys presented motor and attentional deficits that were particularly marked immediately after the lesion. The first day after the operation the animals preferred to use the hand ipsilateral to the lesion. This preference was accom-

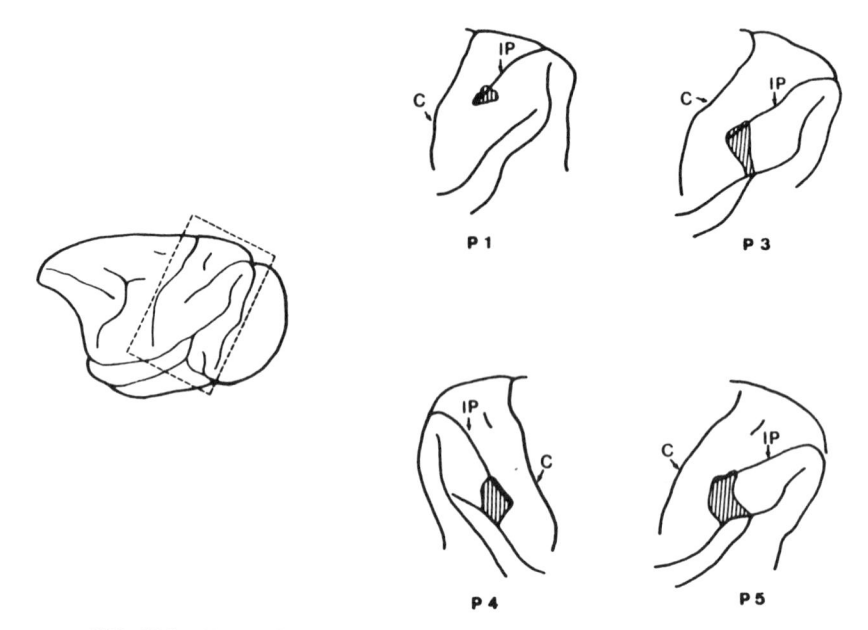

FIG. 13.1. Extent of the lesions in the parietal monkeys. Vertical lines indicate the ablated areas. C = central sulcus, IP = intraparietal sulcus.

panied in monkeys P4 and P5 by hypotonia and a slight decrease in the contralateral hand strength. Monkeys P3, P4, and P5 showed a deficit in opposing the thumb and index finger. No misreaching was observed. A grasping response was easier to elicit from the hand ipsilateral to the lesion than from the opposite one. When the contralateral arm was restrained the animal remained rather indifferent, and even when metallic clips were attached to the arm the reaction was weak. In contrast, the same procedure applied to the ipsilateral arm produced strong attempts to free the restrained arm and rage when the clips were attached.

The response to tactile stimuli applied to the hemiface contralateral to the lesion was reduced. Opening of the mouth or attempts to bite when the lips were stimulated occurred only after a delay and sometimes were absent altogether. This was particularly clear in monkeys P4 and P5. In all monkeys, but especially in these two, the coordinated head–mouth movements necessary to reach the food touching the lips was slower than on the opposite side. This complex sensorimotor act was, however, impaired less than after area 6 lesions (Rizzolatti et al., 1983).

Visual deficits in the peribuccal space were present in all animals. When the monkey fixated a central stimulus, the movement of a piece of food in the visual space ipsilateral to the lesion produced, as in normal animals, an immediate mouth-grasping response, whereas the same stimulus shown contralaterally was ignored. When two stimuli were simultaneously moved one to the right, the other to the left, the one ipsilateral to the lesion was always preferred. The movement of a single stimulus, however, evoked a response on either side. Monkey P1 had no deficit with stimuli presented at the distance of its arms (distant peripersonal space) or further from its body. The other three monkeys showed a clear preference for ipsilateral stimuli, also when they were shown at 30 cm. At variance with animals with frontal eye-field lesions, who do not explore the contralateral hemispace (Crowne, Yeo, & Steel Russel, 1981; Latto & Cowey, 1971; Rizzolatti et al., 1983), the parietal animals oriented spontaneously to both sides of the space. Furthermore, they responded promptly to far stimuli. However, monkeys P4 and P5 showed a modest preference for ipsilateral stimuli with double simultaneous stimulation of the far space.

The symptoms observed the first day after surgery tended to disappear with time. Monkey P1 was tested for the last time 15 months after the surgery. There was still an absolute preference for visual stimuli ipsilateral to the lesion when presented in the peribuccal space and a marked preference for the use of the ipsilateral hand. Monkey P5, tested 21 months after the lesion, also preferred ipsilateral stimuli, in both peribuccal and distant peripersonal space. No differences were found for far stimuli. Monkey P4, tested after 13 months, showed only a clear hand preference. Monkey P3 was sacrificed after 27 days, when most of the initial symptoms were still present.

In conclusion, the attentional disturbances after damage to area 7b were exclusively or predominantly limited to the peripersonal space. This suggests that the inferior parietal lobule is subdivided in regions that control different sectors of the external space.

Frontal Monkeys

The two monkeys of this group were both operated on the right side. Preoperatively, one of them (VRD1) did not show any obvious preference for right or left stimuli; the other (ROS4) strongly preferred stimuli on the left.

Neurologic Testing

The effect of unilateral ablations of postarcuate cortex have been previously described by us in Macaca irus (Rizzolatti et al., 1983). The deficits found in the two monkeys of this study (Macaca nemestrina), although in their essence similar to those previously described, were much less severe. Thus, the preference for the ipsilateral hand was marked, but the reluctance to move the contralateral hand was not observed. Similarly, the typical incapacity to organize the coordinated head–mouth movement was absent, although this movement toward the contralateral hemispace was slower than that in the opposite direction. The attentional deficits were also less marked. Visual neglect could be demonstrated only with a double stimulation, whereas the response was practically normal with a single stimulus. Tactile neglect in response to face stimulation was almost absent, but a deficit was present with stimulation of the contralateral hand. Tactile stimulation of the proximal parts of the arms yields normal responses. In spite of the sparse neurological deficits the animals were tested in the behavioral fixation and saccade tasks.

Behavioral Saccade Task

Albeit similar at neurological testing, the two animals markedly differed in their responses in the saccade task. Briefly, whereas monkey VRD1 showed clear signs of neglect, monkey ROS4 behaved basically identically to before surgery. Because the histological reconstruction of the lesions is not yet available we cannot give a satisfactory explanation for the discrepancy. The data of VRD1 are presented here in some detail. Obviously, they need confirmation in more monkeys.

Perimetry. There was no deficit in the capacity of the animal to orient and respond to visual stimuli in both hemifields. The ocular movements were normal.

Double Stimulation with Symmetrical Stimuli. In this experiment two stimuli were simultaneously presented in homologous points of the visual field, one on the right, the other on the left of the fixation point. The stimuli were presented in blocks. In each block two pairs of stimuli were alternated, with the central stimulus alone (fixation task) presented in one-third of the trials. The two stimuli of a pair dimmed simultaneously and the animal was rewarded if it released the bar during the dimming. The reward was given regardless of which of the two stimuli the animal fixated. Each pair of stimuli was presented 50 times. Because only perimeter 1 (near) and 3 (far) were used systematically, only the data pertaining to these perimeters are presented here.

The number of correct responses (bar releases) was 85.6% in perimeter 1 and 86.7% in perimeter 3. The number of correct trials (trials in which the animal maintained the fixation and made a precise saccade to the target) was 69.5% in perimeter 1 and 82.2% in perimeter 3. Both with stimuli at 10 cm and with stimuli at 150 cm there was a marked preference for the stimulus on the right side of a pair. This stimulus was responded to in 89.5% of the correct trials in perimeter 1 and in 85.1% in perimeter 3.

Double Stimulation with Asymmetrical Stimuli. In this experiment the preference of the animal to respond to right stimuli was counteracted by presenting pairs of stimuli asymmetricaly located in respect with the fixation point. The stimulus in the neglected field was closer to the vertical meridian than the one in the normal field. The rationale for this arrangement was to increase the retinal salience of the stimulus in the neglected hemifield to compensate for the decrease

13. SELECTIVE SPATIAL ATTENTION 259

of perceptual clearness due to neglect. Six positions were tested. The following pairs of stimuli were used: (1) left: azimuth 20°, elevation −10°; right: azimuth 30°, elevation −10°; (2) left: 10°, −10°; right: 30°, −10°; (3) left: 10°, 10°; right: 30°, 10°; (4) left: 10°, −10°; right: 40°, −10°. Pairs 1 and 4 were tested 160 times, pairs 2 and 3, 80 times.

The number of correct responses ranged between 95.6% and 97.5% in perimeter 1 and between 96.2% and 100% in perimeter 3. The number of correct trials ranged between 92.5% and 96.2% in perimeter 1 and between 95.0% and 100.0% in perimeter 3.

As is shown in Table 13.1a, regardless of the degree of retinal advantage of the left stimuli, the monkey always chose the stimulus on the right in the

TABLE 13.1
Percentage of Choices toward the Indicated Side
in the Double Stimulation Experiments after Right Postarcuate Lesions

(a) *Double Stimultion with Asymmetrical Stimuli*

| | Peripersonal Space || Far Space ||
Left Retinal Advantage	Left Hemifield	Right Hemifield	Left Hemifield	Right Hemifield
10°	0	100	53,8	46,2
20° (upper field)	0	100	71,1	28,9
20° (lower field)	0	100	73,8	26,2
30°	1,3	98,7	94,3	5,7

(b) *Double Asymmetrical Stimulation with Eccentric Fixation*

| | | Peripersonal Space || Far Space ||
		Left Stimulus	Right Stimulus	Left Stimulus	Right Stimulus
Right hemispace	upper pair	1,6	98,4	100	0
	lower pair	3,2	96,8	100	0

(c) *Double Stimulation with Stimuli in the Same Visual Hemifield*

| | | Peripersonal Space || Far Space ||
		Left Stimulus	Right Stimulus	Left Stimulus	Right Stimulus
Right hemifield	upper pair	2,8	97,2	100	0
	lower pair	7,4	92,6	100	0
Left hemifield	upper pair	0	100	0	100
	lower pair	0	100	0	100

peripersonal space. In contrast, in the far space the stimulus on the left was preferred.

These data indicate a strong hemineglect limited to the peripersonal space. They also show that the preference for the right stimuli in the far space described in the previous section was very weak. This weak preference can be attributed either to the presence of a few neurons in the postarcuate cortex related to the far space and destroyed by the lesions or to an inadvertent small damage to the adjacent area 8.

Double Asymmetrical Stimulation with Eccentric Fixation. When the animal fixates eccentrically while its head is fixed, the stimuli presented on the right of the (eccentric) fixation point are on the right side of the head midline and on the right side of the fovea; the stimuli located between the center of the perimeter and the eccentric fixation point are on the right of the head midline and therefore in the right hemispace, but on the left of the fovea. In the next experiment the animal fixated a point 20° to the right of the center of the perimeter. Two stimuli were presented in the right hemispace, simultaneously, either 10° above or 10° below the horizontal meridian. Of the two stimuli one was 20° to the right, the other 10° to left of the eccentric fixation point. If the neglect is a disturbance coded in terms of retinal coordinates, the animal will choose the stimulus on the right of the fixation, as it does when it fixates centrally; if the neglect is coded in terms of body coordinates, the left stimulus will be chosen because of its greater retinal salience. The experimental procedure was the same as in previous experiments. The two pairs of stimuli were tested 240 times in perimeter 1 and 80 times in perimeter 3.

The number of correct responses on perimeter 1 was 94.2% and 95% for the upper and lower pair of stimuli, respectively. The number of correct trials was 80% and 77.9%. On perimeter 3 correct responses and trials were more than 93% in both the testing situations. The most striking result was a clear dissociation between the animal's behavior in the peripersonal and in the far space. In the peripersonal space the animal preferred the right stimuli, whereas in the far space it preferred those near the midline. The data are shown in Table 13.1b.

These results seem to indicate that hemi-inattention is related to retinal coordinates. However, an alternative interpretation of the findings is that neglect does not concern the right and the left side of the retina or of the body, but rather it is a disturbance that gives salience to that stimulus that is most ipsilateral to the side of the lesion, regardless of whether the stimuli are located in the right or left hemispace. This hypothesis was tested in the next experiment.

Double Stimulation with Stimuli in the Same Visual Hemifield. The experiment was subdivided in four blocks. In two of them the two stimuli were presented on the right of the fixation point, in two on the left of fixation point. Two pairs of stimuli were used. Their location in each hemifield was the following: (1) azimuth 10°, elevation 10°; azimuth 30°, elevation 10°; (2) azimuth 10°, elevation −10°; azimuth 30°, elevation −10°.

Each pair of stimuli was presented 180 times in the peripersonal space, 120 times in the far space. The testing procedure was identical to that of the previous experiments.

The number of correct responses ranged between 86.7% and 95% with stimuli in the peripersonal space and between 94.2% and 98.3% in the far space. The correct trials were respectively 81.4% (right hemifield) and 79.9% (left hemifield) in the peripersonal space, 95.8% (right hemifield) and 97% (left hemifield) in the far space.

The results are shown in Table 13.1c. With stimuli presented in the *right hemifield,* there was a clear dissociation between the animal's behavior in the peripersonal and far space. In the peripersonal space the animal constantly preferred the most distal stimulus. In the far space the animal preferred the stimulus closer to the midline. This is the behavior of normal animals in both peripersonal and far space. The recordings of the eye movements showed that with stimuli in the peripersonal space the animals sometimes made the saccades directly toward the distal stimulus, sometimes briefly fixated the proximal stimulus and then made a saccade to the distal stimulus, as if it were magnetically attracted by it.

The response in the *left hemifield* was invariably to the proximal stimulus, regardless of whether the stimuli were in the peripersonal or far space.

In conclusion, this experiment shows that the preference for the right stimuli in the experiment with an eccentric fixation was not because neglect is linked to a retinal representation, but rather because neglect produces a preference for the most ipsilateral stimulus to the side of the lesion in both the visual hemifields.

DISCUSSION

Orienting to visual stimuli consists of covert and overt components. The first are represented by a shift of attention toward the stimulus location, the second by behavioral changes such as eye movements or various postural changes (see Posner, 1978). In an animal with a foveate retina, the link between attention and eye movements is very strict. There are various instances, however, when the two aspects are dissociated. An example is the case when a stimulus is very close to the mouth. In this condition the monkey frequently grasps the food without fixating it. Similarly, arm-reaching movements, although usually preceded by fixation of the stimulus, are sometimes executed with the animal looking straight ahead. Our data show that after lesions of the cortical areas that control movements in the animal's peripersonal space, there is an attention deficit mostly restricted to this space. The attentional deficit is demonstrated by the lack of general responsiveness to stimuli presented near the animal and by the absence of ocular orienting responses. The data of VRD1 are very important in this respect because they have clearly shown that in this animal there was no impairment in ocular motility and yet a clear hemi-inattention for the peripersonal space. Thus, the attention deficit could not be attributed to the type of motor response used to demonstrate it.

A model that may explain these data is one that assumes that each area that organizes overt responses in space (premotor areas) is also endowed with the capacity to produce covert attentional responses. Area 8, 7a, and superior colliculus, all centers whose neuronal activity (Bushnell, Goldberg, & Robinson, 1981; Goldberg & Bushnell, 1981; Lynch, 1980; Mountcastle, Lynch, Georgopoulos, Sakata, & Acuna, 1975; Sakata, 1982; Wurtz & Mohler, 1976; Wurtz, Goldberg, & Robinson, 1980) is related to eye movements, are also the centers that shift attention when the stimuli are in the far extrapersonal space. Areas 6 (postarcuate cortex) and 7b, whose neurons are related to head and arm movements (Hyvarinen, 1982; Leinonen & Nyman, 1979; Leinonen, Hyvarinen, Nyman, & Linnankoski, 1979; Rizzolatti, Scandolara, Gentilucci, & Camarda, 1981; Rizzolatti, Scandolara, Matelli, & Gentilucci, 1981a; Rizzolatti, Scandolara, Matelli, & Gentilucci, 1981b), focus attention to the peripersonal space. Finally, if a stimulus is in the distant peripersonal space both oculomotor centers and those controlling reaching movements are involved. It is clear that according to this multicentric model of attention there is no unique "master" center responsible for shifting attention. Second, it is maintained that the shifting of attention is closely linked with the programming of motor acts in space. Third, no prominence is given to oculomotor centers except in the sense that in everyday life most stimuli that attract attention first appear in the far extrapersonal space.

The first point of the multicentric model is confirmed by the lack of a syndrome so severe and enduring as should occur after a lesion of any "master" center. The very severe neglect that sometimes is observed after an acute vascular accident in man recedes over time, and, even in the most acute phase, a dissociation may be present between the capacity of paying attention to visual, somatosensory, and auditory stimuli (Benton, 1979; De Renzi, 1982). An extremely important argument against the idea that the right parietal neglect in humans is due to a lesion of a putative attention master center derives from some recent experiments of Posner and his colleagues (Posner, Walker, Friedrich, & Rafal, 1984). Posner et al. measured the reaction times to visual stimuli presented in the hemifield ipsilateral and contralateral to the lesion in parietal patients. They found that if a cue indicated that a stimulus was to appear in the normal hemifield, but the stimulus actually appeared in the neglected field, the patients showed a marked reaction time lengthening. In contrast, if the locus of the stimulus was correctly indicated by the cue, the reaction times were affected very little. Thus, there is no doubt that these patients could actively move their attention after parietal lesions. This is very likely because the other areas controlling attentional shift can compensate the lack of parietal neurons.

Another argument against the master role of the parietal lobe stems from the similarity between a basic disturbance found in parietal patients and monkeys with a postarcuate lesion. This disturbance consists in the marked, almost compulsive preference for stimuli ipsilateral to the lesion. In the case of VRD1 this was found not only when the stimuli were one on the right and the other on the left of the fixation point, but also when they were both in the same hemifield, even in that ipsilateral to the lesion ("normal" hemifield). A similar preference for ipsilateral stimuli has been described in classical literature on parietal neglect and stressed as one of the basic deficits in these patients by Kinsbourne (1977) and more recently by De Renzi (1983). It is obvious that if the same basic deficits are found after parietal and postarcuate lesions it is difficult to assert that only the first cortical center "controls" the attention.

A last point that deserves some comment is the issue of why there is such a strong preference for ipsilateral stimuli in unilateral inattention. Kinsbourne (1977) suggested that this is due to an imbalance in the lateral orienting tendency. This hypothesis is satisfactory for explaining the ipsilateral preference in the case of stimuli presented one on the right, the other on the left of a fixation point, but it requires additional assumptions for the case when both are in the same hemifield. To account for this one might postulate that the saccadic ocular movements result from a simultaneous activation of two centers or groups of centers, one shifting the gaze in one direction, the other in the opposite. Although this mechanism is possible, we are not aware of any empirical evidence in its favor. Furthermore, in the case of a deficit in such a mechanism one would expect ocular errors (hypermetria) when a single stimulus is presented to hemi-inattentive patients or animals. Nothing of this kind is observed.

An alternative explanation for the strong ipsilateral preference many lie in the fact that the premotor cortical areas have, besides a contralateral representation of the visual field, also a representation of the ipsilateral one, the former being stronger and more complete. In the postarcuate cortex of the monkey, for example, 29% of the neurons have exclusively contralateral visual fields, 2% ipsilateral fields, 69% bilateral fields (Rizzolatti, Scandolara, Matelli, & Gentilucci, 1981b). In these last neurons, contralateral responses are often stronger and never weaker than the ipsilateral ones. Moreover, the bilateral visual fields are always around the midline, extending laterally variously according to the neuron. As a consequence of this arrangement the most lateral part of the visual space is represented almost exclusively in one hemisphere, the central part in both, with the region around the vertical meridian being almost equally subdivided between the two hemispheres. In the case of lesion of one hemisphere the whole visual field will be affected but with a gradient of severity going from a maximum in the extreme contralateral hemifield to a minimum in the extreme ipsilateral field. If it is accepted that the salience of a stimulus and the capacity of shifting attention actively is a function of the number of neurons available and of the strength of their excitation, the ipsilateral preference may be accounted for on the basis of the anatomofunctional properties of the premotor areas.

ACKNOWLEDMENTS

This research was supported in part by NIH Grant # 1 RO1 NS 19206–01A1 and in part by a grant from Italian CNR.

REFERENCES

Benton, A. (1979). Visuoperceptive, visuospatial, and visuoconstructive disorders. In K. M. Heilman & E. Valenstein (Eds.), *Clinical neuropsychology* (pp. 268–307). New York: Oxford University.

Bushnell, M. C., Goldberg, M. E., & Robinson, D. L. (1981). Behavioral enhancement of visual responses in monkey cerebral cortex: I. Modulation in posterior parietal cortex related to selective visual attention. *Journal of Neurophysiology, 46,* 755–772.

Crowne, D. P., Yeo, C. N., & Steele Russel, I. (1981). The effects of unilateral frontal eye field lesions in the monkey: Visual motor guidance and avoidance behaviour. *Behavioural Brain Research, 2,* 165–187.

De Renzi, E. (1982). *Disorders of space exploration and cognition.* London: Wiley.

De Renzi, E. (1983). *Disturbi dell'attenzione.* Paper presented at the Italian Neuropsychological Society, Parma.

Friedland, R. P., & Weinstein, E. A. (1977). Hemi-inattention and hemisphere specialization: Introduction and historical review. In E. A. Weinstein & R. P. Friedland (Eds.), *Advances in neurology* (Vol. 18, pp. 1–31). New York: Raven.

Fuchs, A. F., & Robinson, D. A. (1966). A method for measuring horizontal and vertical eye movement chronically in the monkey. *Journal of Applied Physiology, 21,* 1068–1070.

Goldberg, M. E., & Bushnell, M. C. (1981). Behavioral enhancement of visual responses in monkey cerebral cortex: II. Modulation in frontal eye fields specifically related to saccades. *Journal of Neurophysiology, 46,* 773–787.

Goldberg, M. E., & Wurtz, R. H. (1972). Activity of superior colliculus in behaving monkey. II. Effect of attention on neuronal responses. *Journal of Neurophysiology, 35,* 560–574.

Heilman, K. M. (1979). Neglect and related disorders. In K. M. Heilman & E. Valenstein (Eds.), *Clinical neuropsychology* (pp. 268–307). New York: Oxford University.

Heilman, K. M., & Watson, R. T. (1977). Mechanisms underlying the unilateral neglect syndrome. In E. A. Weinstein & R. F. Friedland (Eds.), *Advances in neurology* (pp. 93–105). New York: Raven.

Hyvarinen, J. (1982). *The parietal cortex of monkey and man. Studies of brain function* (Vol. 8, p. 202). Berlin: Springer.

Judge, S. J., Richmond, B. J., & Chu, F. C. (1980). Implantation of magnetic search coils for measurement of eye position: An improved method. *Vision Research, 20,* 535–538.

Kinsbourne, M. (1977). Hemi-neglect and hemisphere rivalry. In E. A. Weinstein & R. P. Friedland (Eds.), *Advances in neurology: Hemi-inattention and hemisphere specialization* (Vol. 18). New York: Raven.

Latto, R., & Cowey, A. (1971). Visual field defects after frontal-eye-field lesions in monkey. *Brain Research, 30,* 1–24.

Leinonen, L., & Nyman, G., II (1979). Functional properties of cells in anterolateral part of area 7 associative face area of awake monkeys. *Experimental Brain Research, 34,* 321–333.

Leinonen, L., Hyvarinen, J., Nyman, G., & Linnankoski, I. I. (1979). Functional properties of neurons in lateral part of associative area 7 in awake monkeys. *Experimental Brain Research, 34,* 299–320.

Lynch, J. C. (1980). The functional organization of posterior parietal association cortex. *Behavioral and Brain Sciences, 3,* 485–534.

Mesulam, M.-M. (1981). A cortical network for directed attention and unilateral neglect. *Annals of Neurology, 10,* 309–325.
Mountcastle, V. B., Lynch, J. C., Georgopoulos, A., Sakata, H., & Acuna, C. (1975). Posterior parietal association cortex of the monkey: Command functions for operations within extrapersonal space. *Journal of Neurophysiology, 38,* 871–908.
Posner, M. I. (1978). *Chronometric exploration of mind.* Hillsdale, NJ: Lawrence Erlbaum Associates.
Posner, M. I., Walker, J. A., Friedrich, F. J., & Rafal, R. D. (1984). Effects of parietal injury on covert orienting of visual attention. *Journal of Neuroscience, 4,* 1863–1877.
Rizzolatti, G. (1983). Mechanisms of selective attention in mammals. In J.-P. Ewert, R. R. Capranica, & D. J. Ingle (Eds.), *Advances in vertebrate neuroethology* (pp. 261–297). London: Plenum.
Rizzolatti, G., Matelli, M., & Pavesi, G. (1983). Deficits in attention and movement following the removal of postarcuate (area 6) and prearcuate (area 8) cortex in macaque monkeys. *Brain, 106,* 655–673.
Rizzolatti, G., Scandolara, C., Gentilucci, M., & Camarda, R. (1981). Response properties and behavioral modulation of "mouth" neurons of the postarcuate cortex (area 6) in macaque monkeys. *Brain Research, 255,* 421–424.
Rizzolatti, G., Scandolara, C., Matelli, M., & Gentilucci, M. (1981a). Afferent properties of periarcuate neurons in macaque monkeys. I. Somatosensory responses. *Behavioural Brain Research, 2,* 125–146.
Rizzolatti, G., Scandolara, C., Matelli, M., & Gentilucci, M. (1981b). Afferent properties of periarcuate neurons in macaque monkeys. II. Visual responses. *Behavioural Brain Research, 2,* 147–163.
Robinson, D. A. (1963). A method of measuring eye movement using a scleral search coil in a magnetic field. *IEEE Transactions on Bio-Medical Engineering, 10,* 137–145.
Sakata, H. (1982). Spatial properties of visual fixation neurons in posterior parietal associative cortex of the monkey. *Journal of Neurophysiology, 43,* 1654–1672.
Titchener, E. B. (1966). Attention as sensory clearness. In P. Bakan & D. Van Nostrand (Eds.), *Attention: An enduring problem in psychology.* Princeton: Princeton University Press.
Wurtz, R. H. (1969). Visual receptive fields of striate cortex neurons in awake monkeys. *Journal of Neurophysiology, 32,* 727–742.
Wurtz, R. H., & Mohler, C. W. (1976). Enhancement of visual responses in monkey striate cortex and frontal eye fields. *Journal of Neurophysiology, 39,* 766–772.
Wurtz, R. H., Goldberg, M. E., & Robinson, D. L. (1980). Behavioral modulation of visual responses in the monkey: Stimulus selection for attention and movement. In J. M. Sprague & A. N. Epstein (Eds.), *Progress in psychobiology and physiological psychology* (Vol. 9, pp. 43–83).

IV SENSORY SYSTEMS AND SELECTION: VISION

14 Attending to the Spatial Frequency and Spatial Position of Near-Threshold Visual Patterns

Norma Graham
Columbia University

Patricia Kramer
Institute for Vision Research, SUNY College of Optometry

Nancy Haber
Columbia University

ABSTRACT

Results from extrinsic-uncertainty, primary-with-probes, and concurrent experiments using near-threshold visual patterns differing in spatial frequency or spatial position suggest: (a) Typical observers can attend to and give direct reports from selected ranges of spatial frequency and spatial position in the sense of basing their responses on appropriate subsets of visual mechanisms. (b) This selective attention may sometimes occur early enough to block the unmonitored mechanisms' outputs from influencing conscious perception. (c) Observers in these near-threshold tasks can also attend to the whole range without losing any information from any subpart of the range. (The largest number of far-apart spatial frequencies or spatial positions used was five or three, respectively, however.)

INTRODUCTION

Receptive-Field Model

In the current model of near-threshold pattern vision (reviewed in Graham, 1981), there are multiple mechanisms—the physiological substrate for which might be single neurons in the visual cortex. These mechanisms' receptive fields are potentially located at different places in the visual field (i.e., sensitive to different spatial positions), of different sizes and orientation (i.e., sensitive to different ranges of spatial frequency and orientation), and so on. For the quantitative prediction of near-threshold results, the following assumptions are commonly made:

1. The mechanisms' outputs are noisy or variable, with different mechanisms' outputs being probabilistically independent (uncorrelated).
2. Visual patterns of very different spatial frequency and/or spatial position (and/or orientations) are thought to excite completely disjoint subsets of these mechanisms that do not interact with one another in any way at near-threshold contrasts.
3. The observer's decision variable (in the sense of standard signal-detection theory) in detection experiments is the maximum of the outputs from all the mechanisms—for example, the observer says "yes" if and only if this maximum is greater than some criterion.
4. In simple-stimulus identification experiments—in which a stimulus containing a single value on the relevant dimension is presented on each trial and the observer's task is to say which of several possible values was presented—the observer's response is the value that corresponds to the mechanism producing the maximum output.

Monitored Mechanisms

Several aspects of this current model will undoubtedly be modified before it does a perfect job of accounting for near-threshold pattern vision although the model does an extremely good job as is. The present chapter discusses one such modification: the observer is assumed to "pay attention to" only a subset of the mechanisms in the sense that the decision in 3 or 4 above is based only on the outputs from that subset rather than of all the outputs. The mechanisms in that subset are said to be "monitored." Note that, for the present, very little is implied about the stage at which this selective attention occurs.

EXTRINSIC-UNCERTAINTY EFFECTS

Detection and identification performances are worse when an observer is uncertain about the spatial frequency or spatial position of a simple visual pattern—because trials of several different values are randomly intermixed (uncued intermixed condition)—than when he or she is certain because only trials of that one stimulus can occur on each block (alone condition). No such extrinsic-uncertainty effect occurs for intermixing contrasts, however, at least not within the range possible in detection experiments.

14. NEAR-THRESHOLD VISUAL PATTERNS 271

Although over several sessions a particular observer may seem to show a larger uncertainty effect at one spatial frequency than another, overall no consistent effect of spatial frequency is found in the range we have tested (from .67 to 18 c/deg with occasional excursions higher).

These extrinsic-uncertainty effects cannot be explained by assumptions 1 through 4 just described, but they can be explained quantitatively with the following additions:

5. The subsets monitored in the alone conditions for stimuli containing very far-apart values (e.g., grating patches of very different spatial frequencies) contain no mechanisms in common.

6. In an intermixed condition, when an observer knows that any one of several stimuli might be presented, he or she monitors the union of the subsets monitored in alone conditions for those several stimuli.

With these modifications, the observer should do worse in intermixed conditions than in alone conditions because, in the intermixed, he or she must monitor more probabilistically independent mechanisms that add noise or "false alarms" (as they are not sensitive to the stimulus on any particular trial). Note that this predicted performance decrement is entirely attributed to probabilistically independent noise sources and does NOT arise from an inability to monitor many mechanisms nor from any degradation of a mechanism's output when other mechanisms are monitored along with it. The decrement might better be viewed as an increment, therefore; the observer's performance is predicted to be better in the alone than in the intermixed conditions because he or she is able to selectively monitor appropriate mechanisms and thus avoid many false alarms.

The magnitude of the uncertainty effects in the detection of patterns of different spatial frequency and spatial position turn out to be quantitatively consistent with the preceding assumptions (necessarily elaborated to include reasonable probability distributions, a necessity that does not arise for the concurrent experiments of the next section; see Sperling, 1984, for further discussion of this point).

References for the previous statements about spatial frequency include: Davis, Kramer, and Graham, 1983; Graham, Robson, and Nachmias, 1978; Kramer, 1984; Shaw, 1984; Yager, Kramer, Shaw, and Graham, 1984. References for spatial position and contrast include Davis et al., 1983, and others' work—for example, Cohn and Lasley, 1974. Some individual differences are discussed in Yager et al., 1984.

Intrinsic Uncertainty

Although considerable flexibility in monitoring is assumed by assumptions 5 and 6, perfect monitoring is not. In fact, the subset monitored for any simple stimulus may contain not only informative mechanisms (those sensitive to the stimulus—

for example, mechanisms at the correct spatial position, spatial frequency, and orientation for a grating patch) but also noninformative mechanisms. Incorporating such intrinsic uncertainty, in fact, allows prediction of several additional features of detection data beyond those mentioned here (Nachmias & Kocher, 1970; Pelli, 1981).

Compound Stimuli

Recently we measured the detectability of compound gratings containing two spatial frequencies and of the components by themselves in an alone condition (where trials of only one pattern appeared in a given block) and in an intermixed condition (where trials of the components and the compound were randomly intermixed). The compound was very slightly less detectable in the intermixed condition than when it was alone. Because the same mechanisms are likely to be monitored both in the intermixed condition and in the condition when the compound is alone, this small uncertainty effect is puzzling. It may result from a switch between the maximum-output rule (assumption 3) in the intermixed condition and an analogous sum-of-outputs rule in the compound-alone condition (Kramer, 1984).

Effects of Auditory Cues

Auditory precues eliminate these extrinsic-uncertainty effects—producing equivalent detection performance in intermixed and alone conditions—if the cues come 500 to 750 milliseconds (msec) before the first interval in a two-interval forced-choice trial (Davis et al., 1983; Kramer, 1984). (Observers report that precued intermixed stimuli are more salient than alone stimuli; this suggests that nonasymptotic measures of performance—e.g., speeded measures—might have shown better performance in precued conditions than in alone. Percent correct detection is, however, equal in the two conditions.)

As the time of the cue is moved later in the trial, the improvement produced (relative to the uncued intermixed condition) decreases, although some remains even for cues 500 msec after the end of the second interval (Kramer, 1984—for intermixed spatial frequencies).

Direction of Motion

Somewhat oddly, the extrinsic-uncertainty effects are larger and the efficacy of cues in reducing them less for different directions of motion than for different spatial frequencies or spatial positions (e.g., Ball & Sekuler, 1981). Perhaps the eye-movement system is implicated.

CONCURRENT EXPERIMENTS

If monitoring is as flexible as assumed previously (assumptions 4 and 5) and if mechanisms' outputs are distinguishable upstream (assumptions 4, 5, and 6), then an observer might be able to simultaneously attend to two spatial frequencies or two spatial positions in a compound pattern and report on each one individually without loss (further assuming memory load and response competition are negligible).

Suppose, for example, we present the observer with: a blank, a low spatial frequency by itself, a high spatial frequency by itself, or both. Suppose we ask him or her two questions: (a) Is the low spatial frequency present? (b) Is the high spatial frequency present? The answer to each question might be a simple yes or no or it might be a confidence rating. We can formalize the first paragraph's argument as:

7. The decision variable used to answer the question about a particular component in a concurrent experiment (e.g., a particular spatial frequency) is the maximum of the outputs from all the mechanisms sensitive to that component.

To compare the model's predictions to results, compute a d' value for each of the two questions and for each of the nonblank patterns by comparing—in the ordinary fashion of signal-detection theory—the answers to that particular question on nonblank pattern trials with the answers on blank trials. For example, for the low-frequency question and the high-frequency-alone stimulus, the d' value would be calculated as follows: The probability of saying "yes, the low frequen-

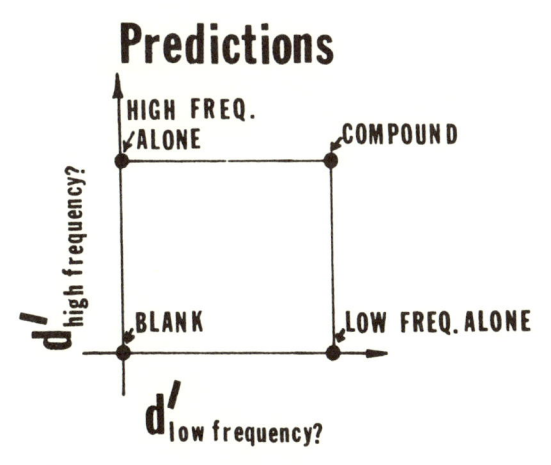

FIG. 14.1. Predicted results from concurrent experiments.

cy is present" in response to the high-frequency-alone stimulus is the hit rate, and the probability of "yes, the low frequency is present" in response to the blank is the false-alarm rate; then the false-alarm and hit rates are converted to standard normal deviates (z scores) and subtracted to get the d' value.

Figure 14.1 shows the predicted d' from one question plotted against the predicted d' from the other. The predicted results are a rectangle of points with that for the blank stimulus at the origin, that for the compound stimulus in the upper right, and those for the simple component stimuli at the other corners (Nachmias, 1974).

Also, because the independent mechanisms' outputs are assumed probabilistically independent, the correlation between the answers to the two questions across repetitions of the same stimulus (henceforth called an interresponse correlation) is predicted to be zero.

Spatial Frequency

Results for an experiment using far-apart spatial frequencies (2.5 and 7.5 c/deg) are shown in Fig. 14.2 for separate replications (different symbols) at several levels of contrast (from Haber, 1976; see details in appendix here). Also, the interresponse correlations were small and scattered around zero except that, for the blank stimulus, positive correlations were regularly observed (median around .2 in this study). Note that the small size of the interresponse correlations means that the d' value for one question will be much the same whether conditionalized on a yes to the other question, conditionalized on a no to the other question, or unconditionalized (as here).

The results in Fig. 14.2 are for long (760 msec) presentations of the gratings. Even with presentations as short as 20 msec, however, the results are the same (unpublished data from two sessions with observer LH run at the same time and using the same procedures as the results at longer durations reported in Hirsch, Hylton, & Graham, 1982).

In summary, the results for far-apart spatial frequencies are approximately as predicted. (See also Nachmias, 1974; Hirsch, 1977; Hirsch et al., 1982; Olzak, 1981).

Spatial Position

To my knowledge, there have been three concurrent experiments on the spatial-position dimension using: three far-apart spots (Wickelgren, 1967); two far-apart lines (unpublished experiment by Nachmias, 1966; details in appendix here); two adjacent but wide patches of a medium spatial-frequency (5 c/deg) grating (Kramer, 1978; details in appendix here). The durations in these three studies were all quite short (7 msec to 125 msec).

14. NEAR-THRESHOLD VISUAL PATTERNS   275

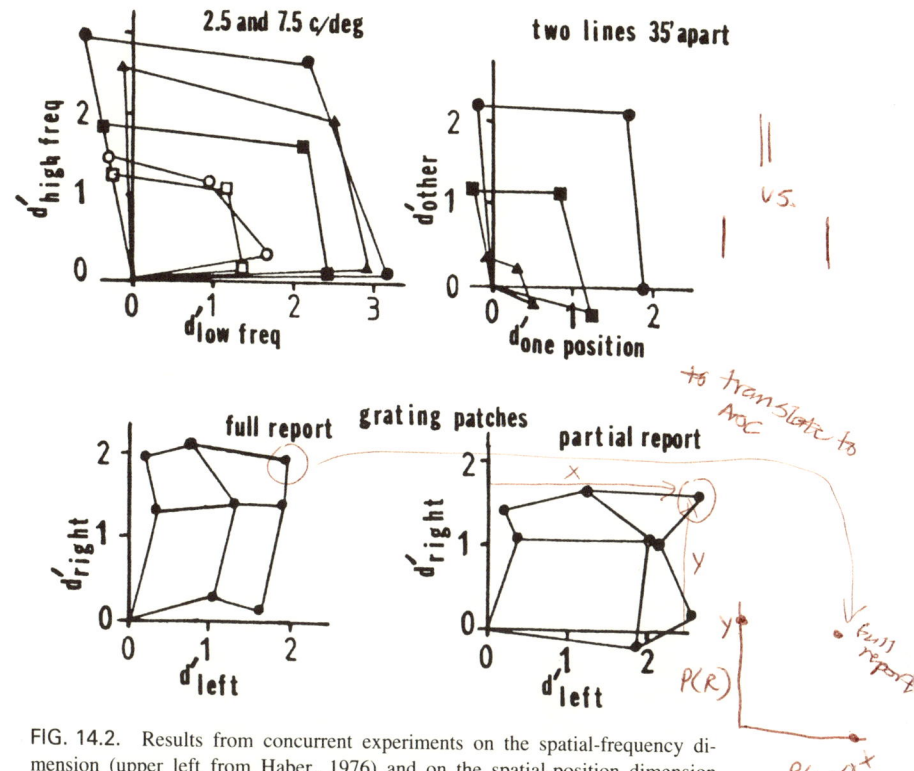

FIG. 14.2. Results from concurrent experiments on the spatial-frequency dimension (upper left from Haber, 1976) and on the spatial-position dimension (upper right, unpublished results from Nachmias, 1966; lower panels from Kramer, 1978).

The three spatial-position studies produced results for far-apart positions very like those predicted—that is, approximate rectangles on d' versus d' plots and little correlation between two responses. Figure 14.2, upper right, shows three replications (at different contrast levels) for two thin lines separated by 35 minutes of visual angle (from Nachmias, 1966). The lower part of Fig. 14.2 shows two sets of results for adjacent grating patches (from Kramer, 1978). Here nine stimuli—three contrast levels at each of the two positions—were used so the predicted results form a rectilinear 3 × 3 array.

Suppose an observer is unable to monitor mechanisms sensitive to both components simultaneously (violating assumption 6) or is unable to answer two questions each trial as well as one (violating assumption 7 because of response competition or memory load, for example). An observer would then perform better when only asked about one component each trial (single-question or partial-report or focused-attention condition; bottom right in Fig. 14.2) than when asked about both (two-question or full-report or divided-attention condition;

bottom left in Fig. 14.2). In fact, however, performance in the two-question condition is not generally worse than in the single-question condition, providing further evidence that the observer can monitor mechanisms for both components simultaneously without loss (and also give direct reports about both simultaneously).

Slight Deviations from Predictions—Interactive Mechanisms or Modified Higher Processing?

Although the results of concurrent experiments are much as predicted, small but systematic deviations of three kinds have been observed: The left and/or bottom edges of the nominal rectangle may lean inward ("confusion") or outward (a "negative influence" of one component on the other). Second, the upper right data point (the d' values for the compound) is often inside the parallogram calculated by adding the d' values for the simple components. Third, as mentioned previously, the interresponse correlations are sometimes not zero.

One class of explanation for these small deviations postulates interactions among the mechanisms themselves: inhibition (or excitation) to account for negative influences (or confusion) and shared noise sources to account for interresponse correlations (Hirsch et al., 1982; Nachmias, 1974; Olzak, 1981).

Another class of explanation elaborates the assumptions (5, 6, and 7) about further processing of the mechansims' outputs. Perhaps, for example, the signal-detection criterion to which a decision variable is compared is not constant over trials but changes depending on the values of both decision variables. Or perhaps—due to intrinsic uncertainty—some of the same mechanisms are contributing to the decision variables for both of two far-apart simple stimuli. Or perhaps the observer's response is not based on anything as simple as the maximally responding mechanism in a subset; instead, perhaps, some rather complicated function from the full set of all mechanism's outputs is calculated (as an optimal observer would do; for discussions of optimality, see Sperling & Dosher, in press; Watson, 1983).

Basis for Selection

The basis for selective monitoring when expecting a certain simple stimulus—as in the extrinsic-uncertainty experiments—need not be the same as when trying to extract information about one simple stimulus from the ongoing perception of several—as in the compound stimulus trials of these concurrent experiments (e.g., Kahneman & Treisman, 1984). The satisfactory predictions here for both experiments' results, however, suggest that in this situation the basis is the same or very similar. This basis might be said to be the component spatial frequencies or spatial positions. More precisely, it is the subsets of mechanisms corresponding to (having receptive fields that are sensitive to) these component stimuli.

Similarly, the successful predictions suggest that the basis for attending to a compound stimulus is its component spatial frequencies or spatial positions (more precisely, the union of the subsets corresponding to these components; see assumption 6). Some modification of this last statement may prove necessary to account for the extrinsic-uncertainty effect for the compound grating, however. Although interpreted above as the effect of a simple change in decision rule, this effect could also result from the intrusion either of a broad bandwidth mechanism (which is more sensitive to the compound than to either component) or of some higher-order entity specialized for the compound (a "node" or an "object file"; e.g., Kahneman & Treisman, 1984). At present, all these interpretations are equally unsupported.

HEARSAY EVIDENCE

Conscious Rejection

The results so far reported have little bearing on whether the selective monitoring occurs early, late, or sideways in some hypothetical processing. Very late (postconscious) selection might seem to be suggested by three of these results, however:

1. The small size of the extrinsic-uncertainty effects suggests that an observer is perfectly able to attend simultaneously to mechanisms sensitive to several spatial frequencies or spatial positions without loss.
2. The concurrent-experiment results suggest that an observer can directly report about at least two or three spatial frequencies or spatial positions separately without loss.
3. Postcues reduce the extrinsic-uncertainty effect.

These three results might suggest the following scenario: The observer's perceptions always reflect the outputs from all mechanisms because there is no limitation to his or her capacity to attend to all of them simultaneously. (For example, in a block where he or she knows that only 9 c/deg gratings are being presented, he or she might consciously perceive something that looks like a 2 c/deg grating whenever the maximal output from the subset of mechanisms sensitive to 2 c/deg just happens to be high—in shorthand, he or she "sees" a false alarm by the 2 c/deg mechanisms.) The observer then consciously realizes that some of what is seen corresponds to stimuli that are definitely not present (e.g., the 2 c/deg false alarm) and so consciously ignores these percepts when making his or her response. In accord with this scenario of conscious rejection of false alarms, observers report that occasionally they do consciously see and then reject "wrong" percepts (percepts having the characteristics of unexpected stimuli—

e.g., at the wrong place or wrong time or wrong spatial frequency or wrong orientation).

Preconscious Selection

Observers also report, however, that such conscious rejections of "wrong" percepts are very rare. They report that, in general, they see only percepts corresponding to expected stimuli. These introspective reports suggest that—in, for example, the alone or precued intermixed conditions of extrinsic-uncertainty experiments—selective filtering is occurring early enough that the outputs of the unmonitored mechanisms do not contribute to conscious perceptions.

The following story, related to us independently by several people, supports this suggestion. While debugging a program or calibrating equipment, you try to display a grating. You keep turning up the contrast far beyond the usual value, quite bewildered by the absence of the grating. Suddenly you do see a grating: It is actually far above threshold (perhaps a log unit) but of a quite different spatial frequency than you had intended. (There is a second and unsurprising point to this story: Even when the unmonitored mechanisms are filtered out before conscious perception, a large enough output will break into consciousness.)

PRIMARY-PLUS-PROBE EXPERIMENTS

Another result, although certainly not conclusive evidence in favor of preconscious selection, lends credence to its possibility. Perhaps an observer can be coaxed into monitoring mechanisms sensitive for one spatial frequency (the primary) and then presented with other spatial frequencies (probe spatial frequencies). To this end, an unbalanced-intermixed condition was used in which most trials were of the primary spatial frequency (known to the observer beforehand) but enough were of probe frequencies to be able to estimate the probes' detectability. One interval of each two-interval forced-choice trial always contained a blank field and the other the sinusoidal grating; the observer's task was to indicate which interval contained the grating even if it was not of the primary frequency. The detectability at each spatial frequency was also measured in an alone condition.

The hoped-for tuning of the uncertainty effect was found (Davis & Graham, 1981). For example, when a primary of 4 c/deg was presented on 95% of the trials, the detectability of 4 c/deg was as high as when alone but the detectability of 1 c/deg and 16 c/deg probes went down to chance (a loss in d' of almost 2— much larger than the loss in the ordinary extrinsic-uncertainty experiments described earlier). Detectability of closer probes was decremented also, although not so completely. When two primaries were used (1 and 16 c/deg), there were two peaks in the tuning function at these two frequencies (Davis, 1981).

If the observers were following instructions—and they say they were—these results strongly suggest that observers in the unbalanced intermixed blocks did not consciously perceive (at least not as well as usual) the patterns that stimulated unmonitored mechanisms.

Although too strong a conclusion about bandwith cannot be drawn, the following can be said: The spatial-frequency dependence of uncertainty effects—in both ordinary and primary-plus-probe experiments—is consistent with the idea that the selectively monitored mechanisms are the same ones that account, for example, for the spatial-frequency bandwidth in summation or adaptation experiments (Davis & Graham, 1981; Yager et al., 1984).

PERCEPTION OF COMPLEX VISUAL STIMULI

Global–Local Studies

In visual-search studies using suprathreshold global–local stimuli—large forms made up of small forms where all forms are easily discriminable from a blank field—an observer's ability or inability to attend to different ranges of spatial frequency is sometimes discussed. Three caveats should be considered, however, before comparing the near-threshold studies discussed here and the suprathreshold visual-search (global–local) studies.

First, too hasty an identification between low versus high spatial frequencies and global versus local structure must be avoided. As shown in Fig. 14.3, information about the identity of the global form is typically present in all spatial-frequency ranges (at least when retinal inhomogeneity is ignored).

Second, comparison of asymptotic performance measures like d' to reaction times (as measured in many suprathreshold studies) must be done with great care; reaction times reflect not only asymptotic performance levels but also processing speeds and the observer's willingness to trade accuracy for speed.

Third, both alternatives of a typical suprathreshold discrimination (e.g., is the small form *E* or *H?*) overlap heavily in spatial position, spatial frequency, and orientation as well as both being far above threshold. According to the multiple-receptive-field model of pattern vision, therefore, many of the same mechanisms produce large outputs in response to both alternatives. (A potential exception to this statement is the discrimination between orientations of blobs in the interesting global–local forms constructed by Hughes, Layton, Baird, & Lester, 1984.) With such substantial overlap, any rule (like assumptions 3 and 4 earlier) that simply compares maximal outputs from subsets of mechanisms to each other or to criteria may be close to optimal for near-threshold tasks but will be very far from optimal for such suprathreshold discriminations. Presumably, therefore, our nervous systems undertake further and more complicated processing of the mechanisms' outputs in order to make the suprathreshold discriminations.

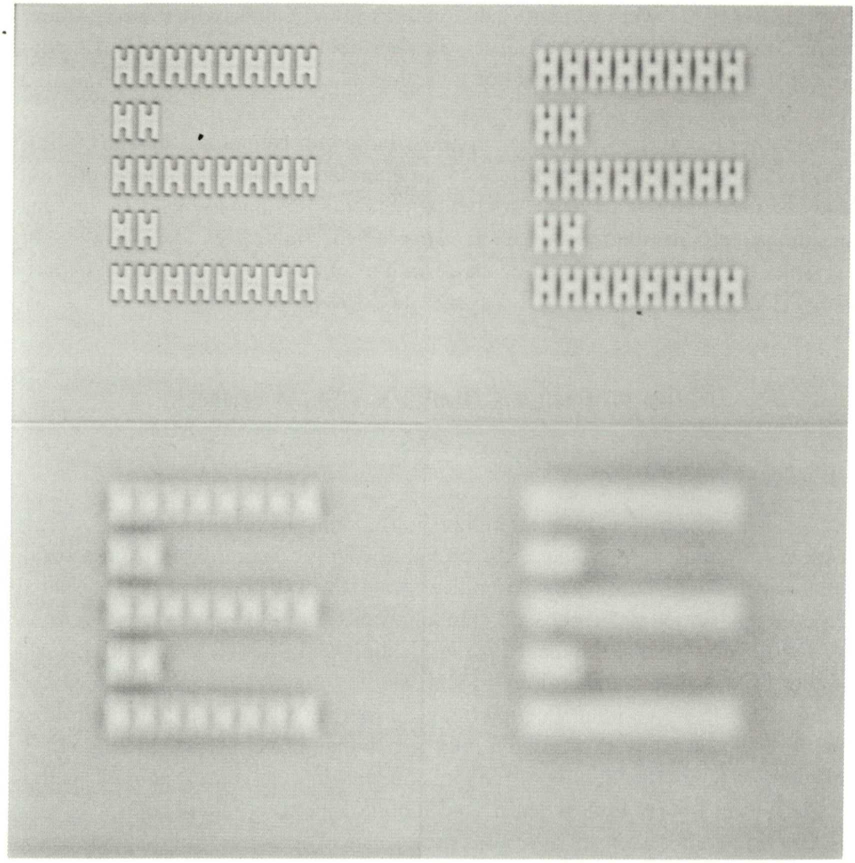

FIG. 14.3. Spatial-frequency filtered versions of an original image (not shown) in which the small *H*s were uniform white on a dark background. Upper left version contains spatial frequencies greater than 32 cycles per large *E*, upper right contains 16 to 32 cycles/*E*, lower left contains 8 to 16 cycles/*E*, and lower right contains 4 to 8 cycles/*E*. These images were provided by James R. Bergen of the RCA David Sarnoff Research Center using the LaPlacian Pyramid technique (with $a = .375$) of P. J. Burt and E. H. Adelson, IEEE Transactions on Communications, 1983, Vol. Com–31, 4, 532–540. The reproduction has undoubtedly distorted these images somewhat, but not so much as to mislead the reader.

In light of this third caveat, the conclusion that observers in the near-threshold experiments can monitor all relevant mechanisms simultaneously and without loss should not be expected to generalize to typical suprathreshold tasks. It seems entirely plausible that, in the complicated calculations required to make suprathreshold discriminations effectively, only some of the mechanisms' outputs can be dealt with simultaneously. One might even argue that preconscious selection occurs in near-threshold experiments—although the observer has the capacity to consciously reject false alarms in those tasks—only because in more ordinary situations costs are incurred if all mechanisms' outputs are allowed upstream.

Basis for Suprathreshold Selection

On the other hand, the conclusion that an observer can selectively attend to the spatial-frequency or spatial-position components of near-threshold patterns (more precisely, can monitor the corresponding subsets of mechanisms) seems more likely to generalize to suprathreshold tasks. Few would argue about selectively attending to spatial position, but selectively attending to spatial frequency or "scale" of objects—that is, to mechanisms with a given size of receptive field—is more controversial.

The objection might be raised, for example, that we do not see patches of sinusoidal gratings in complex visual scenes. However, just as component tones can be "heard out" in musical chords but not in speech, the component sinusoids in suprathreshold compound gratings can easily be "seen out" if the spatial frequencies are a factor of four or five apart. Further, although our immediate, untrained reports of perceptions are, indeed, dominated by objects or by objects at given spatial positions at given times (and experimental results demonstrate objects' importance in controlling attention—e.g., Kahneman & Treisman, 1984), the scale of objects is also quite salient in perception. You can easily decide to "look at" small details or at large structures (as in Julesz's 1980 zoom-lens analogy). Indeed, the conclusion here that either low or high spatial-frequency components of simple near-threshold patterns can be monitored with equal facility accords with the conclusion that either global or local cues in suprathreshold patterns can be attended with equal facility (Hughes et al., 1984; Ward, 1982).

Selective Attention To Avoid False Alarms

Commonly discussed adaptive functions of selective attention include the prevention of: perceptual overload, memory overload, and paralysis resulting from response competition (e.g., Kahneman & Treisman, 1984). In visual scenes of the everyday world, many important components—very high spatial frequencies at the fixation point, not so very high spatial frequencies a few degrees out—are at or below their contrast threshold, a range where noise is widely believed to limit vision. Suprathreshold vision may also be noise limited in many cases (e.g., Pelli, 1981). The avoidance of visual false alarms—which contributes to prevention of perceptual overload although little mentioned under that rubric—is, therefore, an adaptive function of selective attention that could be of considerable importance in ordinary visual perception.

ACKNOWLEDGMENTS

This research was partially supported by NSF grants BNS–76–18839 to Norma Graham and BNS–83–11350 to Dean Yager.

We are grateful to Jacob Nachmias for making available his unpublished experimental results and to James R. Bergen for the spatial-frequency filtered images in Fig. 14.3. We also thank Elizabeth T. Davis, Frances K. Graham, and two anonymous referees for their helpful comments on an earlier draft.

APPENDIX: CONCURRENT EXPERIMENTS

Spatial Frequency and Spatial Position of Grating Patches

Details of equipment can be found in Hirsch et al. (1982). Vertical sinusoidal gratings were presented on a CRT screen seen through an aperture in an illuminated circular surround approximately matching the screen in mean luminance and hue. In the spatial-frequency (spatial-position) experiments, the aperture was 6.2° wide by 4.75° high (5.25 × 4°) at a viewing distance of 129 cm (150 cm) at a mean luminance of 10 cd/m-squared (1.9 ft-L). The contrasts of the two components were chosen to roughly equate their detectability.

Viewing was binocular with natural pupils and normal spectacle corrections.

After each trial, the observer pushed two buttons to indicate the answers (yes or no) to the questions about whether each of the two components was present. There was two-alternative feedback (correct versus incorrect).

Spatial-Frequency Experiments (Haber, 1976). The gratings (of 2.5 and 7.5 c/deg) filled the CRT screen. There was no fixation point. The overall phase of the patterns was randomized from trial to trial to prevent the use of spatial position as a clue to identify. The relative phase in the compound was held constant throughout a session and haphazardly randomized across sessions. The stimuli were exposed for 760 msec (with abrupt onset and offset). There were 125 trials per session per stimulus (per point on the graph).

Spatial-Position Experiments (Kramer, 1978). The two simple stimuli were adjacent gratings patches each containing 13 cycles of a 5 cycle/degree grating. When both patches were present they formed a continuous grating across the display. Marks on the surround above and below the stimulus indicated the division between the two patches. The observer was instructed to fixate at this division. Each stimulus was presented for 125 msec with abrupt onsets and offsets. In each randomly ordered block of trials, there was a total of 40 presentations of each of the nine stimuli (three contrast levels including zero at each of two positions). Two blocks were run each day to constitute a session. Eight full-report sessions were run on observer TS at the same contrast levels (average results for all 640 trials per stimulus shown in lower left Fig. 14.2). Four sessions on a second observer, PK, yielded very similar results. Observer TS also ran six additional single-question (partial-report) control sessions in which she answered only one of the two questions in each session.

Variations. Several variations were tried by Haber (1976) with several observers: nine (3 × 3) stimuli, 2.5 paired with 4.2 c/deg, confidence-rating answers, answers of "blank, low, high, both" rather than answers to questions about components, four-alternative feedback (blank, low, high, both) as in Hirsch et al. (1982), and no feedback. Results were always similar to those shown, but with some variation in the extent to which the three deviations (see main text) appeared.

Improvement in discriminability across sessions was never seen with 2.5 and 7.5 c/deg although it was with 2.5 and 4.2 c/deg.

Spatial Position of Lines (Unpublished Data, Nachmias, 1966)

Two, thin parallel lines were separated by about 60, 35, or 5 minutes. At the intermediate separation, three different intensities were used (producing the three sets of results shown in the upper right of Fig. 14.2). The bright vertical test lines (about 1.5 minutes wide × 4 degrees high) were flashed for 50 msec on a large continuously present adapting field in a Maxwellian view apparatus. The display was seen monocularly in Maxwellian view through a 2 mm artificial pupil. There was a black fixation point (subtending about 10 minutes) in the center of the adapting field. One line was presented 10 minutes to the right of the fixation point. The other line was further from the fixation point. Feedback was given.

There were approximately 300 trials per stimulus (per point in the figure). The results at the largest separation were like those shown. The results for very close lines were quite different, however, showing considerable confusion between the positions (just as there is considerable confusion between close spatial frequencies; see Hirsch et al., 1982).

REFERENCES

Ball, K., & Sekuler, R. (1981). Cues reduce direction uncertainty and enhance motion detection. *Perception and Psychophysics, 30*(2), 119–128.

Cohn, T. E., & Lasley, D. J. (1974). Detectability of a luminance increment: Effect of spatial uncertainty. *Journal of the Optical Society of America, 64,* 1715–1719.

Davis, E. T. (1981). Allocation of attention: Uncertainty effects when monitoring one or two visual gratings of noncontiguous spatial frequencies. *Perception and Psychophysics, 29,* 618–622.

Davis, E. T., & Graham, N. (1981). Spatial frequency uncertainty effects in the detection of sinusoidal gratings. *Vision Research, 21,* 705–712.

Davis, E. T., Kramer, P., & Graham, N. (1983). Uncertainty about spatial frequency, spatial position, or contrast of visual patterns. Perception and Psychophysics, 33, 20–28.

Graham, N. (1981). Psychophysics of spatial-frequency channels. In M. Kubovy & J. Pomerantz (Eds.), *Perceptual organization* (pp. 215–262). Hillsdale, NJ: Lawrence Erlbaum Associates.

Graham, N., Robson, J. G., & Nachmias, J. (1978). Grating summation in fovea and periphery. *Vision Research, 18,* 815–825.

Haber, N. (1976). *Correlation of noise sources and bandwidth estimates: An analysis of a multiple-channels model of visual form perception.* Unpublished master's essay, Columbia University, New York.

Hirsch, J. (1977). *Properties of human visual spatial frequency selective systems: A two-frequency two-response recognition paradigm* (Doctoral dissertation, Columbia University, New York).

Hirsch, J., Hylton, R., & Graham, N. (1982). Simultaneous recognition of two spatial-frequency components. *Vision Research, 22,* 365–375.

Hughes, H. C., Layton, W. M., Baird, J. C., & Lester, L. S. (1984). Global precedence in visual pattern recognition. *Perception and Psychophysics, 35*(4), 361–371.

Julesz, B. (1980). Spatial frequency channels in one-, two-, and three dimensional vision: Variations on a theme by Bekesy. In C. Harris (Ed.), *Visual coding and adaptability.* Hillside, NJ: Lawrence Erlbaum Associates.

Kahneman, D., & Treisman, A. M. (1984). Changing views of attention and automaticity. In R. Parasuraman & R. Davies (Eds.), *Varieties of attention* (pp. 29–61). New York: Academic.

Kramer, P. (1978). *Simultaneous recognition of two spatial positions.* Unpublished Master's essay, Columbia University, New York.

Kramer, P. (1984). *Summation and uncertainty effects in the detection of spatial frequency.* Ph.D. dissertation, Columbia University, New York.

Nachmias, J. (May, 1974). *A new approach to bandwidth estimation of spatial-frequency channels.* Presented at Association for Research in Vision and Ophthalmology, Sarasota, Florida, and personal communication.

Nachmias, J., & Kocher, E. C. (1970). Visual detection and discrimination of luminance increments. *Journal of the Optical Society of America, 60,* 3, 382–389.

Olzak, L. (1981). *Inhibition and stochastic interactions in spatial pattern perception.* Ph.D. dissertation, University of California at Los Angeles.

Pelli, D. (1981). *Effects of visual noise.* Ph.D. dissertation, Cambridge University, England.

Shaw, M. (1984). Consequences for coding variability of the spatial distribution of attention: A fundamental difference between pattern and luminance detection. In H. Bouma & D. Bowhuis (Eds.), *Attention and performance X.* Hillsdale, NJ: Lawrence Erlbaum Associates.

Sperling, G. (1984). A unified theory of attention and signal detection. In R. Parasuraman & D. R. Davies (Eds.), *Varieties of attention.* New York: Academic.

Sperling, G., & Dosher, B. (in press). Strategies and optimization in human information processing. In K. Boff, J. Thomas, & L. Kaufman (Eds.), *Handbook of perception and performance.* New York: Wiley.

Ward, L. M. (1982). Determinants of attention to local and global features of visual forms. *Journal of Experimental Psychology: Human Perception and Performance, 8,* 562–581.

Watson, A. B. (1983/April). *Detection and recognition of simple spatial forms.* Moffett Field, CA: NASA Technical Memorandum 84353.

Wickelgren, W. A. (1967). Strength theories of disjunctive visual detection. *Perception and Psychophysics, 2*(8), 331–337.

Yager, D., Kramer, P., Shaw, M., & Graham, N. (1984). Detection and identification of spatial frequency: Models and data. *Vision Research. 24,* 1021–1036.

15 Smooth Eye Movements as Indicators of Selective Attention

Eileen Kowler
Carolina Zingale
Rutgers University

ABSTRACT

Saccades (voluntary high velocity rotations of the eye) are often used as overt indicators of shifts of visual attention even though attention shifts and saccades are not always coincident. Smooth eye movements may provide more accurate indicators because they are involuntary, but are, nevertheless, affected by cognitive factors. We first review the evidence that selective attention affects smooth eye movements. A recent experiment by Kowler, van der Steen, Tamminga, and Collewijn (1984) showed that subjects could select one of two full-field, identical, superimposed patterns of randomly positioned dots, one stationary and the other moving, as the target for smooth eye movements. There was virtually no influence of the background on smooth eye movement velocity. Effective selection of the target was due to attention and not stimulus variables because target and background were physically identical. We now report that performance of a concurrent visual task (detection of the disappearce of dots from either the stationary or the moving field) was faster and more accurate when dots disappeared from the target than from the background. This result would not be predicted from the differences in the retinal velocities of target and background because the retinal velocity of the background was low enough (about 1 deg/sec) so that visual acuity and contrast sensitivity were not impaired. We conclude that the smooth oculomotor subsystem and the visual system share the same attentional mechanism. This implies that smooth eye movements provide accurate indicators of selective attention during performance of a visual task with stationary and moving stimuli.

INTRODUCTION

Saccades—voluntary high velocity rotations of the eye used to look from place to place—are often used as overt indicators of cognitive processes. Many investigators have used saccades to make inferences about how people read (e.g., McConkie & Rayner, 1975), memorize pictures (e.g., Loftus, 1972; Noton & Stark, 1971), or solve problems (e.g., Just & Carpenter, 1975; Suppes, Cohen, Laddaga, Anliker, & Floyd, 1983). These inferences about cognitive processes were based on the assumption that each saccade reflects a shift in attention to a new portion of the visual display.

This assumption is troublesome. Saccades may reflect attention shifts but they do not always do so. Observers can change attended locations without making saccades, or make saccades without changing the attended location (Klein, 1980; Kowler & Steinman, 1977, 1979c; Sperling & Reeves, 1980). Thus, measurements of saccades may not reveal where the observer attends, nor over how large an area she attends, at any given moment.

Smooth eye movements may be better indicators of attention. Smooth eye movements are the relatively slow eye movements used to track smoothly moving targets, and, as has been known since 1959, maintain the line of sight on stationary targets (Nachmias, 1959; 1961; Steinman, Cunitz, Timberlake, & Herman, 1967; Steinman, Haddad, Skavenski, & Wyman, 1973). Smooth eye movements, unlike saccades, are not under voluntary control. Observers (with the exception of very rare individuals) cannot make voluntary smooth pursuits in the absence of a smoothly moving stimulus. Similarly, observers cannot voluntarily prevent smooth pursuit (Murphy, Kowler, & Steinman, 1975) or change its direction (Kowler & Steinman, 1979b) when only a moving stimulus is present. The only voluntary control observers have over smooth eye movements is the ability to reduce eye velocity to a fraction of target velocity (Steinman, Skavenski, & Sansbury, 1969).

Despite this lack of voluntary control, smooth eye movements are, nevertheless, influenced by cognitive processes. For example, the expectation that a stationary target will begin to move, or that a moving target will change its path, causes the eye to move smoothly in the direction of the expected motion before the expected motion begins (Kowler & Steinman, 1979a, 1979b, 1981; Kowler, Martins, & Pavel, 1984). Smooth eye movements produced by expectations cannot be initiated voluntarily in the absence of the expectation, and cannot be suppressed voluntarily (Kowler & Steinman, 1979a).

This chapter considers whether smooth eye movements automatically reflect selective attention in the same way that prior research has shown they automatically reflect expectations. We first review the evidence showing that selective attention determines the target for smooth eye movements when the visual field contains both stationary and moving stimuli. Then, a new experiment is described to determine how selection of the target for smooth eye movements affects the processing of visual information from target and background.

THE EFFECT OF SELECTIVE ATTENTION ON SMOOTH EYE MOVEMENTS

Prior Demonstrations

Prior studies have shown that smooth pursuit of a large moving pattern (usually stripes) can be more or less inhibited by the instruction to attend a superimposed stationary reference (Cheng & Outerbridge, 1975; Dodge & Fox, 1928; Dubois & Collewijn, 1979; Fischer & Kornmuller, 1930; Mach, 1906/1959; Murphy et al., 1975; Stark, 1971; Tamminga, 1983). (For related observations with different stimuli, see Collewijn, Curio, & Grusser, 1982; Collewijn & Tamminga, 1984; Ter Braak, 1957). These studies showed that smooth eye movement characteristics are not determined solely by involuntary, automatic processing of all available stimulus motions. Rather, the contribution of some stimulus motions to smooth eye movements can be reduced by selection of the target.

These studies, however, could not determine the effectiveness of selection because all prior studies used target and background stimuli that differed in size, luminance, and retinal location. This meant that the effectiveness of selection could have been confounded with the relative strength of the target and background as stimuli for smooth eye movements. The following section describes an experiment in which the capacity of selection was determined uncontaminated by effects of stimulus strength.

Determining the Capacity of Voluntary Selection

Kowler, van der Steen, Tamminga and Collewijn (1984) studied the effectiveness of selection using identical target and background stimuli. Stimuli were two full-field (76 deg by 87 deg), superimposed patterns of randomly positioned dots. Dot size (7.1 min arc by 9.5 min arc), luminance (8.9 cd/m^2), and density (1 dot/deg^2) were the same in each field. The fields differed only in that one was stationary and the other moved to the left at 70.2 min arc/sec.

On some trials either the stationary or the moving field was presented alone. On other trials the two fields were presented superimposed. Subjects were asked to use smooth eye movements either to maintain the line of sight on the stationary field, or to track the moving field. Two highly experienced eye movement subjects (Han Collewijn and Robert Steinman) were tested to increase the likelihood that best possible performance would be obtained. Trials lasted 3 seconds. Eye movements were recorded with a magnetic field search coil monitor (Collewijn, van der Mark, & Jansen, 1975) with noise level less than 1 min arc.

There was virtually no influence of the background field on smooth eye movements. The effect of the background on mean eye velocity was less than 2% of the velocity of the moving field. The small effect of the background on mean eye velocity represents performance on individual trials and did not result from averaging trials in which the background had large effects, but in opposing directions. These results are illustrated by representative eye movement records in Fig. 15.1 and are summarized by the mean eye velocities shown in Fig. 15.2. For further quantitative details, see Kowler et al. (1984).

The same independence from the background field was observed when: (a) the density of the dots increased to 8 dots/deg^2—a condition that completely eliminated the effect of the background on Collewijn's smooth eye movements—(see Fig. 15.2); (b) the intensity of the target field was reduced sixfold (the dimmest target field that could barely be detected from among the dots of the background); and (c) the intensity of the background field was reduced sixfold.

Note: Saccades in this experiment were rare and unrelated to the presence of the background. This is not surprising because saccades during fixation of stationary or moving targets are voluntary options under the control of the subject (Puckett & Steinman, 1969; Steinman et al., 1967; Winterson & Collewijn, 1976). Accurate fixation and pursuit can be achieved without saccades (Colle-

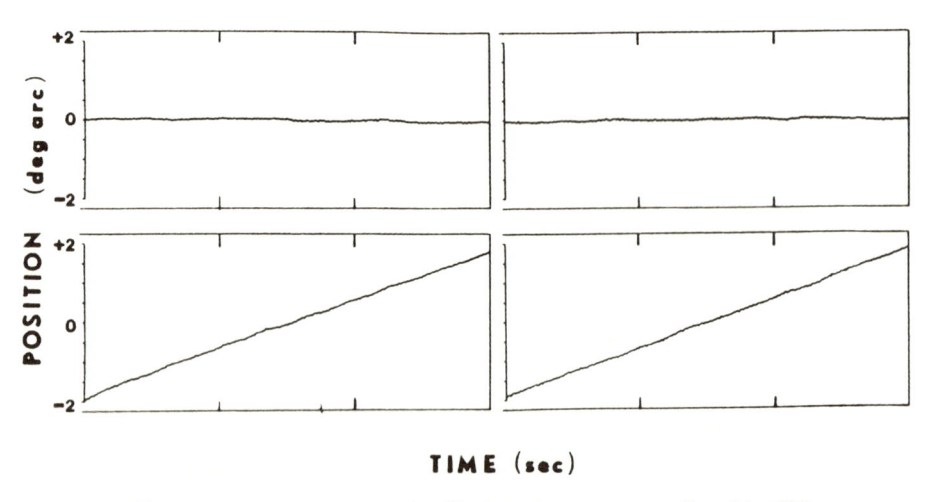

FIG. 15.1. Representative records of horizontal eye movements for subject HC under instructions to maintain the line of sight on the 1 dot/deg^2 stationary (top 2 graphs) or moving (bottom 2 graphs) target field in the presence of the stationary field alone (top left), the moving field alone (bottom left), or both the stationary and moving fields (2 right-hand graphs). Tic marks on the X axis separate 1 sec intervals. Upward deflections of the eye trace indicate movements to the left. Reprinted with permission from *Vision Research, 24,* Kowler, van der Steen, Tamminga and Collewijn, copyright 1984, Pergamon Press, Ltd.

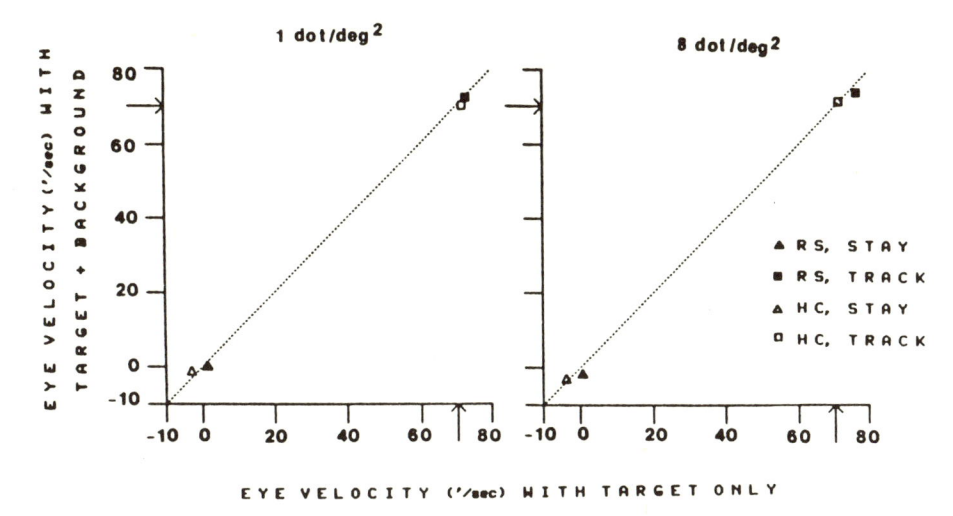

FIG. 15.2. Mean 21 msec eye velocities for subjects HC and RS under the instruction to maintain the line of sight on the 1 dot/deg² (left graph) or the 8 dot/deg² (right graph) target field presented either alone (abscissa) or with the superimposed background field (ordinate). Instructions were to maintain the line of sight on the stationary field (*STAY*), or on the moving field (*TRACK*). Each mean velocity is based on 40 trials for HC and 30 for RS. Standard errors are smaller than the plotting symbols. Negative values on the axes indicate rightward velocities. The arrow indicates the velocity of the moving field. Velocities falling on the dotted diagonal line indicate no effect of the background. Velocities falling above the line, when the stationary field was the target, indicate smooth eye movements in the direction of the moving background. Velocities below the line, when the moving field was the target, indicate smooth eye movements slowed by the stationary background. Reprinted with permission from *Vision Research, 24*, Kowler, van der Steen, Tamminga, and Collewijn, copyright 1984, Pergamon Press, Ltd.

wijn & Tamminga, 1984; Kowler, Murphy, & Steinman, 1978; Steinman et al., 1973).

In summary, selective attention determines the target for smooth eye movements. Involuntary mechanisms in the smooth oculomotor subsystem do not automatically average the velocity of all retinal motions. The role of involuntary mechanisms is limited to determining the velocity of the eye once a target is chosen by the subject.

Kowler et al.'s (1984) results raise the following question: Does selection of the target for smooth eye movement also determine the information available for visual processing? To answer this question we examined how well subjects could make visual judgments about target and background. Finding visual judgments to be more accurate for the target than for the background would suggest that selection of the target for smooth eye movements and selection of perceptual information are the same process.

THE EFFECT OF SELECTION OF THE TARGET FOR SMOOTH EYE MOVEMENTS ON VISUAL PROCESSING

The Visual Task

Stimuli were similar to those used by Kowler et al. (1984): two identical, superimposed fields of randomly positioned dots. During a trial a subset of randomly chosen dots disappeared from either the stationary or the moving field. The subjects did not know in advance which field would lose the dots. They had to press a button as soon as they detected the disappearance, and at the end of the trial, had to identify the field that lost the dots.

Subjects were instructed to choose one of the fields as the target for smooth eye movements. The specific instructions were the same as those used by Kowler et al. (1984), namely: (1) *Stay:* subjects were instructed to use smooth eye movements to maintain the line of sight on the stationary field, and (2) *Track:* subjects were instructed to use smooth eye movements to track the moving field. Note that these instructions constrained eye velocity and not eye position. Before each trial subjects chose where to look within the designated field. They started trials when their choice was made and they were ready to stay or to track. Once trials started, however, subjects were asked not to make saccades to look around the field, but rather to use smooth eye movements exclusively to stay or to track (Puckett & Steinman, 1969; Steinman, Haddad, Skavenski, & Wyman, 1973).

Instructions to stay or to track were alternated every 10 trials. To determine whether visual performance was better for the target for smooth eye movements we measured: (a) the eye movements; (b) the accuracy of detection and identification; and (c) the reaction time of the detection report.

Trials were also run in which instructions to stay or to track were not given. In these trials subjects were allowed to move their eyes in whatever way they felt would lead to the best performance on the visual task. These trials were included to find out whether following explicit instructions to select the target for smooth eye movements interfered with visual performance.

Eye movements were also measured when no concurrent visual task was performed. This was done to find out whether performance of the visual task interfered with effective selection of the target for smooth eye movements. For these trials dots disappeared, as they did in the main experiment, but subjects did not report their disappearance.

Rationale for Choice of Stimulus and Task

The stimulus and the task were designed so that differences between visual performance with target and background fields could be attributed to effects of selective attention and not to extraneous factors. Specifically:

15. SMOOTH EYE MOVEMENTS AND SELECTIVE ATTENTION   291

1. Target and background fields were physically identical, as they were in Kowler et al.'s (1984) experiment. This was done so that any differences between visual performance with target and background fields could not be attributed to differences in their physical characteristics.

2. Each dot that disappeared was selected at random without regard to its location within a field, nor to the locations of the other selected dots. As a result the distribution of the retinal locations of the removed dots was the same for the target and background fields. This procedure was used so that any advantage in detectability at particular retinal locations (such as the fovea) would apply equally to target and background.

3. The velocity of the moving field was low (about 1 deg/sec). A low velocity minimized the possibility that detection of the disappearance of dots would be impaired by the reduction of retinal contrast caused by smearing of dots from the background field across the retina. Visual acuity (Westheimer & McKee, 1975) and contrast sensitivity (Murphy, 1978; Steinman, Levinson, Collewijn, & van der Steen, 1985) are not impaired by retinal image velocities less than about 2 deg/sec.

Details of Methods

Three subjects were tested. Two were highly experienced eye movement subjects, Kowler (EK) and Collewijn (HC). The third, Zingale (CZ), was an inexperienced eye movement subject having previously served in one study concerned with saccades.

Dots were contained in a 5.2 deg by 5.2 deg region, displayed on a CRT (Tektronix 608, P4 phosphor), and viewed through a collimating lens. Each field contained 50 dots (i.e., 1.9 dots/deg^2). Dot luminance was set to 2 log units above foveal threshold. The velocity of the moving field was 65 min arc/sec for HC, 60 min arc/sec for CZ, and 57 min arc/sec for EK. Motion was always rightward. When dots from the moving field reached the edge of the display they were immediately relocated to the other edge and continued moving across.

Dots disappeared at a randomly selected time during the middle 2 sec of the 3 sec trial. Dots never disappeared during the first 500 msec of the trial because during smooth pursuit mean eye velocity is not close to target velocity until 500 msec after motion-onset (Kowler & McKee, 1984). Dots never disappeared during the last 500 msec of the trial because the eye begins to slow down in response to the expectation that a moving target will stop (Kowler & Steinman, 1979b).

The locations of the dots in each field were chosen randomly on each trial to discourage responses based on a well-formed memory for the pattern rather than on detection of dot disappearance.

Dots did not disappear on about 10% of the trials. These were catch trials included to encourage subjects to wait until they saw the disappearance before responding. Subjects HC and EK never responded on the catch trials; CZ responded on one. On all other trials dots were equally likely to disappear from either the stationary or the moving field. The number of dots that disappeared (10 for HC, and 5 for both CZ and EK) was empirically determined to produce about 60% to 70% correct responses. Feedback was given after each trial to encourage best performance.

Horizontal movements of the right eye were measured with a Generation IV SRI Double Purkinje Image Tracker (Crane & Steele, 1978). Noise level was 0.7'. The head was stabilized with a dental biteboard.

Eye velocity was computed for 50 msec intervals around the time the visual judgment was made—specifically, from 200 msec before the dots disappeared until 100 msec before the detection response. Fifty msec eye velocities occurring before and after dot disappearance were averaged separately. The rare intervals containing saccades were discarded.

The Effectiveness of Voluntary Selection during Performance of a Visual Task

The visual task did not interfere with selection of the target for smooth eye movements. Mean eye velocities were about the same for trials in which the concurrent visual task was and was not performed. In both cases the effect of the background was small. This was true for the mean eye velocities both before and after the disappearance of the dots. These results are shown in Table 15.1.

The effective selection was not due to the averaging of trials in which the background had large effects in opposing directions. Distributions of 50 msec eye velocities, shown in Fig. 15.3, were centered around the velocity of the target field. The variability of the velocities is similar to that observed without backgrounds (Kowler & Steinman, 1979a; Kowler et al., 1984).

Effective selection now makes it reasonable to ask whether visual judgments were better for the target field.

Visual Judgments were More Accurate for the Target Field

A correct report was defined as the correct detection of the disappearance of dots and correct identification of the field that lost the dots. The top graphs in Fig. 15.4 show the proportion of correct reports. The abscissa shows correct reports when dots disappeared from the stationary field, the ordinate from the moving field. The closed circle shows performance under the stay instruction, when the stationary field was the target. The triangle shows performance under the track instruction, when the moving field was the target. If visual performance did not depend on the selection of the target for smooth eye movements, the two points would superimpose. If, on the other hand, visual performance was more accurate

15. SMOOTH EYE MOVEMENTS AND SELECTIVE ATTENTION

TABLE 15.1
Mean 50 Msec Eye Velocities in Minarc/Sec
for Subjects HC, CZ, and EK[a]

	HC Moving = 65'/s		CZ Moving = 60'/s		EK Moving = 57'/s	
	Mean	N	Mean	N	Mean	N
Before						
Stay + visual task	3.9 (38.0)	131	−1.0 (15.9)	189	2.1 (15.0)	168
Track + visual task	64.6 (44.5)	142	58.9 (16.3)	174	51.6 (17.4)	180
Stay only	[b]		1.6 (13.0)	160	2.4 (13.5)	167
Track only	[b]		56.7 (14.6)	176	53.6 (15.5)	152
After						
Stay + visual task	7.7 (38.0)	411	.1 (15.6)	573	2.0 (15.2)	391
Track + visual task	66.6 (35.1)	457	59.2 (16.6)	491	49.0 (16.7)	563
Stay only	[b]		.4 (13.8)	1380	.2 (13.5)	1387
Track only	[b]		63.3 (16.6)	1485	50.9 (15.7)	1215

[a]Measured while they maintained the line of sight on the stationary field (*Stay*) or on the moving field (*Track*), both with and without performance of a concurrent visual task. Velocities are shown for 200 msec *before* the disappearance of the dots, and, for the interval from dot disappearance until the subject's report (*after*). The velocity of the moving field (*moving*) used for each subject is also shown. Negative velocities indicate leftward motion.

[b]Subject HC was not tested under this condition.

Note: Standard deviations are in parentheses. The number (*N*) of 50 msec velocities on which each mean is based is also shown.

for the target field, then (1) the proportion of correct reports for the moving field would be higher under the track than under the stay instruction, and (2) the proportion of correct reports for the stationary field would be higher under the stay than under the track instruction.

Figure 15.4 shows that visual performance was more accurate for the target field than for the background field for all 3 subjects. The differences between the proportion of correct reports for the target and the background fields were largest for EK. Differences were smallest for HC with the moving field. He did well detecting the disappearance of dots from the moving field regardless whether the moving field was target or background. But he did not do well detecting the disappearance of dots from the stationary field when it was background. This means that HC easily makes visual judgments about moving targets while staying in place, but has trouble making judgments about stationary targets while engaged in smooth pursuit.

EK's performance was unusual in that she was worse than chance when dots disappeared from the moving background. Most of these errors were incorrect identifications. The proportion of trials in which she correctly identified the field that lost the dots, given a correct detection, was only .35. Identification below

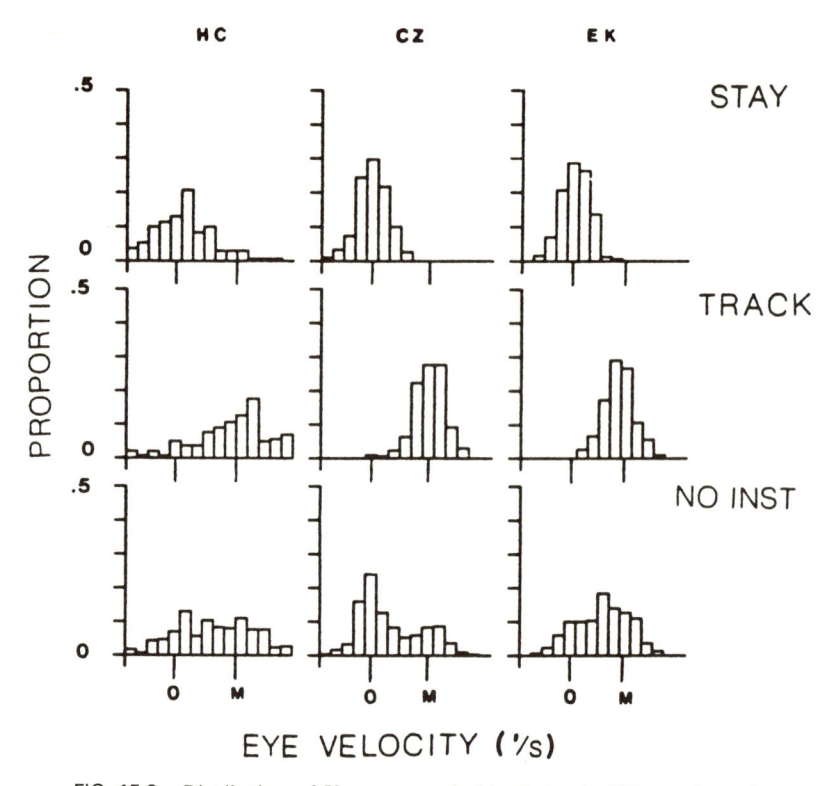

FIG. 15.3. Distributions of 50 msec eye velocities during the 200 msec interval before the disappearance of dots for subjects HC, CZ, and EK under instructions to maintain the line of sight on the stationary field (*STAY*) or on the moving field (*TRACK*), and under no eye-movement instructions (*NO INST*). Velocities to the right of 0 on the abscissa are in the direction of the moving field. The velocity of the moving field for each subject is shown by the tic mark labeled *M*. Bins are 12 min arc wide. Distributions under instructions to stay or track were based on 130 to 190 velocities; distributions under no instruction, on 250 to 320 velocities. A portion (10%) of HC's velocities were greater than the highest velocity bin and are not shown.

chance (.5) suggests that EK saw an illusion in which dots disappearing from the moving background instead seemed to disappear from the stationary target.

Reaction Times were Faster for the Target Field

The bottom graphs in Fig. 15.4 show the mean reaction times for the correct reports. Note that faster reaction times are shown on the top or on the righthand side of the axes. This was done so that the axes in the graphs of reaction time and the axes in the graphs of proportion correct both show performance improving as points move to the right or up.

15. SMOOTH EYE MOVEMENTS AND SELECTIVE ATTENTION 295

Detect and Identify

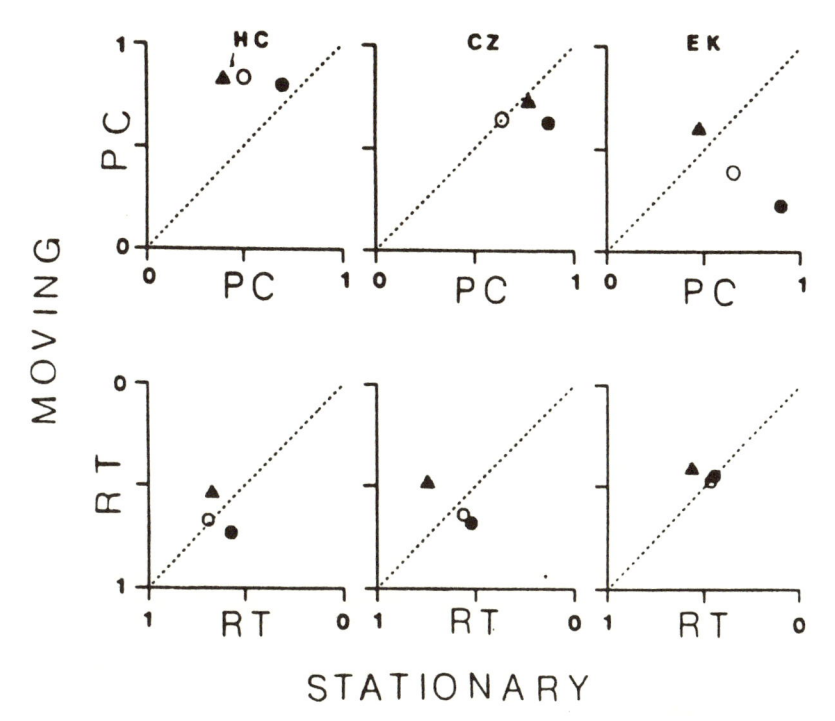

FIG. 15.4. Proportion correct (PC) detections and identifications, and mean reaction time (RT) in seconds for correct reports for subjects HC, CZ, and EK under instructions to maintain the line of sight on the stationary target field in the presence of the moving background (closed circles) or on the moving target field in the presence of the stationary background (triangles). The abscissa shows performance when dots disappeared from the stationary field, the ordinate from the moving field. The open circles show performance when no eye-movement instructions were given. The dotted lines represent the locus of points in which the proportion of correct reports or the mean reactions times were the same for the stationary and the moving fields. Each proportion correct is based on about 25 trials. Standard errors for reaction times are smaller than the plotting symbols.

Mean reaction times, like the proportion of correct reports described in the prior section, show that performance was better with the target field. Specifically, mean reaction times for detecting the disappearance of dots were faster for the target field than for the background field. Differences between reaction times for the target and the background were smallest for EK, the subject who showed the largest differences between the proportion correct reports with the target and the background. Also, HC's reaction times with the moving field, unlike his proportion of correct reports with the moving field, differed depending on whether the moving field was target or background. His mean reaction time was about 200 msec faster when dots disappeared from the moving target than when they disappeared from the moving background. These results suggest that the subjects may have set different criteria for trading off the speed for the accuracy of their reports.

Visual Performance Without Instructions to Stay or to Track

Distributions of eye velocities when subjects were not given a specific eye movement instruction, but instead were told to move their eyes in any way that they felt would lead to the best visual performance. are shown in Fig. 15.3. The distributions appear to combine the eye velocity distributions measured under instructions to stay and to track, but the form of the combination differed among the subjects. CZ's distribution had two peaks, one near 0 min arc/sec and one near the velocity of the moving field. EK's distribution peaked at a velocity between 0 and the velocity of the moving field. HC's distribution showed no clear peak.

Performance on the visual task was consistent with these eye velocities in that it reflected the combination of the instructions to stay and track. Performance for each field, when subjects chose their own eye movement patterns, usually fell between performance for that field when it was the target and when it was the background (see Fig. 15.4). The only exception to this was CZ's accuracy with the stationary field. She did worse when no instruction was given than when the stationary field was the background.

These results show that the visual consequences of instructions to stay or to track were the same regardless of whether these instructions were imposed by the experimenter or were chosen by the subject.

These results also have implications for the role of saccades in the detection of dot disappearance. Saccades were rare when subjects were instructed to stay or to track. Saccades were more frequent when subjects were permitted to choose their own eye movement patterns. The increase in saccade frequency, however, did not improve visual performance in agreement with prior work on the role of the saccades in a counting task (Kowler & Steinman, 1977, 1979c).

CONCLUSIONS

Selective attention determines the target for smooth eye movements when the visual field contains both stationary and moving stimuli. The eye follows the stimulus chosen by the subject. The background stimulus has virtually no effect on the eye movements (Kowler et al., 1984). Such independence from backgrounds is not achieved by subjects voluntarily choosing to move the eye at one or another velocity. Subjects do not have such voluntary control over their smooth eye movement velocity (Kowler & Steinman, 1979a; Steinman et al., 1969). Instead, independence from backgrounds is achieved by voluntary selective attention to the chosen target.

Investigators of perceptual and cognitive processes sometimes take the influence of attention on smooth eye movements for granted (e.g., Neisser & Becklin, 1975). But understanding how selective attention operates on the smooth oculomotor subsystem is no simple matter. Models of smooth eye movements have no provision for such effects. On the contrary, most models assume that smooth eye movements depend on processing of all retinal motion signals (e.g., Lisberger, Evinger, Johanson, & Fuchs, 1981; Rashbass, 1961). This assumption is convenient for relating the eye movements to the underlying physiology because both eye movements and neural firing rates can be described as a function of retinal motion. Effects of selective attention destroy this convenience. Incorporating selective attention into physiological research requires that experimenters know which target the animal selects. Incorporating selective attention into oculomotor models also requires modelers to explain how neurons in the oculomotor system process information from only the selected target. Oculomotor modelers have postponed consideration of such admittedly difficult questions (Robinson, 1984; Steinman, 1984).

In an attempt to better understand how attention operates on the smooth oculomotor subsystem we asked whether the visual and smooth oculomotor systems share the same attentional mechanism. Our results suggest that they do. We found that visual judgments about the target for smooth eye movements were faster and more accurate than judgments about the background. These results, however, must be interpreted cautiously for the following reason:

The retinal velocity of the background was higher than the retinal velocity of the target because eye velocity closely approximated the velocity of the target (which was either 0 or about 1 deg/sec). The retinal velocity of the background, therefore, was low enough (1 deg/sec) so that reductions in the visibility or discriminability of the dots would not be expected on the basis of prior work (Murphy, 1978; Steinman et al., 1985; Westheimer & McKee, 1975). It is possible, however, that the ability to detect the disappearance of dots is impaired even by the low retinal velocities we used because of some, as yet unknown, reason. The stimuli used in the prior work differed considerably from our dot displays.

Compatibility of Visual and Oculomotor Tasks

Certain visual tasks interfere with each other in that performance of both at the same time is worse than performance of either by itself (cf. Sperling, 1984). We found no such interference between the visual and oculomotor tasks we used. Selection of the target for smooth eye movements was not impaired by the concurrent visual task. Similarly, performance of the visual task was not impaired by attempting to follow explicit eye movement instructions to fixate the stationary or the moving field.

Smooth Eye Movements as Indicators of Selective Visual Attention

We found that smooth eye movements limited visual performance in that visual judgments about the target for smooth eye movements were faster and more accurate than visual judgments about the background. Assuming, as we have, that these results were not due to differences in retinal velocity, how can the superior visual performance for the target be explained?

One possibility is that visual thresholds are lower for the target than for the background. We think this explanation is unlikely. Work by Shaw (1984) has shown that effects of attention on the detection of light can be attributed to adjustments of decision criteria rather than to genuine changes of visual thresholds.

Adjustments of decision criteria could explain our results. Subjects may have raised their criterion for detecting the disappearance of dots from the background. A higher criterion could explain the greater proportion of trials in which subjects failed to detect the disappearance of dots from the background, and the longer reaction times for the correct detection responses.

An explanation for our results in terms of changes of the decision criterion would show that selection of the target for smooth eye movements prevented subjects from independently setting a criterion that would have been optimal for the visual task. Instead, only one decision may have been possible—selecting the target—and that single decision constrained both the eye movements and the visual reports. This outcome would make smooth eye movements accurate indicators of decisions subjects make while performing a visual task involving stationary and moving stimuli.

ACKNOWLEDGMENTS

This research was supported by Grant AF00085 from the Air Force Office of Scientific Research, Air Force Systems Command. We thank H. Collewijn, M. Kubovy, and S. Sternberg for useful suggestions, and R. Tandon for technical assistance. The authors' address is the Department of Psychology, Rutgers University, New Brunswick, NJ 08903.

REFERENCES

Cheng, M., & Outerbridge, J. S. (1975). Optokinetic nystagmus during selective retinal stimulation. *Experimental Brain Research, 23,* 129–139.

Collewijn, H., Curio, G., & Grusser, O. J. (1982). Spatially selective visual attention and generation of eye pursuit. *Human Neurobiology, 1,* 129–139.

Collewijn, H., & Tamminga, E. P. (1984). Human smooth and saccadic eye movements during voluntary pursuit of different target motions on different backgrounds. *Journal of Physiology, 351,* 217–250.

Collewijn, H., van der Mark, F., & Jansen, T. C. (1975). Precise recording of human eye movements. *Vision Research, 15,* 447–450.

Crane, H. D., & Steele, C. S. (1978). Accurate three-dimensional eye tracker. *Applied Optics, 17,* 691–705.

Dodge, R., & Fox, J. C. (1928). Optic nystagmus—I. Technical introduction with observations in a case with central scotoma in the right eye and external rectus palsy in the left eye. *Archives of Neurology and Psychiatry, 20,* 812–823.

Dubois, M. F. W., & Collewijn, H. (1979). Optokinetic reactions in man elicited by localized retinal motion stimuli. *Vision Research, 19,* 1105–1115.

Fischer, M. H., & Kornmuller, A. E. (1930). Optokinetisch ausgeloste Bewegungswahrnehmungen und optokinetischer Nystagmus. *Journal of Psychology and Neurology, 41,* 273–308.

Just, M. A., & Carpenter, P. (1975). Eye fixations and cognitive processes. *Cognitive Psychology, 8,* 441–480.

Klein, R. (1980). Does oculomotor readiness mediate cognitive control of visual attention? In R. Nickerson (Ed.), *Attention and performance VIII* (pp. 259–276). Hillsdale, NJ: Lawrence Erlbaum Associates.

Kowler, E., Martins, A. J., & Pavel, M. (1984). The effect of expectations on slow oculomotor control: Anticipatory smooth eye movements depend on prior target motions. *Vision Research, 24,* 197–210.

Kowler, E., & McKee, S. P. (1984). The precision of smooth pursuit. *Investigative Ophthalmology and Visual Science (Supplement), 25,* 262.

Kowler, E., Murphy, B. J., & Steinman, R. M. (1978). Velocity matching during smooth pursuit of different targets on different backgrounds. *Vision Research, 18,* 603–605.

Kowler, E., & Steinman, R. M. (1977). The role of small saccades in counting. *Vision Research, 17,* 141–146.

Kowler, E., & Steinman, R. M. (1979a). The effect of expectations on slow oculomotor control—I. Periodic target steps. *Vision Research, 19,* 619–632.

Kowler, E., & Steinman, R. M. (1979b). The effect of expectations on slow oculomotor control—II: Single target displacements. *Vision Research, 19,* 633–646.

Kowler, E., & Steinman, R. M. (1979c). Miniature saccades: Eye movements that do not count. *Vision Research, 19,* 105–108.

Kowler, E., & Steinman, R. M. (1981). The effect of expectations on slow oculomotor control-III: Guessing unpredictable target displacements. *Vision Research, 21,* 191–203.

Kowler, E., van der Steen, J., Tamminga, E. P., & Collewijn, H. (1984). Voluntary selection of the target for smooth eye movements in the presence of superimposed full-field stationary and moving stimuli. *Vision Research, 24,* 1789–1798.

Lisberger, S. G., Evinger, C., Johanson, G. W., & Fuchs, A. F. (1981). Relationship between eye acceleration and retinal image velocity during foveal smooth pursuit in man and monkey. *Journal of Neurophysiology, 46,* 229–249.

Loftus, G. (1972). Eye fixations and recognition memory for pictures. *Cognitive Psychology, 3,* 525–551.

Mach, E. (1906/1959). *Analysis of sensations* (p. 143). New York: Dover.

McConkie, G., & Rayner, K. (1975). The span of the effective stimulus during fixations in reading. *Perception and Psychophysics, 17,* 578–586.

Murphy, B. J. (1978). Pattern thresholds for moving and stationary gratings. *Vision Research, 18,* 521–530.

Murphy, B. J., Kowler, E., & Steinman, R. M. (1975). Slow oculomotor control in the presence of moving backgrounds. *Vision Research, 15,* 1263–1268.

Nachmias, J. (1959). Two-dimensional motion of the retinal image during monocular fixation. *Journal of the Optical Society of America, 49,* 901–908.

Nachmias, J. (1961). Determiner of the drift of the eye during monocular fixation. *Journal of the Optical Society of America, 51,* 761–766.
Neisser, U., & Becklin, R. (1975). Selective looking: Attending to visually specified events. *Cognitive Psychology, 7,* 480–494.
Noton, D., & Stark, L. (1971). Scanpaths in saccadic eye movements while viewing and recognizing patterns. *Vision Research, 11,* 929–942.
Puckett, J. W., & Steinman, R. M. (1969). Tracking eye movements with and without saccadic correction. *Vision Research, 9,* 695–703.
Rashbass, C. (1961). The relationship between saccadic and smooth tracking eye movements. *Journal of Physiology, 159,* 326–338.
Robinson, R. A. (1985). *The systems approach to eye movements.* Paper presented at the Workshop on the Systems Approach in Vision, Amsterdam, August, 1984.
Shaw, M. (1984). Division of attention among spatial locations: A fundamental difference between detection of letters and detection of luminance increments. In M. Posner (Ed.), *Attention and performance X.* Hillsdale, NJ: Lawrence Erlbaum Associates.
Sperling, G. (1984). A unified theory of attention and signal detection. In R. Parasuraman & D. R. Davies (Eds.), *Varieties of attention* (pp. 103–181). New York: Academic.
Sperling, G., & Reeves, A. (1980). Measuring the reaction time of an unobservable response. In R. Nickerson (Ed.), *Attention and performance VIII* (pp. 347–360). Hillsdale, NJ: Lawrence Erlbaum Associates.
Stark, L. (1971). The control system for versional eye movements. In P. Bach-y-Rita, C. Collins, & J. E. Hyde (Eds.), *The control of eye movements* (pp. 363–428). New York: Academic.
Steinman, R. M. (1985). *The need for an eclectic, rather than systems, approach to the study of the primate oculomotor system.* Paper presented at the Workshop on the Systems Approach in Vision, Amsterdam, August, 1984.
Steinman, R. M., Cunitz, R. J., Timberlake, G. T., & Herman, M. (1967). Voluntary control of microsaccades during maintained monocular fixation. *Science, 155,* 1577–1579.
Steinman, R. M., Haddad, G. M., Skavenski, A. A., & Wyman, D. (1973). Miniature eye movement. *Science, 181,* 810–819.
Steinman, R. M., Levinson, J. Z., Collewijn, H., & van der Steen, J. (1985). Vision in the presence of known natural retinal image motion. *Journal of the Optical Society of America, A, 2,* 226–233.
Steinman, R. M., Skavenski, A. A., & Sansbury, R. V. (1969). Voluntary control of smooth pursuit velocity. *Vision Research, 9,* 1167–1171.
Suppes, P., Cohen, M., Laddaga, R., Anliker, J., & Floyd, R. (1983). A procedural theory of eye movements in doing arithmetic. *Journal of Mathematical Psychology, 27,* 341–369.
Tamminga, E. P. (1983). *Human fixation and voluntary pursuit: The interaction between central and peripheral motion stimuli.* Unpublished doctoral dissertation, Erasmus University, Rotterdam.
Ter Braak, J. W. G. (1957). "Ambivalent" optokinetic stimulation. *Folia Psychiatrica, Neurologica et Neurochirurgica Neerlandica, 60,* 131–135.
Westheimer, G., & McKee, S. P. (1975). Visual acuity in the presence of retinal image motion. *Journal of the Optical Society of America, 65,* 847–850.
Winterson, B. J., & Collewijn, H. (1976). Microsaccades during finely guided visuomotor tasks. *Vision Research, 16,* 1387–1390.

16 Interactive Processes in Perceptual Organization: Evidence from Visual Agnosia

Glyn W. Humphreys
M. Jane Riddoch
Philip T. Quinlan
Birkbeck College, London University

ABSTRACT

Theories of object perception differ in their accounts of how descriptions of global properties of objects are derived, and of how such descriptions are coordinated with local structural properties. These issues were investigated by examining the performance of a visual agnosic patient on three tasks requiring response to either the local or global properties of visual patterns. This patient appears able both to derive and to maintain independent local and global descriptions of form. Further, his global form descriptions are determined only by the position of the local elements, not their nature (e.g., their texture). In contrast, normal subjects are unable to maintain independent local and global form descriptions; also, their global descriptions specify the texture of the local elements in addition to their positions. The implications of these results for understanding object perception, and how object perception may break down following brain damage, are discussed.

INTRODUCTION

What are the processes involved in the internal representation of object structure? One approach to this question has been to suggest that object perception is mediated by the pick up of local features such as lines and edges at particular orientations (Rumelhart & Siple, 1974; Sutherland, 1968). It may be that these local features are mapped directly onto object representations without their prior coding into larger structural units (such as angles and vertices; Rumelhart & Siple, 1974), or that they are coded into larger units, up to and including the whole object, with each unit defined in terms of the spatial relations between its lower-order parts (e.g., Palmer, 1977; Selfridge & Neisser, 1960). Both these views hold that the ontogeny of our structural representations of objects proceeds from descriptions of local features to descriptions of more global units.

Alternatively, early visual processing can be conceptualized as performing the independent analysis of a limited range of spatial frequencies (e.g., Campbell & Robson, 1968). According to this position, low spatial-frequency information is processed concurrently with high spatial-frequency information, and, because of the former's faster rise time and/or its shorter integration time, it may even become available earlier in any developing percept (e.g., Breitmeyer & Ganz, 1977). If we associate low spatial-frequency information with global stimulus characteristics and high-spatial frequency information with local stimulus characteristics (e.g., Broadbent, 1977), this position holds that global and local properties of objects are processed independently and in parallel, and that the processing of global properties may be completed first.

Three pieces of evidence are pertinent to the contrast between the approaches just-described, though none is unequivocal:

1. *Object superiority and object–line effects.* The first is that line segments can be detected more accurately when part of a unitary, three-dimensional line drawing relative to when part of a less unitary, flat design (i.e., the object-superiority effect; e.g., Weisstein & Harris, 1974), and even relative to when the line is presented in isolation (i.e., the object–line effect; e.g., Williams & Weisstein, 1978). These results suggest that the availability of a unitary, three-dimensional object description in some way facilitates the processing of a local line segment: a conclusion that contradicts the argument that global structural descriptions are determined by local descriptions. However, the object–superiority effect and the object–line effect are both obtained using data-limited stimuli, and they can be reversed when stimuli are not data limited and subjects are required to make speeded identification responses (Klein, 1978; Widmayer & Purcell, 1982). It seems possible, therefore, that the object description does not facilitate the processing of the local line segment, but rather the recovery of the segment under degraded conditions. Facilitation of the recovery process may occur even if the availability of the object description is itself consequent upon the partial activation of local feature information.

2. *Emergent features.* A second piece of evidence is that object processing can be affected by structural properties additional to those defined by relations between independent local features. For instance, using simple geometrical figures as stimuli, Palmer (1977, 1978) demonstrated a high degree of conformity in the way subjects rate the "goodness" of parts within figures, that "good" parts can be verified more efficiently than "bad" parts, and that subjects detect differences between two figures more quickly when there is a difference in the "good" rather than "bad" part of the figures, even if the local feature changes are the same in the two cases. These results illustrate that object representations contain "emergent" features based on interrelations between parts of the object.

However, to date most studies have examined the mediating role of emergent features in object recognition rather than the time course of their processing. Consequently, it is not clear whether emergent features arise subsequent to the processing of local features or whether they are derived concurrently (and perhaps, independently). Overall, the results contradict the argument that object perception involves *only* the direct mapping of local features onto object representations (cf. Rumelhart & Siple, 1974), but not the argument that the more global (emergent) features are themselves determined by local feature descriptions.

3. *Global advantage and global-to-local interference effects.* The third piece of evidence is the finding of an advantage when subjects respond to the identity of an object's global structure relative to when they respond to the identity of a constituent part. For instance, Navon (1977, Experiment 3) briefly presented subjects with compound letters (large global letters composed from smaller, local letters) in one of the quadrants of an oscilloscope, and subjects pressed one key if the target letter was an *H* and another if it was an *S*. In one case, the target was the local letter and in another it was the global letter. When subjects responded to the global letter, the local letter could be the same (congruent condition), it could be related to the opposite response (incongruent condition), or it could be unrelated to a response (neutral condition). The same conditions obtained by varying the identity of the global letter when subjects responded to the local letter. Navon found that responses to the global letter were faster than responses to the local letter; also the global letter interfered with responses to the local letter in the incongruent condition, relative to the neutral condition. There were no effects of the identity of the local letter on responses to the global letter. From this pattern of results, Navon (1977) has argued that global structural descriptions may be available to response processes earlier than local structural descriptions. Once again, though, the data do not necessitate the view that local and global properties of objects are derived independently. The global advantage could occur either because descriptions of global properties are made available first by early visual processes (Navon, 1977), or because such descriptions capture attention more easily than descriptions of local properties (Grice, Canham, & Boroughs, 1983). If the global advantage is mediated by attentional mechanisms, it remains possible for descriptions of global properties to be determined by descriptions of local properties.

From the preceding analysis, it seems that descriptions of global properties of objects play a functional role in object perception, but it is unclear whether such properties are derived from local feature descriptions or whether local and global properties are derived independently. Also, if local and global descriptions are derived independently, we know little about how they are coordinated.

One approach to understanding these issues further is to investigate performance when a global form can be defined independently of the structural identity of its constituent elements. This would occur when the identity of a global form is based solely on the positions of its elements—for instance, as when four elements placed at equidistant locations define a global square, irrespective of their identities. Pomerantz (1981, 1983) terms this a Type P part–whole relationship, and distinguishes it from a Type N relationship in which the global form is dependent on the nature as well as the position of local elements (i.e., their structure, size, density, and texture). In a stimulus with only a Type P part–whole relationship, the global identity is defined independently of local element identities; thus, evidence for an effect of global structure on responses to local elements in such a stimulus would suggest that local and global form descriptions are derived separately.

In this chapter, we present evidence suggesting that Type P and Type N part–whole relationships can be separated, and that they produce independent effects in tasks requiring responses to the structural identity of local stimulus features. The major thrust of our argument is based on the performance of a visual agnosic patient who appears to be sensitive to Type P part–whole relationships (where the global form is determined by the position of local elements alone), but not to at least some Type N relationships (where the global form is determined by the nature of the local element descriptions). The performance of this patient was examined on three tasks; in the first two, responses had to be made to the structural identity of local parts of stimuli (Experiments 1 and 2); in the third, responses could be made using local position information (Experiment 3). The contrast between the patient's performance on these tasks suggests that Type P and Type N part–whole relationships have separate functional roles in object perception.

The Patient

The detailed case history of the patient, H. J. A., is presented elsewhere (Humphreys & Riddoch, 1984; Riddoch & Humphreys, in preparation). H.J.A. (born in 1920) suffered a stroke in April, 1981, which resulted in marked, modality-specific deficits in visual perception. In particular, he had severe difficulties in visually recognizing real common objects (including faces), photographs, and line drawings; he also had achromotopsia. Drawing and writing skills were left relatively intact. There was a superior altitudinal field defect of both the left and right visual fields, with intact lower fields. Visual acuity was normal.

Examination of H. J. A.'s object recognition indicated that his ability to identify objects correctly was dependent on the identification of salient local features (Humphreys & Riddoch, 1984), suggesting that he could pick up local feature descriptions. Further, H. J. A. experienced no difficulties in moving around his environment; he could both avoid objects and reach appropriately for them. This suggests that he could pick up information about global object structure (Riddoch & Humphreys, in preparation). These suggestions, and the relationship between H. J. A.'s processing of local and global structures, were examined more analytically in tasks measuring his reaction times (RTs) to identify local and global properties of objects.

EXPERIMENT 1: PROCESSING COMPOUND LETTERS

Method

Apparatus. The presentation of the stimuli, timing, and data collection were under the control of an APPLE II Europlus microcomputer. Two response keys were interfaced with the Apple and RTs, contingent upon button presses, were measured from the onset of the target stimulus.

Materials. Both the global and the local figures could be either an *H*, an *S*, or an *O* (see Navon, 1977, Experiment 3). Global letters were 6.9 cm (7°55') in height and 4.1 cm (4°41') in width. The global letters were located 5 cm below a central fixation point, which was itself 1.2 cm below the top of the screen. A fixation cross was presented at the top of the screen to ensure that the stimuli fell within H. J. A.'s intact visual fields. On a given trial a global letter could appear either to the left or the right side of the screen, and the distance between these two positions was 5 cm. The vertical component of the global letter could be made up of a maximum of seven local elements, and the horizontal component could be made up of six local elements.

Procedure. Each trial began with the presentation of the fixation cross for 500 msec. This was then offset and the target letter was presented until a response was made.

Each subject participated in two blocks of trials. In one block they pressed one button if the local elements in the compound letter were *S*s and the other button if they were *H*s (respond local). In this case, an *O* was never present at the local level. The global letter could either be congruent with the local response, incongruent, or neutral. In the other block of trials, subjects pressed one button if the global letter was an *S* and the other button if it was an *H*. In this case, an *O* was never present at the global level. The local letter was then either congruent, incongruent, or neutral with respect to the global response. Each block contained 120 trials, 40 in each condition. The order of the conditions was randomized for each block. Prior to each block there was a short practice session of 20 trials. H. J. A. always responded to *S* with his preferred hand. The order of the blocks was allocated on a random basis.

To ensure that the present displays produced a normal global advantage (cf. Kinchla & Wolfe, 1979; Martin, 1979; Pomerantz, 1983), 10 control subjects with normal vision also participated. Their age range was from late teens to mid-30s.

Results and Discussion

Control Data. The mean RTs to global stimuli in the congruent, neutral, and incongruent conditions were 504, 509, and 538 msec; the mean RTs to local stimuli in the same conditions were 588, 632, and 694 msec. The range of RTs to global stimuli in the neutral condition was 346 to 636 msec; to local stimuli in the neutral condition, it was 545 to 747 msec. There was no effect of condition on responses to global letters—$F(2,18) = 3.01$, $p > .05$—whereas there was a reliable condition effect on responses to local letters—$F(2,18) = 28.9$, $p < .001$. For local letters, RTs in the neutral and incongruent conditions were reliably slower than in the congruent condition—both $p < .01$. RTs in the incongruent condition were slower than in the neutral condition—$p < .01$. Low error rates were recorded, and the errors followed the same trends as the RT data.

The preceding results replicate those obtained by Navon (1977) and confirm that, under the present display conditions, there is both a global advantage in the neutral condition and a global-to-local interference effect.

H. J. A.'s Data. The mean correct RTs for H. J. A. to global stimuli in the congruent, neutral, and incongruent conditions were 644, 608, and 616 msec. Error rates of 2.5% were made in each case. Mean correct RTs to local stimuli in the same conditions were 932, 925, and 936 msec; error rates were 2.5%, 0%, and 0%, respectively. Analysis of these data[1] showed only that H. J. A. responded faster to global than to local letters—$F(1, 230) = 57.81$, $p < .001$. However, there was no condition effect and no condition $\times$ target letter interaction, both $F < 1.0$.

H. J. A.'s performance contrasts markedly with that of the control subjects. Even though his overall RTs are faster to global than to local structural descriptions, he shows no global-to-local interference. It is unlikely that this result is due to his relatively slow RTs or to a weak overall global advantage. His RTs to global stimuli fell within the normal range and the RT differences between his responses to global and local forms were at least as large as those present in the data of any of the control subjects.

The advantage to global forms demonstrated by both H. J. A. and the controls in the neutral condition may be due either to the early availability of global form descriptions (Broadbent, 1977; Navon 1977), or to their relative discriminability under the present display conditions (Pomerantz, 1983). H. J. A.'s results are important in showing that the global advantage is not in itself sufficient to generate global-to-local interference.

---

[1] In all the analyses of H. J. A.'s RT data, each RT was treated as a separate subject.

The pattern of data demonstrated by H. J. A. suggests that he is able both to process and to maintain local and global properties as independent form descriptions; this facilitates his selective attention to local descriptions despite the evidence indicating that they become available relatively late in any processing sequence. However, if local and global form descriptions are derived independently, we must explain why normal subjects manifest global-to-local interference and why H. J. A. does not. For instance, interference cannot be due solely to response competition occurring automatically between local and global form descriptions; if this were the case, H. J. A. should show a larger interference effect than normals given his large global advantage in the neutral condition. A more viable account is that interference in normals reflects a failure to attend selectively between independently derived local and global form descriptions, perhaps because they have information, such as a coherent texture description, that inhibits attention to local elements. H. J. A. may avoid interference if he fails to achieve such a texture description. This argument is expanded further following Experiment 2.

EXPERIMENT 2: VISUAL SEARCH AGAINST HOMOGENEOUS DISTRACTORS

In order to examine H. J. A.'s processing of local and global stimulus properties in more detail, his performance in a visual search task was investigated. Under particular circumstances, such as when targets and distractors differ on the basis of a salient, disjunctive feature (such as line orientation), the time taken by subjects to detect the presence of a target can be relatively unaffected by the number of distractors present: specifically, RT–display size functions are non-linear and may even be flat (e.g., Treisman & Gelade, 1980; Treisman, Sykes, & Gelade, 1977). This suggests that, in these cases, subjects process the elements in the display in parallel and respond from some description at the level of the whole display. This description may specify, for example, the presence of a disparate element against a background of distractors.

In other cases, such as where the target is specified by a conjunction of features, subjects typically carry out linear searches of displays (e.g., Treisman & Gelade, 1980). That is, they treat each element present as a separate object. Under these circumstances, then, subjects respond on the basis of local form descriptions, where each element is described as a local form relative to the global description of the whole display.

According to the preceding argument, responses based on properties defined across the whole display and responses based on local properties can be distinguished by analyzing RT–display size functions in visual-search tasks. Responses based on whole-display properties describe nonlinear functions; responses based on local properties describe linear functions.

In Experiment 2, the visual-search functions of H. J. A. and of control subjects were obtained in a task in which subjects had to detect the presence of an inverted *T* (the target) against a display of upright *T*s. In this task targets and distractors differ only in the spatial arrangement of their component lines; subjects must, therefore, search for a conjunction of features (cf. Treisman et al., 1977; see also Beck, 1966, 1967). From this, it might be expected that subjects would have to treat each element as a separate object, precipitating linear search functions. However, in pilot work we established that nonlinear search functions could obtain if the display elements were presented in a good configuration and/or were sufficiently close.[2] This is confirmed in the present data. These nonlinear search functions are dependent on the relative position and size of the elements (Humphreys et al., in preparation), and thus reflect a Type N part–whole relationship. Accordingly, the inverted *T* versus upright *T* search task seemed particularly appropriate for investigating H. J. A.'s visual-search functions.

Method

Apparatus. The apparatus was the same as in Experiment 1.

Stimuli. The stimuli consisted of various numbers of capital *T*s .7 cm in height and .5 cm in width. In half the patterns the *T*s described regular polygons, drawn as if inscribed by a circle 4.2 cm (4°49′) in diameter. With patterns of four letters the *T*s described a square, with patterns of 6 and 10 letters the *T*s described a hexagon and a decagon, respectively. Letters were positioned as an intersection of two sides. The interelement distance varied across the three polygons, but all letters were equidistant from the center of the inscribing circle.

With irregular patterns, letters were positioned at random between the circumference of the 4.2 cm diameter inscribing circle and the circumference of a second larger circle, 8.4 cm in diameter. Thus, the center-element distance for irregular patterns was never smaller than the center-element distance for regular patterns. Three basic irregular patterns were generated as counterparts to the three regular polygons composed of 4, 6, and 10 letters.

On half the trials for each regular and irregular display size, the patterns consisted of upright *T*s (same patterns); on the other half one of the upright *T*s was replaced by an inverted *T* (different patterns). The position of the inverted *T* was balanced over all the positions present in the different patterns.

---

[2]In subsequent research work we have attempted to separate these two factors. The evidence suggests that it is the interelement spacing, rather than the goodness of the configuration, that determines whether search functions are linear or nonlinear (Humphreys, Riddoch, & Quinlan, in preparation).

Procedure. There were 136 patterns: 48 four-letter patterns, 48 six-letter patterns, and 60 ten-letter patterns. There were equal numbers of same and different patterns for regular and irregular displays. The conditions were randomly ordered for each subject.

On each trial a fixation cross appeared for 500 msec, followed immediately by the display, which remained for 10 sec or until the subject responded. Contingent feedback was presented after each response and was followed by an intertrial interval of 2 seconds. The test session lasted about 30 minutes, and was proceeded by a short practice session.

There were 10 control subjects, whose ages ranged from early 20s to mid-30s. Half these subjects responded same with their preferred hands and half responded same with their nonpreferred hands. H. J. A. responded same with his preferred (right) hand and different with his nonpreferred (left) hand.

Results and Discussion

Control Data. Analysis of variance on the RT data revealed reliable main effects of response type—$F(1,9) = 9.89, p < .05$—regularity, $F(1,9) = 47.42, p < .05$—and number of characters—$F(2,18) = 11.95, p < .01$. The only statistically significant interaction was between regularity and number of characters—$F(2,18) = 8.24, p < .05$.

Same patterns were responded to faster than different patterns and regular patterns were responded to faster than irregular patterns. The interaction between regularity and number of characters was examined in further detail using separate analyses for regular and irregular patterns.

For regular patterns, neither the linear nor quadratic components of the RT–display size functions approached significance—$F(1,9) = .98$ and $F(1,9) = 1.01$, both $p > .05$. Also, RTs to regular patterns of 4, 6, and 10 characters did not differ.

For irregular patterns, there was a reliable linear component in RT–display size function—$F(1,9) = 15.27, p < .01$. The quadratic component was not significant—$F(1,9) = 4.25, p > .05$. RTs to irregular patterns of 4 and 6 letters did not differ, whereas RTs to patterns of 10 characters were slower than RTs to patterns of four and six characters—both $p < .01$.

Only a few errors were recorded and there was no sign of a speed–accuracy trade-off.

The mean correct RTs and percent errors made by the control subjects and by H. J. A. are given in Table 16.1.

There are two important findings with normal subjects here. One is that same responses are faster than different responses. The second is that RTs to regular patterns did not increase linearly as a function of the number of elements present in the displays. In fact, RTs to 10-character displays were only 21 msec slower

TABLE 16.1
The Mean Correct RTs (msec) and Percent Errors
Made by the Control Subjects and by H.J.A. in Experiment 2

| | Same ||||||| Different |||||||
| | Regular ||| Irregular ||| Regular ||| Irregular |||
	4	6	10	4	6	10	4	6	10	4	6	10
Control Subjects
RTs	601	567	586	638	641	794	619	648	672	665	675	805
% error	.1	.2	.1	.2	.2	.5	.2	.3	.3	.3	.2	.5
H.J.A.
RTs	1148	1304	1501	1284	1677	2127	1175	1201	1198	1158	1162	2078
% error	.0	8.3	16.7	8.3	8.3	25	8.3	25	58.3	16.7	25	58.3

than RTs to four-character displays, indicating a search rate of 3.5 msec per item, which is within the range typically found for search for a salient disjunctive feature target (Kahneman, Treisman, & Burkell, 1983; Treisman & Gelade, 1980). The latter result suggests that subjects could detect the presence of targets using a description at the level of the whole display in the regular condition. From this experiment alone we cannot identify the display factors underlying this effect, because regular and irregular displays differed in at least three ways: Regular displays described a good, canonical figure; the characters were evenly spaced; and the characters all fell within the same (relatively small) distance from the center of the screen. Nevertheless, the result is important in demonstrating that nonlinear search functions can obtain for targets composed of a feature configuration (cf. Treisman & Gelade, 1980; Treisman et al., 1977) under particular display conditions. One possibility is that the presence of an inverted T in regular arrays gave rise to an emergent feature, which was detected irrespective of the number of distractors present (cf. Treisman & Paterson, 1984). Against this is the finding that same (target-absent) responses were faster than different (target-present) responses, which is contrary to the typical finding that the presence of emergent and/or disjunctive features is detected prior to their absence (Treisman & Gelade, 1980; Treisman & Paterson, 1984). The evidence for fast same responses here suggests that subjects can respond using information aggregated across the whole display—that is, they respond using some form of texture description. In the present task, the decision whether the target was present or absent would correspond to a description specifying a consistent or an inconsistent texture.[3]

Linear increases in RTs as a function of the number of characters were found for irregular patterns. There was a 152 msec RT increase across the character set sizes used (a search rate of 25.33 msec per item), which is close to those previously obtained in searches for a conjunction target in randomly plotted displays (Treisman & Gelade, 1980). This is consistent with the argument that, with irregular patterns, subjects search each item serially, and respond on the basis of the description of a local element. The only finding that is contrary to this argument is that RTs to displays of six characters were not reliably slower than RTs to displays of four characters. However, it must be remembered that in the present displays, interelement distance varies relative to the number of characters present. With six-character displays the interelement distances were smaller than with four-character displays. If the critical factor influencing whether search functions depart from linearity is the interelement spacing, then nonlinear search functions might even be observed with irregular patterns (Humphreys et al., in preparation). For instance, if texture descriptions arose with more of the six-character irregular displays than the four-character displays, then only small

---

[3]Our thanks to John Duncan for pointing this out.

RT differences might obtain between these conditions. Even so, texture descriptions arose primarily with only regular displays.

H. J. A.'s Data. For the RT data there were reliable main effects of response type (same vs. different)—$F(1,101) = 5.7$, $p < .05$—regularity—$F(1,101) = 19.2$, $p < .001$—and number of characters—$F(2,101) = 18.3$, $p < .001$. The only statistically significant interaction was between regularity and the number of characters—$F(2,101) = 8.3$, $p < .01$. The effects of the number of characters on regular and irregular patterns were analyzed separately.

For regular patterns, RTs increased linearly as a function of the number of characters present—$F(1,54) = 4.38$, $p < .05$. RTs to 10-character displays were slower than those to 6- and 4-character displays—$p < .05$ and $p < .01$, respectively.

For irregular patterns there was also a reliable linear increase in RTs as a function of the number of characters—$F(1,54) = 28.73$, $p < .001$. RTs to 10-character displays were slower than to 6- and 4-character displays—both $p < .01$. RTs to 6-character displays were slower than to 4-character displays—$p < .01$.

H. J. A. made a high proportion of errors. Nevertheless, the effects of pattern regularity and number of characters on the error data followed those found with the RT data: Performance was better on regular than irregular arrays and for both array types performance decreased as a function of the number of characters. However, unlike the RT results, accuracy was better on same than on different trials. This suggests a speed–accuracy trade-off on different trials, such that if he failed to find a target within a set time period he responded same.

In subsequent studies we have confirmed that both the preceding RT and accuracy data are relatively stable, and that practice does not produce qualitative changes in H. J. A.'s performance.

These findings demonstrate that H. J. A. is sensitive to pattern regularity but that he manifests linear search functions for both regular and irregular patterns. There is a dissociation between the effects of regularity on the speed of search and whether or not RT–display size functions are linear. If the flat, nonlinear searches of regular arrays performed by normal subjects are signatures of a global texture description, it seems that H. J. A. is unable to achieve this description. In its absence, H. J. A. carries out a linear search and responds on the basis of a local element description. Interestingly, the speed of this search is affected by pattern regularity. This pattern information seems to be dependent on the position of the local elements (i.e., a Type P part–whole relationship), but it is insufficient to enable H. J. A. to respond to the pattern as a single object—that is, H. J. A.'s global description tells him where the local elements are but not what they are. In order to detect whether a target is present, H. J. A. must search at a local level of description. These results are consistent with the argument that H. J. A. is sensitive to Type P but Type N part–whole relationships.

EXPERIMENT 3: SUBITIZATION

We have argued that H. J. A. can pick up some information that specifies regularity; however, the global information he has available cannot be used to detect an inverted *T* against a background of upright *T*s. The question arises whether he might be able to use his global description of the display directly when the task does not require information about the nature of local elements. For instance, could H. J. A. use his global description to identify the number of elements present? There is evidence suggesting that normal subjects can use the global description presented by a canonical figure to judge directly the number of items present (Mandler & Shebo, 1982). In this case, the RT to make the numerosity judgment stays relatively flat as a function of the number of elements present. Because a numerosity judgment would not require H. J. A. to know the identity of the local elements, it seemed an appropriate task with which to assess the optimal conditions under which he might use a global description to respond to a display.

Method

The apparatus was the same as in Experiments 1 and 2.

There were two variables: regularity of pattern (regular and irregular) and the number of characters (2, 3, 4, 5, and 6). Displays were composed of upright letter *T*s .7 cm in height and .5 cm in width. Regular patterns were positioned around the circumference of a circle 4.2 cm (4°49′) in diameter, so that their display characteristics matched those of the regular patterns in Experiment 2. Irregular patterns were plotted at random except for the constraint that the total distance of the elements from the center of the screen was the same as for regular patterns.

Subjects were informed of the nature of the displays and were asked to name the number of items as quickly as possible. Each trial began with a 500 msec presentation of a fixation cross at the top of the screen, followed by the display for 200 msec.[4] The intertrial interval was 3 sec. There was a short period of practice trials prior to the experimental trials. There were 32 trials for each character display size for both regular and irregular patterns.

Control subjects had normal or corrected-to-normal vision and their ages ranged between 20 and 40 years of age.

Results and Discussion

Control Data. Analysis of the RT data revealed reliable main effects of regularity and number of characters $F(1,20) = 44.54$ and $F(4,20) = 33.06$, both $p < .001$—and a reliable regularity × number of characters interaction—

---

[4] A 200 msec display was used here to prevent the contamination of numerosity judgments by saccadic eye movements.

$F(4,20) = 10.82, p < .001$. This interaction demonstrates that the number of characters had a stronger effect on RTs to irregular patterns than RTs to regular patterns. RTs to regular patterns of two, three, and four characters departed from linearity—$F(1,5) = 3.75$ and 2.87, both $p > .05$—for linear and quadratic components; RTs to irregular patterns of the same set size increased linearly as a function of the number of characters—$F(1,5) = 39.58, p < .0025$. Thus, over the present set sizes, the time taken by normal subjects to judge the number of characters present in irregular arrays increases linearly, at a rate of about 54 msec/character. This suggests that some form of fairly rapid serial counting process was used. For regular arrays of up to four characters subjects judge the number of items directly from the global description; in this case, RTs are relatively constant over the number of characters present. RTs were somewhat increased for regular arrays containing five and six characters. This probably indicates that the global descriptions of these arrays were perceptually similar, requiring subjects to take some extra time to discriminate the arrays before stating the number of characters they contained (see also Mandler & Shebo, 1982).

Analysis of the error data revealed reliable main effects of regularity—$F(1,5) = 11.12, p < .05$—and number of characters—$F(4,20) = 16.63, p < .001$. The interaction was not reliable, $F(4,20) = 1.45, p > .05$. More errors were made to irregular than regular arrays, and the error rate increased as a function of the number of characters.

The mean correct RTs and percent errors made by the control subjects and H. J. A. are given in Table 16.2.

H. J. A.'s Data. H. J. A. was able to maintain relatively error-free performance when there were less than five items present. For set sizes five and six substantial proportions of errors were made, with more errors occurring with irregular than regular patterns.

TABLE 16.2
The Mean Correct RTs (Msec) and Percent Errors
by the Control Subjects and by H.J.A. in Experiment 3

	Regular					Irregular				
	2	3	4	5	6	2	3	4	5	6
Control Subjects										
RTs	431	466	453	534	574	451	503	578	655	677
% error	0	0	0	7.3	26	1	0	8.1	17.7	31.3
H.J.A.										
RTs	557	606	569	747	732	623	647	726	818	787
% error	0	3.1	3.1	25	31.3	0	9.4	3.1	34.3	50

For H. J. A.'s RT data, there were reliable main effects of pattern regularity and number of characters—$F(1,259) = 23.45$ and $F(4,249) = 21.31$, both $p < .001$. However, the regularity × number of characters interaction was nonsignificant—$F(4,259) = 1.22$, $p > .05$.

Although the preceding analysis failed to show a regularity × number of characters interaction, inspection of the data suggests that for set sizes two, three, and four there was a relatively flat RT function for regular but not irregular patterns. Indeed, for these set sizes there was a reliable regularity × number of characters interaction—$F(2,186) = 5.34$, $p < .001$. RTs increased linearly with set sizes two to four for irregular patterns—$t(93) = 3.32$, $p < .0025$—whereas the RT–set size function was nonlinear for regular patterns (both the linear and the quadratic trends were nonsignificant). This result is important because it is the first to demonstrate that H. J. A. can show nonlinear RT functions to multielement displays, given an appropriate task. For arrays of up to four items, H. J. A. was able to respond directly to a regular pattern if one was present. When the pattern was irregular, he demonstrated a linear search function, suggesting that performance was based on a serial counting process. Interestingly, H. J. A.'s search rate for irregular arrays was 41 msec/character, which is slightly faster than that found in our normal control subjects. H. J. A. also showed an increased error rate, indicating that he may have used a less conservative response criterion than the controls. Similarly to the controls, H. J. A. showed relatively slow RTs even for regular arrays of five and six characters, presumably due to the perceptual similarity of our regular patterns at these set sizes. Overall, it seems that H. J. A. performs relatively normally on the numerosity-judgment task. This appears to be because this task, unlike those used in Experiments 1 and 2, only requires knowledge about the number of elements present in particular patterns, and it requires no knowledge about their nature.

Interestingly, in a similar study to Experiment 3, Kinsbourne and Warrington (1962) reported that patients with deficits specific to the perception of simultaneously presented forms can have intact subitization ability. They suggest that this is because such patients manifest deficits only in simultaneous form-identification tasks, and subitization does not require form identification. Can H. J. A.'s deficits be accounted for in similar terms? Much recent evidence suggests that normal subjects cannot identify visual stimuli simultaneously (e.g., Duncan, this volume; Humphreys, in press); therefore, the deficit in the perception of simultaneously presented stimuli must be attributed to abnormalities in attention-switching mechanisms (cf. Friedman & Alexander, 1984). However, the contrast between the nonlinear and linear search functions to regular patterns demonstrated by normal subjects and by H. J. A. in Experiment 2 seem to reflect a qualitative difference in the nature of the form descriptions available, rather than the speed of switching attention. Second, without further modification the attention-switching account does not provide a ready explanation of H. J. A.'s performance with compound letters. H. J. A. has global information available prior to local information; if attention is captured by the earliest available information, impaired switching of attention should produce large global interference; if attention is not captured by the earliest available information it is difficult to explain the normal global-interference effect. Third, Kinsbourne and Warrington did not measure RTs so we cannot tell whether their patients could respond directly to global-form information; they may have responded accurately by using a serial counting process (cf. performance with irregular arrays here). If this were the case, then their patients would be unlike H. J. A. Fourth, contrary to H. J. A., Kinsbourne and Warrington's patients suffered no apparent deficits in the identification of single objects. To account for H. J. A.'s deficit in attention-switching terms, we must assume that his performance in the present tasks is independent of his object-recognition impairments.

GENERAL DISCUSSION

We have presented data showing that H. J. A. can process both local and global properties of visual forms. However, his global form descriptions seem to specify only the positions of local elements (i.e., Type P part–whole information) and contain no useful information about their nature (Type N information). This is perhaps most clearly demonstrated by Experiment 2, in which subjects searched for an inverted T in arrays of upright Ts. H. J. A.'s visual search is sensitive to array regularity, indicating the pick-up of global form information. However, whereas normal subjects showed nonlinear functions with regular arrays, H. J. A. showed linear search functions (with slopes lower than those with irregular arrays). This suggests that normal subjects have global descriptions of regular arrays that indicate the presence or absence of a disparate local element; because they also showed faster same than different responses, these global descriptions seem to specify texture information aggregated across the local elements. In contrast, H. J. A.'s global description specifies only local element positions, not their texture. Thus, in order to detect the presence of a disparate element he must treat each display character as a separate perceptual object using a serial search strategy.

The evidence on H. J. A.'s processing of compound letters (Experiment 1) supports the view that his global form descriptions lack information derived from local elements. H. J. A. showed much shorter latencies to global than to local forms, yet, unlike normal subjects, there was no effect of global letter identity on local responses. It may be that, for normal subjects, global texture information inhibits attention to local elements, precipitating global-to-local interference effects. For H. J. A. the absence of texture information may facilitate attention to local descriptions.

Experiment 3 demonstrated that H. J. A. could judge directly the number of characters present in regular arrays with discriminable global descriptions (i.e., patterns with fewer than five elements). This indicates that he can respond directly to global form descriptions in an appropriate task. The important property of the numerosity judgment task seems to be that it requires no knowledge of local element identities; only their positions are important.

The data, then, suggest that global form descriptions dependent on local element positions and those dependent on the nature of the local elements (e.g., their texture) are derived independently and are functionally separated in the case of H. J. A. It may be that, in the absence of Type N part–whole information, global descriptions are difficult to coordinate with local element information, leading to wide-ranging difficulties in perceptual organization (e.g., in cases where grouping and segmentation are determined by local structures). This may underlie H. J. A.'s difficulties in object recognition. We believe it is unlikely that the abnormalities demonstrated by H. J. A. in the present tasks reflect specific difficulties in letter recognition (or the recognition of particular symbols); although all the tasks used letter stimuli, they demand general processes in pattern recognition (e.g., those involved in determining position regularity and texture descriptions). An account of H. J. A.'s deficit in terms of a breakdown in these processes provides a parsimonious description of both the present results and his visual agnosia.

ACKNOWLEDGMENTS

This research was conducted while the first and third authors were supported by Grant No. HR 8457/1 from the E.S.R.C, and while the second author was supported by a DHSS research fellowship. Presentation of the paper was supported by travel grants from the E.S.R.C. and from *Brain*. We would like to thank both H. J. A. and his wife for all their effort in making this research possible. Access to H. J. A. was kindly provided by Mary Hill and Dr. J. Patten. John Duncan provided helpful comments on the research.

REFERENCES

Beck, J. (1966). Effect of orientation and of shape similarity on perceptual grouping. *Perception and Psychophysics, 1,* 300–302.
Beck, J. (1967). Perceptual grouping produced by line figures. *Perception and Psychophysics, 2,* 491–495.
Breimeyer, B., & Ganz, L. (1977). Temporal studies with flashed gratings: Inferences about human transient and sustained channels. *Vision Research, 17,* 861–865.
Broadbent, D. E. (1977). The hidden preattention process. *American Psychologist, 32,* 109–118.
Campbell, F., & Robson, J. G. (1968). Application of Fourier analysis to the visibility of gratings. *Journal of Physiology, 197,* 551–566.
Friedman, R. B., & Alexander, M. P. (1984). Pictures, images and pure alexia: A case study. *Cognitive Neuropsychology, 1,* 9–24.
Grice, G. R., Canham, L., & Boroughs, J. M. (1983). Forest before trees? It depends where you look. *Perception and Psychophysics, 33,* 121–128.

Humphreys, G. W. (in press). Attention, automaticity and autonomy in visual word processing. In D. Besner, T. G. Waller, & G. E. Mackinnon (Eds.), *Reading research: Advances in theory and practice*. New York: Academic.

Humphreys, G. W., & Riddoch, M. J. (1984). Routes to object constancy: Implications from neurological impairments of object constancy. *Quarterly Journal of Experimental Psychology, 36A*, 385–415.

Humphreys, G. W., Riddoch, M. J., & Quinlan, P. T. (in preparation). *Regularity, texture and visual search*.

Kahneman, D., Treisman, A., & Burkell, J. (1983). The cost of visual filtering. *Journal of Experimental Psychology: Human Perception and Performance, 9*, 510–522.

Kinchla, R. A., & Wolfe, J. M. (1979). The order of visual processing: "Top-down," "bottom-up," or "middle-out." *Perception and Psychophysics, 25*, 225–231.

Kinsbourne, M., & Warrington, E. K. (1962). A disorder of simultaneous form perception. *Brain, 85*, 461–486.

Klein, R. (1978). Visual detection of line segments: Two exceptions to the object superiority effect. *Perception and Psychophysics, 24*, 237–242.

Mandler, G., & Shebo, B. J. (1982). Subitizing: An analysis of its component processes. *Journal of Experimental Psychology: General, 111*, 1–22.

Martin, M. (1979). Local and global processing: The role of sparsity. *Memory and Cognition, 7*, 479–484.

Navon, D. (1977). Forest before trees: The precedence of global features in visual perception. *Cognitive Psychology, 9*, 353–385.

Palmer, S. E. (1977). Hierarchical structure in perceptual representation. *Cognitive Psychology, 9*, 441–474.

Palmer, S. E. (1978). Structural aspects of visual similarity. *Memory and Cognition, 6*, 91–97.

Pomerantz, J. R. (1981). Perceptual organization in information processing. In M. Kubovy & J. R. Pomerantz (Eds.), *Perceptual organization* (pp. 141–180). Hillsdale, NJ: Lawrence Erlbaum Associates.

Pomerantz, J. R. (1983). Global and local precedence: Selective attention in form and motion perception. *Journal of Experimental Psychology: General, 112*, 516–540.

Riddoch, M. J., & Humphreys, G. W. (in preparation). *Deficits in object perception in a case of associative visual agnosia*.

Rumelhart, D. E., & Siple, P. A. (1974). Process of recognizing tachistoscopically presented words. *Psychological Review, 81*, 99–118.

Selfridge, O., & Neisser, U. (1960). Pattern recognition by machine. *Scientific American, 203*, 60–68.

Sutherland, N. S. (1968). Outlines of a theory of visual pattern recognition in animals and man. *Proceedings of the Royal Society* (London), *B171*, 297–317.

Treisman, A., & Gelade, G. (1980). A feature-integration theory of attention. *Cognitive Psychology, 12*, 97–136.

Treisman, A., & Paterson, R. (1984). Emergent features, attention and object perception. *Journal of Experimental Psychology: Human Perception and Performance, 10*, 12–31.

Treisman, A., Sykes, M., & Gelade, G. (1977). Selective attention and stimulus integration. In S. Dornic (Ed.), *Attention and performance V* (pp. 333–362). Hillsdale, NJ: Lawrence Erlbaum Associates.

Weisstein, N., & Harris, C. S. (1974). Visual detection of line segments: An object-superiority effect. *Science, 186*, 752–755.

Widmayer, M., & Purcell, D. G. (1982). Visual scanning of line segments: Object superiority and its reversal. *Bulletin of the Psychonomic Society, 19*, 353–354.

Williams, M. C., & Weisstein, N. (1978). Line segments are perceived better in a coherent context than alone: An object–line effect. *Memory and Cognition, 6*, 85–90.

17 Imagery and Language Processing: A Neuropsychological Approach

Stephen M. Kosslyn
Harvard University

Rita S. Berndt
University of Maryland Medical School

Timothy J. Doyle
Harvard University

ABSTRACT

A computerized task battery was constructed to assess the efficacy of specific processes used in *image generation, inspection, maintenance*, and *transformation*. This battery was designed to test patients with *aphasia*, allowing investigation of the relationship between language and imagery. The feasibility of this use of the battery was demonstrated by testing two aphasics, a Broca's and a Wernicke's. The results were consistent with claims that the left hemisphere has a significant role in mental imagery.

INTRODUCTION

Until recently, the common wisdom was that imagery is a right-hemisphere activity, and language is primarily a left-hemisphere activity (e.g., see Bryden & Ley, 1983; Erlichman & Barrett, 1983; Springer & Deutsch, 1981). If this notion had held sway, an investigation of possible dissociations between imagery and language ability would have been of questionable interest. But there has long been reason to doubt the common wisdom. Indeed, John Hughlings Jackson (1874/1958) believed that imagery was bilateral, but that "the left is the side for the automatic revival of images, and the right the side for their voluntary revival—for recognition" [p. 142]. In addition, he claimed that the left hemisphere is critical for the use of imagery in thinking, as is evident in the aphasic, who "can bring two images into coexistence—existence in one unit of time—but cannot, without speech, organize the connection, if it be one of difficulty"

319

[p. 142]. By "organize the connection" Jackson seems to have meant "make sense out of" or "understand the implications of" the imaged information.

The claim that both hemispheres are involved in imagery has received surprisingly strong support during the past few years: First, Erlichman and Barrett (1983), in their review of the neuropsychological literature on imagery, discovered that in general imagery is not systematically correlated with either right- or left-hemisphere processing. They concluded that the evidence most strongly supports the view that imagery is carried out bilaterally. Second, in her analytic review of types of imagery deficits, Farah (1984) discovered that there was, in fact, a strong relationship between damage to one cerebral hemisphere and inability to form mental images (but not inability to engage in other imagery activities, such as image transformation). However, the critical locus was on the *left* side, not the right!

Third, perhaps the strongest support for bilateral processing in imagery comes from recent studies of imagery in the isolated cerebral hemispheres of split-brain patients (Kosslyn, Holtzman, Farah, & Gazzaniga, in press). Indeed, the *left* hemisphere of two split-brain patients was *better* than the right at tasks requiring that images of separate parts be arranged together, although both hemispheres were equally good at forming images of single parts and at holding and inspecting imaged objects. For example, in one of Kosslyn et al.'s experiments, names of animals were lateralized to the left or right visual field, ensuring that they were presented to only the right or left cerebral hemisphere, respectively. In one task, a split-brain patient was asked to decide whether the ears of the named animal did or did not protrude above the top of its skull (as do the ears of a German Shepherd dog, but not the ears of an ape). The left hemisphere was almost perfect in its judgments, whereas the right was at chance. In contrast, when asked to decide whether the named animal was bigger or smaller than a goat, both hemispheres performed virtually perfectly. In the first task, two parts had to be related correctly; in the second, only the overall shape was necessary, not the arrangements among parts. Both tasks require imagery, but only the first requires that parts be added to the basic form.

Kosslyn et al. (in press) ascribed the importance of the left hemisphere in generating multipart images to a process that makes use of *descriptions* of part relationships (e.g., of the relationship between an animal's ears and its head), and claimed that this particular component imagery process is more efficient in the left hemisphere (at least in right-handed males). In contrast, the other components of the image-generation process appear to be equally effective in both hemispheres. The notion that descriptions are used in left hemisphere processing is consistent with Jackson's view, but we have augmented his conception of image formation. Rather than viewing images as "automatic" consequences of hearing words, we view them as being actively constructed—with descriptions of part-relationships being used to construct multi-part images.

However, to implicate the use of "descriptions" in a process is not to implicate language: The type of "description" used in arranging parts into an image need not be the same as any of the representations used in language processing per se. Rather, such descriptions could be like the abstract "propositional" descriptions of part relationships apparently used in perceptual processing, which are not also used in language (perhaps being like the descriptions used in computer vision systems; see Winston, 1975).

Given the empirical findings, then, it is important to ask whether different components of imagery processing are localized differently in the brain and, if so, whether those that are more efficient in the left hemisphere also are used in language processing.

THE IMAGERY TASK BATTERY

In order to investigate these issues, we needed to study the neuropsychology of imagery in a systematic fashion. In order to do so, we constructed a task battery, which is administered on the Apple Computer. The battery was constructed in an effort to satisfy certain requirements; we have made some initial progress in satisfying these requirements, as is briefly described in this chapter.

Desiderata for an Imagery Task Battery

Ecological Validity. We wanted to test those aspects of imagery that are central to performing most "real-life" imagery tasks. For example, consider how you decide which boxes and pieces of luggage can be crammed into a car's trunk when you go on vacation. Many people report imaging the suitcases, "seeing" how they would fit into the trunk, and mentally rotating them to "try out" various fits, all the while maintaining images of other bags that seem best placed in specific locations. Such tasks involve: (a) image generation—you first generate an image of some of your luggage; (b) image maintenance—the images of previously considered suitcases must be retained as you image new ones fitting into the available "space"; (c) image scanning—the image often must be scanned across, as one searches for a part, property, or object; (d) image rotation—the object in the image often must be transformed, such as by being rotated, as one examines it from different angles. Our battery assesses the processing used to carry out each of these four abilities.

Precision. As in the Kosslyn, Brunn, Cave, and Wallach (1984) study of individual differences, each of the tasks should be accompanied by a process model derived from a general theory. Without such a model it would be impossible to assess the efficacy of different processing components in brain-damaged populations. We wanted tasks that could be scored to assess the importance of only selected components of imagery processing.

Validity. We wanted tasks that would naturally require imagery and that could be validated to do so. We took advantage of the literature on imagery to devise tasks using methodologies that had, for the most part, already been so validated.

Practicality. We wanted tasks that were simple enough to be practical for testing brain-damaged subjects.

Preliminary Examination of Two Aphasics

In order to demonstrate the feasibility of our approach, and to begin examining the relationship between language deficits and imagery processing, we tested two aphasic patients on the battery. We are particularly interested in any hints as to whether language processing is involved in imagery, as Jackson suggested. If processing of descriptions is primarily left-hemisphere based, the Kosslyn (1980) theory leads us to make specific predictions about imagery deficits following left-hemisphere damage. Briefly, we are led to expect that left-hemisphere damage will disrupt image generation and image rotation (which purportedly require processing of stored descriptions), but not to expect deficits in image maintenance and scanning (which purportedly do not require processing of stored descriptions). If such processing of descriptions makes use of specific linguistic mechanisms, we may obtain different results from subjects who have different language deficits.

Subjects. Two patients with left-hemisphere brain damage were tested, as were a group of nine college students. The college students were tested as a baseline, although the disparity in their ages and those of the patients precludes any strict comparison. The brain-damaged patients previously had been extensively tested for verbal ability and language skills, providing us with grounds for useful comparison of imagery and verbal/language skills (see Kosslyn, Berndt, & Doyle, 1984). Patient J. E. is a right-handed male who was 47 years old at the time of testing. J. E. had a massive resection of the left parietal-occipital lobe in 1979. A CT scan obtained in 1981 documents a large area of left-hemisphere damage, including the posterior parietal lobe, a portion of the occiptal lobe, and the superior posterior temporal lobe. He exhibits many of the classic symptoms associated with Wernicke's aphasia, including comprehension difficulties. In addition, he is severely dyslexic and dysgraphic. Patient F. M. is a right-handed male who was 40 years old at the time of testing. He suffered a left-hemisphere cerebrovascular accident in 1980, which resulted in a right hemiparesis and moderately severe non-fluent aphasia. A CT scan obtained in 1982 shows an infarction of the entire anterior temporal lobe, the contiguous posterior inferior frontal lobe (Broca's area) and the inferior parietal lobe. Underlying white matter and lateral basal ganglia appear to be involved. F. M. exhibits many of the classic symptoms associated with Broca's aphasia: Speech production is very effortful, with reduced rate, dysprosody and severe dysarthria, but language comprehension is only moderately impaired. His reading shows the pattern known as "deep dyslexia," and his writing is effortful with many spelling errors.

The control subjects were tested in a single session, which lasted approximately 1 1/2 hours. The brain-damaged subjects were tested in three sessions, each lasting between approximately 45 minutes and 1 hour. All subjects were paid for their time, and all subjects were tested individually.

IMAGE GENERATION

Imagery processing apparently invokes different combinations of members of a set of underlying *processing modules* (see Kosslyn, Brunn, Cave, & Wallach, 1984). A processing module is a "black box" that performs a specific transformation on input, thereby carrying out one component of an information-processing task. Any given module may be used in numerous tasks, and any given task may require numerous modules. Thus, a subject could fail at one task not because of a task-specific deficit, but because of a disruption in a module used in multiple tasks. We must have a theory of the modules used in carrying out a task if we are to make inferences about processing from how well a subject performs the task. The Kosslyn (1980) theory of imagery specifies a set of processing modules used in imagery, and that theory guided construction and scoring of the present battery (see chapter 5, Kosslyn, 1980).

According to the theory, three modules are used in generating images from information stored in long-term memory. The PICTURE module activates individual "packets" of information stored in long-term memory (which correspond to the overall shape envelope or to individual parts). When any object is imaged, the first form generated by the PICTURE module is a "skeletal image." This is a vague shape envelope capturing the general form of an object. If more detail is to be added, other modules must be used. According to the theory, the PUT processing module is used if multiple representations are to be amalgamated into a single image. The PUT processing module looks up and interprets a description of how parts are to be arranged. For example, in generating a detailed image of a car, it might look up "front wheel" and discover the location description "under front wheelwell." In order to use such a description, a third module, which is called the FIND processing module, is used. The FIND module executes a top-down pattern-recognition process; it is used whenever one "inspects" an image, "looking" for a part. In image generation, the FIND module is used to locate the "foundation part" on the already-imaged parts or objects (i.e., where the new part belongs—"front wheelwell' in the example; we assume that relations among parts are described using a local coordinate system). The PUT processing module uses the output from the FIND processing module (e.g., the location on the skeletal image of the front wheelwell) plus the description of the relation ("under") to compute parameter values for the PICTURE processing module, which it provides to this module, allowing the new part to be imaged in the correct relation to the foundation part.

Rather than pull apart the image-generation processing modules, which are always used if a complex image is formed, we designed a test to measure how well they work together. Our measure of image-generation ability involves comparing performance on two tasks. One of our tasks is very similar to the perception condition in Podgorny and Shepard's (1978) experiment. Subjects see a block letter displayed in a 4 × 5 grid (by selectively filling in cells), two x marks appear in the grid, and the subject decides whether both fall on the figure. If both xs are on the figure, the subject presses one key; if not, he or she presses another. The computer records the responses and response times. These data are useful primarily as a baseline for the imagery task, as will be discussed in the section on scoring.

In the imagery task, a pattern is not presented in the grid; instead, the lower-case version of the letter appears below the grid (which does not physically resemble the upper-case version—such as j and h), and two xs appear in the grid 1 sec after the letter cue. The subject's task is to decide whether both xs would have fallen on the letter if it had been in the grid; the subjects are familiarized with the appearance of the letters in the grid before the experiment begins. One sec is enough time for a patient to recognize the cue and move his or her eyes up to the grid, but not enough time to form the image. The logic here is that if the image is not fully formed when the xs are presented, additional time will be required to finish generating it before the comparison phase can begin. Thus, the response times in this task reflect in part the speed with which the image can be generated.

Previous research has demonstrated that this task requires forming an image to perform and has validated this derived estimate of image-generation time. Briefly, Kosslyn and Provost (1984) examined the differences in the estimates of time to generate images of different letters. They found, replicating past work (see Chapter 6 of Kosslyn, 1980), that more time was taken to image more complex forms (e.g., G and J versus L and C). Furthermore, the estimates of the differences in generation time obtained with this method were virtually identical to those found when subjects were asked simply to press a button after they had generated images of the letters. In addition, Kosslyn and Provost provided evidence that the images were formed a segment at a time, which in theory implciates the use of all three image-generation modules. They showed that the time to decide whether the image covered an x mark depended on which segments were covered, with more time being taken for segments progressively further along the sequence in which segments of the letters are usually drawn. Control experiments showed that this result was not an artifact of postgeneration scanning or experimenter-demand effects, and the magnitude of the effect was as expected if each segment was imaged individually in sequence.

We realized that our aphasic subjects would be working at a disadvantage because of the difficulties they had in reading letters. Thus, we presented these subjects with only four "patterns" to learn: the letters *J, G, H,* and *L.* To avoid confusion during these sessions we referred to the stimuli only as patterns, not as letters. The trick here was first to teach the subjects to remember the patterns, and then to associate each pattern with an—to them—arbitrary symbol, either *j, g, h,* or *l.* Following the pattern-learning procedure, the brain-damaged subjects were told that they were to perform the probe-judgment task only when the stimulus cue was the *j* or the *h;* if cued by a *g* or *l,* the subject was simply to press the space bar to continue. This last manipulation was included so that we might receive an indication of how well the subjects could discriminate among the letter cues; good performance on the null response trials would demonstrate at least a rudimentary ability to discriminate the cues from each other. Indeed, neither subject committed more than one error on these trials (i.e., by failing to press the space bar). The judgment task was explained to the brain-damaged subjects using paper and pencil examples. (For further details on the method, procedure, or results for this or the following tasks, see Kosslyn, Berndt, & Doyle, 1984.)

Process Model and Scoring

In the imagery condition, the subject encodes the lower-case cue (not an imagery process), and accesses a description of the upper-case version. The PICTURE processing module images the first stroke. The PUT processing module then looks up the relation between it and the second stroke, invokes the FIND processing module to locate the foundation part on a previously imaged stroke, and uses this information to set the PICTURE processing module so that the next stroke is imaged in the correct relative location. This procedure is repeated until all parts are imaged. Following this, the *x* marks are encoded into the image via the LOAD module. The LOAD module forms an image from external input. After the input is so encoded, the FIND module compares the locations of the *x* marks to those of segments of the image. (See Kosslyn et al., 1984, for a description of the procedure used to formulate this and the following models.)

In the perceptual condition, only the LOAD and FIND modules (for comparison of pattern and *x* marks) are used. Thus, these times include the time to encode the *x*s, to compare them to the representation (perceptual, in this case) of the figure, to reach a decision, and to respond. By subtracting these "perceptual baseline" times from those from the imagery task, then, we derive an estimate of the speed of image generation.

Summary of Preliminary Results

The results from this and the following two tasks are summarized in Table 17.1. We began by analyzing data from the imagery condition; for purposes of comparing data from the control and the brain-damaged subjects, only responses from the j and h probes were considered. There were no significant differences between the subjects in accuracy. Given the differences in the procedure between the brain-damaged and normal subjects, this comparison is only interesting because of the relatively good performance of both patients. In contrast, the analysis of the response times revealed a significant difference between subjects (see Table 17.1). Examining the means, it appears as if F. M. was slower but more

TABLE 17.1
Results from Testing One Wernicke's Aphasic (J. E.), One Broca's Aphasic (F. M.), and College Students[a]

	Image Generation		
	J. E.	F. M.	Controls
Imagery condition	4.300	4.446	1.433
	(10)	(0)	(8.8)
Perceptual condition	.936	1.691	.772
	(2.5)	(0)	(3)

	Image Maintenance		
	J. E.	F. M.	Controls
Simple patterns			
Brief delay	2.770	1.770	1.444
	(7.5)	(0)	(6.6)
Long delay	3.132	2.101	1.433
	(0)	(5)	(6.1)
Complex patterns			
Brief delay	4.022	2.222	2.232
	(27.5)	(15)	(21.5)
Long delay	5.450	3.621	2.353
	(32.5)	(37.5)	(19.8)

	Scanning	
	J. E.	Controls
Focus	2.811	.948
	(20)	(6.3)
Opposite	3.747	1.347
	(20)	(15.7)

[a]Times are in sec; numbers in parentheses are error rates.

accurate, exhibiting a speed–accuracy tradeoff; however, the lack of significant differences in the accuracy rates belies such a tradeoff.

The results from the perceptual baseline task revealed that all subjects performed remarkably well; there were no significant differences in the analysis of error rates. In contrast, the analysis of the response times indicated that there were differences among the subjects, as is evident in Table 17.1.

We conducted the perceptual task primarily as a baseline to control for encoding, judgment, and response processes. Thus, we computed an estimate of image-generation error rate and time by subtracting the baseline error rates and times from the corresponding trials in the imagery task. This difference, then, should more accurately reflect image-generation performance per se. The analysis of the error rates revealed that there was no overall difference among the subjects. The analysis of the response times indicated a significant difference among the subjects, with derived times of 3.364, 2.755, and .661 sec for J. E., F. M., and the control subjects, respectively. When we compared only the two brain-damaged subjects, we did not find a significant difference in times.[1]

The significantly slower generation times are, of course, as expected in light of the previous results with split-brain patients, indicating a left-hemisphere role in multipart image generation. And, these very stimuli had been shown by Kosslyn and Provost (1984) to be generated a part at a time.

IMAGE MAINTENANCE

We have used a variant of the image-generation task to assess subjects' imagery "memory capacity." Now, however, we wish to eliminate the image-generation components and require use of the REGENERATE module, which boosts levels of activation of the image, preventing it from fading immediately (see Kosslyn, 1980). In this test we first ask subjects to study grids that contain a pattern; the pattern is displayed by randomly filling in one-fifth of the cells in the grid. We let the subjects study each display until they have memorized it, at which point they press a button. The computer then removes the filled squares—leaving only the empty grid. Following this, two x marks appear, and the subject must indicate whether or not both xs fell in cells that had been filled by the pattern. Given the Kosslyn and Provost demonstration that images are generated in the x-mark evaluation task previously described, images presumably must be maintained in order to perform this task.

Four versions of this "image-maintenance" test are administered in the battery; they differ in the complexity of the grid (4 × 5 or 5 × 7, with 20% of the

---

[1] All significant differences had a p value less than .05. See Kosslyn, Berndt, & Doyle (1984) for details about the statistical analyses.

cells being filled in both cases) and in the length of time between the removal of the figure and the presentation of the *x* marks (500 or 5000 msec). On half the trials, both *x*s fall in cells formerly occupied by the pattern, and on half of the trials one of the *x*s falls in a cell formerly empty (and hence presumably not occupied by the image). Subjects press one key if both *x*s fell on the imaged pattern, or another if both did not.

With the brain-damaged subjects, we first verbally described the task and then used pencil and blank 4 × 5 grids to illustrate the nature of the trials. Each subject was shown a grid with a pattern penciled in, then was shown a grid with two *x* marks, and then was shown two grids superimposed in order to explain the nature of the task.

Process Model and Scoring

The LOAD processing module is used to encode the to-be-imaged pattern. The REGENERATE module is used to maintain the image until the probes are encoded, again via the LOAD module. The FIND module compares the locations of the *x* marks to the filled cells in the image. By subtracting the times and errors in the simple condition from those in the complex condition, we assess the relative efficacy of the REGENERATE module at retaining additional material. By subtracting the results in the brief-delay condition from those in the long-delay condition, we assess the relative efficacy of the REGENERATE module at retaining images over time. According to the theory, only the REGENERATE module is placed under additional strain in one of these conditions compared to the other.

Summary of Preliminary Results

Comparing the differences between the pair of conditions previously noted, there was no difference in the effect of complexity on the accuracy of the different subjects. However, there was a significant difference in the effect of delay, as is evident in Table 17.1. This difference was somewhat peculiar, however: For the short delay, F. M. actually did better than the others, but for the long delay, he was the worst of the lot!

We also analyzed the response times. Comparing the times from the simple brief-delay condition with those from the complex brief-delay condition revealed that there were significant differences in the subjects' abilities to maintain images, with complexity affecting J. E. more than F. M., and both patients more than the controls. In addition, delay affected both patients more than the control subjects, but there was no significant difference between the patients. Because pairs of conditions are being compared, these effects cannot be ascribed to the general impairment of response time observed with the brain-damaged subjects.

These results, then, are not as predicted by the Kosslyn (1980) theory. According to this theory, descriptions are not processed in order to maintain images, and hence we did not expect left-hemisphere damage to impair this ability. So far, the data are consistent with the claim that left-hemisphere damage disrupts imagery in general.

IMAGE SCANNING

This task is like the previous ones in that a grid is shown. In this task, however, the grid is shaped something like a square donut, with a hole in the center, and only three cells are filled in at random. The subject studies the grid until he or she has memorized the filled cells, and then presses a button. At that point the filled cells are emptied and a cue appears for 20 msec. In this task, the cue is either an x or an o that falls in a single cell. If the cue is an x, the subject is simply to indicate whether or not that cell was filled. If it is an o, he or she is to indicate whether the corresponding cell on the opposite side of the donut was filled. "Opposite" means diagonal if the cue falls in a corner cell; otherwise, it means directly across, through the middle of the donut.

In earlier work on image scanning (see Kosslyn, 1980), it has repeatedly been found that increasingly more time is required to scan increasingly greater distances across an image. The donut was generated as large as possible on the monitor, to prevent subjects from being able to "see" all of it clearly at the same time in the image; thus, it subtended about 35° of visual angle.

The brain-damaged subjects first were shown blank grids like those used in the task. Patterns were penciled in, and the two probe types were illustrated. The most difficult aspect of the procedure to explain to these subjects was the difference between x and o trials; paper and pencil trials were used until each subject could make the correct response six times in a row (three x probes, three o probes). Half of the test trials were x probes and half were o probes, and half of each probe type were "true" and half were "false."

Process Model and Scoring

The LOAD module is used to encode the input pattern, but now the image must be retained for only the briefest amount of time before the probe appears, minimizing the role of the REGENERATE processing module. The FIND module is used immediately if an x appears. If an o appears, this leads to the SCAN module's being used to shift attention, and the FIND module's being used when attention is shifted across the donut. (Note that some other, nonimagery processing must occur to interpret what x and o mean.) By subtracting x times from o times, then, we obtain an estimate of scan time. If indeed more time is required to scan further distances, we have validation for this task.

Summary of Preliminary Results

The first result here worthy of note is that patient F. M. could not be brought to perform the task. He could not even reliably perform it when the stimuli remained physically present; thus, the deficit is not specific to imagery. This patient appeared to have special difficulty with relational terms, and we could never seem to make the instructions clear to him. Indeed, we spent approximately 45 min (over three separate days) trying to teach him the task, to no avail.

The accuracy results from patient J. E. and our control subjects thus were analyzed without data from F. M. There was no significant difference in accuracy between J. E. and the control subjects. Most importantly, the analysis of the scan times revealed that J. E. did not scan across the image significantly more slowly than did the controls. In general, x probes were responded to faster than o probes, revealing the usual effects of having to scan across an image.

The failure to find significant differences in scan time is of interest partly because it shows that J. E. is not simply slower in general than the control subjects. In addition, this null finding is of interest in contrast to the tasks for which our measures revealed significant differences among subjects.

IMAGE ROTATION

Finally, our image-rotation task is a modified version of one originally reported by Shepard and Metzler (1971). They showed subjects pairs of block-like forms, and asked if the blocks were the same shape irrespective of orientation. They found that response times increased linearly with the angular disparity of the stimuli, suggesting that one was "mentally rotated" into congruence with the other. In our task, two-dimensional forms are generated by selecting six cells in a grid at random, with the constraint that they form a single connected shape. The frame and extra cells are eliminated, producing shapes like two-dimensional analogs of those used by Shepard and Metzler (1971).

In this task, a pair of stimuli are presented side by side, with the left always being upright (i.e., the longest axis is aligned vertically). The right stimulus is presented at one of 10 orientations; half the time it is identical to the left one, and half the time it is a mirror reversal. Only two-dimensional rotations are allowed in this task, and a "true" trial was defined as one in which one form can be rotated in the picture plane so that it is congruent with the other. At the corresponding tops of both stimuli were asterisks, which minimized the task of discovering the relative orientations of the figures so that one can know which direction to begin rotation (subjects typically rotate "the short way around"). The two stimuli together subtended about 20° of visual angle.

The brain-damaged subjects were first shown cut-out figures that could be physically manipulated to illustrate the various orientations used in the test trials.

We demonstrated that some figures were identical once one had been rotated into alignment with the other, whereas other figures were different. The task was to decide whether two figures were identical when they were aligned; in the task itself, we explained, the subjects would not be able to actually move the patterns, but would have to do so "in their heads." We also explained that only rotations in the picture plane were permitted: Any movement was allowed so long as the figure remained flat on the table, or "on the screen" in the actual tests; three-dimensional movements (lifting the cut-out off the table or the figure off the screen) were not permitted in this task. We further explained this constraint by showing how a left and a right hand resting flat with palms down could not be rotated into congruence if they remained flat on the table. Once the subject could perform four trials correctly, when actually allowed to move the cut-outs, he or she was then given the computer-generated practice trials followed by the actual test trials. The test trials included an equal number of stimuli at 10 different relative orientations (at 36° intervals), and an equal number of the stimuli at each orientation were "true" and "false."

Process Model and Scoring

The LOAD module is used to form an image of the figure on the right, and the FIND module is used to locate the top (i.e., the part with the asterisk). The image is then rotated, using the ROTATE module to perform the transformation itself and the FIND module to monitor progress. The theory posits that whenever the ROTATION processing module is used, the FIND processing module must also be used to monitor the image's progress (and stop the ROTATION processing module when the image has been transformed far enough). Thus, the speed of mental rotation is in fact a joint function of the efficiency of the two processing modules (see Chapter 8 of Kosslyn, 1980).

In addition, according to the theory, descriptions of shapes are used to realign the parts of the shape as they become scrambled during rotation—that is, the ROTATION module purportedly moves a part at a time. Because there is noise in the system, the parts are not moved precisely the same "distance" at any given iteration of the movement operation. Thus, the parts become misaligned. If the misalignment is small enough, a description of the correct shape can be used to realign them. (If the parts are moved too large a "distance," they will not be able to be realigned; hence, images are transformed gradually, in a series of small increments.) In this case as well, then, the descriptions used in processing might be stored or processed primarily in the left hemisphere. If so, then left-hemisphere damage might result in some impairment of mental-rotation ability.

The variable of most interest here is the amount of the increase in time when stimuli are presented at increasingly disparate orientations. This measure allows us to assess the efficiency of the ROTATION and FIND processing modules independently of the other processing modules used in the task.

Summary of Preliminary Results

Except for errors on "true" trials for the control group, the error rates did not systematically increase with angle. The analysis of response times revealed large differences in the rotation rates for the different subjects. As is illustrated in Fig. 17.1, the brain-damaged subjects rotated much more slowly than did the controls (i.e., their rotation slope is much steeper in Fig. 17.1); however, there was no significant difference in the rotation rates for the two brain-damaged subjects. Times varied systematically with angle, replicating the now-familiar hallmark of "mental rotation" originally reported by Shepard and Metzler (1971).

Although the results leave no question that these patients can perform mental rotation, they revealed that they are dramatically slower than are normal controls. Because we are examining slopes here, and not simply overall times, the measure is less sensitive to the general impairment of the brain-damaged subjects. It is remarkable that even in the face of considerable additional training, left-hemispere damage slows down the rate of rotation relative to normal subjects. In addition, there is some evidence that left-hemisphere damage may sometimes disrupt the control people normally have over the direction of rotation: F. M.'s response times suggest that he had a tendency (evident for "false" pairs) to rotate in only one direction, even if it was the "long way around," whereas the other subjects appear to have rotated the shortest way around (as is suggested by the peak response times at 180°).

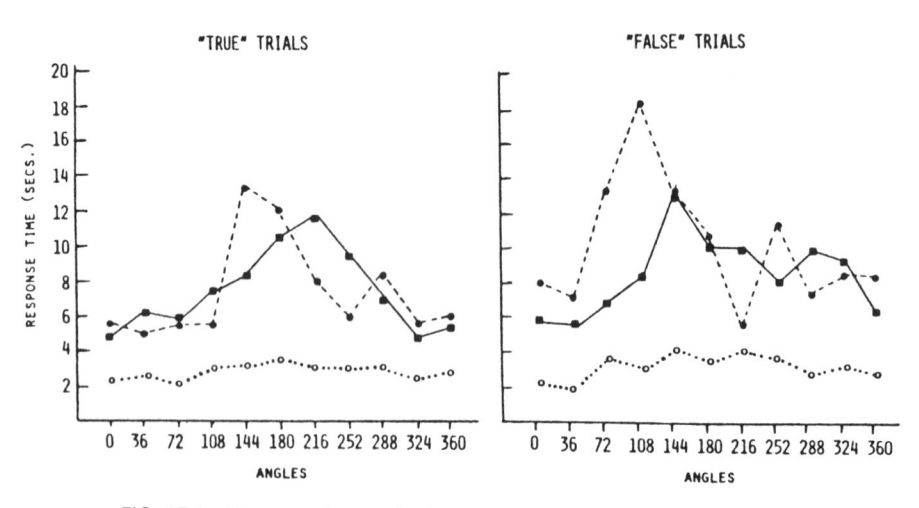

FIG. 17.1. Response-time results from the mental-rotation task.

GENERAL DISCUSSION

Clearly, the imagery task battery can be used to test aphasic subjects. Even with our very preliminary explorations, we have collected some intriguing data about the effects of left-hemisphere damage on imagery. The evidence that left-hemisphere damage may disrupt image generation and rotation is of particular interest because it is consistent with the idea that descriptions are used in this sort of processing. Presumably, descriptions of the relations among parts are either stored or processed primarily in the left hemisphere. This notion makes sense if processing of descriptions is at all language related; our subjects clearly are language impaired. Note, however, that even though the subjects have very different language deficits, there was no dramatic difference between them in these tasks. This result may suggest that the imagery deficits were not directly a consequence of damage to language processing modules. Alternatively, this result may indicate that some of the same language processing modules (whatever they may be) were damaged in the two patients, and it is these modules that also are used in imagery; in this case, damage to other language modules (different ones for the different patients) resulted in the differences in observed behavioral deficits.

In contrast to generation and rotation, the Kosslyn (1980) theory posits that neither image maintenance nor image scanning requires use of stored descriptions. Thus, it is of interest that we *did* find a decrement in image maintenance. It is worth noting that this finding is consistent with one reported by Kosslyn, Brunn, Cave, and Wallach (1984) in their study of individual differences, who found that performance on image maintenance tasks is correlated with scores on verbal abilities tests. Perhaps verbal or descriptive strategies are used to maintain visual patterns in an image. If so, then our findings may suggest that left-hemisphere damage disrupts such strategies, which become increasingly useful with complex stimuli or stimuli maintained over longer periods in short-term memory.

The present study is admittedly exploratory. The main message is that a task battery like the present one can profitably be used to systematically study the effects of brain damage on mental imagery. If cases can be found showing selective dissociations for the separate imagery abilities, and between imagery abilities and specific language abilities, such data will provide a new and powerful foundation for theorizing about imagery per se.

ACKNOWLEDGMENTS

This research was supported by ONR contracts N00014–82–C–0166 and N00014–83–K–0095 awarded to the first author and NINCDS Grant R01–NS 21065 awarded to the University of Maryland Medical School. R. S. B. is supported by NINCDS Grant K04–

NS-00851. The authors are grateful to the Department of Hearing and Speech at the Good Samaritan Hospital, Baltimore, Maryland, for referring these patients to us. We would also like to thank B. Gordon, M.D., for interpreting F. M.'s CT scan and for reviewing J. E.'s postoperative records.

REFERENCES

Bryden, M. P., & Ley, R. G. (1983). Right hemisphere involvement in imagery and affect. In E. Perecman (Ed.), *Cognitive processing in the right hemisphere* (pp. 111–123). New York: Academic.

Erlichman, H., & Barrett, J. (1983). Right hemisphere specialization for mental imagery: A review of the evidence. *Brain and Cognition, 2,* 55–76.

Farah, M. J. (1984). The neurological basis of mental imagery: A componential analysis. *Cognition, 18,* 245–272.

Jackson, J. H. (1874/1958). On the nature of the duality of the brain. In J. Taylor (Ed.), *Selected writings of John Hughlings Jackson* (Vol. 2) (pp. 129–145). London: Staples.

Kosslyn, S. M. (1980). *Image and mind.* Cambridge, MA: Harvard University.

Kosslyn, S. M., Berndt, R. S., & Doyle, T. J. (1984). *Dissociations between imagery and language* (ONR Tech. Rep. No. 5) Cambridge, MA: Harvard University.

Kosslyn, S. M., Brunn, J., Cave, K. R., & Wallach, R. W. (1984). Individual differences in mental imagery: A computational analysis. *Cognition, 18,* 195–243.

Kosslyn, S. M., Holtzman, J. D., Farah, M. J., & Gazzaniga, M. S. (in press). A computational analysis of mental image generation: Evidence from functional dissociations in split-brain patients. *Journal of Experimental Psychology: General.*

Kosslyn, S. M., & Provost, D. (1984). *Sequential processes in image generation: An objective measure.* Harvard University manuscript.

Podgorny, P., & Shepard, R. N. (1978). Functional representations common to visual perception and imagination. *Journal of Experimental Psychology: Human Perception and Performance, 4,* 21–35.

Shepard, R. N., & Metzler, J. (1971). Mental rotation of three-dimensional objects. *Science, 171,* 701–703.

Springer, S. P., & Deutsch, G. (1981). *Left brain, right brain.* San Francisco: W. H. Freeman.

Winston, P. H., (Ed). (1975). *The psychology of computer vision.* New York: McGraw-Hill.

V SENSORY SYSTEMS AND SELECTION: AUDITION

18 The Importance of Transients for Maintaining the Separation of Signals in Auditory Space

Ervin R. Hafter
Thomas N. Buell
University of California, Berkeley

ABSTRACT

In addition to providing a map of the acoustic world, binaural hearing may play a role in selectivity, allowing the listener to attend to certain messages in the presence of others. Binaural detection is strongly dependent on information contained in the signal's onset. Thus, knowledge about the direction of a source may rely more on memory than on the continual processing of ongoing information. Some questions raised by this notion are: How and when does the auditory system sample the spatial environment? How does it differentiate old, unvarying sounds from new? How does it know when a source moves in space? In this chapter, answers to these questions are discussed in the light of results which suggest that at a fairly low level in the auditory system, multiple bands are monitored for changes in level that might accompany the start of a new signal or a variation in the old one. Such changes can cause the system to resample the binaural inputs, updating its spatial map according to information present at the time of the restart.

INTRODUCTION

There seems little question but that we selectively attend to specific auditory signals in the presence of many, and do it quite well. A singer is understood despite intense competition from the orchestra; a threatening bus is detected in a busy street; we are able to hold conversations in that noisiest and most difficult of backgrounds, the one that lends its name to the "cocktail-party" effect (Cherry, 1961). In the last volume of this symposium, Darwin (1984) spoke of the special importance of stimulus onsets for separating speech-like stimuli in the frequency domain. In this chapter, we too stress the importance of onsets, but here the emphasis is on their possible role in sound localization.

The auditory system parses stimuli on the basis of both frequency (Bregman & Pinker, 1978) and the directions from which sounds emanate. The first is made possible by mechanical filters in the cochlea that compute a running Fourier Transform, assigning spectral components to separate neural channels. This analysis does not necessarily solve the problem of selectivity. Because the spectral representation of ongoing speech is a weighted harmonic series, the interleaving of frequencies from competing messages requires additional information to tell which components go with which signal. A probable solution is for the central nervous system to keep track of dynamic changes of amplitude denoting, as common elements, those that vary in unison (McAdams, 1980).

SOUND LOCALIZATION

In addition to analyzing what is said, the listener may compute the location of the speaker in space. It is obvious that localization might help an animal escape from danger or find a prey, depending on the urgencies of the moment, but what may be of equal importance is its usefulness for communication in a noisy environment. For many years, psychoacousticians have known that spatial separation of a signal from interference can reduce masking. The binaural Masking-Level Difference or MLD is the difference between thresholds found with diotic (same at both ears) signals in diotic noise and those cases in which signal and mask differ from one another along an interaural dimension. The MLD can be dramatic, as great as 15 decibels for tonal signals in white noise. Although it is common to point to this release from masking as evidence that spatial hearing adds to the "cocktail-party" effect, one must be cautious when generalizing from detectability to comprehension. Indeed, attempts to mimic the MLD by measuring the effects on speech intelligibility instead of thresholds have found much smaller values.

The auditory sense of space primarily depends on comparison of the inputs to the two ears. Separated by the width and acoustic impedance of the head, the ears receive different versions of each stimulus. The separation per se produces Interaural Differences of Time (IDTs) due to differences in the paths traveled from the source to the two sides of the head. These grow in magnitude up to about 500 Hz, after which they are reasonably constant (Kuhn, 1977). In addition, there are Interaural Differences of Intensity (IDIs) produced by the acoustic shadow of the head on the distal ear. IDIs are extremely small at low frequencies but grow with frequency throughout the auditory range. These two cues, plus those derived from direction-dependent frequency responses of the external ears, create the complex cross-spectrum from which the binaural nervous system determines a signal's location.

For nearly 100 years, Rayleigh's (1907) "duplex theory" of sound localization has dominated thought on binaural hearing. It says that interaural time is of value only at the low-frequency end of the spectrum, an idea conceived to deal with the fact that for higher frequencies, the ambiguities presented by phase delays of 180° and more render the temporal cues unusable. In strong support of this half of the duplex theory (the other half being the view that high frequencies are localized by differences of intensity) has been the fact that interaural delays in low-frequency tones produce a lateral shift of the auditory image, whereas in high-frequency tones they do not.

It has long been known that the duplex theory cannot be entirely true, because listeners hear interaural delay in high-frequency noise and in brief clicks, regardless of their frequency content. During the past 10 years, it has become evident that the model is, at best, restricted to pure tones. Spurred by the pioneering work of Henning (1974), it has been shown that for complex signals such as Amplitude-Modulated (AM) sinusoids, interaural delays are readily detected in the high-frequency regions of the spectrum, as long as the signal's envelope varies at a rate that is not too high (Bielek, 1981; Dye & Hafter, 1984; Hafter & Dye, 1983; Hafter, Dye, & Nuetzel, 1980; Hafter, Dye, & Wenzel, 1983; Hafter & Wenzel, 1983; Henning, 1974; Henning, 1980; Henning & Ashton, 1981; McFadden & Moffitt, 1977; McFadden & Pasanen, 1976; Nuetzel & Hafter, 1976; Nuetzel & Hafter, 1981; Young & Carhart, 1974). Our current work on onsets began as part of an attempt to bridge this gap, hoping to determine the feature(s) of neural processing that prevent the use of temporal cues in tones but not in AM and noise. For the most part we have used a stimulus that is a form of AM. Here, a listener is asked to detect an interaural difference of time in a train of high-frequency acoustic clicks.

TRAINS OF HIGH-FREQUENCY CLICKS

A band-pass click can be made by passing a brief impulse through a filter of the desired bandwidth. The top panel of Figure 18.1 shows an example of one such stimulus, plotted as a function of both time and frequency. In practice, we generate these clicks in the time domain by multiplying a carrier frequency, here a 4000-Hz cosine, by the impulse response of the desired filter. The filter used in this particular example is Gaussian, with ± 1 sigma including a duration of .46 msec; however, the basic results have been shown to obtain with other types of filters. Numbers produced by multiplying the sinusoid by the weighting function are stored in a computer and presented via 14-bit Digital-to-Analog conversion at a sampling rate of 50 kHz. The middle panel of Figure 18.1 shows an example of a continuous train of clicks such as those in Fig. 18.1. In this example, the clicks are repeated at a rate of 250 times/sec, giving a separation between peaks or Interclick Interval (ICI) of 4 msec. For all of these experiments, the carrier

Signal Spectra

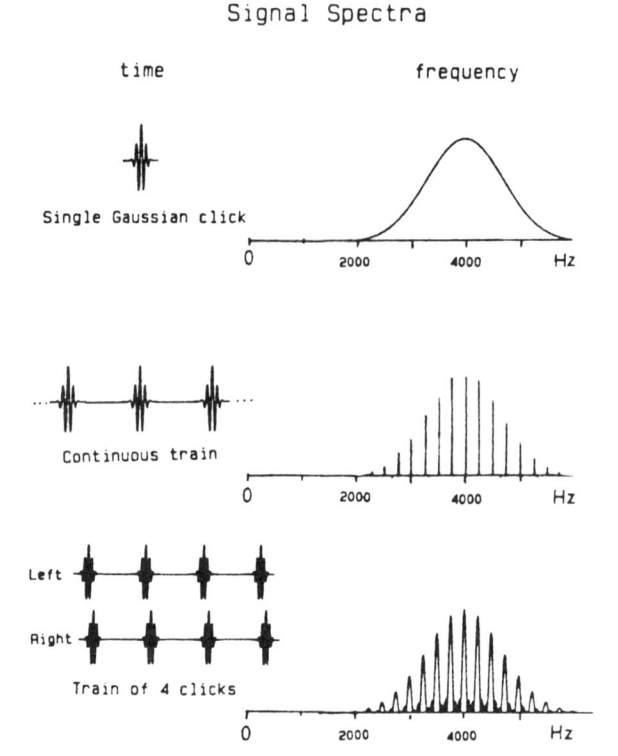

FIG. 18.1. Temporal waveforms and amplitude spectra for 4000 Hz Gaussian clicks (see text). For trains of clicks, the interclick interval is 4 msec. The bottom panel shows dichotic trains used to determine the detectability of interaural differences of time. Here, interaural delay is 200 μs.

frequency of the individual click is an integer multiple of the repetition rate. Note that the largest component is at the carrier frequency, with others falling at integer multiples of the rate, 1/ICI. These others are often called the side bands of modulation. The respective amplitudes of the various components are determined by the Gaussian weighting function that produced a single click.

In the frequency domain, a continuous periodic signal such as that shown in the middle panel of Fig. 18.1 is represented by a line spectrum. This means that energy resides only in the carrier and its side bands. The bottom panel of Fig. 18.1 shows an example of a train of realizable length. It depicts a dichotic signal of the kind that might be presented to a subject, delayed to the right ear by an IDT of 200 μs. Note that limiting the train to a finite number—in this case, four clicks—spreads energy into the regions between spectral lines. The relative amplitudes of components at each ear are unaffected by the interaural delay; rather, what results is a linear shift of phase in the interaural cross-spectrum.

Interaural thresholds are measured using two-alternative, forced-choice psychophysics. Each alternative consists of dichotic clicks that contain an IDT that leads either to the left ear or right. These produce intracranial images heard, respectively, on the left and right sides of the subject midline. The two alternatives are presented in sequence, with the choice of which comes first determined at random. It is the task of the observer to indicate the direction of movement. Feedback is given as to the correctness of the response. By including an appropriate masking noise, one can eliminate potential cues produced at low frequencies by distortion in the apparatus or the auditory system of the listener. This ensures that performance is based on information in the intended regions of the spectrum. With trains such as these, trained subjects readily produce thresholds (ΔIDTs) as low as 10 to 20 μs.

INTERAURAL VARIABILITY

Imagine what we would find if we could present a click to the two ears at exactly the same instant while recording electrophysiologically from a binaural cell in the central nervous system of the listener. Variability in the states of neurons from cochlea to recording site would guarantee that what began as simultaneity would be seen at our hypothetical cell as having led to one side or the other. It is this temporal "noise" that, when added to the temporal "signal" or IDT, prevents perfect performance. With no interaural difference in the stimuli, the jitter in the monaural channels produces a distribution of interaural differences with a mean of 0 and a standard deviation of δ_{IDT}. Let us define threshold as that difference that produces a d' of 1.00. Then, from signal-detection theory, one may argue that psychophysical decisions based only on information available to this hypothetical central neuron should produce a threshold equal to δ_{IDT}.

A binaural signal is apt to evoke responses in the activities of many binaural neurons. If we assume that the statistics of monaural channels feeding these central units are alike, we can expect that for M such channels, the standard error of the mean should be $\delta_1 = \delta_{IDT}/M^{(.5)}$. The subscript 1 refers to the fact that data carried by these neurons were evoked by the presentation of a single click. With real subjects, we do not have access to the activity of single neurons, but only the results of the stimulus averaged across the M channels. The threshold measured with one click, ΔIDT_1, provides a direct estimate of the standard error of that average.

The fundamental logic of our experiments derives from an argument used by Houtgast and Plomp (1968) to study the effects of stimulus duration. We assume that as long as the length of a train of clicks does not exceed the memory of the system, each successive click may act as a separate stimulus, adding samples to the pool of IDTs + interaural noise in much the way that parallel channels each contribute information for a single click. As with the proliferation of channels, additional stimuli should reduce error and lower the threshold. More precisely, if multiplying the number of clicks in a train by n increases the information transmitted by n, it will decrease the standard deviation of the mean error by a factor of $n^{(.5)}$. Consequently, where the interaural threshold for one click is ΔIDT_1, the threshold for n clicks becomes

$$\Delta IDT_n = \frac{\Delta IDT_1}{n^{(.5)}} . \tag{18.1}$$

The more useful, logarithmic form of this expression,

$$\log \Delta IDT_n = \log \Delta IDT_1 - .5 \log n, \tag{18.2}$$

shows a linear relation between the log threshold and log n, with an intercept of log ΔIDT_1 and a slope of $-.5$. This prediction for long ICIs is shown by the dashed line in Fig. 18.2, which represents an upper limit of performance, with every click adding equally to the perception of laterality. Obviously, for extremely short ICIs, the high-frequency limitations of the duplex model should prevail, if for no other reason than that the spectral lines become so separated in frequency (see Fig. 18.1) that each of them falls into its own cochlear filter and the stimulus is turned into a set of separate tones. In that extreme case, extra clicks add nothing to the information derived from the first and so the slope of the log-log plot becomes 0. Of greatest interest to us has been the transition zone from wide separations in the envelope to small; thus, listeners have been asked to localize in a variety of binaural conditions with ICIs ranging from 1 to 15 msec

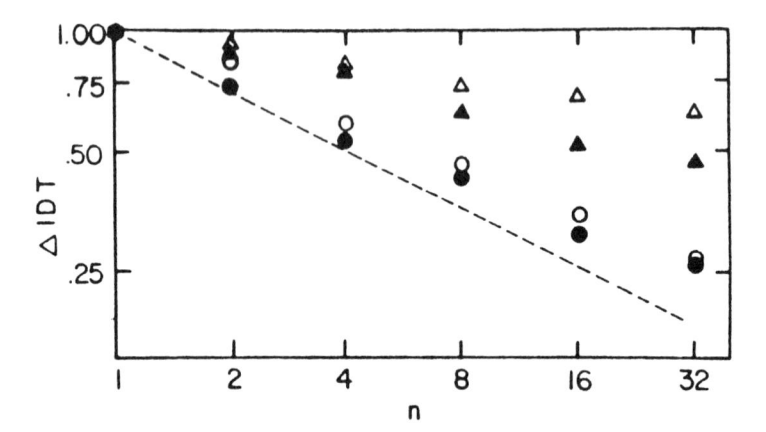

FIG. 18.2. A logarithmic plot of the relative thresholds for interaural differences of time, ΔIDTs, as a function of the numbers of clicks in a train, n. The parameter is the interclick interval: 1 msec, open triangles; 2 msec, filled triangles; 5 msec, open circles; and 10 msec, filled circles. The dashed line has a slope of $-.5$. The data are from four subjects, each a relative threshold for that listener's result for one click (Hafter & Dye, 1983).

and for n ranging from 1 to 48. The data plotted in Fig. 18.2 are a sample from one such experiment (Hafter & Dye, 1983), showing thresholds obtained with clicks centered at 4000 Hz and with ICIs of 1, 2, 5, and 10 msec. The form of these data is typical, best fit by a family of lines whose absolute slopes decrease with ICI. More recent work has found a linear relation between such slopes and ICI, reaching the limiting value of $-.5$ for ICIs in the region of 10 to 12 msec.

POST ONSET EFFECTS: A FORM OF SATURATION

In trying to understand the underlying mechanism(s) responsible for data such as those in Fig. 18.2, we have studied several models of processes that might account for the failure to encode information at high rates (Hafter & Dye, 1983). They include: (a) neural refractoriness that might leave some of the auditory units in an absolute refractory period during presentation of a click; (b) bandwidth limitations set by auditory filters that, by attenuating the magnitudes of adjacent spectral components, reduce the depth of amplitude modulation; (c) serial correlation of the internal noise that might make successive samples of the internal noise added to signals nonindependent. In modeling each of these possibilities, we have found that none is sufficient to describe the basic result. In each case, the effect of reducing ICIs is to reduce performance by a fixed percentage. For example, in the case of refractoriness, if the average length of the refractory periods were greater than $2 \times$ ICI but less than $3 \times$ ICI, the information in about half of the clicks would be lost, a treatment akin to multiplying n by 1/3. One can see from Eq. 18.2 that this would change the intercept, increasing all log thresholds by the constant amount log 2, but leaving the slopes at $-.5$. Instead, the data are better fit by

$$\log \Delta IDT_n = \log \Delta IDT_1 - .5k \log n, \ 0 \leq k \leq 1. \tag{18.3}$$

Taking the antilogarithm gives

$$\Delta IDT_n = \frac{\Delta IDT_1}{n^{(k)(.5)}}. \tag{18.4}$$

In the discussion of multiple neural channels, we suggested that performance with a single click would be based on the responses of M parallel channels. In order to account for the relation in Eq. 18.4, we propose a number N, which is the total number of information-bearing neural events evoked in M potential channels by n clicks. This says that the denominator of Eq. 18.4 is N. The lack of knowledge about M does not prevent plotting the functional relation between N and n as a proportion and, in doing so, we obtain a compressive (exponent $<$ 1) power function of the number of stimuli with an exponent (k) that diminishes with interclick interval:

$$N \propto n^{(k)} \quad 0 \leq k \leq 1. \tag{18.5}$$

Note that a strong assumption of this model is that the binaural neural events evoked by any one click are equivalent in informational value to those evoked by any other. By further assuming that the loss due to short ICIs is in the relative number of events evoked by successive clicks in the train, we can compute the effectiveness of each click by subtraction, comparing performance with a train of length n to that with a length of $n - 1$, and so on. Applying this idea to Eq. 18.5 predicts that the number of neural events and hence the information elicited on the jth click, $N(j)$, can be found from the series

$$N = \sum_{j=1}^{n} N(j) \propto \sum_{j=1}^{n} [(j)^{(k)} - (j - 1)^{(k)}]. \tag{18.6}$$

In this form, the model shows that for fast click rates that produce values of k less than 1, each click in a train evokes fewer neural events than the one before. At first glance, a loss of effectiveness in response to the ongoing stimulus does not seem surprising because "adaptation," as defined by a greater tendency to fire at the onset of a stimulus than to the sustained portion, is a well-documented property of primary auditory neurons (Kiang, Watenabe, Thomas, & Clark, 1965). However, a close look at the pattern of firing times of primary fibers does not reveal a power function as described by Eq. 18.5. Smith and his colleagues (Smith & Brachman, 1982; Smith & Zwislocki, 1975) have examined poststimulus time (PST) histograms for the firing rates of such neurons, using signals comparable in durations to ours. They have found that even though the initial portions of the evoked firing rates are reasonably well fit with a negative exponential, this quickly gives way to a steady state in which the rate of firing is a constant percentage of the response to the onset. Constant rates mean stationary processes—that is, functions that do not change over time. As shown in Hafter and Dye (1983), limitations produced by refractoriness, bandwidth, and nonindependence should produce, in the steady state, stationary responses not unlike those reported for the auditory nerve. All should lead to slopes of a log threshold, log n plot that approach $-.5$. However, this is quite different from a nonstationary process of the kind described by Eq. 18.6. The proposed decline of information throughout the stimulus duration suggests that for binaural performance, there is an additional limitation beyond that seen in the firing patterns of the auditory nerve. Thus, we have been cautious about using the term *adaptation*, choosing instead to ascribe the power-function losses shown here to a process we call *saturation*. Everyday experience tells us that we do monitor continuous sounds. However, the results here suggest that our ability to determine from which direction these sounds emanate relies heavily upon their onsets and that this reliance is itself a function of the rate of stimulation.

POST ONSET SATURATION AS THE PRIMARY LIMITING FACTOR IN LOCALIZATION

Perhaps one should not be surprised at the special importance given to onsets. Work with so-called "binaural precedence" (Lindemann, 1983a, 1983b; Wallach, Newman, & Rosenzweig, 1949; Zurek, 1980) suggests that secondary arrivals caused by reflections in an echoic environment may have little effect on directional percepts established by the "first wavefront" (Blauert, 1984). What is not clear is whether the listener "knows" the direction of a sustained, unmodulated sound and, if so, how? One possibility is that in a direct sense, he or she does not; rather, directional information is held in memory, with the initial wave marking its location. If true, this raises the further question, how does the auditory system know when to stop remembering one direction and start encoding another? Obviously, this is a problem for moving sounds and, of course, it relates directly to initial questions about the ability to attend selectively by using the spatial dimension to maintain a separation between potentially competing messages. These are difficult questions and as yet, no one has any really good answers to them. However, because we believe that postonset saturation plays a major role in these processes, we have continued to study this limitation on high-frequency modulation in hopes of elucidating its underlying mechanisms. Before presenting new data that directly address the issue of how the system recognizes change, we briefly describe experiments designed to better define the biological bases of the model in Eq. 18.5.

INTERACTION WITH OTHER PARAMETERS

Effects of Stimulus Level

The primary dependency in the power functions shown here is on ICI or its inverse, stimulus rate. The faster the click rate, the more quickly the flow of information is cut off. One might postulate an interaction with stimulus level in which more intense clicks would produce faster saturation. In order to address this question, lateralizations based on IDT were obtained at 20, 40, and 60 dB SPL in a paradigm otherwise like that used to produce the data in Fig. 18.2. It is well known that binaural thresholds improve with level, a finding that was repeated. More important, however, was the lack of an interaction between level and the parameters n and ICI. The result of raising the level was to produce a family of parallel lines, displaced in the direction of lower thresholds but unaffected in slopes (Dye & Hafter, 1984). This suggests that even though higher levels may entrain more neurons (increase M), the mechanism described by Eq. 18.5 holds true across all such units.

Effects on Detection of IDI

If the basic effect found with interaural delay is unaffected by signal level and so presumably identical in all neurons, it raises questions about the ubiquity of the underlying mechanism; perhaps the saturation affects all localization. Because the traditional duplex theory is clearly wrong when applied to AM, we decided to look more closely at performance with interaural differences of intensity to see how well the rules of transient effectiveness found with IDTs would apply. Using stimuli much like those in Fig. 18.1, except with the interaural delay set to 0 and the cue to be detected an interaural difference of intensity, we found the same effect as that shown in Fig. 18.2: Decreasing ICIs result in shallower slopes (compare Hafter & Dye, 1983, to Hafter et al., 1983). This suggested that the postonset saturation might be a general principle, applicable to all binaural detection.

THE NEURAL SITE OF THE SATURATION

Within Frequency Bands?

Explanations of the similarity of functions found with both temporal and intensive cues range from postulation of a mechanism very early in the auditory system, where it might restrict post onset coding of all information fed to binaural centers, to one very high in the system, where it might act on the reconstructed complex percept. In order to help distinguish these possibilities, we have attempted to determine the neural site of the operation, using psychophysics to study neuroanatomy. To do so, one needs to find interactions between the function of interest and variation along a dimension whose site of activity is known. The first such question was, "Is the reduction of successive information something that happens across frequency bands, acting on the total percept, or is it within bands, restricted to like spectral components?" To answer this, we pre-

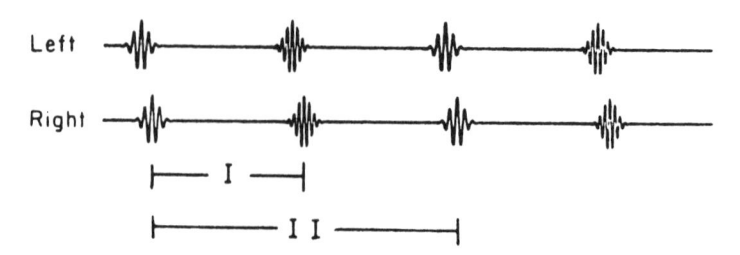

FIG. 18.3. Waveforms from trains of dichotic clicks that alternate in carrier frequency. The carrier frequencies are 4000 Hz and 6000 Hz. The interclick interval labeled I is between dissimilar clicks; that labeled II is between clicks of the same carrier frequency.

sented trains of dichotic clicks like those shown in Fig. 18.3. Here, the carrier frequency of successive clicks was alternated between 4000 Hz and 6000 Hz in order to see, from the slopes of the log threshold, log n functions, whether the amount of saturation would reflect the spacing between successive clicks, regardless of spectral content, ICI_I, or between clicks of the same carrier frequency, ICI_{II}. The results of this study clearly support the within-channel prediction, with slopes matching those found with only a single carrier of 4000 Hz or 6000 Hz and ICI_{II} (Hafter & Wenzel, 1981).

Across IDT and IDI?

The next "anatomical" question asked concerned the similarity between log threshold, log n plots for interaural time and intensity. Might this be due to a single mechanism acting on both? Here, unlike the trains shown in Fig. 18.3, the division is by type of interaural cue, with clicks alternating between IDTs and IDIs. Small differences in procedure were needed because of the complexity of the stimulus; for example, rather than trying to choose comparable interaural differences in the mixed conditions, the IDTs and IDIs were held constant and the effects of increasing n were measured in d'. Essentially, though, the logic of the experiment was the same as with alternating carrier frequencies. The results, however, were just the opposite. Borrowing the terminology used in the preceding discussion, the "effective" spacing was ICI_I—that is, between adjacent clicks—regardless of the type of interaural information (Hafter & Wenzel, 1983).

Before or After Binaural Interaction?

The twin findings that post onset saturation occurs within limited-frequency channels but across both types of interaural information lend support to the notion that the process occurs in the auditory periphery, perhaps suppressing post onset information prior to binaural interaction. As a direct test of this hypothesis, trains were generated with clicks differing from one another in the amount of IDT contained in each. It is generally felt that different IDTs stimulate different "binaural" neurons (e.g., Rose, Gross, Geisler, & Hind, 1966). Thus, if clicks with one value of the delay reduced the effectiveness of clicks with a different value, it would imply that the interaction was occurring prior to the separation into specific binaural channels. To help answer this question, we tested for detection of IDT with a set of "preconditioning" clicks, with a large IDT set to lead *always* to the left side, at the beginning of the trains in both intervals. Predictions of the hypothetical number N were made in the following manner: Consider the condition with six preconditioning clicks followed by three clicks, each containing the IDT to be detected. If saturation occurs after binaural interaction, the three usable clicks should be unaffected by the large-IDT clicks at the beginning; in this case, predictions from Eq. 18.6 should sum over values of *j* from 1 through 3. Conversely, if saturation occurs in the monaural channels prior to binaural interaction, the preconditioning clicks should reduce the effectiveness of the usable ones, and the appropriate fit to the equation should sum over values of *j* from 7 through 9. The data agree with the latter prediction, further reinforcing the view that the loss of effectiveness past onset is the result of a peripheral mechanism (Hafter & Buell, 1984).

Neural Site: Speculation

It is well documented that cells in the superior olivary complex of the brain stem respond to interaural differences (Tsuchitani, 1977). Thus, the experiments presented imply that the post onset saturation is preolivary. We can think of no psychophysical test to see whether or not the mechanism is in the auditory nerve, though the uniformity of firing rates to long stimuli reported for auditory nerve fibers by Smith and Brachman (1982) suggest that it is not there. By default, this leaves the second-order cochlear nucleus (CN) (more specifically the ventral CN where fibers are known to be less primary-like) as the expected neural site of our psychophysical results. It will certainly be interesting if this exercise in anatomical speculation from behavioral testing turns out to have merit.

SOME CONSEQUENCES OF A BINAURAL SYSTEM THAT RECEIVES ONLY TRAINSIENTS

The fact that any frequency, when modulated, can convey temporal information is comforting, because most "real-world" sounds (e.g., speech) are amplitude modulated and one expects sensory mechanisms to be attuned to "ecologically valid" stimuli. We note, however, that for modulations above about 80 to 100 Hz, binaural information beyond the onset is to some extent attenuated, to the point that virtually none of its is useful for modualtions above about 500 to 600 Hz. So how does the auditory system keep track of the direction of an ongoing signal? How does it know when the signal terminates? How does it follow the movement of a source from one location to another? How does it maintain the integrity of the source in the presence of others? Although it is easy to say that these functions must be the job of a higher-order process that oversees the whole of spatial hearing, here we examine the questions in the context of peripheral mechanisms of saturation and offer some new data that suggest ways in which at least some of these problems might be solved.

Tracking the location of a continuous signal need not be a problem if the direction, once computed, is simply held in memory. This, of course, begs the second question: how to erase the spatial memory once established? One possibility is that signals are followed continuously in channels that bypass binaural interaction. In order to test for such continuous tracking, we presented stimuli similar to those in the localization experiments only—in this case, identical to the two ears. Listeners were asked to discriminate small differences in the ICI, making the task a study of envelope pitch. For localization, trains with ICIs of 2.5 msec engender little or no added performance when lengthened beyond the onset. For envelope pitch, however, the log ΔICI versus log n plots for an ICI of 2.5 msec produced terminal slopes of $-.5$ (Richards & Hafter, 1983). This is not to say that there were no onset effects but simply that the slopes for large values of n showed a critical difference between the two tasks, with nonbinaural information being monitored throughout a train. This reinforces the view that there is a separate monaural system that monitors the entire signal. It does not prove that this supplies the message to "clear" binaural memory, but it adds feasibility to the argument. We skip discussions of sensitivity to source movement until after the presentation of a new set of experiments.

ATTEMPTS TO DISCOVER WHAT CONSTITUTES AN ONSET

Recovery After a Gap

Having described the effects of rate-induced saturation on localization and having considered its potential neural site, we have set about trying to understand how it works. The data presented here concern the question: What does it take to get the system to resample the binaural environment? In other words, what sorts of stimulus configurations will function as onsets?

These experiments began with an attempt to see how long it takes to get full recovery after a saturation-inducing stimulus is removed. To this end, we first presented a train of 1, 6, 12, or 24 dichotic clicks with an ICI of 2.5 msec and found the usual high degree of saturation. In subsequent conditions, the trains of 12 and 24 were segregated into groups of six by the insertion of temporal gaps. The intention was to end the saturation momentarily, thus allowing the clicks coming after a gap to transmit information as though they were at the beginning of a new train. It was argued that recovery from saturation would be indicated if the train of 12 were broken into halves by a gap of sufficient duration to produce a threshold equal to $1/\sqrt{2}$ of that found for an unbroken train of length six. Similarly, for a train of length 24 broken into four equal parts, recovery would be indicated if the ΔIDT was $1/\sqrt{4}$ of the ΔIDT for the unbroken train of six. Predictions and data from this experiment are shown in Fig. 18.4. The dashed line drawn through the intercept at the threshold for one click shows the slope of $-.5$ indicative of no saturation. The solid points and the solid line fitted through them show the thresholds for unbroken trains of 1, 6, 12, and 24 clicks. The short dashed line drawn through that function at $n = 6$ also has a slope of $-.5$. It

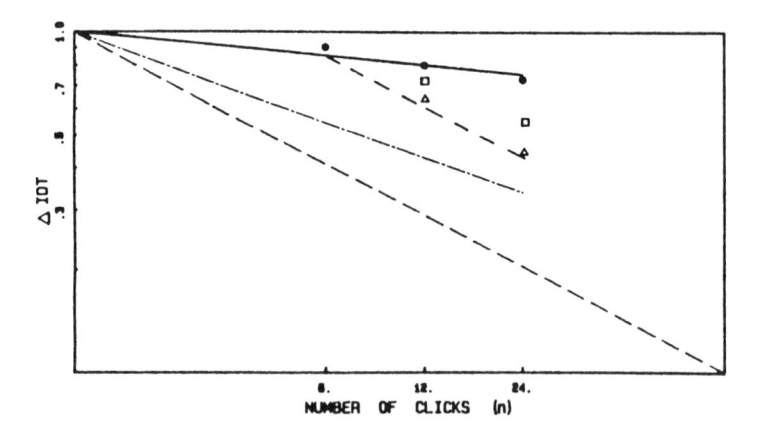

FIG. 18.4. Logarithmic plots of thresholds for interaural differences of time as a function of n. The filled cirlces and fitted solid line are for unbroken trains of clicks with an ICI of 2.5 msec. Performance with trains broken into two or four groups of six clicks each are shown for gaps of 5 msec (squares) and 7.5 msec (triangles). The dashed lines have slopes of $-.5$. The alternating dots and dashes indicate performance for unbroken trains with an ICI of 7.5 msec (slope = $-.34$). These are averaged data from four listeners. Each is a relative threshold for that listener's result for one click.

shows the predicted thresholds for performance based on the sums of information derived from either two or four sets of equally effective trains of length six. Squares show the results of the 5 msec gaps; the triangles are for gaps of 7.5 msec.

From the figure, one sees that the larger breaks were sufficient to obtain the required slope and our first supposition was that the saturation is the result of a rapid process, able to achieve complete recovery with gaps as small as 7.5 msec. However, a surprising result occurred when we asked these same listeners to localize trains with a constant ICI of 7.5 msec. Those data are represented by the line with alternating dots and dashes. Note that its slope is shallower than the $-.5$ implied by the recovery with sets of six. Clearly, 7.5 msec per se was inadequate separation for independence of the successive clicks. Somehow, grouping of the stimuli had made the gap more effective.

Recovery Initiated by Change

Faced with the fact that an interval that is too short to allow for optimal processing when between individual clicks is sufficient when between groups, we sought a different explanation for the implied recovery found with gaps. Suppose that the gap had produced recovery not by the decay of saturation but rather by an active trigger than caused the system to resample the binaural environment? Consider the effect of these gaps in the frequency domain in which the result is a splatter of energy into bands relatively unaffected by the unbroken train. Although the total amount so spread is relatively small, the bands into which it is placed are relatively quiescent and so the signal-to-noise ratio can be considerable. In the discussion surrounding Fig. 18.1, we point to the fact that relatively quiet areas between the spectral lines receive energy from the act of turning the train on and off. During the duration of any repetitive stimulus, a change must produce transient splatter of this kind. One might argue that it was this sudden appearance of sound in the quiet bands that triggered a restart—that is, a reappraisal of the IDT.

In order to study the spectral-splatter hypothesis, we have recently completed a pilot study. Here, listeners were asked to detect an IDT in an unbroken train of 48 clicks with an ICI of 2.5 msec. Simultaneous with the middle of the train, they received a brief (7.5 msec) burst of a 1000 Hz tone of low sound-pressure level. The tone was the same in both intervals. Obviously, a brief tone burst is reasonably wideband, but the overlap between the spectrum of the burst and that of the train was minimal. The only purpose of the tone was to flash energy into quiescent bands, perhaps awakening the auditory system with the message, "Hey, there's something new out there!" The data thus far are encouraging, with the 1000 Hz tone reducing localization thresholds for a train of 4000 Hz clicks. The magnitude of the reduction is less than that found with a 7.5 msec gap, but that is not disturbing because we really have no notion yet about the optimal parameters for getting the system to resample. Indeed, with a 7.5-msec burst of noise that divided the train into two parts, we have been able to obtain a $\sqrt{2}$ reduction in the threshold, as might be expected with complete recovery.

Spectral Change as a Clue to Movement

The precise rules for what is sufficient to trigger a restart are still to be found. Nevertheless, the idea that a "new" sound may cause the auditory system to resample binaural space may help to answer some of the questions raised in this discussion. For example, it may give a clue to the problem of how a listener recognizes when a source moves. Displacement of a steady-state stimulus, even one as simple as a pure tone, creates a momentary shift in phase at each ear. These shifts create a kind of Doppler effect, represented in the frequency domain by a spread of energy into adjacent bands. Perhaps it is this small splatter that tells the system to resample the binaural environment and so allows for replacement in memory of the moved-from location with the moved-to.

SUMMARY

The idea that auditory channels grow quiet during sustained stimulation reminds one of the reduced response to stationary images on the retina (Riggs, Ratliff, Cornsweet, & Cornsweet, 1953), only there, reappearance requires movement of the retinal image itself. In contrast, our data suggest that binaural function may be reactivated by sounds that are not directly a part of the image to be localized. What is more, the reactivation seems to be controlled by mechanisms that are both universal, in the sense that any frequency will do, and active at the level of the site of saturation, where top-down analyses are not required.

The message that we would like to leave is of a relatively quiescent binaural system that is limited in the information that it receives by rapidly adapting monaural gates in the periphery. Sounds may be monitored throughout their durations for features such as their pitch, but if so this is by channels that bypass the processes of binaural interaction. However, binaural processing shows the result of saturation at rates of modulation so low that it seems unlikely that the locations of most sounds are monitored continuously. Rather, information garnered from the onset plus that derived during a triggered restart probably mark the location of the source in memory, holding it until the signal is moved or terminated.

We have not really answered the question with which this chapter began— namely, how well does localization help the listener to separate disparate messages presented at the same time? In showing that onset coding can be especially important for disentangling messages differentiated by spectral cues, Darwin (1984) says, and we agree, that, "More attention should be paid to the dynamic response of the perceptual system. Short-term adaptation provides one simple mechanism for giving special significance to components that are simultaneous" [p. 208]. Perhaps the fact that the binaural system is also responsive to transients will open the way to discovery of spectral–directional interactions that use the episodic nature of signals such as speech to place new bits onto the appropriate streams in memory, while releasing analytic processes in the auditory periphery to scan the environment for change.

ACKNOWLEDGMENTS

We are indebted to Jack Gallant and Virginia Richards for the excellent advice and help they gave in preparing this manuscript. Support for the research came from a grant from the National Institutes of Health.

REFERENCES

Bielek, K. H. (1981). *Spectrale Dominanz bei der interauralen Signalanalyse.* Unpublished diploma thesis, Rhur-University, Bochum. Cited in J. Blauert, Lateralization of jittered tones. *Journal of the Acoustical Society of America, 70,* 694.

Blauert, J. (1984). *Spatial hearing: The psychophysics of human sound localization.* Cambridge, MA: MIT Press.

18. IMPORTANCE OF TRANSIENTS IN AUDITORY SPACE 353

Bregmann, A. S., & Pinker, S. (1978). Auditory streaming and the building of timbre. *Canadian Journal of Psychology, 32,* 19–31.

Cherry, C. (1961). *On human communication.* New York: Science Editions.

Darwin, C. J. (1984). Auditory processing and speech perception. In H. Bouma & D. G. Bouwhuis (Eds.), *Attention and performance X* (pp. 197–209). Hillsdale, NJ: Lawrence Erlbaum Associates.

Dye, R. H., Jr., & Hafter, E. R. (1984). The effects of intensity on the detection of interaural differences of time in high-frequency trains of clicks. *Journal of the Acoustical Society of America, 75,* 1593–1598.

Hafter, E. R., & Buell, T. N. (1984). Onset effects in lateralization denote a monaural mechanism. *Journal of the Acoustical Society of America, 76,* S91.

Hafter, E. R., & Dye, R. H., Jr. (1983). Detection of interaural differences of time in trains of high-frequency clicks as a function of interclick interval and number. *Journal of the Acoustical Society of America, 73,* 644–651.

Hafter, E. R., Dye, R. H., Jr., & Nuetzel, J. M. (1980). Lateralization of high-frequency stimuli on the basis of time and intensity. In G. van der Brink & F. A. Bilsen (Eds.), *Psychophysical, Physiological, and Behavioural Studies in Hearing* (pp. 393–400). Delft: Delft.

Hafter, E. R., Dye, R. H., Jr., & Wenzel, E. (1983). Detection of interaural differences of intensity in trains of high-frequency clicks as a function of interclick interval and number. *Journal of the Acoustical Society of America, 73,* 1708–1713.

Hafter, E. R., & Wenzel, E. M. (1981). Lateralization of trains of clicks having alternating center frequencies. *Journal of the Acoustical Society of America, 70,* S30.

Hafter, E. R., & Wenzel, E. M. (1983). Lateralization of transients presented at high rates: Site of the saturation effect. In R. Klinke & R. Hartmann (Eds.), *Hearing–physiological basis and psychophysics* (pp. 202–208). New York: Springer-Verlag.

Henning, G. B. (1974). Detectability of interaural delay in high-frequency complex waveforms. *Journal of the Acoustical Society of America, 55,* 84–90.

Henning, G. B. (1980). Some observations on the lateralization of complex waveforms. *Journal of the Acoustical Society of America, 68,* 446–454.

Henning, G. B., & Ashton, J. (1981). The effect of carrier and modulation frequency on lateralization based on interaural phase and interaural group delay. *Hearing Research, 4,* 185–194.

Houtgast, T., & Plomp, R. (1968). Lateralization threshold of a signal in noise. *Journal of the Acoustical Society of America, 44,* 807–812.

Kiang, N. Y., Watanabe, T., Thomas, E. C., & Clark, L. F. (1965). Discharge patterns of single fibers in the cat auditory nerve *MIT Res. Monogr.* (No. 35). Cambridge, MA: MIT Press.

Kuhn, G. F. (1977). Model for the interaural time differences in the azimuthal plane. *Journal of the Acoustical Society of America, 62,* 157–167.

Lindemann, W. (1983a). The extension of binaural crosscorrelation modelling by a mechanism of lateral inhibition. *Journal of the Acoustical Society of America, 74,* S85.

Lindemann, W. (1983b). General discussion. Following R. M. Stern & S. J. Bachorski (aus.), Dynamic cues in binaural perception. In R. Klinke & R. Hartmann (Eds.), *Hearing–physiological basis and psychophysics* (pp. 209–214). New York: Springer-Verlag.

McAdams, S. (1980). Spectral fusion and the creation of auditory images. In M. Clynes (Ed.), *Music, mind and brain: The neurophysiology of music* (pp. 279–298). New York: Plenum.

McFadden, D., & Moffitt, C. M. (1977). Acoustic integration for lateralization at high frequencies. *Journal of the Acoustical Society of America, 61,* 1604–1608.

McFadden, D., & Pasanen, E. (1976). Lateralization at high frequencies based on interaural time differences. *Journal of the Acoustical Society of America, 59,* 63–69.

Nuetzel, J. M., & Hafter, E. R. (1976). Lateralization of complex waveforms: Effects of fine structure, amplitude, and duration. *Journal of the Acoustical Society of America, 60,* 1339–1346.

Nuetzel, J. M., & Hafter, E. R. (1981). Lateralization of complex waveforms: Spectral effects. *Journal of the Acoustical Society of America, 69,* 1339–1346.
Rayleigh, Lord. (1907). On our perception of sound direction. *Philosophical Magazine, 13,* 214–232.
Richards, V. M., & Hafter, E. R. (1983). Effect of duration on pitch discrimination of complex signals. *Journal of the Acoustical Society of America* (Suppl. 1), *74,* S70.
Riggs, L. A., Ratliff, F., Cornsweet, J. C., & Cornsweet, T. N. (1953). The disappearance of steadily fixated test objects. *Journal of the Optical Society of America, 43,* 495–501.
Rose, J. E., Gross, N. B., Geisler, C. D., & Hind, J. E. (1966). Some neural mechanisms in the inferior colliculus of the cat which may be relevant to the localization of a sound source. *Journal of Neurophysiology, 29,* 288–314.
Smith, R. L., & Brachman, M. L. (1982). Adaptation in auditory-nerve fibers: A revised model. *Biological Cybernetics, 44,* 107–120.
Smith, R. L., & Zwislocki, J. J. (1975). Short-term adaption and incremental response of single auditory-nerve fibers. *Biological Cybernetics, 17,* 169–182.
Tsuchitani, C. (1977). Functional organization of lateral cell groups of cat superior olivary complex. *Journal of Neurophysiology, 40,* 296–318.
Wallach, H., Newman, E. B., & Rosenzweig, M. R. (1949). The precedence effect in sound localization. *American Journal of Psychology, 62,* 315–336.
Young, I. L., Jr., & Carhart, R. (1974). Time-intensity trading functions for a pure tone and a high-frequency AM signal. *Journal of the Acoustical Society, 56,* 605–611.
Zurek, P. M. (1980). The precedence effect and its possible role in the avoidance of interaural ambiguities. *Journal of the Acoustical Society of America, 67,* 952–964.

19 Selective Attention and Stimulus Processing: Reflections in Event-Related Potentials, Magnetoencephalogram, and Regional Cerebral Blood Flow

R. Näätänen
University of Helsinki

ABSTRACT

The present chapter focuses on stimulus processing during selective attention by examining physiological studies of brain activity—mainly studies involving event-related potentials (ERPs), but also important supplementary evidence provided by measurements of the regional cerebral blood flow and of the magnetic fields surrounding the head. On the basis of these physiological studies, sensory processing during selective attention in multichannel stimulus situations can be divided into two categories: (a) task-unrelated, basic, high-speed processing of physical stimulus features per se, which occurs automatically, preconsciously, and in parallel, and is not influenced by selective attention; (b) task-related, selective, sensory processing of physical stimulus features, which is a manifestation of selective attention at the sensory level. This selective sensory processing is conducted by means of a voluntarily maintained neuronal representation of the specific physical features of the stimulus to be attended, called the attentional trace, which acts as a fast, accurate, and efficient mechanism for recognizing these stimuli. The rejected stimuli, however, appear to receive full processing of their physical attributes per se, which can be inferred from the physiological data available. This processing is the task-unrelated, basic, processing described in (a).

INTRODUCTION

As early as a century ago everybody knew what attention was, if one is to believe William James (1890). The subjective experience of selective attention is indeed familiar to all of us. Yet, explaining the underlying selection process continues to be an exceedingly difficult undertaking, despite intensive research efforts. The secret is, perhaps, concealed by virtue of its being an integral part of the immense mystery of how a material system, our brain, can have subjective experience and consciousness.

One way to understand selective *attention* is first to try to understand selective *inattention*—that is, how extensively the unattended stimuli are processed. In fact, to clarify this question seems to have been one of the most important objectives of much of the research that has been conducted in this area. Moreover, the fate of material belonging to an unattended channel is a major bone of contention among the different attention theories that have been proposed. Behavioral research has not been able to settle this controversy, there being strong data in favor of both the early-selection (Broadbent, 1970) and the late-selection (Deutsch & Deutsch, 1963; Norman, 1968) theories. The first aim of this chapter is to examine the event-related potential (ERP) literature and some magnetoencephalographic work that pertains to the problem of how extensively unattended stimuli are processed. Thereafter, I consider a possible mechanism that may perform certain types of stimulus selection.

PROCESSING OF UNATTENDED STIMULI AND ERPS

This review concentrates on the auditory ERP, because most ERP work on attention has used auditory stimuli. An auditory ERP is composed of a sequence of negative and positive waves, peaks, or deflections. The latter do not generally represent any unitary brain event (generator process), but are rather composed of temporally overlapping components of the same or opposite polarity. An ERP *component* should be understood as a contribution of some single generator process (for instance, activation of some brain center) to the total waveform. ERP deflections are peaks and troughs of this waveform.

A discrete auditory stimulus, such as a brief tone pip, first elicits cochlear and brainstem potentials recordable from the scalp. These deflections are, however, of very low amplitude and must be averaged over many hundreds, or even thousands, of stimuli in order to be resolved clearly. The brainstem auditory response consists of six or seven small deflections, all occurring well within the first 10 msec from stimulus onset (Picton, Stapells, & Campbell, 1981). These deflections probably reflect the arrival of sensory inflow in the various auditory nuclei in the cochlea and brainstem.

The auditory brainstem potentials provide a means of testing theories of selective attention that propose a selective peripheral gating (Hernández-Peón, Scherrer & Jouvet, 1956). Such theories predict that the impulse inflow in the afferent pathways carrying information about the unattended sensory stimuli should be partially or totally blocked. This appears not to be the case, in general (Picton et al., 1981). However, because the processing of physical stimulus features of a sound certainly continues after the brainstem potentials have occurred and involves more rostral brain structures, the brainstem potentials may not provide a valid measure for the magnitude of stimulus processing received by unattended stimuli. The same appears to be true also with regard to the early cortical components, which probably reflect the arrival of sensory input to the respective primary sensory receiving areas. Also these components seem to be insensitive to selective attention. However, good ERP evidence on this point is only available for the somatosensory modality (Desmedt & Robertson, 1977).

The large N1 deflection, which occurs approximately with a peak latency of 100 msec (see Fig. 19.1), does not provide any definitive evidence with regard to the processing of unattended stimuli, particularly in view of the conflicting claims as to the attentional sensitivity of the underlying generator process(es) (for reviews, see Hillyard, 1981; Näätänen, 1982; see also Donald, 1983). Moreover,

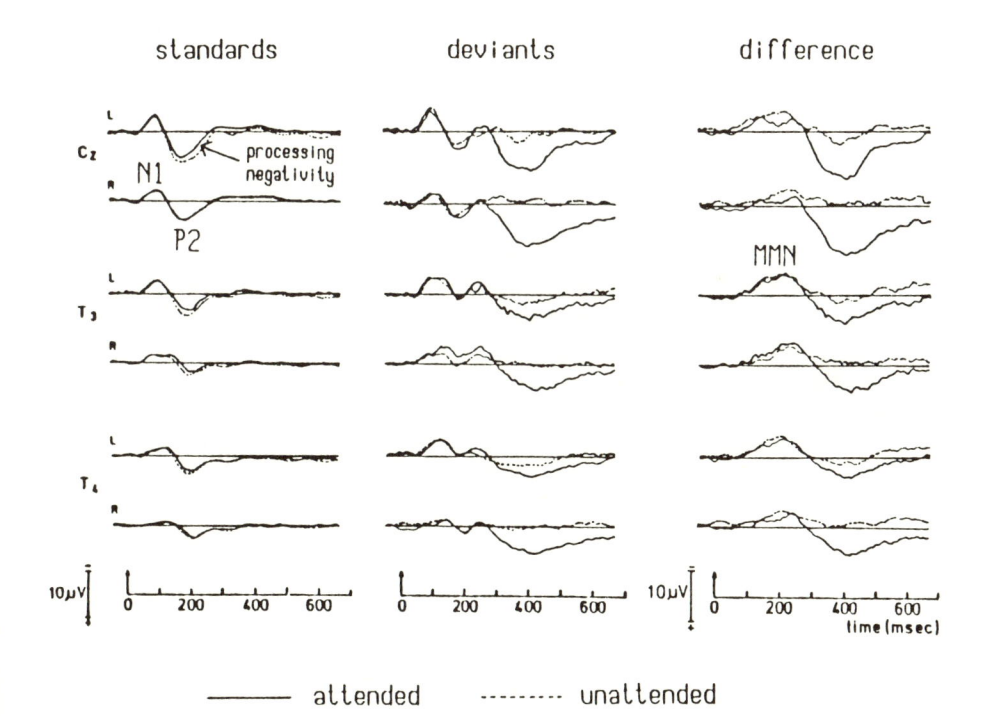

FIG. 19.1. Vertex (Cz), left-temporal (T3), and right-temporal (T4) ERPs to standards and deviants in a dichotic-listening situation, separately when stimuli were attended and when they were unattended. The processing negativity is seen as the negative displacement of the attended-standard trace relative to the unattended-standard trace. The difference curves (ERPs to standards subtracted from those to deviants) are shown on the right. MMN refers to the mismatch negativity. (From Näätänen, Gaillard & Mäntysalo, 1980. Reproduced with permission of Elsevier/North-Holland Biomedical Press.)

data involving P3, a late positive deflection usually peaking at 300 to 500 msec, appear to be impossible to interpret with regard to processing received by unattended stimuli (Näätänen, 1975, 1982).

MISMATCH NEGATIVITY

Fortunately, there is one component of the auditory ERP that provides a way to explore the processing of unattended stimuli. This component, the so-called *mismatch negativity,* was isolated by Näätänen, Gaillard, and Mäntysalo (1978, 1980) from the N2 deflection (Ford, Roth, Dirks, & Kopell, 1973; Simson, Vaughan, & Ritter, 1977; Snyder & Hillyard, 1976; Squires, Squires, & Hillyard, 1975). In Fig. 19.1, data are presented illustrating a mismatch negativity. The subject performed a dichotic-listening task under instructions to discriminate and count silently occasional pitch changes ("deviant stimuli") in the sequence of tones delivered to a designated ear and to ignore the concurrent sequence presented to the other ear. With constant interstimulus intervals (ISI) of 800 msec, stimuli were delivered through earphones either to the left or right ear in random order. The left-ear "standard" and deviant stimuli were of 1000 Hz and 1150 Hz, respectively, and those for the right ear were of 500 Hz and 575 Hz, respectively.

The right side of Fig. 19.1 presents difference curves in which the same-latency data points of the ERP to the standards were subtracted from those of the ERP to the deviants. This operation reveals that in reference to the ERP produced by the standards, that elicited by the deviants discloses a negative shift with an onset latency of approximately 100 msec and duration of some 200 msec. This is the mismatch negativitiy, and it was very similar for the attended and unattended inputs. In contrast, the late positive shift was observed only in response to the attended input (the target effect). This differential positivity, as well as the processing negativity (the negative displacement of the ERPs to the attended standards in relation to those to the unattended standards discussed later), indicate that the subject was indeed selectively attentive.

The authors suggested that the mismatch negativity reflects a physiological mismatch process, an automatic basic sensory process that is unaffected by the direction of attention. Näätänen et al. (1978) had previously obtained similar data both for frequency deviations and intensity deviations; the mismatch negativity was insensitive to attention in those data, too.

In the same vein, the deviant stimuli in a binaural stimulus sequence elicited a similar mismatch negativity when they were the targets to be detected or when all the auditory stimuli were to be ignored, the subject reading a book (e.g., Näätänen et al., 1982; Sams, Alho, & Näätänen, 1984). Instead of reading, we have also used a difficult visual performance task—namely, a computer game—

to make sure that the subject is ignoring the auditory stimuli. The mismatch-negativity amplitudes were very similar to those obtained during reading.

It is clear that the mismatch negativity must be somehow related to a deviation in a sequence of repetitive stimuli, because counterbalancing of tone frequencies has removed the possibility of a frequency-specific potential. Now, there are two alternative ways of interpreting the mismatch negativity:

1. The mismatch negativity is elicited because the deviant stimulus activates a different group of afferent neurons having different receptive fields from those activated by the standard stimulus. This could be called the "release-from-refractoriness" explanation (see Thompson, Berry, Rinaldi, & Berger, 1979).

2. The mismatch negativity is produced by a genuine comparison process in which the input from the deviant stimulus is compared to some neuronal representation of the standard stimulus (the "comparison explanation").

The following observations support the latter interpretation:

1. The mismatch negativity can be elicited even by stimuli that differ from the standards only by being of a lower intensity (see Näätänen & Michie, 1979; Snyder & Hillyard, 1976).

2. There is no mismatch negativity to the first stimulus of a stimulus sequence (for a review, see Näätänen & Gaillard, 1983). A large mismatch negativity should be elicited by the first stimulus if the mismatch negativity to a change in stimulus were due to release from refractoriness. It is N1 that behaves in accordance with the release-from-refractoriness hypothesis. N1 is largest to the first stimulus in a sequence and habituates rapidly within the first few stimulus repetitions; there is a strong stimulus generalization of this habituation (Butler, 1968; Fruhstorfer, 1971; Picton, Woods, & Proulx, 1978).

3. The mismatch negativity, at least to an auditory frequency deviation, has different temporal characteristics and scalp distribution from those of the evoked *N1* wave (Sams et al., 1984).

4. An intermodal deviant stimulus (an auditory stimulus among somatosensory standards) seems to elicit no mismatch negativitiy (Näätänen, Sams, & Alho, in press).

5. The relationship between the magnitude of stimulus change and the mismatch-negativity amplitude approaches a step (all-or-none) function (Näätänen, Simpson, & Loveless, 1982; Sams, Paavilainen, Alho, & Näätänen, submitted; the data of Ford, Roth, & Kopell, 1976, could also be interpreted in this way) rather than increasing linearly or exponentially, which would be predicted by the release-from-refractoriness hypothesis.

6. The mismatch-negativity latency and duration, rather than amplitude, are continuous functions of the magnitude of stimulus deviation; both become short-

er with increasing deviation (for a review, see Näätänen & Gaillard, 1983). According to the release-from-refractoriness hypothesis, the reverse effect would be predicted—that is, amplitude rather than latency should be influenced by the magnitude of stimulus change.

For these reasons I regard the mismatch negativity as being generated by an intramodal comparison type of cerebral event and not merely reflecting the fact that two different stimuli elicit two different responses. This implies the existence of some short-duration neuronal representation of the repetitive (standard) stimulus in the human brain. A mismatch negativity is generated when the sensory input from a deviant stimulus does not correspond to this neuronal representation. The latter must very accurately represent the physical stimulus features (at least of the auditory stimulus frequency), because even slightly deviant stimuli, but not standards, elicit a mismatch negativity (see Fig. 19.2).

The decay time of the neuronal representation for auditory pitch seems to be on the order of 10 sec. This was studied by Mäntysalo and Näätänen (in preparation) by varying the ISI, which was held constant within each block. The standards were tones of 950 Hz and the deviants (occurring with $p = .1$) were similar tones of 1150 Hz, all stimuli delivered to the right ear. The ISIs used were 1, 2, 4, and 8 sec. The mismatch negativity was largest for the shortest ISI and only a very small mismatch negativity was elicited by the deviants when the ISI was 8 sec. The mismatch-negativity amplitude and decay were unaffected by whether the subject paid attention to or ignored the auditory stimuli. In a pilot study in our laboratory, no mismatch negativity was elicited by the deviants when the ISI was 15 sec, even though the magnitude of deviation was very great (standards of 1000 Hz and deviants of 2000 Hz, or vice versa).

The results involving probability effects on the mismatch negativity also illustrate the short duration of the assumed neuronal representations of past stimuli. The smaller the probability of the deviant stimulus, the larger is the mismatch negativity that is elicited (Näätänen, Sams, Järvilehto, & Soininen, 1983). However, this relationship appears to be entirely mediated by the sequence of the preceding stimuli over the last few seconds (Sams, Alho, & Näätänen, 1983; Sams et al., 1984); the global probability has no independent influence. Consistently, a mismatch negativity can even be obtained when the two stimuli are equiprobable; a stimulus change in this situation after a few repetitions of the other stimulus results in a distinct mismatch negativity (Sams et al., 1983).

It is probable that even a single presentation of a stimulus leaves a neuronal representation in the system involved: Even a standard succeeding a deviant tone elicited a (small) mismatch negativity (Sams et al., 1984). On the other hand, if that deviant stimulus happened to be succeeded by another deviant, the mismatch negativity elicited by this "second deviant" was considerably smaller than the

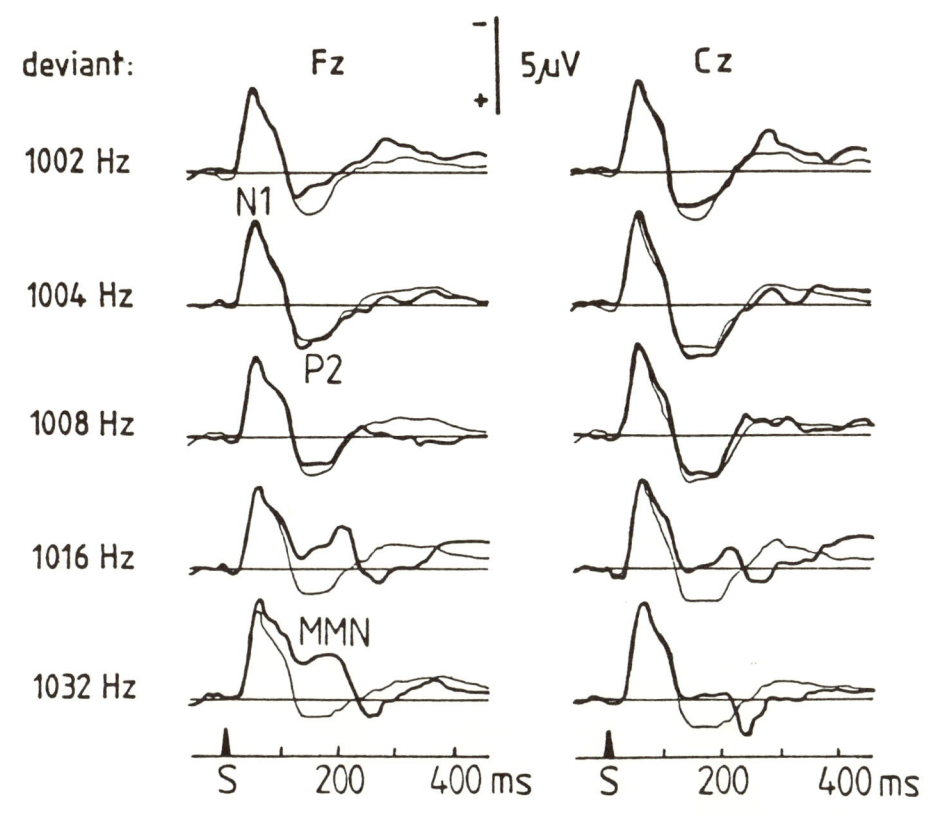

FIG. 19.2. Frontal (Fz) and vertex (Cz) ERPs to standards ($p = .8$) and deviants ($p = .2$) in an ignore condition. The frequency of the standards was 1000 Hz. The frequency of the deviants, varied between the blocks, is indicated on the left. MMN refers to the mismatch negativity (from Sams et al., submitted).

mismatch negativity to the "first deviant." This pattern of results suggests that at the moment of the delivery of the stimulus after the "first deviant," both the standard and deviant have neuronal representations in the system involved (for parallel neuronal representations of two stimuli, see also Näätänen et al., 1978, 1980).

On the basis of the aforementioned studies, it can be suggested that each stimulus leaves a short-duration neuronal representation of its physical features somewhere in the brain. This trace decays in a few seconds but is kept alive or strengthened by repetitions of this stimulus in close succession. If a physically different stimulus of the same sensory modality is presented during the life span of this trace, a mismatch negativity is elicited. It appears parsimonious, then, to attribute the mismatch negativity to a change in this system of neuronal representations. For a suggestion as to how a neuronal population could develop a representation of a physical stimulus feature with the characteristics inferred from the mismatch-negativity data, see Näätänen (1984).

Generator of the Mismatch Negativity

Where in the brain might such neuronal representations be located? Hari, Hämäläinen, Ilmoniemi, Kaukoranta, Reinikainen, Salminen, Alho, Näätänen, and Sams (1984) made an attempt to localize the mismatch-negativity generator process by recording magnetoencephalographic (MEG) responses to deviant auditory stimuli (1030 Hz) presented among standard stimuli (1000 Hz) while the subject was reading a book. A magnetic mismatch response was observed to occur in parallel with an electric mismatch negativity recorded in the same situation. Importantly, the magnetic mismatch response reversed its polarity when the recordings above the anterior and the posterior parts of the Sylvian fissure were compared, indicating that the response was generated somewhere in the peri-Sylvian cortex. Detailed mappings of the magnetic response over the lateral surface of the head performed in two subjects made it possible to localize the generator source with a rather high precision. In both subjects, the magnetic mismatch response was generated in the auditory primary cortex; this was also the probable principal site of generation of the electric mismatch negativity. It seems reasonable to infer that the neuronal representation of the previous stimulus resides where the mismatch process occurs (see Näätänen, 1984).

Consistently, as mentioned previously, there appears to be no mismatch negativity to intermodal deviant stimuli (such as infrequent auditory stimuli among frequent somatosensory stimuli). Further evidence for a high degree of specificity of the neuronal representations is provided by dichotic-listening studies in which neuronal representations seem to develop separately for the left-ear and the right-ear inputs. The deviants within each ear appear to elicit a mismatch negativity only with respect to the same-ear standard that differs in frequency and not with respect to the opposite-ear standard of a different frequency (compare the results of Näätänen et al., 1978 and 1980).

Interpretation of the Mismatch Negativity

The apparent insensitivity of the mismatch negativity to attentional manipulations suggests that the assumed neuronal representations code physical stimulus features to an equally elaborated degree, both when the stimuli are attended and when they are not attended. This means that the physical stimulus features represented in these neuronal traces must have been analyzed to the same extent by the sensory system in both cases. Otherwise, there could not be an accurate neuronal representation of physical features even for the unattended stimuli.

Additionally, the time course of the decay of these traces appears to be the same for the attended and unattended stimuli (Mäntysalo & Näätänen, in preparation).

Moreover, the neurophysiological comparison process reflected by the mismatch negativity probably occurs similarly both for the attended and unattended stimuli, thereby implying that it is preattentive in nature. Näätänen et al. (1978) suggested that the mismatch negativity reflects a preperceptual, physiological representation of stimulus change—that is, a brain process that in itself does not involve a conscious discrimination of the change. Apparently, the mismatch-negativity generator process exemplifies genuinely automatic and parallel high-level information processing that occurs outside conscious awareness, but whose outcomes may intrude therein. Hence, the functional significance of this generator process in information processing might be in turning attention to changes in unattended stimulus sequences (passive attention) and providing internal representations of such changes for their poststimulus examination and evaluation.

Näätänen et al. (in press) proposed that the short-duration neuronal representations probed by deviant stimuli form the neurophysiological basis for the short-duration memory called the sensory register or preattentive store (for a review, see Crowder, 1976), the "echoic" memory in audition (Neisser, 1967). This form of memory is characterized as an attention-independent, large-capacity system that holds raw sensory data and decays rapidly, usually outside of conscious experience (see Kroll, 1975). The sensory information held in this memory appears to be in a fully processed form with respect to physical stimulus features; auditory stimuli are represented with respect to their pitch, intensity, and so on, as are stimuli in our percepts. This concept of the preattentive store is consistent with inferences involving this memory derived from the mismatch-negativity data.

In summation, the following picture emerges from the ERP findings: All the discrete sensory stimuli receive a rapid and complete processing of their physical features. This is an automatic and parallel preconscious processing that is not influenced by the direction of attention. Hence, there is no efferent, or top-down, control of these processes; for instance, stimulus set (Broadbent, 1970) of the subject has no influence on these processes. Thus, the brain, as a result of these processes, obtains sensory information of the same quality irrespective of the direction of attention. When attention is directed to a stimulus source, even very slight outcomes of these preattentive processes, such as those usually associated with low-intensity stimuli, can reach consciousness. On the other hand, attention directed elsewhere at the moment of stimulation can be caught only by considerably more robust outcomes of preconscious processing. Discrete stimuli capture attention particularly well against an "empty" or homogeneous background (see Broadbent, 1982), as do changes in the repetitive elements of the environment.

Possibly all the sensory information produced by preconscious processing is stored for a while at the level of the primary cortical sensory areas in the form of precise neuronal representations. Thus, sensory memory might be located in cerebral systems that are usually understood as receiving and analyzing sensory inputs (see also Deutsch, 1975; Näätänen, 1984). Hence sensory storage would occur separately within each sensory modality and would mainly involve the contralateral cerebral hemisphere.

Only sensory data are stored in this short-duration sensory memory, there being no representation for meanings, interpretations, expectancies, and so on. Neither these factors nor the direction of attention affect the accuracy and strength of representations and their decay times. On the other hand, these factors must be crucial for storing and maintaining information in further memory systems. Thus, the neurophysiological evidence reviewed strongly suggests the existence of a passive, sensory-register type of memory that is strictly separable from other types of memory.

The system of neuronal sensory representations of past stimuli is in a state of continuous flux, with new traces being added and older ones perpetually decaying and vanishing. However, when a stimulus corresponding to some existing trace occurs, this trace receives sensory reinforcement through the match process and is consequently refreshed and strengthened. On the other hand, when the input from a deviant stimulus arrives, the trace system experiences an abrupt change: The emergence of a new neuronal representation while the previous one was still active appears to generate a mismatch negativity. (It is not clear to what extent a different stimulus actually erases the existing trace; in any case, the erasing cannot be complete. See Sams et al., 1984.) In the schema proposed here, the mismatch-negativity generator process is capable of alerting the limited-capacity system that an environmental change has occurred, if the change is large enough—that is, the mismatch-negativity generator process is strong enough to exceed some internal threshold varying as a function of a number of factors.

When there are no abrupt stimulus changes, the information in the sensory register is usually only potential, or latent, and could be characterized as being outside the limited-capacity system, but is apparently transferable to the latter almost instantaneously. Therefore, large amounts of detailed information may enter the limited-capacity system even during very short periods of attention switching, providing the controlled processing with an excellent information base and bringing this information into contact with semantic analyzers and long-term memory.

Consequently, the present position is that if the "unattended channel" really is unattended—that is, if no attention switchings occur—only automatic processing of physical stimulus features takes place, and the outcome of this processing does not automatically activate semantic and other representations stored in some higher memory systems (see also Treisman, 1964). However, the point is made elsewhere (Näätänen, in revision) that the "steering system" of the brain is such that attention switchings necessarily occur quite frequently, and that these switchings are either self-induced or stimulus triggered ("passive attention"). An example of the latter is attention switching caused by the mismatch-negativity generator process exceeding some threshold. This means that every now and then we actually do take a brief, and very informative, sample from the "unattended channel," despite our determined intention to concentrate only on the "attended channel."

MECHANISMS OF SELECTIVE ATTENTION

So far I have only discussed attention-independent processing—that is, processing that occurs in the same fashion whether or not the subject attends to the stimulus source. What, then, does selective attention affect? Much of the processing required in our typical experiments can be characterized as *task-related processing*. This is usually controlled, limited-capacity processing that occurs in addition to the basic, automatic processing of the physical stimulus features—that is, *task-unrelated processing*. Task-related processing is specific to, and hence varies according to, the requirements of task. This form of analysis is often slow compared to the task-unrelated analysis of physical stimulus features. With practice, however, task-related analyses can become highly *automatized* (Schneider & Shiffrin, 1977; Shiffrin & Schneider, 1977) and perhaps can use some automatic kinds of processes as subroutines as well (see the following discussion).

The question arises, however, whether some task-related processing can take place at the sensory level or does all the task-related processing occur beyond the level of the sensory systems. In other words, can selective attention also induce intrasensory changes in processing or does selective attention only affect postsensory events? This, of course, resembles the early- versus late-selection controversy of the attention theories (see also Johnston & Dark, 1982).

A multitude of recent ERP data on selective attention indicates that selective attention or task demands affect sensory processing, most notably in high-load, multichannel situations. (This sensory processing is not, however, the same as that involving the basic sensory analysis; see the following discussion). Näätänen (1982) proposed that selective attention to one of two or more competing stimulus sequences is dependent on an "attentional trace" in the sensory cortical regions. This trace essentially is a *voluntarily* maintained neuronal representation of the physical features of the stimulus to be attended (not to be confused with the involuntary neuronal representations of past stimuli). The attentional trace serves as a tool for fast recognition of sensory input with desired physical features (the matching input) for further processing and response along with task requirements. Subjectively, during the attentional trace there is a vivid mental image of the stimulus to be attended; only at those moments when the subject actually has this image is there an attentional trace in his or her sensory systems. The attentional trace was, in fact, assumed to form the neurophysiological basis of this percept-kind of image.

The attentional trace was suggested to be based on the sensory information stored in the sensory register. Thus, in order to be able to attend selectively to some stimulus, the subject has first to receive this stimulus a few times. Hence, one of the neuronal representations of the sensory register, strengthened by frequent presentations of the corresponding stimulus, is chosen for the sensory-data basis of the attentional trace. This choice, however, does not change the passive neuronal representation involved, judging from the unchanged mismatch negativities to the deviant stimuli. Rather, this choice means information transfer; the sensory information contained by the passive neuronal representation is "read" by the limited-capacity system to develop the corresponding attentional trace—that is, to "tune" the respective part of the sensory receiving system according to the specific sensory attributes of the stimulus to be attended. Another reason to regard these two stimulus representations, the active and the passive, as separate physiological mechanisms is their opposite functions: Whereas the attentional trace responds best to the matching stimuli (see the following discussion), the passive neuronal representation is sensitive to mismatching stimuli; the matching stimuli only strengthen it, but elicit no response (Näätänen, in revision).

These proposals are based on the behavior of the "processing negativity" described by Näätänen et al. (1978; see also Näätänen & Michie, 1979) in a series of experiments that represented modifications of Hillyard, Hink, Schwent, and Picton's (1973) short-ISI dichotic-listening paradigm. In the latter study, the authors obtained their pioneering "N1 effect" of selective attention—that is, the amplitude of the N1 *component* was claimed to be enhanced by selective attention. On the other hand, Näätänen and his colleagues, using longer ISIs than Hillyard and his colleagues, found a protracted negativity, the "processing negativity," that started at 150 msec from stimulus onset—that is, on the descending slope of N1—and lasted several hundreds of msec. This negativity was a separate, endogenous component associated with selective attention. The authors concluded that under short-ISI conditions the processing negativity may overlap the N1 component and hence make it appear larger. It is still controversial whether Hillyard's effect was indeed a genuine N1 effect—that is, an enhancement of the N1 generator process, or an early part of the processing negativity (Donald, 1983; Hansen & Hillyard, 1980; Hillyard, 1981). Possibly, selective auditory attention affects both these components in parallel.

Näätänen (1982) characterized the processing negativity as being generated by a cerebral matching process between the sensory input and the attentional trace. For a schematic illustration, see Fig. 19.3, which represents a situation in which equiprobable tones of 2500 Hz, 2000 Hz, and 1500 Hz are presented (binaurally) in random order. The longest and largest processing negativity is

ATTEND 2500 Hz

— 2500 Hz
······ 1500 Hz
— 500 Hz

Difference:
— 2500 - 500 Hz
······ 1500 - 500 Hz

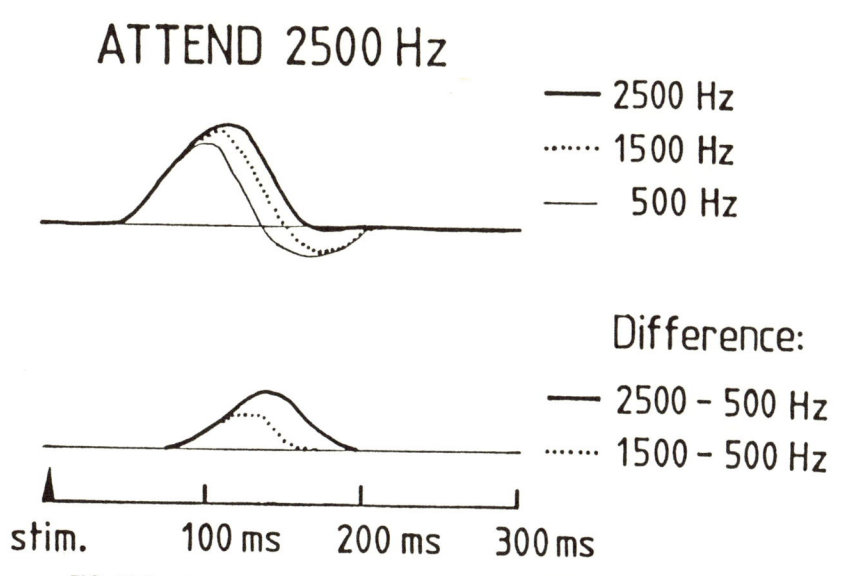

stim.   100 ms   200 ms   300 ms

FIG. 19.3. *Top:* A schematic illustration of the processing negativity presenting ERPs to 2500 Hz, 1500 Hz, and 500 Hz tones when the subject is attending to the 2500 Hz tones. *Bottom:* The difference waves obtained by subtracting the 500 Hz ERP from the 2500 Hz and the 1500 Hz ERPs, respectively.

generated by the stimulus to be attended, that of 2500 Hz, but some processing negativity is generated even by the unattended stimuli (see Alho, Sams, Paavilainen, & Näätänen, submitted). In general, the processing negativity is longer and larger to a particular stimulus the more similar it is to the attended (Näätänen, 1982; in revision). The system described is able to carry out even fine discriminations. Alho et al. presented a sequence of equiprobable tone pips of 480, 500, and 521 Hz, instructing the subject to count one of the tone pips. The counted tone pips elicited the largest processing negativity. This result suggests that the attentional trace is indeed a highly accurate neuronal representation of the physical features of the stimulus to be attended. The degree of discrimination accuracy demonstrated approaches that revealed by the passive neuronal representation in its mismatching function (Fig. 19.2), further supporting the previously presented claim that the latter representation serves as the sensory-information source for the attentional trace.

There are several reasons for regarding the attentional trace and the matching process between it and the sensory input as intrasensory rather than postsensory processes:

1. The early phase of the processing negativity appears to be generated in modality-specific sensory areas (see Desmedt & Robertson, 1977; Harter &

Guido, 1980; Michie, 1984; Renault, Baribeau-Braun, Dalbokova, & El Massioui, in press).

2. The onset latency of the processing-negativity differential (the difference wave; see Fig. 19.3) can be as short as 50 msec or even less (McCallum, Curry, Cooper, Pocock, & Papakostopoulos, 1983; Okita, 1979). This suggests that there must be an attentionally selective state, treating stimuli differentially, at the sensory level (the attentional trace)—otherwise, such an early onset latency appears impossible (see Hillyard et al., 1973).

3. In regional cerebral blood-flow studies, increased blood flow can be observed in the sensory-specific cortical regions corresponding to the stimulus to be attended. For instance, when Roland's (1981) subjects attended for 40 sec to a possible weak touch on the tip of their index fingers (no stimuli were given), blood flow increased 25% in the contralateral somatosensory finger area (and in the surrounding cortex as well). Smaller increases occurred in the superior prefrontal and midfrontal regions together with lesser increases in the middle part of the posterior parietal region. There was, in addition, a diffuse increase involving the frontal and parietal association areas. When attention was directed to the upper lip, blood flow increased in the contralateral somatosensory mouth area and in the other regions just mentioned.

The processing negativity at least in the auditory modality has also a later, frontal component (Hansen & Hillyard, 1980). This might indicate the existence of a frontal activation focus during selective attention. Possibly this frontal focus reflects the voluntary, limited-capacity activity maintaining the attentional trace in the sensory-specific regions (see Näätänen, in revision). This is supported by a second blood-flow focus, which was found in the frontal cortex during selective attention (Roland, 1981, 1982). Significantly, this frontal focus, involving certain well-defined parts of the frontal cortex, seems to be the same in various selective-attention situations involving different sensory modalities (Roland, 1982). Risberg and Prohovnik's (1983) blood-flow study indicated that the right frontal cortex might be more important in the control of selective attention than the left frontal cortex.

OVERVIEW

The ERP evidence reviewed in this chapter points to the existence of a cerebral sensory system that processes the physical features of stimuli in a manner uninfluenced by selective attention. Such processing is automatic, parallel, and preconscious, and it provides the brain with accurate physical stimulus information. This information may be consciously experienced—that is, it may give rise to conscious percepts—mainly depending on the direction of attention and on the magnitude of the transient neurophysiological response caused by the sensory input to the sensory systems (and presumably to some nonspecific systems as well).

It was further proposed that in addition to these phasic responses of the sensory sytems, a more sustained neuronal representation for physical stimulus features starts to develop upon arrival of the sensory input in the sensory cortical areas. In the case of auditory pitch, the magnetoencephalographic data reviewed suggest that the system representing physical features of past stimuli is probably located in the primary auditory cortex. These neuronal representations might form the neurophysiological basis of the memory called sensory memory, precategorical store, or sensory register. This storage function is independent of attention. A mismatch process, reflected by the mismatch negativity, in the precategorical store is capable of "calling" the limited-capacity system (see also Öhman, 1979).

In addition to this automatic, task-unrelated processing, we also invoke task-related processing when the situation requires it, and even this latter processing can in part be sensory. However, these task-related influences on the sensory events do not involve the basic sensory events. Selective attention manifests itself rather by producing temporary sensory mechanisms or functions for selection of specific, relevant, stimuli; these selection mechanisms are called attentional traces. Essentially, these are voluntarily maintained neuronal stimulus representations corresponding to the physical features of the stimulus to be attended. These traces, located in the sensory-specific areas, explain the high speed and efficiency of a stimulus-set kind of selective attention and performance. The attentional-trace system is biased toward recognizing a certain stimulus, as if tonically asking whether an incoming sensory input is this stimulus or not. Hence, the sensory systems additionally perform task-related sensory analysis, as opposed to the task-unrelated, stimulus-determined, sensory analysis that the sensory systems are continuously performing irrespective of the direction of attention (Fig. 19.4). However, the sensory neuronal populations participating in the two forms of processing are probably somewhat different (see Näätänen, in revision).

The attentional trace is thus suggested to be the physiological mechanism that subserves stimulus-set kind of selection. The processing-negativity data reviewed demonstrate, however, that the fast discrimination performed by this mechanism is much more accurate than what appears to be consistent with the previous views of stimulus set, which suggest the latter to operate only on rough physical differences. Moreover, whereas those views imply termination of processing of rejected stimuli, the present view holds that their processing is completed with regard to the basic physical attributes, selection involving only entry to temporary *task-related* processing stages maintained for task performance. Hence, selective attention cannot facilitate, or lack of it inhibit, the cerebral

```
                                          |  POST-SENSORY
                           SENSORY        |   ANALYSIS
                                          |  & CONTROL
                           ANALYSIS       |  PROCESSES
```

TASK-UNRELATED ('BASIC') SENSORY ANALYSIS	Peripheral sensory analysis	PERMANENT FEATURE-DETECTION SYSTEM -parallel -automatic -pre-attentive	'What?'
TASK-RELATED (MATCH-MISMATCH) SENSORY ANALYSIS		TEMPORARY FEATURE-RECOGNITION SYSTEM (ATTENTIONAL TRACE) -sequential -controlled -conscious	'Whether or not this? If this, then...'

→
t

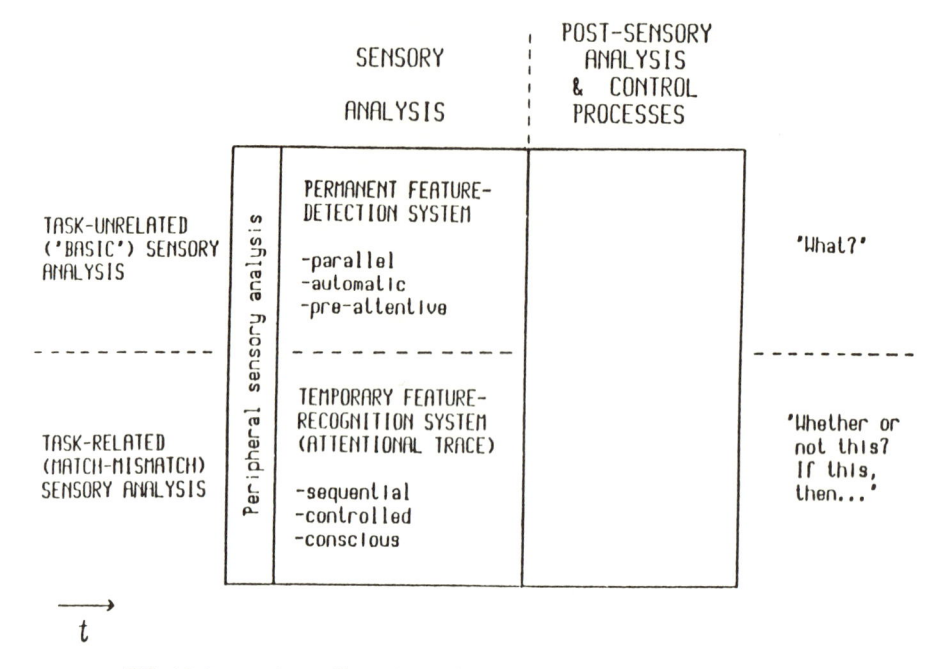

FIG. 19.4. A schema illustrating task-unrelated and task-related sensory processing. The schema proposes that selective attention in these kinds of situations is manifested by the emergence of a temporary feature-recognition system (the attentional trace) in the cerebral sensory systems. This mechanism is maintained by the limited-capacity system (control processes), which receives information of the occurrence of the wanted stimulus by means of the attentional-trace mechanism and can immediately subject this stimulus to preprepared further-processing stages or release the response held facilitated. This task-related sensory analysis occurs in parallel with the task-unrelated ("basic") sensory analysis and storage without affecting them but drastically reducing the chances of the outcomes' of the task-unrelated sensory processing entering the postsensory analysis.

accumulation (and retaining) of sensory data from environmental events. The latter feature of the present theory is more in line with the late-selection than the early-selection theories.

ACKNOWLEDGMENTS

This chapter was prepared during my visit with Professor F. K. Graham at the Waisman Center, University of Wisconsin, and has greatly gained from the stimulating discussions with her and her associates, Drs. B. Anthony and S. A. Hackley and with Dr. S. Orrman. In preparing the final form, I wish to acknowledge the very useful comments of Professor S. A. Hillyard, Professor M. I. Posner, and Dr. A. W. K. Gaillard, as well as the help of my colleague P. Paavilainen in producing the manuscript and the figures. This work was supported by the Academy of Finland.

19. SELECTIVE ATTENTION AND STIMULUS PROCESSING

REFERENCES

Alho, K., Sams, M., Paavilainen, P., & Näätänen, R. *Magnitude of pitch separation and the selective-attention effect on the ERP.* Manuscript submitted for publication.

Broadbent, D. E. (1970). Stimulus set and response set: Two kinds of selective attention. In D. I. Mostofsky (Ed.), *Attention: Contemporary theory and analysis* (pp. 51–60). New York: Appleton-Century-Crofts.

Broadbent, D. E. (1982). Task combination and selective intake of information. *Acta Psychologica, 50,* 253–290.

Butler, R. A. (1968). Effects of changes in stimulus frequency and intensity on habituation of the human vertex potential. *The Journal of the Acoustical Society of America, 44,* 945–950.

Crowder, R. G. (1976). *Principles of learning and memory.* Hillsdale, NJ: Lawrence Erlbaum Associates.

Desmedt, J. E., & Robertson, D. (1977). Differential enhancement of early and late components of the cerebral somatosensory evoked potentials during forced-paced cognitive tasks in man. *Journal of Physiology, 271,* 761–782.

Deutsch, D. (1975). The organization of short-term memory for a single acoustic attribute. In D. Deutsch & J. A. Deutsch (Eds.), *Short-term memory* (pp. 108–151). New York: Academic.

Deutsch, J. A., & Deutsch, D. (1963). Attention: Some theoretical considerations. *Psychological Review, 70,* 80–90.

Donald, M. W. (1983). Neural selectivity in auditory attention: Sketch of a theory. In A. W. K. Gaillard & W. Ritter (Eds.), *Tutorials in ERP Research: Endogenous components* (pp. 37–77). Amsterdam: North-Holland.

Ford, J. M., Roth, W. T., Dirks, S. J., & Kopell, B. S. (1973). Evoked potential correlates of signal recognition between and within modalities. *Science, 181,* 465–466.

Ford, J. M., Roth, W. T., & Kopell, B. S. (1976). Auditory evoked potentials to unpredictable shifts in pitch. *Psychophysiology, 13,* 32–39.

Fruhstorfer, H. (1971). Habituation and dishabituation of human vertex response. *Electroencephalography and Clinical Neurophysiology, 30,* 306–312.

Hansen, J. C., & Hillyard, S. A. (1980). Endogenous brain potentials associated with selective auditory attention. *Electroencephalography and Clinical Neurophysiology, 49,* 277–290.

Hari, R., Hämäläinen, M., Ilmoniemi, R., Kaukoranta, E., Reinikainen, K., Salminen, J., Alho, K., Näätänen, R., & Sams, M. (1984). Responses of the primary auditory cortex to pitch changes: Neuromagnetic recordings in man. *Neuroscience Letters, 50,* 127–132.

Harter, M. R., & Guido, W. (1980). Attention to pattern orientation: Negative cortical potentials, reaction time, and the selection process. *Electroencephalography and Clinical Neurophysiology, 49,* 461–475.

Hernández-Peón, R., Scherrer, H., & Jouvet, M. (1956). Modification of electrical activity in the cochlear nucleus during attention in unanesthetized cats. *Science, 123,* 331–332.

Hillyard, S. A. (1981). Selective auditory attention and early event-related potentials: A rejoinder. *Canadian Journal of Psychology, 35,* 85–100.

Hillyard, S. A., Hink, R. F., Schwent, V. L., & Picton, T. W. (1973). Electrical signs of selective attention in the human brain. *Science, 182,* 177–180.

James, W. (1890). *The principles of psychology* (2 vols.). New York: Holt.

Johnston, W. A., & Dark, V. J. (1982). In defence of intraperceptual theories of attention. *Journal of Experimental Psychology: Human Perception and Performance, 8,* 407–421.

Kroll, N. A. (1975). Visual short-term memory. In D. Deutsch & J. A. Deutsch (Eds.), *Short-term memory* (pp. 108–151). New York: Academic.

Mäntysalo, S., & Näätänen, R. (in preparation). *Inter-stimulus-interval and the mismatch negativity of the event-related potential.*

McCallum, W. C., Curry, S. H., Cooper, R., Pocock, P. V., & Papakostopoulos, D. (1983). Brain event-related potentials as indicators of early selective processes in auditory target localization. *Psychophysiology, 20*, 1-17.

Michie, P. T. (1984). Selective attention effects on somatosensory event-related potentials. In R. Karrer, J. Cohen, & P. Tueting (Eds.), *Brain and information: Event-related potentials. Annals of the New York Academy of Sciences, 425* (pp. 250-255). New York: New York Academy of Sciences.

Näätänen, R. (1975). Selective attention and evoked potentials in humans—a critical review. *Biological Psychology, 2*, 237-307.

Näätänen, R. (1982). Processing negativity: An evoked-potential reflection of selective attention. *Psychological Bulletin, 92*, 605-640.

Näätänen, R. (1984). In search of a short-duration memory trace of a stimulus in human brain. In L. Pulkkinen & P. Lyytinen (Eds.), *Essays in Honour of Martti Takala. Jyväskylä Studies in Education, Psychology and Social Science* (pp. 22-36). University of Jyväskylä.

Näätänen, R. (in revision). Theory of auditory selective attention based on event-related brain potentials in man. *The Behavioral and Brain Sciences*.

Näätänen, R., & Gaillard, A. W. K. (1983). The orienting reflex and the N2 deflection of the ERP. In A. W. K. Gaillard & W. Ritter (Eds.), *Tutorials in event related potential research: Endogenous components* (pp. 119-141). Amsterdam: North-Holland.

Näätänen, R., Gaillard, A. W. K., & Mäntysalo, S. (1978). Early selective attention effect on evoked potential reinterpreted. *Acta Psychologica, 42*, 313-329.

Näätänen, R., Gaillard, A. W. K., & Mäntysalo, S. (1980). Brain potential correlates of voluntary and involuntary attention. In H. H. Kornhuber & L. Deecke (Eds.), *Motivation, motor and sensory processes of the brain: Electrical potentials, behaviour and clinical use. Progress in brain research, 54* (pp. 343-348). Amsterdam: Elsevier.

Näätänen, R., & Michie, P. T. (1979). Early selective attention effects on the evoked potential. A critical review and reinterpretation. *Biological Psychology, 8*, 81-136.

Näätänen, R., Sams, M., & Alho, K. (in press). The mismatch negativity: the ERP sign of a cerebral mismatch process. *Electroencephalography and Clinical Neurophysiology* (Supplement).

Näätänen, R., Sams, M., Järvilehto, T., & Soininen, K. (1983). Probability of deviant stimulus and event-related brain potentials. In R. Sinz & M. R. Rosenzweig (Eds.), *Psychophysiology 1980* (pp. 397-405). Jena: VEB Gustav Fischer Verlag and Amsterdam: Elsevier.

Näätänen, R., Simpson, M., & Loveless, N. E. (1982). Stimulus deviance and evoked potentials. *Biological Psychology, 14*, 53-98.

Neisser, U. (1967). *Cognitive psychology*. New York: Appleton-Century-Crofts.

Norman, D. A. (1968). Towards a theory of memory and attention. *Psychological Review, 75*, 522-536.

Öhman, A. (1979). The orienting response, attention, and learning: An information-processing perspective. In H. D. Kimmel, E. H. Van Olst, & J. F. Orlebeke (Eds.), *The orienting reflex in humans* (pp. 443-471). Hillsdale, NJ: Lawrence Erlbaum Associates.

Okita, T. (1979). Event-related potentials and selective attention to auditory stimuli varying in pitch and localization. *Biological Psychology, 9*, 271-284.

Picton, T. W., Stapells, D. R., & Campbell, K. B. (1981). Auditory evoked potentials from the human cochlea and brainstem. *The Journal of Otolaryngology, 10*, 1-41.

Picton, T. W., Woods, D. L., & Proulx, G. B. (1978). Human auditory sustained potentials. II. Stimulus relationships. *Electroencephalography and Clinical Neurophysiology, 45*, 198-210.

Renault, B., Baribeau-Braun, J., Dalbokova, D., & El Massioui, F. (in press). Differential topographical analysis of auditory components in a selective attention task. *Electroencephalography and Clinical Neurophysiology* (Supplement).

Risberg, J., & Prohovnik, I. (1983). Cortical processing of visual and tactile stimuli studied by non-invasive rCFB measurements. *Human Neurobiology, 2*, 5-10.

Roland, P. E. (1981). Somatotopical tuning of postcentral gyrus during focal attention in man. A regional cerebral blood flow study. *Journal of Neurophysiology, 46*, 744-754.

Roland, P. E. (1982). Cortical regulation of selective attention in man: A regional cerebral blood flow study. *Journal of Neurophysiology, 48,* 1059–1077.

Sams, M., Alho, K., & Näätänen, R. (1983). Sequential effects on the ERP in discriminating two stimuli. *Biological Psychology, 17,* 41–58.

Sams, M., Alho, K., & Näätänen, R. (1984). Short-term habituation and dishabituation of the mismatch negativity of the ERP. *Psychophysiology, 21,* 434–441.

Sams, M., Paavilainen, P., Alho, K., & Näätänen, R. *Auditory frequency discrimination and event-related potentials.* Manuscript submitted for publication.

Schneider, W., & Shiffrin, R. M. (1977). Controlled and automatic information processing: I. Detection, search, and attention. *Psychological Review, 84,* 1–66.

Shiffrin, R. M., & Schneider, W. (1977). Controlled and automatic information processing: II. Perceptual learning, automatic attending, and a general theory. *Psychological Review, 84,* 127–189.

Simson, R., Vaughan, H. G., & Ritter, W. (1977). The scalp topography of potentials in auditory and visual discrimination tasks. *Electroencephalography and Clinical Neurophysiology, 42,* 528–535.

Snyder, E., & Hillyard, S. A. (1976). Long-latency evoked potentials to irrelevant, deviant stimuli. *Behavioural Biology, 16,* 319–331.

Squires, N. K., Squires, K. C., & Hillyard, S. A. (1975). Two varieties of long-latency positive waves evoked by unpredictable auditory stimuli in man. *Electroencephalography and Clinical Neurophysiology, 38,* 387–401.

Thompson, R. F., Berry, S. D., Rinaldi, P. C., & Berger, T. W. (1979). Habituation and the orienting reflex: The dual-process theory revisited. In H. D. Kimmel, E. H. Van Olst, & J. F. Orlebeke (Eds.), *The orienting reflex in humans* (pp. 21–60). Hillsdale, NJ: Lawrence Erlbaum Associates.

Treisman, A. M. (1964). Selective attention in man. *British Medical Bulletin, 20,* 12–16.

20 Comparisons Across Paradigms: An ERP Study

Anthony W. K. Gaillard
Cornelis J. Verduin
Institute for Perception TNO

ABSTRACT

Event-related brain potentials (ERPs) were obtained in three experimental conditions, representing three tasks often used in ERP research. The aim of the present study was to make a direct comparison between the ERP components elicited by the three tasks, using the same experimental procedures. It was argued that comparisons across paradigms might lead to erroneous conclusions, because these comparisons are usually based on different studies, varying in the use of procedures, the type of stimuli and responses, and so on.

Two negative components were obtained, an early negativity (*EN*) and an N2 component. These components were thought to reflect an early (stimulus encoding) and a late (stimulus classification) discrimination process. The *EN* is related to the processing negativity observed in selective-attention tasks and the *N2* is contrasted with the mismatch negativity, a cortical correlate of a preattentive mismatch process.

INTRODUCTION

In the early 1970s researchers examining the relationships between psychological processes and event-related brain potentials (ERPs) concentrated on the effects of psychological factors on the amplitude and latency of the peaks of the ERP. Later, it became evident that the waves produced by psychological processes were not strictly related to the peaks of the ERP and a distinction was made between endogenous and exogenous components (Donchin, Ritter, & McCallum, 1978; Gaillard & Ritter, 1983). Exogenous components are evoked by events outside the central nervous system and their variance is primarily determined by the physical characteristics of the stimulus. Endogenous components are not directly affected by the physical parameters of the stimulus and the variance of their amplitudes and latencies is primarily determined by the psychological processes invoked by stimulus events and the instructions assigned to them. Depending on the task requirements, endogenous components may vary over a considerable time range. For example, the processing negativity, originally regarded as an enhanced *N1* component (latency 100 msec), is now reported to have peak latencies up to 200 to 300 msec (Näätänen, 1982). Also, the classical positive wave P300 was so called because it was thought that its latency would vary around 300 msec. Now several studies have reported similar waves with latencies up to one sec (Mulder, Gloerich, Brookhuis, Van Dellen, & Mulder, 1984).

The large and still increasing number of endogenous components has raised the question of how to define a component and what criteria should be used to decide whether two ERP waves can be regarded as representing the same component. When one accepts that endogenous components may vary considerably in time, they can no longer be defined as occurring strictly in a certain time period, as is the case with exogenous components.

A component may also be defined in terms of its assumed underlying neurophysiological mechanism. In this definition the distribution on the scalp is the critical factor in deciding whether or not two ERP waves represent the same component. If two waves have the same scalp distribution, they are assumed to be generated by the same neurophysiological mechanism.

It is also possible to define an endogenous component in terms of the psychological factors that determine its occurrence. In this approach the amplitude and latency are investigated as a function of task variables, which are known to be related to a certain psychological process (for example, on the basis of RT studies). The psychological process reflected in the component can then be inferred from the pattern of the effects of the task variables. This approach has some similarity to the additive factor method, used to identify stages of processing (Sternberg, 1969).

As in RT research we are not so much interested in the ERP as an absolute measure but we are interested in its relative changes in latency and amplitude as a function of task variables. These changes may be associated with the processes assumed to be involved in the manipulation of these variables. As with the measurement of RT, there are factors, such as conduction time, that are assumed to be constant for all conditions and do not play a role when conditions are compared. In ERP research it has always been a major concern to ascertain that the exogenous components do not change between experimental conditions. This can be established by keeping the physical characteristics of the task constant. Even then, comparisons between conditions may be difficult because the summation of exogenous and endogenous components results in complex waveforms in which the experimental effects are sometimes difficult to disentangle. This has led to the now common practice of subtracting ERP waveforms from each other. The effects of the experimental manipulations can be better observed in the difference waveforms because the exogenous components are now removed. Subtractions may be done between ERPs obtained in the same block of trials (frequent vs. infrequent, attended vs. unattended) or in different blocks of trials. It is also possible to make subtractions with ERPs obtained in control conditions, in which subjects ignore the stimuli and are usually given another task to ensure that they do not pay attention to the stimuli.

One important factor that hampers the progress in evaluating the psychological significance of endogenous components is that they are usually obtained in quite different paradigms. Even when the same task is used, there may be considerable differences in the manipulation of task variables, the procedures (instructions, training, etc.), and the stimulus and response characteristics. Moreover, most investigators tend to concentrate on one or two components obtained in one particular paradigm. Thus, comparisons between components are very often comparisons between paradigms and even between investigators. This makes it extremely difficult to review the area and to decide whether a particular wave obtained by one investigator is in fact the same component as the one obtained by another investigator who uses a somewhat different paradigm. Comparisons between paradigms are necessary to establish the psychological significance of endogenous components and to examine their generalizability, reliability, and validity. This issue also is relevant to human performance research; there the question may be raised about the extent to which differences between models of information processing are caused by the particular paradigms used. A related issue is whether an information-processing model based on a particular paradigm can be generalized to other task configurations or to task performance in real-life situations.

The aim of the present study was to compare the endogenous components obtained in three RT tasks. A direct comparison within the same study using the same subjects, stimuli, procedures, and so on, would demonstrate more clearly similarities and differences in the latencies and amplitudes of the endogenous components.

The three experimental conditions used in the present study were devised to represent three tasks often used in ERP research: an odd-ball task, a memory-comparison task, and a localization task. The choice of these conditions was based on three earlier studies (Gaillard & Lawson, 1984; Gaillard & Van Arkel, in press; Lawson & Gaillard, 1981) that all used syllables as stimuli.

The odd-ball task involves the discrimination of two stimuli, a frequent one and an infrequent one. In the ERP to the infrequent stimulus, a large negative wave (*N2*) is followed by a large positive wave (*P3*). This *N2–P3* complex is largely reduced or absent in the ERP to the frequent stimulus. The peak latency of *N2* varies between 200 msec and 500 msec, depending on the difficulty of the discrimination. This has been shown in a number of studies, which mostly used pitch discriminations (see Fitzgerald & Picton, 1984; Näätänen & Gaillard, 1983; Ritter, Vaughan, & Simson, 1983).

In memory-comparison tasks subjects search for stimuli designated as targets from among several nontargets (Sternberg, 1969). In two previous studies (Gaillard & Lawson, 1984; Gaillard & Van Arkel, in press) there were one, two, or four targets. Targets and nontargets were presented with equal probability, which resulted in a high (50%, 25%, or 12.5%) stimulus probability for each target and a low (6.25%) probability for each of the eight nontargets. A large N2 was found in the ERP to the nontarget, whereas this component was reduced or absent in the ERP to the target. The peak latency of N2 was increased the larger the size of the memory set (i.e., the number of targets). N2 peak latency was also larger for nontargets than for targets.

In contrast, the onset latency of *N2* was hardly affected by either set size or discriminability. However, both peak and onset latency were shorter in the odd-ball than in the memory-comparison task. In the present study the "difficult"-discrimination condition of the odd-ball task in the Lawson and Gaillard study is compared with the one-target condition of the memory-comparison task in the Gaillard and Van Arkel study. It was expected that the discrimination between two stimuli would be faster than the selection of one stimulus from among several stimuli, and that therefore the onset and peak latency of *N2* would be shorter.

In the third experimental condition of the present study subjects had to localize whether stimuli were presented to the left or to the right ear. It was expected that localization would enable a faster processing of the stimuli as compared to the other two conditions. Space localization is generally regarded as providing the largest separation between channels. Processing negativity reflecting the early processing in selective-attention tasks is also most prominent when attended and unattended stimuli differ in spatial location (Hillyard, Munte, & Neville, this volume; Näätänen, 1982).

So far, early negativities, similar to the processing negativity, have received little attention by ERP researchers using RT tasks. In most studies just reviewed no evidence was found for such a component. These early negativities may have remained unnoticed because they appear to be largely insensitive to stimulus probability. An enhanced amplitude in the ERP to the infrequent stimulus would have helped to detect these early components. Another related factor may have been the lack of an appropriate reference, comparable to the unattended channel in selective-attention tasks. In RT tasks an early negative wave was only observed by Ritter, Vaughan, & Simson (1983). The existence of this wave, called *NA*, was shown by subtracting ERPs obtained in a simple RT task from the ERPs obtained in the experimental conditions. In the present study there were two control conditions: a simple RT condition and a passive listening condition, in which the subject read an article and ignored the stimuli.

METHOD

The subjects were 9 male adults (mean age 24 years; range 19 to 28). They were seated in a sound-attenuated and electrically-shielded room. The EEG was recorded from three midline positions (Fz, Cz, Pz). Electrodes attached to the ear were linked for reference. Miniature electrodes were taped to the infra- and supraorbital ridge of the left eye for the monitoring of eye movements with the electrooculogram (EOG). An electrode attached just above the nose bridge served as ground. After amplification (time constant 6 sec; high frequency cut-off 30 Hz) EEG and EOG signals were digitized (one sample per 2 msec) online and stored on tape for further analysis.

Audio tapes were generated with the aid of a computer that programmed order and timing of the stimuli, which were nine consonant–vowel syllables ($k\epsilon$, $t\epsilon$, $p\epsilon$, etc.). The interstimulus interval was randomly either 2, 2.5, 3, 3.5, or 4 sec. The syllables were presented via headphones and the intensity of the vowel was 65 dB (rms SPL).

Subjects were run in three experimental conditions, the order of which was balanced across subjects: *Odd-ball* condition (ODD), with two stimuli, a frequent (93.75%) and an infrequent one (6.25%); *Phonetic* discrimination (PHON), with one frequent (50%) and eight infrequent (6.25%) stimuli; and *Localization* condition (LOC), with one frequent and eight infrequent stimuli occurring with the same probabilities as in the PHON condition. In the ODD and in the PHON conditions the stimuli were presented binaurally. In the LOC condition, however, stimuli were always presented to one ear and the infrequent stimuli always to the other ear. Ear of presentation of the frequent and infrequent stimuli was balanced across subjects. Thus, the ODD and the PHON condition differed in the number of infrequent stimuli (one vs. eight), although the probability of a given infrequent stimulus was kept constant. In the PHON condition stimuli had to be discriminated on the basis of their phonetic features, and in the LOC condition on the basis of their localization. In all three conditions the subjects were instructed to respond as quickly as possible by pressing one of two buttons; they responded with one hand to the frequent and with the other hand to the infrequent stimuli. The relationship between stimulus type (frequent/infrequent) and response side (left/right hand) was the same in each condition and was balanced across subjects. In the LOC condition the relationship between ear of presentation (left/right) and response side (left/right hand) was compatible.

ERPs also were obtained in two control conditions that were given after the experimental conditions: a simple RT condition, in which subjects responded to a sequence of the same syllable, and a reading condition, in which the subjects were instructed to ignore the stimuli and to read an interesting article. In both conditions the syllables were binaurally presented and they were given in separate sequences in which one syllable occurred 100% of the time.

Because the RTs and ERPs may be different for the different syllables, averages were computed for each syllable separately. The results are based on two syllables (kε,tε), which have similar ERPs and RTs. The syllable kε was the frequent stimulus and tε was one of the infrequent stimuli. Averaging of the ERPs started 120 msec before and ended 580 msec after stimulus onset. Trials containing incorrect responses, EEG or EOG artifacts were excluded from the analysis. Amplitudes and latencies of the ERP peaks were obtained through peak detection. In addition, the data were reduced to 35 data points by averaging over 10 successive samples, yielding averages over 20-msec periods. Two types of analysis of variance (ANOVA) were carried out on the RT, the latencies, the amplitudes, and the data points. The factors in the first ANOVA were conditions (PHON, ODD, LOC), probability (frequent-Kε, infrequent-tε) and derivation (Fz, Cz, Pz). The second ANOVA was done for each condition separately and had stimulus probability and derivation as factors. Unless otherwise stated, only effects are reported when their *p*-value is smaller than .01.

RESULTS

Figure 20.1 presents the averaged ERPs elicited by the frequent and by the infrequent stimulus, separately for the experimental conditions and for the derivations. A *P1–N1–P2* complex is present in the ERPs for all conditions as is a late positive wave (*P3*), in particular in the Pz derivation. A second negative wave (*N2*) is most prominent in the PHON and ODD conditions, in particular to the infrequent stimulus. Both *N2* and *P3* are more spread out in the PHON condition, which suggests a larger variability in the processing of the stimuli.

The ANOVAs carried out on the data of the control conditions yielded no statistical significant differences between kε and tε.

N1 latency was somewhat longer [$F(1,8) = 6.9; p < .03$] for the infrequent than for the frequent stimulus (126 and 122 msec, respectively). *N1* amplitude was larger in the LOC condition than in the other conditions [$F(2,16) = 8.4; p < .003$] and larger for the infrequent than for the frequent stimulus [$F(1,8) = 6.9; p < .005$]. As can be seen in Fig. 20.1, the latter effect is most prominent at Fz and Cz [$F(2,16) = 5.6; p < .01$]. In the ANOVAs per condition the probability effect did not reach significance for either the ODD or the PHON condition. ANOVAs carried out on the data points (i.e., averages over 20 msec periods) demonstrated that the probability effect in the LOC condition was significant for the three periods between 120 and 180 msec after stimulus onset.

N2 amplitude is larger for the infrequent than for the frequent stimulus, in particular for the ODD and PHON conditions [$F(2,16) = 13.9; p < .001$]. *N2* latency in the ERP to the infrequent stimulus was longer [$F(2,16) = 4.5; p < .03$] in the PHON than in the ODD condition (271 and 264 msec). *N2* latency

20. COMPARISONS ACROSS PARADIGMS 381

was longer for the infrequent than for the frequent stimulus. This effect was small (5 msec) in the ODD condition [$F(1,8) = 9.7; p < .014$] and large (12 msec) in the PHON condition [$F(1,8) = 29; p < .001$]. In the ANOVAs on the data points the probability effect in the ODD condition was significant ($p < .002$) for the periods 240–260 msec and 260–280 msec. In the PHON condition this effect also reached significance in the 240–260 msec period, but continued to be significant until 400 msec after stimulus onset (see Fig. 20.2). In the LOC condition an *N2* is only clearly present at Fz; in this condition no dif-

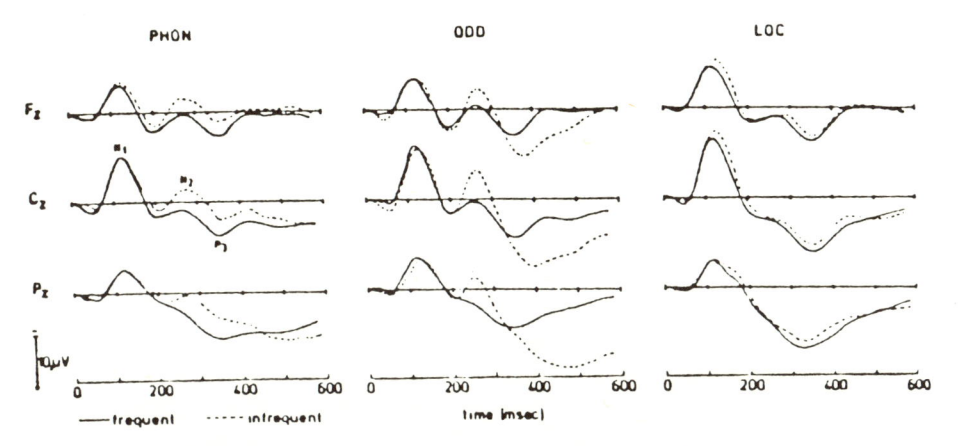

FIG. 20.1. ERPs elicited by the frequent and the infrequent stimuli, as a function of conditions and derivations.

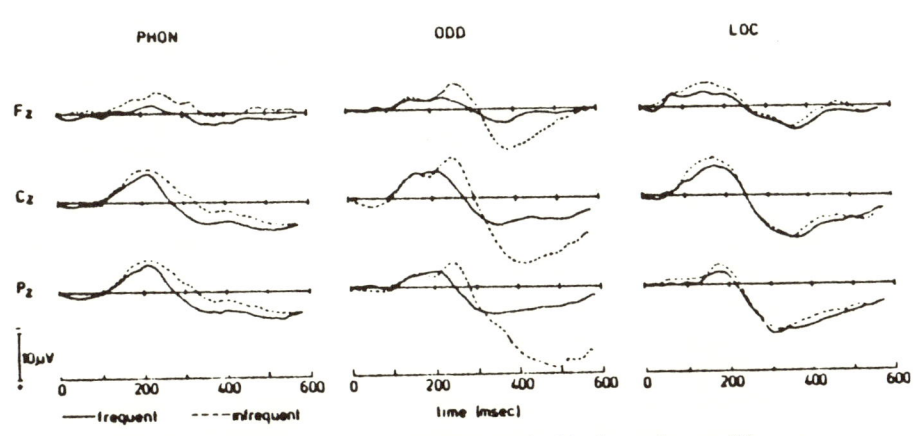

FIG. 20.2. Difference waveforms. ERPs obtained in the reading condition are subtracted from the ERPs obtained in the experimental conditions, separately for frequent and infrequent stimuli, and for the derivations.

ferences were found between frequent and infrequent stimuli for either *N2* latency, *N2* amplitude or for the data points in this time range.

The interaction between probability and conditions was significant for both the latency ($F(2,16) = 6.8; p < .007$) and the amplitude of *P3* ($F(2,16) = 15.8; p < .001$). The latency of *P3* was longer for the infrequent than for the frequent stimulus; this difference was hardly present in the LOC condition (3 msec) and was large in the PHON (19 msec) and ODD conditions (37 msec). There was no difference in *P3* amplitude between the frequent and infrequent stimuli in the LOC and PHON conditions, whereas there was a large difference in the ODD condition (9.1 µV).

Figure 20.2 presents the same data as in Fig. 20.1, but now the ERPs obtained in the reading condition are subtracted from the ERPs in the experimental conditions. In these difference waveforms an early negativity (*EN*) was observed that was most prominent in the LOC condition, in particular for the infrequent stimulus. This *EN* component started earlier in the LOC condition (60 msec) than in the other conditions (100 msec). In the difference waveform of the infrequent stimulus in the ODD-condition two negative peaks could be observed: an *EN* reaching a peak at the same latency (160 msec) as in the LOC condition and an *N2* component with a peak latency of 250 msec. The *EN* in the difference waveforms of the frequent stimulus in the ODD and PHON conditions reached its peak quite late (205 msec), whereas no clear *N2* peak could be observed. The peak latency of *EN* was hard to detect for the infrequent stimulus in the PHON-condition (also in the individual waveforms), because it did not reach a clear peak, but appeared to continue in an *N2* deflection, which also had no clear peak (see Fig. 20.2). It can also be seen in Fig. 20.2 that the scalp distribution of *EN* is fronto-central in the LOC condition, whereas it is parieto-central in the PHON condition.

To examine further the characteristics of the *N2* component difference waveforms were computed in which the ERP to the frequent stimulus was subtracted from the ERP to the infrequent stimulus. In these difference waveforms the onset latency of *N2* was about the same in the ODD as in the PHON condition (220 msec), whereas the peak latency was shorter in the ODD condition (260 msec) than in the PHON condition (300 msec). The scalp distribution of *N2* in the difference waveforms (infrequent minus frequent) was much more parietal than in the original ERPs. Although to a lesser extent, this also was the case in the difference waveforms, where the reading ERPs were subtracted (see Fig. 20.2).

In general, the RTs showed the same picture as *P3* latency. The effect of conditions [$F(2,16) = 46; p < .001$] and of probability ($F(1,8) = 59; p < .001$), as well as their interaction [$F(2,16) = 28; p < .001$]. In the LOC-condition the difference between the frequent (311 msec) and the infrequent stimulus (324 msec) was small, whereas this difference was large in the PHON condition (453 and 502 msec) and very large in the ODD condition (332 and 444 msec).

DISCUSSION

In their review Näätänen and Gaillard (1983) discuss two components in the *N2* time range. An early component, the mismatch negativity (*MMN*), is assumed to reflect an automatic mismatch process, which occurs after a physical stimulus change. The later component (*N2*) is assumed to reflect stimulus classification, a stage in the chain of information processing (see also Ritter, Vaughan, & Simson, 1983). *N2* is found for various types of discriminations involving tones, flashes, speech sounds, letters, or words. In contrast, the *MMN* is only found in stimulus configurations, where an automatic discrimination can be made on the basis of separate physical features (e.g., pitch, intensity, location, etc.). A second requirement for its occurrence is a homogeneous, repetitive stimulus background, which is assumed to be necessary for the maintenance of a neuronal representation. When the stimulus presented does not match with this representation, an automatic mismatch process occurs that is reflected in the *MMN* (see also Näätänen, this volume).

In the present study no differences were found in the LOC condition between the ERP to the frequent and that to the infrequent stimulus, except for the *EN* component superimposed on the descending limb of the *N1* component. The *N2* component may have been largely reduced, because localization enabled an early discrimination that made later processing hardly necessary. However, because the mismatch process is assumed to occur automatically, the *MMN* was expected to be elicited by the infrequent stimulus even when its processing was not necessary to perform the task. The 50% probability of the frequent stimulus may not have been sufficient to build up a neuronal representation. This interpretation is supported by a study of Ritter, Simson, and Vaughan (1983), in which subjects were presented with a sequence of words, which were presented once only. An N2 was obtained when the words had to be categorized; no N2 was found when the subjects were instructed not to process the stimulus content of the words and to respond with a simple RT to the words. However, when the sequence only consisted of two stimuli, a clear negative wave was observed in the infrequent ERP, although the subjects were again instructed not to process the stimulus content. These results support the idea that a homogeneous background is necessary to elicit the *MMN*. It appears that a *MMN* did not occur in the present experimental conditions, not even in the ODD condition, which is the most often used configuration to obtain the MMN. It appears that the phonetic difference between the frequent and infrequent stimulus was too complex and not salient enough to trigger an automatic mismatch process.

In the present study a large *N2* was elicited by the infrequent and a small one by the frequent stimulus in the ODD and PHON conditions. In the LOC condition *N2* was very small for both types of stimuli. Because the infrequent stimuli were presented with the same probability in the three conditions, these results suggest that there is no straightforward relationship between stimulus probability and the characteristics of *N2*. The results also are difficult to explain in terms of the probability of the stimulus class, because this probability is the same (50%/-50%) in the LOC as in the PHON condition.

One interpretation of the present results is that N2 reflects the process of stimulus classification, which occurs after stimulus encoding (see also Ritter, Vaughan, & Simson, 1983). Stimulus classification is assumed to be an important aspect of the discrimination process in the ODD and PHON conditions, whereas it plays a minor role in the LOC condition. In the latter condition the two stimulus classes can be separated on the basis of their location in the earlier encoding stage, which makes processing of the stimulus content unnecessary. In the other two conditions subjects will expect the frequent stimulus and compare the stimulus presented with that expectation. *N2* appears to reflect this comparison process, which is more elaborate and elicits more physiological activity in the case of a mismatch (i.e., with an infrequent or a nontarget stimulus). This explains why *N2* is larger and its latency longer for infrequent or nontarget stimuli as compared to frequent or target stimuli. Thus, stimulus probability seems only to affect *N2*, when this probability plays a role in the classification process.

This interpretation of N2 is supported by previous studies. In an odd-ball task stimulus discriminability was manipulated by varying the number of features, which separated the frequent from the infrequent stimulus (Lawson & Gaillard, 1981). N2 latency was shorter, in the case of three features ($k\epsilon$ vs. $b\epsilon$), than when there was only one feature ($k\epsilon$ vs. $t\epsilon$). The latter condition was the same as the present ODD condition, except that the interstimulus interval was constant and a selective RT rather than a choice RT was used. These differences may have resulted in the shorter onset and peak latency of N2 in the Lawson and Gaillard study as compared to the present ODD condition. In the Lawson and Gaillard study no systematic differences were found between a phonetic ($k\epsilon/t\epsilon$) and an acoustic (10 dB difference) discrimination. The effects of discriminability on *N2* have been found in several other studies for both pitch and intensity discriminations (see Fitzgerald & Picton, 1984; Näätänen & Gaillard, 1983, for reviews).

In memory-comparison tasks (Gaillard & Lawson, 1984; Gaillard & Van Arkel, in press) *N2* latency was longer and its amplitude was larger with increasing set size and for nontargets as compared to targets. Moreover, when the four items of the memory set share a common feature *N2* decreases in both latency and amplitude (Gaillard & Lawson, 1984). In the Gaillard and Van Arkel study it was shown that *N2* decreased in both latency and amplitude as a function of learning under consistent mapping (i.e., the memory set consisted of the same syllables over repeated sessions).

Similar findings were obtained by Ritter and coworkers for the visual modality. In an odd-ball task *N2* latency increased with the difficulty of a physical discrimination and was longer for semantic than for physical discriminations

(Ritter, Simson, & Vaughan, 1983). In a memory-comparison task two variables were varied at two levels (Ritter, Simson, Vaughan, & Macht, 1982). Stimulus encoding was made more difficult by degrading the characters used with a mask. The difficulty of the stimulus classification was manipulated by the type of distractor used. In one condition, subjects searched for four letters and in the other condition for any digit; the nontargets were letters in both conditions. N2 latency was affected by degradation and by the type of distractor (letters in letters versus digits in letters).

These results suggest that *N2* reflects stimulus classification and is associated with discrimination and memory comparison on a cognitive level, whereas the *MMN* reflects a mismatch process that operates at an unconscious and preattentive level. The MMN and N2 appear to be reflections of two related mechanisms that operate in a similar way but at different levels. Both components reflect a discrimination process involving a mismatch to an unexpected stimulus and both are most prominent to unexpected or rare stimuli. There are, however, also important differences between the two components:

1. The MMN only occurs when the infrequent stimulus differs on a "salient" physical dimension from a homogeneous background. In contrast, N2 can also be obtained when the infrequent stimulus belongs to a different stimulus class defined by instructions.

2. The mismatch process underlying the MMN is automatic and not under voluntary control. *N2* reflects controlled processing and the relevant stimulus class may be activated in working memory voluntarily and consciously.

3. In contrast to the N2, the MMN is not sensitive to attention instructions and can also be obtained under passive conditions.

The early negativity (EN) observed in the present study is regarded as a separate wave rather than as an enhancement of the *N1* component. The EN is superimposed on the *N1* component, in particular in the LOC condition. The N1 component in the reading condition has a shorter latency (118 msec), whereas EN has a much slower rise and decay time (compare Fig. 20.1 and Fig. 20.2) and reaches its peak latency (160 msec or later) well after the peak latency of N1 (125 msec in the experimental conditions).

Our interpretation of the EN is that it reflects stimulus encoding, which is assumed to be nearly absent in the reading condition and to be earlier and more elaborate in the LOC condition than in the other conditions. The larger EN to the infrequent stimulus may be caused by a bias toward the frequent stimulus adopted by the subject in the other conditions. This bias is also reflected in the faster RT to the frequent stimulus in the LOC condition. As was already mentioned with respect to *N2,* stimulus probability appears only to have an effect on a component when this probability influences the processing reflected in that component. This may also explain why the early negative wave (NA) found by

Ritter et al. (1982; Ritter, Simson, & Vaughan, 1983) was not affected by the probability of a stimulus or stimulus class. In Ritter et al. (1982), for example, the task variable (degradation) that affected *NA* was varied between blocks of trials. When degradation would have been changed from trial to trial with a biased probability, an enhanced *NA* might have been obtained to the less probable stimuli.

The EN found in the present study appears to be quite similar to the *NA* observed by Ritter and coworkers. The latency of NA increased when the stimuli were more complex (one of two symbols vs. four letter words; Ritter, Simson, & Vaughan, 1983) or when they were degraded with a mask (Ritter et al., 1982). In a third study (Simson, Ritter, & Vaughan, in press) subjects received a sequence, in which the same stimulus was presented 100% of the time; they were falsely instructed, however, that there would be infrequent stimulus changes, to which a different response had to be made. In this LIE condition a clear *NA* component was obtained, as compared to a simple RT condition, in which subjects were told that one stimulus would be presented 100% of the time. The interpretation of this result is that in the LIE condition subjects actively process each stimulus in the expectation that a stimulus change might occur.

The *NA* component observed by Ritter and coworkers and the *EN* in the present study appear to belong to a family of early negative waves, which reflect the encoding of perceptual characteristics. Processing negativity reflecting early "channel" selection in selective-attention tasks also belongs to this family. This interpretation of *EN* is supported by a recent study (Mäntysalo & Gaillard, unpublished data) using the same syllables in a selective-attention task, in which subjects counted an infrequent stimulus. *EN* was larger in a dichotic-listening situation as compared to monaural listening. The latter task was similar to the present PHON condition. The *EN* was, in turn, larger in the monaural condition than in a reading condition or in a condition in which all stimuli had to be counted, which made processing of the stimuli unnecessary as in a simple RT task. These results strongly suggest that *EN* is similar to the processing negativity and that the processing involved in selective listening may call upon the same mechanism as the localization of stimuli in a choice RT task.

The *EN*, and also *NA*, is larger in tasks involving a discrimination than in control conditions (reading, simple RT, counting all stimuli), because in the latter conditions the processing of the stimulus content is not necessary to perform the task. The peak latency of these early components is delayed when more time is needed for encoding more complex stimuli. In the studies of Ritter and coworkers both the onset and peak latency of *N2* were prolonged with degraded or more complex stimuli. These effects were, however, as large for the *NA* latency. This suggests that the variables affecting the process underlying *NA* had no additional effect on the process underlying *N2*, and also that the processing reflected in *N2* could only begin after the earlier processing had been completed. Also the present results provide evidence for the notion of an early versus late stage of processing (encoding and stimulus classification). In the LOC condition the localization of the stimuli made later processing hardly necessary; this resulted in a large *EN* and a small *N2*. In the PHON and ODD conditions the encoding process is the same, but the classification of the stimuli is different. The ERPs in both conditions are quite similar until the onset of *N2*. Also, previous experiments and studies by other investigators (e.g., Fitzgerald & Picton, 1984) generally show that the effects of discriminability and set size only start after the onset latency of *N2*. Thus, the ERPs were quite similar until the onset of *N2*—that is, the moment in time at which the ERPs to infrequent stimuli start to deviate from the ERPs to frequent stimuli, and nontarget ERPs from target ERPs. These results suggest that these task variables do not affect stimulus encoding, nor the moment that stimulus classification begins, but only the way in which the stimuli are classified after encoding.

In conclusion, the present results clearly show that it is indeed hazardous to make comparisons across paradigms, at least between different experiments. As was discussed earlier the differences between the results of two previous experiments were partially caused by the way the tasks were administered and did not reflect differences in the way information was processed in the two tasks. The direct comparison of the tasks in one study, however, facilitated the interpretation of the results and helped to clarify the psychological significance of two endogenous components of the ERP. The present study also illustrates that the ERP technique can be used to investigate the timing of processing events. Although the resolution of this timing is still rather inprecise (around 20 msec), it provides information which is hard, if not impossible, to obtain with other techniques.

ACKNOWLEDGMENTS

This work was partially supported by a fellowship from the Royal Society (UK) and by the MRC Applied Psychology Unit, Psychophysiology Section, Cambridge (UK), where the first author was on study leave. The authors wish to thank J. Th. Eernst and A. J. Krul for their technical and statistical assistance, and John Duncan, Risto Näätänen, Walter Ritter, and Annice Ryder for their helpful comments on earlier versions of this chapter.

REFERENCES

Donchin, E., Ritter, W., & McCallum, W. C. (1978). Cognitive psychophysiology: The endogenous components of the ERP. In E. Callaway, P. Tueting, & S. H. Koslow (Eds.), *Event-related brain potentials in man* (pp. 349–411). New York: Academic.

Fitzgerald, P. G., & Picton, T. W. (1984). Event-related potentials recorded during the discrimination of improbable stimuli. *Biological Psychology, 17,* 241–276.

Gaillard, A. W. K., & Lawson, E. A. (1984). Evoked potentials to consonant–vowel syllables in a memory scanning task. In R. Karrer, J. Cohen, & P. Tueting (Eds.), Brain and information: Event-related potentials. *Annals of the New York Academy of Sciences, 425,* 204–209.

Gaillard, A. W. K., & Ritter, W. (Eds.) (1983). *Tutorials in ERP research: Endogenous components.* Amsterdam: North-Holland.

Gaillard, A. W. K., & Van Arkel, A. E. (in press). Learning effects on ERPs in a memory comparison task. *Electroencephalography and Clinical Neurophysiology* (Supplement).

Lawson, E. A., & Gaillard, A. W. K. (1981). Mismatch negativity in a phonetic discrimination task. *Biological Psychology, 13,* 281–288.

Mulder, G., Gloerich, A. B. M., Brookhuis, K., Van Dellen, H. J., & Mulder, L. J. M. (1984). Stage analysis of the reaction process using brain-evoked potentials and reaction time. *Psychological Research, 46,* 15–32.

Näätänen, R. (1982). Processing negativity: An evoked-potential reflection of selective attention. *Psychological Bulletin, 92,* 605–640.

Näätänen, R., & Gaillard, A. W. K. (1983). The orienting reflex and the N2 deflection of the event-related potential (ERP). In A. W. K. Gaillard & W. Ritter (Eds.), *Tutorials in ERP research: Endogenous components* (pp. 119–141). Amsterdam: North-Holland.

Ritter, W., Simson, R., & Vaughan, H. G., Jr. (1983). Event-related potential correlates to two stages of information processing in physical and semantic discrimination tasks. *Psychophysiology, 20,* 168–179.

Ritter, W., Simson, R., Vaughan, H. G., Jr., & Macht, M. (1982). Manipulation of event-related potentials manifestations of information processing stages. *Science, 218,* 909–911.

Ritter, W., Vaughan, H. G., Jr., & Simson, R. (1983). On relating event-related potential components to stages of information processing. In A. W. K. Gaillard & W. Ritter (Eds.), *Tutorials in ERP research: Endogenous components.* (pp. 143–158). Amsterdam: North-Holland.

Simson, R., Ritter, W., & Vaughan, H. G., Jr. (in press). Effects of expectation on negative potentials during visual processing. *Electroencephalography and Clinical Neurophysiology.*

Sternberg, S. (1969). The discovery of processing stages: An extension of Donders' method. In W. G. Koster (Ed.), *Attention and performance II* (pp. 276–315). Amsterdam: North-Holland.

VI ATTENTION AND MOTOR CONTROL

21 Information Encapsulation and Automaticity: Evidence from the Visual Control of Finely Timed Actions

Peter McLeod
Oxford University

Carmel McLaughlin
Ian Nimmo-Smith
MRC Applied Psychology Unit, Cambridge, England

ABSTRACT

Experiment 1 suggests that people compute the time for an approaching object to arrive with an informationally encapsulated processor—that is, one that operates directly on its input, in this case the retinal array, without using evidence from other sources of knowledge. The computation is shown in Experiment 2 to have an extremely low temporal variation: It has a standard deviation of 5 msec. We suggest that the low variability arises precisely because the process generating it *is* informationally encapsulated. The process performs a specific, autonomous calculation and hence takes a fixed time. A process that integrates a range of sources of information would produce relatively greater variability.

This suggestion links observed reduction in variability after prolonged practice to theoretical proposals that changes with practice are caused by gradual specialization of the processes involved. We further suggest that theorists who propose a shift from general to specific resources to account for changes of attentional demand as a result of practice could strengthen this interpretation by demonstrating accompanying reduction in the temporal variability of the responses emerging from these processes.

INTRODUCTION

Much of our lives is spent producing finely timed actions that are geared to approaching objects. We either wish to make an action in time to avoid a collision, or, as when we pick up an object, we time the action in order to ensure a precise collision. This chapter explores the visual cues used to time actions based on relative motion between ourselves and approaching objects and examines the kind of perceptual–motor processing involved. The experiments are consistent with Lee's (1980) contention that the estimate of time to contact required by such actions is obtained from a specific computation based on the expanding retinal array associated with an approaching object, and does not require interaction of visual input with the knowledge about the world that is required to compute distances and velocities. We found that the temporal variability of the time-to-contact computation is extremely low: a standard deviation of 5 msec. We suggest that such remarkably low variability comes about *because* the computation is performed by a specific, dedicated processor, uninfluenced by other cognitive activities. A computation influenced by a range of cognitive inputs will inevitably lead to trial to trial variability in the time taken to perform it because the process will concatenate the variability of the inputs. In contrast, a fixed computation on a specific input, uninfluenced by other sources of information, might be expected to produce output with much greater temporal regularity.

Following Fodor (1983) we call processes that are uninfluenced by general cognitive resources informationally encapsulated. Fodor proposes that this lack of external influence is a defining characteristic of one of the two sorts of computational process that he believes are represented in the cognitive system. Although Fodor does not make this claim, we suggest that an empirical distinguishing characteristic of an informationally encapsulated process will be the low temporal variability of its output.

In the first part of the chapter we describe the observations that lead us to believe that the production of actions based on time to contact estimation is informationally encapsulated, and demonstrate that these estimates have a very low temporal variability. Then we show that the idea that information encapsulation leads to low temporal variability can be used to tie up a common observation and a popular idea about how information processing changes following extensive practice. The observation is that performance becomes much less variable with practice. The idea, represented in a variety of forms in different theories, is that practice leads to the development of specific devices or programs for carrying out actions. If such devices are informationally encapsulated—that is, if they are capable of producing appropriate output on the basis of a specific input only, needing no interaction with general-purpose cognitive facilities—then it follows from the argument in the first paragraph that practice will lead to reduction in variability.

We then propose that this idea could be used to develop a converging line of attack on the distinction proposed in attention theory by Schneider and Shiffrin (1977), and many others, between automatic and attention-demanding processes. Automatic processes develop after extensive practice with fixed S–R relationships and they are hypothesized to perform specific operations independent of any general cognitive resource. In contrast, nonautomatic processes must be used early in practice to link S and R because no specific device for forming the link exists; they will continue to be used if the S-R links are not consistent and they use general-purpose computational facilities. Clearly automatic processes fit the description of informationally encapsulated processes. Most authors using the automatic/nonautomatic distinction have concentrated on distinguishing between the two modes of control on the basis of their different attentional demands. We suggest that an alternative way of plotting the development of automaticity would be by demonstrating the gradual reduction of variability of the output of processes that were hypothesized to be under automatic control.

Time to Contact from the Visual Array

Central to the argument of this chapter is the idea that the timing information required to link actions to approaching objects is computed by a specialized processor without recourse to any general computational resources. Lee (1980) has demonstrated how, in principle, this could be done. As an object approaches an observer its image on the retina expands. Lee has shown that, if the relative velocity of object and observer remain constant, the time at which they will collide (the time to contact) is given by the ratio of the size of the retinal image to the rate at which the image is expanding.[1] The crucial point about the observation is that although time to contact *is* available from the expanding optic array in isolation, many other quantities, such as the distance or the velocity of the object, are not. Objects at different distances, moving at different velocities, can give rise to the same retinal array. These ambiguities can only be resolved by the application of knowledge about the visual world.

For many actions that people wish to make relative to approaching objects, such as avoiding collisions or executing an action like closing the hand at the moment of collision, time to contact information is adequate. In the first case an action is required before contact time; in the second an action must be produced at contact time, or, as in the case of an act like catching a ball, at a specific time before contact (Alderson, Sully, & Sully, 1974). In each case time to contact provides the necessary information for performing the task, irrespective of the relative velocity of responder and object or their distance apart. Time to contact information could come from a processor that performs a specific operation on the optic array and is uninfluenced by other computations. Thus, the computation of time to contact is potentially informationally encapsulated—it can be calculated from raw stimulus information without top-down influences. Of course, if the observer *does* wish to know the velocity of the approaching object, or when it will arrive at some point in space other than him- or herself, this will require a

---

[1]In our experiments, in which the "object" is a ball accelerating under gravity, the relative velocity of observer and ball is not constant as required by the analysis in Lee (1980). However, Lee, Young, Reddish, Lough, and Clayton (1983) have demonstrated that in such situations the observer appears to base actions on successive estimates of the ball's velocity, each computed by taking the ratios of the instantaneous image size and velocity.

different sort of computation involving knowledge and inference about the world to disambiguate the various possible interpretations of the retinal image.

EXPERIMENT 1A

If actions linked to the approach of objects are controlled by a computation of the ratio of retinal image size and retinal image velocity, then the straightforward prediction can be made that such actions should be performed as accurately with one eye as with two, because the only information required is available monocularily. (This is not strictly true because with two eyes the observer has two samples of the information available and could thus, in theory, do better than with either sample in isolation. We come to this in the results.) The first experiment, therefore, sets up a simple test of Lee's hypothesis by requiring subjects to execute an action based on the time of arrival of an approaching object, and compares their accuracy when they perform the test with both eyes open and with only one eye open. If time to contact is taken directly off the retinal array the absence of binocular cues should not harm performance. On the other hand, if timing is controlled by, for example, estimates of velocity and distance, binocular cues would presumably aid performance.

Subjects

These were nine members of the staff and subject panel of the Applied Psychology Unit (APU), Cambridge, aged 22 to 66 years. There were six males and three females.

Method

Squash balls (firm black rubber balls with a diameter of 4.2 cm) were dropped from a point 6.7 m above the ground toward the subject. The balls were dropped down a fixed plastic tube 1 m in length to ensure that they fell on the same spatial trajectory on each trial. The subject held the handle of a rectangular metal bat 30.5 cm long, 16.2 cm wide, and .25 cm thick. With this the subject made a horizontal swing[2] at the ball as it dropped past, keeping the bat blade (i.e., the 16.2 cm face) vertical. The task was to hit the ball into a square target with 2 m sides 1.8 m in front of the subject. Balls that hit the ground before reaching the target or that failed to reach the target were counted as misses. In other words the

---

[2]Subjects were free to swing the bat at any height they liked, provided they kept the bat horizontal. Swinging below eye height introduces a delay between the time when the ball reaches the eye (which would be the time given by the time-to-contact computation) and the time when the ball reached the bat. It is conceivable that more successful hitters were better able to use this delay, by adjusting swing height, to compensate for errors caused by, for example, treating the velocity of the ball as constant when in reality it was accelerating.

subject was required to impart considerable horizontal momentum to the ball as it passed.

The experimental situation effectively eliminated spatial uncertainty because the ball always fell on the same trajectory. The subject's problem was a relatively pure temporal one—to intercept the flight path at the correct time to achieve a coincidence of bat and ball. The temporal problem facing the subject can be estimated from the following considerations: The bat face must reach the path of the ball after the ball passes the top of the bat but before it passes the bottom of the bat. The bat must, therefore, reach this position during a time window given by the length of time it takes the ball to fall past the bat. This time is given roughly[3] by:

$$\text{time window} = \frac{\text{width of bat} + \text{diameter of ball}}{\text{velocity of ball}}.$$

A crucial point that follows from this equation is that by varying the width of the bat the experimenter can vary the width of the time window available to the subject while keeping other parameters, such as flight time and ball velocity, constant.

Procedure

Subjects practiced briefly with bats of varying widths (16.2 cm, 10.1 cm, 5.1 cm, or 2.6 cm) until they found one with which they were achieving approximately 50% hits. They then tried to hit a series of 10 balls dropped at intervals of about 5 to 10 secs with an audible warning from the experimenter just before each one was dropped. They repeated this sequence three times, once with both eyes open, once with the left eye occluded, and once with the right eye occluded. The first 30 swings (i.e., three blocks of 10) were treated as practice. The subject then proceeded to produce nine further runs of 10 swings, three each in the three viewing conditions (binocular, monocular [right], monocular [left]). The percentage of successful swings in each of the three conditions over the 90 drops was recorded. The ordering of blocks of 10 swings across viewing conditions was randomized across subjects.

---

[3]The inclusion of the full diameter of the ball in this calculation will lead to an overestimate of the time window available to the subject. However, if the ball diameter is excluded from the calculation, this implies that only swings that reach the flight path of the ball while the center of the ball is between the upper and lower extremities of the bat will count as hits. This is unlikely. An uncertain proportion of swings that make contact with the ball either below or above its center will probably reach the target and be designated "hits." The inclusion of the full diameter is a conservative measure to ensure that we do not overestimate the fineness of the subject's timing. Because the ball width remains constant, any inaccuracy becomes proportionately smaller with the larger bat widths.

Results

Table 21.1 shows the between-subject median percentage of hits with the right eye only [$P(R)$], the left eye only [$P(L)$], and with binocular viewing [$P(B)$]. It can be seen that there is a small improvement of binocular vision over monocular. Does this mean that the subject can use binocular cues? The problem is that even if the subject used only monocular cues, binocular viewing would yield two estimates of arrival time and some combination of these would yield a better estimate than either alone. It is uncertain what principle the visual system might use for evidence combination, but a possible procedure would be to treat the two eyes as producing independent samples of the time to contact and combine them, weighting each by the inverse of its variance—that is, to combine the two

TABLE 21.1
Hit Probabilities under Conditions
of Temporal Uncertainty with Left, Right,
or Both Eyes Open[a]

$P(L)$	$P(R)$	$P(B)$	Prediction of $P(B)$ from Independence Model
.53	.5	.57	.68

[a]The independence model predicts $P(B)$ by combining the estimates obtained from the two eyes in isolation.

estimates, giving greater weight to the estimate coming from the more accurate eye (see Appendix). Such a procedure was performed for each individual, giving an estimate of the probability of a hit with binocular viewing that a subject could achieve by combining the estimates provided by each eye. The intersubject median value of this estimated $P(B)$ is shown in Table 21.1. This is better than subjects actually achieved with two eyes, although a Wilcoxon matched-pairs comparison of the individual values of $P(B)$ actual and $P(B)$ estimated from $P(R)$ and $P(L)$ shows no significant difference between them ($N = 9$, $T = 11$, $p > .15$).

A more conservative way of combining evidence might be to see whether the probability of a hit with both eyes is any better than the probability of a hit with the better of the subject's individual eyes. A Wilcoxon test across subjects shows that $P(B)$ is not significantly better than the better of $P(R)$ and $P(L)$ ($N = 9$, $T = 17.5$, $p > .5$).

Thus, on the results of this experiment there are no grounds for assuming that binocular cues are used in estimating time to contact. The data are consistent with the idea that this value is obtained by a direct computation on the retinal array.

EXPERIMENT 1B

It is possible that binocular cues *were* being used in Experiment 1A but that the procedure was insufficiently sensitive to pick them up. Experiment 1B is a control, the result of which makes such a conclusion unlikely. The temporal uncertainty of Experiment 1A was converted into spatial uncertainty.

The squash ball was thrown by an experimenter toward a square target area 1.2 m wide and 1.2 m high to one side of the subject. The subject had a square bat with 5 cm sides with which he or she tried to intercept the ball. There was no requirement to do anything other than intercept it. Thus, there was little temporal uncertainty. All the subject had to do was to get the bat into the path of the ball before it arrived. Thus, time to contact information was of little importance. However, there was considerable spatial uncertainty. The subject must compute on which of a wide range of possible trajectories the ball was travelling.

Subjects

The subjects were 10 members of the APU staff and subject panel, male and female, aged between 20 years and 42 years.

Procedure

The procedure was the same as for Experiment 1A except that the ball was projected horizontally toward the subject rather than being dropped toward him or her. As before the subject had 10 practice attempted interceptions with bin-

TABLE 21.2
Hit Probabilities under Conditions
of Spatial Uncertainty with Left, Right,
or Both Eyes Open[a]

P(L)	P(R)	P(B)	Prediction of P(B) from Independence Model
.43	.45	.77	.60

[a]The independence model predicts $P(B)$ which could be obtained by combining the estimates obtained from the two eyes in isolation.

ocular viewing, right eye only and left eye only, followed by nine blocks of 10 attempted interceptions spread across the three viewing conditions.

Results

The data are shown in Table 21.2. They are the between-subject median hit rate with right eye only [$P(R)$], with left eye only [$P(L)$], and with both eyes [$P(B)$]. It can be seen that the probability of hitting the ball with binocular viewing is now substantially better than with only one eye. Following the same procedure used in Experiment 1A an estimate of $P(B)$ based on combining the evidence from the left and right eyes was made. The median between-subject value of this estimate is shown in Table 21.2. A Wilcoxon test on the individual values of $P(B)$ actual and $P(B)$ estimated shows that subjects perform reliably better ($p < .02$) with two eyes than they could by combining monocular cues. Following the same procedure as in Experiment 1A the subjects' individual $P(B)$s were compared with the better of their two monocular hit probabilities. Every subject did better with both eyes than with the better of the two single eyes.

The observer clearly makes use of binocular cues in judging the spatial trajectory of the ball as it approaches. What these cues might be is not the concern of this chapter, although a convincing account of why computation of the direction of the ball's trajectory would benefit from binocular cues is given by Regan, Beverley, and Cynader (1979). The crucial point for us is that the experimental technique used in Experiment 1A is clearly capable of picking up the use of binocular cues. Therefore, the failure to find them during the temporal judgments of Experiment 1A suggests that they were not being used.

EXPERIMENT 2

Whatever mechanism is computing the time of arrival of the ball in Experiment 1A presumably produces a distribution of estimates on different trials that is centered on the real time of arrival but has a certain trial-to-trial variability. Success or failure on any given trial will be determined by whether the discrepancy between the computed and the real time of arrival is less than or greater than the time window that the subject's bat size allows for a hit. The degree of timing accuracy that the individual can achieve overall across a range of trials will be determined by the shape of this distribution of estimates. The narrower it is, the more successful the subject will be. Experiment 2 is a development of the procedure used in Experiment 1A designed to measure the shape of the distribution of time-to-contact estimates directly. Each subject performs the ball-hitting task of Experiment 1A with a range of bat sizes (always with binocular vision). By converting bat size to time window and plotting hit probability against time window one can get an estimate of the shape of the temporal output variability of the process computing time to contact. In fact, it will be a conservative estimate of the variability of the process because there will also be some variance associated with the motor response of hitting the ball. It will at least give an upper bound for the variability of the temporal computation.

This chapter argues that time to contact is computed by an informationally encapsulated processor. We also suggest that the temporal output variability of computations from encapsulated processes will be markedly less than that of processes resulting from more general computations. So, in Experiment 2, as well as looking at the variability of estimates of time of arrival as demonstrated in the hitting experiment, we look at the variability of the output of a comparable process for which there is no reason to believe that an encapsulated processor might exist. A condition felt to meet this criterion required the subject to watch the flight of the ball and to press a button when it passed a point in space, the roof of a building clearly visible against the sky behind the flight path of the ball. It was about 1.6 m above and 1.6 m in front of the observer.

In most respects the requirements of this task are similar to but, if anything, easier than the ball hitting. The crucial respect in which the processes leading to these two actions might differ is that hitting the ball requires the computing of the time of arrival of an object *at* the observer, whereas the visual coincidence judgment requires the computing of time of arrival at a point other than the observer. Time of arrival at the observer can be computed directly from the retinal image. For time to arrive at an arbitrary position on the retinal array no simple computation will do. The image of the ball will expand as it approaches the line of sight between observer and building but there is no simple function involving properties of this expanding array that will predict when the ball will reach the line of sight. Either a calculation involving the position and velocity of the ball is required (both of these properties drop out of the equation if, and only if, time of arrival at the observer is being calculated) or, more likely, the brain will simply try to register the moment of coincidence as the ball reaches the top of the building. Visual coincidence, the coming into line of two objects in the outside world, occurs continuously and is generally of no interest to the observer. There is no reason to believe that any special-purpose computing facilities would exist to register such events. On the other hand, there is every reason to believe that a special processor will have developed for calculating time to contact because this is a piece of information of the utmost significance to the individual. Indeed, it is difficult to think of any single piece of visual information with greater survival value than the time when an approaching object will reach the observer.

Subjects

These were nine members of the APU staff or subject panel, seven male and two female, aged 24 to 66 years. Two subjects had already performed in Experiment 1A.

Method

The experiment consisted of two parts, ball hitting and visual-coincidence judgment. The ball hitting followed the design of Experiment 1A. The subject first had 20 swings with a 16.2 cm bat, followed by 10 swings each with a 10.1 cm and a 5.1 cm bat. Following this practice session the subject had nine blocks of 10 swings, three blocks with each bat width. The order of swinging with the three widths was varied between subjects. The data used for analysis are the probabilities of scoring a hit with each bat width over the last nine blocks.

Filming of the ball's trajectory showed that the speed of the ball at the bat was 10 m/sec. Given this speed, the bat widths correspond to time windows of ± 10 msec, ± 7 msec, and ± 4.5 msec.

For the visual-concidence judgment the subject watched the ball drop as in the hitting experiment, but, instead of hitting it, the subject pressed a button as it passed a clearly visually defined point in space. The balls were dropped at intervals of about 5 sec with an auditory warning before each one. The ball triggered a photocell as it fell, starting a timer that was stopped when the subject pressed the button. The assumption is that the real flight time is a constant and the range of times produced on the timer gives the variability of the subject's estimates of this time. The subject had 20 practice trials followed by three blocks of 20 trials with a short pause between blocks.

Procedure

Four of the subjects performed the visual-coincidence judgment first and five performed the ball hitting first.

Results

The probability of a time-to-contact estimate falling within a given time window around the correct value (i.e., an estimate that would have produced a hit with the center of the bat) is given by the percentage of hits with a bat width corresponding to that time window. To obtain a comparable figure from the visual-coincidence judgment a mean estimate was computed for each individual subject by averaging all of their estimates. Then, the percentage of estimates falling within ± t msec of that value was computed, separately for each subject, using their own average as the "real" coincidence time. The two distributions are shown in Fig. 21.1.

The group medians are shown as well as the range of scores achieved by the best and worst subjects. It is immediately obvious that the two distributions are quite different. Time to arrive at the observer is computed with astonishing accuracy. Sixty-six percent of the estimates fall within ± 5 msec of the correct value and 88% within ± 10 msec. Two of the subjects can achieve 100% hits with a bat that gives a time window of ± 10 msec. Estimates of time to arrive at a point in space other than the observer are much more variable; ± 30 msec is required to catch 66% of the estimates, and nearly ± 60 msec to catch 88%. The time-to-contact estimation is about six times less variable than the visual-coincidence judgments. Another indication of how different the processes generating these two estimates are is the lack of overlap between the individual scores in the two conditions. The worst subject at producing time-to-contact estimates is about half as variable as the best person at producing visual-coincidence judgments.

We are assuming that the difference between the variability of the estimates of time of arrival produced by the two conditions of this experiment are caused by the difference in the underlying process generating the responses—a special-

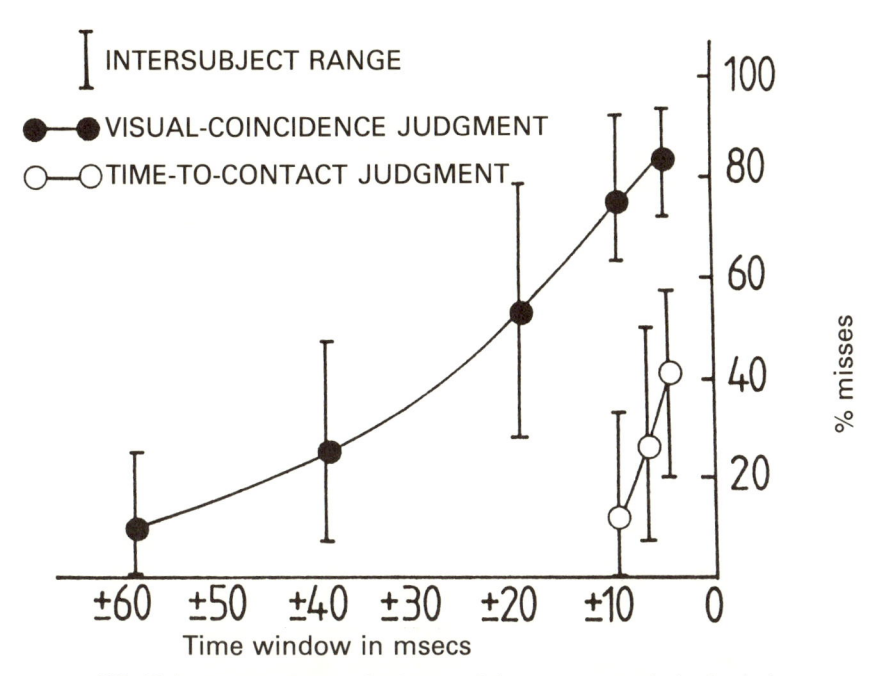

21. INFORMATION ENCAPSULATION AND AUTOMATICITY 401

FIG. 21.1. The distribution of estimates of time to contact and visual coincidence. The data are the intersubject medians. The intersubject range is shown.

purpose dedicated processor for computing time of arrival at the observer, and a general-purpose processor for computing time of arrival at an arbitrary point in space. It is possible that procedural differences in the experiment are the real underlying cause. The main difference between the two conditions is that feedback is available when hitting the ball but not when judging visual coincidence. However, the feedback available in the ball-hitting condition is not as good as it might appear from reading a description of the experiment. Although feedback is available to the subject following a hit, it is generally impossible for subject or experimenter to tell whether a miss was too early or too late. Thus, feedback will tell whether the observer is right or wrong, but will be of no assistance in showing how to change following an error.

It is possible that there is some variability in the real flight time of the ball and this needs to be taken into account in assessing the variability of the subjects' estimates of visual coincidence. The ball dropping was repeated with the subject's microswitch on the ground in the flight path of the ball with a thin metal plate over the switch. Thus the arrival of the ball physically triggered the microswitch. Under these conditions over 80% of the flight times fell within ± 5 msec of the median time. Although there is some variability in flight time, it is clearly too small to account for the differences found between the two sets of temporal estimates generated in this experiment.

DISCUSSION

Lee has shown that the information in the expanding retinal array is sufficient to compute a quantity, time to contact of an approaching object, without reference to other knowledge sources. Although the present experiment is not a direct test of Lee's hypothesis, the fact that binocular cues do not help in making judgments about time to contact is consistent with the claim that people can use the retinal-array computation rather than necessarily having to estimate the distance and velocity of the approaching object and perform some computation based on these values to control their action. We have also shown that the temporal variability of the time to contact estimates is very low, and much lower than that achieved with a visual estimate for which no simple retinal array calculation exists. The hypothesis we are going to propose is that there is a direct link between these two observations. The reason *why* the temporal variability of the estimtes is so low is precisely because they emerge from a single autonomous processor that performs one fixed and invariant calculation without having to integrate input from other sources. The corollary of this is that when a process is influenced by a range of inputs it will inevitably produce a temporally variable output because the values and timing of the various inputs will vary from trial to trial.

We apply the hypothesis that low variability is the behavioral consequence that accompanies the process of informational encapsulation to two related areas of theorizing in information processing. We first use the hypothesis to try and tie together the common observation that practice leads to reduced variability with various theoretical proposals about the changes in information processing that occur with practice. Second, we suggest that the hypothesis generates a plausible line of evidence that could be used to try to understand the changes in attentional demand that occur as a task becomes "automatic."

Variability, Practice, and Specific Processors

Just how low the variability of the time-to-contact estimates is can be gathered by comparison with estimates of the temporal variability of other processes. Standard deviations of 100 msec or more are common in simple laboratory tasks involving manual reaction to visual stimuli. However, in some circumstances variability can be much lower. The chief distinguishing characteristics of processes that produce output with a very low temporal variability seem to be extensive practice and/or a task that could be reasonably considered as being driven by a specific process (such as a timer) or generated by the running off of a specific motor program. Hopkins and Kristofferson (1980) showed that after 80,000 trials one subject could produce a tap 461 msec after a warning signal with a standard deviation of 7 msec. Their subjects started the task with a standard deviation of around 60 msec. Perhaps 80,000 trials is an indication of the length of time required to isolate a specific timer from any external influences. Tyldesley and Whiting (1975) claim that expert table-tennis players can produce forehand drives with a temporal consistency of ± 4 msec. Presumably such an action is driven by a specific motor program that, when triggered, runs off without interaction with other sources. A motor program is a perfect example of an informationally encapsulated device. By definition it is not influenced by any external sources. Once triggered it runs off in a deterministic, ballistic fashion. These figures presumably demonstrate the intrinsic variability that remains when an informationally encapsulated response is triggered. They are similar to the figures we obtained in Experiment 2. Thus, it appears that a temporal standard deviation of ± 5 msec, which our subjects achieved, although remarkable, is not unique. It can be achieved in situations in which practice has allowed a specific processor or program to develop to control the action.

Most theorizing about changes with practice has concentrated on trying to model the observed improvement in mean speed, and ignored changes in variability (e.g., Crossman, 1959; Kolers, 1975; Newell & Rosenbloom, 1981; Seibel, 1973). However, there are some theoretical proposals that would fit the ideas advanced here. Crossman (1959) proposed that when initially presented with a task a large number of potential information-processing operations can be used by the subject. The subject gradually discovers by trial and error which are inefficient, because they lead to slow responses, and rejects them. Thus the pool of possible mechanisms for linking S to R becomes narrowed down to the fastest. Crossman was interested in the predictions this sort of model made for the rate of improvement of a skill with practice. However, it also predicts a steady decrease in variability with practice via the gradual setting up of a fixed computational route from input to output.

In a rather different context Broadbent (1977) has proposed a mechanism that could lead to the prediction of reduced variability via informational encapsulation that we are suggesting. Broadbent proposes a two-level system for the control of actions, with a passive lower level that converts input to output by fixed computations and an active higher level that is capable of changing the parameters of the lower-level device if the lower level fails to respond appropriately to input. Learning is the gradual adjustment of the lower-level parameters to appropriate values. During the learning phase the lower level will produce temporally variable output as a range of parameters for its computations are tried. Once optimum values are achieved the lower level will be effectively informationally encapsulated because there will be no further interaction from the higher level. Its operations will be fixed and its output will show minimal temporal variability. An idea proposed by Rabbitt (1981) would also explain reduction in variability with practice. Rabbitt suggests that in reaction-time tasks practice leads to more subtle control of movements on a speed-error trade-off function. Early, the subject makes unnecessarily large adjustments to his or her response criteria following errors but gradually learns to make much finer adjustments. Thus, the overall variability of RTs will be reduced by practice.

Both these ideas fit into the framework presented here. They suggest that the effect of practice is to reduce the need for interaction between general high-level resources and low-level specific resources as the low level gradually acquires the correct parameters for coping with its task. This is the process we are referring to as information encapsulation. We suggest that an observable change in performance that would accompany this hypothesized change in the organization of information processing is a reduction in temporal-output variability of the process.

Attention, Automaticity, and Information Encapsulation

The relationship proposed between information encapsulation and temporal variability might provide a means of understanding the changes in information processing that accompany the development of automaticity. The concept of automaticity as a description, or, more optimistically, as an explanation of task performance, is widespread; examples can be found in areas as diverse as dual task performance, visual search, reading, and motor control.

Classic examples in dual task performance are Solomons and Stein (1896) and Bryan and Harter (1899). They used the concept of the automaticity of one of the tasks to explain why people could read and listen simultaneously, or converse while typing telegraphic messages, respectively. More recently Bahrick and Shelley (1958) used the increasing ability to perform two tasks simultaneously as an index of the degree of automaticity the tasks had achieved. Lucas and Bub (1981) have suggested that the demonstration by Hirst, Spelke, Reaves, Caharack, and Neisser (1980) that people could learn to perform semantic operations on simultaneous visual and auditory inputs should be seen in terms of the automaticity of the tasks. The common point about all these observations is that a gradual reduction of interference between simultaneously performed tasks is found after extensive practice, and that authors wish to attribute this difference to a shift in information processing from a form that requires attention to one that does not. This latter form is called automatic. The same concept of automaticity has been used in reading (Laberge & Samuels, 1974) and ubiquitously in motor skills to describe the gradual decrease in attentional demand of the task with practice. The same account has been used by Schneider and Shiffrin (1977; Shiffrin & Schneider, 1977) to describe the changes in information processing that take place with practice in visual search. They suggest that after extensive practice with a constant S–R relationship the processing required to produce the correct response when the stimulus is presented gradually changes from a general computational resource, which can be used for mapping any stimulus onto any response, to a specific resource that can only be used for mapping that particular stimulus onto its appropriate response.

The constructs from these different areas all fit the idea of gradual information encapsulation. Early in practice with an unknown task, a wide range of general computational resources are brought to bear. However, as the task becomes learned, the process of mapping stimulus to response is gradually taken over by more and more specific processes that need no input from general resources. In all these areas the chief concern of the authors has been to try to model and measure the changes in demand for attention that accompany changes in performance. If we are right that the underlying change is one of information encapsulation, and we are also correct in assuming from our own experiments that information encapsulation of a process leads to a reduction in the temporal variability of its output, then we have a new line of attack on understanding the changes involved. We would predict that at least some of the changes described as the development of automaticity should be accompanied by a reduction in temporal variability. For those that are, we can be encouraged to believe that their automaticity is information encapsulation.

APPENDIX

The probability of a hit, P, is related to the estimated time to contact, T, by the formula:

$$P = Prob(T - e \leq To \leq T + e)$$

where To is the actual time to contact and e represents the maximum time error that will still result in a hit. If T is normally distributed with mean To and standard deviation σ, then σ can be estimated by inverting the preceding formula:

$$\hat{\sigma} = \frac{2}{e}\Theta^{-1}\left(\frac{1-P}{2}\right).$$

From $P(L)$ and $P(R)$ we obtain estimates for the variances $\hat{\sigma}^2(L)$ and $\hat{\sigma}^2(R)$. If $T(L)$ and $T(R)$ are statistically independent with common mean To and variance $\sigma^2(L)$ and $\sigma^2(R)$, then the combined estimate $T(B) = [\sigma^{-2}(L)T(L) + \sigma^{-2}(R)T(R)]/[\sigma^{-2}(R) + \sigma^{-2}(L)]$ is optimal according to several criteria. Using the estimates $\hat{\sigma}^2(R)$ and $\hat{\sigma}^2(L)$ and the first formula we obtain our estimate of $P(B)$ with optimal combination of independent data from the two eyes.

REFERENCES

Alderson, G., Sully, D., & Sully, H. (1974). An operational analysis of a one-handed catching task using high speed photography. *Journal of Motor Behavior, 6,* 217–226.

Bahrick, H. P., & Shelley, C. (1958). Time sharing as an index of automatization. *Journal of Experimental Psychology, 56,* 288–298.

Broadbent, D. E. (1977). Levels, hierarchies, and the locus of control. *Quarterly Journal of Experimental Psychology, 29,* 181–203.

Bryan, W. L., & Harter, N. (1899). Studies of the telegraphic language: The acquisition of a hierarchy of habits. *Psychological Review, 6,* 345–375.

Crossman, E. R. F. W. (1959). A theory of the acquisition of speed skill. *Ergonomics, 2,* 153–166.

Fodor, J. (1983). *The modularity of mind: An essay on faculty psychology.* Cambridge, MA: MIT Press.

Hirst, W., Spelke, E., Reaves, C., Caharack, G., & Neisser, U. (1980). Divided attention without alternation or automaticity. *Journal of Experimental Psychology: General, 109,* 98–117.

Hopkins, G. W., & Kristofferson, A. B. (1980). Ultra-stable stimulus–response latencies: Acquisition and stimulus control. *Perception and Psychophysics, 27,* 241–250.

Kolers, P. A. (1975). Memorial consequences of automatized encoding. *Journal of Experimental Psychology: Human Learning and Memory, 1,* 689–701.

Laberge, D., & Samuels, S. J. (1974). Towards a theory of automatic information processing in reading. *Cognitive Psychology, 6,* 293–323.

Lee, D. N. (1980). Visuo-motor coordination in space-time. In G. E. Stelmach & J. Requin (Eds.), *Tutorials in motor behavior* (pp. 281–295). Amsterdam: North-Holland.

Lee, D. N., Young, D., Reddish, P., Lough, S., & Clayton, T. (1983). Visual timing in hitting an accelerating ball. *Quarterly Journal of Experimental Psychology, 35,* 333–347.

Lucas, M., & Bub, D. (1981). Can practice result in the ability to divide attention between two complex language tasks? Comment on Hirst et al. *Journal of Experimental Psychology: General, 4,* 495–498.

Newell, A., & Rosenbloom, P. S. (1981). Mechanisms of skill acquisition and the law of practice. In J. R. Anderson (Eds.), *Cognitive skills and their acquisition* (pp. 1–55). Hillsdale, NJ: Lawrence Erlbaum Associates.

Rabbitt, P. M. A. (1981). Sequential reactions. In D. Holding (Ed.), *Human skills* (pp. 153–175). Chichester: Wiley.

Regan, D., Beverley, K. I., & Cynader, M. (1979). The visual perception of motion in depth. *Scientific American, 241,* 136–151.

Schneider, W., & Shiffrin, R. M. (1977). Controlled and automatic information processing: I. Detection search and attention. *Psychological Review, 84,* 1–66.

Seibel, R. (1963). Discrimination reaction time for a 1,023 alternative task. *Journal of Experimental Psychology, 66,* 215–226.

Shiffrin, R. M., & Schneider, W. (1977). Controlled and automatic human information processing: II. Perceptual learning, automatic attending and a general theory. *Psychological Review, 84,* 127–190.

Solomons, L. M., & Stein, G. (1896). Normal motor automatism. *Psychological Review, 3,* 492–512.

Tyldesley, D. A., & Whiting, H. T. A. (1975). Operational timing. *Journal of Human Movement Studies, 1,* 172–177.

22 The Role of Position of Gaze in Movement Accuracy

B. Biguer
M. Jeannerod
C. Prablanc
Laboratoire de Neuropsychologie Expérimentale

ABSTRACT

How are head-, hand-, and eye-position information combined in directing the hand to an eccentric target? This chapter reports two sets of experiments conducted on normal subjects during visual pointing. The first series records latencies of eye, head, and hand movement and of EMG commands following target presentation. The results indicate a temporal grouping of segmental motor programs for target-oriented actions. The second set measures pointing errors when the head is fixed or free to move. A significant advantage occurs in the latter condition. The implications of these results for views of central integration of signals from eye, head, and hand are discussed.

INTRODUCTION

Reconstructing the position of a visual target in body-centered coordinates, a necessary condition for reaching that target by hand, implies that signals resulting from eye position relative to the head and from head position relative to the body are monitored centrally. However, the nature of these eye- and head-position signals and their contribution to the accuracy of hand movements are still poorly understood. The work of Prablanc, Echallier, Komilis, and Jeannerod (1979) has shown that availability of an eye-position signal is not in itself sufficient to accurately guide hand movements to a target. In those experiments in which subjects had to point their forefingers at small visual targets appearing in the peripheral visual field in the dark (i.e., without visual feedback from the moving hand) large pointing errors were recorded. The important point was that, whether subjects kept their gaze fixated at the center of the display or whether they were allowed to move their eyes in order to fixate the targets, had relatively little influence on the magnitude of the pointing errors.

Only a few indications are available in the literature that head-position signals might be a cue for monitoring target position and, therefore, for guiding hand movements (Cohen, 1961; Loemker, 1930; Marteniuk, 1978). Further experiments are thus clearly needed to document this point.

A solution to these problems first requires a complete description of the coordination of eye, head, and hand movements during pointing at a visual target. From this description a temporal structure should arise revealing which signals are likely to be used at the programming level for improving hand accuracy. Studies of eye–head coordination have shown that, although in the overt sequence the eye movement usually precedes that of the head (Whittington, Hepp-Reymond, & Flood, 1981), activation of the neck muscles occurs some 20 to 40 msec prior to the beginning of the eye movement (Bizzi, Kalil, & Tagliasco, 1971; Warabi, 1977). In other studies dealing with eye–hand coordination, the overt hand movement has been shown to lag behind the eye-movement by 60 to 100 msec (Angel, Alston, & Garland, 1970; Megaw & Armstrong, 1973; Prablanc et al., 1979). This delay seems to match the typical delay of about 100 msec between contraction of agonist arm muscles and the resulting limb displacement. From these data one gains the impression that the commands forwarded to the different muscular groups involved in pointing are clustered within a relatively short span of time. Definite conclusions, however, can only be drawn from a recording of the complete set of events in the same subjects and during the same sessions.

In the present chapter, we report a series of experiments on visual pointing in normal subjects. In the first set of experiments the latencies of eye, head, and arm movements during pointing at a target and of the EMG discharges of corresponding neck and arm muscles have been measured with respect to target presentation. Results provided a clear picture of the temporal organization of the action of pointing (Biguer, Jeannerod, & Prablanc, 1982). In the second set of experiments, the pointing error of hand movements has been measured as a function of target position in conditions in which the head was either fixed or free to move. A significant improvement in accuracy was observed in the latter condition. These results are discussed in light of available cues for the encoding of target position during coordinated eye and head movements.

THE TEMPORAL PATTERN OF EYE, HEAD, AND ARM MOVEMENTS DURING POINTING AT A VISUAL TARGET

In 1982, Biguer et al. published a preliminary report on eye-, head-, and arm-movement latencies during the action of pointing. These results have now been completed by control experiments.

Methods

Five normal, right-handed adult subjects participated in the initial experiment. Subjects were seated in front of the experimental display (Fig. 22.1), with their trunks fixed with seat belts. Electroluminescent diodes (LEDs) were placed on the top plane (1). Subjects could see the LEDs through a semireflecting mirror (2) and point at their virtual image projecting on a semicircular table (3). Turning the room lights on or off controlled whether subjects could see their hands during pointing.

Horizontal eye movements of both eyes were recorded by the electrooculogram technique (EOG) using Beckman electrodes. The recording system was equipped with a counter-drift device and had a bandpass from DC to 30 Hz. Horizontal head movements were recorded by means of a low-weight helmet secured to the subject's head. The helmet was connected to a low-torque potentiometer by a cardan device. Angular position of the right hand was recorded by way of a thimble attached to the subject's forefinger. Position was monitored when the thimble was in contact with the semicircular table (3 in Fig. 22.1). The table was covered with an isotropic resistive paper fed by a current distributed concentrically. A logic pulse was generated by the recording device each time the thimble left contact with the table (at the onset of movement) and each time it again came in contact with the table (at the end of movement).

Electromyographic (EMG) activity of the biceps brachialis of the right arm and of the right posterior neck muscles (splenius capitis, splenius cervicis, and semispinalis capitis) was recorded bipolarly (Venables & Martin, 1967) using Beckman surface electrodes. EMG was displayed either directly (0 to 300 Hz bandpass) or as a rectified signal by using a continuous mean voltage technique.

LEDs used as targets were presented along a semicircular line at 50 cm from the subject's egocenter. One of the targets was in the subject's sagittal plane and is thus referred to as the "central target." The other LEDs were located at 10°, 20°, 30°, and 40° to the left and to the right of the central target. Targets always stepped from the central position to a randomly selected peripheral position and remained on for 3 sec. The interstimulus interval was 5 sec with a random variation of 1 sec.

Subjects were instructed to track the targets by eye, head, and hand as quickly and accurately as possible. At the beginning of a trial the central target was on. Subjects had to keep their fingers pointed to it and to fixate it by eye until another target appeared. Each target was presented 10 times. Arm movements performed by the subjects consisted of raising the arm and making a rotation at the shoulder joint and an extension at the elbow joint.

Each subject participated in two sessions. In one session the room lights were turned on. Subjects could see their hands prior to and during their movements. In the other session, room lights were turned off and only the targets were visible.

Time was measured between the onset of each target and the following events: ocular saccade, head movement (as recorded by the potentiometer), hand move-

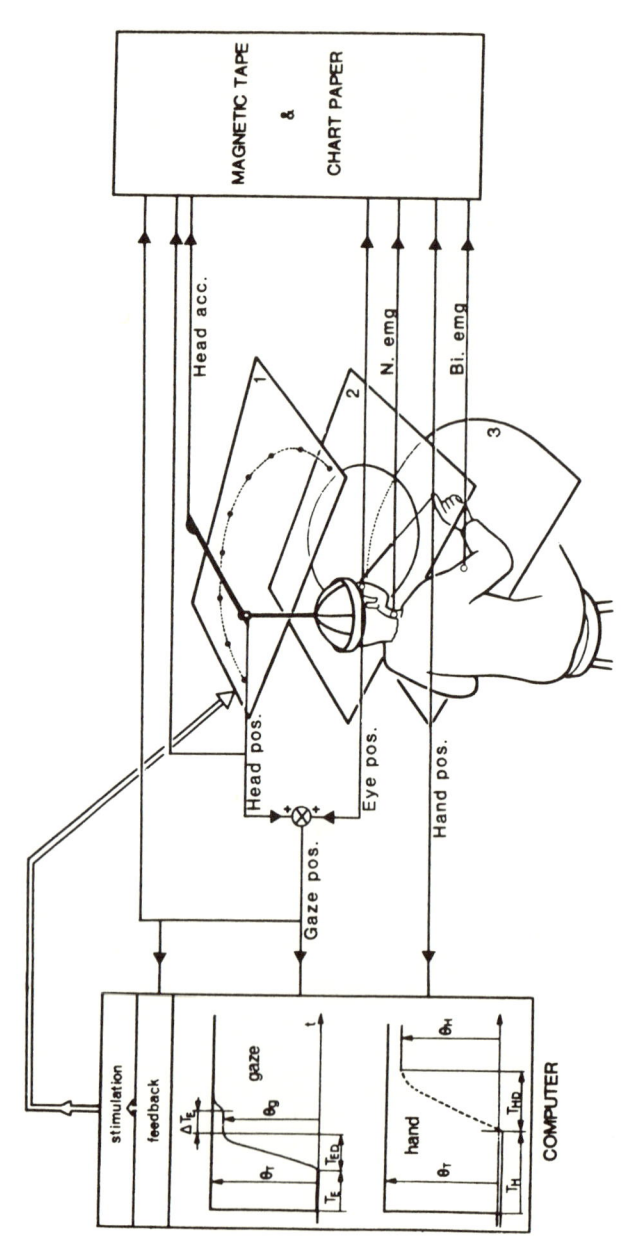

FIG. 22.1. Experimental set-up used in the experiment. On surface 1 are attached the LEDs along a semicircular line centered on the subject's head. The subject sees the targets on surface 3 through the mirror on surface 2. The schematized recordings on the left represent the gaze and hand responses to a target step θ_T. On these records is indicated the timing of the logical pulses generated by the computer at the beginning and at the end of each movement. For further explanations, see the text.

ment (as signaled by the first digital pulse), biceps EMG, and neck EMG. The biceps muscle was selected because it is involved in initial raising of the whole arm and forearm. For EMG the relevant measure was a rise of the rectified EMG signal corresponding to about 15% of the maximum amplitude reached by this signal on each trial.

Only responses directed at targets appearing on the right side of the central target have been considered for analysis. The reason for excluding from analysis responses directed at targets on the left side was biomechanical. Pointing with the right arm to the left side normally involves torsion of the body. Because in our experiment subjects had their trunks fixed with seat belts this could have produced exaggerated pointing errors.

Results

The ocular saccade was consistently found to be the leading event in the pointing sequence for all five subjects. Its latency tended to increase slightly but significantly ($p < .001$, F-test; see Table 22.1) with distance of target from the midline, in agreement with previous findings (Bartz, 1962; Prablanc & Jeannerod, 1974; White, Eason, & Bartlett, 1962).

The onset of the head movement lagged behind that of the eye movement. In this experiment, however, the latency of head movements was found to be longer for targets close to the midline (351 msec for a 10° target; see Table 22.1) than

TABLE 22.1
Mean Latency of the Overt Segmental Movements (Gaze, Head, Hand) and of the Corresponding EMG Activation (Neck and Biceps)[a]

	\multicolumn{4}{c}{No Visual Feedback Condition}	\multicolumn{4}{c}{Visual Feedback Condition}
	Eccentricity (Deg.)							
	10	20	30	40	10	20	30	40
Gaze	197.30	214.11	231.37	244.11	188.86	206.00	233.09	259.67
	(25.96)	(32.64)	(30.38)	(35.99)	(22.78)	(30.53)	(40.41)	(49.21)
Neck EMG	195.79	192.85	212.67	214.09	204.81	201.02	218.09	225.53
	(37.33)	(38.39)	(33.95)	(40.91)	(38.85)	(39.37)	(53.29)	(43.02)
Biceps EMG	219.19	211.55	213.98	218.55	221.24	208.62	222.87	238.69
	(43.20)	(39.01)	(35.09)	(45.55)	(38.91)	(38.07)	(49.36)	(41.29)
Head	358.12	337.72	330.52	313.98	351.71	340.36	309.60	305.73
	(58.77)	(52.24)	(61.47)	(53.58)	(73.56)	(58.54)	(39.22)	(51.35)
Hand	358.67	345.50	353.50	344.63	347.50	374.79	352.33	359.13
	(49.78)	(37.01)	(43.06)	(57.42)	(25.73)	(34.15)	(34.55)	(52.38)

[a]The sessions were performed in a closed-loop condition (i.e., with visual feedback from the moving hand, and in open-loop condition (i.e., without visual feedback from the moving hand).

for more remote targets (e.g., 305 msec for a 40° target). This point was subjected to verification in a control experiment (see the next section). Finally, the onset of arm movements had a constant latency of about 350 msec over the full range of target distances (Glencross, 1972; Lagasse & Hayes, 1973; Rosenbaum, 1980).

This pattern of a serial ordering of eye, head, and arm movements during pointing broke down when EMG activation, rather than onset of movements, was used as an index for latency. The latency of either biceps or neck EMG was found to remain within 200 to 220 msec and to be uninfluenced by target distance from the midline (see Table 22.1). Difference in latency between the two muscle groups did not exceed 17 msec, a value that did not reach statistical significance.

Biceps and neck EMG latencies appeared to be slightly shorter than those of eye movements. This difference was significant ($p < .05$) for targets located at 40° but not for targets located at 20° or 30°. Finally, for targets located at 10° the pattern reversed and eye-movement latencies were systematically shorter than those of biceps and/or neck EMG. It should be pointed out that EMG of extraocular muscles was not recorded in this experiment. Therefore, a constant value of about 7 msec should be subtracted from eye-movement latency in order to get a more realistic picture of muscular activation during pointing. This value of 7 msec has been estimated in the monkey to correspond to duration of isometric contraction time of extraocular muscles (Fuchs & Luschei, 1970; Robinson, 1970). It can be assumed that a similar value also holds for humans.

Another important result from this experiment was that latencies of either movements or EMG activations were not affected by whether subjects could see their hands during pointing or not (see Table 22.1).

Control Experiments

Results reported in the previous section raised two simple questions. The first question was about the relation of head-movement latencies to target distance. Because arm-movement latencies do not vary as a function of target distance, it could be expected that head-movement latencies for targets located at 10° or 20° should be the same as for targets located at 30° or 40°. The longer latencies for targets close from the midline (10° or 20°) were attributed to difficulty in detecting the real onset of head movements. Head movements directed at a 10° target can be very small (see the next section) and consequently have a slower rise time than movements of a larger amplitude. This point was verified by using a more sensitive detection of movement.

The second question was whether biceps EMG was a sufficiently sensitive index for establishing the timing of motor commands to the arm during pointing. Pointing movements as those recorded here also involve initial raising of the whole arm and abduction at the shoulder joint. For this reason, EMG activity of shoulder extensor muscles might have given a more accurate picture of motor commands.

An experiment was run with two more subjects using the same procedure and a similar apparatus as in the previous one. Only the condition without visual feedback from the hand was used. Head movements were recorded using a highly sensitive accelerometer (EGA.5D, Entran) attached to the helmet. The EMG activity of the deltoid muscle was recorded on the right side.

Latencies of eye and arm movements were found to follow the same trend with respect to eccentricity as in the previous experiment. Head movements, however, were found to have a latency shorter by about 40 to 45 msec over the full range of target distances (e.g., 310.6 msec [70.5] at 10°; 270.8 [60.9] at 40°) (see Fig. 22.2, left). This resulted in a relationship of head-movement latency as a function of target distance very similar to that previously observed—namely, head-movement latency tended to decrease when the target was more distant from the midline. A similar result has been reported by Uemura, Arai, and Shimazaki (1980) also using an helmet-mounted device containing terrestrial magnetic sensors.

Results concerning EMG latencies were closely similar to those reported in the previous experiment. EMG activation of the deltoid tended to lag behind that of the neck muscle group by about 15 msec. Both muscle groups lagged behind the eye movement for targets close from the midline and lead it for more remote targets (see Fig. 22.2, right).

Discussion

Our results stress the fact that the neural commands forwarded to different moving segments (e.g., eye, head, shoulder, arm) implicated in the same act of pointing are generated in parallel. Such a synergy of motor commands has an obvious advantage (with respect to a serial type of organization) in achieving a faster mobilization of the motor ensemble related to the goal. One possibility to explain the synergy is that the commands would be released by a signal from a common generator. This signal would have to carry information as to the location of the target on a body-centered map of visual space. Such a requirement could be met by a feed foward signal issued from the eye-movement generator, because eye movements are likely to be coded in spatial, rather than in retinal, coordinates (Mays & Sparks, 1980). This hypothesis, however, was not completely confirmed by the data. First, EMG latencies for biceps, deltoid, and neck muscles can be clearly shorter than eye-movement latency, even if the 7 msec isometric contraction time of extraocular muscles is subtracted. Second, if commands were produced by a common generator one should expect a high degree of correlation between EMG latencies and eye-movement latencies. Such a correlation was found to be rather weak, either in the first experiment using biceps EMG

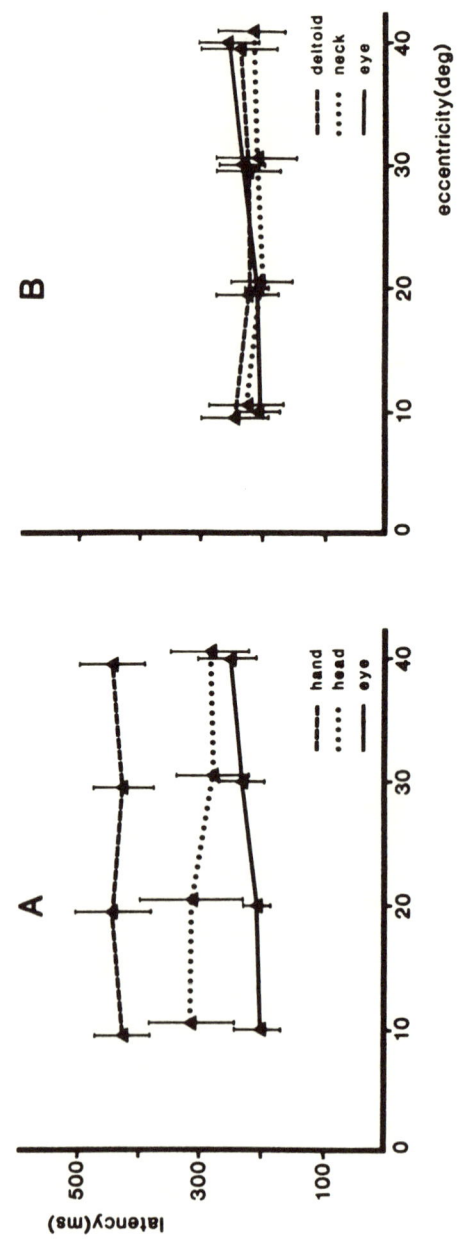

FIG. 22.2. Mean latency of overt segmental movements and of the corresponding EMG activation. (A) Mean latency (in msec) and standard deviation for eye, head, and hand movements as a function of target eccentricity (in degrees of arc). (B) Mean latency and standard deviation for eye movement, neck, and deltoid EMG.

(Biguer et al., 1982) or in the control experiment using deltoid EMG. In the latter case, the eye-movement latency–deltoid latency, eye-movement latency–neck latency, and deltoid latency–neck latency correlation coefficients were $r = .42$, $r = .47$, and $r = .38$, respectively.

The relative synchrony of neural commands for eye, head, and arm muscles may also have an important implication for eye–hand coordination and pointing accuracy in producing a correlative sequence of the overt movements. This point was tested in the following set of experiments.

THE CONTRIBUTION OF COORDINATED EYE AND HEAD MOVEMENTS IN HAND-POINTING ACCURACY

Methods

Five normal, right-handed subjects (different from those of Experiment 1) participated in this experiment. The apparatus previously described (Fig. 22.1) was used. Horizontal eye movements and finger position were recorded as in Experiment 1. Head movements were recorded using the accelerometer. In addition to latency of eye, head, and arm movements, the duration of these movements was also measured. The position of the gaze in space (i.e., the sum of eye and head positions) was computed electronically. Two other temporal parameters were measured: TIHH, the time interval between the end of the head movement and the end of hand movement, and TIGH, the time interval between the end of the gaze movement and the end of the hand movement.

The final head position relative to the target, the final eye position relative to the head, and the final position of the hand relative to the target were all separately calculated. The absolute values of angular distance between final hand position and target position were averaged for each target. This mean value represented the *absolute error* (AE) of hand position. In a separate calculation, each value of hand position was assigned a (+) or a (−) depending on whether it overshot or undershot target position, respectively. The averaged value of those measurements for each target represented the *constant error* (CE) of hand position.

Subjects were instructed to point "as quickly and accurately as possible" to randomly selected peripheral targets. Each trial started from the central target. Experiments were performed in the dark, so that no visual reafference from the hand was available at any time of the movement. Two experimental sessions were run for each subject: one in which the head was free to move (head-free condition) and one in which the head was fixed (head-fixed condition).

The head-fixed condition was achieved by simply asking the subjects not to move their heads. Fulfillment of this instruction was ascertained on recordings of the head-movement signal. Trials in which the head had moved were discarded. Each session involved five presentations of each target.

Results

Latency of Movement

Data on eye-, head-, and hand-movement latency fully confirmed those obtained in the previous section. For this reason, they are not developed further here (see Biguer, Prablanc, & Jeannerod, 1984).

In addition, eye- and hand-movement latencies were not affected by whether the head was fixed or free to move.

Duration of Movements

An analysis of variance with two main factors (target position × head condition—fixed or free) was used.

Target eccentricity had a highly significant effect on the duration of gaze movement ($F_{3,192} = 279.15$, $p < .001$) (see Fig. 22.3). In the head-free condition, the duration of gaze movement was found to vary from 38.40 msec (s.d., 7.86) for movements directed at the target located at 10° to 110.93 msec (s.d., 28.97) for movements directed at the target located at 40°. The duration of eye movement when the head was immobile was not significantly different from the duration of gaze movement in the head-free condition.

Target eccentricities also had a significant effect on head-movement duration ($F_{3,80} = 20.76$; $p < .001$) (see Fig. 22.3). Indeed, the duration of head movement increased with target eccentricity. Although subjects were instructed to orient their gaze "as quickly as possible," the maximum head velocity remained relatively low, varying from 35 deg/sec for a target located at 10° to 87 deg/sec for a target located at 40° from the midline.

Finally, target eccentricity significantly influenced hand-movement duration ($F_{3,192} = 16.08$, $p < .001$), which increased with target eccentricity. Experimental conditions did not significantly affect the duration of hand movement ($F_{1,192} = 2.07$ NS), although there was a slight increase in the head-fixed condition (see Fig. 22.3). A large intersubject variability of hand-movement duration was observed.

TIHH and TIGH

The TIHH—that is, the time interval between the end of the head movement and that of the hand movement—was found to increase with target eccentricity. The mean value of TIHH varied from 110 msec to 160 msec for targets located at 10° and 40°, respectively.

The TIGH corresponds to the time interval between the end of the gaze movement and that of the hand movement. In the head-free condition, the end of gaze movement was measured when the gaze position had reached the target position. At this time, however, the eye and the head were still moving in opposite directions, due to the fact that the eyes were stabilized on the target by the vestibuloocular reflex.

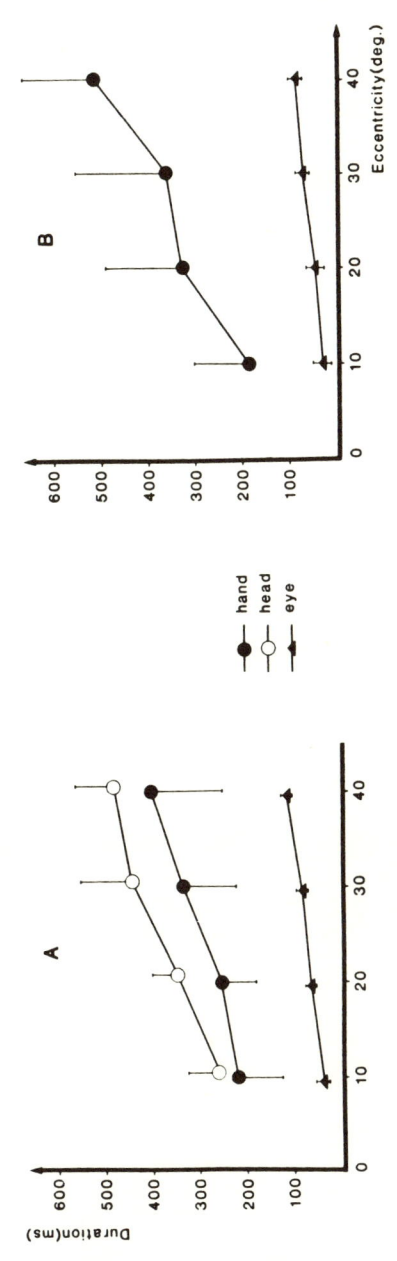

FIG. 22.3. Mean duration of the eye, head, and hand movements as a function of target eccentricity in head-free condition (A) and head-fixed condition (B).

The TIGH increased with target eccentricity. Its mean value varied from 243 to 375 msec for targets located at 10° and 40°, respectively. The fixation of the head did not significantly affect these values.

Accuracy of Movements

Gaze Movement. In the head-fixed condition, the gaze movement was represented by the eye movement alone, whereas in the head-free condition, eye and head movements combined to produce gaze orientation. In both conditions, the eye movement toward targets beyond 20° often consisted of two saccades: The first saccade reached about 90% of the required movement amplitude. It was followed by a corrective saccade, which aligned the fovea with the target.

The amplitude of the head movement was usually hypometric with respect to the target (see Fig. 22.4) (see also Uemura et al., 1980). For instance, the mean

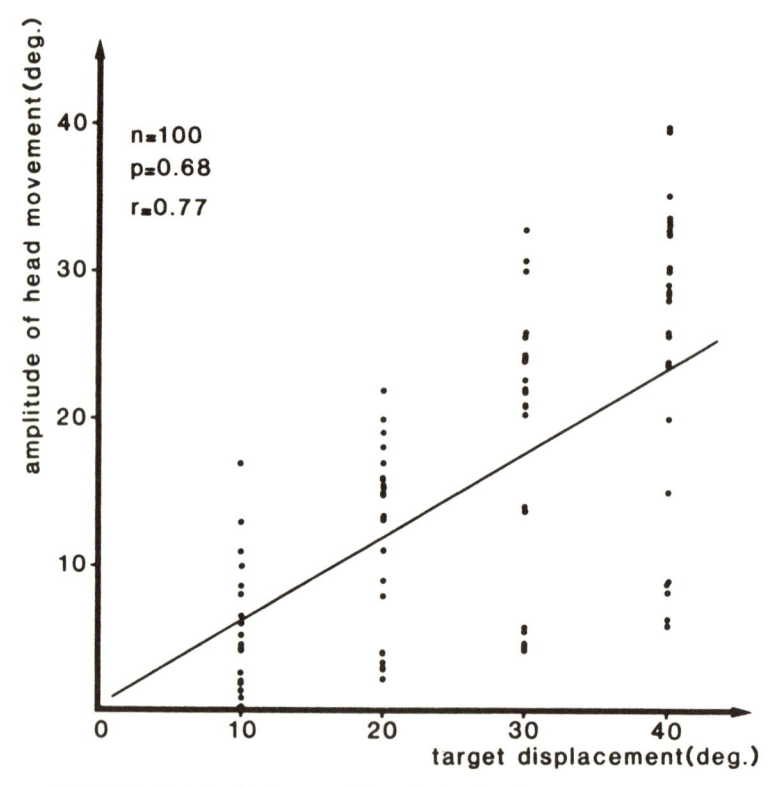

FIG. 22.4. Relationship between the amplitude of head movement (in degrees of arc) and the target displacement from the midline. Each point of the scatter represents an individual trial for five subjects in the head-free condition (n = total number of individual trials; p = slope of regression line; r = correlation coefficient).

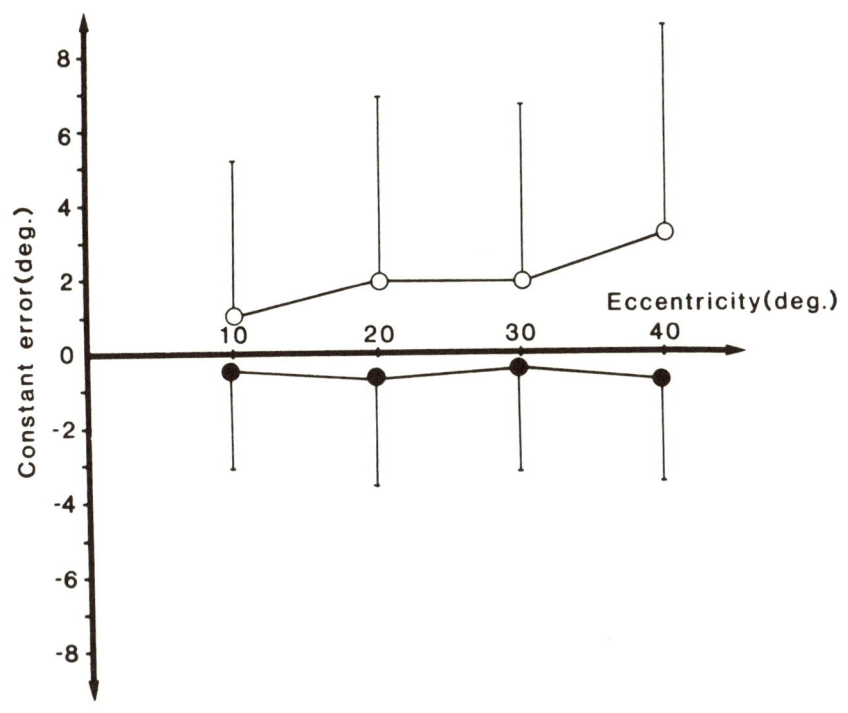

FIG. 22.5. Mean constant pointing error (CE) in degrees of arc as a function of target eccentricity. Open circles = head-fixed condition; filled circles = head-free condition (from Biguer et al., 1984).

final head position was 5.02° (s.d. 4.4°) for targets located at 10° from the midline and 12.3° (s.d., 6), 19.92° (s.d., 8.5), and 25.29° (s.d., 10.5) for targets located at 20°, 30°, 40° from the midline, respectively. The amplitude of head movement nevertheless correlated positively ($r = .77$, $p < .001$) with target position. This hypometry meant that, even in the head-free condition, a large amount of the distance to the target (about 40% on the average) was covered by a displacement of the eye alone. Consequently, the head axis at the end of the gaze displacement was almost never aligned with the position of the target.

Hand-Pointing Movement. An analysis of variance with two main factors (target position × head condition) was used for both the constant error (CE) and the absolute error (AE) of hand pointings.

In the head-fixed condition, hand movements globally overshot the targets. The degree of hypermetry increased slightly with target eccentricity (see Fig. 22.5). The mean CE varied from +1.07° for the target located at 10° to +3.23° for the target located at 40°, and the ANOVA indicated that the main effect for target eccentricity was significant ($F_{3,80} = 13.11$; $p < .001$). In fact, partly due to the large variability of the subjects' responses in the head-fixed condition, it was found that both the CE and its standard deviation increased significantly only beyond 30° of target eccentricity (t test, $p < .01$). This point has important implications for the discussion of the results.

In the head-fixed condition the AE of the hand-pointing movement also increased with target eccentricity, but mainly for targets located beyond 30° (Fig. 22.6). The ANOVA for AE revealed that the main effect of target eccentricity was significant ($F_{3,80} = 22.60, p < .001$).

One of the subjects, though showing similar results to the others up to 30°, had, at 40°, a decrease of CE as well as AE, contrarily to the others. He also showed a great variability in his responses. Nevertheless, he had similar responses to the others in the head-free condition.

In the head-free condition, the mean value of CE was close to $-.5°$ irrespective of target eccentricity (see Fig. 22.5). In addition, the standard deviations remained at about the same level for all targets and were smaller than in the head-fixed condition. The ANOVA for CE in the head-free condition revealed that the main effect of target eccentricity was not significant ($F_{3,80} = .43$, NS).

In addition, in this condition, the mean AE also remained practically constant through different spatial positions of the target (see Fig. 22.6). There was no significant variation of the AE of hand-pointing movement with target eccentricity ($F_{3,80} = 1.78$, NS).

Comparison of the responses obtained in the two head conditions showed that the CE as well as the AE differed according to whether subjects had their heads fixed or free to move. The head condition had a significant effect on subjects' responses for both CE ($F_{1,192} = 35.78, p < .001$) and AE ($F_{1,192} = 48.90, p < .001$). In addition, the head condition effect was not independent of target eccentricity, because the target eccentricity × head condition interaction was highly significant ($F_{3,192} = 8.10, p < .001$). In fact, comparison of mean AE values for each target eccentricity between the two head conditions (t test) showed that the accuracy of hand movement differed mainly for the target located at 40° from the midline—the subjects were more accurate in the head-free condition.

Three other aspects of the findings are worth reporting. First, there was no correlation between the final head position and the constant error or the absolute error of hand movements in the head-free condition. Second, there was no relationship between the accuracy of hand movement and the final eye position in the orbit. And, finally, no correlation was found between the accuracy of hand movement and the values of either TIHH or TIGH.

Discussion

When the subjects in the present experiment were required to point toward the target with their heads fixed, the results were very similar to those previously obtained by Prablanc et al. (1979), who also used a head-fixed condition to study hand-pointing movements executed in the absence of visual feedback.

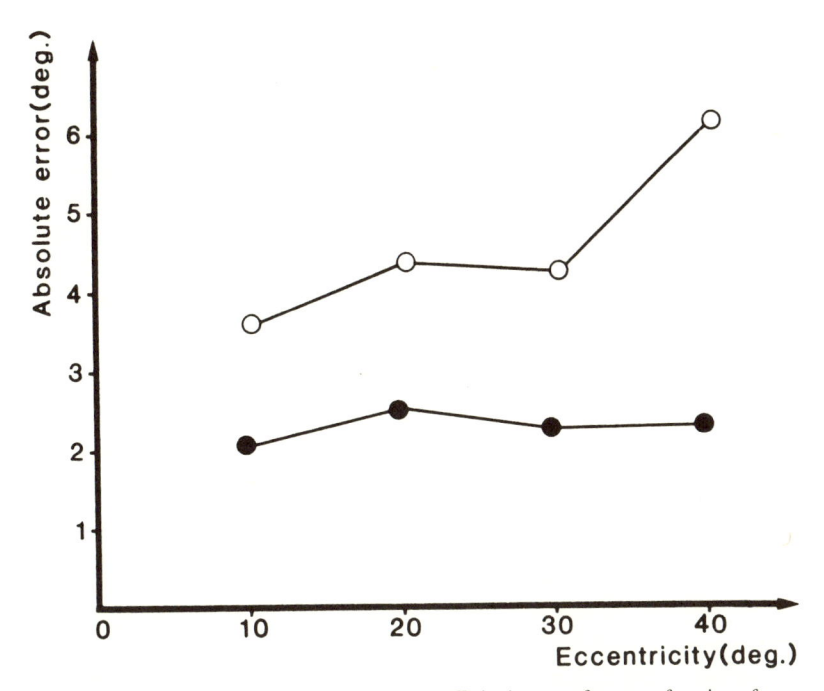

FIG. 22.6. Mean absolute pointing error (AE) in degrees of arc as a function of target eccentricity. Open circles = head-fixed condition; filled circles = head-free condition (from Biguer et al., 1984).

In contrast to the results in the head-fixed condition, when the subjects were free to move their heads, they made smaller pointing errors and the amplitude of these errors did not vary as a function of target eccentricity. The difference in accuracy between the two conditions, however, was statistically significant only for targets located 40° from the midline. Even though accuracy was improved when subjects were allowed to move their heads, there was no change in the temporal parameters of the limb movements. The latency and the duration of the movements varied little from one condition to the other and, if anything, were slightly shorter in the head-free condition.

There are a number of possible explanations for the improvement in pointing accuracy that was observed when subjects were allowed to move their heads as well as their eyes. One explanation involves the suggestion that there is a considerable synergistic advantage in having the head, eyes, and limbs move together during a pointing movement. Another explanation centers on the possibility that more information about the position of the target can be obtained when the head as well as the eyes are free to move. Moreover, the two explanations are not mutually exclusive.

Because pointing and reaching movements made with the hand and arm are normally accompanied by movements of both the head and eyes, programming of such movements may be more "efficient" (and thus more accurate) when the subject produces all of the components of the normal sequence than when he or she is required to inhibit one component (head movement) while producing the others. This is congruent with the fact that commands related to all three components are released synchronously, as shown by Experiment 1. It is possible that at some level in the central nervous system the signals generated by head movements may facilitate the organization of target-directed hand movements. The time available between the end of the head movement and the end of the hand movement is compatible with the required kinesthetic reaction time described in the literature (Chernikoff & Taylor, 1952; Glencross, 1977; Higgins & Angel, 1970; Vince, 1948). Although such explanations might account for the overall improvement in accuracy that was observed in the head-free condition, they do not explain why the accuracy of the pointing movements in the head-fixed condition was so much poorer for targets located at 40° of eccentricity than for targets located closer to the midline. Nevertheless, the possibility remains that some of synergistic advantage could have been at work in the head-free condition.

Another explanation is based on the possibility that kinesthetic receptors in the neck could have adapted so much in the head-fixed condition that the information they provided about the position of the head could have become severely degraded. As a consequence, information about the position of the eye with respect to the body would not have been as accurate in this condition as in the head-free condition in which the head was being moved regularly from trial to trial. In a different context Paillard and Brouchon (1968) have shown that the position of the limb can be more accurately perceived when the limb is moved actively by the subject than when it is moved passively or is maintained in one position for a long period of time. They also suggested that the kinesthetic receptors in the limb would be much less adapted (and thus more sensitive) during the active as opposed to the passive or stationary conditions. Thus, if eye position (with respect to the body and visual space) was an important determinant of final limb position in the present experiment, then pointing in the active (head-free) condition would be expected to be more accurate than pointing in the stationary (head-fixed) condition. Although this explanation can account for the overall difference in accuracy between the two conditions, like the synergy explanations described earlier, it cannot explain why pointing to 40° targets in the head-fixed condition was so much less accurate than pointing to targets closer to the midline.

One final explanation, however, can account for the large differences in accuracy observed during pointing to very eccentric targets in the two conditions. It too suggests that the error inherent in the mechanisms for encoding target position in body-centered space is reduced when the head as well as the eyes are allowed to move. This hypothesis assumes that the absolute error of the pointing movement is the sum of encoding errors that are present in the information obtained about eye position and head position, as well as variability in the motor programming and control of limb and hand movements. The hypothesis makes the additional assumption that the error in monitoring eye position remains constant up to a limiting angular displacement of the eye within the orbit. Thus, for targets within this limit (up to 30° or so from the midline axis of the head) no head movement is required. Beyond this limit, however, the error would increase sharply if no head movement occurred. The same argument can be made for the error in monitoring head position relative to the body—that is, beyond a certain angular displacement of the head, errors in monitoring head position would increase sharply.

The encoding-error explanation just outlined assumes that any information about gaze position that affects the motor programming of the limb movement takes place after the movement of the limb has been initiated. Such an assumption is necessary because we know that the eye-movement onset and the EMG bursts related to head and arm movements directed at the same target are nearly synchronous and not sequential.

According to this explanation, it can be suggested that precise information about target location is necessary not only prior to the movement but also during the movement itself in order to produce an on line correction of the motor program. Recent experiments by Prablanc, Goodale, Pelisson, Biguer, and Jeannerod (1984) seem to confirm this point.

ACKNOWLEDGMENTS

We thank M. Rouvière for kindly typing the manuscript and S. Bello for assistance with the illustrations.

REFERENCES

Angel, R. W., Alston, W., & Garland, H. (1970). Functional relations between the manual and oculomotor systems. *Experimental Neurology, 27*, 248–257.

Bartz, A. E. (1962). Eye movement latency, duration and response time as a function of angular displacement. *Journal of Experimental Psychology, 64*, 318–324.

Biguer, B., Jeannerod, M., & Prablanc, C. (1982). The coordination of eye, head and arm movements during reaching at a single visual target. *Experimental Brain Research, 46*, 301–304.

Biguer, B., Prablanc, C., & Jeannerod, M. (1984). The contribution of coordinated eye and head movements in hand pointing accuracy. *Experimental Brain Research, 55*, 462–469.

Bizzi, E., Kalil, R. E., & Tagliasco, V. (1971). Eye-hand coordination in monkeys: Evidence of centrally patterned organization. *Science, 173*, 452–454.

Chernikoff, R., & Taylor, F. V. (1952). Reaction time to kinesthetic stimulation resulting from sudden arm displacement. *Journal of Experimental Psychology, 43*, 1–8.

Cohen, L. A. (1961). Role of the eye and neck proprioceptive mechanisms in body orientation and motor coordination. *Journal of Neurophysiology, 24*, 1–11.

Fuchs, A. F., & Luschei, E. (1970). Firing patterns of abducens neurons of alert monkeys in relationship to horizontal eye movements. *Journal of Neurophysiology, 33,* 382–392.

Glencross, D. J. (1972). Latency and response complexity. *Journal of Motor Behavior,* 4, 251–256.

Glencross, D. J. (1977). Control of skilled movements. *Psychological Bulletin, 84,* 14–29.

Higgins, J. R., & Angel, R. W. (1970). Correction of tracking errors without sensory feedback. *Journal of Experimental Psychology, 84,* 412–416.

Lagasse, P. P., & Hayes, C. C. (1973). Premotor and motor reaction time as a function of movement extent. *Journal of Motor Behavior, 5,* 25–32.

Loemker, K. K. (1930). Certain factors determining the accuracy of a response to the direction of a visual object. *Journal of Experimental Psychology, 13,* 500–518.

Marteniuk, R. G. (1978). The role of eye and head positions in slow movement execution. In G. E. Stelmach (Ed.), *Information processing in motor control and learning.* (pp. 267–288). New York: Academic.

Mays, L. E., & Sparks, D. L. (1980). Saccades are spatially, not retinocentrally coded. *Science, 208,* 1163–1165.

Megaw, E. D., & Armstrong, W. (1973). Individual and simultaneous tracking of a step input by the horizontal saccadic eye movement and manual control systems. *Journal of Experimental Psychology, 100*(1), 18–28.

Paillard, J., & Brouchon, M. (1968). Active and passive movements in the calibration of position sense. In S. J. Freedman (Ed.), *The neuropsychology of spatially oriented behavior* (pp. 37–55). Homewood, Ill.: Dorsey.

Prablanc, C., Echallier, J. F., Komilis, E., & Jeannerod, M. (1979). Optimal response of eye and hand motor systems in pointing at a visual target. I. Spatio-temporal characteristics of eye and hand movements and their relationships when varying the amount of visual information. *Biological Cybernetics, 35,* 113–124.

Prablanc, C., Goodale, M. A., Pelisson, D., Biguer, B., & Jeannerod, M. (1984). Visual control of reaching movements without vision of the limb. *Investigative Ophtalmology and Visual Science,* 25(3), 221 (Suppl.).

Prablanc, C., & Jeannerod, M. (1974). Latence et précision des saccades en fonction de l'intensité, de la durée et de la position rétinienne d'un stimulus. *Revue d'E.E.G. et de Neurophysiologie Clinique, 3,* 484–488.

Robinson, D. A. (1970). Oculomotor unit behavior in the monkey. *Journal of Neurophysiology, 33,* 393–404.

Rosenbaum, D. A. (1980). Human movement initiation: Specification of arm, direction and extent. *Journal of Experimental Psychology: General, 109,* 444–474.

Uemura, T., Arai, Y., & Shimazaki, C. (1980). Eye–head coordination during lateral gaze in normal subjects. *Acta Oto-Laryngology, 90,* 191–198.

Venables, P. H., & Martin, I. (1967). *A manual of psychophysiological methods.* New York: Wiley.

Vince, M. A. (1948). Corrective movements in a pursuit task. *Quarterly Journal of Experimental Psychology, 1,* 85–106.

Warabi, T. (1977). The reaction time of eye–head coordination in man. *Neuroscience Letters, 6,* 47–51.

White, C. T., Eason, C., & Barlett, N. R. (1962). Latency and duration of eye movements in the horizontal plane. *Journal of Optical Society of America, 52,* 210–213.

Whittington, D. A., Hepp-Reymond, M. C., & Flood, W. (1981). Eye and head movements to auditory targets. *Experimental Brain Research, 41,* 358–363.

23 Eye Movement Control Following Corpus Commissurotomy in Humans

Jeffrey D. Holtzman
Cornell University Medical College

ABSTRACT

Surgical transection of the corpus callosum in humans, so-called *split-brain* surgery, restricts each hemisphere's vision to the contralateral hemifield, and impairs each hemisphere's ability to control the ipsilateral limbs. Nevertheless, visual-motor behavior remains remarkably well integrated in these patients. In order to account for the integrity of visual-motor control following callosal surgery, two predictions were made concerning the control of eye movements. First, it was predicted that each hemisphere has access to some visual information from the ipsilateral hemifield for eye movements that is not available perceptually, or that is not of sufficient resolution necessary to identify a stimulus. Second, it was predicted that each disconnected hemisphere can generate both contraversive and ipsiversive lateral eye movements.

The results of three experiments verified these predictions. Experiments 1 and 2 demonstrated that each hemisphere has access to visual information from the ipsilateral hemifield for eye movements, albeit this information is of relatively crude spatial resolution. Experiment 3 demonstrated that each hemisphere can generate both leftward and rightward eye movements. Taken together, these results support a *dominant hemisphere* account of oculomotor control following callosal surgery in which visually based lateral eye movements in either direction can be managed by a single hemisphere.

INTRODUCTION

Surgical transection of the corpus callosum in humans, so-called *split-brain* surgery, has dramatic consequences for both perceptual and motor function. Perhaps the most striking effects of callosal surgery are for visual perception, where, at least for tachistoscopic visual stimulation, each hemisphere's visual space is limited to the contralateral hemifield. The left hemisphere perceives only right visual field stimulation, whereas the right hemisphere perceives only left field stimulation. Likewise, each hemisphere has preferential control over the contralateral limbs, although for motor control, the effects of hemispheric disconnection are less pronounced. For example, although each disconnected hemisphere is profoundly limited in its ability to control the musculature of the ipsilateral fingers, both retain weak control of the musculature of the ipsilateral arm (for review, see Gazzaniga, 1970).

Surprisingly, this perceptual and motor independence of the disconnected hemispheres, which is so readily apparent under controlled laboratory procedures, is virtually undetectible in the normal environment. Commissurotomy patients direct action within the environment with little overt difficulty or hesitation; they do not fail to notice objects on one side of space, nor do they appear to be under the control of two independent behavioral systems. This discrepancy between the normally integrated behavior of the commissurotomy patient and the behavioral dissociations observed under laboratory conditions underlies the basic question addressed in this chapter. Namely, what are the mechanisms by which behaviors from two perceptually disconnected hemispheres are integrated?

Consider the manner in which the hemispheres might interact to control behavior. One possibility is that all behavior is controlled by a single dominant hemisphere. Based on studies of perception following split-brain surgery, this account would predict that commissurotomy patients would have difficulty responding to objects in the hemifield ipsilateral to the dominant hemisphere. For example, if the left hemisphere controlled behavior, a failure to notice and difficulty avoiding objects on the left side of space would be expected. But, commissurotomy patients make no such complaints regarding either visual field.

An alternative possibility is that the control of behavior shifts between the hemispheres depending upon each hemisphere's response priorities to various environmental contingencies. This account predicts a disorder of motor function when the hemispheres attempt to execute conflicting responses. Such interhemispheric rivalry should be particularly detrimental for the control of eye movements, where the hemispheres share access to a common musculature. In this context, imagine a situation in which the right hemisphere chooses a target to fixate 5 deg to the left of fixation, while, at the same time, the left hemisphere chooses a target 3 deg to the right of fixation. Accordingly, a 5 deg leftward eye movement is programmed by the right hemisphere; a 3 deg rightward eye movement is programmed by the left hemisphere. How is this conflict resolved? A clearly unsatisfactory solution would be a compromise in which the two motor commands sum, a 2 deg leftward eye movement results, and neither target reaches the fovea. Summation of this kind has been reported by Robinson and Fuchs (1969) in monkeys when the frontal eye fields of the two hemispheres are simultaneously stimulated. Nevertheless, although anomolous vertical nystagmus has been reported in commissurotomized monkeys (Pasik, Pasik, Valciukas,

& Bender, 1971), there is no evidence of oculomotor dysfunction following corpus commissurotomy in humans.

Thus, each of these accounts of behavioral control is inadequate, each for a different reason. *Hemispheric dominance* predicts a perceptual disorder that is not seen after callosal surgery. *Shifting hemispheric control* predicts a motor deficit that is not observed. The present studies represent an attempt to resolve this paradox by examining motor responses of commissurotomy patients to visual stimulation. Saccadic eye movements were selected for study because, for the reasons previously outlined, they should be particularly sensitive to disruption if the hemispheres do not cooperate in specifying the direction of gaze. Moreover, saccades are preprogrammed, ballistic, and, for the most part, voluntary in nature (see Leigh & Zee, 1983), so there is little ambiguity in specifying what constitutes a response.

The coherent real-world behavior of commissurotomy patients leads to two predictions concerning oculomotor control following callosal surgery. The first is that each separated hemisphere has access to visual information from the ipsilateral hemifield for eye movements that is not available perceptually, or that is not of sufficient resolution necessary to identify a visual stimulus. In other words, callosal surgery does not completely abolish each hemisphere's representation of the ipsilateral hemifield, as would be concluded based on the evaluation of perceptual function in the laboratory. The second prediction is that each hemisphere is capable of generating both ipsiversive and contraversive lateral eye movements. If these predictions are correct, then the dominant hemisphere account of behavioral control becomes more plausible (*e.g.*, each hemisphere now has an integrated representation of the visual world, plus the capacity to direct behavior into either hemifield). It should be emphasized, however, that the veracity of both predictions is critical to this account. For example, if the isolated left hemisphere has access to vision from the left visual field, but only the right hemisphere can generate leftward eye movements, little would be accomplished in minimizing potential interhemispheric conflict in specifying the direction of gaze. On the other hand, if each hemisphere can generate eye movements in either direction, but only can perceive stimuli in the contralateral hemifield, then the functional equivialence of a cortical hemianopia would be expected.

The purpose of Experiments 1 and 2 was to ascertain what visual information, if any, each hemisphere can glean from the ipsilateral visual field for oculomotor control (additional data from these studies appear in Holtzman, 1984). Once established, it was possible in Experiment 3 to ascertain unambiguously whether each hemisphere can generate eye movements into the ipsilateral hemifield.

GENERAL METHODS

Subjects. One extensively studied commissurotomy patient, J. W., participated in these experiments. J. W.'s neurological history is described in detail elsewhere (Sidtis, Volpe, Wilson, Rayport, & Gazzaniga, 1981). Briefly, he is a

31-year-old right-handed male who suffered, since age 17, from a seizure disorder that could not be managed with antiepileptic drugs. In 1979, he underwent a two-stage microneurosurgical section of his corpus callosum (Wilson, Reeves, & Gazzaniga, 1978). The posterior body and splenium were sectioned first. Eight weeks later the callosal section was completed by dividing the anterior body, genu and rostrum. The anterior commissure was left intact. NMR revealed complete callosal transection with intended sparing of the anterior commissure (Gazzaniga, Holtzman, Gates, Deck, & Lee, 1984).

A second patient, V. P., also participated in most of these studies. Although her results were very similar to those of J. W., they will not be presented here because recent NMR findings (Gazzaniga, Holtzman, Gates, Deck, & Lee, in preparation) raise the possibility that some callosal fibers in the region of her splenium and rostrum were inadvertently spared.

Apparatus. To record eye movements, the observer's head was held by a bite-board and forehead rest, and the position of the right eye (left occluded) was monitored by a double Purkinje-image eye tracker developed and described by Cornsweet and Crane (1973). This system provides continuous analog voltage outputs for the horizontal and vertical components of eye position with less than 4 min of arc noise. Computer-controlled visual displays were presented on a Hewlett-Packard 1310 oscilloscope equipped with a p15 phosphor (decays to less than 10% in 3 microsec) and viewed from a distance of 1 meter. Visual displays had a luminance of approximately 3.3 cd/m². The experimenter could visually monitor the observer's eye movements on an oscilloscope located outside the eye tracker room.

During the experiments, the eye tracker output was sampled every 2 msec by computer and stored on magnetic tape for subsequent analysis. The computer program used a velocity criterion to detect the beginnings and ends of saccades. The onset of a saccade was indicated when, over an 8 msec interval, the eye reached a velocity of 28 deg/sec. An end of saccade was indicated when the eye velocity fell below this value.

EXPERIMENT 1

This experiment examined whether each disconnected hemisphere has access to visual information from the ipsilateral hemifield for the control of saccadic eye movements.

Methods

Conditions and Procedure. Examples of the two experimental conditions are depicted in Fig. 23.1. On all trials, two matrices of four X's were displayed on either side of a central fixation stimulus. The nearest edge of each matrix was

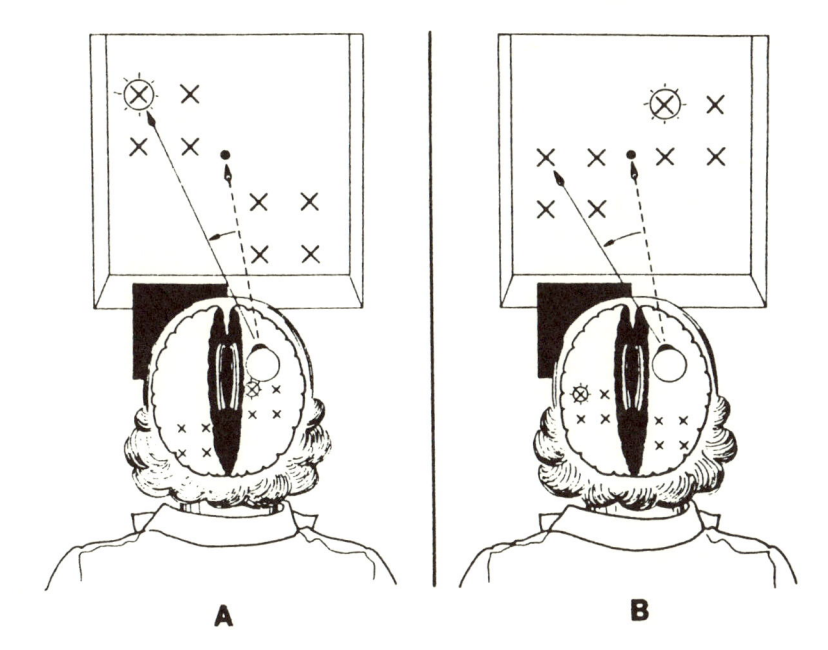

FIG. 23.1. Example of conditions in Experiment 1. On within-field trials (A), the eye moved to the stimulus that was surrounded by the probe; on between-field trials (B), the eye moved to the corresponding stimulus in the other hemifield. Each matrix of 4 X's subtended 2 × 2 deg for visual angle; the nearest edge of each matrix was 1.5 deg from the vertical midline. On each trial, the vertical offsets of the matrices varied randomly in 1 deg steps, so that the vertical positions of the matrices were unpredictable from trial to trial (reprinted from Holtzman, 1984).

always displaced 1.5 deg from the vertical midline, whereas the vertical position of each matrix was varied from trial to trial. There were seven possible vertical positions, which varied in one degree steps, one of which was randomly selected for each visual field on each trial. Shifting the matrices insured that the vertical offset of a particular matrix could not be inferred from spatial memory built up across trials.

Each trial began with a period of central fixation in which just the eight X's were displayed. A probe circle then briefly surrounded one of the X's, one second elapsed, and a tone sounded. On *within-field* trials (Fig. 23.1A), J. W. was required to move his eyes at the tone to the figure that had been surrounded by the probe. Thus, for the within-field trial depicted in Fig. 23.1A, the upper left X in the LVF is probed and an eye movement to this stimulus is required. It was predicted that, because both the target and probe appeared in the same hemifield, J. W. would have no difficulty localizing the target on these trials.

This was not the case for *between-field* trials, as depicted in Fig. 23.1B. In this example, the probe stimulus appears in the RVF and an eye movement to the homologous target in the unprobed LVF is required. Accurate performance on this trial requires that at least one of two conditions be met, depending on which hemisphere generates the eye movement: If the eye movement is generated by the contralateral right hemisphere, then the right hemisphere must be able to localize the probe in the ipsilateral RVF. If the eye movement is generated by the ipsilateral left hemisphere, then it must be able to localize the target matrix in the ipsilateral LVF. Whereas these explanations differ with respect to which hemisphere generates the eye movement, both require that at least one hemisphere have access to visual information from the ipsilateral hemifield. Hence, if callosal surgery completely abolishes each hemisphere's representation of the ipsilateral hemifield, then performance in the between-field condition should not differ significantly from chance.

Finally, in order to insure that each matrix remained lateralized to one visual field for the initial period of central fixation, a trial was interrupted and both matrices were extinguished if the eye deviated .5 deg from central fixation before the tone sounded. The displays reappeared and the trial continued when the eyes returned to center.

Within-field and between-field trials were run in counterbalanced blocks of 10 trials with approximately 2 min rest between blocks. A total of 480 trials were collected—120 trials for each of the four conditions.

Results and Discussion

Data Analysis. All analyses were restricted to the first eye movement after the tone because, subsequent to this, it could not be assumed that each matrix was lateralized to a single hemisphere. Both the accuracy and latency of J. W.'s eye movements were analyzed. Two analyses of eye movement accuracy were performed. The first analysis computed the proportion of trials in which the first eye movement after the tone terminated closer to the target stimulus than to any of the remaining stimuli, i.e., *correct trials*. The second analysis computed the absolute distance between the end point of the first eye movement and the target stimulus. For these analyses, 19 trials were not analyzed because an eye movement failed to occur at the tone, or the eye moved into the wrong hemifield. An additional 15 trials were excluded from the analysis of latencies because eye movement latency exceeded 2 sec. For all analyses, *hemisphere* refers to the hemisphere contralateral to the probed field. Thus, for the purposes of analysis, it was assumed that all responses were generated by the probed hemisphere.

Results. The proportion of "correct" trials appears for each condition in Fig. 23.2A. Several aspects of these data bear mentioning. First, for all conditions, J. W. localized the target on significantly more than one quarter of the trials (z values ranged from 3.65 to 11.68; $p < .01$ and $< .001$, respectively). Second, within a hemisphere, fewer between-field responses terminated closest

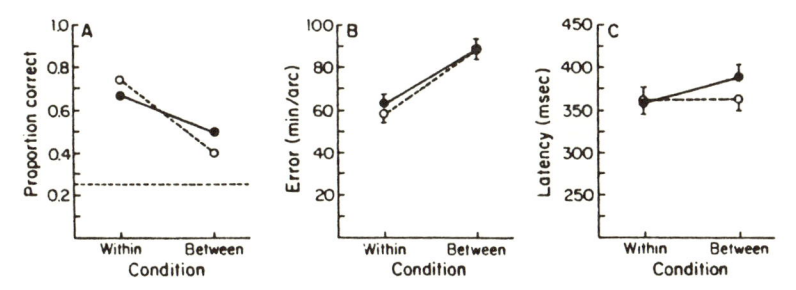

FIG. 23.2. Results of Experiment 1 for the left (solid circles) and right (open circles) hemispheres. (A) Proportion of trials in which the first eye movement after the tone terminated closest to the target stimulus. (B) Average distance between the endpoint to the first eye movement after the tone and the target stimulus. (C) Average latency of the first eye movement after the tone. Error bars represent one standard error of the mean.

to the target stimulus than did within-field responses ($X^2_{(1)}$ = 6.24 and 24.76; p < .05 and < .001 for the left and right hemispheres, respectively). Third, within a condition, there were no significant differences between the hemispheres ($X^2_{(1)}$ = .83 and 2.69; n.s. for the within and between-field conditions, respectively). Finally, it should be pointed out that J. W. had a tendency to execute multiple eye movements to reach the target, particularly for the larger vertical offsets. This was seen even on within-field trials, where there is little doubt that the target stimulus was correctly identified. Because the present analysis focused exclusively on the end position of the *first* eye movement following the tone, J. W.'s eye movement strategy resulted in a large number of responses scored "incorrect".

A similar pattern of results was obtained when eye movement error was calculated, as can be seen in Fig. 23.2B. A two-way ANOVA (Condition × Hemisphere) revealed a highly significant main effect of condition ($F(1,458)$ = 32.65; p < .001) and a non-significant main effect of hemisphere or condition by hemisphere interaction.

An additional analysis of eye movement accuracy computed the product-moment correlation between the vertical position of the target and the vertical position of the eye for the first saccade following the tone. Thus, this analysis was concerned exclusively with the unpredictable aspect of the visual displays—their vertical offset—and thereby with the *sensory* information required of each hemisphere to accurately localize the target. The results of this analysis, presented in Table 23.1, indicate that vertical eye and target positions were highly correlated for all conditions.

Finally, the latencies of the first saccade following the tone were analyzed, as can be seen in Fig. 23.2C. Unlike eye movement accuracy, a two-way ANOVA (Condition × Hemisphere) of eye movement latency revealed that none of the main effects or interaction were significant, although, as Fig. 23.2C indicates,

TABLE 23.1
Correlations and Slopes of the Regression
Lines between the Vertical Component of the
Target Stimulus and the Vertical Component
of the Initial Eye Movement Following the
Tone for the Left and Right Hemispheres

	r	Slope	N
Within-Field			
Left	.91	.81	117
Right	.92[a]	.92	115
Between-Field			
Left	.79	.65	116
Right	.80	.72	113

[a] All correlations are significant at $p < .001$.

there was a tendency for the right hemisphere to respond faster than the left in the between-field condition.

Discussion. How is the target localized when the probe and target stimuli appear in different hemifields, i.e., on between-field trials? In this experiment, the vertical position of each matrix was randomly varied on each trial, yet vertical eye and target positions were highly correlated. Moreover, an eye movement to the target stimulus occurred on significantly more than one fourth of the between-field trials. Thus, these results strongly imply that each hemisphere has access to some visual information from the ipsilateral hemifield, which is the first of the two predictions about eye movement control previously outlined.

However, it is not clear which hemisphere generates the eye movements on between-field trials. For example, for the between-field trial depicted in Fig. 23.2B, the LVF eye movement to the target X could be generated by the *ipsilateral* left hemisphere—the hemisphere that receives the RVF proble. Conversely, it could be generated by the *contralateral* right hemisphere—the hemisphere that receives the LVF target matrix. For the former explanation, the left hemisphere requires visual information regarding the location of the matrix in the ipsilateral LVF. For the latter explanation, the right hemisphere requires visual information regarding the location of the probe in the ipsilateral RVF. Thus, these results do not resolve the question of which hemisphere is generating between-field responses.

Finally, although the present results imply that each hemisphere has access to some visual information from the ipsilateral hemifield for eye movements, they also imply that this information is of relatively crude spatial resolution. Otherwise, eye movements on within-field and between-field trials should have been of comparable accuracy. To the contrary, eye movements were consistently more accurate on within-field trials, where integration of the two visual fields was not required. In the next experiment, the ability of each hemisphere to resolve detail in the ipsilateral visual field was assessed.

EXPERIMENT 2

Experiment 2 was designed in such a way that eye movements on between-field trials only would be accurate if each hemisphere had a detailed and integrated sensory map of both visual fields. Some of these results have been reported elsewhere (Holtzman, 1984).

Methods

Conditions and Procedure. The two experimental conditions for this study are illustrated in Fig. 23.3. On each trial, four figures were randomly shuffled among four locations in each 2 deg square matrix, so that the position of a particular figure was unpredictable from trial to trial. The nearest edge of each matrix was 1.5 deg from the vertical midline, and each figure subtended approximately .25 deg of visual angle. The two matrices of figures always were positioned symmetrically about the horizontal and vertical meridians. Analogous to the previous study, on each trial, following a period of central fixation, during which just the eight figures were displayed, a probe stimulus (one of the four shapes) appeared briefly centered in one of the arrays. One second then elapsed and the tone sounded, at which time J. W. was required to move his eyes to the stimulus that matched the probe. As in the previous experiment, if the eye moved .5 deg from central fixation before the tone sounded, the matrices disappeared until the eyes returned to center.

Within-field trials (Fig. 23.3A) were those in which J. W. moved to the stimulus that matched the probe, in the field in which the probe appeared; between-field trials (Fig. 23.3B) were those in which he moved to the corresponding stimulus in the opposite field. Thus, this procedure is very similar to that used in Experiment 1, except that accurate performance in this experiment required the resolution of .25 deg figures.

Within-field and between-field trials were run in counterbalanced blocks of 10 trials. A total of 80 within-field and 200 between-field trials were collected. Trials in which the probe appeared in the LVF and RVF were equally represented.

Results and Discussion

Data Analysis. Both the accuracy and latency of J. W.'s eye movements were analyzed. For the analysis of accuracy, 11 trials were not analyzed because an eye movement failed to occur at the tone, or the eye moved into the wrong

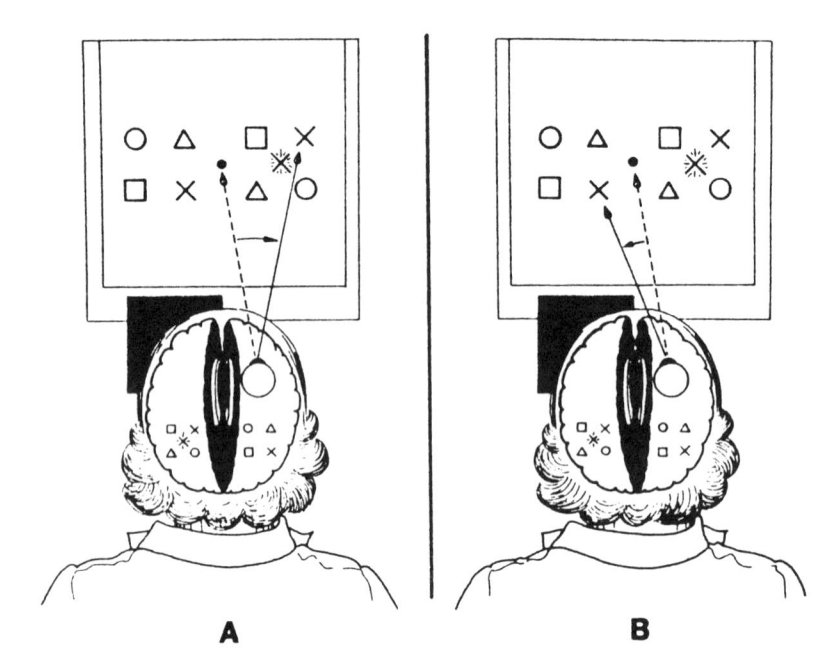

FIG. 23.3. Example of conditions in Experiment 2. On within-field trials (A), the probe appeared centered in one of the arrays and the eye moved to the corresponding stimulus in the field in which the probe appeared; on between-field trials (B), the eye moved to the corresponding stimulus in the opposite field. Each matrix of four figures subtended 2 × 2 deg of visual angle; each figure within a matrix subtended approximately .25 deg of visual angle. The nearest edge of each matrix was 1.5 deg from the vertical meridian. The matrices always were positioned symmetrically about the horizontal and vertical meridians. On each trial, the four figures in each matrix were randomly shuffled so that the position of a particular figure was unpredictable from trial to trial (reprinted from Holtzman, 1984).

hemifield. An additional 13 trials were excluded from the analysis of latency because eye movement latency exceeded 2 sec. The results of these analyses are summarized in Fig. 23.4.

Results. The proportion of trials in which the first eye movement after the tone terminated closest to the target stimulus appears for each condition in Fig. 23.4A. Unlike the previous findings, there is no evidence here that J. W. was able to localize the target on between-field trials: The proportion of correct between-field responses did not exceed .25 for either hemisphere ($z = -.37$ and .17; $p > .1$ for the left and right hemispheres, respectively), although J. W. was quite accurate on within-field trials ($z = 10.22$ and 8.76; $p < .001$ for the left and right hemispheres, respectively).

Eye movement latencies are summarized in Fig. 23.4B, where the general pattern of results resembled that obtained in Experiment 1, and some of the differences reached significance. A two-way ANOVA (Condition × Hemisphere) revealed significant main effects of condition ($F(1,253) = 13.82$; $p < .001$) and a marginally significant effect of hemisphere ($F(1,253) = 3.59$; $p = .056$). The hemisphere by condition interaction was not significant.

Discussion. Whereas the results of Experiment 1 implied that each hemisphere of the commissurotomy patient has access to some sensory information from the ipsilateral visual field, the results of the present study confirm that this information is of relatively limited spatial resolution. It will be recalled that two explanations were proposed to account for the accuracy of between-field responses in Experiment 1. The first account was that these responses were generated by the hemisphere *ipsilateral* to the target matrix based on its ability to localize the target matrix in the ipsilateral visual field. The second account was that between-field responses were generated by the hemisphere *contralateral* to the target matrix based on its ability to localize the probe stimulus in the ipsilateral visual field. Thus, the former account requires that each hemisphere can localize a 2 × 2 deg matrix in the ipsilateral visual field; the latter account requires that each hemisphere can localize a .25 deg probe in the ipsilateral hemifield.

The results of Experiment 2 clearly favor the first explanation, where only relatively crude ipsilateral vision is required. However, a critical aspect of this

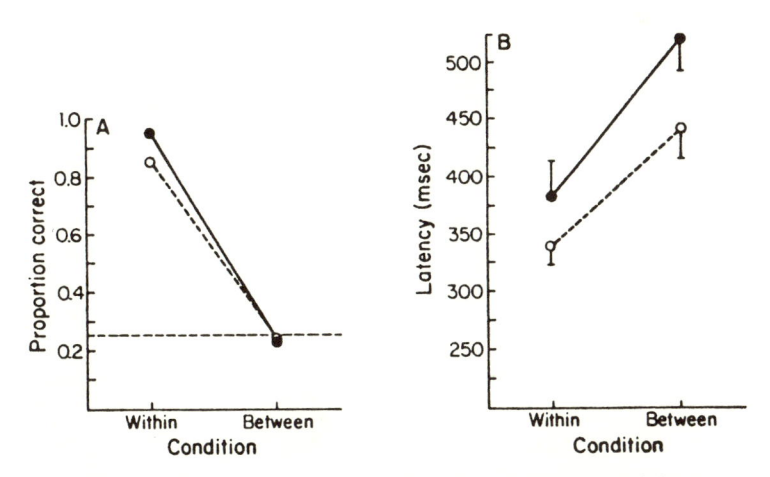

FIG. 23.4. Results of Experiment 2 for the left (solid circles) and right (open circles) hemispheres. (A) Proportion of trials in which the first eye movement after the tone terminated closest to the target stimulus. (B) Average latency of the first eye movement after the tone. Error bars represent one standard error of the mean.

account is each hemisphere's ability to generate eye movements into the ipsilateral visual field, something that these studies have yet to demonstrate conclusively. Given the results of Experiment 2, this now can be assessed unambiguously. Experiment 2 demonstrated that each hemisphere is unable to discriminate .25 deg shapes in the ipsilateral hemifield so that, when a hemisphere is instructed to direct the eyes to a particular shape in the ipsilateral field, and the location of that shape is unpredictable from trial to trial, the eyes are no more likely to move to the correct stimulus than to any other stimulus. In other words, neither hemisphere is able to resolve both the probe stimulus in one field and the target array in the other—the visual fields are functionally disconnected for these stimuli.

Hence, for the stimuli used in Experiment 2, it can be assumed that the probe stimulus is strictly lateralized to the contralateral hemisphere. If, on between-field trials, the probed hemisphere also is informed of the location of the corresponding ipsilateral target figure, then the ability of each hemisphere to generate ipsiversive eye movements can be assessed. In Experiment 3, this was accomplished by leaving each hemifield's array of figures unchanged from trial to trial—the square always appeared in the upper left corner of each matrix, the circle in the bottom right corner, and so on. J. W. was told that the figures would remain in the same positions throughout the study, and that, if he had any difficulty "seeing" any figures, he could rely on his spatial memory in generating his eye movements.

EXPERIMENT 3

Methods

Conditions and Procedure. All aspects of this study were identical to Experiment 2, except that the four figures in each visual field did not change their locations from trial to trial. A total of 40 trials were collected for each of the four conditions.

Results

Data Analysis. Both the accuracy and latency of J. W.'s eye movements were analyzed. For the analysis of accuracy, five trials were not analyzed because an eye movement failed to occur or the eye moved into the wrong visual field. An additional six trials were excluded from the analysis of latencies because eye movement latency exceeded 2 sec. The results of these analyses are summarized in Fig. 23.5.

Results. The proportion of trials in which J. W.'s first eye movement after the tone terminated closest to the target stimulus appears for each condition in Fig. 23.5A. The results are quite clear: J. W. is now able to localize the target

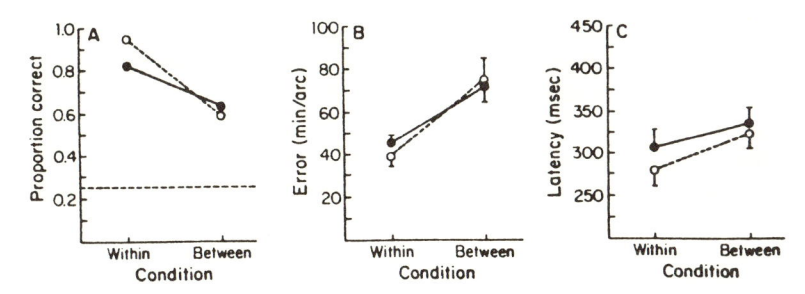

FIG. 23.5. Results of Experiment 3 for the left (solid circles) and right (open circles) hemispheres. (A) Proportion of trials in which the first eye movement after the tone terminated closest to the target stimulus. (B) Average distance between the endpoint to the first eye movement after the tone and the target stimulus. (C) Average latency of the first eye movement after the tone. Error bars represent one standard error of the mean.

stimulus on between-field trials ($z = 5.43$ and 4.90; $p < .001$ for the left and right hemispheres, respectively). For the reasons just outlined such a result only is possible if each hemisphere is able to generate eye movements to specific locations in the ipsilateral visual field.

Additional analyses and comparisons yielded results similar to those obtained in the prior experiments. Hence, significantly more within-field eye movements terminated closest to the target stimulus than did between-field responses ($X^2_{(1)} = 3.71$ and 13.74; $p = .052$ and $p < .001$ for the left and right hemispheres, respectively), and, within a condition, performance was quite similar for the two hemispheres ($X^2_{(1)} = .14$ and 2.86; n.s. for between-field and within-field responses, respectively).

Figure 23.5B presents a summary of eye movement error. Once again, a two-way ANOVA (Hemisphere × Condition) revealed that between-field responses were less accurate than within-field responses ($F(1,152) = 23.57$; $p < .001$), whereas no significant main effect of hemisphere or hemisphere by condition interaction was obtained.

Finally, Fig. 23.5C presents a summary of eye movement latency. Although the same general pattern of results obtained in the previous studies is present here—between-field responses had longer latencies than did within-field responses, left hemisphere responses had longer latencies than did right hemisphere responses—only the main effect of condition approached significance ($F(1,146) = 3.07$; $p = .078$).

GENERAL DISCUSSION

The present findings support two general conclusions concerning the control of saccadic eye movements following callosal surgery. First, each hemisphere has access to some visual information from the ipsilateral hemifield for oculomotor control. Representation of the ipsilateral hemifield appears to be of relatively crude spatial resolution; sufficiently detailed so that each hemisphere could localize a 2 deg square matrix in the ipsilateral field, but not precise enough to identify .25 deg shapes. Second, each hemisphere can direct the eyes into either visual field. Analogous to vision, ipsiversive responses tended to be less accurate than contraversive responses. Unfortunately, it can not be concluded that this represents a true motor apraxia; inaccurate ipsiversive eye movements simply may have reflected impoverished ipsilateral vision. Data consistent with this latter interpretation was obtained in a similar study from our laboratory in which a hemianopic subject, B. H., was required to move her eyes to the remembered locations of targets in her blind field based on visual cues that appeared in her intact field (Holtzman, Volpe & Gazzaniga, 1984). This can be regarded as a control condition in which the callosal connections between motor areas are left intact, but all ipsilateral vision is eliminated. Overall, the blind field versus intact field performance of B. H. was relatively worse than the between-field versus within-field performance of J. W. (average increase in error = 108% for B. H., 74% for J. W.). This result would be anticipated if the relative inaccuracy of J. W.'s ipsiversive eye movements was due primarily to impoverished ipsilateral vision.

One obvious question is whether each hemisphere's representation of the ipsilateral visual field for eye movements also is available for perceptual function. This appeared to be the case in the present context, where additional observations of J. W. (Holtzman, 1984) revealed that he also could perform *perceptual* interfield comparisons of the locations of the two matrices used in the eye movement studies. Similarly, Trevarthen and Sperry (1973) describe two additional commissurotomy patients who could perceptually integrate the visual fields for continuous peripheral visual stimulation (+/− 30 deg), and Johnson (1984) reports that one of these patients (N. G.) even could perform interfield perceptual comparisons of briefly flashed stimuli, a capacity clearly lacking in J. W. (e.g., see Holtzman & Gazzaniga, in press; Sidtis, Volpe, Holtzman, Wilson, & Gazzaniga, 1981).

The only empirical evidence suggesting that different visual information may be used for motor control and perceptual function in these patients was a study of covert orienting by Holtzman, Sidtis, Volpe, Wilson, and Gazzaniga (1981). Here, despite their ability to shift attention across the visual midline, commissurotomy patients were unable to perceptually compare the relative locations of two briefly flashed X's, one appearing in each field. However, as the results of Experiment 3 clearly demonstrate, such interfield orienting could have been mediated by spatial memory, and need not have required perceptual integration of the visual fields. In all, there is little evidence, if any, to suggest that a dissociation exists between visual information for motor control and perceptual function following corpus commissurotomy.

The other conclusion of these studies is that each hemisphere of the commissurotomy patient is capable of generating both ipsiversive and contraversive saccadic eye movements. Thus, when a visual cue was lateralized to a single hemisphere, say to the left hemisphere via right field stimulation, J. W. directed his eyes to the corresponding target stimulus either in the probed right hemifield (i.e., a contraversive saccade), or in the unprobed left field (i.e., an ipsiversive saccade). Moreover, apart from a small right hemisphere advantage for eye movement latency, the performance of the two hemispheres was virtually identical. Ipsiversive saccades also have been reported in commissurotomy patients by Trevarthen (1974), and they are consistent with unilateral lesion studies of both humans (Guitton, Buchtel and Douglas, 1982; Troost, Weber & Daroff, 1972) and animals (Latto & Cowey, 1971a, 1971b; Schiller, True & Conway, 1980). Although it cannot be argued from the present results that ipsiversive saccades are exclusively under cortical control, it is clear from these findings that there is a strong cortical influence on the generation of visually based saccadic eye movements. Hence, when the hemispheres are disconnected for the perceptual resolution of detail, as they were in Experiment 2, they also appear to be disconnected for the generation of eye movements based on the discrimination of such detail.

Overall, the present results are consistent with the dominant hemisphere account of behavioral control following callosal surgery previously outlined. The availability of relatively crude ipsilateral vision, coupled with the capacity to generate both contraversive and ipsiversive eye movements, would permit a single hemisphere to control behavior without overt signs of sensory or motor impairment. It should be emphasized, however, that it is highly unlikely that a particular hemisphere maintains exclusive control of behavior outside of the laboratory. Numerous studies of commissurotomized humans and animals have demonstrated that control can readily shift between the hemispheres based on a variety of factors including task type (e.g., Levy, Trevarthen & Sperry, 1972), hand preference (e.g., Trevarthen, 1962), and reward contingencies (e.g., Gazzaniga, 1971). There is no reason to assume that such factors do not influence behavior in the normal environment. Although the present results may help explain how a single disconnected hemisphere can manage behavior so effectively, the mechanism by which unilateral control is maintained and the manner in which it ultimately is relinquished remain a mystery.

ACKNOWLEDGMENT

Preparation of this chapter was supported by NIH Grants 17936 and 15053.

REFERENCES

Cornsweet, T. N., & Crane, H. D. (1973). Accurate two-dimensional eye tracker using first and fourth Purkinje images. *Journal of the Optical Society of America, 63,* 1192–1193.
Gazzaniga, M. S. (1970). *The bisected brain.* New York: Appleton-Century-Crofts.
Gazzaniga, M. S. (1971). Changing hemisphere dominance by changing reward probability in split-brain monkeys. *Experimental Neurology, 33,* 412–419.

Gazzaniga, M. S., Holtzman, J. D., Gates, J., Deck, M. D. F., & Lee, B. C. P. (in preparation). *NMR evaluation of corpus callosotomy in humans.*

Gazzaniga, M. S., Holtzman, J. D., Gates, J., Deck, M. D. F., & Lee, B. C. P. (1984 October). *NMR verification of surgical section of the corpus callosum and presence of the anterior commissure.* Paper presented to the Society for Neuroscience.

Guitton, D., Buchtel, H. A., & Douglas, R. M. (1982). Disturbances of voluntary saccadic eye movement mechanisms following discrete unilateral frontal lobe removals. In G. Lennerstrand, D. S. Zee, & E. L. Keller, (Eds.), *Functional basis of ocular motility disorders* (pp. 497–499). New York: Pergamon.

Holtzman, J. D. (1984). Interactions between cortical and subcortical visual areas: Evidence from human commissurotomy patients. *Vision Research, 24,* 801–813.

Holtzman, J. D., & Gazzaniga (in press). Enhanced dual task performance following corpus commissurotomy in humans. *Neuropsychologia.*

Holtzman, J. D., Sidtis, J. J., Volpe, B. T., Wilson, D. H., & Gazzaniga, M. S. (1981). Dissociation of spatial information for stimulus localization and the control of attention. *Brain, 104,* 861–872.

Holtzman, J. D., Volpe, B. T., & Gazzaniga, M. S. (1984 February). *Deficits in visual-motor control despite intact subcortical visual areas.* Paper presented at the American Academy of Neurology 36th Annual Meeting.

Johnson, L. E. (1984). Bilateral visual cross-integration by human forebrain commissurotomy subjects. *Neuropsychologia, 22,* 153–166.

Latto, R. and Cowey, A. (1971a). Visual field defects after frontal eye-field lesions in monkeys. *Brain Research, 30,* 25–36.

Latto, R., & Cowey, A. (1971b). Fixation changes after frontal eye-field lesions in monkeys. *Brain Research, 30,* 25–36.

Leigh, R. J., & Zee, D. S. (1983). *The neurology of eye movement.* Philadelphia: Davis.

Levy, J., Trevarthen, C., & Sperry, R. W. (1972). Perception of bilateral chimeric figures following hemispheric deconnection. *Brain, 95,* 61–78.

Pasik, P., Pasik, T., Valciukas, J. A., & Bender, M. B. (1971). Vertical optokinetic nystagmus in the split-brain monkey. *Experimental Neurology, 30,* 162–171.

Robinson, D. A., & Fuchs, A. F. (1969). Eye movements evoked by stimulation of frontal eye fields. *Journal of Neurophysiology, 32,* 637–648.

Schiller, P. H., True, S. D., & Conway, J. L. (1980). Deficits in eye movements following frontal eye-field and superior colliculus ablations. *Journal of Neurophysiology, 44,* 1175–1189.

Sidtis, J. J., Volpe, B. T., Holtzman, J. D., Wilson, D. H., & Gazzaniga, M. S. (1981). Cognitive interactions after staged callosal section: Evidence for transfer of semantic activation. *Science, 212,* 344–346.

Sidtis, J. J., Volpe, B. T., Wilson, D. H., Rayport, M., & Gazzaniga, M. S. (1981). Variability in right hemisphere language function after callosal section: evidence for a continuum of generative capacity. *Journal of Neuroscience, 1,* 323–331.

Trevarthen, C. B. (1962). Double visual learning in split-brain monkeys. *Science, 136,* 258–259.

Trevarthen, C. B. (1974). Analysis of cerebral activities that generate and regulate consciousness in commissurotomy patients. In S. J. Dimond & J. G. Beaumont (Eds.), *Hemisphere function in the brain.* London: Elek Science.

Trevarthen, C. B., & Sperry, R. W. (1973). Perceptual unity of the ambient visual field in human commissurotomy patients. *Brain, 96,* 547–570.

Troost, B. T., Weber, R. B., & Daroff, R. B. (1972). Hemispheric control of eye movements. I. Quantitative analysis of refixation saccades in hemispherectomy patient. *Archives of Neurology, 27,* 441–448.

Wilson, D. H., Reeves, A., & Gazzaniga, M. S. (1978). Division of the corpus callosum for uncontrollable epilepsy. *Neurology, Minneapolis, 28,* 649–653.

24. Stimulus Selection and Conditional Response Mechanisms in the Basal Ganglia of the Monkey

Robert H. Wurtz
Laboratory of Sensorimotor Research, National Eye Institute

ABSTRACT

In both humans and monkeys rapid or saccadic eye movements move the eye from one part of the visual field to another, frequently in association with shifts of attention. The neural mechanisms related to stimulus selection for such shifts of attention or initiation of saccadic eye movements have been investigated in awake, behaving monkeys. When the monkey uses a stimulus as the target for a saccadic eye movement, the response of the cells to that stimulus is enhanced. The change in discharge of single cells in one structure within the basal ganglia of monkeys, the pars reticulata of the substantia nigra, illustrates the characteristics of the enhanced visual response, particularly in relation to the initiation of movement. These experiments on the substantia nigra also show that one overt response, the saccadic eye movement, can involve different neural circuitry depending on the conditions under which the saccade is made. Some cells in this structure discharge in relation to saccades to a target that must be remembered but not in relation to saccades to visual targets or to saccades made spontaneously in either the light or the dark. Selective alteration of the neural transmitter that conveys the signal from this structure to the next, the superior colliculus, alters the monkey's ability to make saccades to remembered targets more than to visual targets.

INTRODUCTION

Many of the attention and performance characteristics seen in people can also be seen in old-world monkeys, and these monkeys offer the added possibility of directly investigating the neural events related to these behavioral phenomena.

One way in which monkeys are particularly similar to humans is in the types of eye movements they make, including the rapid or saccadic eye movements that move the eye from one part of the visual field to another. These saccadic eye movements are closely associated with shifts of attention, although such shifts can occur in the absence of eye movements (Posner, 1980; Wurtz, Goldberg, & Robinson, 1980). My colleagues and I have investigated the single-cell events in the monkey that might be related to the selection of visual stimuli and the initiation of saccadic eye movements to these stimuli.

This chapter concentrates on two major points that can be made by considering one area of the brain. The first point concerns the neural mechanism related to stimulus selection; the response of a cell to a stimulus can be enhanced when that stimulus is used in some way by the monkey. After a review of the methods used and the findings in a number of brain areas, the general characteristics of the enhancement effect can be described in an area recently studied. The second point relates to the neural mechanism underlying the initiation of the same behavioral response made under different conditions; a saccade can have different neural mechanisms depending on the condition under which it is made. The area of the brain used to illustrate both of these phenomena is the substantia nigra pars reticulata of the basal ganglia.

STIMULUS-SELECTION MECHANISMS

The behavioral methods used in these experiments allow analysis of the sensory properties of cells within the brain, the change in properties when a particular stimulus is chosen as the trigger or target for a movement, and the relation between these properties and the movement itself. Figure 24.1 outlines these basic behavioral methods. We train the monkey to fixate on a small spot of light for several seconds (FP in Fig. 24.1A), and while it is doing so, a second spot of light, the receptive-field stimulus (RF in Fig. 24.1A), is projected onto the screen in front of it. This second stimulus is used to analyze the receptive field of a particular cell in the brain. The methods we use for single-cell recording, recording eye movement, control of behavior, and analysis of single-cell data have been described previously (Hikosaka & Wurtz, 1983a). In the task shown in Fig. 24.1A, the response of the cell to visual stimulation is not dependent on the monkey's use of the visual stimulus because the monkey is rewarded for detecting changes at the fixation point and can be regarded as reflecting the "passive" response of the cell. Figure 24.1B illustrates the behavioral method used to require the monkey to use the visual stimulus, in this case as the target for a rapid or saccadic eye movement. When the monkey makes a saccade to that stimulus, we can say that it must have used the stimulus, and we can then look for any increase or decrease in the response of a single cell under study related to this use. In order to say whether such changes in cellular discharge are related only to

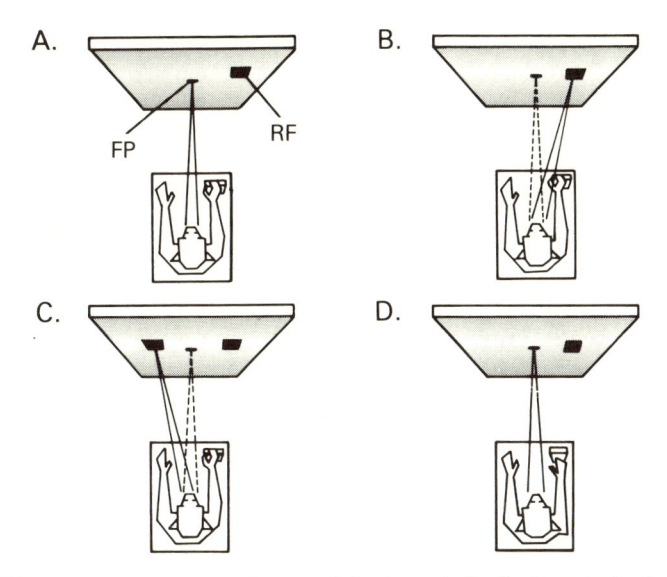

24. STIMULUS SELECTION AND RESPONSE MECHANISMS   443

FIG. 24.1. Behavioral paradigms used for the analysis of enhanced visual responses seen during stimulus selection. In A, the monkey fixates on a spot of light (FP) and a second visual stimulus (RF) is used to map the visual receptive field of the cell under study. In B, the paradigm is modified so that the monkey is required to make a saccade to the visual stimulus and thereby demonstrate any change in visual response related to use of the stimulus. In C, the effect of selective use of the target is determined. Two targets appear simultaneously, a receptive-field stimulus as in B and a control stimulus in the other visual field. If an enhanced visual response is related to saccades to the receptive-field stimulus only, spatial selectivity is demonstrated; if the enhancement is related to saccades to the control stimulus as well, only a general affect, such as arousal or activation, is indicated. In D, the dependence of any response modulation on the specific behavioral response is shown. In this experiment the monkey does not make saccadic eye movements to the stimulus but instead responds to a change in the stimulus by reaching toward it or releasing a bar. Dependence of the enhancement effect on the response is interpreted as stimulus selection for the initiation of movement whereas enhancement that is independent of the response is interpreted as a possible correlate of selective spatial attention.

one part of the visual field, the behavioral paradigm shown in Fig. 24.1C is necessary. In this paradigm, when the target light in the receptive field comes on, another light also comes on in the opposite visual field. In a series of trials, the monkey is rewarded for making saccades to the stimulus in the receptive field; in another series of trials, the monkey is rewarded for making saccades to the control stimulus. If the response of the cell shows enhancement only when the monkey makes saccades to the receptive-field stimulus, the stimulus selection is clearly spatially selective. If enhancement occurs when the monkey makes saccades both to the receptive-field stimulus and the control stimulus, then no such selectivity is evident and the enhancement is probably more appropriately described as related to arousal rather than any selective process. Finally, it is necessary to determine whether, in the case of selective enhancement, the enhancement is specifically dependent on the occurrence of a saccadic eye movement. To determine this, the monkeys are required to look at the fixation point and not make an eye movement to the visual stimulus, but, instead, to respond to a change in the visual stimulus by releasing the bar or reaching toward the visual stimulus (Fig. 24.1D). If the visual enhancement is independent of the movement made by the monkey, we have interpreted this enhancement as related to selective visual attention. If, however, the enhanced response is dependent on the monkey's saccade to a visual target, then we would say that this is probably not a correlate of attention but rather a correlate of the initiation of movement. Note, however, that in both of these cases the visual enhancement is *selective,* in the one case independent of movement, in the other case dependent on movement.

A series of experiments, summarized elsewhere (Wurtz, Goldberg, & Robinson, 1980, 1982), have shown that cells in different areas of the brain show different types of visual enhancement when these methods are used. In the occipital cortex, cells in both the primary visual area (striate cortex or V1) and the second visual area (V2) show enhancement that is best described as a nonspecific arousal effect; no selective enhancement is observed (Robinson, Baizer, & Dow, 1980; Wurtz & Mohler, 1976a). In striking contrast, Bushnell, Goldberg, & Robinson (1981) found selective enhancement in the parietal cortex that is response independent, and this visual enhancement is argued to be a correlate of visual spatial attention. In contrast, cells that show selective visual enhancement but are dependent on the occurrence of saccadic eye movements made to the visual stimulus are found in the superior colliculus (Goldberg & Wurtz, 1972; Wurtz & Mohler, 1976b), in the frontal eye fields (Goldberg & Bushnell, 1981; Wurtz & Mohler, 1976a), and most recently in the substantia nigra pars reticulata (Hikosaka & Wurtz, 1983a).[1] Enhancement of response has also been tested in the inferior temporal area (Richmond, Wurtz, & Sato, 1983) and areas of prestriate cortex (Fischer & Boch, 1981; Fischer, Boch, & Bach, 1981), as well as with visual discriminations, but this is beyond the scope of the present discussion (see Wurtz, Richmond, & Newsome, 1984).

One structure, the pars reticulata of the substantia nigra, has been investigated recently (Hikosaka & Wurtz, 1983a, 1983b, 1983c, 1983d, 1985a, 1985b) and illustrates several general points about the enhancement effect associated with the initiation of movement. This structure is part of the basal ganglia, a group of

---

[1]The test for movement specificity (Fig. 24.1D) has not been done for the substantia nigra. For present purposes, the close relationship of the structure to initiation of movement shown by single-cell and lesion studies prompts placement of these cells into the movement-related category.

24. STIMULUS SELECTION AND RESPONSE MECHANISMS 445

anatomically related nuclei located primarily in the diencephalon and mesencephalon, that are related to the initiation and modulation of movement (see DeLong & Georgopoulos, 1981, for review). This structure becomes of interest in relation to the initiation of eye movements if one looks at neural processing at successively increasing distances back into the nervous system from the final oculomotor pathway. Figure 24.2 shows the location of cells near the final pathway, those cells that are related to initiation of saccadic eye movements in the horizontal and vertical planes that are concentrated in the pontine reticular formation (PPRF) and mesencephalic reticular formation (MRF), respectively. These motor structures provide the burst of activity and the continuous discharge (the pulse and step) that eventually reach the eye muscles to move the eye from one part of the visual field to another and hold it there. Projecting directly to these structures is the superior colliculus (SC), the last premotor area above the PPRF and MRF where a topographically organized map of visual and movement-related neuronal activity is found. The superior colliculus is a laminated structure and one set of these layers, the intermediate gray and white layers, has cells that

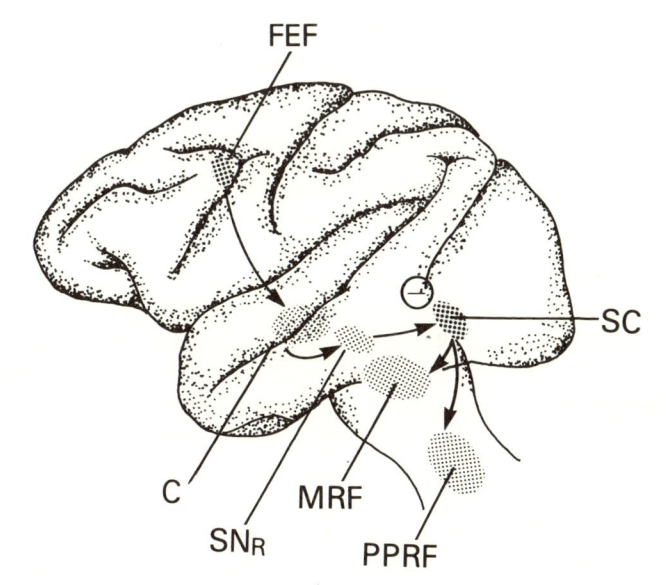

FIG. 24.2. Illustration of the location of substantia nigra pars reticulata (SNr) in a pathway related to control of saccadic eye movements. View is from the side of the brain. Shaded areas represent structures within the brain except FEF, which is on the surface of the cerebral cortex. Connection is from SNr to the superior colliculus (SC), which in turn projects to the oculomotor areas in the mesencephalic and pontine reticular formations (MRF, PPRF). The inhibitory connection from the substantia nigra to the superior colliculus is indicated by the minus sign in the circle. Projections from frontal cortex, including frontal eye fields (FEF), through the caudate nucleus (C) to the SNr are also indicated.

discharge before saccadic eye movements. For this and other reasons (see Wurtz & Albano, 1980) it is believed that the superior colliculus is related to the initiation of saccadic eye movements. One of the major anatomical inputs to the layers within the superior colliculus in which these "movement" cells are located is the pars reticulata of the substantia nigra (SNr). The input from the substantia nigra pars reticulata, along with that from the frontal eye fields (FEF), in the frontal cortex, are probably the most prominent input to the movement cell layers in the superior colliculus. Analysis of the substantia nigra, therefore, represents an attempt to back one step further into the nervous system to analyze the visual and motor processing preceding eye movements.

As indicated in Fig. 24.2, the substantia nigra might lie on a pathway that extends from the frontal cortex, including the frontal eye fields, through the caudate nucleus (C), to the substantia nigra, then to the superior colliculus, and finally to the brainstem oculomotor areas. As becomes evident later, this anatomical relation of the substantia nigra to frontal cortex is consistent with similarities between cell activity in substantia nigra and some functions postulated to be dependent on frontal cortex.

There are, in fact, two parts of the substantia nigra, the pars reticulata, which we consider here, and the pars compacta, which we do not. The pars compacta is the dopamine-rich structure that modulates activity of the striatum of the basal ganglia. We have found that the pars reticulata is probably the most important output pathway of the basal ganglia for the initiation of saccadic eye movements. (For convenience, the substantia nigra pars reticulata is referred to subsequently as the substantia nigra.) A transmitter used by cells in the substantia nigra is likely to be γ-amino butyric acid (GABA) (see Hikosaka & Wurtz, 1983c, 1985a, for discussion). GABA is an inhibitory transmitter, so that the substantia nigra is likely to inhibit activity of the superior colliculus.

The key characteristic of all substantia nigra neurons studied so far is shown in Fig. 24.3A: They have high discharge rates, frequently reaching 80 to 100 impulses per second. The response of these cells is a decrease in discharge rate following, for example, the onset of a visual stimulus (Fig. 24.3A). The signal these cells convey is a pause in the high discharge rate. Given the evidence that the effect of the substantia nigra on the superior colliculus is inhibitory, a pause in discharge rate in the substantia nigra should lead to a reduction of inhibition on the superior colliculus. This should produce or facilitate an increase in discharge rate within the superior colliculus at the same time that a decrease in discharge rate occurs in the substantia nigra; such a reciprocal relation between these two structures has been shown to occur (Hikosaka & Wurtz, 1983d).

The receptive-field stimulus for substantia nigra neurons need not be very specific: Small spots of light are as effective as oriented stimuli, colored stimuli, or moving stimuli. Receptive fields are generally large with a gradient of response intensity moving from the center to the edge of the field, and the receptive fields are centered in the visual field contralateral to the side of the brain in which

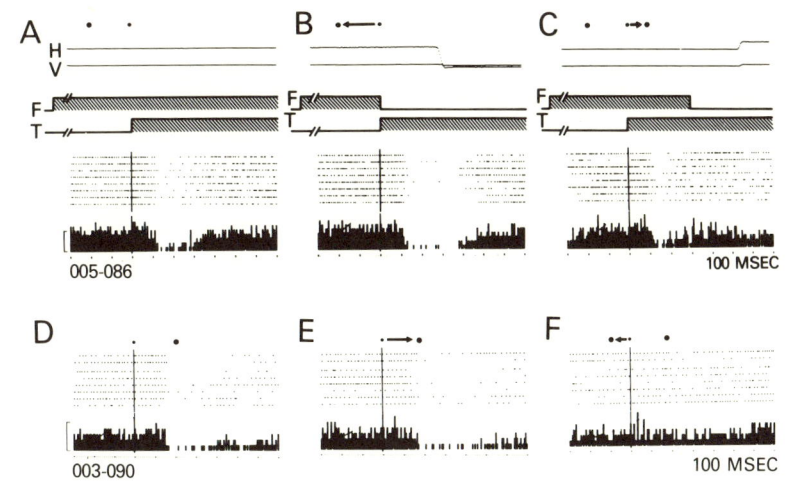

24. STIMULUS SELECTION AND RESPONSE MECHANISMS 447

FIG. 24.3. Enhanced visual response of cells in substantia nigra when the monkey uses the visual stimulus as the target for saccadic eye movements. In A, the response while the monkey looks at the fixation point (F) is a decrease in discharge rate following onset of the visual stimulus (T). In B, this decrease is enhanced when the monkey makes saccades to the visual target (as indicated by the horizontal, H, and vertical, V, eye-movement traces), but not in C, when the monkey makes saccades to another stimulus in the ipsilateral field. In D, E, and F, the response of a different cell is shown in which an enhanced response is evident when the monkey makes saccades to the visual target (compare saccade condition, E, with fixation condition, D) but a decreased response occurs with saccades to the control target in the other visual field (compare saccade to control target, F, with that during fixation, D). Saccades to the control target in the ipsilateral field were made 300 msec after the target in the receptive field came on in order to reveal any response to the control target; simultaneous onset of the control target and receptive-field target produced the same effect. The target point was 20° into the contralateral visual field, the control point was 10° into the ipsilateral field for both cells, but the cells were studied on different sides of the brain so that contralateral in A, B, C is in the opposite field from that in D, E, F.

Cell discharge is indicated by the dots, cell discharge on successive stimulus presentations is indicated by successive lines on the dot pattern, and the sum of these individual discharges is shown on the histogram. Calibration for the histogram is 100 discharges/sec/trial; bin width is 12 msec. Time between scale marks is indicated in the lower right corner; cell number is in the lower left corner. Subsequent figures use the same convention.

the cells are recorded. In all these respects the receptive fields and stimulus specificity of substantia nigra neurons are similar to those found in other movement-related areas such as the superior colliculus and the frontal eye fields.

An example of the enhanced visual response seen in substantia nigra cells when the monkey uses the receptive-field stimulus is shown in Fig. 24.3. Fig. 24.3B shows the neuronal response when the monkey used the stimulus in the contralateral visual field as the target for saccadic eye movements: The decrease in discharge is prolonged—that is, the response is enhanced. Note that because the response of the cells is a decrease in discharge rate, the enhanced response is a greater and more prolonged *decrease* in discharge rate. This enhancement is spatially selective because when the monkey made saccades to a control target in the ipsilateral visual field (Fig. 24.3C) no response enhancement occurred.

In areas studied so far, the superior colliculus and frontal eye fields, when the control stimulus is the target for the saccade, the visual response is nearly the same as the response when the monkey is simply fixating and the visual stimulus comes on. In Fig. 24.3C, when the saccades were made to control targets, the response returned to the level observed when the monkey was simply fixating (Fig. 24.3A). Other cells in the substantia nigra, however, show a decrease in response when the monkey uses the target in the other visual field, as shown for another cell in Fig. 24.3D to 24.3F. The response shows some enhancement when the monkey used the stimulus in the receptive field (Fig. 24.3E compared with Fig. 24.3D) but the response when the monkey used the target in the other visual field is actually reduced below the level evident when the monkey was fixating (Fig. 24.3F compared to Fig. 24.3D). This "push–pull" effect, an increase with use of the stimulus, a decrease with use of another stimulus, is so far unique. It indicates that visual processing can be incremented in areas of use relevant to a current movement and decremented in the other visual-field areas that are not relevant to the current movement. It might be that this bidirectional effect is specifically related to an area whose output is exclusively or largely inhibitory; other areas studied, in which the bidirectional effect is not observed, have outputs that are probably in large part excitatory.

One of the functions of the enhanced response that was originally considered by Goldberg and Wurtz for cells in the superior colliculus (Goldberg & Wurtz, 1972) is that use of the stimulus reverses the decrement in neural response that occurs with repetitive stimulation. This habituation has been particularly striking for the visual responses in the substantia nigra. For many cells, repetition of the same stimulus at the same point in the visual field produces a habituation of response in less than 10 stimulus presentations. Furthermore, this habituation is dependent on intertrial interval. For example, the response of cells in the substantia nigra when the intertrial interval is .5 sec is less than when the intertrial interval is 2 sec (see Hikosaka & Wurtz, 1983a, Fig. 12). But the response when the stimulus is the target for a saccade is about the same for both the short and long interstimulus intervals. Thus, the relative enhancement is larger as habituation becomes greater. When the habituation is reversed, as the monkey makes saccades to the visual stimulus, the maximum response enhancement is frequently not instantaneous but builds up over a number of trials. A similar effect is seen in the superior colliculus (Goldberg & Wurtz, 1972; Wurtz & Mohler, 1976b).

Many substantia nigra cells respond to auditory stimuli instead of, or as well as, to visual stimuli. We have thus had an opportunity to determine whether an auditory response might also show enhancement when the monkey used that auditory stimulus as the target for saccadic eye movements. The response of the substantia nigra cells to an auditory stimulus is a decrease in discharge rate, just as it is to a visual stimulus, and the response enhancement is also a longer-lasting decrease in discharge rate, just as it is for a visual response. The auditory-response enhancement is reversed when the monkey stops making saccades to the auditory stimulus, and this reduced enhancement occurs over a number of trials.

CONDITIONAL RESPONSE MECHANISMS

The cells in the substantia nigra with visual responses are likely to be part of the neural mechanism related to the initiation of visually guided saccadic eye movements. Consistent with this view is the intermingling with these visual cells of other cells whose discharge is synchronized not to the onset of visual targets but to the saccades made to the visual targets. This relation to visual stimuli and the initiation of saccades to visual targets is similar to the prominence of visual function seen in the frontal eye fields and superior colliculus.

Other cells in the substantia nigra show a change in discharge rate related to saccades made not to visual targets but to those to the position of remembered targets. In order to demonstrate this phenomenon, a different paradigm was used; this is shown schematically in Fig. 24.4A. In this task, the monkey was given a cue as to the location of the target for the subsequent saccade by flashing a 50 msec spot of light during the fixation period. The monkey was required to continue fixating for several seconds beyond that time because any eye movement away from the fixation point would cancel the trial. Not until the fixation point went off was the monkey allowed to make a saccade to the remembered target position. If the saccade was to the location of the previously flashed target the monkey would be able to see the target when it reappeared, detect the dimming of the target, and be rewarded for this detection. Fig. 24.4A shows the response of a cell to a flashed stimulus when the monkey made saccades to the location of the remembered target. In contrast, Fig. 24.4B shows the lack of response to the flashed stimulus when the monkey was not required to make a saccade to it.

Other cells in substantia nigra show a decrease in discharge rate associated with the saccades made to remembered targets but not when the monkey made saccades to targets that were still present. Still other cells show a combination of these reponses, as indicated in Fig. 24.5. In this case the cell discharge decreased after the stimulus onset and stayed at this decreased level until the onset of the saccade to the remembered target (indicated by the tick mark in the dot pattern). Thus, this cell preserves information about the necessity of making a saccade to a remembered target.

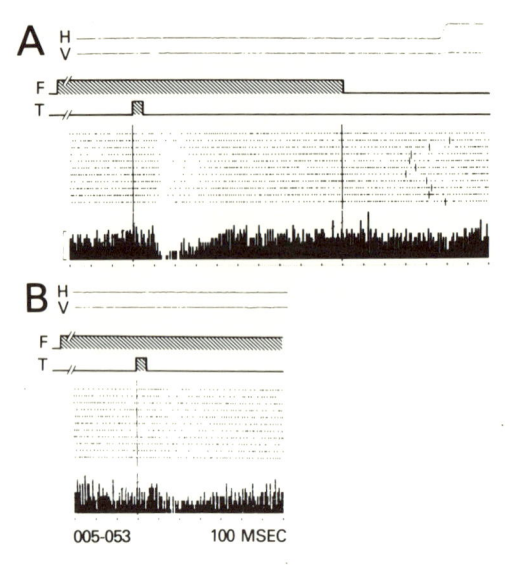

FIG. 24.4. Response of a substantia nigra cell to a remembered visual target. The schematic drawing above A shows the sequence of stimuli and eye movements in this experimental task. A flash of light (T) during the fixation period (F) identified the location to which the monkey was required to make a saccadic eye movement *after* the fixation point went off. The monkey was rewarded if this subsequent saccade brought the fovea near the target because it could then detect the return of the target and its subsequent dimming (not shown). The eye movement to the target location was not permitted until after the fixation point went off; sample eye-movement traces are shown. The time at which the monkey made the saccade to the stimulus on each trial is indicated by the tick marks on each line. In A, when the monkey had to remember the location of the stimulus, the cell responded to the flashed visual stimulus. In B, when the monkey did not make a saccade to the visual stimulus but continued to fixate, no such response to the visual stimulus is evident.

This class of cells has been referred to as related to saccades to remembered targets, but this is intended to describe the operational conditions under which the experiment was done. A more general interpretation of their response might be that the cells are related to the initiation of eye movements when such movements are made in the absence of direct sensory control.

Thus, in this area of substantia nigra we find cells responding to visual stimuli, with saccades made to visual targets, to visual stimuli that must be remembered as the target location for a future saccade, and with the saccades made to these remembered targets. It is particularly striking that cells in this area do not discharge in relation to saccades made spontaneously in the light or dark. This is in contrast to cells in the superior colliculus, where such discharge in relation to spontaneous eye movements is the rule rather than the exception (Wurtz & Goldberg, 1972). Cells discharging in relation to saccades to visual targets have also been found in the superior colliculus (Mohler & Wurtz, 1976) and in the frontal eye fields (Bruce & Goldberg, 1984) as well as in the substantia nigra. However, discharge related to saccades to remembered targets is also seen in the frontal eye fields (Bruce & Goldberg, 1984) but is not as prominent as in substantia nigra. This raises the possibility that the pathway that includes the substantia nigra is particularly related to the initiation of saccades made under this condition.

That such response segregation might occur is a testable hypothesis because the projection from the substantia nigra is largely to one structure, the superior colliculus. By facilitating or blocking this pathway it should be possible to alter the transmission of the signal related to the initiation of saccades from substantia nigra to the superior colliculus. Such an alteration would affect the signal related to saccades to visual targets as well as saccades to remembered targets. But if the signal from the substantia nigra related to saccades to remembered targets is particularly important, the alteration should be more damaging for saccades to remembered targets than those to visual targets. By using an agonist of the transmitter in the substantia nigra to superior colliculus pathway, muscimol, it is possible to produce just such an alteration. Injection of muscimol into the intermediate layers of the superior colliculus should produce tonic inhibition of the colliculus cells, and the phasic pause in activity, which signals a saccade, should be eliminated.

We compared the monkey's ability to make saccadic eye movements to visual targets and to remembered targets before and after such an injection of mus-

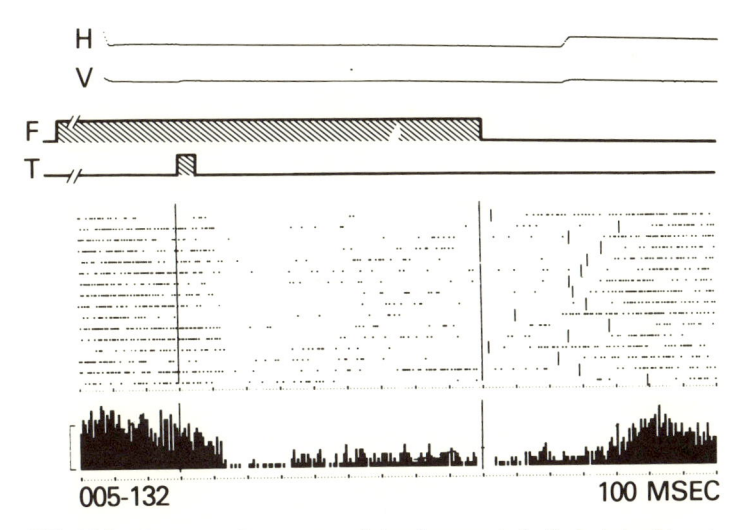

FIG. 24.5. Response of a neuron persisting from onset of a flashed visual target until the saccade to the location of the target. Onset of 50 msec target is indicated by T; onset of the saccade, by the vertical tick mark on each line.

cimol. Figure 24.6 shows saccades made to targets 10° away from the fixation point in eight different directions before the injection of the muscimol (Figs. 24.6A and C) and to the same targets after the injection of muscimol (Figs. 24.6B and D). The injection would be expected to affect movements to the left visual field, because cells at the point of injection were related to saccades to the left and stimulation at the point of injection produced saccades to the left. For saccades to visual targets there is a slight change in the trajectory after the injection (Fig. 24.6B) as compared to before (Fig. 24.6A), and there is also an increase in the latency of the saccade and a decrease in peak velocity (not seen in the figure). However, saccades to the location of remembered targets after the injection (Fig. 24.6D) are more severely disrupted compared to the saccades before the injection (Fig. 24.6C). Saccades to the remembered targets even before the injection do not have the precision and smooth trajectory that saccades

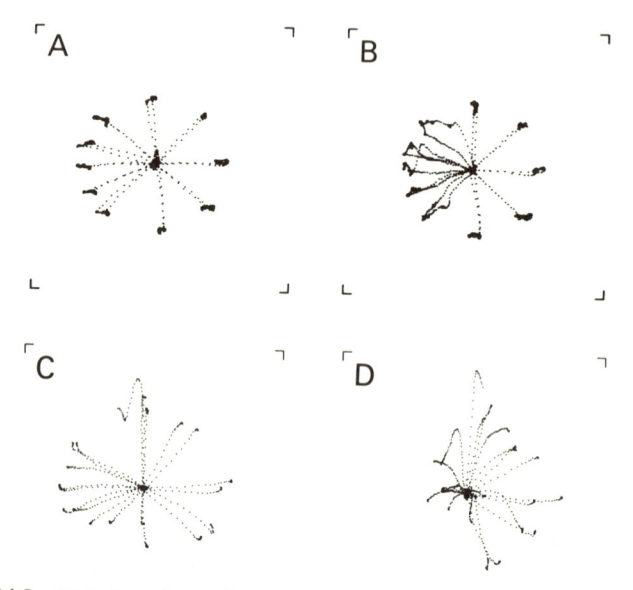

FIG. 24.6. Trajectory of saccadic eye movements before (A and C) and after (B and D) an injection of a transmitter agonist into the superior colliculus. The transmitter is GABA, the agonist is muscimol, and the part of the visual field affected by the injection is in the left hemifield. A shows the saccades made to visual targets 10° away from the fixation point. The targets were spaced at 45° intervals around the circle and two saccades were made to each target. B shows that the monkey can still make saccades to the same target configuration following injection of muscimol into the intermediate layers of the right superior colliculus. C shows two saccades made to the *location* of each remembered target before an injection of muscimol and D shows the attempts to make eye movements after the same injection. C and D show only the first saccade attempted to each target; subsequent saccades are not shown. Saccades to the location of the remembered target following this injection (D) are more severely disrupted than are saccades to visual targets (B).

to visual targets do, but after the injection saccades to the location of the remembered target are frequently not made at all or look as if they were deflected from the location of the previously present target. The effects of the muscimol on the saccades to the remembered targets are more severe than those on the saccades to visual targets. The frequency of saccades made to the left visual field spontaneously in the dark is also reduced following the muscimol injection.

This differential effect of the muscimol on saccades to remembered targets is consistent with the view that the substantia nigra is particularly important for the initiation of saccades to remembered targets. These experiments also demonstrate that the same saccadic eye movement can be governed by different neural mechanisms depending on the condition under which the saccadic eye movement is made.

CONCLUSION

The first conclusion to be drawn from these experiments is that the selection of sensory input, as indicated by enhanced visual responses of single cells, occurs at all the premotor steps in the oculomotor system so far examined: the superior colliculus, the frontal eye fields, and the substantia nigra pars reticulata. This is not surprising because a saccade can move the eye in only one direction at a time, and stimuli must be selected from the large range of possible stimuli in the normal environment. The presumed effect of the enhancement is an increase in the effectiveness of a particular set of sensory stimuli in one part of the visual field, as opposed to stimuli in other parts of the visual field (Wurtz, Goldberg, & Robinson, 1980). This increase in effectiveness, then, should lead to an increase in the probability that cells with an enhanced visual response achieve access to the motor output.

The second conclusion is that one overt response—in the case of these experiments, saccadic eye movements—can be demonstrated to have different neural circuitry depending on the conditions under which the response is made. It is not only the movement made, but the behavioral condition under which it is made, that determines the neural structures involved in initiation. In the case of saccades to remembered targets, the covert nature of the neural responses that persist during the period between a cue stimulus and the initiation of the movement might be of particular relevance to those concerned with the covert orienting of attention.

ACKNOWLEDGMENTS

The work described in this chapter is derived from a series of experiments done in collaboration with Okihide Hikosaka who is now at Toho University, Tokyo, Japan (Hikosaka & Wurtz, 1983a, 1983b, 1983c, 1983d, 1984a, 1984b). This particular organization and presentation is the responsibility of the author. Figures are largely modified from the detailed reports of the experiments that appeared in the *Journal of Neurophysiology*.

REFERENCES

Bruce, C. J., & Goldberg, M. E. (1984). Primate frontal eye fields: I. Single neurons discharging before saccades. *Journal of Neurophysiology*,

Bushnell, M. C., Goldberg, M. E., & Robinson, D. L. (1981). Behavioral enhancement of visual responses in monkey cerebral cortex: I. Modulation in posterior parietal cortex related to selective visual attention. *Journal of Neurophysiology, 46,* 755–772.

DeLong, M. R., & Georgopoulos, A. P. (1981). Motor functions of the basal ganglia. In V. B. Brooks (Ed.), *Handbook of physiology, section 1: The nervous system* (Vol. 2, Part 2, pp. 1017–1061). Bethesda, Md.: Am. Physiol. Soc.

Fischer, B., & Boch, R. (1981). Enhanced activation of neurons in prelunate cortex before visually guided saccades of trained rhesus monkeys. *Experimental Brain Research, 44,* 129–137.

Fischer, B., Boch, R., & Bach, M. (1981). Stimulus versus eye movements: Comparison of neural activity in the striate and prelunate visual cortex (A17 and A19) of trained rhesus monkey. *Experimental Brain Research, 43,* 69–77.

Goldberg, M. E., & Bushnell, M. C. (1981). Behavioral enhancement of visual responses in monkey cerebral cortex. II. Modulation in frontal eye fields specifically related to saccades. *Journal of Neurophysiology, 46,* 773–787.

Goldberg, M. E., & Wurtz, R. H. (1972). Activity of superior colliculus in behaving monkey: II. The effect of attention on neuronal responses. *Journal of Neurophysiology, 35,* 560–574.

Hikosaka, O., & Wurtz, R. H. (1983a). Visual and oculomotor functions of monkey substantia nigra pars reticulata. I. Relation of visual and auditory responses to saccades. *Journal of Neurophysiology, 49,* 1230–1253.

Hikosaka, O., & Wurtz, R. H. (1983b). Visual and oculomotor functions of monkey substantia nigra pars reticulata. II. Visual responses related to fixation of gaze. *Journal of Neurophysiology, 49,* 1254–1267.

Hikosaka, O., & Wurtz, R. H. (1983c). Visual and oculomotor functions of monkey substantia nigra pars reticulata. III. Memory-contingent visual and saccade responses. *Journal of Neurophysiology, 49,* 1268–1284.

Hikosaka, O., & Wurtz, R. H. (1983d). Visual and oculomotor functions of monkey substantia nigra pars reticulata. IV. Relation of substantia nigra to superior colliculus. *Journal of Neurophysiology, 49,* 1285–1301.

Hikosaka, O., & Wurtz, R. H. (1985a). Modification of saccadic eye movements by GABA-related substances. I. Effect of muscimol and bicuculline in the monkey superior colliculus. *Journal of Neurophysiology, 53,* 266–291.

Hikosaka, O., & Wurtz, R. H. (1985b). Modification of saccadic eye movements by GABA-related substances. II. Effects of muscimol in the monkey substantia nigra pars reticulata. *Journal of Neurophysiology, 53,* 292–307.

Mohler, C. W., & Wurtz, R. H. (1976). Organization of monkey superior colliculus: Intermediate layer cells discharging before eye movements. *Journal of Neurophysiology, 39,* 722–744.

Posner, M. I. (1980). Orienting of attention. The VIIth Sir Frederick Bartlett Lecture. *Quarterly Journal of Experimental Psychology, 32,* 3–25.

Richmond, B. J., Wurtz, R. H., & Sato, T. (1983). Visual responses of inferior temporal neurons in the awake rhesus monkey. *Journal of Neurophysiology, 50,* 1415–1432.

Robinson, D. L., Baizer, J. S., & Dow, B. M. (1980). Behavioral enhancement of visual responses of prestriate neurons in the rhesus monkey. *Invest. Ophthalmol. Vis. Sci., 19,* 1120–1123.

Wurtz, R. H., & Albano, J. E. (1980). Visual-motor function of the primate superior colliculus. *Ann. Rev. Neurosci., 3,* 189–226.

Wurtz, R. H., & Goldberg, M. E. (1972). Activity of superior colliculus in behaving monkey: III. Cells discharging before eye movements. *Journal of Neurophysiology, 35,* 575–586.

Wurtz, R. H., Goldberg, M. E., & Robinson, D. L. (1980). Behavioral modulation of visual responses in the monkey: Stimulus selection for attention and movement. *Prog. Psychobiol. Physiol. Psychol. 9,* 43–83.

Wurtz, R. H., Goldberg, M. E., & Robinson, D. L. (1982). Brain mechanisms of visual attention. *Sci. Am. 246*(6), 124–135.

Wurtz, R. H., & Mohler, C. W. (1976a). Enhancement of visual response in monkey striate cortex and frontal eye fields. *Journal of Neurophysiology, 39,* 766–772.

Wurtz, R. H., & Mohler, C. W. (1976b). Organization of monkey superior colliculus: Enhanced visual response of superficial layer cells. *Journal of Neurophysiology, 39,* 745–765.

Wurtz, R. H., Richmond, B. J., & Newsome, W. T. (1984). Modulation of cortical visual processing by attention, perception, and movement. In G. M. Edelman, W. M. Cowan, & W. E. Gall (Eds.), *Dynamic aspects of neocortical function.* New York: Wiley.

25 Attention and Coding Effects in S–R Compatibility Due to Irrelevant Spatial Cues

Carlo Umiltà
Università di Parma, Italy

Roberto Nicoletti
Università di Padova, Italy

ABSTRACT

In choice reaction time, when the speed of response depends on the spatial relationships between the location of the command stimulus and that of the response, two types of S–R compatibility must be distinguished—namely, spatial compatibility and the so-called Simon effect. The former is present if the location of the stimulus provides the relevant cue for choosing the correct response. The latter is present if the stimulus provides a locational cue that is not necessary for choosing the correct response.

Two hypotheses have been advanced to explain these compatibility effects. One suggests that there is a tendency to orient attention toward the stimulated side and, because of this, the response located on that same side is favored. The other hypothesis is based on the concept of a correspondence, or lack of it, between the spatial codes of the stimulus and response. Response latency is shorter when they are the same than when they are different.

Recently we (Nicoletti, Anzola, Luppino, Rizzolatti, & Umiltà, 1982) have shown that for spatial compatibility the coding hypothesis only is tenable. That is not surprising because the task requires the encoding of the relative positions of stimuli and responses. This is not true of the Simon effect, in which the position of the stimulus does not provide any information concerning the correct response. Therefore, it is possible that the coding hypothesis holds true for spatial compatibility whereas the Simon effect depends on the orienting of attention.

The results of the four experiments reported here clearly support the coding hypothesis also for the Simon effect. The results of this series of experiments also suggest that subjects are faster in directing attention to the right than the left visual hemifield.

INTRODUCTION

In choice reaction time (RT) the type of stimulus–response (S–R) pairing is of paramount importance in determining the speed of response. This phenomenon is known as *S–R compatibility* (Fitts, 1951) and those pairings that yield the shortest RTs are said to be the most compatible ones (see, e.g., review in Teichner & Krebs, 1974). When the property of S–R pairing that brings about compatibility is the spatial relationship between the stimulus and the response, two types of compatibility can be distinguished—namely, spatial compatibility and the Simon effect (see Nicoletti et al., 1982; Nicoletti & Umiltà, 1984; Simon, Sly, & Vilapakkam, 1981; see also Hedge & Marsh, 1975, who proposed the term Simon effect).

Spatial compatibility is observed when the location of the stimulus provides the relevant cue for selecting the correct response. For example, in a condition in which the right or left position of the stimulus requires a response with the right or left key, RTs are faster when the spatial locations of stimulus and response correspond (right–right and left–left) than when they do not (right–left and left–right). The Simon effect is observed when the stimulus provides a locational cue that is not required for selecting the correct response. For example, even if it is color that indicates the side of the correct response (e.g., red light–right key and green light–left key), RTs are faster when the positions correspond (i.e., stimulus and response are both on the right or left side) than when they do not (i.e., the stimulus appears on one side and the key is located on the other side).

Two hypotheses have been advanced to explain compatibility due to S–R spatial relationships. One (Simon, 1968, 1969) asserts a basic natural tendency to respond toward the source of the command stimulus. When the side of the stimulus does not match the side of the response, comparatively longer RTs are obtained because the inappropriate response tendency must be inhibited. In contrast, when the two sides correspond, RTs are shorter because the basic response tendency is consistent with the required response. This is basically an attentional explanation as attested by the fact that Simon (see, e.g., 1969, p. 175) likened the natural tendency to respond toward the stimulus source to an orienting reaction. The command stimulus would provide a directional cue that tends to elicit a response on its same side (see, e.g., Simon, Hinrichs, & Craft, 1970, p. 101).

Simon (see Craft & Simon, 1970; Simon, Craft, & Small, 1971) also showed that the effect was due to the directional cue supplied by the stimulus rather than the eye or ear stimulated per se. This finding renders unlikely an explanation based on absolute spatial proximity between stimulus and response. More direct evidence against the spatial-proximity hypothesis was later gathered by Nicoletti et al. (1982, Experiment 2) and Nicoletti & Umiltà (1984, Experiment 3) for spatial compatibility.

The second explanation (Brebner, Shepard, & Cairney, 1972; Hedge & Marsh, 1975; Nicoletti et al., 1982; Nicoletti & Umiltà, 1984; Wallace, 1971) is in terms of the correspondence, or lack of it, between the spatial codes that define the S-R pairing. When a stimulus is presented, a spatial code would be formed and compared to the spatial code of the response. Response latencies are faster when the two codes are the same than when they are different.

In essence, the main difference between the two hypotheses is that Simon's proposal stresses the importance of the side of stimulation in relation to an egocentric reference axis, which can be the body midline, the head midline, or the vertical retinal meridian. By contrast, the hypothesis put forward by Wallace points to the other stimulus as the external reference location according to which the position of the command stimulus is coded as right or left in relative terms. Of course, the same reasoning also applies to the response. Accordingly, from now on we use the term *side* to indicate the right-left location of the stimulus or response in relation to one or more of the egocentric reference axes and the term *relative position* to indicate the right-left location of one stimulus or response with respect to the other stimulus or response.

Recently, by employing experimental manipulations very similar to that described for Experiment 2 of the present study, Nicoletti et al. (1982) have shown that for spatial compatibility only the coding hypothesis is tenable. That study, however, could not provide evidence concerning the Simon effect because in it the relative position of the stimulus always indicated the position of the correct response. A tendency to react toward the side of the stimulus cannot be discarded on the basis of results obtained when the subject is required to form and use the relative spatial codes appropriate for each S-R pairing. It may well be that the coding hypothesis holds true for spatial compatibility whereas the Simon effect depends on an asymmetrical response tendency.

In the present study the relevant stimulus property was color and the coding of stimulus position was not necessary for choosing the correct response. The first experiment replicated the basic finding—that is, the Simon effect. The purpose of the other experiments was to discriminate between the two hypotheses mentioned earlier. In the second experiment the two stimuli were presented both on the right or left side with respect to the three reference axes and the subjects operated two keys located both on that same side. If the determining factor is the tendency to react in the direction of the command stimulus, no compatibility effect is to be expected because the two stimuli should cause a response tendency that is identical for the two responses, which are both emitted on the compatible side. By contrast, if what matters are the spatial codes of the S-R pairing, one should expect a compatibility effect attributable to the encoding of the relative positions. That is, because stimuli and responses can still be discriminated in terms of right and left relative positions, S-R pairings that share the same code should yield faster RTs than those demanding the use of two different codes.

EXPERIMENT 1

Experiment 1 was essentially a repetition of those previous experiments that had shown the Simon effect. The relevant property of the command stimulus was color and the subject had to choose the correct response on the basis of it. Stimulus location did not convey any task-relevant information. It was predicted, however, that this irrelevant feature should influence response latency.

Method

Subjects. Ten students between the ages of 20 and 25 years served as paid subjects. All were right handed, had normal or corrected-to-normal visual acuity, had normal color vision, and were naive as to the purpose of the experiment.

Apparatus and Procedure. The experiment took place inside a sound-proof cubicle. The subjects sat in front of a translucent screen. The head was positioned in an adjustable head-and-chin rest, so that the distance between the eyes and the screen was about 90 cm. The apparatus was indirectly illuminated from above and the luminance of the ambient light was about 6 cd/m^2. The fixation point was a black patch subtending a visual angle of 1° square in the center of the screen. In each hand the subjects held a brass cylinder equipped with a push button and positioned 15 cm to the right and left of the body midline. The stimuli (duration 100 msec and luminance about 25 cd/m^2) were two well-circumscribed circular lights, one red and the other green, subtending 1.5° of visual angle. They were generated by two projectors with color filters and were projected 9.5° to the right or left of the fixation point. An acoustic warning signal preceded the light by an interval of 1 sec. From the warning signal to the execution of the response the subjects had to maintain their gaze on the fixation point, and eye position was continuously monitored by a television camera that allowed a deflection of about 1° to be reliably detected. Interstimulus interval was 3 sec. Interval timing was achieved with interval generators and response latencies were recorded to the nearest msec through an electronic counter that was started with the onset of the light stimulus and stopped by pressing the switch.

There were two experimental sessions on two consecutive days, each preceded by informal practice trials. Experimental trials were given in two blocks (80 trials each) separated by a 2 min rest period. Side of presentation and light color were determined according to a quasirandom sequence that allowed a maximum of three consecutive trials of the same type. Therefore, in each block there were 20 right–red stimuli, 20 left–red stimuli, 20 green–right stimuli, and 20 green–left stimuli. The subjects were instructed to press one button for the red light and the other for the green light as fast as possible with their thumbs. In one session the hands were kept in the normal uncrossed position whereas in the other they were crossed at midforearm (right hand on the left side of the body, left hand on the right side). Color-key assignment was counterbalanced between subjects and hand position (i.e., uncrossed or crossed) across sessions and within subjects. Half of the 320 trials were compatible in the sense that the stimulus commanded a response with the key located in spatial correspondence with it. The remainder were incompatible because the stimulus commanded a response with the key located on the opposite side. The instructions were given in terms of red and green lights and stressed both speed and accuracy. With the exception of the practice trials, no feedback was given about speed or accuracy. Errors, including the very few eye movements, were discarded and replaced at the end of the block.

Results and Discussion

Errors were about 4% for compatible and 6% for incompatible trials and were not submitted to statistical analysis. The correct mean RTs were entered in a three-way within-subjects analysis of variance. The factors were stimulus side (right or left; but also, right or left visual hemifield [VHF]), response side (right or left), and responding hand (right or left).

The main factor stimulus side and the interaction between stimulus side and response side were significant—$F(1,9) = 7.29$, $p < .05$, and $F(1,9) = 100.52$, $p < .001$, respectively. They showed that the stimuli were responded to faster when presented in the right than the left VHF for nine of the 10 subjects (373 msec versus 378 msec), and the stimulus on the right side yielded faster RTs when the response was on the right than on the left side (362 msec versus 384 msec), whereas the left stimulus yielded faster RTs with the left than the right response position (368 msec versus 389 msec). The interaction thus showed a 22 msec compatibility effect, which was present for every subject. The effect was almost identical for the two hand arrangements: 21 msec when the hands were in the normal uncrossed position and 23 msec when they were crossed.

The advantage of the right over the left VHF can be interpreted in two ways. An explanation in terms of hemispheric specialization would point to a left-hemisphere prevalence for detecting the presence of the light and/or discriminating its color. An explanation in terms of an attentional asymmetry would indicate that the subjects have a bias to orient attention to the right VHF. The discussion of these tentative interpretations is postponed to Experiment 4.

Of greater interest was the highly significant interaction that showed that compatible S–R pairings were processed faster than incompatible ones. It is also apparent that what mattered was the relationship between response side and stimulus side whereas that between stimulus side and responding hand had no effect. This latter finding is also in accordance with a number of previous studies (for spatial compatibility see Anzola, Bertoloni, Buchtel, & Rizzolatti, 1977; Brebner et al., 1972; Nicoletti et al., 1982; Nicoletti, Umiltà, & Ladavas, 1984; for the Simon effect see Simon et al., 1970; Wallace, 1971). In the present experiment the locus of the command stimulus did not provide any relevant information as for the position of the correct response; hence, it can be concluded that the Simon effect was successfully replicated. After replicating the basic finding, we went on with an experiment that was aimed at discriminating between the two explanations proposed for it.

EXPERIMENT 2

In Experiment 1 the two hypotheses made similar predictions because side and relative position were confounded. They make different predictions, however, when both responses as well as both stimuli are located on the same side.

The hypothesis of a tendency to respond in the direction of the stimulus predicts that there will be no compatibility effect. This is because, when stimuli and responses occur on the same side in relation to the egocentric reference axes, even though each stimulus and each response is still on the right or left of the other, there should no longer be a differential orientation. For example, if both stimuli are to the left of the midline, they will produce an equal orientation to the left side where both responses take place. In contrast, the coding hypothesis predicts the occurrence of a compatibility effect because right and left relative positions can still be discriminated. This is because the crucial factor for compatibility is the correspondence between the relative positions of stimuli and responses even within the same hemispace.

By following this line of reasoning Experiment 2 replicated Experiment 1, with the only difference being that the two stimuli and the two responses were always on the same side in relation to all egocentric axes.

Method

Subjects. Twelve new subjects selected as before participated in the experiment.

Apparatus and Procedure. The apparatus was that already described for Experiment 1 except that the two light stimuli were shown in the same VHF, 5° and 24° to the right or left of the fixation point, and the two cylinders were positioned on the corresponding side, 8 cm and 38 cm to the right or left of the body midline.

The procedure was similar to that of the previous experiment with the following exceptions: The two sessions did not differ for hand arrangement—the hands were always in the uncrossed position. In each session there were two blocks of 80 trials, one with stimuli and responses on the right side and the other with stimuli and responses on the left side. In other words, side of both stimulation and responding was blocked, with stimuli and responses always occurring in the same hemispace. The order of conditions was counterbalanced within subjects and across sessions. Overall, 160 trials were compatible and 160 incompatible with reference to the relative positions of stimuli and responses. As in the previous experiment, only color identified the locus of the correct response.

Results and Discussion

The errors (about 4% overall and equally distributed between compatible and incompatible trials) were not analyzed. The correct mean RTs were submitted to a three-way within-subjects analysis of variance in which the factors were side (right or left; i.e., the side where the stimuli were presented and the responses emitted), relative position of the stimulus (right or left), and relative position of the response (right or left; but also, right or left responding hand).

Only two sources proved significant—namely, the interaction between side and relative position of the stimulus and that between relative positions of stimuli and responses—$F(1,11) = 58.48$, $p < .001$, and $F(1,11) = 23.40$, $p < .001$, respectively. Both interactions were present in 11 subjects.

The first interaction was clearly unrelated to compatibility. It merely showed that the more peripheral stimuli—that is, the right in the right VHF and the left in the left VHF—were responded to more slowly than the less peripheral ones—that is, the right in the left VHF and the left in the right VHF (289 msec and 298 msec vs. 280 msec and 281 msec). The other interaction was much more interesting because it showed a compatibility effect due to relative positions. The right stimulus yielded faster RTs with the right than with the left response (268 msec vs 296 msec), whereas the left stimulus yielded faster RTs with the left than with the right response (281 msec vs 302 msec). Overall the compatibility effect, which was shown by every subject, was of 25 msec—that is, very close to that found in Experiment 1.

It is clear that the results of Experiment 2 support the coding hypothesis and disprove the hypothesis of a tendency to respond toward the source of stimulation. In an earlier study (Nicoletti et al., 1982) we had demonstrated that spatial compatibility depends on the comparison of the codes that describe the relative positions of stimuli and responses. Now this explanation can be extended to the Simon effect. However, before reaching a definitive conclusion, it seemed appropriate to gather further evidence by testing another prediction of the coding hypothesis.

EXPERIMENT 3

According to the coding hypothesis compatibility effects always occur, provided that right and left relative positions can be distinguished for both stimuli and responses. Conversely, they must disappear if the stimuli or the responses are no longer distinguishable in terms of right and left relative positions. One very important feature of the preceding experiments was that the two lights came from easily distinguishable locations. A crucial test of the hypotheses could be performed, however, if the stimuli were presented from a single location, thus eliminating any relative positional information. In Experiment 3 the subjects had to emit discriminative right–left responses to red and green lights that were shown in the same position, either to the right or left of fixation. In this manner the location where the stimuli were shown was blocked and no relative position could be discriminated. Thus, according to the coding hypothesis, no compatibility effect should emerge. On the other hand, sidedness information was still available because the lights were shown to the right or left side in relation to the egocentric axes. Thus, according to the response-tendency hypothesis, compatibility effects should still be present.

Method

Subjects. Twelve new subjects selected as before took part in the experiment.

Apparatus and Procedure. The apparatus was that already employed for Experiment 2 but now the subject had to turn his or her head about 15° to the right or left in relation to the body midsagittal plane to fixate a mark positioned halfway between the two locations where the stimuli were shown. This modification was introduced to eliminate those retinal effects that had been observed in the previous experiment.

The procedure was different from that of the preceding two experiments because now the red and green lights appeared in the same position. Half of the subjects fixated to the right of the midline in the first session and to the left in the second whereas the others followed the inverse order. In each session there were two blocks of 80 stimuli, one on each side of fixation, and order was counterbalanced within subjects and across sessions. In other words, for two blocks all of the stimuli came from only one position on one side of fixation, whereas for the other two blocks the position on the other side of fixation was used. Half of the 320 trials were compatible (e.g., a red stimulus on the right of fixation required a response with the right hand) and the remainder were incompatible (e.g., a green stimulus shown in the same location required a response with the left hand).

Results and Discussion

The errors were about 5% in compatible trials and 6% in incompatible trials. The correct RTs were submitted to a three-way within-subjects analysis of variance with the following factors: side of the body where stimuli and responses occurred (right or left), stimulus side (right or left VHF), and responding hand (right or left; but also, right or left relative position of the response).

There was only one significant source, the interaction between stimulus side (or VHF) and responding hand—$F(1,11) = 15.32$, $p < .005$—which showed that, contrary to expectations, compatible trials were faster than incompatible ones. Stimuli to the right of fixation yielded faster RTs with the right than the left hand (299 msec vs. 309 msec), whereas stimuli to the left of fixation yielded faster RTs with the left than with the right hand (306 msec vs. 313 msec). Examination of individual data showed that 10 subjects had the "compatibility effect." Overall the effect was of 8 msec—that is, significantly smaller (see *Results* of Experiment 4) than that found in the two previous experiments.

Taken at face value, such an outcome is contrary to the prediction of the coding hypothesis because now the stimuli could not be encoded according to their right and left relative positions. However, the effect might be due to the directness of the anatomical connections between the receiving hemiretinae and the responding hand (see, e.g., Anzola et al., 1977; Berlucchi, Crea, Di Stefano, & Tassinari, 1977; Berlucchi, Heron, Hyman, Rizzolatti, & Umiltà, 1971). The significant interaction was that between VHF of stimulation and responding hand; therefore, it is likely to reflect the fact that ipsilateral responses were mediated within a single hemisphere whereas contralateral responses required transfer of information from one hemisphere to the other. This explanation is not appropriate for the findings of either Experiment 1 or 2. In fact, in the former the effect did not depend on the hand that emitted the response (see the crossed-hand manipulation) and in the latter the two stimuli were projected to the same VHF (i.e., hemisphere). It must be pointed out, however, that an interhemispheric transmission time of the order of 8 msec does not fit satisfactorily with previous estimates, which have always been in the range of 2 to 5 msec if not contaminated by compatibility effects (see review in Bashore, 1981).

Another interpretation could be that the propensity to respond toward the side of the stimulus can emerge only when relative locational cues are absent. If this is the case, it is also apparent that the sidedness effect is much smaller than a true compatibility effect.

A third, perhaps more convincing, interpretation would be that the subject formed a code for the VHF where the stimulus appeared and compared it with the code of the response (see Ladavas & Moscovitch, 1984, for a similar suggestion). Therefore, that found here would be a special case of the Simon effect. Probably the effect was small because it depended on the comparison of two heterogeneous codes, one specified in relative terms (i.e., that for the response) and the other in relation to the vertical retinal meridian (i.e., that for the stimulus).

Unfortunately, there is a further interpretation that, if proved true, might cast doubt on the coding hypothesis. It has been suggested (Bowers, Heilman, & Van den Abell, 1981; Bradshaw, Nathan, Nettleton, Pierson, & Wilson, 1983; Morais, 1978; Pierson, Bradshaw, & Nettleton, 1983; but see Ladavas & Moscovitch, 1984, for a different point of view) that sidedness effects depend heavily on the orientation of the head with respect to the body and head turning could either destroy the sense that space is divided into right and left sides (Bradshaw et al., 1983) or cause incompatibility between VHF and hemispace (Bowers et al., 1981). It can be argued, therefore, that Experiment 3 showed a typical Simon effect whose reduced size is attributable to the fact that head and body were not aligned as they were in the preceding experiments. The last experiment addressed this issue.

EXPERIMENT 4

So far, the coding hypothesis can easily account for the results of Experiments 1 and 2 but has difficulties in accommodating the outcome of Experiment 3. The hypothesis of a tendency to respond toward the side of the stimulus has no problems in explaining the results of Experiment 1 and can interpret the smaller effect found in Experiment 3 as due to the fact that the head was not aligned with the body. It does have problems in explaining the results of Experiment 2 because in it stimuli and responses were always on the same side.

Let us now imagine a condition identical to that of Experiment 3, with the only difference being that the stimuli become again discriminable in terms of right–left relative positions. The coding hypothesis predicts that the Simon effect should be as large as that observed in Experiments 1 and 2. By contrast, the hypothesis of a tendency to respond toward the stimulus side must predict an effect comparable to that found in Experiment 3. This was the condition chosen for Experiment 4. It was also aimed at testing the interpretations proposed for the right-VHF superiority found in Experiment 1.

Method

Subjects. Twelve new subjects selected as before participated in the experiment.

Apparatus and Procedure. The usual apparatus was employed and the procedure exactly replicated that of Experiment 2, with the only notable difference being that the subjects had to fixate, by turning the head about 15° to the right or left, a mark placed halfway between the two stimulus positions. Therefore, Experiment 4 differed from Experiment 3 only because now relative locational cues were again present.

Results and Discussion

The errors were about 5% overall and were equally distributed between compatible and incompatible trials. The correct mean RTs were entered in a three-way within-subjects analysis of variance whose factors were the side of the body where stimuli and responses occurred (right or left), stimulus relative position (right or left; but also, right or left VHF), and relative position of the response (right or left; but also, right or left responding hand).

Two sources proved significant—namely, the main effect of stimulus relative position (or field of stimulation) and the interaction between stimulus and response relative positions—$F(1,11) = 14.46$, $p < .01$, and $F(1,11) = 25.01$, $p < .001$, respectively. The first indicated that RTs were faster in the right than in the left VHF (332 msec versus 344 msec). The effect was present in 11 subjects. The second source demonstrated that right stimuli yielded faster RTs with the right than the left response (315 msec versus 352 msec), whereas the opposite was true for the left stimuli (335 msec versus 350 msec). Also the advantage of compatible over incompatible trials was present in 11 subjects.

Overall, the compatibility effect was of 26 msec—that is, very similar to that observed in Experiments 1 and 2 (22 msec and 25 msec, respectively) and markedly larger than that of Experiment 3 (8 msec). In order to test the difference in the size of the compatibility effect among the four experiments, a one-way between-subjects analysis of variance was carried out. It showed that experiments differed—$F(3,42) = 4.79$, $p < .01$. Successive pairwise Newman-Keuls tests confirmed that the effect was of the same magnitude in Experiments 1, 2, and 4, but significantly smaller in Experiment 3 (all $ps < .05$).

The outcome of the present experiment demonstrated that, as long as the two stimuli can be distinguished in terms of right and left relative positions, the Simon effect does not diminish when the head is rotated in relation to the body. Therefore, the results of Experiment 3 cannot be attributed to the lack of alignment between head and body. The best explanation seems to be one that ascribes the effect found in Experiments 1, 2, and 4 on one side and that found in Experiment 3 on the other to different mechanisms. The former is a true Simon effect due to the coding of the relative positions of stimuli and responses. The latter can be due to the directness of the anatomical connections, or to a propensity to respond toward the side of the stimulus, or to the encoding of the VHF of stimulation.

The advantage for the right VHF, which was present in Experiment 1 and absent in Experiments 2 and 3, was observed again here. In the present experiment, as well as in Experiment 1, field of stimulation was random, whereas it was blocked in the other two experiments. It appears that the right-VHF advantage manifests itself when attention has to be reoriented to one of the two VHFs on each trial and vanishes when attention can be allocated permanently to one VHF. If there is a basic tendency to orient attention to the right side of the space, as was first suggested by Heilman and Watson (1977) and then confirmed by several other studies (Bertelson, 1982; Bradshaw et al., 1983; Mazzucchi, Cattelani & Umiltà, 1983; Pierson et al., 1983), it is not surprising that this bias becomes apparent when the VHF in which the stimulus will appear is not known in advance. By contrast, an interpretation of the right-VHF advantage in terms of a left-hemisphere specialization is at odds with the results of those studies that have shown a right-hemisphere superiority for color discrimination and stimulus detection (see reviews in Bradshaw & Nettleton, 1983; Davidoff, 1982) and cannot explain why the effect is restricted to nonblocked presentations.

GENERAL DISCUSSION

In those tasks that show the spatial-compatibility effect (see, e.g., Anzola et al., 1977; Nicoletti et al., 1982; Nicoletti & Umiltà, 1984; Simon, 1969) the subject is explicitly required to encode the relative positions of the stimuli. When a stimulus appears, it is its location in relation to the other that indicates the correct response. The responses are also defined according to their relative positions. Response latency depends on presence or lack of concordance between the spatial codes associated to stimuli and responses (Nicoletti et al., 1982; Nicoletti & Umiltà, 1984) because an S-R pairing that lacks such concordance requires a translation from the stimulus code to the response code that will consume more time than if the concordance were present (Teichner & Krebs, 1974).

In those tasks that show the Simon effect (see, e.g., Simon, 1968; Wallace, 1971; and the experiments reported here) the subject does not have to process the position of the stimulus because it is a nonlocational feature that indicates the position of the correct response. Therefore, it is not readily apparent why response latency should still depend on the spatial aspects of the S-R pairing.

The interpretation proposed by Simon (1968, 1969) is in terms of a tendency to respond on the perceived side of the stimulus, which does not necessarily coincide with the actual side of stimulation (Simon, Small, Ziglar, & Craft, 1970), and ascribes the compatibility effect to the stage of response selection (Simon, Acosta, & Mewaldt, 1975; Simon, Acosta, Mewaldt, & Speidel, 1976). In essence, what Simon (1968, 1969; see also Heilman & Valenstein, 1979, for a similar suggestion and Nicoletti et al., 1982, for a thorough discussion) proposed was an attentional hypothesis. The subject covertly orients him- or herself to the side of apparent origin of the stimulus, thus bringing about an attentional bias that favors the response located on the corresponding side. In other words, if the correct response is on the side where attention is first allocated, it is immediately selected and consequently yields faster RTs than a response that is on the other side and requires an extra time for the reorienting of attention. This interpretation is based on the spatial relationships of both the stimulus and the response with an egocentric reference axis.

Wallace (1971; see also Nicoletti et al., 1982) proposed an explanation of the Simon effect in terms of the correspondence, or lack of it, between the code that defines the position of the stimulus and the code that defines the position of the response. This interpretation indicates the stage of S-R translation (see, e.g., Teichner & Krebs, 1974) as that where the Simon effect occurs. Basically, it is suggested that, upon presentation of the stimulus, two spatial codes are automatically formed: one, which is necessary for performing the task, describes the position in space of the response; the other, which is not demanded by the task, describes the position in space of the stimulus. The two codes are then compared and when they are the same RTs are faster than when they are different. This is because only in the latter case a translational process must take place. Because in a two-choice RT paradigm the two discriminative responses are always defined, either explicitly or implicitly, in relation to each other, it is the relative positions of stimuli and responses that bring about the Simon effect.

It is apparent from the preceding reasoning that the two hypotheses differ about whether or not the Simon effect depends on relative locational cues. The attentional hypothesis predicts that response latency is faster when S–R pairings occur on the same side in relation to a given reference axis than when they cross that axis. In contrast, the coding hypothesis predicts that response latency is faster when the S–R pairings involve the same relative positions than when they do not.

In brief, Simon's hypothesis refers to the spatial relationships between the locus of the command stimulus and one of several reference axes—namely, the body midline, the head midline, or the vertical retinal meridian. Instead, for Wallace's hypothesis, the relevant reference point is the locus of the other stimulus.

In Experiment 1 each stimulus could be described as to the right or left in relation to any of the just-described reference points. By contrast, in Experiment 4 only three were available (i.e., the head midline, the vertical retinal meridian, and the other stimulus) and in Experiment 2 only the position of the other stimulus could be used as a reference point. In spite of this, the compatibility effect did not diminish from Experiment 1 to Experiments 2 and 4. However, when, in Experiment 3, the position of the other stimulus was eliminated, whereas the head midline and the vertical retinal meridian could still be used, the compatibility effect was greatly reduced or disappeared altogether. The much smaller effect observed could be attributed to anatomical connectivity or to a tendency to respond toward the side of the stimulus or to the encoding of the stimulated VHF. In conclusion, it is clear that the results of the present study pointed unambiguously to the encoding of the relative stimulus position as the major factor in producing the Simon effect.

ACKNOWLEDGMENTS

This research was supported by funds from the Consiglio Nazionale delle Ricerche and the Ministero della Pubblica Istruzione to the first author. The authors thank Professor G. Rizzolatti for helpful discussion of the experiments. Requests for reprints should be sent to Carlo Umiltà, Istituto di Fisiologia Umana, Università di Parma, via A. Gramsci, 14, 43100 Parma, Italy.

REFERENCES

Anzola, G. P., Bertoloni, G., Buchtel, H. A., & Rizzolatti, G. (1977). Spatial compatibility and anatomical factors in simple and choice reaction time. *Neuropsychologia, 15*, 295–302.

Bashore, T. R. (1981). Vocal and manual reaction time estimates of interhemispheric transmission time. *Psychological Bulletin, 89*, 352–368.

Berlucchi, G., Crea, F., Di Stefano, M., & Tassinari, G. (1977). Influence of spatial stimulus–response compatibility on reaction time of ipsilateral and contralateral hand to lateralized light stimuli. *Journal of Experimental Psychology: Human Perception and Performance, 3*, 505–517.

Berlucchi, G., Heron, W., Hyman, R., Rizzolatti, G., & Umiltà, C. (1971). Simple reaction times of ipsilateral and contralateral hand to lateralized visual stimuli. *Brain, 94*, 419–430.

Bertelson, P. (1982). Lateral differences in normal man and lateralization of brain function. *International Journal of Psychology, 17*, 173–210.

Bowers, D., Heilman, K. M., & Van den Abell, T. (1981). Hemispace–VHF compatibility. *Neuropsychologia, 19*, 757–765.

Bradshaw, J. L., Nathan, G., Nettleton, N. C., Pierson, J. M., & Wilson, L. E. (1983). Head and body hemispace to left and right III: Vibroctatile stimulation and sensory and motor components. *Perception, 12*, 651–661.

Bradshaw, J. L., & Nettleton, N. C. (1983). *Human cerebral asymmetry.* Englewood Cliffs, NJ: Prentice-Hall.

Brebner, J., Shepard, M., & Cairney, P. (1972). Spatial relationships and S–R compatibility. *Acta Psychologica, 36*, 1–15.

Craft, J. L., & Simon, J. R. (1970). Processing symbolic information from a visual display: Interference from an irrelevant directional cue. *Journal of Experimental Psychology, 83*, 415–420.

Davidoff, J. (1982). Studies with non-verbal stimuli. In J. G. Beaumont (Ed.), *Divided visual field studies of cerebral organisation* (pp. 29–55). London: Academic.

Fitts, P. M. (1951). Engineering psychology and equipment design. In S. S. Stevens (Ed.), *Handbook of experimental psychology* (pp. 1287–1340). New York: Wiley.

Hedge, A., & Marsh, N. W. A. (1975). The effect of irrelevant spatial correspondence on two-choice response-time. *Acta Psychologica, 39*, 427–439.

Heilman, K. M., & Valenstein, E. (1979). Mechanisms underlying hemispatial neglect. *Archives of Neurology, 5*, 166–170.

Heilman, K. M., & Watson, R. T. (1977). Mechanisms underlying the unilateral neglect syndrome. In E. A. Weinstein & R. F. Friedland (Eds.), *Hemi-inattention and hemispheric specialization* (Advances in Neurology Series, Vol. 18, pp. 93–106). New York: Raven.

Ladavas, E., & Moscovitch, M. (1984). Must egocentric and environmental frames of reference be aligned to produce spatial S–R compatibility effects? *Journal of Experimental Psychology: Human Perception and Performance, 10*, 205–215.

Mazzucchi, A., Cattelani, R., & Umiltà, C. (1983). Hemispheric prevalence in acoustical attention. *Brain and Cognition, 2*, 1–11.

Morais, J. (1978). Spatial constraints on attention to speech. In J. Requin (ed.), *Attention and performance VII* (pp. 245–260). Hillsdale, N.J.: Lawrence Erlbaum Associates.

Nicoletti, R., Anzola, G. P., Luppino, G., Rizzolatti, G., & Umiltà, C. (1982). Spatial compatibility effects on the same side of the body midline. *Journal of Experimental Psychology: Human Perception and Performance, 8*, 664–673.

Nicoletti, R., & Umiltà, C. (1984). Right–left prevalence in spatial compatibility. *Perception and Psychophysics, 35*, 333–343.

Nicoletti, R., Umiltà, C., & Ladavas, E. (1984). Compatibility due to the coding of the relative position of the effectors. *Acta Psychologica, 57*, 133–143.

Pierson, J. M., Bradshaw, J. L., & Nettleton, N. C. (1983). Head and body space to left and right, front and rear I: Unidirectional competitive auditory stimulation. *Neuropsychologia, 21,* 463–473.

Simon, J. R. (1968). Effect of ear stimulated on reaction time and movement time. *Journal of Experimental Psychology, 78,* 344–346.

Simon, J. R. (1969). Reactions toward the source of stimulation. *Journal of Experimental Psychology, 81,* 174–176.

Simon, J. R., Acosta, E., & Mewaldt, S. P. (1975). Effect of locus of warning tone on auditory choice reaction time. *Memory and Cognition, 3,* 167–170.

Simon, J. R., Acosta, E., Mewaldt, S. P., & Speidel, C. R. (1976). The effect of an irrelevant directional cue on choice reaction time: Duration of the phenomenon and its relation to stages of processing. *Perception and Psychophysics, 19,* 16–22.

Simon, J. R., Craft, J. L., & Small, A. M., Jr. (1971). Reaction toward the apparent source of an auditory stimulus. *Journal of Experimental Psychology, 89,* 203–206.

Simon, J. R., Hinrichs, J. V., & Craft, J. L. (1970). Auditory S–R compatibility: Reaction time as a function of ear–hand correspondence and ear–response–location correspondence. *Journal of Experimental Psychology, 86,* 97–102.

Simon, J. R., Sly, P. E., & Vilapakkam, S. (1981). Effects of compatibility of S–R mapping on reactions toward the stimulus source. *Acta Psychologica, 47,* 63–81.

Simon, J. R., Small, A. M., Jr., Ziglar, R. A., & Craft, J. L. (1970). Response interference as an information processing task: Sensory versus perceptual factors. *Journal of Experimental Psychology, 85,* 311–314.

Teichner, W. H., & Krebs, M. J. (1974). Laws of visual choice reaction time. *Psychological Review, 81,* 75–98.

Wallace, R. J. (1971). S–R compatibility and the idea of a response code. *Journal of Experimental Psychology, 88,* 354–360.

VII DIVIDING AND SUSTAINING ATTENTION

26 Toward a Model of Attention and the Development of Automatic Processing

Walter Schneider
University of Illinois

ABSTRACT

A model for the development of automatic processing is briefly described in this chapter. The model is a quasineural one in which information processing is done through the transmission of vectors between visual, lexical, semantic, and motor processing units. Controlled processing involves gating of the output power of vectors to perform matches and to release response vectors. As subjects practice consistent tasks, associative learning enables an input vector to evoke an output vector and priority learning determines the power with which a vector is transmitted. Automatic processing involves a cascade of vector transmissions in which the output power of each transmission is determined by the priority learning. The transition from controlled to automatic processing takes place in four phases. Empirical illustrations of this transition are described.

INTRODUCTION

A fundamental question in attention and learning is "What is the microstructure of skill development?" This chapter briefly presents an explicit microstructure illustrating the qualitative and quantitative changes in processing associated with the development of skill.

It is generally agreed that the acquisition of almost any cognitive or motor skill involves profound changes with practice. These changes have impressed researchers since the earliest days of psychology (James, 1890; Solomon & Stein, 1896). Consider, for example, the changes that occur while learning to type. At first, effort and attention are devoted to the smallest movement or minor decision, and performance is slow and error-prone. After extensive training, long sequences of movements or cognitive processes are carried out with little attention. The changes are striking enough that performance of the task seems qualitatively different before and after practice.

A number of researchers have interpreted the qualitative differences between novice and skilled performers as being the result of two qualitatively different forms of information processing (James, 1890; LaBerge, 1976; Logan, 1978, 1979; Neumann, 1984; Norman, 1976; Posner & Snyder, 1975; Schneider & Fisk, 1983; Shiffrin & Schneider, 1977). In this chapter the two forms are referred to as controlled and automatic processing. *Controlled processing* is characterized as a slow, generally serial, effortful, capacity-limited, subject-controlled processing mode that must be used to deal with novel or inconsistent information (see Schneider & Fisk, 1983). *Automatic processing* is a fast, parallel, fairly effortless process that is not limited by short-term memory capacity, is not under direct subject control, and performs well-developed skilled behaviors.

At present we have no detailed representation of how the practice changes occur. The models in the literature are generally verbal descriptions of the qualitative changes observed in performance. For example, James described the transition from conscious control to automatic, habitual behaviors (1890). A number of researchers (e.g., LaBerge, 1976; Norman & Shallice, 1980; Shiffrin & Schneider, 1977) discuss the shift from controlled to automatic processing. J. R. Anderson (1982) discusses the shift from an interpretive processing of knowledge to a compiled processing. Pew (1966, 1974) characterizes practice as changing the level of conscious control. MacKay (1982) suggests that practice increases the linkage between nodes. Adams (1971) interprets practice effects as shifting from carefully monitored closed-loop control to a more automatic open loop. These proposals, however, are too vaguely stated to allow detailed simulations of the learning effects in a simple search.

MODEL OVERVIEW

The rationale for the present model comes from three sources: the attention literature, neurophysiology, and communication theory. The attention literature illustrates the shift from serial to parallel processing and the inability to directly control automatic processing (see Schneider & Fisk, 1983; Shiffrin & Schneider, 1977). The present model illustrates how continuous improvements in associative strength and message gain (see the next section) can shift processing from a serial to a parallel mode. The present model also predicts the importance of consistent practice in developing fast, efficient processing (see Schneider & Fisk, 1983).

The neurophysiological literature suggests the structure of the model. Cortical information transmission occurs when a population of neurons (e.g., a hypercolumn) sends a set of firing rates (e.g., a vector of activation) to another population. This set of firing rates of the output neurons can be modulated as a set (e.g., chandelier modulation of pyramidal cell output; see Szentagothai, 1977). Learning in the physical system occurs after this set of firing rates comes into a population and a second burst is output (Levy & Steward, 1983). The evidence for vector transmission for modulation of vector output power and vector burst mediated association supports the central concepts of the model.

Communication theory provides optimality considerations regarding how best to allocate transmission time in a network of vector transmission units (see Van der Meulen, 1977). Communication theory theorems indicate that if the brain optimally processes information there should be two modes of transmission: a serial, time-sharing, control-process-type mode and a parallel, automatic-process-type mode (see Schneider, 1984).

The present model assumes that processing is done by the transmission of messages between specialized processing units. For example, a semantic choice–reaction-time task (e.g., respond to animal words) would require at least three transmissions. A visual unit transmits visual features to a semantic unit. The semantic unit makes an associative translation to the semantic code and transmits that to a motor unit. The motor unit makes an associative translation of the semantic code to a muscle code and transmits that message to produce a response.

In the model, controlled processing is conceived of as a limited central-processing mechanism that gates the transmission of messages between units and compares the received messages. The development of automatic processing is the result of two types of learning. The first, *associative learning,* is the mechanism by which one message is associatively translated to another message. The second type of learning, *priority learning,* is the mechanism by which a unit determines how strongly to transmit a message. The unit-specific message priority determines the strength of the automatic message transmission. Automatic processing occurs when priority and associative learning are sufficiently advanced to allow a sequence of transmissions without any controlled-process gating of the information.

The model predicts that the transition from controlled to automatic processing should occur in four phases. The transition between phases is done in a continuous manner depending on subjects' strategies, workload, and skill acquisition. Phase 1 requires memory preloading of message units and controlled-processing gating of transmissions. Phase 2 involves Phase 1 operations plus, on some trials, the automatic transmission of messages evokes a response. Phase 3 involves automatic processing with controlled-process gating's assisting in the transmission of messages. Phase 4 involves pure automatic processing of messages without controlled processing.

STRUCTURE OF THE MODEL

The processing is done by the transmission of vectors between a large number of processing units. The vector transmission could be represented as the frequency of firing a set of neurons (e.g., cortical hypercolumns). For example, a visual unit might transmit a vector that codes dot locations. The letter E might be represented as vector of 1s and 0s on a 4 × 6 dot matrix (i.e., E = 1111 1000 10000 1111 1000 1111). Similarly, a semantic unit vector codes semantic features (e.g., size, function, category, etc.) and a motor unit codes muscle groups.

The received vector is transformed through an association matrix. The association matrix could be implemented as the set of strengths of connections between the output neurons from one unit and the input neurons to a receiving unit. The transmission of the E vector of the visual unit would evoke a character vector (e.g., 10001101 . . . representing letter, not digit, not consonant, vowel, not sound a, sound e . . .). Such an association matrix can encode many associations by storing in the connective strengths the additions of all the individual associations. J. A. Anderson (1977, 1983; Anderson, Silverstein, Ritz, & Jones, 1977) has illustrated how such matrices can produce associative translations (see also the following discussion of associative learning).

The transmission of vectors amounts to the sending of messages between units. The received vector of a unit is the summation of all the individual vectors (component by component) transmitted to the unit. The clarity of a message is determined by the signal-to-noise ratio (S/N) of the received vector. The S/N is determined by the power of the signal vector divided by the summed power of all the nonsignal vectors. This representation allows the prediction of the detection sensitivity of a receiving unit (d') and the reaction time necessary to receive a message.

Attention is the gating of processing units that influences the power of the transmitted vectors. The output power of a vector is determined by two components. The power of the processing unit can be thought of as the variance of the firing rate of the output neuron. The first is a "central" *controlled-process gain*, G_{cpu}.[1] It is assumed that a central mechanism sends a scalar, G_{cpu}, to unit u, which influences the power of the transmitted vector. The second component determining the power is the *automatic-process gain*, $G_{ap\mu\lambda}$. The automatic gain is specific to a given unit μ transmitting message λ. When a unit has a message to transmit, the unit-encoded priority of the message determines the automatic gain for that message. The actual total output power is assumed to be determined by a scalar function of the automatic- and controlled-process gains [$f(G_{cpu}, G_{ap\mu\lambda})$].

---

[1]The term *central* here refers to a level of processing that controls the cooperative interaction of a population of units. It may be truly central in the sense of one system of the whole cortex. Or it may be partially differentiated in the sense of units for vision, audition, motor control, and so on. Also, there may not be a true center, but rather the net effect of interactions between units.

In the current model, I assume the function is simply the addition of the automatic- and controlled-process gain ($G_u = G_{cpu} + G_{apµλ}$). To illustrate, suppose that a visual unit transmits a vector to the semantic unit indicating that the word CAT has appeared. If the automatic gain for the word CAT in the visual unit has a power of 4 and the controlled-process gain for the visual unit is at a power of 5, the transmitted vector would have a power of 9 times that of the initial vector (e.g., if the vector is [−6,0,+6] with an average power or variance of 24, after gain control of 9, the vector is [−18,0,+18]—because the power squares the elements of the vector, each element of the vector is multiplied by the square root of the power—and an average power of 216).

Controlled processing is accomplished through modifications of the controlled-process gain of units and assessment of the degree of activity of units. The degree of activity is defined as the average power or variance of a received message. The mechanism for changing the controlled-process gain allocated to units is represented as a sequence of steps of a program (see Fig. 26.2) or a series of productions (cf. J. R. Anderson, 1983). These productions amount to "if–then" rules for assessing the degree of activity of a given unit and changing the allocated power of units.

CATEGORY-SEARCH PROCEDURE

The transition from controlled to automatic processing is illustrated with examples from a category-search experiment. A typical procedure for a category-search experiment involves: (a) presentation of a short list of memory-set categories to memorize (typically one to four); (b) presentation of a short list of probe words that may or may not be exemplars from the target categories; and (c) a subject response, indicating whether any of the members of the probe words are members of the target categories held in memory. In a "yes–no" variant of the procedure, the subject makes a "yes" response if there is a match between a presented probe word and a memorized target category, and a "no" response if none of the probe words match any of the target categories. In such an experiment reaction times increase linearly with the number of comparisons. The data are generally interpreted to reflect a serial, self-terminating comparison process (see Fisk & Schneider, 1983).

A critical variable in category search is whether the target and distractor sets are *variably* or *consistently* mapped. In a variably mapped (VM) condition, a word that requires a "yes" response on one trial may require a "no" response on the next (e.g., in searching for ANIMALS, the subject may respond "yes" to the word CAT on Trial 1, then, while searching for VEHICLES on Trial 2, respond "no" to the word CAT). In such conditions subjects utilize a serial, slow (200 msec per category), self-terminating comparison process. Performance shows little, if any, change in comparison time as a function of practice

(Fisk & Schneider, 1983). In a consistently mapped (CM) condition, the subject always responds to a given category in the same way (e.g., whenever the subject sees the word CAT, he or she responds by pushing the button with an index finger). Search in CM procedures shows substantial change with practice (see Fig. 26.4). The processing becomes fast (2 msec per category), parallel, and fairly effortless (Fisk & Schneider, 1983).

Phase 1—Controlled Processing with Memory Preload (VM Search)

In Phase 1, controlled processing modifies the output power of given vectors and identifies matches on the basis of how changes in the gain influence the degree of activity of particular units in the system. Phase 1 processing is exhibited during initial practice or in tasks in which the stimuli are variably mapped.

Figure 26.1 illustrates the structure of the model for performing Phase 1 category search. The subject must compare two probe words to two semantic categories and respond with a positive or negative response. It is assumed that before the probe words are presented, the subject is given instructions to preload lexical memory (or working memory) with the category vectors of TREE and ANIMAL, and to preload motor response memory with the vectors for pressing buttons with the index finger and the middle finger. When the visual probe

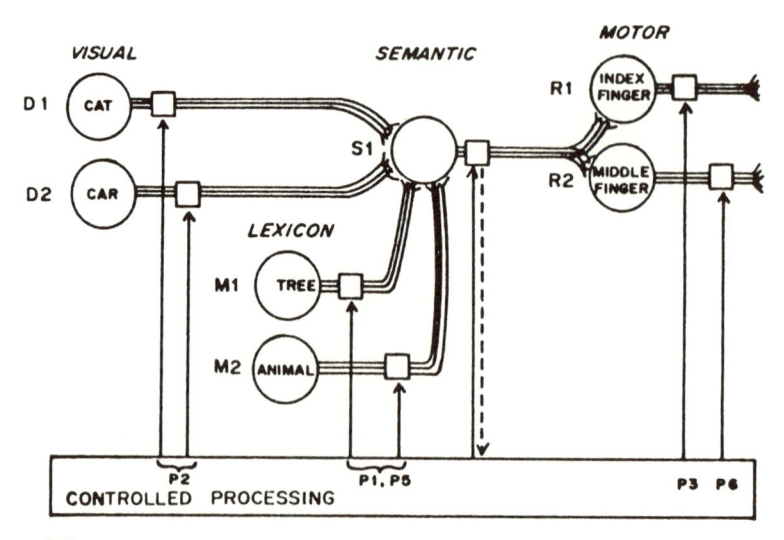

FIG. 26.1. Structure of controlled-processing search. The units (circles) (D1, D2, S, M1, M2, R1, R2) transmit vector messages (words in the circles) with a power determined by controlled-processing gating (upward arrows and boxes). The received power of a vector is reported to the controlled-processing system (downward dashed arrow). See Fig. 26.2 for operations of controlled processing.

Controlled Processing Operations

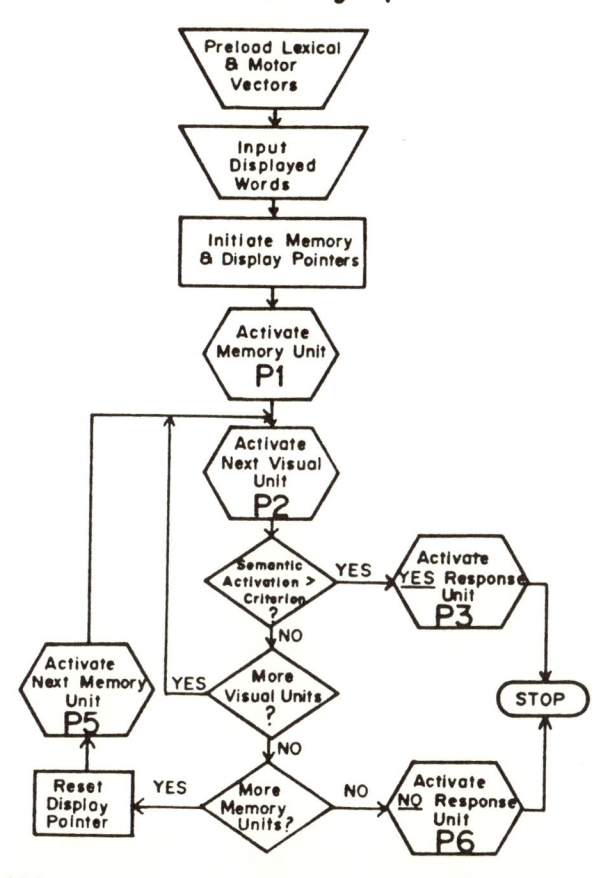

FIG. 26.2. Flow chart of controlled-processing operations during VM category search. The trapezoid shapes represent input to the system; the hexagonal shapes represent controlled-process gating of vector transmissions, the diamonds are conditional tests, and the rectangles are internal controlled-process operations. The P numbers refer to controlled-processing gating referred to in Figs. 26.1 and 26.3.

stimuli are presented, the display units activate the vectors for the visual representations of the words CAT and CAR. Controlled processing manipulates the gains of the various vectors in order to perform a category-comparison match and motor response.

Figure 26.2 illustrates the controlled-processing operations.[2] Controlled processing maintains information about the goal states in the search, which units have been activated, and the degree of activation of units. Controlled processing does not directly send messages between units; instead it modulates the power of messages transmitted between units.

The degree of match between any two vectors is determined by the evoked power or variance of a received vector. To illustrate, when the gain of the first display unit (D1) is increased, the vector for CAT is transmitted to the semantic unit (see Fig. 26.1). When the gain of the second memory unit (M2) is increased, the vector for ANIMAL is also transmitted to the semantic unit. The received vector is the sum of the two individual vectors (D1 GD1 + M2 GM2). The variance or power of the received vector is equal to

$$\sigma^2(D1G_{D1} + M2G_{M2}) = \sigma_{D1}^2 G_{D1}^2 + \sigma_{M2}^2 G_{M2}^2 + 2\rho_{D1M}^2 \sigma_{D1} G_{D1} \sigma_{M2} G_{M2} \qquad (26.1)$$

In the equation, σ is the standard deviation, σ^2 is the variance, ρ is the correlation between the two vectors, and G represents the gain. The controlled system identifies a match if the correlation between the two vectors is greater than some criterion (e.g., rho > .3).[3] The manipulations of gain of processing units enable the assessment of the correlation between vectors. Thus the output representations of any two vectors can be compared (e.g., by comparing the received variance in a visual imagery unit, the system could determine what the degree of physical match would be between the word *CAT* and the lexical unit of ANIMAL, or, by comparing the received variance in the semantic unit, the degree of semantic similarity can be assessed).

Figure 26.3 illustrates the simulated activity patterns during a variably mapped category search. The reader is encouraged to match up Figs. 26.2 and 26.3 with the following text. It is assumed that before the trial begins, the M1, M2, R1, and R2 units are loaded with the appropriate vectors. During preloading the subject interprets the instructions, gating messages to activate vectors in appropriate units (e.g., the instructions to respond with an ''index finger'' would activate the appropriate vector in the motor unit M1). These vectors are decaying with a halflife of 5 sec. When the probe words CAT and CAR are presented, their vectors are evoked in D1 and D2. At 350 msec after display presentation, the first memory unit is activated (P1), transmitting the TREE vector. This results in an additional increase in activation of the semantic unit. At 400 msec, the first display unit is activated (P2), gating the activity of the first display unit. This results in an increase in the activation of the semantic unit. From 400 to 550 msec, the received variance in the semantic unit (S) of the summed vector of D1 + M1 is compared to the criterion (see Eq. 26.1). At 550 msec, the variance is

---

[2]The controlled-processing operations can be represented as a set of productions (cf. J. R. Anderson, 1983) in which P1 to P6 (Figs. 26.2 and 26.3) are productions that fire one at a time. However, in contrast to Anderson-type productions, the present productions gate messages but do not directly send messages.

[3]Because the controlled processing system sets GD1 and GM2, and if the vectors are normalized vectors, the correlation can be calculated from the variance of the summed vector.

26. DEVELOPMENT OF AUTOMATIC PROCESSING 483

still below criterion and the comparison is terminated with a mismatch (P4). At 600 msec, the next visual unit is activated (P2), deactivating vector D1 and increasing the power of vector D2. This results in a decrease in the semantic activation from D1 and an increase in the semantic activation from D2. At 750 msec, there is another mismatch between the display and the category vector (P4). At 800 msec, the next memory-set item is activated (P5). This results in a decrease in the semantic activation due to the deactivation of TREE and an increase due to the activation of ANIMAL. At 850 msec, the first visual display

UNIT	DISPLAY	MEMORY	RESPONSE
1	CAT	TREE	PRESENT
2	CAR	ANIMAL	ABSENT

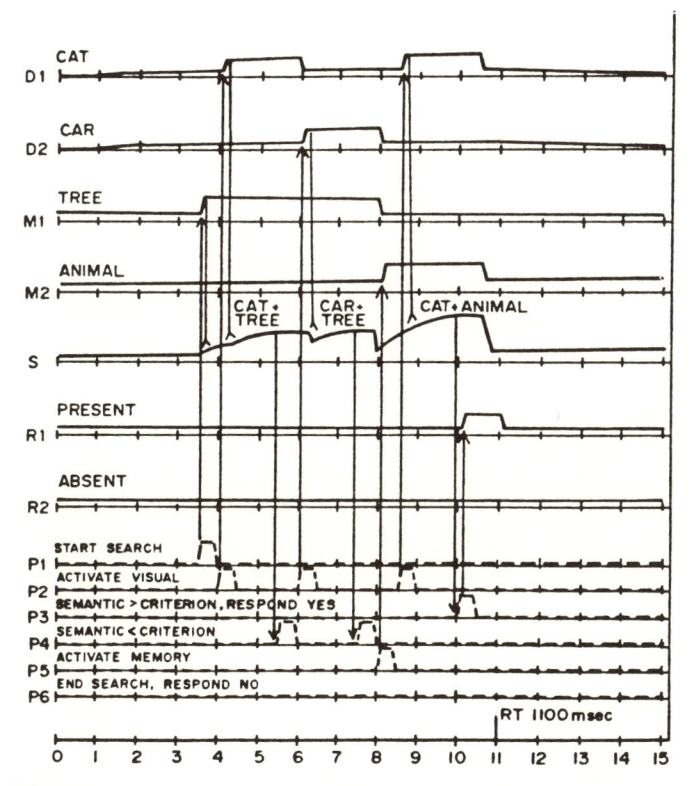

FIG. 26.3. Simulated activity patterns during a variably mapped category search. The middle of the figure illustrates the output activities of units in the system. The bottom of the figure illustrates controlled-process gating of vector transmissions (see Fig. 26.2). The upward lines indicate changes in gain, the downward solid lines indicate the effects of vector transmission, and the downward arrows indicate the report of the received variance from the semantic unit to the controlled-processing system. The bottom axis of the figure indicates elapsed time in 100 msec intervals. See text for a discussion of the sequence of operations.

item is once again activated (P2). This results in an increase in the semantic activation. If we assume that the semantic factor evoked by the word CAT correlates .5 with the semantic vector evoked by the word ANIMAL, the activity in the semantic unit would be 1.5 times greater than would be expected by the activation of two orthogonal vectors (e.g., the activation of CAT and TREE). This increased activity relative to criterion results in the activation of Response 1 vector (P3) at 1000 msec, resulting in the pressing of the TARGET PRESENT button. The response occurs at 1100 msec.

The sequence of operations shown in Fig. 26.3 illustrates a serial self-terminating comparison process with a 200 msec comparison time per category. Note that there are many switches of gains within the processing system. To the extent that such changes in gains are effortful for the subject, this processing represents an effortful procedure.

At this stage of training, any events that either disrupt the preloaded memory vectors or disrupt the operations of the controlled-processing system result in degradation of performance. In variably mapped search conditions, such degradations of performance are observed. For example, in a letter-search task, increasing the memory load of a secondary task interacts with the search memory load, and results in a degradation of performance (Fisk & Schneider, 1983; Logan, 1979). In dual-task conditions, occupying the controlled-processing system by performing a digit search results in substantial degradation of performance of a concurrent variably mapped letter-search task (Schneider & Fisk, 1982a, 1982b) and category-search task (Schneider & Fisk, 1983).

In a variably mapped condition, subjects' performance is expected to remain in Phase 1 even after extended training. The learning mechanisms (see Learning section) influence performance when there is a consistent relationship between the messages that are sent from one unit to another. In a variably mapped condition, this consistency is not maintained, and hence little, if any, learning is expected to occur (see Fisk and Schneider, 1983). In a category-search experiment (Schneider & Aldrich, 1984) the slope for trials 97 to 192 was 224 msec per condition; for trials 769 to 864, the slope was 208 msec with no significant change in slope.

The performance in Phase 1 of the model illustrates the primary characteristics of novice and variably mapped performance. Performance is slow, serial, and effortful. Performance degrades with increases either in memory load or in processing load and there is little benefit for variably mapped processing.

Phase 2—Controlled and Automatic Processing (CM)

Phase 2 processing is exhibited in the early development of a skill in which the subject is making consistent responses to stimuli. Phase 2 processing is defined as the cooccurrence of two types of processing. The first type of processing is the Phase 1 controlled shifting of gain and memory preloading. The second type of processing is automatic processing. Automatic processing develops such that when the target semantic vector is transmitted, the semantic vector will associatively evoke the index-finger response. The reaction times are assumed to be a mixture of responses from the controlled and automatic processing mode. The observed positive reaction times should be the minimum of the two reaction-time distributions.

Associative and Priority Learning. Automatic processing develops as a function of two types of learning mechanisms. The associative learning mechanism modifies the unit-to-unit associative matrix such that a stimulus vector will evoke an appropriate response vector. This involves a Hebb-type synaptic learning mechanism. J. A. Anderson (1977, 1983; Anderson et al., 1977) has illustrated how vector-to-vector learning might occur. The interconnections between the elements of the stimulus vectors and response vector change such that the stimulus evokes the response. The equation for change is:

$$\text{delta } A = c(R - AS)ST \tag{26.2}$$

where A is the associative matrix, R the response vector, S the stimulus vector, ST the transposed stimulus vector, c a learning constant, and *delta A* the change in the strength of the association. Such an associative system can reliably store about as many associations as there are elements of the vector (see Anderson, 1977, 1983). The associations are robust to noise and can produce appropriate responses when only a part of the learned input pattern is presented (Kohonen, 1984).

The associative learning mechanisms require that there be a consistent relationship between the message transmissions in order to develop discriminative associations. To illustrate, assume that the semantic vector of ANIMAL is transmitted to the motor units. If the ANIMAL vector is always transmitted before the index finger responds, the ANIMAL vector will come to associatively evoke the index-finger response. However, if on half the trials the ANIMAL vector is transmitted immediately before an index-finger response and on half the trials it is transmitted immediately before a middle-finger response, the ANIMAL vector will not be able to evoke a discriminative response between these two output vectors. In that case, the controlled processing system would still need to resolve which response to output in a manner described in Phase 1 processing.

The priority learning mechanism tunes the unit's transmission so that important messages are transmitted at high gain and unimportant messages at low gain. Eq. 26.3 and 26.4 illustrate how the automatic gain for a given message changes after a hit and correct rejection.

after hit

$$G_{ap(i+1)} = G_{api} + CH(G_{apmax} - G_{api}) \tag{26.3}$$

after correct rejection

$$G_{ap(i+1)} = G_{ap} + CR(G_{apmin} - G_{api}) \tag{26.4}$$

where G_{apmax} is the maximum automatic gain for a vector, G_{apmin} is the minimum automatic gain for a vector, CH is the proportional increase in gain after a hit, i is the trial number, and CR is the proportional decrease in gain after a correct rejection. The predicted reaction time as a function of consistent practice produces a power-law-type practice curve (see Schneider, 1984).

If there is a consistent relationship such that certain vectors always result in hits and other vectors always result in correct rejections, the priority learning changes will tune the network so that only stimuli that result in hits evoke transmissions. As a result of this tuning, the target stimuli become foreground and "pop out" of the display. The distractor stimuli become background and, in a sense, disappear from the display. This type of popping-out effect is frequently reported by well-practiced subjects in search experiments (see Shiffrin & Schneider, 1977). In a variably mapped situation each stimulus has the same probability of hits and correct rejections. Hence, there is no differential priority between stimuli and the priority learning mechanism cannot discriminate which messages to transmit. When the priority mechanisms cannot filter the stimuli, it is necessary for the controlled-processing mechanism to continue to operate as in Phase 1. Search data illustrate the degree of consistency effect—that is, as consistency decreases, the amount of automatic-processing development decreases (Schneider & Fisk, 1982b).

Controlled processing operates as a training mechanism for the development of automatic processing. Controlled processing allows slow, serial, and accurate processing of the stimulus situation. By the use of the memory preloading mechanism, any vector can be compared to a second vector and the results of the comparison allow releasing of a third vector. The comparison activates input and output vectors, enabling the associative matrix to develop.

Controlled-processing-induced gain shifts initiate local activation patterns that can produce associative learning. Priority learning occurs following a controlled process transmission. Immediately after a hit or a correct rejection occurs, each unit has a decaying trace of the vector it transmitted. The unit modifies the priority (Eqs. 26.3 and 26.4) of automatic gain for that last-transmitted vector.

A number of empirical phenomena are indicative of Phase 2 processing. Automatic-processing detections are expected to occur at first in situations in which controlled processing is particularly slow. Poorly developed automatic processing transmits vectors at weak power. Weak automatic processes will finish before controlled processing only when many controlled-processed comparisons must be made. Thus, there should be a flattening of the reaction-time function for higher memory-set sizes. With practice, the automatic processing should become faster and, hence, the function should flatten at smaller and smaller memory-set sizes. Figure 26.4 illustrates the positive reaction-time functions for a category-search experiment. The first three replications (96 trials each) were variably mapped (blocks 1 to 3) and these replications show the expected lack of change in slope in variably mapped practice. On the fourth

26. DEVELOPMENT OF AUTOMATIC PROCESSING 487

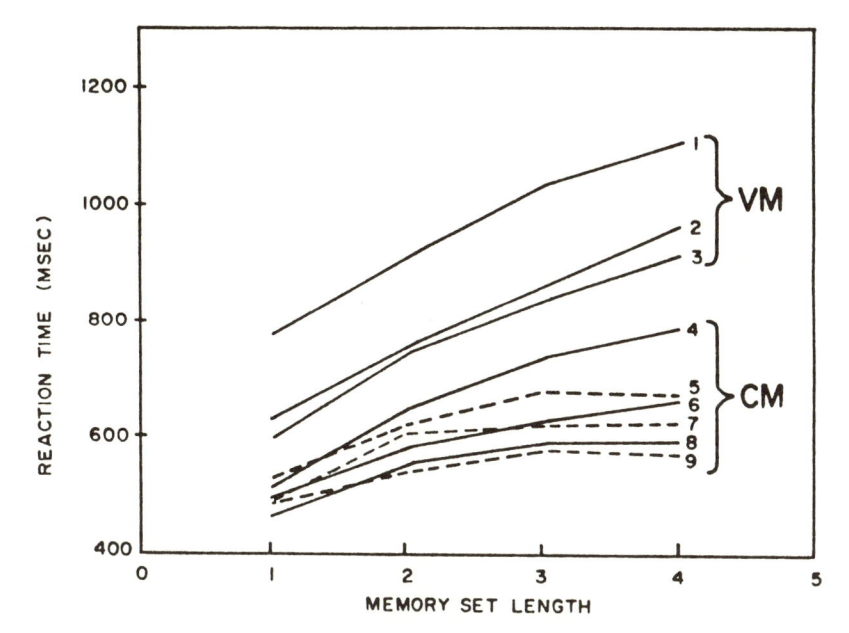

FIG. 26.4. Positive response-reaction times for category-search memory-set size 1 to 4 categories and a single probe word. Replications of 96 trials with 8 positive probes per category. The first three replications were variably mapped, the last six consistently mapped. Note the flattening for the higher memory-set sizes (Schneider & Aldrich, 1985).

replication, the mapping became consistent. Note that by the fifth replication, the reaction times for memory-set size 3 and 4 were equivalent.

Phase 2 processing is a mixture of automatic and controlled processing. Controlled processing is still sensitive to memory and resource-load effects. If the subject must perform other tasks requiring memory or controlled-processing resources, performance will deteriorate. As practice proceeds, the automatic processing becomes faster and can complete before the controlled-processing mechanism.

Phase 3—Automatic Processing with Controlled-Processing Assist

Phase 3 processing is exhibited when sufficient associative and priority learning has occurred such that vectors can evoke vectors without memory preloading. In Phase 3 the memory-comparison mechanism is eliminated. The controlled-processing sequential operations (Fig. 26.2) are no longer necessary. The vector-evoking process substitutes for the vector-comparison process. To illustrate, at this stage of practice the transmission of the ANIMAL vector from the semantic to the motor unit (see Fig. 26.1) will associatively evoke the index-finger response. However, controlled-processing gain is still required in order to have the ANIMAL vector transmitted with sufficient power to overcome the background noise and evoke the index-finger response vector. The controlled-processing system is assisting the automatic-processing system by allocating the additional power. The complex sequential operations of Phase 1 controlled processing (see Fig. 26.2) are replaced by a single Phase 3 operation of "allocate gain to the display (D1,D2), semantic (S), and motor (M1,M2) units." In this stage, the subject attends to the task in general. For example, in learning to operate a manual transmission, this phase would require the trainee to attend generally to the motor task but not require rehearsal of specific patterns.

Phase 3 processing makes two predictions that have been empirically demonstrated. First, as Phase 3 processing develops there should be a shift from serial to parallel processing. Reaction time, mean, and variance data show a shift to parallel processing in consistently mapped search (see Fisk & Schneider, 1983; Schneider & Shiffrin, 1977, Appendix G). Second, there should be little performance decrement for removal (e.g., through secondary task) of the memory set (except possibly for the very first small memory sets). After extensive CM training subjects can search equally well whether the memory set is presented or not (see Fisk & Schneider, 1983; Schneider & Aldrich, 1985; Schneider & Fisk, 1982a, 1982b).

Whether subjects operate in Phase 2 or Phase 3 is probably dependent on the subjects' strategy (i.e., which controlled-processing operation the subjects activate). Even after Phase 3 processing may be effective, subjects may still choose a strategy of preloading the memory vectors and performing the serial category search exhibited in Phases 1 and 2. In some of our experiments a few subjects have exhibited serial controlled-processing-type search after many sessions of consistent practice. When these subjects were encouraged to "let go" of the category search, their performance frequently shifted to exhibit behavior suggestive of automatic processing (see Schneider & Fisk, 1983).

Phase 4—Automatic Processing

Phase 4 processing will occur in well-practiced, consistently mapped tasks. In Phase 4 processing, the associative and priority learning mechanisms have sufficiently developed such that one vector will evoke a follow-on vector without controlled processing. The processing diagram for Phase 4 processing would be simply the visual units outputting to the semantic unit and the semantic unit outputting to a motor unit (basically the top row of Fig. 26.1 with no controlled processing inputs). Figure 26.5 shows the activation patterns that would be indicative of the automatic processing of the category search experiment. When the words CAT and CAR are presented, they are assumed to evoke the appropriate patterns in the visual display units, D1 and D2. When the display units are

26. DEVELOPMENT OF AUTOMATIC PROCESSING   489

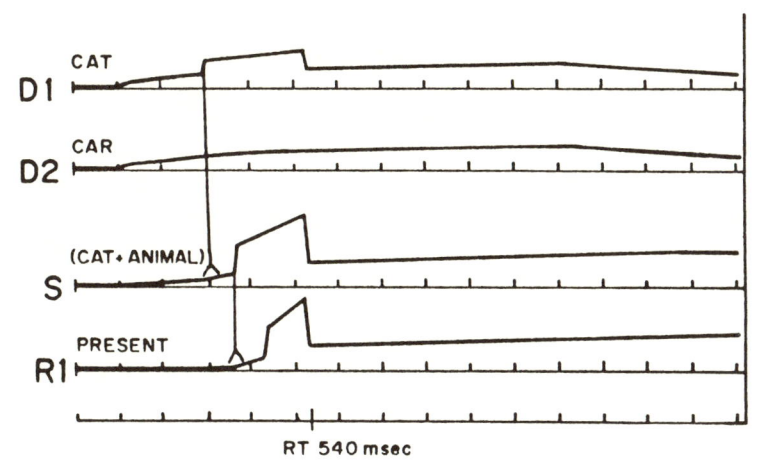

FIG. 26.5. Activity pattern, Phase 4 processing (see caption for Fig. 26.3 for specifications). The gain increases (D1, S, R) are now the result of automatic gain determined by priority learning.

sufficiently activated (e.g., have d' over 2), they identify on which vector to transmit. The word CAT is transmitted at a high gain (Gap = 3), becoming foreground information from the display. The distractor stimulus, CAR, is transmitted on a low automatic grain (e.g., Gap = 1), resulting in its being background information and not influencing the later processing stages. The transmission of the CAT vector at 400 msec activates the semantic representation for ANIMAL. Once this activation exceeds a criterion threshold (at 450 msec), the unit identifies the automatic gain with which to transmit that message and transmits the message for a brief period of time. The transmission of the ANIMAL vector to the response unit results in evoking the index-finger response vector. When this vector exceeds criterion, its automatic gain is determined and that vector is transmitted on, causing the response. This cascade of three transmissions results in a response at 540 msec. The transmission cycle includes associative translation of the received message, assessment of gain, and transmission at the specified gain. Note the complete absence of controlled-processing operations during Phase 4 operations.

Empirically, Phase 4 processing is characterized as being robust to the elimination of the controlled-processing resources. After sufficient CM practice, subjects can perform reliable automatic detection while performing a concurrent high workload controlled-processing search (Fisk & Schneider, 1983, 1984; Schneider & Fisk, 1982a, 1982b, 1983, 1984).

Phase 4 processing may not operate effectively if the stimuli are severely degraded. If the input vector is severely degraded, a unit cannot identify the vector sufficiently to determine the automatic gain for the vector. To minimize noise in the system, the unit should *not* transmit a noisy signal. This would predict that consistently mapped stimulus processing of highly degraded stimuli should not exhibit Phase 4 performance. A number of researchers (Hoffman, Simons, & Houck, 1983; Shaw, 1983; Shaw, Mulligan, & Stone, 1983) have shown that consistent processing of severely degraded stimuli does not show the parallel, capacity-free processing associated with automatic processing.

Even after Phase 4 processing has developed, controlled processing can be used to enhance message transmission. Increasing the power of a message will enhance that message, resulting in reduced transmission time and fewer errors. However, total network communications might be hindered by allocating a Phase 4 process additional power. This can occur for one of two reasons. First, giving greater power to one message may interfere with the other messages (see Schneider, 1983). Second, allocating power to an automatic process may preclude allocating the power to a different message that requires it (this assumes that controlled processing can influence the gain of only a limited number of units).

Note that there is no clear transition between Phase 3 and Phase 4 processing. I might operationally define Phase 4 processing in dual-task paradigms if two conditions are met. First, performance on the automatic task must be reliable (e.g., > 95% of single-task performance level), while the subject is fully engaged in a high resource load controlled-processing task. Second, the subject must maintain the controlled-processing performance at a level comparable (e.g., within 90%) to the single-task level. Note that the reaction times of the automatic processing might still be substantially increased due to the secondary task's prohibiting controlled-processing assist.

SUMMARY

The present model provides a description for the transition from controlled to automatic processing. The transition is assumed to occur continuously through four phases. The proposed phases are: (a) controlled processing with memory preload; (b) controlled and automatic processing; (c) automatic processing with controlled assist; and (d) automatic processing. Controlled processing involves the gating of vectors and the assessment of match between vectors. Automatic processing involves a cascade of vector transmissions in which the output power of each transmission is determined by the message unit specific priority. When subjects consistently transmit messages, associative learning causes one message to evoke a new message in a receiving unit; and priority learning determines which messages are transmitted. The present model is sufficiently detailed to allow quantitative simulations of many practice, attention, and search phenomena. Future work will present these fits and novel predictions.

ACKNOWLEDGMENT

This research was supported in part by funds from the Office of Naval Research, Personnel and Training Contract N000-14-84-K-0008 (NR 154-527) and National Institute of Mental Health Grant 5 R01 MH 31425-04.

Reprint requests should be sent to Walter Schneider, Department of Psychology, University of Illinois, 603 E. Daniel Street, Champaign, IL 61820.

REFERENCES

Adams, J. A. (1971). A closed-loop theory of motor learning. *Journal of Motor Behavior, 3,* 111–150.
Anderson, J. A. (1977). Neural models with cognitive implications. In D. Laberge & S. J. Samuels (Eds.), *Basic processes in reading* (pp. 27–90). Hillsdale, NJ: Lawrence Erlbaum Associates.
Anderson, J. A. (1983). Cognitive and psychological computation with neural models. *IEEE Transactions on Systems, Man, and Cybernetics, SMC–13,* 799–815.
Anderson, J. A., Silverstein, J. W., Ritz, S. A., & Jones, R. S. (1977). Distinctive features, categorical perception, and probability learning: Some applications of a neural model. *Psychological Review, 84,* 413–451.
Anderson, J. R. (1982). Acquisition of cognitive skill. *Psychological Review, 89,* 369–406.
Anderson, J. R. (1983). *The architecture of cognition.* Cambridge, MA: Harvard University Press.
Fisk, A. D., & Schneider, W. (1983). Category and word search: Generalizing search principles to complex processing. *Journal of Experimental Psychology: Learning, Memory and Cognition, 9,* 177–195.
Fisk, A. D., & Schneider, W. (1984). Memory as a function of attention, level of processing, and automatization. *Journal of Experimental Psychology: Learning, Memory, and Cognition, 10,* 181–197.
Hoffman, J. E., Simons, R. F., & Houck, M. R. (1983). Event-related potentials during controlled and automatic target detection. *Psychophysiology, 20,* 625–632.
James, W. (1890). *Principles of psychology* (Vol. 1). New York: Holt.
Kohonen, T. (1984). *Self-organization and associative memory.* New York: Springer-Verlag.
LaBerge, D. (1976). Perceptual learning and attention. In W. K. Estes (Ed.), *Handbook of learning and cognitive processes* (Vol. 4, pp. 237–273). Hillsdale, NJ: Lawrence Erlbaum Associates.
Levy, W. B., & Steward, O. (1983). Temporal contiguity requirements for long-term associative potentiation/depression in the hippocampus. *Neuroscience, 8,* 791–797.
Logan, G. D. (1978). Attention in character-classification tasks: Evidence for the automaticity of component stages. *Journal of Experimental Psychology: General, 107,* 32–63.
Logan, G. D. (1979). On the use of a concurrent memory load to measure attention and automaticity. *Journal of Experimental Psychology: Human Perception and Performance, 5,* 189–207.
MacKay, D. G. (1982). The problems of flexibility, fluency, and speed-accuracy trade-off in skilled behavior. *Psychological Review, 89,* 483–506.
Neumann, O. (1984). Automatic processing: A review of recent findings and a plea for an old theory. In W. Prinz & A. F. Sanders (Eds.), *Cognition and motor processes* (pp. 255–293). Heidelberg: Springer-Verlag.
Norman, D. A. (1976). *Memory and attention: An introduction to human information processing.* New York: Wiley.
Norman, D. A., & Shallice, T. (1980). *Attention to action: Willed and automatic control of behavior* (Tech. Rep. 8006). La Jolla, CA: University of California, San Diego, Center for Human Information Processing.

Pew, R. W. (1966). Acquisition of hierarchical control over the temporal organization of skill. *Journal of Experimental Psychology, 71,* 764-771.

Pew, R. W. (1974). Levels of analysis in motor control. *Brain Research, 71,* 393-400.

Posner, M. I., & Snyder, C. R. R. (1975). Attention and cognitive control. In R. L. Solso (Ed.), *Information Processing and cognition: The Loyola symposium* (pp. 55-85). Hillsdale, NJ: Lawrence Erlbaum Associates.

Schneider, W. (1983, November). *A simulation of automatic/controlled processing predicting attentional and practice effects.* Paper presented at the meeting of the Psychonomic Society, San Diego, California.

Schneider, W. (1984, April). *The crisis and challenge of attention.* Paper presented at ONR Contractors Meeting, New Haven, Connecticut.

Schneider, W., & Aldrich, K. (1984). *Practice effects in category search and the development of parallel search.* Manuscript submitted for publication.

Schneider, W., & Fisk, A. D. (1982a). Concurrent automatic and controlled visual search: Can processing occur without resource cost? *Journal of Experimental Psychology: Learning, Memory and Cognition, 8,* 261-278.

Schneider, W., & Fisk, A. D. (1982b). Degree of consistent training: Improvements in search performance and automatic process development. *Perception and Psychophysics, 31,* 160-168.

Schneider, W., & Fisk, A. D. (1983). Attention theory and mechanisms for skilled performance. In R. A. Magill (Ed.), *Memory and control of action* (pp. 119-143). New York: North-Holland.

Schneider, W., & Fisk, A. D. (1984). Automatic category search and its transfer. *Journal of Experimental Psychology: Learning, Memory, and Cognition, 10,* 1-15.

Schneider, W., & Shiffrin, R. M. (1977). Controlled and automatic human information processing. I. Detection, search, and attention. *Psychological Review, 84,* 1-66.

Shaw, M. L. (1983). Division of attention among spatial locations: A fundamental difference between detection of letters and detection of luminance increments. In H. Bouma & D. G. Bonwhuis (Eds.), *Attention and performance X* (pp. 109-122). Hillsdale, NJ: Lawrence Erlbaum Associates.

Shaw, M. L., Mulligan, R. M., & Stone, L. D. (1983). Two-state versus continuous-state stimulus representations: A test based on attentional constraints. *Perception and Psychophysics, 33,* 338-354.

Shiffrin, R. M., & Schneider, W. (1977). Controlled and automatic human information processing. II. Percetual learning. *Psychological Review, 84,* 127-190.

Solomon, L. M., & Stein, G. (1896). Normal motor automation. *Psychological Review, 3,* 492-512.

Szentagothai, J. (1977). The neuron network of the cerebral cortex: A functional interpretation. *Proceedings of the Royal Society of London B, 201,* 219-248.

Van der Meulen, E. C. (1977). A survey of multi-way channels in information theory: 1961-1976. *IEEE Transactions on Information Theory, IT-23,* 1-37.

27 Sustained Attention: A Multifactorial Approach

Raja Parasuraman
The Catholic University of America

ABSTRACT

Decrements over time in sustained attention (vigilance decrement) have been attributed to filtering, reduced tonic arousal, neural habituation, and related factors. A recent taxonomic approach to vigilance suggests that multiple factors may play a role in vigilance decrement. Furthermore, the factors that account for performance changes over time (vigilance decrement) may differ from those influencing the overall level of performance (vigilance level). This chapter examines the role of four factors—tonic arousal, capacity limitations, target expectancy, and neural habituation—in the explanation of the vigilance decrement and the level of vigilance. The results of three experiments suggest a multifactor model of sustained attention in which the level of vigilance is related to tonic arousal, and the vigilance decrement to expectancy or capacity, depending on the event rate and other task parameters defining different classes of vigilance task. Arousal and neural habituation do not appear to play a significant role in vigilance decrement.

INTRODUCTION

Human attention can be simultaneously efficient and inefficient. The ability to focus on a single source of information in the presence of other competing sources, as exemplified by the "cocktail-party" phenomenon (Cherry, 1953), is clearly a significant achievement of biological adaptation. Yet the efficiency of selective attention may be accompanied by inefficiency in divided attention (attending to many sources at once), or *sustained* attention (attending to a source for a prolonged, unbroken period of time). Deficits in divided attention are generally found when target events occur simultaneously on two or more channels (Moray, 1975). Sustained attention deficits are most prominent when both target and nontarget events occur rapidly, irrespective of the number of channels monitored. The *vigilance decrement*, which refers to the decline in the detection rate of critical targets over time, is most marked in such high-event rate tasks (Davies & Parasuraman, 1982; Parasuraman, 1979, 1984b; Warm & Jerison, 1984).

The vigilance decrement has been attributed to the build-up of response inhibition (N. H. Mackworth, 1950), fluctuations in target expectancy (Baker, 1959; Colquhoun & Baddeley, 1964), "filtering" of task-relevant information (Broadbent, 1958), reduction in observer arousal (Corcoran, 1965), variations in the quality of "observing responses" (Jerison, 1970), and neural habituation (J. F. Mackworth, 1969). As recent reviews have pointed out, no single one of these theories can account for the major findings on vigilance in the literature (Davies & Parasuraman, 1982; Loeb & Alluisi, 1984; Warm, 1977). However, a recent taxonomic approach to vigilance suggests that multiple factors may play a role in vigilance decrement, depending on the event rate and other task parameters defining different classes of vigilance task (Parasuraman, 1979, 1984b). In addition, a distinction must be made between the vigilance decrement over time and the overall level of vigilance. These two facets of vigilance performance may or may not be influenced by the same factors. Thus, multiple theoretical explanations may be needed to account for different aspects of performance on different classes of vigilance task.

TAXONOMY OF VIGILANCE

Parasuraman (1976, 1979; Parasuraman & Davies, 1977) suggested an initial classification of tasks by event rate, target discrimination type (successive or simultaneous discrimination, sensory or cognitive), sensory modality (visual or auditory), and source complexity (single or multisource). Other investigators also have pointed to event rate (Posner, 1975; Warm & Jerison, 1984) and target discrimination type (Davies & Tune, 1970; Warm, Dember, & Lanzetta, 1984) as important task dimensions.

The taxonomic approach has led to improved generalizations of the effects on vigilance of factors such as time on task (Levine, Romashko, & Fleishman, 1973; Parasuraman, 1979), individual differences (Davies & Parasuraman, 1982, Chapter 6), and noise (Smith, 1984). Event rate and target discrimination type (successive or simultaneous discrimination), for example, are important in distinguishing between sensitivity and criterion shifts over time on task (Parasuraman, 1979). The vigilance decrement in detection rate or speed is generally accompanied by a decrease in the false detection rate. Thus, vigilance may decline because the observer's ability to discriminate targets, or perceptual sensitivity (d'), decreases over time. On the other hand, sensitivity may remain stable and an increase in the response criterion (β) may account for the decrement in the detection rate and false-alarm rate.[1]

In Parasuraman's (1979) study a distinction was made between *successive-* and *simultaneous-*discrimination vigilance tasks. In successive-discrimination tasks, targets have to be distinguished from a nontarget reference represented in recent memory, because nontarget and target features are presented successively. In contrast, in simultaneous-discrimination tasks, target and nontarget features are provided within the same stimulus event. Parasuraman (1979) showed that a sensitivity decrement over time occurred only for the successive-discrimination vigilance tasks when the event rate was high (greater than 24 per min), irrespective of sensory modality.[2] In the low event-rate tasks, sensitivity remained stable, and the vigilance decrement was associated with an increase in response criterion over time (see Parasuraman, 1984b, for a review).

The effects of event rate on the overall level of performance also differ as a function of target discrimination type. Lanzetta (1984) found that the deleterious effects of event rate on detection rate occurred at a lower event rate for a visual successive-discrimination task (12 to 24/min) than for a visual simultaneous-discrimination task (24 to 48/min). The results were interpreted in terms of the greater processing load imposed by the successive task.

The results of these studies suggest that the factors influencing both the vigilance decrement and the overall level of vigilance performance vary with the class of vigilance task being performed. In high event-rate tasks, sensitivity may fall because the limited-capacity attentional system (Kahneman, 1973; Moray, 1967) cannot devote resources consistently to target discrimination for a prolonged period. This possibility is explored further in Experiment 3 in this chapter. In tasks showing changes in the criterion, the decrement may reflect adaptations in observer expectancy for targets (Vickers & Leary, 1983) or the use of probability-matching strategies (Craig, 1978). (See Davies & Parasuraman, 1982, Chapter 4, for a detailed explanation of expectancy theories.)

The taxonomic analysis suggests a role for both target expectancy and capacity limitations in the explanation of vigilance decrement, depending on the type of vigilance task. However, alternative explanations have also been put forward. J. F. Mackworth (1969) suggested that the sensitivity decrement reflects increased

---

[1]The demonstration of criterion or sensitivity shifts does not depend solely on the use of parametric signal-detection theory measures such as d' or β (whose use depend on assumptions that may be violated), but can be demonstrated using nonparametric measures (Craig, 1978), robust ROC-based measures (Parasuraman, 1979), or reaction-time measures (Parasuraman & Davies, 1976). (See Davies & Parasuraman, 1982, Chapters 3 to 5, for a review.)

[2]The conclusion that only successive-discrimination tasks show sensitivity decrement is consistent with early findings of a greater increase over time in sensory "thresholds" with successive than with simultaneous-discrimination threshold procedures (Bakan, 1955; Berger & Mahneke, 1954).

neural habituation at high event rates. Welford (1978) linked criterion shifts in vigilance tasks to a reduction in arousal over time. Buck (1966) also proposed that the vigilance decrement occurs only for difficult targets and results from lowered arousal. Three experiments that attempt to distinguish between these different explanations of the vigilance decrement, and in addition examine their role in the level of vigilance, are briefly reported in this chapter. The neural habituation theory is examined first.

EXPERIMENT 1: HABITUATION OF ERPS AND VIGILANCE DECREMENT

The effects of event rate on performance in vigilance tasks were linked to the concept of habituation by J. F. Mackworth (1969). Habituation refers to the reduction in intensity of a physiological or behavioral response with repeated stimulation (Thompson & Spencer, 1966). In examining the habituation of the EEG alpha desynchronization response, Sharpless and Jasper (1956) first suggested that the performance decrements found in vigilance tasks might result from habituation. High rates of stimulation have been found to depress detection performance in vigilance tasks (Jerison & Pickett, 1964) and to lead to greater habituation of autonomic and central nervous system responses (Thompson & Spencer, 1966). In linking these two results, J. F. Mackworth (1969) suggested that the repetitious nature of the events in vigilance tasks serves to habituate the neural responses to these events, the rate of habituation being greater for more frequently presented events. As a result, the background neural "noise" increases, leading to a gradual impairment in the observer's ability to detect targets among these events.

Although there is evidence that both EEG alpha desynchronization and various components of the event-related potential (ERP) habituate over time, a direct EEG or ERP test of Mackworth's theory has not been reported (see Gale, 1977). One way to test the theory is to compare the usual "passive" habituation paradigm (in which subjects are given no task) with an "active" detection or vigilance paradigm. According to Mackworth, evoked potentials and "arousal reactions" are necessary for the maintenance of performance in vigilance tasks. Habituation of evoked potentials and the resultant spread of cortical inhibition leads to the initial decrement seen in vigilance tasks. This initial habituation occurs irrespective of whether a task is performed or not. Habituation can be distinguished from processes of fatigue or adaptation by the phenomenon of *dishabituation,* which refers to a restoration in response amplitude following a change in stimulation. In Mackworth's theory, habituation is followed later in the task by dishabituation, which enables the reevocation of arousal reactions so that performance stabilizes, although it remains at a low level. This process occurs only when there is a performance requirement. Under passive conditions, evoked potentials continue to habituate. Thus, the rate of decrement in evoked potential amplitude over the entire period of the task should be greater under passive than under active conditions. Moreover, any difference in the rate of decrement should be greater at fast event rates. These hypotheses were examined in Experiment 1 by investigating the effects of event rate on vigilance performance and on the N1 component of the auditory ERP. This ERP component is an appropriate candidate as it has been shown to satisfy a number of criteria for habituation, including sensitivity to stimulation rate and to a dishabituating stimulus (Callaway, 1973).

Method

Eight subjects were presented with a series of 1000 Hz tones for a continuous period of 30 min at either a slow (20/min) or fast (40/min) event rate. In different conditions subjects were instructed to: (a) listen actively and detect infrequent target tones by depressing a response key; or (b) read a book and ignore all tones. Targets were tones of slightly higher pitch and occurred with a probability of .15. Each subject was tested on all four combinations of event rate and instruction condition, in counterbalanced order. ERPs were recorded from scalp electrodes placed at the vertex (Cz), referred to linked ears. ERPs were averaged separately to nontargets and targets and for each of three consecutive 10 min blocks of trials of the 30 min task. Trials in which the ERP was contaminated by ocular artifacts, as indicated by the EOG, were excluded from the averages.

Results and Discussion

The target detection rate (hits) and the signal detection theory index d' were computed for each 10 min block of trials. Table 27.1 shows the mean hit rates and d' values for the two event rates and for each 10 min block of trials. The hit

TABLE 27.1
Mean Values of Hit Rate and Sensitivity (d')
at Low and High Event Rates
for Consecutive 10 Min Blocks of Trials
for a 30 Min Auditory Discrimination Task[a]

10 Min Blocks	Low Event Rate			High Event Rate		
	1	2	3	1	2	3
Hit rate	.71	.64	.61	.72	.50	.51
d'	2.51	2.54	2.51	2.48	2.10	1.98

[a]Data for the "active" conditions of Experiment 1.

rate declined over trials at both slow and fast event rates, but the decrement was greater for the fast event rate, confirming previous reports (Jerison & Pickett, 1964). Sensitivity declined significantly only for the fast event-rate condition, again confirming previous findings (Loeb & Binford, 1968; Parasuraman, 1979).

Figure 27.1 shows ERPs to nontargets for one subject in the passive and active detection conditions. The auditory ERP waveform shows the prominent vertex potential, which comprises an early negative component with a peak latency of about 100 msec, N1, and a later positive component, P2. The amplitude of the N1 component, measured relative to a 100 msec prestimulus baseline, as well as the N1–P2 amplitude, declined with time on task. The mean values of N1 amplitude are shown in Fig. 27.2, plotted as a function of time on task for all four experimental conditions. The amplitude of N1 declined over the three 10 min blocks of trials, in agreement with previous studies indicating that this ERP component exhibits habituation (Callaway, 1973). The decrement over time in N1 amplitude was greater for the fast than for the slow event rate, but the rate of decrement was the same for active and passive listening conditions. The only difference between the active and passive conditions was in the overall amplitude of N1. As Fig. 27.2 indicates, although as expected habituation was more rapid for the fast event rate, there were no differences in the rate of habituation between the passive listening and vigilance conditions.

J. F. Mackworth's (1969) habituation theory of vigilance is unique in that it is formulated with respect to a specific physiological index, the ERP, rather than in terms of physiological measures in general, as for arousal theory. The specificity of the habituation theory allowed a direct test of the theory in Experiment 1. Nevertheless, the finding that the rate of decrement in ERP amplitude does not

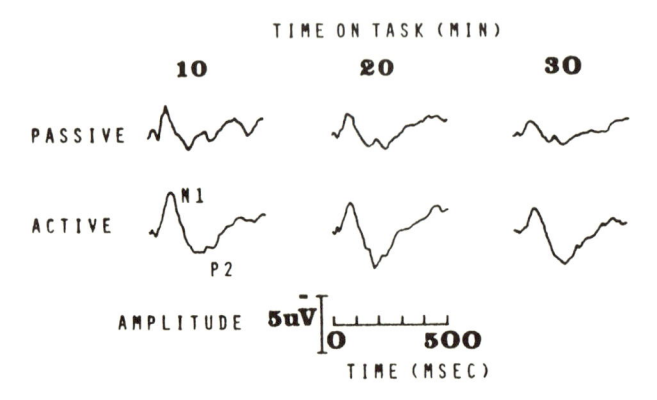

FIG. 27.1. Event-related brain potentials to nontarget tones for consecutive 10 min blocks under passive listening and active detection conditions. Data from Experiment 1.

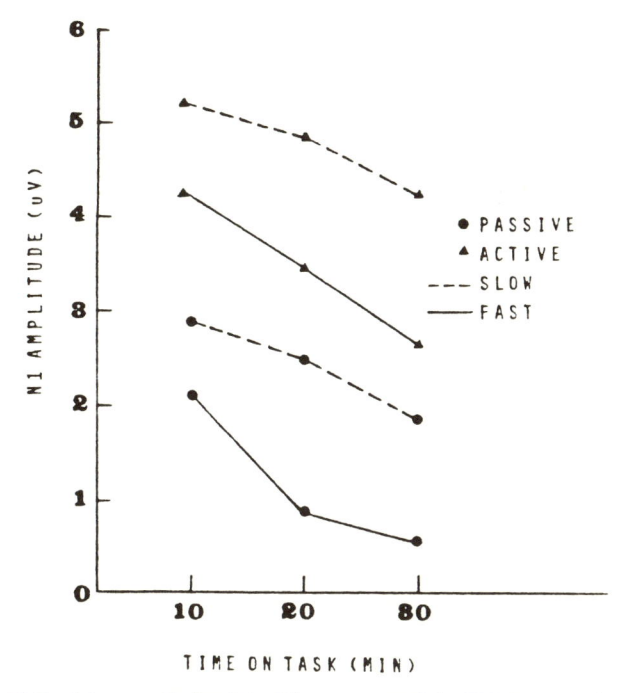

FIG. 27.2. Mean amplitude of the N1 component of the ERP in successive 10 min blocks at slow and fast event rates, and for passive listening and active detection conditions. Data from Experiment 1.

differ between passive and active detection conditions fails to support Mackworth's habituation–dishabituation theory of vigilance decrement. Although sensitivity declined only at the high event rate, and habituation of N1 amplitude was also greater at the high event rate, the pattern of results obtained for the passive condition suggests that neural habituation was not the specific factor causing vigilance decrement in the active condition. A study by Krulewitz, Warm, and Wohl (1975) in which the event rate was changed *during* a vigilance task further supports this view. According to Mackworth's theory, vigilance performance should improve (due to dishabituation) following *any* shift in event rate. However, Krulewitz et al. found that detection performance was primarily affected by the event rate level rather than by the shift per se. Furthermore, when performance did improve (following a shift to a lower event rate), it did so only after subjects experienced the new event rate for about 20 min. Dishabituation is generally characterized as an *immediate* restoration in response amplitude following a change in stimulation (Thompson & Spencer, 1966). This last finding indicates further that the time course of vigilance performance differs markedly from that of habituation and dishabituation processes.

EXPERIMENT 2: TONIC AROUSAL, TIME OF DAY, AND VIGILANCE: THE EFFECTS OF MEMORY LOAD

The arousal theory of vigilance decrement postulates that the vigilance decrement results from a progressive reduction in arousal or alertness due to the repetitive, monotonous nature of vigilance tasks. Buck (1966) proposed a specific form of arousal theory to account for vigilance decrement. He suggested that the vigilance decrement is determined by the relationship of the initial arousal level to some critical level below which performance degradation occurs. The critical level is set by target duration, difficulty, and other task and individual factors. When the critical level is low, as in tasks in which the target is present until detected (e.g., search and so-called "unlimited-hold" tasks), the observer's arousal level will tend to exceed the critical level at all times. A decline in arousal over time will result in an increase in reaction time (RT), but as long as arousal level exceeds the critical level, there is no decrement in detection accuracy. A decrement in both accuracy and speed occurs only when the critical level is high, as in tasks with difficult targets.

Buck's (1966) arousal theory suggests that the performance decrement found with difficult targets may occur due to lowered arousal. Increasing the observer's level of arousal should therefore reduce or eliminate the decrement in detection accuracy. Examination of the effects of time of day provides a means for testing this prediction. Tonic arousal increases from morning to afternoon and early evening as part of the diurnal rhythm (Colquhoun, 1971). According to Buck's theory, therefore, arousal is more likely to exceed the critical level below which performance degradation occurs in the afternoon than in the morning. Hence, the vigilance decrement over time should be greater in the morning than in the afternoon. This hypothesis was examined in Experiment 2 by investigating performance on high event-rate tasks during morning and afternoon testing.[3]

Method

In order to examine the moderating influence of target discrimination type, two tasks lasting 30 min were used: (a) a duration-judgment task in which a decrease in the duration of a repetitively presented 1000 Hz tone had to be detected; (b) a detection task requiring the detection of the same tone in a noise burst. The duration-judgment and detection tasks were matched for the initial level of difficulty. The event rate was 30/min and signal probability was .1 in both tasks. It was hypothesized that task a (successive discrimination) would place an additional demand on short-term memory than task b (simultaneous discrimination).

---

[3] A more detailed description of this experiment appears in Davies, Parasuraman, and Toh (1984).

Thus, on the basis of Parasuraman's (1979) taxonomy, only the duration-judgment task should show a sensitivity decrement over time.[4]

Forty subjects aged 17 to 30 years were randomly assigned to one of the four possible combinations of two testing times, morning (8 to 10 AM) or afternoon/evening (4 to 6 PM), and two tasks (duration judgment or detection). Subjects were required to indicate whether they had detected a target by depressing a response button and also to record their confidence by depressing one of three confidence-rating buttons. Following training, subjects were given a 10 min practice task, and then were tested on the main task.

Results and Discussion

The results are shown in Table 27.2. The ROC-based index d_a was used as a measure of sensitivity (Simpson & Fitter, 1973). There was a small but reliable decrement in sensitivity over time for the duration-judgment task, whereas there was no decline in sensitivity for the detection task. Time of day had no significant effect on performance decrement over time in either task. However, there was a significant interaction between task type and time of day, indicating that time of day had differential effects on the overall level of performance on the two tasks. As Table 27.2 indicates, performance on the detection task increased with time of day, whereas performance on the duration-judgment task decreased.

These results indicate that changes in tonic arousal associated with time of day do not affect the vigilance decrement in high event-rate tasks. Thus, the arousal theory of the decrement was not supported. Evidence was obtained, however, for effects of arousal on the overall level of vigilance. The direction of the time-of-day effect depended on the memory load of the task. Performance on short-term memory tasks and memory-loaded tasks *decreases* from morning to afternoon testing, and there is evidence that increases in arousal impair performance on tasks requiring short-term retention (Folkard, 1979). Thus, the results of Experiment 2 are consistent with the following interpretation: (a) arousal influences the overall level of vigilance; (b) arousal increases with time of day; (c) performance on memory-loaded tasks varies inversely with arousal, whereas performance on nonmemory tasks varies directly with arousal; (d) the duration-judgment task imposes a memory load; (e) hence, changes in arousal from morning to evening, forming part of the diurnal rhythm, are associated with either an improvement or deterioration in the overall level of vigilance, depending on the memory load imposed by the task, but the vigilance decrement is unaffected.

---

[4]Because one of these tasks required a threshold-detection judgment and the other a threshold-temporal discrimination, the two tasks differed in respects other than short-term memory. However, Parasuraman (1979, Experiment 2) found that the memory requirement was more important in determining sensitivity decrement in such tasks.

TABLE 27.2
Mean Values of Sensitivity (d_a)
for Consecutive 10 Min Blocks of Trials
for Two 30 Min Vigilance Tasks
Performed in the Morning or the Afternoon[a]

10 Min Blocks	Duration Task 1	2	3	Detection Task 1	2	3
Morning	1.7	1.9	1.6	1.2	1.9	1.5
Afternoon	1.2	.9	1.0	2.0	2.0	1.9

[a]Data from Experiment 2.

EXPERIMENT 3: PROBING SUSTAINED ATTENTION CAPACITY

As the results of the Experiments 1 and 2 indicate, neither neural habituation nor reduced tonic arousal can account directly for the vigilance decrement over time. A recent finding that the sensitivity decrement can occur in very short time periods (Nuechterlein, Parasuraman, & Jiang, 1983) further supports this view. In most studies reporting sensitivity decrement, the decrement is usually fairly small and occurs over a long period. Typically d' decreases by about .2 to .4 over a 1 hour period. However, Nuechterlein et al. (1983) reported a situation in which large sensitivity declines were obtained after only 5 min in a 8 min task. Subjects had to detect a specified target digit among digit stimuli presented visually at a very fast event rate (60/min). A sensitivity decrement occurred when the digits were highly degraded but not when the digits were moderately degraded or not degraded. In a second experiment, it was found that the decrement was still present after repeated testing on four occasions. The time course of the decrement in Nuechterlein et al.'s (1983) study appears too short to be attributable to a decrement in arousal (in fact, the subjects reported the task to be consistently difficult and stimulating). The results suggest instead that sensitivity decrements result from demands on a limited-capacity attention system that is taxed when the event rate is high and coupled with either a memory or stimulus-encoding load.

The attentional capacity interpretation of sensitivity decrement was examined further in Experiment 3. One way to investigate the attentional demands associated with sensitivity decrement is to use a secondary, probe reaction-time task. Posner and Ogden (see Posner, 1978) and Bowers (1983) used probe RTs to auditory stimuli to examine vigilance performance. In Bowers' (1983) study subjects were required to respond quickly to visual probes while performing a visual discrimination task for 40 min. The primary task event rate was varied over four levels: 5, 15, 25, and 35 events/min. Probe RT was significantly longer for all probes for the fastest event rate than for the other event rates. The motivation behind this study was an experiment reported in Posner (1978) in which auditory probes were responded to *faster* when the event rate in a letter identification was high than when it was low. Bowers (1983) attributed the difference between the two studies to the fact that Posner (1978) used clearly presented and highly learned stimuli–namely, letters–whereas Bowers (1983) used targets that were changes in the length of a line presented briefly on a display. Encoding and identification of letters may pose minimal demands on central capacity. Thus, the overall primary-probe task demand would not exceed operator capacity, and the probes might not have been sensitive to variations in primary task performance.

Method

A modified probe technique was used in the present study. In Bowers' (1983) study, probes were presented continuously for 40 min. In the present experiment, however, probes were presented for 3 min periods only at two different times during the performance of a 30 min primary vigilance task—either early (2 min) or late (22 min). This was to eliminate the possible confounding effects of habituation or automatic processing. The probes were intended to provide "momentary" (i.e., short-term) estimates of available capacity at different points in time during the performance of a vigilance task. A digit-discrimination task similar to that used by Nuechterlein et al. (1983) was used. Subjects had to detect a single target digit among a repetitive series of visually degraded digits by depressing a response key with their right hands. The event rate was either low (15/min) or high (30/min). Targets appeared irregularly with a probability of .1 in each event-rate condition. The probe task consisted of the presentation of 15 1000 Hz tones over a 3 min period. The probes were presented at random intervals with the restriction that a probe could not occur within less than 1 sec of a nontarget and 5 sec of a target in the primary task. Subjects were required to respond to the probes as quickly as possible by depressing a second response key with their left hands. A group of 10 subjects attended for three sessions. In the first session they performed 10 min versions of the slow and fast event-rate vigilance tasks alone and the auditory probe task alone. In the second and third sessions they performed the combined primary and probe tasks at the slow and fast event rates, in counterbalanced order.

Results and Discussion

Fig. 27.3 shows the main results of the study. The sensitivity index d' was computed for each event-rate condition and for three successive 10 min blocks of trials of the 30 min task. As Fig. 27.3A shows, d' declined with time on task for

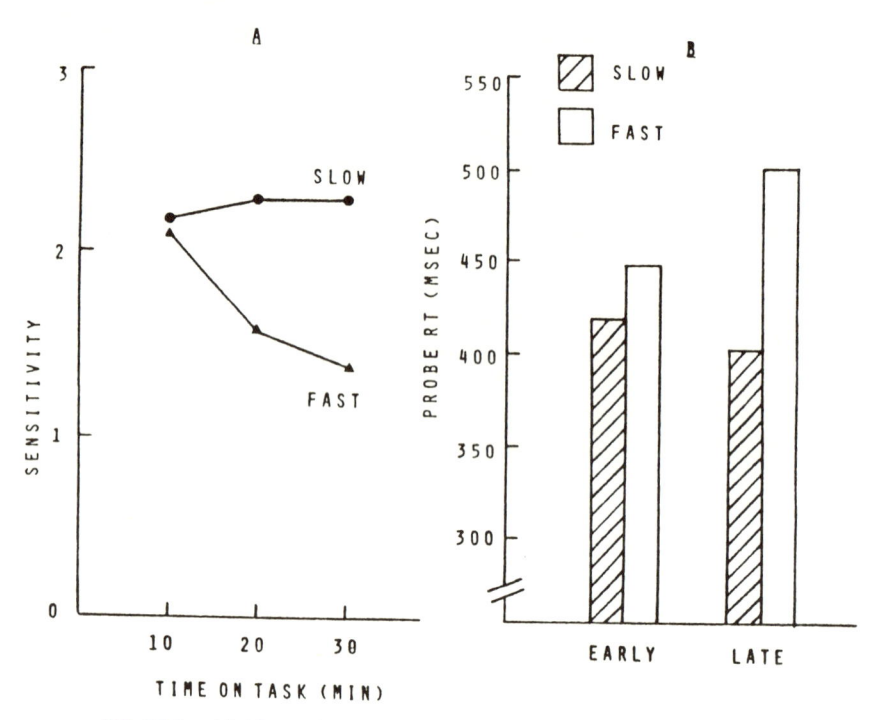

FIG. 27.3. (A) Mean values of sensitivity (d') in consecutive 10 min blocks of a 30 min visual discrimination task at slow and fast event rates. (B) Mean values of reaction time (msec) to auditory probes presented early or late during the primary task, for slow and fast primary-task event rates. Data from Experiment 3.

the high event rate but not for the low event rate. This finding confirms previous findings with this task (Nuechterlein et al., 1983) and other vigilance tasks showing sensitivity decrement at high event rates (Loeb & Binford, 1968; Parasuraman, 1979).

Fig. 27.3B shows the results for the probe task. The mean RT to early (2 min) and late (22 min) probes did not differ for the slow event-rate condition. For the fast event rate, however, RT was significantly longer for late probes than for early probes.

The results are consistent with the study by Bowers (1983), which found that probe RT increased when the primary task event rate was increased from 5/min to 35/min. The present study found a similar result when the event rate was increased from 15/min to 30/min. Both sets of results are consistent with the view that when the event rate is sufficiently high, the demands of the primary task tax central capacity and divert resources away from probe detection. The present study demonstrates that the adverse effects of event rate on probe RT are obtained only late into the vigilance task period, when perceptual sensitivity is lower. These results support a capacity-limitations view of sensitivity decrement in vigilance.

A MULTIFACTOR MODEL OF SUSTAINED ATTENTION

Arousal and the Level of Vigilance

The results of Experiments 1 and 2 clarify the role of the habituation and arousal constructs in vigilance. Although EEG signs of habituation and arousal often seem to parallel changes in vigilance performance, neither neural habituation nor reduced tonic arousal can account for the vigilance decrement. A direct ERP test of J. F. Mackworth's neural habituation–dishabituation theory in Experiment 1 failed to support the theory. Lowered arousal is clearly an outcome of performing a vigilance task, especially if it is prolonged. However, as the results of Experiment 2 indicate, arousal primarily affects the overall level of vigilance rather than the vigilance decrement. The one exception to this conclusion may be when a vigilance task is performed under extremely low arousal conditions—for example, following sleep deprivation or physical fatigue.

Parasuraman (1983, 1984a) recently reviewed the physiological evidence bearing on the arousal theory. In general, many indices of autonomic nervous activation show changes during vigilance performance indicative of a reduction in arousal over time. However, the conclusion that the performance decrement results from such a drop in arousal cannot be drawn with conviction. The difficulty is that physiological arousal declines in many situations of prolonged testing, not just vigilance tasks, and often the changes in arousal are unrelated to behavioral outcomes. Part of the difficulty may be linked to the view, implicit in many of these studies, of arousal as a unitary construct. The development of multistate arousal constructs (Gale, 1977; Hockey, 1984), though still in its infancy, may resolve some of these difficulties.

Expectancy and Vigilance Decrement

The factors controlling the vigilance decrement differ according to the type of vigilance task. In low event-rate tasks, the vigilance decrement is associated with an increase in the response criterion over time. As a number of investigators have pointed out, criterion shifts over time can be linked to expectancy (Colquhoun & Baddeley, 1964; Davies & Parasuraman, 1982, Chapter 4; Williges, 1969). Deese (1955) first pointed out that the course of events experienced by the observer establishes a level of expectancy for targets that in turn influences subsequent detection performance. Deese proposed that as long as the average probability of target occurrence remains low, expectancy for a target remains low, but that as target probability increases, so does expectancy. For an a priori target probability of p, the ideal observer has a response criterion of $(1 - p)/p$ and most human observers will set criteria close to but less than this value. Thus, the observer's response rate will be lower than the target probability. According to the expectancy theory, subjects monitor their responses to formulate their expectancy for future targets. Thus, observers will underestimate the target probability. This results in an upward revision of the response criterion appropriate to the (lower) estimate of target probability. An increase in the criterion results in a lower hit and false-alarm rate, leading to further upward revision of the criterion, and so on, in a "vicious circle" (Baker, 1959; Broadbent, 1971). Although there are alternative explanations of criterion shifts in vigilance (e.g., Vickers & Leary, 1983), all assume that criterion shifts reflect adaptations in the observer's expectancy for critical targets.

Capacity Limitations and Vigilance Decrement

Whereas changes in target expectancy can account for performance changes in low event-rate tasks, a different factor influences the vigilance decrement in high event-rate tasks. In high event-rate tasks in which target discrimination imposes a memory load (Parasuraman, 1979) or a stimulus-encoding load (Nuechterlein et al., 1983), the vigilance decrement results from a sensitivity decrement. As the results of Experiment 3 indicate, the evidence suggests that the sensitivity decrement reflects a loss in attentional capacity over time.

These findings suggest a three-factor model of sustained attention. The level of vigilance is proportional to the level of tonic arousal. However, neither arousal nor neural habituation influence the vigilance decrement. The vigilance decrement results either from adaptations in target expectancy or from capacity limitations, depending on the nature of the task.

The mechanisms underlying the capacity limitations in high event-rate tasks are not fully understood, although some suggestions can be put forward. Fisk and Schneider (1981) have also proposed that the sensitivity decrement results from a decline in the allocation of processing resources to detection over time, but they suggest that only *control* processes draw upon attentional resources. So-called *automatic* processes do not require access to working memory and can be sustained for prolonged periods of time without deficit (see also Schneider & Shiffrin, 1977). Fisk and Schneider compared the effects of time on task on a letter-discrimination task in which targets and nontargets were either drawn from separate sets or variably from the same set. A decrement in sensitivity (A') over a 50 min period occurred only for the "variably mapped" targets, a condition in which automatic processing could not be developed. Vigilance tasks producing sensitivity decrement usually have targets requiring access to working memory, and there is evidence that the sensitivity decrement does not disappear with repeated testing (Binford & Loeb, 1966; Nuechterlein et al., 1983). Hence, the evidence supports the contention that only tasks requiring controlled or effortful processing show sensitivity decrement. Nevertheless, it is not clear that *all* cases of sensitivity decrement can be attributed to control processing and *all* cases of stable vigilance performance to automatic processing.

The view that sensitivity may fall in vigilance tasks because the level of processing resources needed to detect targets cannot be consistently allocated for a prolonged period would carry greater weight if resource demand was evaluated independently. The results of a probe-task measurement of available capacity in Experiment 3 indicate that auditory probes are responded to more slowly when presented late rather than early in a high event-rate task, but time on task does not affect probe RT at low event rates. Results from secondary-task measures are open to criticism on the grounds that primary and secondary tasks may not tap the same pool of resources (McLeod, 1978; Wickens, 1984), or that secondary-task performance might become automatic and thus not depend on allocation of resources (Fisk, Derrick, & Schneider, 1983). The latter criticism at least is not applicable in the present study, because subjects had to respond to only 15 probe trials, at two widely separated periods of time. A further criticism has been that inference of resource demand from measures of task performance can be an exercise in circularity (e.g., see Navon, 1984). Physiological measures, however, may provide independent evaluation of processing resource demand. Isreal, Wickens, Chesney, and Donchin (1980) showed that the amplitude of the P300 component of the ERP elicited by probe stimuli reflected the processing demands of a primary display-monitoring task. However, this technique has not been applied to vigilance. One would predict that P300 to probes presented toward the end of a high event-rate task would be lower in amplitude than P300 for early probes, whereas probe-P300 amplitude would not vary as a function of time on task for a slow event rate. Beatty (1982b) has shown that the amplitude of the evoked pupillary response provides a sensitive index of the aggregate demand for processing resources in a wide range of perceptual and cognitive tasks. Thus, one would expect the evoked pupillary amplitude to be lower at the end of a vigilance task than at the beginning. Beatty (1982a) recorded this result for a 40 min, high event-rate, successive-discrimination task. The sensitivity decrement over time on this task was correlated with a decrease in amplitude of the evoked pupillary response. Beatty (1982a) argued that this was not a result of reduction in arousal over time because the absolute or *tonic* pupillary size, which is a sensitive indicator of tonic arousal (Yoss, Moyer, & Hollenhorst, 1970), did not vary with time on task.

The sensitivity decrement found in high event-rate tasks may reflect a "cost of time sharing" similar to that observed in the performance of dual tasks. Taylor, Lindsay, and Forbes (1967) compared sensitivity (d') in tasks performed singly and in combination and showed that attentional capacity in dual discrimination tasks consumed about 85% of the capacity available when each task was performed alone. They suggested, therefore, that the time-sharing "central processor" consumes about 15% of total capacity. It is interesting to note that the sensitivity decrement found in high event-rate tasks is generally small, of the order of 10% to 15% in d'. Although only one source is monitored in vigilance tasks, this suggests that a cost of time sharing the primary vigilance with other processing activities may develop with time on task. This recalls Jerison's (1970) "observing-response" model of vigilance, although the "cost" can be described generally in terms of time sharing a single task (visual or auditory) with other irrelevant "tasks" (distracting thoughts, environmental noises, etc), rather than in terms of having to observe a visual display. Consistent with this view, McGrath (1963) found that environmental distractors (traffic and machine noise) improved performance on a visual vigilance task at an event rate of 20/min but exacerbated the vigilance decrement at an event rate of 60/min.

These results suggest a much closer link between selective attention and sustained attention, at least for high event-rate tasks, than previously supposed. Broadbent (1971) distinguished between results on divided attention and vigilance by his findings that deficits in divided attention were associated with d' changes (Broadbent & Gregory, 1963a) whereas vigilance decrement was associated with β changes (Broadbent & Gregory, 1963b). This led him to revise his original filter theory as applied to vigilance and to suggest a role for expectancy in vigilance decrement. But, as we have seen, both d' and β changes occur in vigilance tasks, the former being restricted to high event-rate tasks. Thus, the distinction drawn by Broadbent (1971) now has less force. At the same time, as Posner, Cohen, Choate, Hockey, and Maylor (1984) have noted, it is interesting that the d' changes in vigilance tasks occur under the same conditions that lead to improved selectivity in divided attention tasks. Both behavioral (Harvey & Treisman, 1973) and ERP (Hansen & Hillyard, 1984; Parasuraman, 1980) studies suggest that a high event rate is conducive to high selectivity. Although beneficial in the short term, over prolonged periods high event rates are associated with a cost of time sharing that is seen as a drop in perceptual sensitivity.

ACKNOWLEDGMENTS

I thank Paul Nestor, Joel Warm, and an anonymous referee for their comments on a previous draft of this chapter.

REFERENCES

Bakan, P. (1955). Discrimination decrement as a function of time in a prolonged vigil. *Journal of Experimental Psychology, 50,* 387–390.
Baker, C. H. (1959). Towards a theory of vigilance. *Canadian Journal of Psychology 13,* 35–42.
Beatty, J. (1982a). Phasic not tonic pupillary responses vary with auditory vigilance performance. *Psychophysiology, 19,* 167–172.

Beatty, J. (1982b). Task evoked pupillary responses, processing load, and the structure of processing resources. *Psychological Bulletin, 91*, 276–292.

Berger, C., & Mahneke, A. (1954). Fatigue in two simple visual tasks. *American Journal of Psychology, 67*, 509–512.

Binford, J. R., & Loeb, M. (1966). Changes within and over repeated sessions in criterion and effective sensitivity in an auditory vigilance task. *Journal of Experimental Psychology, 72*, 339–345.

Bowers, J. C. (1983). *Stimulus homogeneity and the event rate function in sustained attention.* Unpublished Ph.D. dissertation, University of Cincinnati.

Broadbent, D. E. (1958). *Perception and communication.* London: Pergamon.

Broadbent, D. E. (1971). *Decision and stress.* New York: Academic.

Broadbent, D. E., & Gregory, M. (1963a). Division of attention and the decision theory of signal detection. *Proceedings of the Royal Society, 158B*, 221–231.

Broadbent, D. E., & Gregory, M. (1963b). Vigilance considered as a statistical decision. *British Journal of Psychology, 54*, 309–323.

Buck, L. (1966). Reaction time as a measure of perceptual vigilance. *Psychological Bulletin, 65*, 291–308.

Callaway, E. C. (1973). Habituation of averaged evoked potentials in man. In H. V. S. Peeke & M. J. Herz (Eds.), *Habituation* (Vol. 2, pp. 153–174). New York: Academic.

Cherry, E. C. (1953). Some experiments on the recognition of speech with one and with two ears. *Journal of the Acoustical Society of America, 25*, 975–979.

Colquhoun, W. P. (1971). *Biological rhythms and human performance.* London: Academic.

Colquhoun, W. P., & Baddeley, A. D. (1964). Role of pretest expectancy in vigilance decrement. *Journal of Experimental Psychology, 73*, 153–155.

Corcoran, D. W. J. (1965). Personality and the inverted-U relation. *British Journal of Psychology, 56*, 267–273.

Craig, A. (1978). Is the vigilance decrement simply a response adjustment towards probability matching? *Human Factors, 20*, 441–446.

Davies, D. R., & Parasuraman, R. (1982). *The psychology of vigilance.* London: Academic.

Davies, D. R., Parasuraman, R., & Toh, K. Y. (1984). Time of day, memory load, and vigilance performance. In A. Mital (Ed.), *Trends in ergonomics/human factors* (pp. 9–14). Amsterdam: North-Holland.

Davies, D. R., & Tune, G. S. (1970). *Human vigilance performance.* London: Staples.

Deese, J. (1955). Some problems in the theory of vigilance. *Psychological Review, 62*, 359–368.

Fisk, A. D., Derrick, W., & Schneider, W. (1983). The assessment of workload: Dual-task methodology. *Proceedings of the Human Factors Society, 27*, 229–233.

Fisk, A. D., & Schneider, W. (1981). Control and automatic processing during tasks requiring sustained attention: A new approach to vigilance. *Human Factors, 23*, 737–750.

Folkard, S. (1979). Time of day and level of processing. *Memory and Cognition, 7*, 247–252.

Gale, A. (1977). Some EEG correlates of sustained attention. In R. R. Mackie (Ed.), *Vigilance: Theory, operational performance, and physiological correlates* (pp. 263–283). New York: Theory, Plenum.

Hansen, J. C., & Hillyard, S. A. (1984). Effects of stimulation rate and attribute cuing on event-related potentials during selective auditory attention. *Psychophysiology, 21*, 394–405.

Harvey, N., & Treisman, A. M. (1973). Switching attention between the ears to monitor tones. *Perception and Psychophysics, 14*, 51–59.

Hockey, G. R. J. (1984). Varieties of attentional state: The effects of environment. In R. Parasuraman & D. R. Davies (Eds.), *Varieties of attention* (pp. 449–483). Orlando, FL: Academic.

Isreal, J. B., Wickens, C. D., Chesney, G., & Donchin, E. (1980). The event-related brain potential as an index of display-monitoring workload. *Human Factors, 22*, 211–224.

Jerison, H. J. (1970). Vigilance: A paradigm and some physiological speculations. *Acta Psychologica, 33*, 367–380.

Jerison, H. J., & Pickett, R. M. (1964). Vigilance: The importance of the elicited observing rate. *Science, 143,* 970–971.

Kahneman, D. (1973). *Attention and effort.* Englewood Cliffs, NJ: Prentice-Hall.

Krulewitz, J. E., Warm, J. S., & Wohl, T. H. (1975). Effects of shifts in the rate of repetitive stimulation on sustained attention. *Perception and Psychophysics, 18,* 245–249.

Lanzetta, T. M. (1984). *Effects of stimulus heterogeneity and information processing load on the event rate function in sustained attention.* Unpublished doctoral dissertation, University of Cincinnati.

Levine, J. M., Romashko, T., & Fleishman, E. A. (1973). Evaluation of an abilities classification system for integrating and generalizing human performance research: An application to vigilance tasks. *Journal of Applied Psychology, 58,* 149–157.

Loeb, M., & Alluisi, E. (1984). Theories of vigilance. In J. S. Warm (Ed.), *Sustained attention in human performance* (pp. 179–205). London: Wiley.

Loeb, M., & Binford, J. R. (1968). Variations in performance on auditory and visual monitoring tasks as a function of signal and stimulus frequencies. *Perception and Psychophysics, 4,* 361–366.

Mackworth, J. F. (1969). *Vigilance and habituation.* Baltimore: Penguin.

Mackworth, N. H. (1950). Researches on the measurement of human performance. *Medical Research Council Special Report* (No. 268). London: H.M.S.O.

McGrath, J. J. (1963). Irrelevant stimulation and vigilance performance. In D. N. Buckner & J. J. McGrath (Eds.), *Vigilance: A symposium* (pp. 3–19). New York: McGraw-Hill.

McLeod, P. (1978). Does probe RT measure central processing demand? *Quarterly Journal of Experimental Psychology, 30,* 83–89.

Moray, N. (1967). Where is capacity limited? A survey and a model. *Acta Psychologica, 27,* 84–92.

Moray, N. (1975). A data base for theories of selective listening. In P. M. A. Rabbitt & S. Dornic (Eds.), *Attention and performance V* (pp. 1–16). New York: Academic.

Navon, D. (1984). Resources: A theoretical soup stone? *Psychological Review, 91,* 216–234.

Nuechterlein, K., Parasuraman, R., & Jiang, Q. (1983). Visual sustained attention: Image degradation produces rapid sensitivity decrement over time. *Science, 220,* 327–329.

Parasuraman, R. (1976). *Task classification and decision processes in monitoring behavior.* Unpublished Ph.D. dissertation, University of Aston, Birmingham.

Parasuraman, R. (1979). Memory load and event rate control sensitivity decrements in sustained attention. *Science, 205,* 924–927.

Parasuraman, R. (1980). Effects of information processing demands on slow negative shift latencies and N100 amplitude in selective and divided attention. *Biological Psychology, 11,* 217–233.

Parasuraman, R. (1983). Vigilance, arousal and the brain. In A. Gale & J. Edwards (Eds.), *Physiological correlates of human behaviour: Attention and performance* (pp. 35–55). London: Academic.

Parasuraman, R. (1984a). The psychobiology of sustained attention. In J. S. Warm (Ed.), *Sustained attention in human performance* (pp. 61–101). London: Wiley.

Parasuraman, R. (1984b). Sustained attention in detection and discrimination. In R. Parasuraman & D. R. Davies (Eds.), *Varieties of attention* (pp. 243–271). Orlando, Fla.: Academic.

Parasuraman, R., & Davies, D. R. (1976). Decision theory analysis of response latencies in vigilance. *Journal of Experimental Psychology: Human Perception and Performance, 2,* 569–582.

Parasuraman, R., & Davies, D. R. (1977). A taxonomic analysis of vigilance performance. In R. R. Mackie (Ed.), *Vigilance: Theory, operational performance, and physiological correlates* (pp. 559–574). New York: Theory, Plenum.

Posner, M. I. (1975). Psychobiology of attention. In M. S. Gazzaniga & C. Blakemore (Eds.), *Handbook of psychobiology* (pp. 441–480). New York: Academic.

Posner, M. I. (1978). *Chronometric explorations of mind.* Hillsdale, NJ: Lawrence Erlbaum Associates.

Posner, M. I., Cohen, Y., Choate, L., Hockey, G. R. J., & Maylor, E. (1984). Sustained concentration: Passive filtering or active orienting? In S. Kornblum & J. Requin (Eds.), *Preparatory states and processes* (pp. 49–65). Hillsdale, NJ: Lawrence Erlbaum Associates.

Schneider, W., & Shiffrin, R. M. (1977). Controlled and automatic human information processing: I. Detection, search, and attention. *Psychological Review, 84,* 1–66.

Sharpless, S., & Jasper, H. H. (1956). Habituation of the arousal reaction. *Brain, 79,* 655–680.

Simpson, A. J., & Fitter, M. J. (1973). What is the best measure of detectability? *Psychological Bulletin, 80,* 481–488.

Smith, A. P. (1984). *The effects of noise on sustained detection of specific targets and general categorization of events.* Unpublished manuscript.

Taylor, M. M., Lindsay, P. M., & Forbes, S. M. (1967). Quantification of shared capacity processing. *Acta Psychologica, 27,* 223–229.

Thompson, R. F., & Spencer, W. A. (1966). Habituation: A model phenomenon for the study of the neuronal substrates of behavior. *Psychological Bulletin, 73,* 16–43.

Vickers, D., & Leary, J. N. (1983). Criterion control in signal detection. *Human Factors, 25,* 283–296.

Warm, J. S. (1977). Psychological processes in sustained attention. In R. R. Mackie (Ed.), *Vigilance: Theory, operational performance, and physiological correlates* (pp. 623–644). New York: Theory, Plenum.

Warm, J. S., Dember, W. N., & Lanzetta, T. M. (1984). Cognitive demand and vigilance performance. *Proceedings of the Midcentral Ergonomics/Human Factors Conference, 1,* 179–184.

Warm, J. S., & Jerison, H. J. (1984). The psychophysics of vigilance. In J. S. Warm (Ed.), *Sustained attention in human performance* (pp. 15–59). London: Wiley.

Welford, A. T. (1978). Mental work-load as a function of demand, capacity, strategy and skill. *Ergonomics, 21,* 151–168.

Wickens, C. D. (1984). Processing resources in attention. In R. Parasuraman & D. R. Davies (Eds.), *Varieties of attention* (pp. 63–102). Orlando, FL: Academic.

Williges, R. C. (1969). Within session criterion changes compared to an ideal observer criterion in a visual monitoring task. *Journal of Experimental Psychology, 81,* 61–66.

Yoss, R. E., Moyer, N. J., & Hollenhorst, R. W. (1970). Pupil size and spontaneous pupillary waves associated with alertness. *Neurology, 201,* 545–554.

28 Discrete and Continuous Models of Divided Attention

Jeff Miller
University of California, San Diego

ABSTRACT

Two-alternative forced-choice reaction-time experiments were conducted to determine whether preliminary information about a stimulus can begin to activate responses before recognition of the stimulus has completely finished, as assumed by continuous and denied by discrete models of human information processing. Targets were presented either visually or auditorally, with distractors on the other modality. When the auditory stimulus was a target, a visual stimulus similar to a target served as the distractor. If preliminary information about the visual distractor does activate responses before recognition is complete, it should cause a bias toward the response appropriate for the target to which the distractor is similar. This bias should facilitate responses when the distractor is similar to the visual target consistent with the auditory target (i.e., assigned to the same response) and inhibit responses when the distractor is similar to the inconsistent visual target (cf. Eriksen & Hoffman, 1973). The results suggest that recognition must finish before information about a stimulus begins to influence decisions in a two-choice task, contrary to continuous models. Biasing was not obtained with distractors that were similar to targets either physically or physically and categorically. It was only obtained with distractors that had the same names as targets, but this biasing was consistent with discrete as well as continuous models. Nor was there biasing when distractors shared one defining characteristic with each target, even though one characteristic was perceptually much more discriminable than the other.

INTRODUCTION

Discrete and Continuous Information Processing

A common assumption in the study of human information processing is that processing of most stimuli involves a set of distinct mental processes, sequential and contingent in the sense that the output of one process serves as the input to the next (e.g., Broadbent, 1958). In choice reaction-time (RT) tasks, for example, it is common to distinguish among at least three processes: recognition, which identifies the stimulus; decision, which selects ("activates") the appropriate response; and response execution, which carries out the motor commands necessary for making that response (e.g., Sanders, 1977). A critical theoretical dispute concerns the nature of the overall sequence in which such processes are embedded. Two major classes of models have been suggested, referred to here as continuous and discrete.

Continuous models allow different mental processes in a sequence to operate simultaneously (Eriksen & Schultz, 1979; McClelland, 1979; Norman & Bobrow, 1975; Taylor, 1976; Turvey, 1973). Such models assume that the output of a given process is produced gradually and that a later process can begin its operations based on *preliminary partial output* from the process in question. Thus, as shown in Fig. 28.1a, preliminary information about a stimulus can be used to start decision making before recognition of the stimulus has finished.

Discrete models require an earlier process to finish before a later process can begin, so different processes operate in strict temporal sequence with no overlap (e.g., Sanders, 1977, 1980; Sternberg, 1969a, 1969b). Thus, as shown in Fig.

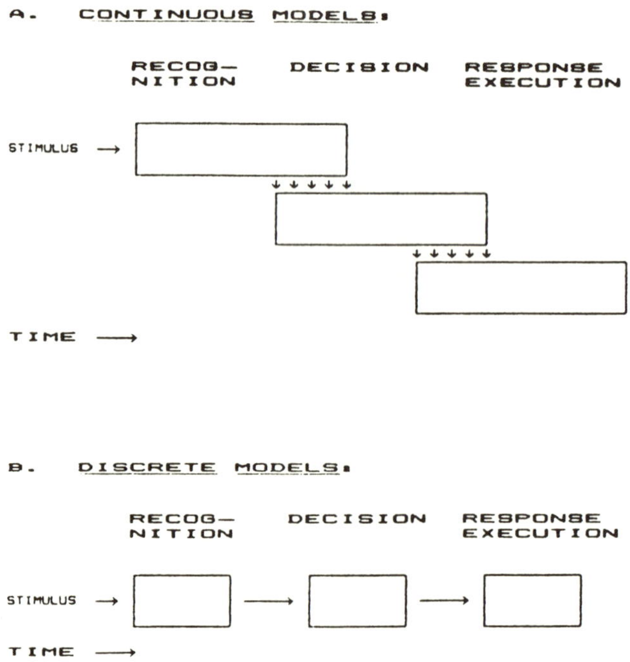

FIG. 28.1. Schematic drawings of continuous and discrete models with three information-processing stages.

28.1b, discrete models require recognition of a stimulus to finish before decision making can begin. Normally, discrete models assume that preliminary partial output about a stimulus is held in a buffer until recognition is finished, at which time a complete identification is transmitted to the next process, though other mechanisms could be used to prevent temporal overlap of recognition and decision processes.

Miller (1982a, 1983) suggested a model intermediate between the continuous and discrete extremes, called the Asynchronous Discrete Coding (ADC) model. The ADC model is based on the idea that stimuli are not always represented as unitary entities, and it assumes that processing is discrete with respect to stimulus codes rather than entire stimuli. For example, suppose that subjects must respond to stimulus letters varying in size as well as name. If these two attributes are represented with two separable internal codes (Garner, 1974), then the ADC model would allow decision making to begin as soon as either attribute had been fully recognized. The model is intermediate between the discrete and continuous extremes, because the decision process cannot use preliminary output that partially specifies size or letter name, as would be allowed by continuous models, but can use preliminary output that partially specifies the stimulus (i.e., identifies one attribute), contrary to discrete models. Of course, the ADC model is only useful if the codes used in representing various sets of stimuli can be identified with sorting tasks, multidimensional scaling of similarity ratings, or other independent behavioral procedures (e.g., Garner, 1974; Posner, 1978).

The distinction between continuous and discrete models has important implications for RT methodology. The relation between process durations and total RT depends critically on whether the processes overlap in time, so the nature of the sequence dictates the appropriate methods for collecting and drawing inferences from RT data (McClelland, 1979; Sternberg, 1969a, 1969b; Taylor, 1976). Unfortunately, the type of sequence may not be invariant, but instead may depend on stimulus set, task, or subject strategy. If so, it will be necessary to investigate individually each situation in which RT is to be used. Though no single type of experiment can discriminate among the models absolutely, it is useful to evaluate the models in a variety of paradigms to discover the range of applicability of each model.

EXPERIMENT 1

This experiment compared continuous, discrete, and ADC models in a two-alternative forced-choice divided-attention task. Visual stimuli were single alphanumeric characters presented at fixation, with one target character assigned to each of two alternative response keys. Auditory stimuli were tones varying in pitch; one tone served as the target for each response. For example, some subjects were required to press a left key if the letter A or the high tone was presented, and a right key if the letter B or the low tone was presented. One of the four possible targets was presented on each trial, together with a distractor stimulus presented on the other modality. The auditory distractor was a medium-pitch tone, and the visual distractor was a nontarget character. Both a tone and a character were presented on every trial, at the same or nearly the same time, and responses were determined by the character on some trials and by the tone on others. Conflicting stimuli (e.g., high tone and letter B) were never presented.

Special visual distractors, each similar to a particular visual target, were used to discriminate among continuous, discrete, and ADC models. Because of the similarity, presenting the distractor would provide the recognition process with some partial evidence (e.g., visual features) suggesting that a particular target had been presented. The critical question is whether this partial evidence causes the decision process to begin (i.e., some response activation to occur) before stimulus recognition is finished, as assumed by continuous (and, for some kinds of stimuli, ADC) models. If so, then the decision process should partially activate the response appropriate for the target indicated by the partial output, producing a bias toward that response. Such bias can be measured through its effect on responses to auditory targets presented on the same trial, as described after discussion of the similarity conditions. Thus, it should be possible to discriminate among continuous, discrete, and ADC models by determining when a distractor biases the decision toward the response appropriate for the target to which it is similar. Three kinds of similarity were examined in this experiment.

1. *Physical-similarity condition.* For one group of subjects each visual distractor was a letter physically similar to a particular target letter (e.g., targets C and T, distractors G and I). Continuous models predict that one of these distractors (e.g., G) should bias the decision toward the response appropriate for the similar target letter (C). The features in the distractor G provide much more perceptual evidence for the target C than for the target T, so preliminary recognition output should indicate that the stimulus is more likely to be a C than a T. If this preliminary output influences decisions, the response appropriate for C should become activated relative to the one appropriate for T.

According to discrete and ADC models, on the other hand, these distractors should not activate responses. A single-letter stimulus is represented with a single abstract or phonemic code (e.g., Conrad, 1964), and these models do not allow the decision process to begin until this code has been fully determined. A fully recognized distractor is irrelevant to the decision, however, so it should not activate either response. In other words, if preliminary output favoring a target is held until distractor recognition is complete, the decision process receives no information that would bias it toward either response.

2. *Physical- and categorical-similarity condition.* For a second group the distractors were similar to targets, both physically and in alphanumeric category. The targets were one letter and one digit (e.g., U and 4), and the distractors were

another physically similar letter and another physically similar digit (V similar to U, 9 similar to 4). Because alphanumeric category is a very salient attribute of character stimuli (e.g., Jonides & Gleitman, 1972), it is assumed that these characters are coded in terms of both identity and category (e.g., "letter U", "digit 4").

With these stimuli, continuous models again predict that distractors will bias responses by virtue of their physical similarity to targets, as described earlier. If anything, the alphanumeric category difference would only increase the effect.

Discrete models again predict that these distractors will not influence responses. Response activation cannot begin until the stimulus has been recognized completely (both category and identity). Because targets are defined by their identities, category can be ignored by the decision process. Thus, no biasing would result from the information that the stimulus is "the letter V," even though the target U is also a letter.

The presence of a category code does allow ADC models to predict biasing with these stimuli, because preliminary category information in ADC models has the same effect as preliminary featural information in continuous models. Stimuli in different categories are physically dissimilar (UV versus 49), so the recognition process could determine the alphanumeric category of a stimulus before it determined stimulus identity. Furthermore, ADC models allow a fully recognized category code to be used by the decision process without waiting for identity. Given this code, the decision should be biased toward the response appropriate for the target of the recognized category, because the a posteriori probability of that response is greater given the category information.

3. *Name-similarity condition.* For a third group the targets were two letters of the same case (e.g., A and B), and the distractors were the opposite-case versions of the same two letters (a and b). This condition was not included to discriminate among models. Instead, it was designed to show that: (a) there are distractors capable of partially activating responses; and (b) the paradigm is sensitive enough to detect such response activation when it occurs. These points must be demonstrated to strengthen the interpretation of null results if no biasing is obtained in the other similarity conditions.

With these stimuli, all three models predict that a distractor will activate the response appropriate for the target of the same name. Names often activate responses with which they are associated, even when the names are clearly irrelevant to the required decision (Eriksen & Hoffman, 1973; Stroop, 1935), so it appears that the decision process cannot completely ignore distractors with target names. Even if the decision process receives the name information after the distractor has been completely identified (name and case) as assumed by discrete models, the decision could still be influenced because of the difficulty of ignoring names of distractors. Of course, if name information were used before case had been identified, as is allowed by continuous and ADC models, it would also have an effect on the decision.

Measurement of Response Activation

If partial response activation is produced by distractors similar to targets, it can be measured through its biasing effect on responses to auditory targets presented on the same trials. An auditory target can require either the same response that would be favored by the partial activation ("consistent trials") or the opposite response ("inconsistent trials"). For example, if C were a target and the distractor G was presented, the trial would be consistent if the tone required the same response as the C, and inconsistent if it required the opposite response. The difference in RT for these two conditions (inconsistent minus consistent) measures the partial response activation produced by the visual distractor, because this activation should facilitate responses on consistent trials and inhibit them on inconsistent trials. Thus, the partial activation produced by a visual distractor can be measured indirectly, much as one might measure wind speed in terms of its effect on travel time for an airplane with constant engine thrust.

A critical assumption of this paradigm is that the response activation produced by the visual distractor will combine with activation produced by the auditory target. If response activations produced by stimuli on different channels are not combined, consistent distractors will not facilitate responses, nor will inconsistent distractors inhibit them. Two main findings support models in which activations are combined across stimulus channels ("coactivation" models; cf. Miller, 1982b). First, there are often large effects of irrelevant information in focused attention tasks (e.g., Eriksen & Schultz, 1979; Logan, 1980). These effects show that response activation from an irrelevant stimulus (or attribute) can influence the response to the relevant one, exactly as expected in the present divided-attention paradigm. Second, responses in divided-attention tasks are especially fast when targets are presented simultaneously on two channels (e.g., Raab, 1962). Detailed analyses of RT distributions suggest that this effect is due to the combination of activation produced by targets on different channels (Miller, 1982b).

An important manipulation in this paradigm is the stimulus onset asynchrony (SOA) between the visual and auditory stimuli (cf., Eriksen & Schultz, 1979). Activations produced by the visual distractor and auditory target must be present at the same time if they are to be combined. Because partial activation resulting from the distractor could be transient, relative timing of the target and distractor presentations is critical. In these studies, a wide range of SOAs was used to try to span the range in which target and distractor coactivation could occur.

Method

Apparatus and Stimuli. Stimuli were presented on an Apple II+ computer that randomized presentation order and recorded responses and RT. The character font was that used by Miller (1982a). Characters were approximately 14 mm high and 5 to 9 mm wide, and they were viewed from a distance of about 60 cm. Auditory stimuli were tones of 56 msec duration and frequencies of about 410, 520, and 680 Hz; subjects practiced discriminating them before testing began. Responses were made by pressing keys on the computer keyboard with the index fingers. For each similarity condition, the assignments of target letters and tones to responses were counterbalanced across subjects.

Subjects and Procedure. Subjects were 96 undergraduate students at the University of California, San Diego, divided equally among similarity conditions. They were tested individually in single 45 min sessions made up of three blocks of 160 trials, excluding warm-up. Each of the four target stimuli was presented eight times at each of five SOAs: $-.3$, $-.2$, $-.1$, $.1$, and $.2$ sec, measured from the onset of the visual stimulus to the onset of the tone. When visual targets were presented, the accompanying tone was always the medium-pitch distractor. When tone targets were presented, the accompanying visual distractor was consistent on half of the trials and inconsistent on the other half.

Each trial began with a 500 msec presentation of a fixation point. One sec after its offset, the first stimulus—either visual or auditory depending on the SOA—was presented. After the appropriate SOA, the second stimulus was presented (unless the subject had already responded). Accuracy feedback was given immediately after the response, and the next trial began approximately 1 sec later. Subjects were instructed to respond as quickly as possible without making too many errors. Any trial on which the subject made an error or responded in less than 150 msec or more than 2 sec was rerun later in the block.

Physical-Similarity Condition. Seven pairs of visually similar letters were used: CG, IT, MN, KR, UV, EF, and OQ. For each subject two pairs were randomly selected for use as stimuli. One letter from each pair was used as a target; the other, as a distractor.

Physical- and Categorical-Similarity Condition. The pairs of visually similar stimuli were UV, 49, EF, and 17. For each subject one pair of letters and one pair of digits were selected as stimuli. One character from each pair was used as a target; the other, as a distractor.

Name-Similarity Condition. Stimuli were the characters A, a, B, b, D, d, E, e, G, g, N, n, R, and r, chosen to minimize physical similarity of upper- and lower-case versions. To prevent subjects from rejecting visual distractors on the basis of a simple size judgment, lower-case letters were nearly the same size as upper-case letters (10 to 14 mm in height). For each subject two letters of the same case were randomly selected as targets, and the opposite cases of these letters were distractors.

TABLE 28.1
Experiment 1: RT as a Function of Similarity Condition,
Target–Distractor Combination, and SOA

Target–Distractor Combination	SOA^a in Sec:				
	−.3	−.2	−.1	.1	.2
Physical Similarity:					
Tone target, consistent distractor	942	879	858	681	630
Tone target, inconsistent distractor	935	883	865	692	621
Visual target, neutral distractor	627	643	672	755	790
Physical and Categorical Similarity:					
Tone target, consistent distractor	919	884	851	684	610
Tone target, inconsistent distractor	895	900	843	684	632
Visual target, neutral distractor	602	623	638	730	750
Name Similarity:					
Tone target, consistent distractor	1025	957	935	766	708
Tone target, inconsistent distractor	1059	1019	975	802	754
Visual target, neutral distractor	718	731	760	849	888

[a]Measured from onset of visual to onset of auditory stimulus.

Results and Discussion

Table 28.1 shows average RT as a function of similarity condition, SOA, and target–distractor combination (auditory target with consistent distractor, auditory target with inconsistent distractor, or visual target). In the name-similarity condition, responses to auditory targets were an average of 44 msec faster with consistent than inconsistent visual distractors, so these distractors did bias responses. In the other two similarity conditions, however, there was virtually no difference in responses for consistent and inconsistent distractors (average differences of 1 msec), and therefore no evidence of response activation.

There was also a large effect of SOA for both auditory and visual targets. Both effects indicate faster responses to targets appearing later relative to distractors, probably due to an attentional shift during the trial. Targets presented before distractors must be processed with divided attention, because the target modality is uncertain. If a distractor comes on first, however, it can be processed and then attention can be concentrated on the other channel. Thus, targets appearing after distractors can be processed with nearly full attention, leading to faster responses.

Analyses of variance (ANOVAs) confirmed the reliability of the effects just described. An overall analysis was computed using subject average RTs to compare conditions with consistent and inconsistent visual distractors, with additional factors of similarity condition and SOA. There were highly reliable main effects of distractor consistency (consistent versus inconsistent)—$F(1,93) = 13$, $MSe = 4,217, p < .01$—and SOA—$F(4,372) = 548, MSe = 6,194, p < .01$—

with a marginally reliable main effect of similarity condition—$F(2,93) = 2.56$, $MSe = 465,757$, $p < .10$. The only significant interaction was that of similarity condition and distractor consistency $F(2,93) = 11$, $MSe = 4,217$, $p < .01$. To examine this interaction further, separate ANOVAs were computed for each similarity condition. In the name-similarity condition, responses were reliably faster with consistent than inconsistent distractors—$F(1,28) = 44$, $MSe = 3,433$, $p < .01$, but this effect was not significant in either the physical- or physical- and category-similarity condition (both $Fs < 1$). Percentages of correct response (PCs) were also computed for each subject and condition, and an ANOVA indicated that responses were more accurate on consistent (97.9%) than inconsistent trials (96.7%)—$F(1,93) = 19$, $MSe = 19.7$, $p < .01$.

In summary, responses were biased when distractors shared the names of targets but not when they shared visual or visual and categorical features. These results suggest that response activation does not begin until the visual stimulus has been fully identified, as claimed by discrete models. Distractors having the same names as targets would activate responses even if response selection did not begin until distractor recognition was finished, as assumed by discrete models, because target names are too salient to ignore completely. If response selection began before distractor recognition was complete, as assumed by continuous and ADC models, distractors physically and/or categorically similar to targets should also have activated responses. With such similarity, preliminary recognition output would favor the presence of a particular target, so, if this output were used by the decision process, the response associated with that target should have been activated. Because biasing did not occur in these conditions, it appears that preliminary stimulus information was not used by the decision process. It must be concluded that, as general models, continuous and ADC models seriously overstate the ability of preliminary perceptual information to influence responses.

The error rates introduce a small complication. Responses were slightly more accurate with consistent distractors than with inconsistent ones, and this effect did not differ significantly across similarity conditions, though it was largest in the name-similarity condition (1.8% versus 1%). It is tempting to interpret the distractor consistency effect in the physical- and physical- and category-similarity conditions as evidence favoring continuous and ADC models. However, if partial output were large enough to produce errors, how could it be too small to influence RT? One would have to assume that partial output varied across trials and was either very large, producing an error, or very small, having no influence on RT. Such all-or-none partial output violates the basic spirit of the continuous and ADC models. The accuracy effect is quite easy to reconcile with discrete models, on the other hand. Discrete models need only assume that the perceptual process mistakenly recognizes a distractor as a target on a small percentage of distractor trials—not an unreasonable assumption in a speeded task with distractors physically similar to targets. Incorrect information about the stimulus would still be transmitted discretely to the decision process, where it would activate a response just as if a target had actually been presented, thereby producing errors on inconsistent trials but not consistent ones.

It should be noted in passing that the biasing observed in the name-similarity condition also provides additional support for coactivation models. This biasing demonstrates another set of conditions under which partial response activations are combined across stimuli, so that multiple stimuli influence the decision to make a single response (cf. Miller, 1982b).

EXPERIMENT 2

This experiment used visual stimuli constructed from two separable stimulus attributes to provide a further test of discrete models against continuous and ADC models. The basic paradigm was identical to that of Experiment 1. Visual stimuli were the upper-case letters S and T varying in size. Each subject's two visual targets were the small version of one letter and the large version of the other (e.g., small S = target for left-hand response; large T = target for right-hand response).

There were two distractor conditions. In the size-neutral distractor condition, a visual distractor was an S or T of medium size. This condition is a conceptual replication of the name-similarity condition in Experiment 1, with the size attribute's replacing case. A distractor with the same name as a target, but a size designating it irrelevant, should activate the response appropriate for that target. Activation could occur after the distractor had been recognized completely, due to difficulty in ignoring stimulus name, and is therefore predicted by discrete as well as continuous and ADC models.

In the size-competing distractor condition, distractors had the same names and sizes as targets, but in opposite combinations (e.g., targets small S and large T, distractors large S and small T). Thus, each distractor shared its name with one target and its size with the other, so the two attributes of a distractor should compete (i.e., activate opposite responses). Perceptually, however, the competing attributes were not equivalent. Sizes were chosen so that the small/large discrimination would take about 75 to 100 msec longer than the S/T discrimination (Miller, 1982a, 1983), so distractors shared an easy-to-discriminate attribute with one target and a difficult-to-discriminate attribute with the other target.

Discrete models predict no *net* response activation in the size-competing condition. Activation does not begin until complete information about a distractor is available (i.e., both letter name and size), and the two attributes of a distractor support opposite responses. Hence, the activation produced by one attribute should negate the activation produced by the other, leaving equal activation of both responses. The two attributes should produce equal amounts of activation, because they are equally relevant to the decision. Because size is just as important to the decision as name, it should be equally difficult to ignore in a distractor. Perceptual discriminability of attributes is irrelevant in discrete models, because response selection starts only after both attributes have been fully recognized, at which point the discrimination is complete.

Unlike discrete models, both continuous and ADC models predict that size-competing distractors should produce more activation of the response appropriate for the target with the same letter name. Because the letter name discrimination is easier than the size discrimination, distractor name can start to influence the decision before competing size information has been recognized. This implies that name can influence decisions longer than size, so it should have a bigger influence on response activation. Perceptual discriminability is important in continuous and ADC models, because response activation can begin as soon as the more easily discriminable attribute has been recognized.

Method

The same apparatus and tones used previously were employed again, with minor changes in procedure. The visual stimuli were the letters S and T for all subjects. SOAs, defined as in the first experiment, were .1, .15, .2, .25, and .3 sec. There were three identical blocks of 200 test trials, equally distributed across SOAs and modality of target, with consistent and inconsistent visual distractors on equal numbers of auditory-target trials. In the instructional phase of the session, subjects were shown all visual stimuli simultaneously to help them learn the size discriminations. There were 24 subjects in the size-neutral condition and 32 in the size-competing condition.

To maximize comparability of distractor conditions, it was necessary to make the size discriminations equally difficult in the two conditions. In the size-competing condition, only two sizes of letters were used, about 18 and 22 mm in height. In the size-neutral condition, three sizes were needed, because the targets were small and large, whereas the distractors were medium sized. In this condition, however, only the small/medium and medium/large discriminations had to be made, because each letter only appeared in two sizes. The difficulty of the small/medium discrimination was matched to the size-competing condition by using the same sizes, 18 and 22 mm. The difficulty of the medium/large discrimination was matched by choosing a large size (about 28 mm in height) to equate the small:medium and medium:large size ratios.

Results and Discussion

Table 28.2 shows average RT as a function of distractor-size condition, target condition, and SOA. In the size-neutral condition, responses to auditory targets averaged 50 msec faster with consistent than inconsistent visual distractors, a reliable difference—$F(1,16) = 39$, $MSe = 22,250$, $p < .01$. PC was also higher for consistent (98%) than inconsistent (95%) distractors—$F(1,16) = 44$, $MSe =$

TABLE 28.2
Experiment 2: RT as a Function of Distractor Size Condition,
Target–Distractor Combination, and SOA

Target–Distractor Combination	SOA[a] in Sec:				
	.1	.15	.2	.25	.3
Size Neutral					
Tone target, consistent distractor	908	922	933	969	986
Tone target, inconsistent distractor	964	964	983	1000	1055
Visual target, neutral distractor	856	855	886	892	914
Size Competing:					
Tone target, consistent distractor	870	850	800	770	725
Tone target, inconsistent distractor	885	842	810	777	737
Visual target, neutral distractor	831	834	835	843	857

[a]Measured from onset of visual to onset of auditory stimulus.

83, $p < .01$. Thus, the size-neutral condition shows that distractors sharing a target name will partially activate the response appropriate for that target, thereby replicating Experiment 1.

In the size-competing condition, the distractor consistency effect on RT was a nonsignificant 7 msec—$F(1,24) = .7$, $MSe = 36,910$, $p > .4$—and the effect on PC was only .13%—$F(1,24) = .08$, $MSe = 95$, $p > .7$. Thus, the activation effect expected from the distractor name was eliminated when distractor size favored the opposite response.

The pattern of results across the two distractor-size conditions supports discrete models and contradicts continuous and ADC models. When distractor size was not associated with either response, distractor name produced considerable biasing. This effect was eliminated when distractor size favored the response opposite that favored by distractor name, even though name could be recognized 75 to 100 msec before size. The results thus suggest that name is not used to begin selecting a response until size information is also available, as assumed by discrete models.

It is possible that the lack of distractor-consistency effect in the size-competing condition is a result of the particular SOAs used, because any advantage for the name attribute would probably be transient. For example, the total activation produced by the size attribute could eventually catch up with that produced by name, even if name started first. To test this hypothesis, an additional 32 subjects were run in this condition with SOAs ranging from $-.4$ to $-.1$ sec. These subjects also showed a nonsignificant 7 msec advantage for consistent over inconsistent distractors—$F(1,24) = 1.2$, $MSe = 24,938$, $p > .25$.

Another possibility is that an averaging artifact concealed a true effect of distractor consistency in the size-competing condition. Suppose that distractor name does produce some response activation, but that size produces even more activation of the opposite response when it becomes available. Net response activation would first favor the target with the distractor name and later favor the target with the distractor size, so both competing consistency effects would be present in RT, though at different SOAs. However, if the optimal SOAs for these competing effects varied across subjects, then they could cancel each other out when results were averaged. The data of blocks 2 and 3 were used to evaluate this possibility. For each subject, the data of block 2 were used to identify the optimal SOAs for name and size activation, and consistency effects at those SOAs in block 3 were noted. Across subjects, however, consistency effects for these selected SOAs were still not reliably different from 0. Another possible averaging artifact is that the relevant processes are stochastic within each subject. For a given subject and SOA, there could be net activation corresponding to name on some trials and size on others, yet, on average across trials, there might be no net activation of either type. If this were the case, the variance of RT within a given subject and condition should be larger in the size-competing condition than in the size-neutral. In the former condition some trials show activation in each direction, but in the latter only one type of activation occurs. Variances of RTs within subjects and conditions did not differ significantly for size-neutral and size-competing subjects, however.

GENERAL DISCUSSION

In two experiments a visual distractor with the same name as a visual target facilitated the response appropriate for that target and inhibited the opposite response, as revealed in RT to an auditory target presented at about the same time. However, responses were not affected by visual distractors that were either physically or physically and categorically similar to targets. Responses were also unaffected by a distractor with the same name as one target and the same size as the opposite target, even though the name attribute was perceptually much more discriminable than the size attribute.

Contrary to both continuous and ADC models, these results provide no evidence that a visual stimulus can start to influence response selection before it has been fully identified. Continuous models predict, incorrectly, that distractors physically similar to targets should partially activate responses. ADC models predict, incorrectly, that responses should be activated by distractors similar to targets both physically and categorically. Both models also predict, incorrectly, that responses should be activated by distractors similar to one target in name and to the other target in size if the name discrimination is easier than the size discrimination. The lack of predicted response activation is particularly significant because activation was obtained when distractors shared names (only) with targets. This effect, though it does not distinguish among the models, shows that the paradigm is sensitive enough to detect partial response activations under some circumstances.

In accordance with discrete models, these results suggest that a visual stimulus must be recognized completely before it begins to influence the decision process, at least in bimodal divided-attention tasks. All of the biasing effects incorrectly predicted by continuous and ADC models depend on the assumption that response activation starts before stimulus recognition is complete; discrete models predict none of these effects. Discrete models can explain the one obtained biasing effect (activation of a response by a distractor having the same name as a target assigned to that response) as a decision effect occurring after distractor recognition is complete. The finding that name biasing is eliminated by a competing size attribute is particularly strong support for discrete models, because name and size were unequally discriminable attributes. The fact that responses are equally activated by unequally discriminable attributes suggests that response selection does not begin until discrimination is complete.

Though the results of the present experiments offer straightforward support for discrete models, such models were contradicted by the results of previous studies that used the same stimuli but different paradigms to compare discrete, continuous, and ADC models. Miller (1982a, 1983) found evidence for ADC models in tasks designed to determine whether preliminary information is used to begin preparing responses before stimulus recognition is completely finished, and Miller (1982c) found evidence for continuous models in focused and divided-attention tasks within the visual modality. Obviously, a more elaborate model will be needed to account for all of these results, and the various studies should be regarded as providing constraints on rather than decisive tests of the models. One possibility is that information processing can shift among the three modes depending on the task, in which case the problem is to determine what sorts of task lead to each type of processing. Another possibility is that a new model, perhaps a modified version of one of the three discussed here, can account for all the results. Further research is obviously needed to provide closure on this issue.

The present results are also relevant to models describing the combination of information from different channels in divided-attention tasks. Like previous findings (e.g., Miller, 1982b), these results are consistent with a model in which multiple stimuli can coactivate a single response. These results also suggest, however, that each stimulus must be fully identified before it can begin to contribute activation. This point resolves an apparent contradiction between the results of Miller (1982b) and Shaw (1980, 1982). Shaw showed that response probabilities in divided-attention tasks are predicted well by models assuming a separate decision about each channel. This finding appears to conflict with coactivation models, because the latter allow the response to receive partial activation from targets on several different channels. The resolution is that the perceptual process makes separate decisions, whereas coactivation occurs in the process of activating a speeded response. Separate decisions about stimuli on different channels correspond to discrete perceptual processing of those stimuli, and models with separate decisions fit accuracy data because the decision process only uses information about fully recognized stimuli. The speed of the response is jointly influenced by several stimuli because the decision process takes all recognized stimuli into account, not because it uses information about partially recognized stimuli.

In summary, the results of the present studies support several conclusions. First, responses can be activated by stimuli presented on several channels, and activations produced by different stimuli are combined into a net activation for each response. Second, response activation can sometimes be produced by distractors that are similar to targets. The conditions under which this occurs suggest the main conclusion: Perceptual analysis of a stimulus must finish completely before that stimulus can begin to activate responses, at least in two-choice divided-attention tasks. Further research is needed to investigate the limits on this last conclusion, particularly because contradicting results have been obtained in other paradigms (Miller, 1982a, 1982c).

ACKNOWLEDGMENTS

This research was supported by a Biomedical Research grant to the Center for Human Information Processing, UCSD, and Academic Research Grant R-G40-G from the University of California. Jennifer Browne, Bancroft Dutton, Todd Fitzpatrick, Sarah Frampton, Lisa Oakes, and Janice Quackenbush assisted in the collection of the data. I would like to thank William P. Banks, Patricia Haden, John Polich, Michael Posner, and two anonymous reviewers for helpful comments on earlier drafts of this manuscript.

REFERENCES

Broadbent, D. E. (1958). *Perception and communication.* New York: Pergamon.
Conrad, R. (1964). Acoustic confusion and immediate memory. *British Journal of Psychology, 55,* 75–84.
Eriksen, C. W., & Hoffman, J. (1973). The extent of processing of noise elements during selective encoding from visual displays. *Perception and Psychophysics, 14,* 155–160.
Eriksen, C. W., & Schultz, D. (1979). Information processing in visual search: A continuous flow conception and experimental results. *Perception and Psychophysics, 25,* 249–263.
Garner, W. R. (1974). *The processing of information and structure.* Hillsdale, NJ: Lawrence Erlbaum Associates.
Jonides, J., & Gleitman, H. (1972). A conceptual category effect in visual search: O as letter or digit. *Perception and Psychophysics, 12,* 457–460.
Logan, G. (1980). Attention and automaticity in Stroop and priming tasks: Theory and data. *Cognitive Psychology, 12,* 523–553.
McClelland, J. L. (1979). On the time relations of mental processes: A framework for analyzing processes in cascade. *Psychological Review, 86,* 287–330.

Miller, J. O. (1982a). Discrete versus continuous stage models of human information processing: In search of partial output. *Journal of Experimental Psychology: Human Perception and Performance, 8,* 273–296.

Miller, J. O. (1982b). Divided attention: Evidence for coactivation with redundant signals. *Cognitive Psychology, 14,* 247–279.

Miller, J. O. (1982c). Effects of noise letters on decisions: Discrete or continuous flow of information? *Perception and Psychophysics, 31,* 227–236.

Miller, J. O. (1983). Can response preparation begin before stimulus recognition finishes? *Journal of Experimental Psychology: Human Perception and Performance, 9,* 161–182.

Norman, D. A., & Bobrow, D. G. (1975). On data-limited and resource-limited processes. *Cognitive Psychology, 7,* 44–64.

Posner, M. I. (1978). *Chronometric explorations of mind.* Hillsdale, NJ: Lawrence Erlbaum Associates.

Raab, D. (1962). Statistical facilitation of simple reaction times. *Transactions of the New York Academy of Sciences, 24,* 574–590.

Sanders, A. F. (1977). Structural and functional aspects of the reaction process. In S. Dornic (Ed.), *Attention and performance VI* (pp. 3–25). Hillsdale, NJ: Lawrence Erlbaum Associates.

Sanders, A. F. (1980). Stage analysis of reaction processes. In G. Stelmach & J. Requin (Eds.), *Tutorials in motor behavior* (pp. 331–354). Amsterdam: North-Holland.

Shaw, M. L. (1980). Identifying attentional and decision-making components in information processing. In R. S. Nickerson (Ed.), *Attention and performance VIII* (pp. 277–296). Hillsdale, NJ: Lawrence Erlbaum Associates.

Shaw, M. L. (1982). Attending to multiple sources of information: I. The integration of information in decision making. *Cognitive Psychology, 14,* 353–409.

Sternberg, S. (1969a). The discovery of processing stages: Extensions of Donders' method. *Acta Psychologica, 30,* 276–315.

Sternberg, S. (1969b). Memory scanning: Mental processes revealed by reaction-time experiments. *American Scientist, 57,* 421–457.

Stroop, J. (1935). Studies of interference in serial verbal reactions. *Journal of Experimental Psychology, 18,* 643–662.

Taylor, D. A. (1976). Stage analysis of reaction time. *Psychological Bulletin, 83,* 161–191.

Turvey, M. T. (1973). On peripheral and central processes in vision: Inferences from an information-processing analysis of masking with patterned stimuli. *Psychological Review, 80,* 1–52.

29 Word Load and Visual Hemifield Shape Recognition: Priming and Interference Effects

Marcel Kinsbourne
Eunice Kennedy Shriver Center and Harvard Medical School

Mark Byrd
University of Toronto

ABSTRACT

In a repeated-measures shape-recognition paradigm, young and old subjects exhibited right-hemisphere–left visual-field (RH–LVF) advantage. The young group showed left-hemisphere–right visual-field (LH–RVF) advantage when primed by a prior light verbal memory load, but both LH–RVF and RH–LVF interference under heavier prior loading. The U-shaped effect of increasing prior load on LH–RVF performance in the young group demonstrates the continuity between priming and interference. At an interfering level of load, the verbal performance itself also suffered interference. In both visual fields interference occurred at an objectively lighter level of prior load in old than in young people and the old group began to make errors in the verbal task at a lighter verbal workload.

Light prior workloads prime neighboring brain areas. In contrast, interference becomes reliably demonstrable at heavier levels of prior workload (perhaps because rehearsal sets up a concurrent dual-task situation) and generalizes across both hemispheres. In the less efficient brain of the elderly, a lighter workload suffices to set up interference. The preceding two-factor account of activation effects on hemisphere performance could also apply to the Yerkes–Dodson relationship between activation levels and performance of the subject as a whole.

INTRODUCTION

As a result of the differential localization of function in the cerebrum, activities that do not utilize common component processes are considered to be represented in anatomically distinct cortical areas (Luria, 1980). This type of organization would appear to be conducive to parallel processing. As long as structural interference (Kahneman, 1973) is avoided by allocating nonconflicting inputs to distinct effectors, it should be possible to perform two or more qualitatively different activities simultaneously. But automatized performance aside, few instances of truly independent concurrent performances have been described (Allport, Antonis, & Reynolds, 1972). More usually, one or both activities are performed less well in the dual- than the single-task condition. This "concurrence cost" (Gopher & Navon, 1980) is sometimes extreme, in that one performance is held in abeyance until the other is completed (Welford, 1952). Depending on the source of the findings they are attempting to organize, theorists have formulated multiple-channel (Allport et al., 1972), allocatable-resource (Moray, 1979), and single-channel (Welford, 1952) theories of capacity limitations. However, a general theory of capacity limitations must encompass all three of the just-described patterns of dual-task interaction, and do so in terms compatible with the known constraints of the neural hardware that subserves cognitive processes in the brain (Kinsbourne, 1980).

The relevant organizational principle appears to be the highly interconnected nature of the neural network (Pribram, 1971). Be it laterally or by recurrent vertical loops, activation can spread from one cerebral area to another. We have proposed that this spread of influence is proportionate to the connectedness of the areas in question. According to their "functional cerebral distance" (FCD) principle, Kinsbourne and Hicks (1978) predict that, if the neural substrate of activity A is known to be more connected to that of B than C, the state of A will influence B more than C.

Most demonstrations of the FCD principle have taken advantage of the well-validated contralateral hemisphere representation of each of paired bilateral input and output processes. Thus, the central representations of lateral inputs or outputs are "closer" to any ongoing categorically related activity in the contralateral than the ipsilateral hemisphere. Whereas conceptually, speaking or thinking in words has no more in common with unrelated right-ear, visual half field, or hand activity than left, neuropsychologically the former are more related ("closer") than the latter. Based on such and analogous considerations, numerous demonstrations of the FCD principle have been accomplished (Kinsbourne & Hicks, 1978) and no contradictory findings (i.e., greater effect on the distant than the near locus) are on record. Examples are the greater interference of movement by one limb with unrelated movement in the ipsilateral limb than the obliquely opposite limb (Kinsbourne, 1973); interference of reciting passages under delayed auditory feedback with right but not left step-tracking arm movement (Briggs, 1975); interference of speech with right more than left arm movement in many studies, though not in left handers (reviewed by Kinsbourne & Hiscock, 1983); interference of spatial tasks with left- more than right-hand performance (MacFarland & Ashton, 1978).

Disparate tasks imposed in rapid succession are also able to facilitate each other under certain conditions. This has been termed priming (though it differs from the well-known within-category class of priming effects). Typical *priming* and interfering secondary tasks differ in numerous ways. But in general, tasks that prime *precede* and tasks that interfere *coincide* with the main task.

Since its first demonstration in 1970, lateralized priming of categorically unrelated responses has typically been accomplished by letting a lateralized (usually verbal) memory load (e.g., Kinsbourne, 1970, 1973) or warning signal (Bowers & Heilman, 1976) precede each main task trial. Priming across blocks of trials has also been demonstrated (Klein, Moscovitch, & Vigna, 1976). Again the priming and primed performances are successive. In contrast, lateralized interference has from the first (Kinsbourne & Cook, 1971) involved the *concurrent* presence of the main and the secondary task (overt or covert verbalization, rehearsal of verbal or visuospatial material). Is this difference in temporal relationship between tasks critical for determining the valence of task interaction?

If this suggestion is to be taken seriously, it must be reconciled with the results of certain studies in which a preceding lateralized task did influence the "closer" main task more, as predicted by the FCD principle, but interfered rather than primed (Boles, 1979; Gardner & Branski, 1976; Geffen, Bradshaw, & Nettleton, 1973; Hellige & Cox, 1976). The work of Hellige and Cox is a case in point. Their research was aimed at determining how subjects' abilities to recognize shapes presented to each visual field are differentially affected by the level of difficulty of a word list presented before each visual trial, and recalled afterwards.

Right-handed subjects recognizing nonverbal shapes usually yield a perceptual asymmetry favoring stimuli presented in the left visual hemifield (LVF). But there is evidence that either hemisphere is capable of performing this type of task. This relative hemispheric specialization for nonverbal shape recognition contrasts with the exclusive (usually left) hemispheric specialization that appears to obtain for language-output processes (Zaidel, 1983). The LVF advantage can be neutralized if steps are taken to activate the left hemisphere. This may be accomplished by imposing, before each trial, a prior task, verbal in nature, that calls for the specialized activity of the left hemisphere. Selective activation for purposes of verbal processing involves, but is not confined to, areas specialized for language functions. It is apt also to spread to other parts of the hemisphere, including those involved in processing visual input (Mazziotta, Phelps, Carson, & Kuhl, 1982). Thus, imposing an unrelated verbal task may improve recognition of shapes presented in the right visual hemifield (RVF). Priming facilitation of RVF may occur at the expense of the RH–LVF performance by trade-off between hemispheres (Kinsbourne, 1973), or independently of the other hemisphere (Hellige & Cox, 1976; Kinsbourne & Bruce, submitted). Hellige and Cox's results were the first to demonstrate definitively that a secondary task imposed prior to the main task can interfere with main performance, if it is difficult enough. They found a U-shaped relationship between LVF performance and level of concurrent verbal load, with enhanced performance at light loads reversed as word load increased. They found no significant effect of load on LVF performance, but there was a trend toward LVF decline with increasing load. Thus, Hellige and Cox made explicit a factor foreshadowed in previous work: Preceding tasks that interfere rather than prime tend to be relatively difficult—that is, they involve a memory load that might not be fully recaptured at posttest unless the subject actively rehearses (Naveh-Benjamin & Jonides, 1984). If the subject continues to rehearse the word list *while* performing the perceptual main task, the word-list procedure becomes concurrent, and aligns with other concurrent dual-task situations in which interference is the outcome. Given this possibility, it becomes important to replicate the Hellige and Cox study, to determine whether subjects whose verbal-memory performances are relatively inferior at a given list length show more interference or fail to show priming, in contrast to better memory-span performers.

The present work focuses on the transition between priming and interference effects exerted by the *same* secondary task at *different* workloads, and its interaction with age as a subject variable. The results bear on the choice between unitary resource, dual (hemispheric) resource, and graduated cross-talk interference models of capacity limitations. A nonverbal-visual main task and a verbal-acoustic secondary task are used. The Hellige and Cox study was limited by its use of a between-subjects design and lack of control for shifting trade-off between tasks across workload. Our study was similar, but with a within-subjects design, and we also performed it with elderly subjects. Beyond determining whether the RVF U-shaped function is replicable, we addressed three issues:

1. As verbal secondary load is increased, does it interfere with the functioning of the right hemisphere as well as the left?
2. Does the task difficulty variable operate similarly among young and old people (though their absolute levels of efficiency at these tasks might differ)?
3. Could the U-shaped curve performance of RVF be due to differential trade-off between the visual and the verbal task at different levels of secondary verbal load?

The first issue addresses claims that the hemispheres tap independent resources (strongly by Friedman & Polson, 1978; more tentatively by Hellige, Cox, & Litvac, 1979). According to this view, processing within one hemisphere cannot compete with processing by the other. Indeed, Friedman and Polson (1978) claim that when one hemisphere is activated, the other is also equally activated, and yet according to them, it does not participate in the cognitive activity. Accordingly, imposing a secondary task on one hemisphere should not interfere with activity programmed by the other. Relevant to the second issue, Craik (1977) found dual-task (division of attention) paradigms particularly sensitive to age-related decrement in performance. It follows that old subjects should behave like young ones with heavier workloads. Specifically, they should exhibit interference under workloads that in young subjects induce priming. The issue of trade-off is a methodological control not formally addressed in previous work.

METHOD

Subjects

Of 40 subjects who participated in this experiment, 20 ranged in age from 15 to 22 (mean age = 18.8 years) and 20 from 61 to 71 (mean age = 65.4 years). All subjects were right handed, as determined by the verbally administered Edinburgh handedness inventory. Additionally, no subject had an immediate family member (parent, child, or sibling) who was/is left handed. The younger subjects were paid volunteer undergraduates. The older subjects were volunteers from a pool of University of Toronto graduates.

Apparatus and Materials

Forty random geometric shapes were selected from those studied by Vanderplas and Garvin (1959). Twenty were 12-point shapes and 20 were 16-point shapes. Ten additional shapes were used during practice trials only. The shapes were presented to the subjects with a Kodak carousel slide projector equipped with a Gerbrands electronic shutter. The shapes were projected onto a Hudson Telescreen facing the subject. Each shape spanned a visual angle of approximately .5° both horizontally and vertically. The near side of the shape was 2° from the center of the viewing screen.

One hundred and twenty nouns from the Thorndike–Lorge (1944) lists were used for the concurrent memory task. They were selected for both high frequency of usage (A or AA ratings) and high imagery according to the Paivio, Yuille, and Madigan (12) norms (mean imagery rating = 7.12). The nouns used on each trial were randomly selected from this pool. Each word was used only once during the experiment.

Procedure

Each subject was told to fixate centrally. A geometric shape would be projected to either the left or the right of the fixation dot. The two visual fields would be tested in random sequence, and therefore the best strategy would be to fixate on the spot at the beginning of each trial. After each form was presented to either the

LVF or RVF, the subject was given a card displaying the form that had just been shown, randomized in with four distractor forms. The subject selected one of the forms on each trial by forced choice.

After the general procedure was explained, each subject was given five LVF and five RFV practice trials in a random order. On each trial the experimenter said "fixate" and then presented the stimulus shape for 15 msec. Immediately after the exposure, a card containing five geometric shapes was placed in front of the subject, who was asked to point to the shape that had been presented on the viewing screen. These 10 trials also served as a means of calibrating exposure time for each subject. If the subject gave fewer than three or more than seven correct responses, the duration was changed to 10 msec or 20 msec, respectively. Five older subjects but no younger ones were excluded for failing to meet minimum shape-recognition requirements. Mean exposure durations used were 13.75 msec (s.d. 3.19) for the young and 16 msec (s.d. 3.08) for the old group.

After the practice series, the subject received 40 experimental trials using the same procedure. Twenty of the shapes were presented to the RVF and 20 to the LVF. Trials were not blocked by memory load, but randomly determined. In addition, the subject performed a concurrent memory task. At the beginning of each trial the subject was read a list of unrelated words and was asked to hold them in memory while performing the visual-recognition task. After the subject had made his or her choice from the set of geometric shapes, he or she was asked to repeat the string of words. The subject was asked to pay equal attention to the visual and verbal tasks, neither of which was described as "secondary." The subject was given zero, two, four, or six nouns to remember on each trial. Each subject had five trials in each hemifield by memory-load condition. An equal number of words was coupled with the shapes presented to each visual field.

RESULTS

The results of the visual-recognition task for both young and old groups are shown in Figs. 29.1 and 29.2. These data were analyzed by a one between-subjects factor (age) and two within-subjects factor (hemifield and memory load) analysis of variance. There were significant main effects of age—$F(1,38) = 7.10$, $p < .01$, $MSe = .15$—hemifield—$F(1,38) = 4.37$, $p < .05$, $MSe = .04$—and memory load—$F(3,114) = 17.00$, $p < .01$, $MSe = .03$. In addition, there was a significant hemifield × memory-load interaction—$F(3,114) = 8.43$, $p. < .01$, $MSe = .03$—with the RVF–LH being more affected by the secondary task than the LVF–RH, and an age × memory-load interaction—$F(3,114) = 3.94$, $p < .01$, $MSe = .03$—with the visual-recognition scores of older individuals being more adversely affected by the increased amount of concurrent memory load than those of their younger counterparts.

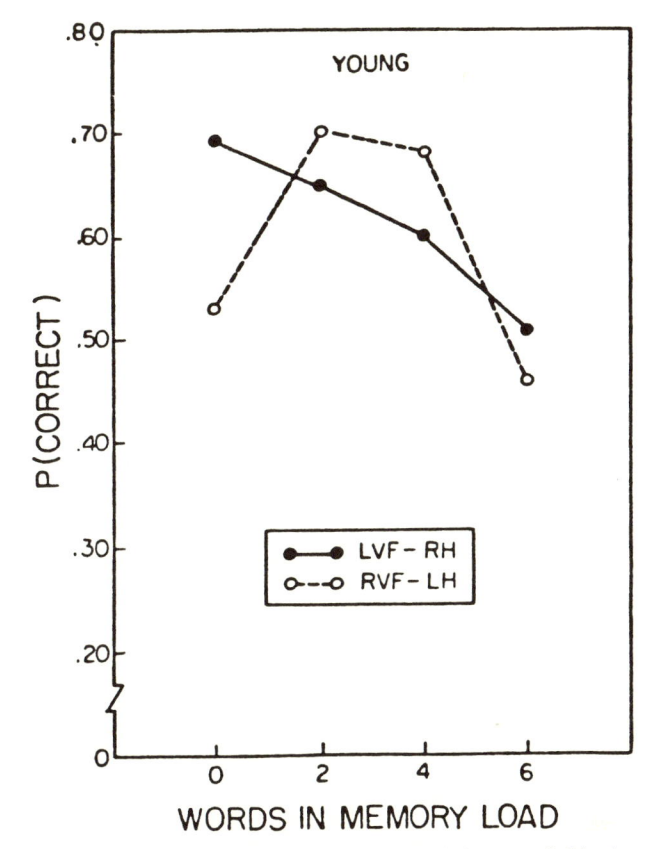

FIG. 29.1. Percent correct shape recognition in relation to verbal load: young group.

A series of specific comparisons for repeated-measures designs were performed. The performance levels within the two hemifields at the 0 memory-load condition were compared to determine whether the expected LVF–RH advantage for spatial material was present. The young group showed a significant LVF–RH advantage in the shape-recognition task—$t(19) = 2.74, p < .05$—as did the older group—$t(19) = 3.28, p < .01$. A trend analysis was performed on the pattern of results for each hemifield for both age groups. In the older subjects, both hemifields displayed significant linear trends with LVF–RH $t(19) = 3.90, p < .01$, and RVF–LH $t(19) = -4.14, p < .01$. The trend analysis for the LVF–RH in the younger subjects showed a similar linear trend—$t(19) = 3.76, p < .01$. However, the RVF–LH showed a significant quadratic trend in the data—$t(19) = -5.67, p < .01$. A specific contrast was performed on the performance levels of the shape-recognition task between zero- and two-word memory-

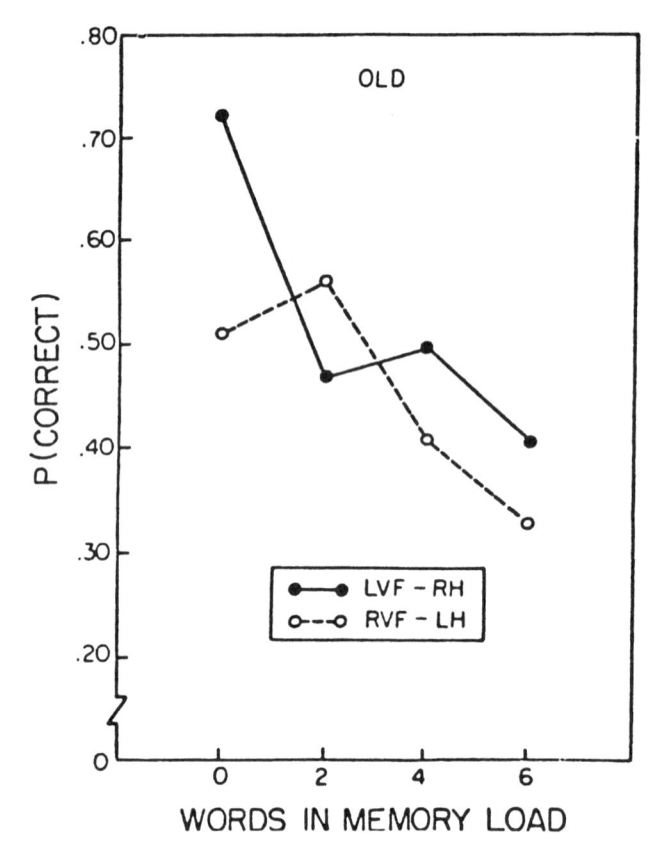

FIG. 29.2. Percent correct shape recognition in relation to verbal load: old group.

load condition for the RVF–LH for both age groups in order to examine the initial effects of left-hemisphere loading by the memory task. In the young group of subjects, this loading produced a significant increase in performance levels on the shape-recognition task—$t(19) = 3.85, p < .01$. However, the same analysis for the oldest group revealed no significant difference in shape-recognition performance levels in the RVF–LH—$t(19) < 1$. Table 29.1 presents the results for specific comparisons of shape-recognition scores between adjacent load levels for each visual field separately. Mean percent of words recalled by list length and visual-field hemisphere for the two groups are shown in Table 29.2.

Differential trade-off cannot account for interference effects in the visual task, as interference with the verbal task occurred in parallel. Nor can it account for the appearance of interference with LVF–RH functioning, as, if anything, concomitant percentage verbal recall was less than during RVF–LH stimulation.

29. PRIMING AND INTERFERENCE EFFECTS   537

TABLE 29.1
Specific Contrasts

	Memory Load	T (df 19)	p
Young Subjects			
LVF–RH	0–2	.893	N.S.
	2–4	.865	N.S.
	4–6	2.651	<.05
RVF–LH	0–2	3.847	<.01
	2–4	.400	N.S.
	4–6	4.067	<.01
Old Subjects			
LVF–RH	0–2	4.324	<.01
	2–4	.719	N.S.
	4–6	1.308	N.S.
RVF–LH	0–2	1.000	N.S.
	2–4	2.595	<.05
	4–6	1.506	N.S.

DISCUSSION

As Hellige and Cox (1976) and Hellige (1978) found, randomized presentation of 12- and 16-point random geometric shapes yield a left visual-field advantage. There were differential effects of verbal loading on the two age groups (see Table 29.3). The U-shaped RVF–LH findings on the young group in essentials replicate Hellige and Cox (1976). The priming effect of verbal load on another left-hemisphere activity was also found by Bruce (1973) and Hellige et al. (1979) in their Experiment 3. It appears not to obtain when the other left-hemisphere activity is also verbal. In that case, there is LH–RVF interference (Geffen et al., 1973) and the LVF–RH findings conform to a U-shaped relationship (Hellige and Cox, 1976, experiment 2). One could regard increasing levels of difficulty of the secondary task as progressively increasing the selective activation of the left hemisphere, with a U-shaped outcome for the hemisphere similar to that usually

TABLE 29.2
Mean Percent of Words Recalled

List Length	2		4		6	
Group	Young	Old	Young	Old	Young	Old
LH–RVF	100	100	100	95	92	69
RH–LVF	100	100	99	94	86	66

TABLE 29.3
Correlations between Visual Fields

Memory Load	Young	p	Old	p
0	.14	(n.s.)	−.09	(n.s.)
2	.19	(n.s.)	.15	(n.s.)
4	.34	(n.s.)	.52	<.05
6	.56	<.05	.64	<.01

described for the operator as a whole. The result offers a guide to the prediction of secondary task effects: facilitating at light and interfering at heavy workloads. The diverse results of previously published studies appear at least partly to reflect unintentional differences in how exacting the secondary task happened to be.

When a concurrent task interferes bilaterally, this could be: (a) because the task involves cognitive structures in both hemispheres; or (b) because, although it utilizes one hemisphere only, it affects the other also, at a distance. That effects at a distance can occur in the tightly connected cerebral network can hardly be denied. But is the present case an instance of such effects?

In favor of (a) is the verbal capability of the right hemisphere, as expressed in certain pathological circumstances (Kinsbourne, 1971; Searleman, 1977; Zaidel, 1976). However, there is no evidence of right-hemisphere participation in verbal-memory performance in intact people. Or perhaps the subjects use imagery to assist them in retention of the imageable nouns they were to remember? If so, this would not, contrary to general belief, implicate the right hemisphere. Imagery of this type appears to be a left-hemisphere function (Ehrlichman & Barrett, 1983). In any case, Hellige and Cox (1976) found no effect of imageability of nouns on the pattern of effect on the perceptual task. (High imagery nouns were used in conformity with materials selected by Hellige and Cox, Experiment 1). In favor of (b) is the obvious potential for effects at a distance in a neural network, and more specifically in the present case the strictly lateralized nature of priming effects, due to the same verbal secondary task at light levels of load. Thus, there is little reason to doubt that expressive verbal tasks are controlled by the left hemisphere only in most right handers. When task difficulty is increased the right hemisphere becomes involved. This could be because of interfering cross-talk from the left (Kinsbourne & Hicks, 1978). Cerebral metabolic measurement should cast light on this hypothesis. In the meantime, we interpret the present data without committing ourselves to this particular mechanism.

The left-hemisphere priming effect considered alone is compatible with the view that a hemisphere is a limited-capacity channel with independent "resources" (Friedman & Polson, 1978; Hellige et al., 1979) in that it showed no tendency to involve the other side. Previous priming demonstrations have similarly shown effects limited to one hemisphere (Kinsbourne, 1970, 1973; Hellige

& Cox, 1976; Kinsbourne & Bruce, submitted). But the significant linear LVF–RH performance decrement with increasing levels of verbal load contradicts this model. At these levels, loading one hemisphere (the left) prejudices efficiency of the other (the right). A detrimental effect of a lateralized secondary task on main performance by the contralateral hemisphere, less than the ipsilateral effect, but none the less significant, is often found in lateralized dual-task interference paradigms (Kinsbourne & Hiscock, 1983). Such an effect becomes greater when either primary (Hicks, Bradshaw, Kinsbourne, & Feigin, 1978) or secondary (Hicks, 1975) task difficulty is increased. Hiscock, Kinsbourne, Samuels, and Krause (submitted) attempted to determine whether ipsilateral and contralateral interference between speech and speeded unimanual finger tapping are quantitatively the same or different. They might be different if hemispheres tap independent resource pools. For instance, ipsilateral interference might be characterized by observable cross-talk between neuronal programs, whereas contralateral interference only derives from conflicting claims to a limited resource. The variability of finger tapping (expressed as the coefficient of variation) was used as a face-valid index of interference. It did not differ between hands in the amount of its increase in the dual-task condition. The same result for variability was obtained by Hiscock and Chipuer (submitted). This outcome offers no support to dual-resource models.

In sharp contrast to the findings of Hellige and Cox (1976), the present study reveals declines in LVF–RH performance with verbal loading; these are particularly steep in the elderly groups. In fact, the 0 to 2 LVF–RV change comparison in the young groups fell short of significance, but given the significant linear tread, it would be formalistic to exclude from consideration the likelihood that even a light load can affect RH function: We accept this on the assumption that our repeated-measure design yielded a more representative outcome in this respect than Hellige and Cox's between-subjects design.

We cannot determine whether interference at light load is *selective* for LVF–RH, because we have no way of telling how much interference in RVF–LH was overridden by the priming effect. However, the LVF–RH decline contemporaneous with RVF–LH improvement in performance is reminiscent of earlier findings suggesting that attentional shifts away from LVF toward RVF contribute to the verbal memory-load priming effect of verbal memory load (Kinsbourne 1970, 1973). Thus, by our interpretation, priming could enhance RVF–LH performance in the present paradigm by rendering the LH a more efficient processer (as supposed by Hellige and Cox), shifting attention rightward, or a combination of these effects.

Light levels of the secondary task exert opposite effects on the functioning of each hemisphere in contrast with the bilateral interference effects due to heavier load. This necessitates a two-factor model. One way of conceptualizing the two factors would be: (a) unilateral (left) hemisphere priming at light levels of verbal load; (b) bilateral interference at heavier levels of load and proportionate to load.

The main divergence of the present findings from the Hellige and Cox result, a significant LVF decrement with increasing load that in their data was a trend that failed to reach significance, leaves this model viable. At a load of six words, at which level the RVF facilitation is no longer present, an appreciable number of errors in the secondary task is first seen.

For elderly subjects, the LVF decrement with increasing load was steeper than among the young. The priming effect of light load in RVF performance was limited to a trend toward improvement from zero- to two-word load that fell short of significance. Beyond two-word loading, RVF performance began to decline, and secondary-task performance also began to show errors. There was no differential trade-off contribution to those hemispheric differences in either group.

Taken literally, this result indicates an absence of the priming effect and thus a qualitative difference between the performance of young and old subjects. But if the crucial manipulation is of secondary-*task difficulty* rather than work load per se, then a priming effect could have been missed because among the elderly subjects a main effect of secondary task detrimental to main-task performance was already evident at a load level of two words (in this sense equivalent to a load of six words in the young). Note the steeper decline of LVF performance in the elderly group between zero- and two-word load. As in the young group, this resulted in higher mean performance in the RVF than LVF at that level of load. In a second experiment, we replicated the zero- and two-word load conditions on a new group of elderly subjects and added an intermediate (one-word) loading condition to determine whether it would generate a priming effect, as did two- and four-word loads in the young. The result was that, as in the case of the zero- to two-word load comparison in the present experiment, the zero- to one-word load comparison yielded an improved performance at one-word load that fell just short of significance ($t = 5.12$, $p < .10$). This second study also revealed a significant zero- to one-word load decrement for LVF–RH. There was a crossover, leaving RVF performance higher than LVF performance at the one-word load level. The interference effect of the secondary task on LVF–RH performance was quite severe, even at the one-word load level. Thus, in both groups imposing light load occasioned changes in LVF and RVF performance in opposite directions.

The pattern of interference in the elderly group is therefore also at odds with the notion that hemispheric resources are independent.

The extent to which a given performance lays claim to "cerebral space" depends on task difficulty. The more difficult the task is, the more of the network it occupies, and the more liable it is to interact with another concurrently programmed unrelated action. Task difficulty is determined not only by the work to be done, but also by the subject's operational efficiency in doing such work. With advancing age, operational efficiency diminishes on a vast array of tasks (Botwinick, 1978). Older persons given a task at a particular workload perform like younger persons do at a lighter work load. The present research illustrates this. Effects evident in the young at a particular level of verbal load already become apparent in the old at a lighter level of load. As a result, the secondary task disproportionately handicaps the elderly. Kinsbourne (1977) has interpreted this phenomenon in terms of a decrease in "functional cerebral distance" in the aged brain. If on account of the general depletion of the neuronal network that attends aging, the functional cerebral space between two active loci diminishes, a concurrent activity that competes for such space becomes disproportionately detrimental to main-task performance.

One may therefore argue that functional cerebral space between control centers is a "resource." If so, it is neither an exclusive ("dedicated") nor a freely shared ("multipurpose") resource. Each cerebral area is more readily available to, and earlier drawn upon by, processes localized close by functionally. But given the questionable explanatory value of the resource concept (Navon, 1984, this volume), we prefer not to use that term.

The RVF effects in the young group may be comparable to the effect of overarousal on performance first described by Yerkes and Dodson (1908). Although the concept that overarousal as such is detrimental to performance (Broadbent, 1971; Malmo, 1959) remains tenable, Näätänen (1973) has given evidence for a two factor view: The ascending limb of the inverted U-shaped function is generated by activation increase, but the descending limb during further increase in activation is a consequence of interference between two tasks, the explicit task that generates the dependent variable of interest, and the "task" of dealing with or accommodating to the variable that generates the high activation level. When Näätänen had subjects perform the main task at a high activation level that was not caused by ongoing influences, but was residual from a previous exertion, they showed no performance decrement. This view aligns the Yerkes–Dodson function, in mechanism as well as configuration, with the U-shaped effect of concurrent verbal load on left-hemisphere shape recognition found in this study. For the case of noise effects on performance, Poulton (1979) has advocated a similar composite model.

We have already mentioned the possibility that the interfering effect of relatively heavy secondary verbal load *preceding* the main task is use of rehearsal during main-task performance to keep the material in mind. Such a strategy might have been initiated at a lighter objective load level by the elderly subjects. But although this hypothesis fits well into a two-factor model as described, rehearsal was neither controlled nor monitored in this or previous studies. Further work will test the prediction of this hypothesis: (a) that having subjects explicitly rehearse during main-task performance is interfering; (b) that having subjects refrain from rehearsing even at heavy loads will minimize interference.

Effects of the secondary task on the two hemispheres are neither independent (as supposed by Friedman & Polson, 1978) nor parallel (as accounts of dual-task performance that ignore the constraints imposed by brain organization would assume).. Priming is limited to one hemisphere; interference ultimately affects both. It remains to be determined whether similar two-factor relationships obtain between more versus less "connected" loci within a hemisphere.

REFERENCES

Allport, D. A., Antonis, B., & Reynolds, P. (1972). On the division of attention: A disproof of the single channel hypothesis. *Quarterly Journal of Experimental Psychology, 24,* 225–235.
Boles, D. B. (1979). Laterally biased attention with concurrent verbal load: Multiple failures to replicate. *Neuropsychologia, 17,* 353–361.
Botwinick, J. (1978). *Aging and Behavior,* New York: Springer.
Bowers, D., & Heilman, K. M. (1976). Material specific hemispheric arousal. *Neuropsychologia, 14,* 147–149.
Broadbent, D. E. (1971). *Decision and stress.* London: Academic.
Briggs, G. G. (1975). A comparison of attentional and control shift models of the performance of concurrent tasks. *Acta Psychologica, 39,* 183–191.
Bruce, R. C. (1973). *The role of attention in perceptual asymmetries.* Unpublished Ph.D. dissertation, Duke University, Durham, NC
Craik, F. I. M. (1977). Age differences in human memory. In J. E. Birren & K. W. Schaie (Eds.), *Handbook of the psychology of aging* (pp. 384–420). New York: Van Nostrand.
Ehrlichman, M., & Barrett, J. (1983). Right hemisphere specialization for neutral imagery: A review of the evidence. *Brain and Cognition, 2,* 55–78.
Friedman, H., & Polson, M. C. (1978). Hemispheres as independent resource systems: Limited capacity processing and cerebral specialization. *Journal of Experimental Psychology: Human Perception and Performance, 7,* 1031–1058.
Gardner, E. B., & Branski, D. M. (1976). Unilateral cerebral activation and the detection of gaps: A signal detection analysis. *Neuropsychologia, 14,* 43–54.
Geffen, G., Bradshaw, J. L., & Nettleton, N. C. (1973). Attention and hemispheric differences in reaction time during simultaneous audio-visual tasks. *Quarterly Journal of Experimental Psychology, 25,* 404–412.
Gopher, D., & Navon, D. (1980). How is performance limited: Testing the notion of central capacity. *Acta Psychologica, 66,* 161–180.
Hellige, J. B. (1978). Visual laterality patterns for pure- versus mixed-list presentation. *Journal of Experimental Psychology: Human Perception and Performance, 4,* 121–131.
Hellige, J., & Cox, P. J. (1976). Effects of concurrent verbal memory on recognition of stimuli from the left and right visual fields. *Journal of Experimental Psychology: Human Perception and Performance, 2,* 210–221.
Hellige, J., Cox, P. J., & Litvac, L. (1979). Information processing in the cerebral hemispheres: Selective hemispheric activation and capacity limitations. *Journal of Experimental Psychology: General, 108,* 251–279.
Hicks, R. E. (1975). Intrahemispheric response competition between vocal and unimanual performance in normal adult human males. *Journal of Comparative and Physiological Psychology, 89,* 50–60.
Hicks, R. E., Bradshaw, G., Kinsbourne, M., & Feigin, D. S. (1978). Vocal-manual trade-offs in hemispheric sharing of human performance control. *Journal of Motor Behavior, 10,* 1–6.
Hiscock, M., & Chipuer, H. *Concurrent performance of rhythmically compatible or incompatible vocal and manual tasks: Evidence for two sources of interference in verbal-manual time sharing.* Manuscript submitted for publication.
Hiscock, M., Kinsbourne, M., Samuels, M., & Krause, A. E. (in press). Effects of speaking upon the rate and variability of concurrent finger tapping in children. *Journal of Experimental Child Psychology.*
Kahneman, D. (1973). *Attention and effort.* Englewood Cliffs, NJ: Prentice-Hall.

Kinsbourne, M. (1970). The cerebral basis of lateral asymmetries in attention. *Acta Psychologica, 33,* 192–201.
Kinsbourne, M. (1971). Cognitive deficit: Experimental analysis. In J. McGaugh (Ed.), *Psychobiology.* New York: Academic.
Kinsbourne, M. (1973). The control of attention by interaction between the cerebral hemispheres. In S. Kornblum (Ed.), *Attention and performance IV.* New York: Academic.
Kinsbourne, M. (1977). Cognitive decline with advancing age: An interpretation. In W. L. Smith & M. Kinsbourne (Eds.), *Aging, dementia and cerebral function.* New York: Spectrum.
Kinsbourne, M. (1980). Single channel theory. In D. H. Holding (Ed.), *Human skill* (pp. 65–89). Chichester, Sussex: Wiley.
Kinsbourne, M., & Bruce, R. C. *Shift in visual laterality within blocks of trials.* Manuscript submitted for publication.
Kinsbourne, M., & Cook, J. (1971). Generalized and lateralized effect of concurrent verbalization on a unimanual skill. *Quarterly Journal of Experimental Psychology, 23,* 341–345.
Kinsbourne, M., & Hicks, R. F. (1978). Functional cerebral space: A model for overflow, transfer and interference effects in human performance. In J. Requin (Ed.), *Attention and performance VII.* Hillsdale, NJ: Lawrence Erlbaum Associates.
Kinsbourne, M., & Hiscock, M. (1983). Asymmetries of dual-task performance. In J. Hellige (Ed.), *Cerebral hemisphere asymmetry: Method, theory and application.* New York: Academic.
Klein, D., Moscovitch, M., & Vigna, C. (1976). Attentional mechanisms and perceptual asymmetries in tachistoscopic recognition of words and faces. *Neuropsychologia, 14,* 55–66.
Luria, A. R. (1980). *Higher cortical functions in man* (2nd ed.). New York: Basic Books.
Malmo, R. B. (1959). Activation: A neuropsychological dimension. *Psychological Review, 66,* 367–386.
MacFarland, K., & Ashton, R. (1978). The lateralized effects of concurrent cognition and motor performance. *Perception and Psychophysics, 23,* 344–349.
Mazziotta, J. C., Phelps, M. E., Carson, R. E., & Kuhl, D. E. (1982). Tomographic mapping in human cerebral metabolism: Auditory stimulation. *Neurology, 32,* 921–937.
Moray, N. (1979). *Mental workload: Theory and measurement.* New York: Plenum.
Näätänen, R. (1973). The inverted-U relationship between activation and performance: a critical review. In S. Kornblum (Ed.), *Attention and performance, IV.* New York: Academic.
Naveh-Benjamin, M., & Jonides, J. (1984). Maintenance rehearsal: A two-component analysis. *Journal of Experimental Psychology: Learning and Memory, 10,* 369–385.
Navon, D. (1984). Resources—a theoretical soup-stone? *Psychological Review, 91,* 216–234.
Poulton, E. C. (1979). Composite model for human performance in continuous noise. *Psychological Review, 86,* 361–375.
Pribram, K. (1971). *Languages of the brain.* Englewood Cliffs, NJ: Prentice-Hall.
Searleman, A. (1977). A review of right hemisphere linguistic capabilities. *Psychological Bulletin, 84,* 503–528.
Thorndike, E. L., & Lorge, I. (1944). *The teacher's word book of 30,000 words.* New York: Columbia University Teachers College, Bureau of Publications.
Vanderplas, J. M., & Garvin, E. A. (1959). The association values of random shapes. *Journal of Experimental Psychology, 57,* 147–154.
Welford, A. T. (1952). The "psychological refractory period" and the timing of high speed performance: A review and theory. *British Journal of Psychology, 43,* 2–19.
Yerkes, R. M., & Dodson, J. D. (1908). The relation of strength of stimulus to rapidity of habit formation. *Journal of Comparative and Neurological Psychology, 18,* 459–482.
Zaidel, E. (1976). Auditory vocabulary of the right hemisphere after brain bisection or hemidecortication. *Cortex, 12,* 191–211.
Zaidel, E. (1983). Disconnection syndrome as a model for laterality effects in the normal brain. In J. Hellige (Ed.), *Cerebral hemisphere asymmetry: Method, theory, and application.* New York: Academic.

VIII ATTENTION TO SYMBOLS AND WORDS

30 The Perceptual Record: A Common Factor in Repetition Priming and Attribute Retention?

Kim Kirsner
John Dunn
University of Western Australia

ABSTRACT

Repetition priming effects are reviewed in this chapter as a function of the stimulus attribute changed between encoding and test. The amount of priming is found to depend on this attribute; it is virtually nil across a change in language, substantially reduced across modality, and largely complete across case and voice. It is argued that these effects and others in the literature are consistent with a multilevel model of perceptual analysis. The usefulness of this model in predicting performance in an incidental attribute-retention task is also explored. A review of the literature reveals attribute memory to be inversely related to priming effects; memory for language is superior to modality, which is superior to both case and voice. This inverse relationship is also found to apply to the effect of intentionality on attribute recall. From these data it is argued that a record of the perceptual analysis of a word both underlies repetition priming across attributes and is accessible to retrieval processes concerned with memory for detail.

INTRODUCTION

The conceptual steps developed in this chapter stand at the junction of perceptual processing and memory. The particular issue we wish to explore concerns the effect of the perceptual analysis of verbal material on subsequent memory for the physical characteristics of this material. Specifically, we argue for the possibility that knowledge of stimulus features is represented and retained in two distinct but closely connected ways: automatically as a record of perceptual analysis of the input, and effortfully as a result of encoding material into episodic memory. The primary impetus for this suggestion is the observation of parallel effects of changing stimulus features on two separate indices of memory: long-term or repetition priming and attribute recognition and recall.

There is now considerable evidence that the prior presentation of a nameable item (e.g., a word or picture) facilitates its subsequent processing even when the two occasions are separated by several hours or days (Scarborough, Cortese, & Scarborough, 1977). We refer to this facilitatory effect as long-term or repetition priming in order to distinguish it from other priming effects (e.g., semantic, phonological) that appear to have different characteristics and to be confined to much smaller lags (Dannenbring & Briand, 1982; Gough, Alford, & Holley-Wilcox, 1981). Repetition priming has been observed in a variety of tasks, such as naming (Morton, 1969), lexical decision (Kirsner & Smith, 1974), and semantic classification (Durso & Johnson, 1979), and appears to be relatively invariant across a range of different study-list conditions that normally affect memory (Jacoby & Dallas, 1981). It has been variously explained as due to the lowered threshold of recognition units in semantic memory (Morton, 1969) or as due to the recapitulation of previously engaged analytic procedures (Kolers, 1979). Whatever the choice of language used, this form of priming serves to demonstrate the existence of an enduring effect of the processing of nameable items.

One characteristic of repetition priming that is of particular interest concerns the amount of facilitation observed as a function of the similarity between items presented in the second or test phase of an experiment and corresponding items presented in the first or priming phase. For example, the subject may hear the word *cheese* spoken in the priming phase and then see the same word printed in the test phase. In this case, any priming that is observed would be across a change in modality, from speech to print. Figure 30.1 summarizes the results of 28 separate experiments that show how the amount of priming depends on the stimulus attribute altered between priming and test phases. In order to allow a comparison of results across a number of different tasks, the amount of priming observed in each experiment has been converted to an index of relative priming (*RP*) by the following formula:

$$RP = \frac{\textit{different form} - \textit{control}}{\textit{same form} - \textit{control}} \tag{30.1}$$

"Same form" refers to the level of performance when the item is repeated in the test phase in exactly the same form as it was presented in the priming phase (e.g., both in the visual modality and printed in lower case). "Different form" refers to the level of performance when the item is presented in the test phase with a change on a single attribute (e.g., from the auditory to visual modality). "Control" refers to the level of performance observed when an item is presented for the first time only in the test phase (i.e., it has not been primed). Fig. 30.1, therefore, plots the amount of facilitation that results from a change in a single attribute relative to the amount of facilitation that results from a change in no

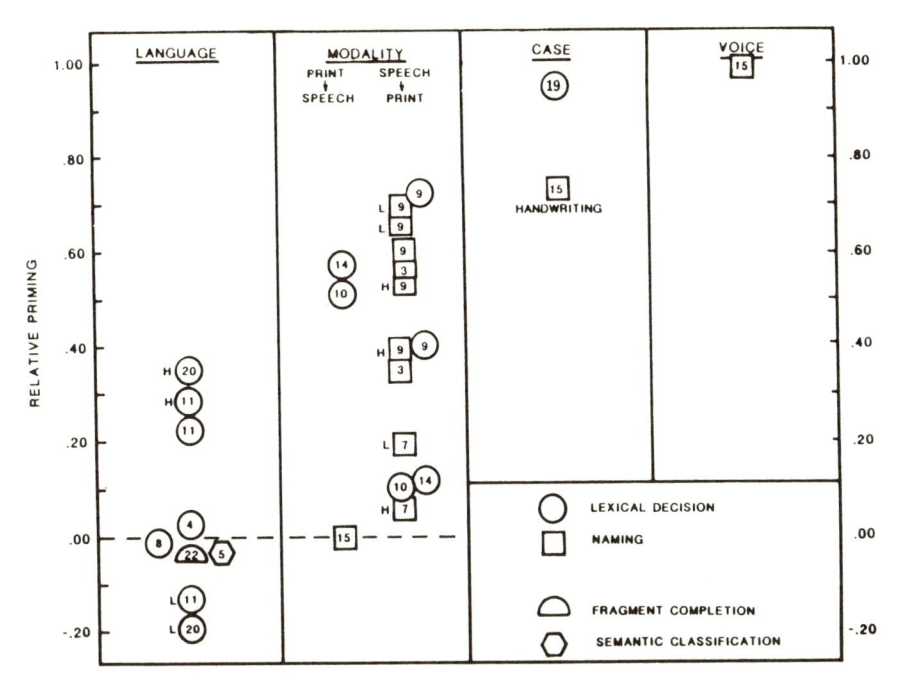

FIG. 30.1. Relative priming in word-identification and classification tasks as a function of attribute and type of task. The ordinate measures the proportion of facilitation observed under interformat conditions relative to intraformat conditions. H = high-frequency and L = low-frequency words used. The enclosed numbers identify cited experiments (e.g., for 1, see Clarke & Morton, 1983).

attribute. For the present purpose, the stimuli have been restricted to words and the attributes to language, modality, case, and voice. The language experiments include transfer between English and French, Hindi, Italian, Spanish, and Turkish, although we exclude words that are cognates (Cristoffanini, Kirsner, & Milech, in preparation) or that differ only in script (Brown, Sharma, & Kirsner, 1984), because these classes of word, unlike other translations, show substantial facilitation across language. The modality comparison is restricted to transfer between spoken and printed words, although comparable data are available for pictures and printed words. Case and voice are used here to refer to transfer between upper- and lower-case print, or between handwriting and print, and between male and female speakers, respectively. In addition, where relevant and in order to avoid confounding with short-term priming effects, the analysis was restricted to treatments with repetition intervals of at least four items or 16 sec.

Inspection of Fig. 30.1 reveals consistent differences in relative priming across the four attributes. There is little or no priming across language (mean RP = .05 ± .09 SD, N = 9); it is substantially reduced across modality (mean RP = .38 ± .24 SD, N = 16); and it is largely unaffected by a change in either case (mean RP = .84 ± .11 SD, N = 2) or voice (mean RP = .98, N = 1).

A MODEL OF PERCEPTUAL ANALYSIS

It has been argued that the occurrence of long-term or repetition priming in words reflects the existence of enduring, unitary representations of these words. In this vein, Morton (1969) has suggested that each word is represented by an abstract unit called a *logogen* that is activated as part of the identification process. It is proposed that this activation temporarily lowers the threshold for subsequent reactivation, resulting in the repetition priming effect. Words that differ in their surface form will prime each other as long as they are both represented by a common logogen, whereas words that map onto different logogens will show no mutual facilitation. Some of the results summarized in Fig. 30.1 conform to these expectations. As a first approximation, a change in the case or voice of a word is irrelevant to the amount of priming observed, whereas the amount of priming across language is effectively nil. Presumably, words that differ in case and voice are represented by a single logogen whereas words in different languages, although they may refer to the same concept, are represented by different logogens.

The logogen model is able to account for the effects of language, case, and voice, but is less readily able to account for the intermediate priming effect found for modality. According to this model, or any single-level model, stimuli map onto either the same or different units, meaning that priming should be all or none. Recently, Kirsner, Milech, and Standen (1983) proposed one way of accommodating the logogen model to the existence of partial priming. They posit two levels of lexical representation: one that is modality specific, and one that is modality independent. Words that differ in neither modality nor language map onto common units at both levels and therefore maximally prime each other. Words that differ in language converge upon no common representation and hence fail to prime each other. Words from the same language that differ in modality map onto separate modality-specific units but common modality-independent units, leading to facilitation from only the latter level of analysis.

The explanation of the pattern of data in Fig. 30.1 offered by Kirsner et al. is not the only one possible. However, it embodies three assumptions that may be necessary to any account of these results and that, in themselves, constitute a generalized model of perceptual analysis:

1. *Abstraction:* A stimulus is processed through multiple levels of abstraction. The initial coding of an item is in terms of its physical characteristics, such as color, shape, position, and size, but it is subsequently mapped onto more abstract representations. For present purposes, it is immaterial whether these levels are described as separate codes (Posner, 1969), units (Kirsner et al., 1983), logogens (Morton, 1979), or access pathways (Allport & Funnell, 1981).

2. *Hierarchy:* Although not demanded by priming data alone, we make the usual assumption that the successively more abstract representations of a given

stimulus form a hierarchy of analysis. Different attributes become irrelevant to an internal description of the stimulus at different levels of the hierarchy. A strong variant of this assumption is that the order in which attributes become irrelevant is fixed across tasks.

3. *Priming:* Activation of a stimulus representation at any level of the hierarchy facilitates subsequent reactivation of that representation for some period of time thereafter.

If these assumptions are made, the data summarized in Fig. 30.1 contribute to an account involving at least two, and possibly four, hierarchically organized levels of representation. At the first level, not directly reflected in the repetition priming data, a stimulus representation is specific to its surface form (case if printed, voice if spoken), as well as to its modality and language. The existence of this level may be inferred from other paradigms involving short-term priming effects (e.g., Cole, Coltheart, & Allard, 1974; Posner, 1969).

At the second level of analysis, the stimulus representation is independent of its surface form. For printed words this may constitute either a name code (Posner, 1969), an abstract-letter identity (Besner, Coltheart, & Davelaar, 1984), or a logogen (Morton, 1969), and is common to the same word printed in either upper or lower case. For spoken words this may represent a level at which aspects of the acoustic code, such as its fundamental frequency, have been normalized prior to further segmental analysis (Krulee, Tondo, & Wightman, 1983). This level is directly reflected by the priming effects summarized in Fig. 30.1, where facilitation is relatively insensitive to minor variations in surface form.

At the third level of analysis, differences in modality, as well as surface form, become irrelevant. At this level, the stimulus may be represented by some kind of language-specific abstract rule that subserves both printed and spoken forms. This level is reflected in the partial repetition effects shown in Fig. 30.1 for transfer between modality.

Beyond the third level, it is possible to envisage a conceptual or semantic level at which words expressing the same idea in different languages converge upon a common representation. There is no evidence that this level is reflected in repetition priming, but it may be inferred from the existence of transient interlingual facilitation that occurs when semantically related translations are presented in a two-word lexical-decision task (Kirsner, Smith, Lockhart, King, & Jain, 1984; Meyer & Ruddy, 1974).

There is currently good evidence to suggest the existence of the first, second, and fourth levels of perceptual processing. It could be argued, though, that there is no compelling reason for the existence of a modality-independent representation because the partial facilitation observed across changes in modality may also be explained in terms of the coactivation on some occasions of the alternate modality-specific representation (Allport & Funnell, 1981; Kirsner & Smith,

1974). Although this possibility cannot be excluded, it is rendered somewhat less plausible by the finding of an interaction between priming across modality and word frequency (Kirsner et al., 1983). Low-frequency words prime to a greater extent than high-frequency words, but Kirsner et al. found this effect to be restricted to differences between the control (words not primed) and different modality conditions. High- and low-frequency words have the same effect across same and different modality conditions. According to the present model this implies that differences between high- and low-frequency words are apparent only at the modality-independent level of representation. On the other hand, to explain this result a coactivation model would have to assume that rare words are more likely than common words to activate their corresponding representation in the other modality—an implication that seems counterintuitive.

ATTRIBUTE RETENTION

In the present model, perceptual analysis is assumed to proceed through a hierarchy of levels of increasing abstraction, and activation of a stimulus representation at any level is assumed to leave an enduring record that facilitates its subsequent reactivation. In essence, this record constitutes a "memory" for any particular perceptual analysis. The question we now pose is this: Can the record of the perceptual analysis of an item be used to aid explicit memory for the physical characteristics of that item? For example, suppose a subject is asked to remember that a presented word was spoken and not printed. Later, the subject is shown a printed version of the word and is asked to specify whether it is now in the same or in a different modality to that in which it was originally presented. One way of solving this problem is in some way to compare the perceptual analysis of the current printed form with the perceptual record of the item when first presented. If the two coincide, it may be concluded that the item was presented in the same modality on both occasions. If there is a divergence of analyses up to and including the modality-specific level, the item must have been presented in a different modality on the first occasion. Thus, in principle at least, problems in attribute retention can be solved without recourse to any explicit, episodic memory for the incidental features of words.

If the consequences of perceptual analysis can be used diagnostically in an attribute-retention task, the "memorability" of a particular attribute should be a function of the level of analysis at which differences in the attribute are resolved. In the case of features, such as case and voice, that are assumed to be resolved early in perceptual analysis, there would be few differences between the patterns of activation of words differing on only these attributes. Consequently, diagnosis of the original case or voice of a word on the basis of its perceptual record will tend to be unreliable. On the other hand, differences in language should be relatively easy to detect as the perceptual analyses of translations are distinct up

30. THE PERCEPTUAL RECORD   553

to and including the modality-independent level of abstraction. It follows from this that if the enduring record of perceptual analysis that is assumed to underlie long-term priming effects can be used to aid explicit memory for detail, there should be a relationship between the level of attribute retention and the attribute concerned that parallels the relationship between level of priming and attribute summarized in Fig. 30.1. Specifically, the greater the amount of priming across an attribute, the less well should it be retained.

Figure 30.2 summarizes the results of 27 experiments that examine the recognition or recall of attributes of words presented under incidental learning conditions. That is, subjects were told that they would be tested on their memories for the words but not for the physical details of the words, designated as either language, modality, case, or voice. The dependent variable in Fig. 30.2 is the proportion of correct attribute judgments given that the word itself was correctly recognized or recalled. Consideration was restricted to studies that minimized the contribution of effortful, elaborative processes or semantic cues to aid attribute memory. All studies presented unrelated words in relative isolation to each other.

The pattern of results summarized in Fig. 30.2 parallels the pattern of priming shown in Fig. 30.1. As expected, the greater the facilitation across an attribute,

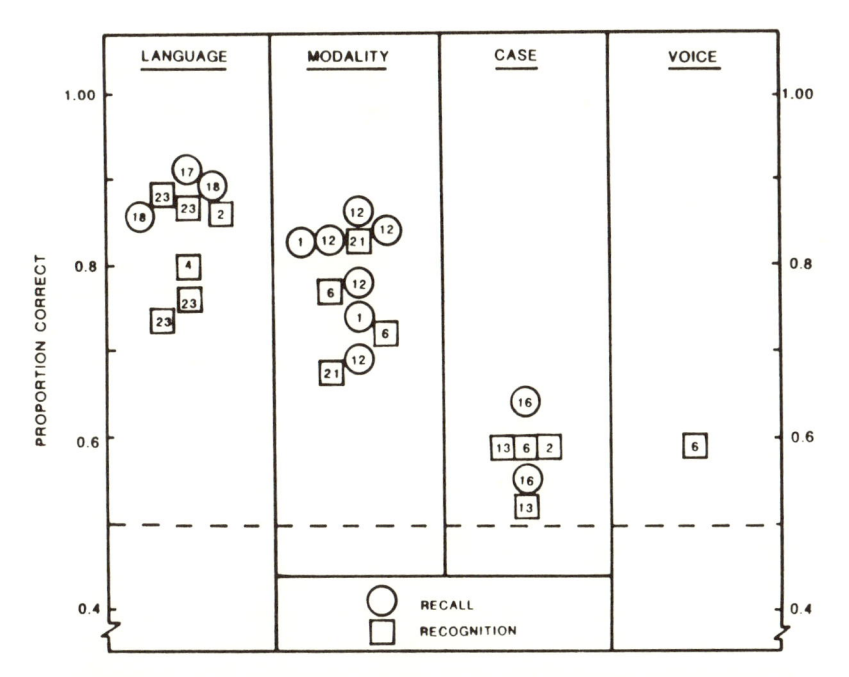

FIG. 30.2. Attribute retention (proportion correct) as a function of attribute and type of test. The enclosed numbers identify cited experiments (e.g., for 1, see Bray & Batchelder, 1972).

and hence the more overlap between perceptual analyses, the poorer is its incidental retention. The mean values summed across experiments are .84 ± .06 SD ($N = 9$) for language, .78 ± .06 SD ($N = 11$) for modality, .59 ± .04 SD ($N = 6$) for case, and .59 ($N = 1$) for voice.

TWO FORMS OF MEMORY

We have suggested that knowledge of the physical characteristics of a stimulus may be available for relatively long periods of time as a direct consequence of its perceptual analysis. Of course, this is not the only way in which such information may be retained. Specifically, attribute data may be stored as a part of an episodic trace of the stimulus and its immediate context. The extent of this memory is assumed to depend on such task-specific features as the kind of instruction given (incidental or intentional learning), the kind of orienting task given during initial study, and the nature of intervening material, as well as organizational strategies available to the subject. Thus, the probability of correctly recovering the status of a stimulus attribute (R_a) will be a function of the probability of recovering this information from either the perceptual record (P_a) or from episodic memory (E). That is:

$$R_a = P_a + E(1 - P_a). \tag{30.2}$$

The variable P is subscripted in order to indicate that its contribution to attribute retention is dependent on the attribute concerned. The differential-attribute effect shown in Fig. 30.2 is assumed to be due entirely to the contribution of perceptual analysis. As a corollary to this, it is also assumed that attributes, in and of themselves, are not differentially encoded into episodic memory. When this does occur—as, for example, when subjects are specifically instructed to remember the modality in which a word is presented—it is a consequence of the demands of the task, not of the attributes themselves. The contribution of P_a is assumed to be fixed across varying tasks and conditions and to be determined solely by the hierarchical nature of perceptual analysis. In this sense, such analysis may be considered to be automatic, whereas the encoding of information into episodic memory is effortful or strategic and its contribution across tasks and conditions, variable.

EXPERIMENT

The model of attribute retention embodied in Eq. 30.2 generates two predictions concerning performance in an attribute-retention task under both incidental and intentional learning instructions. First, under incidental conditions, attribute retention will largely reflect only the assumed structure of perceptual analysis. That is, memory will be best for language, followed by modality, followed by case and voice. Second, if the contribution of episodic memory is increased, by directing subjects to intentionally learn the surface form of each item, the effect on attribute retention will be inversely related to the level of performance under incidental conditions; memory for case and voice will benefit most, followed by modality, followed by language. The experiment described here was designed to test these two predictions.

For comparative purposes, our argument may be contrasted with that developed by Hasher and Zacks (1979). According to Hasher and Zacks, attributes can be divided into two classes: those such as occurrence frequency, temporal information, word meaning, and spatial location, which are automatically encoded into memory, and the remainder, which must be explicitly encoded into memory via effortful, elaborative processing. The present account differs from that proposed by Hasher and Zacks in two ways. The first concerns the manner in which some attribute information may be "automatically" retained. Hasher and Zacks postulate a single memory system to which some attributes have privileged access. In contrast, we propose two kinds of memory for stimulus attributes. Some attribute information will appear to be retained automatically only insofar as its analysis yields a distinct perceptual record.

A second point of departure concerns the status of spatial location. On the basis of a number of results that point to little or no effect of intentionality, concurrent load, and developmental level on memory for spatial location (Mandler, Seegmiller, & Day, 1977; von Wright, Gebhard, & Karttunen, 1975; Zechmeister, McKillip, Pasko, & Bespalec, 1975), Hasher and Zacks have concluded that this attribute is automatically encoded into memory. In our model, however, it seems unlikely that the spatial location of a verbal item would be maintained to a very high level of abstraction. Instead, it may be processed to the same level as case and voice. If so, like case and voice, it should be poorly retained under incidental instructions and show an improvement under intentional instructions.

Method

The experiment consisted of a learning phase, during which subjects were presented with 64 words, followed by a test phase, during which they were presented with 96 pictures. Memory for the words and their attributes was tested with pictures in order to provide a relatively neutral test medium and to exclude or at least minimize solutions based on the direct matching of encoding and test representations. Each stimulus in the learning phase was presented in one of two forms, defined by language (English or Italian), modality (print or speech), case (upper or lower), voice (male or female speaker), and spatial position (left or right). All subjects were informed that they would be given an old/new recognition test of their memories for the names of the words. Attribute-learning conditions varied, being either incidental or intentional.

The entire experimental session lasted approximately 30 min. The learning and test phases lasted 5 min and 15 min, respectively. As there was an interval of approximately 5 min between the two phases, the average period of time between the learning and test presentations was 15 min (range 5 to 25 min). All subjects were tested individually.

Subjects. A total of 120 volunteers acted as subjects. All were aged 35 years or less (mode = 19 years) and were selected from two populations: English–Italian bilinguals ($N = 24$) and English monolinguals ($N = 96$). Bilinguals were so defined by self-report; all spoke Italian at home and had studied the language to at least secondary level. The monolinguals were from an introductory psychology course at the University of Western Australia.

Twelve subjects were randomly allocated to each of 10 groups defined by the factorial combination of the five attributes and two learning conditions, with the necessary proviso that only bilinguals served in the language-relevant conditions.

Because the primary aim of the experiment was to assess memory for attributes given successful recognition of the concept, subjects were discarded and replaced until their observed hit rates in the item-recognition task were significantly greater than their corresponding false-alarm rates (by a one-tailed binomial test, alpha = .05).

Stimuli. The stimuli consisted of 96 concepts: Seventy were selected from the set of 260 described by Snodgrass and Vanderwart (1980), whereas the remaining 26 were selected elsewhere but prepared in the same way. All stimuli were selected from two frequency bands, one having a mean word-frequency count of four per million (range 0 to 9) and the other a count of 123 per million (range 45 to 431).

Each stimulus, whether printed, spoken, or pictured, was recorded on videotape and presented via a TV monitor. During the learning phase, one word was presented every 5 sec and, if printed, subtended 1° to 3° on the horizontal axis. Duration of exposure was approximately 1 sec for both printed and spoken words. All words were presented in English unless language was the relevant attribute, and all were printed unless either modality or voice was relevant. Printed words were presented in upper case unless case was relevant, and spoken words were uttered by a female speaker unless voice was relevant. When spatial position was relevant, stimuli were displaced 3° to either the left or the right of the midpoint of the TV screen. Otherwise, printed words were presented at the center of the screen and spoken words simultaneously to both ears.

Stimuli in the test phase were pictures initially prepared on 5 inch × 8 inch cards and then recorded on videotape. Presentation rate was 1 per 8 sec and stimulus duration was 4 sec. As inspected from a viewing distance of approximately 30 cm, each picture subtended approximately 2° on the vertical and horizontal axes. The first four trials of the learning phase and the first six trials of the test phase drew on a fixed subset of items in all conditions and were treated as practice.

Within each group of 12 subjects, each stimulus appeared equally often as an old item at each level of the attribute being tested (e.g., English or Italian), and as a new item.

Instructions. Subjects learned words in the learning phase under one of two conditions. Under incidental instructions, subjects were told to remember the name of each word, because they were to be given a later recognition test. Although warned that the stimuli would vary on one attribute, these subjects were given no instructions to remember the form in which each word was presented. Under intentional instructions, subjects were told to remember both the name and the form of each word as their memories for both were to be tested in a subsequent recognition test.

Recognition Tests. During the test phase, subjects made two serial responses to each of the 96 pictures. The first was a manual response indicating the status of the presented item (whether old or new), and the second was a verbal response indicating the original value of the relevant attribute (e.g., English or Italian). An "old" item decision was required if the concept depicted by the picture had been presented, as a word, in any form during the learning phase. Otherwise a "new" response was required. Furthermore, in order to assess the relative availability of attribute information given a failure to recognize an old item, subjects were always required to make an attribute decision after each item decision, even though 32 of the test pictures depicted new concepts. All of the words presented in the learning phase also were presented in the test phase.

Picture-Naming Test. Following the recognition test, all subjects were required to name each of the 96 pictures they had previously seen. Bilinguals named each picture in both English and Italian. Whenever the name offered by the subject failed to match the name by which the picture was designated in the original word list, responses to that item were deleted from the analysis of that subject's results. On average, only 9% of responses were so deleted.

Dependent Variables. There are two dependent variables of interest, calculated to control for the effects of guessing and response bias. The first, designated P(item access), estimates the probability of successfully accessing the memory trace of an old item. The second variable, designated P(attribute access/item access), estimates the probability that information about an attribute is available given successful access to the memory trace of the item. Derivations of both measures are outlined in the Appendix.

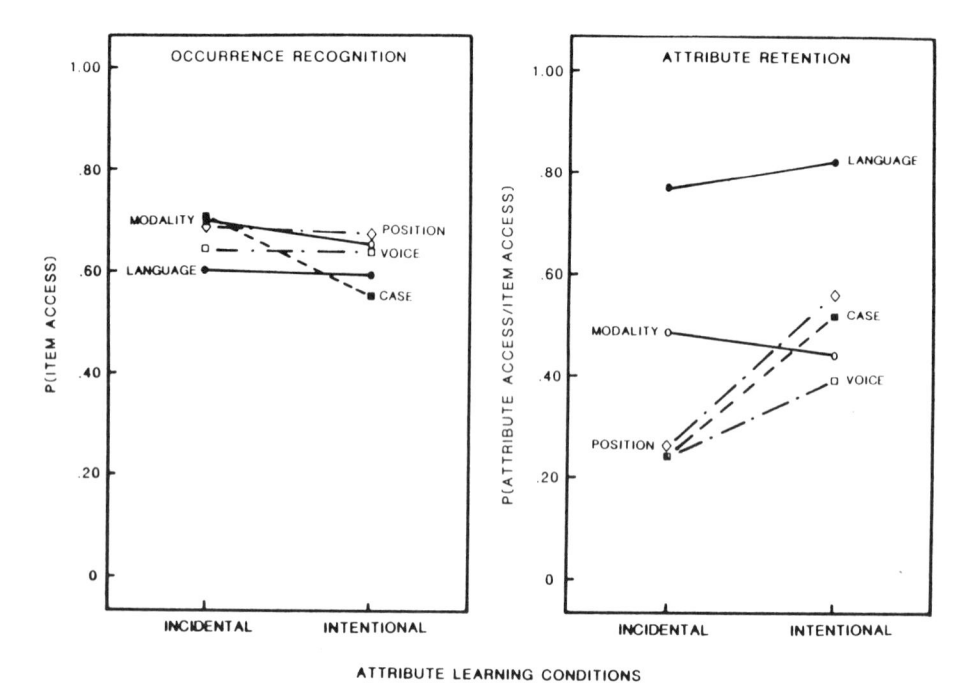

FIG. 30.3. Item and attribute retention as a function of type of attribute and learning condition.

Results

P(item access) is plotted in the left panel of Fig. 30.3 as a function of the tested attribute and learning condition. The data were submitted to a two-way analysis of variance. The factors were attribute (language, modality, case, voice, and position) and learning condition (incidental, intentional). There was no main effect of attribute—$F(4,110) < 1$—and although there was a slight decrement in performance in the intentional condition relative to the incidental condition, this was not significant—$F(1,110) = 2.70$, $MS_w = .021$, $p < .1$. The attribute × learning condition interaction was also not significant—$F < 1$.

P(attribute access/item access) is plotted in the right panel of Fig. 30.3 similarly as a function of attribute and learning condition. Analysis of this measure revealed significant main effects of both attribute—$F(4,110) = 22.77$, $MS_w = .046$, $p < .001$—and learning condition—$F(1,110) = 12.40$, $p < .01$—as well as a significant interaction—$F(4,110) = 2.97$, $p < .05$.

Newman-Keuls tests between the five means in the incidental condition revealed significant differences between language and modality, case, voice, and position, as well as between modality and case, voice, and position. There were no differences between any combination of case, voice, and position.

The model of attribute retention specified by Eq. 30.2 was fitted to the 10 data points plotted in the right panel of Fig. 30.3. This model had six free parameters (an estimate of P_a for each of the five attributes and the difference in E between the incidental and intentional conditions), and accounted for 92.7% of the observed variance—$F(5,4) = 10.13$, $p < .05$.

The overall probability of incorrectly classifying an old item as "new" was .26. Neither the effect of attribute nor learning condition nor the attribute × condition interaction was significant. The overall probability of correctly identifying the original value of an attribute, given a "new" response to an old item, was .54. This value did not differ significantly from chance (.5)—$t(110) = .31$.

DISCUSSION

The results of the experiment confirm the predictions derived from the two-process model outlined earlier. First, the level of attribute retention under incidental conditions was found to depend on the attribute concerned. Memory for language was superior to memory for modality, which, in turn, was superior to memory for either case, voice, or position. This pattern is the same as that summarized in Fig. 30.2 and parallels the pattern of priming effects summarized in Fig. 30.1. The effect of intentionality was to improve attribute retention, but, as predicted by the model, this improvement was inversely related to the level of incidental performance. Memory for case, voice, and position improved to a greater extent than memory for language or modality.

Although the model specified by Eq. 30.2 provided a satisfactory fit to the attribute-retention data summarized in Fig. 30.3, there was no indication of an effect of intention on memory for modality. Lehman (1982) similarly found no effect of instruction on modality retention and suggested that this attribute may by automatically encoded into memory in accordance with the model specified by Hasher and Zacks (1979). As this conclusion rests on a null finding, it must be accepted with caution. According to the current account, only a small effect of intentionality is predicted for modality, and the present between-subjects design may not have had the power to detect this difference.

It also is possible that the observed interaction between attribute and learning condition reflects no more than a ceiling effect—attributes such as language that are well retained incidentally have little room for further improvement under intentional conditions. Although this possibility cannot at present be excluded, it appears unlikely given the margin for improvement evidenced by language (.19) and especially modality (.52).

It has been argued that information concerning the physical attributes of a learned item is available from a record of its perceptual analysis as well as from the explicit retention of the event and its temporal context in episodic memory. This view can be contrasted with the suggestion by Hasher and Zacks (1979) that some fundamental characteristics of an event are automatically retained in episodic memory, whereas other aspects require effortful processing. Within this account, the differential retention of attributes under incidental conditions could be explained in terms of a continuum of automaticity—language is more likely to be automatically encoded, or generally requires less effort, than either case or voice, and so is better retained. Yet, this approach faces two sources of difficulty. The first concerns the status of spatial position. The results of the experiment clearly demonstrate that, under present conditions at least, memory for the spatial position of an item is not automatic—incidental retention was poor and there was a large effect of instruction. Although under other conditions, using different stimuli and definitions of spatial position, the criteria of automaticity may be met, it is difficult to envisage, within the framework offered by Hasher and Zacks, how an attribute can be automatically encoded in some circumstances and effortfully encoded in others. The second source of difficulty concerns the extension of their model to similar effects in other task domains. The value of the model proposed in this chapter is that it provides an independent rationale for and set of predictions concerning performance in an attribute-retention task. Hasher and Zacks' account constitutes a classification scheme for patterns of results found using only this task. It has seemingly few, if any, implications for tasks beyond this domain.

Our aim in this chapter has been to integrate parallel findings across different tasks within a common explanatory framework. The model that has been proposed assumes the existence of two means by which stimulus information may be retained: episodic memory and the perceptual record. Although the application of this distinction to the current context is, we believe, novel, the distinction itself is not. The existence of some record of stimulus encoding has been proposed by Kolers (1973, 1979) as a basis for long-lasting effects of experience, by Marcel (1983) as a basis for conscious perception, and by Gillund and Shiffrin (1984) as a basis for a model of item recognition and recall. Our present contribution is to suggest that such records of perceptual analyses are reflected in both repetition priming and attribute retention.

Given the possibility of two forms of memory for stimulus information, a critical question concerns the extent of their interaction. At one extreme, the perceptual record and episodic memory may be separate systems that contribute independently to attribute retention. If this were so, it should be possible to gain access to some attribute information from the perceptual record in the absence of recognition of the item on the basis of episodic memory. Analogously, Tulving, Schachter, and Stark (1982) found evidence for priming in a fragment-completion task in the absence of explicit word recognition. In the present experiment, however, no such evidence of an independent contribution was found; memory for the attributes of items incorrectly classified as "new" was at chance levels. This suggests that what we have called the perceptual record is accessible only when the item, represented perhaps at the highest level of analysis, is itself accessed in episodic memory.

At the other extreme, only one form of memory may exist. The perceptual record may simply constitute storage within episodic memory of the multiple results of perceptual analysis. Although this version will account for the lack of attribute retention in the absence of item recognition, it less readily accounts for the effects of attribute changes on repetition priming unless a second record of perceptual analysis is also postulated (but see Jacoby, 1983). Resolution of this issue must await future research.

In conclusion, we have proposed the existence of a record of perceptual analysis that underlies repetition priming and is accessible to retrieval processes concerned with memory for detail. We hypothesize that this record is created automatically as a result of the perceptual processing of a stimulus through successive levels of increasing abstraction. Memory for the physical characteristics of a stimulus is based both on this record and the effortful encoding of the stimulus and its context into episodic memory. In this respect, our account differs from that proposed by Hasher and Zacks. Finally, explication of the way in which these two forms of memory may interact awaits further study.

ACKNOWLEDGMENTS

This research was supported by a grant from the Australian Research Grants Scheme. Reprint requests should be addressed to Kim Kirsner, Department of Psychology, University of Western Australia, Nedlands, 6009, Australia.

Appendix

Derivation of P(Item Access) and P(Attribute Access/Item Access)

It is assumed that presentation of an old item enables access to a stored trace of that item with some probability r_i. Given such access, it is assumed that the original status of the attribute concerned becomes available with a further probability r_a. These probabilities are designated P(item access) and P(attribute access/item access), respectively. The following outlines a derivation of each.

Let h_i equal the item hit rate or the probability of calling an old item "old." It is assumed that this is a mixture of the probability of knowing that this is an old item, r_i, and of guessing that it is old, g_i. That is:

$$h_i = r_i + g_i (1 - r_i).$$

Let f_i equal the item false-alarm rate or the probability of calling a new item "old." It is assumed that such an item is never accessed as old (i.e., $r_i = 0$) and consequently will be guessed to be old with a probability g_i:

$$f_i = g_i.$$

Substituting this into the first equation yields the following estimate of P(item access):

$$r_i = (h_i - f_i) / (1 - f_i).$$

Once an old item is successfully accessed, the status of the attribute to be recalled is available with some probability r_a. From the foregoing:

$$P(\text{item access/item hit}) = r_i / h_i;$$
$$P(\text{attribute access/item hit}) = r_i \cdot r_a / h_i.$$

It is assumed that attribute information is either accessed in this way or that the subject guesses its status correctly with a probability g_a. Let h_a equal the probability of correctly recalling the attribute in question given an item hit. From the preceding:

$$h_a = [r_i \cdot r_a + g_a (1 - r_i \cdot r_a)] / h_i.$$

Let f_a equal the probability of incorrectly recalling the attribute in question given an item hit. This must be a guess based on a failure to access attribute information:

$$f_a = [g_a (1 - r_i \cdot r_a)] / h_i.$$

Solving for P(attribute access/item access) yields:

$$r_a = h_i (h_a - f_a) (1 - f_i) / (h_i - f_i).$$

REFERENCES

Allport, D. A., & Funnell, E. (1981). Components of the mental lexicon. *Philosophical Transactions of the Royal Society of London, B295*, 397–410.

Besner, D., Coltheart, M., & Davelaar, E. (1984). Basic processes in reading: Compilation of abstract letter identities. *Canadian Journal of Psychology, 38*, 126–134.

Bray, N. W., & Batchelder, W. H. (1972). Effects of instructions and retention interval on memory of presentation mode. *Journal of Verbal Learning and Verbal Behavior, 11*, 367–374. (1)

Brown, H. L., Sharma, N. K., & Kirsner, K. (1984). The role of script and phonology in lexical definition. *Quarterly Journal of Experimental Psychology, 36A*, 491–506. (2)

Clarke, R., & Morton, J. (1983). Cross-modality facilitation in tachistoscopic word recognition. *Quarterly Journal of Experimental Psychology, 35A*, 79–96. (3)

Cole, R. A., Coltheart, M., & Allard, F. (1974). Memory of a speaker's voice: Reaction time to same- and different-voiced letters. *Quarterly Journal of Experimental Psychology, 26*, 1–7.

Cristoffanini, P., Kirsner, K., & Milech, D. (in preparation). Bilingual lexical representation: The status of English-Spanish cognates. (4)

Dannenbring, G. L., & Briand, K. (1982). Semantic priming and the word repetition effect in a lexical decision task. *Canadian Journal of Psychology, 36*, 435–444.

Durso, F. T., & Johnson, M. K. (1979). Facilitation in naming and categorizing repeated pictures and words. *Journal of Experimental Psychology: Human Learning and Memory, 5*, 449–459.

Gillund, G., & Shiffrin, R. M. (1984). A retrieval model for both recognition and recall. *Psychological Review, 91*, 1–67.

Gough, P. B., Alford, J. A., & Holley-Wilcox, P. (1981). Words and contexts. In O. J. L. Tzeng & H. Singer (eds.), *Perception of print*. Hillsdale, NJ.J: Lawrence Erlbaum Associates.

Harvey, R. (unpublished). *The structure of semantic representation in bilinguals*. Honours thesis, University of Western Australia. (5)

Hasher, L., & Zacks, R. T. (1979). Automatic and effortful processes in memory. *Journal of Experimental Psychology: General, 108*, 356–388.

Hintzman, D. L., Block, R. A., & Inskeep, N. R. (1972). Memory for mode of input. *Journal of Verbal Learning and Verbal Behavior, 11*, 741–749. (6)

Jacoby, L. L. (1983). Perceptual enhancement: Persistent effects of an experience. *Journal of Experimental Psychology: Learning, Memory and Cognition, 9*, 21–38.

Jacoby, L. L., & Dallas, M. (1981). On the relationship between autobiographical memory and perceptual learning. *Journal of Experimental Psychology: General, 110*, 306–340. (7)

Kirsner, K., Brown, H. L., Abrol, S., Chaddha, N. N., & Sharma, N. K. (1980). Bilingualism and lexical representation. *Quarterly Journal of Experimental Psychology, 32,* 585–594. (8)

Kirsner, K., Milech, D., & Standen, P. (1983). Common and modality-specific coding in the mental lexicon. *Memory and Cognition, 11,* 621–630. (9)

Kirsner, K., & Smith, M. C. (1974). Modality effects in word identification. *Memory and Cognition, 2,* 637–640. (10)

Kirsner, K., Smith, M. C., Lockhart, R. S., King, M-L., & Jain, M. (1984). The bilingual lexicon: Language-specific units in an integrated network. *Journal of Verbal Learning and Verbal Behavior, 23,* 519–539. (11)

Kolers, P. (1973). Remembering operations. *Memory and Cognition, 1,* 347–355.

Kolers, P. (1979). Reading and knowing. *Canadian Journal of Psychology, 33,* 106–117.

Krulee, G. K., Tondo, D. K., & Wightman, F. L. (1983). Speech perception as a multilevel processing system. *Journal of Psycholinguistic Research, 12,* 531–554.

Lehman, E. B. (1982). Memory for modality: Evidence for an automatic process. *Memory and Cognition, 10,* 554–564. (12)

Light, L. L., & Berger, D. E. (1974). Memory for modality: Within modality discrimination is not automatic. *Journal of Experimental Psychology, 103,* 854–860. (13)

Mandler, J. M., Seegmiller, D., & Day, J. (1977). On the coding of spatial information. *Memory and Cognition, 5,* 10–16.

Marcel, A. J. (1983). Conscious and unconscious perception: An approach to the relations between phenomenal experience and perceptual processes. *Cognitive Psychology, 15,* 238–300.

Meyer, D. E., & Ruddy, M. E. (1974). *Bilingual word recognition: Organization and retrieval of alternative lexical codes.* Paper presented to the Eastern Psychological Association, Philadelphia.

Monsell, S., & Banich, M. T. (1982). *Lexical priming: Repetition effects across input and output modalities.* Paper presented to the 23rd Annual Meeting of the Psychonomic Society, Minneapolis. (14)

Morton, J. (1969). Interaction of information in word recognition. *Psychological Review, 76,* 165–178.

Morton, J. (1979). Facilitation in word recognition: Experiments causing change in the logogen model. In P. A. Kolers, W. E. Wrolstad, & M. Bouma (eds.), *Processing visible language.* New York: Plenum. (15)

Park, D. C., & Mason, D. A. (1982). Is there evidence for automatic processing of spatial and color attributes present in pictures and words? *Memory and Cognition, 10,* 76–81. (16)

Posner, M. (1969). Abstraction and the process of recognition. In K. W. Spence & J. T. Spence (eds.), *The psychology of learning and motivation* (Vol. 3). New York: Academic Press.

Rose, R. G., & Carroll, J. F. (1974). Free recall of a mixed language list. *Bulletin of the Psychonomic Society, 3,* 267–268. (17)

Saegert, J., Hamayan, E., & Ahmar, H. (1975). Memory for language of input in polyglots. *Journal of Experimental Psychology: Human Learning and Memory, 1,* 607–613. (18)

Scarborough, D. L., Cortese, C., & Scarborough, H. S. (1977). Frequency and repetition effects in lexical memory. *Journal of Experimental Psychology: Human Perception and Performance, 3,* 1–17. (19)

Scarborough, D. L., Gerard, L., & Cortese, C. (1984). Independence of lexical access in bilingual word recognition. *Journal of Verbal Learning and Verbal Behavior, 23,* 84–99. (20)

Siple, P., Fischer, S. D., & Bellugi, U. (1977). Memory for nonsemantic attributes of American Sign Language signs and English words. *Journal of Verbal Learning and Verbal Behavior, 16,* 561–574. (21)

Snodgrass, J. G., & Vanderwart, M. (1980). A standardized set of 260 pictures: Norms for name agreements, image agreements, familiarity, and visual complexity. *Journal of Experimental Psychology: Human Learning and Memory, 6,* 174–215.

Tulving, E., Schachter, D. L., & Stark, H. A. (1982). Priming effects in word-fragment completion are independent of recognition memory. *Journal of Experimental Psychology: Learning, Memory and Cognition, 8,* 336–342.

von Wright, J. M., Gebhard, P., & Karttunen, M. (1975). A developmental study of the recall of spatial location. *Journal of Experimental Child Psychology, 20,* 181–190.

Watkins, M. J., & Peynircioglu, Z. F. (1983). On the nature of word recall: Evidence for linguistic specificity. *Journal of Verbal Learning and Verbal Behavior, 22,* 385–394. (22)

Winograd, E., Cohen, C., & Barresi, J. (1976). Memory for concrete and abstract words in bilingual speakers. *Memory and Cognition, 4,* 323–329. (23)

Zechmeister, E. B., McKillip, J., Pasko, S., & Bespalec, D. (1975). Visual memory for place on the page. *Journal of General Psychology, 92,* 43–52.

31 Dissociable Domains of Selective Processing

William A. Johnston
Veronica J. Dark
University of Utah

ABSTRACT

Relevant and irrelevant words were exposed for 67, 200, or 500 msec before being backward masked. Awareness of relevant words increased sharply with exposure duration. Physical and semantic levels of perceptual processing were measured in terms of identity priming and semantic priming, respectively. A test word was primed by a replica of itself in the former case and by a semantic associate in the latter case. Relevant prime words surpassed irrelevant prime words on both measures, but this effect was confined to longer exposure durations in the case of semantic priming. Controlled processing was measured in terms of recognition accuracy on a delayed test. Relevant words surpassed irrelevant words on this measure, but only at longer durations of original exposure. The semantic-priming data and recognition data described corresponding patterns, but the identity-priming data described a different pattern. As a composite, the data indicate that perceptual processing and controlled processing are dissociable and that selective processing can begin during perceptual processing.

INTRODUCTION

General Framework

This research addresses two main issues: dissociations in processing and the loci of selective processing. We develop these issues in terms of a dual-process conception of stimulus processing. Such a conception distinguishes between two qualitatively distinct domains of processing (e.g., LaBerge, 1975; Marcel, 1983a; Posner & Snyder, 1975; Shiffrin & Schneider, 1977). We refer to these domains as perceptual processing and controlled processing. Perceptual processing yields an internal representation of a stimulus. It can be partitioned roughly into physical processing and semantic processing. The physical properties of the stimulus are encoded during physical processing and the semantic/conceptual properties of the stimulus are encoded during semantic processing. The physical and semantic codes comprise the perceptual representation of the stimulus. This representation is transitory and nonconscious unless it undergoes, or is transformed by, controlled processing. Controlled processing yields a more durable, conscious representation of the stimulus. One way to distinguish empirically between the two general domains of processing is to show that the same manipulation can have differential effects on measures of the two domains.

In principle, dissociations in processing provide a useful tool for localizing the effects of various experimental manipulations. The manipulation of principal concern in this chapter is that of stimulus relevancy. In a focused-attention task, observers are instructed to attend to relevant stimuli and ignore irrelevant stimuli. Do these instructions affect just the controlled processing accorded the two classes of stimuli, or do they affect perceptual processing as well? This question defines the classical issue of the locus of selective attention. Early-selection theories allow selective processing of relevant and irrelevant stimuli to begin during perceptual processing (e.g., Broadbent, 1958; Johnston & Dark, 1982; Kahneman & Treisman, 1984; Treisman, 1964). Late-selection theories claim that as long as the two classes of stimuli are equally clear and familiar they will necessarily receive an equal amount of perceptual processing and can differ only in terms of amount of controlled processing (e.g., Deutsch & Deutsch, 1963; Duncan, 1980; Marcel, 1983a; Shiffrin & Schneider, 1977).

An apparently straightforward way to empirically settle this theoretical controversy is to see if stimulus relevancy has dissociative effects on measures of the two domains of processing. Late-selection theories call for dissociative effects, and early-selection theories allow for corresponding effects. However, before conducting this test, one must first consider whether perceptual processing and controlled processing are in fact, rather than just in principle, empirically dissociable. We briefly review the literature on the empirical dissociability of perceptual processing and controlled processing, and then we outline the rationale behind our test for dissociative effects of stimulus relevancy.

Dissociations in Processing

Dissociative phenomena, especially those involving aware and unaware forms of processing, have attracted considerable empirical and theoretical interest (e.g., Jacoby & Witherspoon, 1982; Kahneman & Treisman, 1984; Nisbett & Wilson, 1977). The dissociative phenomena reported by Marcel (1983b) are of particular relevance to the present research. In some of his experiments (Experiments 4 and 5), Marcel measured the perceptual processing of a *prime* word (e.g., CHILD) in terms of the extent to which it facilitated the speed of a lexical (word/nonword)-decision response to a test word (e.g., INFANT). In one condition, the prime word could be easily seen and control processed. In another condition, the prime was followed by a visual mask at a stimulus-onset asynchrony (SOA) so short that the observers could only guess whether or not a word had even been presented. The priming effect averaged 62 msec in the former condition and 56 msec in the latter condition. Thus, the prevention of controlled processing of the prime word did not affect its potency as a semantic prime. Similar results have been reported by others (e.g., Fischler, 1977; Fowler, Wolford, Slade, & Tassinary, 1981).

These findings support the use of semantic priming as a measure of perceptual processing in studies of dissociations between the two domains of processing. However, other data indicate that semantic priming is affected by controlled processing and, therefore, is suspect as a dissociable measure of perceptual processing. For example, Smith, Theodor, and Franklin (1983) investigated the effect of depth of processing of primes on both semantic priming of lexical decisions and subsequent episodic memory. Depth of processing is regarded as a manipulation of controlled processing, and episodic memory is regarded as a measure of controlled processing (e.g., Fisk & Schneider, 1984). When subjects searched the primes for asterisks or for particular letters, semantic priming was not obtained and episodic memory for the primes was negligible. When subjects named or semantically categorized the primes, both semantic priming and episodic memory were substantial. Similar findings have been reported by others (e.g., Henik, Friedrich, & Kellogg, 1983; Parkin, 1979).

In summary, the literature is ambiguous with respect to a dissociation between semantic-priming potency of a word and measures of controlled processing of the word. On the one hand, studies represented by Marcel (1983b) indicate that semantic-priming potency is not diminished by a manipulation (e.g., backward masking of prime) that curtails a measure of controlled processing of the prime (e.g., detection of prime presentation). On the other hand, studies represented by Smith et al. (1983) indicate that semantic priming is facilitated by a manipulation (e.g., depth of prime processing) that also enhances a measure of controlled processing of the prime (e.g., episodic memory of primes). This empirical ambiguity leaves in doubt the fundamental dissociability of perceptual processing and controlled processing, and it constitutes a caveat with respect to any attempt to use processing dissociations as a tool for localizing the effects of stimulus relevancy.

Selective Processing

Johnston and Dark (1982) measured the semantic-priming potency of relevant and irrelevant words in a focused-attention task. Significant semantic priming was obtained only for relevant words. In the context of the kind of data reported by Marcel (1983b), this finding indicates that stimulus relevancy affects perceptual processing and, therefore, supports early-selection theories. However, in the context of the kind of data reported by Smith et al. (1983), this finding can be attributed to the effect of stimulus relevancy on controlled processing and, therefore, is ambiguous with respect to early- and late-selection theories.

One way to diagnose the effect of stimulus relevancy on semantic priming is to delimit controlled processing and observe whether the effect is diminished. We know of three studies in which this tact was taken. Allport, Tipper, and Chmiel (this volume) curtailed controlled processing of the primes via Marcel's (1983b) backward-masking procedure, and they found uniformly high semantic priming for both relevant and irrelevant stimuli. These data indicate that semantic priming is a dissociable measure of perceptual processing, and they support late-selection theories with respect to the locus of the effects of stimulus relevancy. Hoffman and MacMillan (this volume) curtailed semantic priming via the depth-of-processing procedure of Smith et al. (1983), and they observed a marked reduction in semantic priming for both relevant and irrelevant words. These data contraindicate semantic priming as a dissociable measure of perceptual processing, and they are mute with respect to the locus of effects of stimulus relevancy. Finally, Dark, Johnston, Myles-Worsley, and Farah (1984) curtailed controlled processing by reducing duration of prime exposure (without backward masks). They found a large effect of stimulus relevancy on semantic priming even at durations of prime exposure too short to support recognition memory. These data indicate that semantic priming is a dissociable measure of perceptual processing, and they support early-selection theories with respect to the locus of the effects of stimulus relevancy.

There were many differences in procedure between these experiments, some of which undoubtedly contributed to the differences in the findings. In any event, the available evidence is ambiguous with respect to both the loci of selectivity of processing and the utility of semantic priming as a tool for assessing these loci. The present research attempted to make some progress toward a resolution of this ambiguity.

Experimental Rationale

The present research attempted to measure both perceptual processing and controlled processing of relevant and irrelevant words presented in the course of a focused-attention task. We measured perceptual processing in terms of semantic priming and another priming-like measure described in the next section. We measured controlled processing in terms of recognition memory. The strong dependence of recognition memory on controlled processing was nicely demonstrated by Fisk and Schneider (1984). In addition, we manipulated the opportunity for controlled processing of the words by manipulating word-exposure duration via Marcel's (1983b) backward-masking procedure. Two main questions were asked:

1. Does the direct manipulation of controlled processing affect only measures of controlled processing and not measures of perceptual processing?
2. Does stimulus relevancy affect only measures of controlled processing and not measures of perceptual processing?

The first question addresses the issue of dissociations in processing, and the second question addresses the issue of the loci of selective processing.

Strong support for late-selection theory would be yielded by a positive empirical answer to both questions. This outcome would mean that the two domains of processing are empirically dissociable and that stimulus relevancy affects only the domain of controlled processing. Strong support for early-selection theory would be yielded by a positive answer to the first question but a negative answer to the second question. This outcome would mean that the two domains of processing are empirically dissociable and that stimulus relevancy affects both domains of processing. Hence, if measures of perceptual processing remain intact even when measures of controlled processing are reduced to a minimum, then the presence or absence of an effect of stimulus relevancy on perceptual processing would be fairly decisive with respect to the loci of selective processing.

Unfortunately, a negative answer to the first question would leave in doubt both the empirical dissociability of perceptual processing and controlled processing and, indeed, the validity of two-process theories that distinguish between the two domains of processing. If the direct reduction of controlled processing curtails to an equal extent measures of both domains of processing, then the basic dissociation needed to probe the loci of selective processing would not be present. However, if the direct reduction of controlled processing curtails measures of controlled processing more than measures of perceptual processing, then the two domains would be partially dissociable, and perhaps dissociable enough to shed some light on the loci of selective processing.

Measurement of Physical Processing

Semantic priming was supplemented in the present research by a measure intended to reflect physical, or nonsemantic, aspects of perceptual processing. This measure was used for two main reasons. First, the evidence is ambiguous with respect to the sensitivity of semantic priming to controlled processing. The use of an additional measure of perceptual processing might increase our chances of empirically dissociating perceptual processing from controlled processing. Second, the use of a measure of physical processing would allow us to explore the possibility of selectivity at nonsemantic levels of perceptual processing.

The measure that we chose to serve these purposes is based on the perceptual-fluency, or perceptual-repetition, effect studied by Jacoby (e.g., Jacoby, 1983; Jacoby & Dallas, 1981) and others (e.g., Eich, 1984; Feustel, Shiffrin, & Salasoo, 1983; Kirsner & Smith, 1974). The nature of this effect is that a single prior presentation of a stimulus can enhance the perceptibility of the stimulus if it is repeated in the same experimental context. We refer to this effect as *identity priming*.[1] We used the identity-priming potency of words as our supplementary measure of perceptual processing.

Identity priming appears to serve both of the purposes specified earlier. First, unlike semantic priming, identity priming is not affected by depth-of-processing manipulations of the prime stimulus (e.g., Jacoby & Dallas, 1981). Second, identity priming differs from semantic priming in important ways: It survives long prime-test intervals, it requires that the physical features of the prime be preserved in the test stimulus (e.g., Feustel et al., 1983; Jacoby & Dallas, 1981), and it requires that the processing of the prime be data driven as opposed to conceptually driven (Jacoby, 1983). Thus, the available evidence suggests that this measure both is dissociable from controlled processing and reflects the physical analysis of the prime stimulus.

METHOD

Subjects and Design

The subjects were 90 male and female undergraduate students at the University of Utah. They earned credit toward a higher grade in an introductory psychology course for their participation. The design was a 2 (word relevancy) × 3 (word-exposure duration) factorial with repeated measures on both factors. Measures were taken of identity priming, semantic priming, and recognition memory for both relevant and irrelevant words at all exposure durations. An additional measure, report accuracy, was taken on relevant words to establish that exposure duration affected observers' awareness of the words.

Apparatus and Main Task

The experiment was controlled by a Terak 8510A computer system. Subjects viewed a series of 2136 word pairs. Each word was displayed in one of four cells, which were arranged in the form of a cross. The two horizontal cells shared a common border and the two vertical cells were separated by the two horizontal cells. The display was centered on the screen of a Zenith (Model ZVM121) television monitor. At the approximate viewing distance of 60 cm, the display subtended 1.9° vertically and 5° horizontally. The words were center adjusted in

---

[1] It is perhaps a misnomer to refer to this perceptual-augmentation effect as *priming*. The effect is more likely to be based on episodic retrieval at the time of the second (test) presentation of physical representations established by the first presentation (e.g., Jacoby & Dallas, 1981; Feustel et al., 1983).

the cells. The visual angle was 2.5° between the centers of the two horizontal cells and 1.5° between the centers of the two vertical cells.

Two of the cells were called relevant and the other two cells were called irrelevant. The horizontal cells were relevant for half the subjects and the vertical cells were relevant for the other half. One word in each pair was always in a random one of the relevant cells and the other word was in a random one of the irrelevant cells. Each word was followed by a 33 msec backward mask (row of nine Xs) at SOAs of 67, 200, or 500 msec.[2] The short duration was set at 67 msec because that duration was both easily managed by our computer and very close to the average awareness threshold reported by Marcel (1983b). The two words in a pair were exposed for the same duration. The interval between the masks and the next pair of words was 550 msec. Thus, the SOA for successive word pairs varied from 617 msec for the shortest exposure duration to 1050 msec for the longest. The three exposure durations were represented equally often in the series of word pairs.

For 135 of the word pairs (45 at each exposure duration) a question mark appeared 250 msec after the mask in the cell that had contained the relevant word. The subjects' main task was to monitor the relevant cells and to try to report those relevant words that were followed by a question mark. The subjects were encouraged to guess when they were not sure what the relevant word was. An interval of 3 sec was allowed for the subjects' verbal reports, and then the task was resumed. A 15 sec rest period was provided after approximately every 50 word pairs. The subjects were advised to rest their eyes during these periods. A warning buzzer sounded after 12 sec in each rest period so that subjects could get ready for the resumption of the task.

The subjects served individually. They were seated in a small room across a hall from the experimenter's area. The subjects wore headsets over which 60 db of white noise was generated in order to mask out external noises. The experimenter also wore headsets over which he or she could hear subjects' verbal responses.

Measures

Controlled Processing. Degree of awareness of relevant words was measured in terms of immediate-report accuracy. In addition, amount of controlled processing of both relevant and irrelevant words was measured in terms of subsequent recognition memory. Recognition was tested for 60 words altogether, 10 words for each combination of word relevancy and exposure duration. In

---

[2]The actual durations of stimulus exposure were 33 msec less than the SOAs. Thus, the exposure durations of 67, 200, and 500 msec were really *effective* durations that included 33 msec of iconic storage.

order to guard against a floor effect on recognition performance, each of the 60 words was presented twice under the same conditions of relevancy and exposure duration. The interval between repetitions was filled with a minimum of 15 other word pairs.

The recognition test was given after the completion of the main task. The subjects were not forewarned of this test. The test was a forced-choice one in which each old word appeared next to a new distractor and subjects indicated which word they thought (or guessed) was old by pushing a left- or a right-hand button. The two words appeared on opposite sides of the center of the screen, and the position of the old word (left or right) was determined randomly, with the restriction that old words appear in each position equally often. The test was subject-paced with a 1 sec delay between the response to one pair and the presentation of a new pair. After the recognition test, subjects were debriefed and dismissed.

Semantic Processing. The amount of semantic processing of relevant and irrelevant words in the main task was measured in terms of semantic priming. A word whose semantic processing was to be measured served as a semantic prime for a *test word* that was presented in lieu of what would have been the next word pair in the series. The four-cell display was replaced by a test word on which a random pattern of 300 dots was superimposed. The dots were then removed at the rate of one dot every 20 msec. The subject's task was to verbally identify the test word before it became completely clear. The subject's microphone was linked to the computer by a voice key. As soon as the subject made an identification attempt, the word was fully clarified and stayed that way for 1 sec so that the subject could see if his or her response was correct. The latency of identification was scored by the computer, and accuracy was scored by the experimenter. The main attention task resumed 500 msec after the termination of the test word.

There were 45 test words: five for each of the six combinations of relevancy and prime exposure duration, and 15 that were used to establish a baseline identification latency against which semantic priming could be measured in the six experimental conditions. The baseline test words were preceded equally often by nonprime words at each of the three exposure durations. Altogether, then, there were nine test-word conditions: six entailed priming and three were baseline conditions.

Physical Analysis. The amount of physical analysis of relevant and irrelevant words was measured in terms of identity priming. A word whose physical analysis was to be measured was presented again as a test word after an interval containing at least 10 other events (e.g., word pairs, report trials, and other test words). A new set of 45 test words was needed to measure physical analysis: They were distributed across conditions in exactly the same way as were the test words that were used to measure semantic analysis. That reliable identity priming can be obtained with our word-clarification procedure has been shown by Dark et al. (1984), Johnston, Dark, and Jacoby (1985), and Feustel et al. (1983).

Stimulus Material and List Construction

The words were all nouns three to nine letters in length. The main bulk of the words (filler and nonprime words) were randomly drawn, with replacement, from a pool of 500 words generated from the Kučera and Francis (1967) norms. The report words were also selected from the Kučera and Francis norms but they were used only once. The recognition-test words consisted of 60 pairs of words from the Paivio, Yuille, and Madigan (1968) norms. For a given subject, one word in each pair was old and one was new. What were old words for half of the subjects were distractors for the other half. The words represented a wide range of both frequency and imagery, but the two words in a pair were matched on these dimensions. The assignment of old words to the six combinations of word relevancy and exposure duration was counterbalanced across subjects.

The 45 prime-test pairs that were needed to measure semantic processing were selected from associative and priming norms that we had previously collected on 210 words from 150 University of Utah students. The 45 pairs were arranged into nine sets of five pairs. The sets were matched as closely as possible in terms of normative values of both baseline-identification latency of the test words and amount of semantic priming. Each set was assigned to a different one of the nine (six priming and three baseline) conditions of semantic priming for each subject. The sets were rotated across conditions for different subjects such that each test word served equally often in all nine conditions and each prime word served equally often in all six priming conditions.

The 45 words needed for identity priming were also drawn from our norms. They were arranged in nine sets of five words matched as closely as possible in terms of baseline identification latency. The norms do not provide values of identity priming in terms of which the sets might otherwise have been matched. The nine sets were rotated across the nine identity-priming conditions for different subjects such that each word was represented equally often in each condition.[3]

The main task consisted of a sequence of 2231 events or frames. Of these, the first 150 were considered practice and included 15 report words and five non-primed test words. The remaining 2081 events comprised 1676 filler pairs, the

---

[3]An alternative experimental design would have been to use the same nonprimed baseline for both semantic priming and identity priming. However, this alternative requires a more complicated counterbalancing scheme to control for item effects, and it does not allow for conditions within subjects to be matched in terms of normative values of priming and baseline latencies as closely as they were in our experiment.

135 report words, the 60 twice-presented words for the recognition test, 30 semantic primes, 30 physical primes, and 90 test words (45 for measuring semantic priming and 45 for measuring physical priming). The report words, recognition words, and prime words were each accompanied by a filler word. Words were assigned randomly to positions in the sequence of events with several restrictions in addition to those already mentioned. The three exposure durations were represented across every succession of three report words, the nine conditions of semantic priming were represented across every succession of nine of the test words entailed in these conditions, and the nine conditions of physical priming were represented across every succession of nine of the test words entailed in these conditions. Further, no word in any of the following categories could occur within two positions of another word in any of these categories: report word, recognition word, identity prime word, identity test word, and semantic prime-test pair. Finally, no word in any of these categories could be represented in another category or as a filler word.

RESULTS

The main data are summarized in Fig. 31.1. We report the results for each measure separately. Statistical results were considered significant at $p < .05$.

Controlled Processing

Report Accuracy. As the upper left panel of Fig. 31.1 reveals, report accuracy increased regularly with word-exposure duration—$F(2,178) = 1673.16$, $MS_e = .006$. Although the report accuracy for words exposed for 67 msec was higher than what we expected on the basis of Marcel's (1983b) results, the data clearly show that exposure duration had a strong effect on awareness of the words. Moreover, subjects correctly reported only around 29% of the words that were exposed for 67 msec even though they ventured guesses for 83% of these words. Our own subjective experience with the task was one of not seeing the words in an aware way but of sometimes correctly guessing them anyway (see Allport, 1977). Thus, we suspect that 29% is an inflated estimate of the level of awareness of relevant words exposed for 67 msec.

Recognition Accuracy. Recognition data were lost for five subjects owing to experimenter error. Statistical analyses were conducted on the data for the remaining 85 subjects. The data are summarized in the upper right panel of Fig. 31.1. Recognition accuracy was greater for relevant words than for irrelevant words—$F(1,84) = 43.18$, $MS_e = .031$—and increased with exposure duration—$F(2,168) = 7.03$, $MS_e = .021$. However, these effects were qualified by an interaction—$F(2,168) = 4.99$, $MS_e = .034$. A Newman-Keuls test indicated

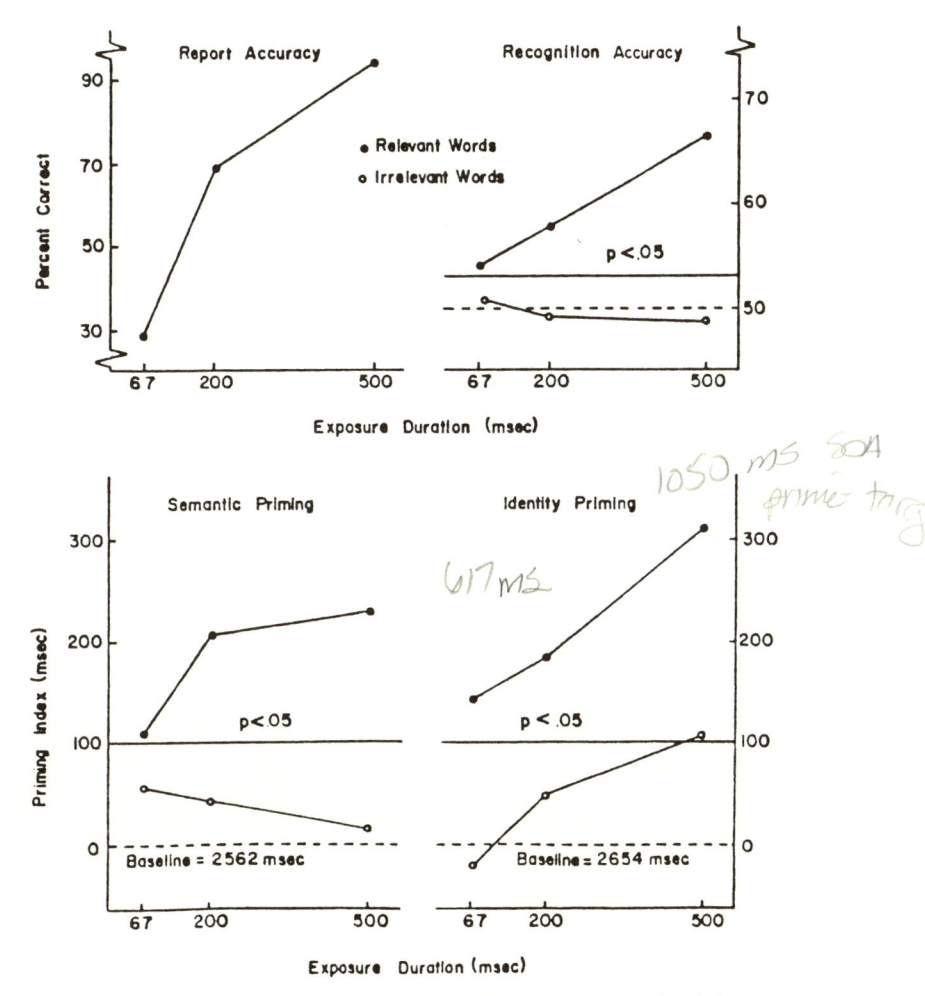

FIG. 31.1. Immediate report accuracy, recognition accuracy, semantic priming, and identity priming as a function of duration of word exposure. (Accuracy data are in terms of percent correct and priming data are in terms of msec below baseline-identification latency. Solid circles indicate data for relevant words, and open circles indicate data for irrelevant words. A solid line running above and parallel to the horizontal axis in a panel indicates the approximate level of the measure needed for statistical significance.)

that recognition increased with exposure duration only for relevant words and increased with relevancy only at the medium and long exposure durations. However, recognition was significantly above chance for relevant words even at the short duration of exposure—$t(84) = 2.94$, $S_e = .016$.

Summary. As a composite, the report-accuracy and recognition-accuracy data suggest that controlled processing is directly dependent on exposure duration for relevant words and is minimal for irrelevant words. Consequently, controlled processing is greater for relevant words than for irrelevant words only when exposure duration is long enough to allow for controlled processing of the relevant words. Report accuracy, which was obtained only for relevant words, increased across exposure durations by a factor of 3.35. The extent to which recognition of relevant words exceeded chance (50%) increased by the almost identical factor of 3.4. This correspondence suggests that the two measures reflect a common process. We now assess the extent to which the variations in our priming measures correspond to the variations in our measures of controlled processing.

Perceptual Processing

Semantic Priming. Identification latency for nonprimed test words did not differ as a function of the duration of exposure of the nonprime words that preceded them—$F(2,178) = 2.01$, $MS_e = 320030$. Therefore, a single identification latency was computed for each subject as the baseline from which semantic-priming indices could be derived. This baseline averaged 2562 msec. A semantic-priming index was computed by subtracting from the baseline a subject's mean latency of identification of primed test words. A positive index means that priming speeded up identification. A priming index was computed for each combination of word relevancy and exposure duration for each subject. Incorrectly identified test words were excluded from these computations. Approximately 85% of the semantic-priming test words were correctly identified. The semantic-priming data are summarized in the lower left panel of Fig. 31.1.

An analysis of variance of the semantic-priming indices revealed a significant effect only for prime relevancy—$F(1,89) = 10.86$, $MS_e = 243093$. Despite the trends evident in Fig. 31.1, neither duration of prime exposure nor the duration-by-relevancy interaction approached statistical significance ($Fs < 1$.). As Fig. 31.1 indicates, significant priming was obtained for relevant words even at short exposures and was not obtained for irrelevant words even at long exposures. In analyses of the simple main effects, exposure duration did not approach statistical significance for either relevant or irrelevant words ($Fs < 1$). However, whereas the effect of prime relevancy was reliable at both the long—$F(1,89) = 7.01$, $MS_e = 297182$—and the medium—$F = 4.15$, $MS_e = 273936$—exposures, it was not reliable at the short exposure duration—$F < 1$. Thus, despite the absence of a significant interaction in the overall analysis, we are inclined to accept the conclusion that the effect of stimulus relevancy increased with exposure duration.

Identity Priming. Identity-priming indices were computed in the same manner as were semantic-priming indices. Again, the lack of a difference between the three baseline conditions ($F < 1$) justified the use of a single baseline (2654 msec). Approximately 82% of the identity-priming test words were correctly identified. The data are summarized in the lower right panel of Fig. 31.1.

An analysis of variance indicated that identity priming increased with both stimulus relevancy—$F(1,89) = 13.05$, $MS_e = 293412$—and exposure duration—$F(2,178) = 3.52$, $MS_e = 268651$—and that there was no tendency for these variables to interact—$F < 1$. The lack of an interaction was confirmed by tests of the simple main effects of stimulus relevancy. Identity priming was greater for relevant than for irrelevant words even at the short duration of exposure—$F(1,89) = 3.99$, $MS_e = 309467$. As Fig. 31.1 indicates, significant priming was obtained for relevant words even at the short duration of exposure and, importantly, even for irrelevant words at the long duration.

Summary. Our two measures of perceptual processing showed only partial correspondence. Both measures increased with stimulus relevancy and, for relevant words, both increased across exposure durations by a factor of about 2.2. Even so, the two measures are dissociated in two important respects. First, the effect of stimulus relevancy obtained even at the shortest exposure duration in the case of identity priming but not in the case of semantic priming. Second, for irrelevant words, identity priming increased across exposure durations to a statistically reliable level, but semantic priming remained low and even decreased slightly. These dissociations suggest that the two priming measures reflect somewhat different processes.

DISCUSSION

As Fig. 31.1 reveals, the semantic-priming data and the recognition data display the same general pattern. Both measures were consistently below the significance line for irrelevant words and above the line for relevant stimuli. In addition, in the case of relevant words, both measures increased across exposure durations. The picture is more one of correspondence than of dissociation, and it is consistent with the argument that semantic priming is sensitive to controlled processing (e.g., Henik et al., 1983; Smith et al., 1983). The picture runs counter to the dissociative effects reported by Marcel (1983b) even though we used his backward-masking procedure to manipulate controlled processing. If we accept this picture as an accurate description of the data, then we must accept the possibility that the effect of stimulus relevancy on semantic priming found in this study and in prior research (e.g., Dark et al., 1984; Johnston & Dark, 1982) is based on controlled processing rather than on perceptual processing. Ancillary evidence for a controlled-processing contribution to semantic priming is that, in a postexperimental interview, 44% of the subjects indicated that they were aware that some of the test words were preceded by semantic primes.

On the other hand, the degree of correspondence between semantic priming and recognition is less than perfect. Duration of exposure of relevant words had a larger (3.4 to 2.2) and more reliable effect on recognition accuracy than on semantic priming. In addition, two 67 msec exposures of a relevant word raised recognition accuracy only 4.7 percentage units above chance, but only one such exposure yielded a semantic-priming index of 105 msec. In terms of absolute level, the latter effect is more impressive than the former. Moreover, using very similar procedures, Dark et al. (1984) found a much more striking dissociation between the two measures. In their study, a reduction in exposure duration of relevant words led to a decrease in recognition memory but actually yielded an increase in semantic priming. Hence, the dissociability of semantic priming and recognition memory remains unclear.

By contrast, the identity-priming data and the recognition data define quite distinguishable patterns. The only correspondence is that both measures increase with exposure duration for relevant stimuli. However, this increase is 35% larger for recognition memory. In addition, although the increase in identity priming might be based on controlled processing, a plausible alternative interpretation is that it is based on data-driven perceptual processing. Physical processing must be to some extent data limited, and our manipulation of exposure duration might well have affected the amount and quality of stimulus data on which physical processing ultimately depends (see Norman & Bobrow, 1975, for a discussion of data- and resource-limited processing).

There are two important dissociations between identity priming and recognition memory. One is that the effect of word relevancy at 67 msec of word exposure was statistically reliable only in the case of identity priming. Two short exposures of a relevant word raised percentage recognition only 4.7 units above chance level, but only one such exposure raised the speed of test-word identification by 141 msec. This large identity-priming index for a briefly flashed word is all the more remarkable considering that the prime-test interval was filled with at least 10 intervening events. The second dissociation between the two measures occurred with respect to irrelevant words exposed for 500 msec. Two long exposures of an irrelevant word failed to raise recognition memory above chance level, but only one such exposure was sufficient to raise identity priming to a statistically significant level. Auxillary evidence that identity priming was not influenced by controlled processing is that none of our subjects indicated awareness of the identity primes in our postexperimental interviews.

These dissociations indicate that identity priming is sensitive to a form of processing that is not reflected in recognition memory. We suggest that this form of processing is perceptual in nature. Thus, the identity-priming data are less ambiguous than the semantic-priming data with respect to both of the main issues to which this research was addressed. A comparison of the identity-priming data with the recognition memory data provides evidence both for a fundamental dissociation between perceptual processing and controlled processing and for the early-selection proposition that perceptual processing is selective.

We offer the following tentative interpretation of our findings: Processing at all levels is selective but data limited. At an exposure duration of 67 msec, irrelevant words received little or no processing of any kind, and relevant words underwent substantial physical processing, some semantic processing, and a small amount of controlled processing. As exposure duration was increased, physical processing increased regularly for both relevant and irrelevant words, but semantic and controlled processing increased only for relevant words. Identity priming reflected the variations in physical processing, recognition accuracy reflected the variations in controlled processing, and semantic priming reflected composite variations in both semantic processing and controlled processing. Because identity priming appears to be less sensitive to controlled processing than semantic priming, we recommend that it be considered for use in future studies of dissociations between perceptual processing and controlled processing.

We address a final comment to our failure to reduce report accuracy to a nil level even with a 67 msec duration of word exposure. Not only does this failure conflict with Marcel's (1983b) data, but it provides a lingering thread of evidence with which to salvage a late-selection interpretation of our findings. Specifically, one can argue that 67 msec allowed for some controlled processing of relevant words, not enough to support a relevancy effect in terms of either recognition memory or semantic priming, but enough to support an above-zero level of report accuracy and a relevancy effect in terms of identity priming.

One way to more firmly resolve the issue might be to reduce exposure duration even further. The problem with this procedure is that it is also likely to reduce the quality of the stimulus data well below the data limits of physical processing. An alternative procedure might be to reduce report accuracy to a chance level by adding a second task, one that diverts enough controlled processing from the words that those exposed for relatively short durations cannot be reported. If a relevancy effect on identity priming were still evident under these conditions, then a late-selection interpretation of the data would be more difficult to salvage.

ACKNOWLEDGMENTS

We thank Jann Farah, Marina Myles-Worsley, and Jay Brummett for their help in conducting this experiment.

REFERENCES

Allport, D. A. (1977). On knowing the meaning of words we are unable to report: The effects of visual masking. In S. Dornic (Ed.), *Attention and performance VI* (pp. 505–553). Hillsdale, NJ: Lawrence Erlbaum Associates.

Broadbent, D. E. (1958). *Perception and communication*. London: Pergamon Press.

Dark, V. J., Johnston, W. A., Myles-Worsley, M. M., & Farah, M. J. (1984). *Levels of selection and capacity limitations*. Manuscript submitted for publication.

Deutsch, J. A., & Deutsch, D. (1963). Attention: Some theoretical considerations. *Psychological Review, 70*, 80–90.

Duncan, J. (1980). The locus of interference in the perception of simultaneous stimuli. *Psychological Review, 87*, 272–300.

Eich, E. (1984). Memory for unattended events: Remembering with and without awareness. *Memory & Cognition, 12*(2), 105–111.

Feustel, T. C., Shiffrin, R. M., & Salasoo, A. (1983). Episodic and lexical contributions to the repetition effect in word identification. *Journal of Experimental Psychology: General, 112*, 309–349.

Fischler, I. (1977). Associative facilitation without expectancy in a lexical decision task. *Journal of Experimental Psychology: Human Perception and Performance, 3*, 18–26.

Fisk, A. D., & Schneider, W. (1984). Memory as a function of attention, level of processing, and automatization. *Journal of Experimental Psychology: Learning, Memory, and Cognition, 10*(2), 181–197.

Fowler, C. A., Wolford, G., Slade, R., & Tassinary, L. (1981). Lexical access with and without awareness. *Journal of Experimental Psychology: General, 110*, 341–362.

Henik, A., Friedrich, F. J., & Kellogg, W. A. (1983). The dependence of semantic relatedness effects upon prime processing. *Memory & Cognition, 11*, 366–373.

Jacoby, L. L. (1983). Remembering the data: Analyzing interactive processes in reading. *Journal of Verbal Learning and Verbal Behavior, 22*, 485–508.

Jacoby, L. L., & Dallas, M. (1981). On the relationship between autobiographical memory and perceptual learning. *Journal of Experimental Psychology: General, 3*, 306–340.

Jacoby, L. L., & Witherspoon, D. (1982). Remembering without awareness. *Canadian Journal of Psychology, 36*, 300–324.

Johnston, W. A., & Dark, V. J. (1982). In defense of intraperceptual theories of attention. *Journal of Experimental Psychology: Human Perception and Performance, 8*, 407–421.

Johnston, W. A., Dark, V. J., & Jacoby, L. L. (1985). Perceptual fluency and recognition judgments. *Journal of Experimental Psychology: Human Learning and Memory, 11*, 3–11.

Kahneman, D., & Treisman, A. (1984). Changing views of attention and automaticity. In R. Parasuraman & R. Davies (Eds.), *Varieties of attention* (pp. 22–61). New York: Academic.

Kirsner, K., & Smith, M. C. (1974). Modality effects in word identification. *Memory & Cognition, 2*, 637–640.

Kučera, H., & Francis, W. N. (1967). *Computational analysis of present-day American English*. Providence: Brown University.

LaBerge, D. (1975). Acquisition of automatic processing in perceptual and associative learning. In P. M. A. Rabbitt & S. Dornic (Eds.), *Attention and performance V* (pp. 50–64). New York: Academic.

Marcel, A. J. (1983a). Conscious and unconscious perception: An approach to the relations between phenomenal experience and perceptual processes. *Cognitive Psychology, 15*, 238–300.

Marcel, A. J. (1983b). Conscious and unconscious perception: Experiments on visual masking and word recognition. *Cognitive Psychology, 15*, 197–237.

Nisbett, R. E., & Wilson, T. D. (1977). Telling more than we can know: Verbal reports on mental processes. *Psychological Review, 84*, 231–259.

Norman, D. A., & Bobrow, D. G. (1975). On data-limited and resource-limited processes. *Cognitive Psychology, 7,* 44–64.

Paivio, A., Yuille, J. C., & Madigan, S. A. (1968). Concreteness, imagery, and meaningfulness values for 925 nouns. *Journal of Experimental Psychology Monograph Supplement, 76*(1, Pt. 2).

Parkin, A. J. (1979). Specifying levels of processing. *Quarterly Journal of Psychology, 31,* 179–195.

Posner, M. I., & Snyder, C. R. R. (1975). Attention and cognitive control. In R. L. Solso (Ed.), *Information processing and cognition: The Loyola symposium* (pp. 55–85). Hillsdale, NJ: Lawrence Erlbaum Associates.

Shiffrin, R. M., & Schneider, W. (1977). Controlled and automatic human information processing: II. Perceptual learning, automatic attending, and a general theory. *Psychological Review, 84,* 127–190.

Smith, M. C., Theodor, L., & Franklin, P. E. (1983). The relationship between contextual facilitation and depth of processing. *Journal of Experimental Psychology: Learning Memory and Cognition, 9,* 697–712.

Treisman, A. M. (1964). Verbal cues, language and meaning in selective attention. *American Journal of Psychology, 77,* 206–219.

32 Is Semantic Priming Automatic?

James E. Hoffman
Frank W. MacMillan
University of Delaware

ABSTRACT

The time to decide that a letter string (e.g., "doctor") is a word is reduced when it is preceded by a related word ("nurse"). At least some component of this semantic priming effect is thought to be automatic and therefore free of attentional limitations. The present series of experiments investigated this claim by engaging subjects in an attention-demanding activity at the time of presentation of the prime word. The results indicated that the usual semantic priming effect could be eliminated and in some cases reversed ("negative priming") if encoding processes on the concurrent task occurred in close temporal proximity to the prime word. Delaying this encoding process resulted in priming for both attended and unattended prime words. Semantic priming appears to be a "weakly" automatic process. It can occur for both attended and unattended words but can be suppressed by simultaneous memory encoding of other information.

INTRODUCTION

William James (1890) once claimed that "everyone knows what attention is." A few years later, Titchener (1908) noted that once experimental psychologists began investigating the topic, they unleashed a whole "hornets' nest" of new problems. And recently, Kinchla (1980) reported that the hornets are still on the wing.

One could claim with equal conviction that everyone knows what practice can do, for everything from hitting a tennis ball to becoming literate. Recent research on automatization, however, raises the possibility of another invasion of stinging insects. The distinction between well-practiced skills that are automatic and unfamiliar tasks that depend on attention are so striking as to virtually demand an explanation in terms of qualitatively different processes. Perhaps the clearest statement of this difference is offered by Schneider and Shiffrin (1977) and Shiffrin and Schneider (1977), who draw a distinction between "automatic processes" that do not use attention and controlled processes that do. Recent research, however, suggests that at least some kinds of attention may play a role in several tasks thought to be automatic.

In the area of visual search, Schneider and Shiffrin (1977) suggested that performance is automatic when search time is relatively independent of the number of items in the display. There are several difficulties in accepting this "zero-slope" criterion as an unambiguous sign of automaticity. First, this ideal is rarely, if ever, met. As pointed out by Eriksen and Spencer (1969), Kinchla (1974), and Duncan (1980), even an ideal observer should show some effect of set size. Increases in the number of inputs increases the probability of false alarms and therefore lowers d'. Attention can only be invoked as an explanation of set-size effects if their magnitude exceeds that predicted by an ideal observer model (Sperling, 1984). Shaw (1984) reported that after 34 sessions of searching for the same target set, subjects had greater set-size effects than would be predicted for an ideal observer. Therefore, there appears to be a limited-capacity process playing a role in well-practiced and presumably automatic search tasks.

In addition to set-size effects, patterns of dual-task interference provide a criterion for evaluating automaticity. If two tasks suffer when performed together relative to single-task control levels, then one may conclude that they are competing for some limited commodity. Hoffman, Nelson, and Houck (1983) recently showed that a search task meeting several criteria for being automatic was nonetheless susceptible to dual-task interference. The pattern of interference effects suggested that the search process requires access to the spatial attention system. Diverting attention away from the location of the targets made them difficult to detect and easy to ignore. Kahneman and Treisman (1984) report similar results for the task of reading common words.

The preceding results appear to rule out the claim that the entire task of reading a word or detecting a familiar target can be done without any attention. It is still possible, however, that these stimuli are processed to a semantic level without attention; one could maintain that all the tasks reviewed so far are limited in fairly "late" stages involved with decisions and responses. One might, therefore, look to "indirect" measures of processing that reflect these earlier levels of representation. This is precisely the reasoning used by Johnston and Dark (1982) in a recent study that provided the main impetus for the present investigation. They review evidence suggesting that semantic priming reflects relatively "early" processing levels that are separate from the limited-capacity system or "working memory" that is thought to be the source of attentional limitations by automaticity theorists (Shiffrin & Schneider, 1977). One kind of finding that is consistent with this view is Marcel's (1983) report that words that are pattern masked so that they cannot be identified nonetheless produce normal semantic priming. If semantic priming is also affected by variations in spatial attention, then one could conclude that attention is operating relatively early in the processing system.

Johnston and Dark (1982) report a clever experiment showing that words presented in an "attended" channel produce greater priming than unattended words. Given the claim that priming is a "pure" measure of early processing, this result offers valuable evidence on the site of attention. It is consistent with the claim that subjects filter unattended material so that it only weakly activates the lexical system. They also suggest that unattended material may be actively inhibited.

The Johnston and Dark results are a convincing demonstration of early attentional effects only to the degree to which priming provides a "pure" measure of automatic activation of the semantic network. Unfortunately, there is considerable evidence that priming is not only produced by automatic, spreading activation but that it is also influenced by limited-capacity, strategic processes that reflect subjects' active expectations about the relation between prime and target (Neeley, 1976; Posner & Snyder, 1975). Presumably, attended words in the Johnston and Dark study would have access to these limited-capacity processes, an advantage denied to unattended words. Thus, the priming advantage of attended words may reflect, to an unknown degree, the contributions of late, limited-capacity processes. Johnston and Dark considered this to be an unlikely possibility, partly because very few subjects were aware of a semantic relationship between the prime and target words in their experiment. Nonetheless, it seemed worthwhile to create a paradigm specifically designed to prevent strategic processing of the prime word.

EXPERIMENT 1

The first experiment was designed to assess the influence of spatial attention on semantic priming while blocking the access of prime words to "late," limited-capacity processes. The sequence of events on each trial is illustrated in Fig. 32.1. The prime word is presented in the center of the display and is surrounded by a "near" and "far" array of alphanumeric characters. There are three conditions. In the attend-prime condition, the subject is instructed to silently read the prime word. This display is followed approximately 1 sec later by a letter string on which the subject performs a lexical decision. This condition should indicate whether we can obtain semantic priming when the subject attends to the prime word.

In the "attend-near" condition, the subject is required to search the array closest to the prime word in order to determine the position of a digit. The

FIG. 32.1. The sequence of events occurring on each trial in Experiment 1. A prime word is presented at the center of the display along with two arrays: one located close to the prime ("near") and the other remote ("far"). In the search conditions, the subject is required to determine the location of a digit in either the near or far arrays. Following an ISI of 1130 msec, a letter string is presented requiring a speeded lexical decision.

"attend-far" condition is similar except that the subject must search the outer array for the target. The purpose of the search tasks is to occupy the subject with a demanding task during the interval between the prime and lexical decision string, thus preventing the subject from engaging in "strategic processing" of the prime word. The attend-near condition should allow greater sharing of spatial attention than the far condition because previous research has shown that the attentional field forms a gradient around the attended position, with forms within about 1° of visual angle being processed to a semantic level (Eriksen & Hoffman, 1973; Hoffman & Nelson, 1981; Shaffer & LaBerge, 1979). A filtering view would predict greater priming for the near than the far condition.

Method

Subjects. Subjects were 24 undergraduates (11 males and 13 females) at the University of Delaware; they were paid for serving in a single session.

Apparatus and Stimuli. Prime and target words were three to eight letters in length and subtended 3° of visual angle. The near array was a rectangle 1.49° × 4.23° in size centered on the fixation point. The corresponding dimensions for the far array were 6.17° × 4.23°. All stimuli were presented on an Apple II microcomputer equipped with a millisecond timer.

Procedure. Each session consisted of three blocks of 72 trials corresponding to the attend-prime, attend-near, and attend-far conditions. Each trial consisted of the sequence of events shown in Fig. 32.1. The prime and search arrays shared identical onsets and were shown for 64 msec and 128 msec, respectively. The prime word was preceded and followed by masks. A lexical decision string was presented 1130 msec later and the subject was required to make a speeded yes/no judgment as to whether or not the string was a word. Responses were made via the computer keyboard. In the search conditions, the subject was then required to choose one of four positions as having contained a digit. The target digit was chosen at random from the set {56789}. Distractor letters came from the set {ACDEFHIJMP}.

Half of the trials consisted of nonwords. Of the remaining 36 trials, 18 consisted of words that were related to the prime and 18 were unrelated pairs. Related pairs were chosen from the norms provided by Palermo and Jenkins (1964) and Postman and Keppel (1970) as well as pairs used by Meyer and Schvaneveldt (1971). Finally, these sources were supplemented from pairs agreed upon by the laboratory staff to produce a total pool of 108 pairs of related words.

Words were never repeated during the session for any subject. In addition, different lists were counterbalanced among the different conditions for different subjects so that a given lexical decision word appeared as a member of both a related and an unrelated pair in each condition. This procedure ensured that any differences in priming in different conditions could not be attributed to characteristics of the particular lexical decision strings.

Results and Discussion

Error rate on the search task was 6.2% and 11.7% for the attend-near and attend-far conditions, respectively. This difference was significant—$F(1,23) = 13.6, p < .05$—and shows, not surprisingly, that the search task was more difficult when the array was positioned on less sensitive foveal areas. More importantly, the high accuracy indicates that subjects were performing the search task as required by the instructions.

Median reaction times for correct lexical decision trials are shown in Table 32.1. Planned comparisons contrasted related and unrelated pairs for each instructional condition. First, in the attend-prime condition, lexical decisions were faster when preceded by an associated prime than an unrelated word—$F(1,23) = 11.7, p < .05$. This simply replicates the well-known semantic priming effect. Requiring subjects to search either the near or far arrays for a target at the time of prime presentation completely eliminated this facilitory effect—both $Fs < 1$.

The error rates in the lexical decision task are also shown in Table 32.1. In the attend-prime condition, there was an accuracy advantage when the lexical decision string was preceded by a related word—$F(1,23) = 9.3, p < .05$. Similar to the case with reaction time, this difference was eliminated when the subject was searching the near array—$F < 1$. Surprisingly, facilitation was reinstated in the attend-far condition—$F(1,23) = 7.3, p < .05$. These results are opposite to what would be expected on the basis of a spatial-attention mechanism. Recall that we predicted more facilitation for the attend-near condition because this arrangement should have allowed greater sharing of attention with the prime word.

What are the differences between the two search conditions that mediate these differences in priming? One possibility is suggested by the lexical decision time

TABLE 32.1
Median Reaction Time (Msec) and Percent Error Rate
for the Lexical Decision Task in Experiment 1
as a Function of Attention Condition
and the Relationship between Prime and Target

Attention Condition	Prime/Target Relationship	Median	Error Rate
Attend prime	Associated	523	4.2
	Unassociated	547	8.3
	Nonword	597	8.3
Attend near	Associated	547	6.0
	Unassociated	549	4.3
	Nonword	614	7.0
Attend far	Associated	558	3.5
	Unassociated	564	7.5
	Nonword	628	5.5

data. Table 32.1 shows that subjects were slightly slower in the search conditions than in the attend-prime condition, suggesting that the search task was more difficult than simply remembering the prime word. This greater difficulty, in turn, means that subjects are more likely to still be engaged in the search task when the lexical decision string appears. In addition, this delay was greater for the far condition than the near, which is commensurate with the slower transmission times and poorer acuity that accompanies increasing retinal eccentricity. These considerations lead to the following tentative hypothesis: Semantic priming will be eliminated when memory encoding occurs in close temporal proximity to the prime word. The obvious exception is when it is the prime word itself that is being encoded. This hypothesis would explain the greater priming obtained in the attend-far condition as being due to the delay in locating and encoding the position of the target.

EXPERIMENT 2

These considerations led to a change in paradigm. The prime display consisted of two words, one above and one below the fixation point. This display was preceded, at an ISI of 96 msec, by two arrows pointing to one of the two words. In the "word condition," the subject was instructed to report the cued word. In the "letter-search" condition, the subject determined whether a target letter was present in the cued word. The prime display was followed 650 msec later by a letter string, on which the subject performed a lexical decision. Finally, the subject reported either the cued word or the presence/absence of the target letter.

The logic behind this arrangement is similar to that of Experiment 1. The cue position controls the location of attention. The requirement to perform a letter search is designed to prevent strategic processing of the prime word as a whole. This Experiment provides a more sensitive manipulation of spatial attention because, even in the search condition, attended words should be in the center of the attentional field. If spatial attention modulates semantic priming even in the letter-search condition, then one might have some confidence in concluding that these attentional effects do not reside in later, strategic processes.

Method

Subjects. Subjects were 36 undergraduates at the University of Delaware (17 males and 19 females); they were paid for participating in a single session. All subjects were right handed and had normal or corrected-to-normal vision.

Apparatus and Stimuli. These were identical to Experiment 1 with the following exceptions: The prime display now consisted of two words, one above and one below the fixation point. The vertical separation between the centers of the two strings was 1°.

Procedure. The sequence of events on each trial was as follows: The two prime words were preceded by a pair of arrows with an ISI of 96 msec. The display was shown for 64 msec and no masks were employed. The lexical decision string was presented 650 msec later. Following the lexical decision, subjects were prompted for a decision regarding the prime display. In the attend-word condition, they were shown one word and had to indicate whether or not it was the cued word. On negative trials, the choice word was taken from the to-be-ignored position. Positive and negative instances were shown equally often.

In the search condition, the sequence was preceded by a display of a single letter. Subjects were to search the cued word and determine whether the target letter was present. They indicated this decision after making their lexical decisions. Target letters occurred on half the trials and were never present in the to-be ignored word.

Each session consisted of two blocks of 48 trials, corresponding to the word-report and letter-search conditions. Each block consisted of an equal number of word and nonword trials for the lexical decision task. Within the word trials, three categories were of interest: In the "associated-cued" condition, an associate of the lexical decision word occurred in the cued position. The uncued position contained an unassociated word. In the "associated-uncued" condition, the related word occurred in the uncued position. In the "unassociated" condition, unassociated words were presented in both positions. These three conditions were each represented by eight trials in a block.

As in Experiment 1, different lists were constructed and counterbalanced among subjects so that a given lexical decision word occurred in the associated-cued, associated-uncued, and unassociated conditions equally often for both the word-report and letter-search conditions.

Results and Discussion

Error rates on the "secondary task" of reporting the cued word or searching it for a letter were 6.4% and 8.4%, respectively, and did not differ according to the nature of the cued word. These relatively low error rates indicate that subjects were performing the assigned tasks.

The median reaction times for correct trials on the lexical decision task are shown in Table 32.2. In the word condition, subjects were faster at deciding that a string was a word when it was preceded by an associated word in the attended position (associated-cued) than when neither prime word was related to the target (unassociated)—$F(1,35) = 5.7, p < .05$. This is the expected semantic facilitation effect. Moving the related word to an unattended position (associated-uncued) completely eliminated this priming effect—$F < 1$. It is interesting to note that an examination of *mean* RTs revealed an "inhibition effect" of 21 msec in which the associated-uncued condition was slightly slower than the unassociated condition. This effect was, however, of only marginal significance—$F(1,35) = 3, p < .09$. Overall, our results are in agreement with those of Johnston and Dark (1982) in showing that more priming is obtained for attended words than unattended words.

An answer to the question of whether this priming advantage is due to early filtering or late, strategic processing is provided by the letter-search data. Having a related word in the attended position still produces a small but marginally

TABLE 32.2
Median Reaction Time (Msec) and Percent Error Rate
for the Lexical Decision Task in Experiment 2
as a Function of Attention Condition
and the Relationship between Prime and Target

Attention Condition	Prime/Target Relationship	Median	Error Rate
Attend word	Associated-Cued	555	6.1
	Associated-Uncued	593	7.8
	Unassociated	580	8.2
	Nonword	632	7.0
Attend letter	Associated-Cued	597	5.0
	Associated-Uncued	616	4.5
	Unassociated	613	6.7
	Nonword	664	6.0

significant facilitation in lexical decision relative to the case in which the word occurs in a to-be-ignored position—$F(1,35) = 3.5$, $p < .066$. Thus, if we are right in assuming that subjects cannot engage in strategic processing of the prime word when they are engaged in letter search, these results indicate that semantic priming is affected by spatial attention without the contribution of later controlled processing.

Notice that our paradigm does not require an immediate response to the search task, which raises the possibility that subjects may be reading the word and searching it for the target letter after performing the lexical decision. If this were the case, then it might not be surprising that we obtained priming for the attended word, even in the letter-search condition. It is unlikely that all subjects are following this strategy because lexical decisions in the letter-search condition are significantly slower than in the word condition, as would be expected if subjects were still engaged in the search task at the moment of prime presentation. A possibility that is more difficult to reject is that a subset of subjects are simply reading the word in the search condition and that these subjects are responsible for the semantic priming that we observed. We evaluated this possibility by computing the correlation between the overall difference in RT between the search and word conditions and the amount of semantic facilitation obtained in the search condition. This correlation should be negative if semantic priming is only obtained for subjects who adopt the strategy of reading the word and searching it later. The correlation was $-.05$, which was not significantly different from zero.

The present data show no semantic facilitation for words falling outside the focus of spatial attention. One might be tempted to conclude that unattended words are not processed to the semantic level, a position compatible with "early filtering" positions. Two considerations, however, suggest caution in accepting this conclusion. First, the results are at odds with Experiment 1, which showed semantic priming for to-be-ignored words. This result was only observed in error rates in the attend-far condition. The present experiment did not produce any significant effects of priming on error rates, but there was a hint of semantic processing of the unattended word in the reaction-time data. This consisted of a small (21 msec in mean RT) "negative-priming" effect in which subjects were slower with a related word in an unattended position than when there were no related words in the display. This effect was not statistically reliable ($p < .09$) but it may be a weak manifestation of negative-priming effects that have been observed in other experiments. Underwood and Thwaites (1982), Lupker and Katz (1981), and Allport, Tipper, and Chmiel (this volume), among others, have found negative-priming effects although the range of conditions employed by these different investigators makes comparisons somewhat tenuous.

We can expand our original simultaneous encoding hypothesis in the following way: When subjects encode information into memory, they engage an inhibitory process that suppresses to-be-ignored representations. This inhibition process may extend to semantically related material and slow down its later access.

The longer this inhibition process is delayed, the more facilitation accrues in memory representations for both attended and unattended material.

The simultaneous-encoding hypothesis accounts for the present results in the following way: In the first experiment, encoding is delayed in the attend-far condition, allowing activity to accumulate in the node representing the prime word. This activation manifests itself as a facilitation in accuracy in the lexical decision task. In contrast, the attend-near condition allows rapid encoding in the search task and, consequently, inhibition of the prime word. This inhibition is transitory and, at an ISI of 1130 msec, there is no trace of priming, either positive or negative.

In the second experiment, the lexical decision word is presented close enough in time (650 msec) to the prime word to observe some remnants of the inhibition process in the form of negative priming. The letter-search condition is more difficult than the word-report condition and therefore its encoding is delayed sufficiently to allow some facilitation of the attended word to accumulate before inhibition is applied. For the unattended word in the search condition, we may be seeing something like a balance between inhibition and excitation that results in an absence of priming, either positive or negative.

It is interesting to compare the present results with three other related studies. Henik, Friedrich, and Kellogg (1983), Smith (1979), and Smith, Theodor, and Franklin (1983) found that performing a letter search on a prime word eliminated the semantic priming of a subsequently presented test word. One of the studies presented by Smith (1979), however, did find significant accuracy priming under these conditions whereas the present study found priming in RT. It may be that the critical variable determining whether one obtains RT or accuracy priming in the letter-search task is the ISI between prime and target words. The present study used a short ISI of 650 msec whereas Henik et al. (1983), Smith (1979), and Smith et al. (1983) used relatively long ISIs (> 1500 msec).

EXPERIMENT 3

The foregoing considerations suggest that *accuracy* priming should be obtained in the search condition of Experiment 2 at long ISIs. Experiment 3 replicated Experiment 2, but with increases in the ISI between prime display and lexical decision target to 1500 msec. The main prediction was that accuracy priming would be obtained for both attended and unattended words in the search condition.

Method

Subjects. Subjects were 36 undergraduates at the University of Delaware (10 males and 26 females); they were paid for their participation in a single session. All other details of apparatus, stimuli, and procedure were identical to those in Experiment 2 with the exception of the ISI between prime and target display, which was increased from 650 to 1500 msec.

Results and Discussion

Error rates on the word report and search tasks averaged 6.7% and 8.3%, respectively, and did not vary with the nature of the prime-target relationship.

The median RT for correct trials is shown in Table 32.3. The difference between associated-cued and associated-uncued conditions in the word-report condition was marginally significant—$F(1,35) = 3.4$, $p < .08$. None of the effects of prime type approached significance in the letter-search condition—all $Fs < 1$. These results replicate the RT pattern of the previous experiment in showing no priming produced by an unattended word. In addition, the requirement to perform a letter search on a word eliminates semantic priming, a result in agreement with Smith (1979), Smith et al. (1983), and Henik et al. (1983) who used comparably long ISIs.

The error rates in the lexical decision task are of primary interest in this Experiment and are also shown in Table 32.3. First, consider the case when subjects are instructed to read the cued word. They are significantly more accurate when an associated word occurs in the attended position than when it occurs in an unattended position—$F(1,35) = 5.7$, $p < .05$. This pattern is similar to that observed in the RTs. The situation is different when the task is letter search. Both the associated-cued and associated-uncued conditions are more accurate than the case in which related words do not occur in either position—$F(1,35) = 13.8$, $p < .05$, and $F(1,35) = 4.6$, $p < .05$, respectively.

TABLE 32.3
Median Reaction Time (Msec) and Percent Error Rate
for the Lexical Decision Task in Experiment 3
as a Function of Attention Condition
and the Relationship between Prime and Target

Attention Condition	Prime/Target Relationship	Median	Error Rate
Attend word	Associated-Cued	589	4.2
	Associated-Uncued	611	8.4
	Unassociated	608	7.0
	Nonword	678	4.4
Attend letter	Associated-Cued	598	2.8
	Associated-Uncued	593	4.2
	Unassociated	597	8.0
	Nonword	670	5.0

The results of Experiment 3 confirm that prime words in unattended positions are processed to the semantic level. This result was obtained only when subjects were in the search condition at relatively long ISIs. These conditions appear to be similar to those in Experiment 1, which revealed the same result. In both cases, unattended words produced semantic priming in error rates in those conditions in which memory encoding would be delayed relative to the time of presentation of the prime word. The implications of this result for the nature of semantic priming are explored in the following final discussion.

FINAL DISCUSSION

The set of experiments reported here was designed to reveal the influence of attention on semantic priming, a process thought to have some automatic component. First, the results are suffcient to reject a "strong" version of automaticity for this task. Requiring subjects to read one word eliminated the semantic priming produced by another, to-be-ignored word. Thus, semantic priming appears to be vulnerable to interference from other ongoing mental activities, a clear violation of the claim of automaticity.

There appears to be two components to the effect of attention on semantic priming. First, words that fall within the focus of spatial attention produce more priming than unattended words, even when a letter-search task prevents access to later, strategic processing. These results are in agreement with the results and conclusions of Johnston and Dark (1982) in showing that spatial attention plays a role in semantic priming.

There is also a second factor influencing the magnitude of semantic priming. At long SOAs between prime and target, even words within the focus of attention failed to produce semantic priming in RT when subjects performed a letter search on the word. We did, however, find evidence of semantic facilitation in error rates, a result also reported by Smith (1979) for a similar task.

These results suggest that the degree of semantic processing of to-be-ignored material is related to the memory-encoding operations being conducted on attended material, a position we call the *simultaneous encoding hypothesis*. This states that all words, attended and unattended, initially access semantic representations in long-term memory. If the subject simultaneously encodes information about display aspects other than the word, a suppression mechanism is applied to all active memory nodes. This suppression is capable of affecting associated concept nodes as well. The suppression mechanism can be manifested in two ways. At short ISIs between prime and lexical decision, words that are related to the ignored word may produce longer lexical decision times than unrelated words. This "negative priming" was observed in a weak form in the present experiment but has been observed by many previous investigators, primarily when a word or picture is to be ignored (Allport et al., this volume; Lupker & Katz, 1981; Underwood & Thwaites, 1982).

When encoding of information other than the prime word is delayed, the inhibition process is delayed and activation of long-term memory representations accumulates for both attended and unattended material. Activation by to-be-ignored words occurred in two experiments reported here, but only in terms of *accuracy* of the lexical decision. We do not yet know if accuracy and RT reflect different aspects or stages in the lexical decision process but, in any case, these accuracy effects have occasionally been observed in other studies. Smith (1979) found that requiring subjects to perform a letter search on a word eliminated semantic priming in RT. A semantic-facilitation effect was still observed in the accuracy of the decision. In addition, Zimba and Blake (1983) showed that prime words in a suppressed eye do not produce RT priming. Their data do show an accuracy advantage for these words although no statistical analysis of these data was reported.

A more recent report by Allport et al. (this volume) shows consistent negative priming from pictures that subjects are to ignore. Interestingly, in a condition in which display durations are too short for accurate report of either the attended or unattended pictures, negative priming was eliminated and replaced by facilitation. This finding is consistent with the simultaneous encoding hypothesis advanced here because failure to encode the attended picture would eliminate the suppression mechanism and result only in the facilitation effect. They only observed negative priming, however, when subjects responded to complex target pictures consisting of two overlapping shapes. Further work is required to determine whether these different manifestations of negative priming reflect a single underlying mechanism.

The simultaneous encoding hypothesis is obviously post hoc and too vague to be considered as a model of the effects of attention on priming. It does, however, offer a good heuristic for organizing the present data as well as several findings reported by others in the priming literature. It suggests that semantic priming is not a "module" free of top-down influence, as suggested recently by Fodor (1983). Priming appears to be a "weakly automatic" process in terms of the scheme of Kahneman and Treisman (1984). Priming will occur passively without the benefit of attention but it can be influenced by other simultaneous mental activities. Thus, priming appears to be similar to other "automatic" activities in being vulnerable to dual-task interference (Hoffman et al., 1983; Kahneman & Treisman, 1984).

A final comment concerns the methodological implications of the present experiments. First, error rates in priming studies may reveal effects when RT measures do not. Second, the time interval between prime and lexical decision may be important in determining whether negative priming effects are observed as well as whether accuracy or RT will be the more revealing measure. Finally, when priming is examined in dual-task situations, the relative onset of encoding operations may be a critical factor in the amount of priming observed.

ACKNOWLEDGMENT

This research was supported by the Army Research Office under contract No. DAAG 29–83–K–0049.

REFERENCES

Duncan, J. (1980). The locus of interference in the perception of simultaneous stimuli. *Psychological Review, 87,* 272–300.
Eriksen, C. W., & Hoffman, J. E. (1973). The extent of processing of noise elements during selective encoding from visual displays. *Perception and Psychophysics, 14,* 155–160.
Eriksen, C. W., & Spencer, T. (1969). Rate of information processing in visual perception: Some results and methodological considerations. *Journal of Experimental Psychology Monograph, 79,* 1–16.
Fodor, J. (1983). *The modularity of mind.* Cambridge, MA: MIT Press.
Henik, A., Friedrich, F. J., & Kellogg, W. A. (1983). The dependence of semantic relatedness effects upon prime processing. *Memory and Cognition, 11,* 366–373.
Hoffman, J. E., & Nelson, B. (1981). Spatial selectivity in visual search. *Perception and Psychophysics, 30,* 283–290.
Hoffman, J. E., Nelson, B., & Houck, M. R. (1983). The role of attentional resources in automatic detection. *Cognitive Psychology, 51,* 379–410.
James, W. (1890). *The principles of psychology.* New York: Holt.
Johnston, W. A., & Dark, V. J. (1982). In defense of intraperceptual theories of attention. *Journal of Experimental Psychology: Human Perception and Performance, 8,* 407–421.
Kahneman, D., & Treisman, A. (1984). Changing views of attention and automaticity. In R. Parasuraman, R. Davies, & J. Beatty (Eds.), *Varieties of attention* (pp. 29–61). New York: Academic.
Kinchla, R. A. (1974). Detecting target elements in multielement arrays: A confusability model. *Perception and Psychophysics, 15,* 149–158.
Kinchla, R. A. (1980). The measurement of attention. In R. S. Nickerson (Ed.), *Attention and performance VII* (pp. 215–238). Hillsdale, NJ: Lawrence Erlbaum Associates.
Lupker, J. S., & Katz, A. N. (1981). Input, decision, and response factors in picture–word interference. *Journal of Experimental Psychology: Human Learning and Memory, 7,* 269–282.
Marcel, A. J. (1983). Conscious and unconscious perception: Experiments on visual masking and word recognition. *Cognitive Psychology, 15,* 197–237.
Meyer, D. E., & Schvaneveldt, R. W. (1971). Facilitation in recognizing pairs of words: Evidence of a dependence between retrieval operations. *Journal of Experimental Psychology, 90,* 227–234.
Neely, J. H. (1976). Semantic priming and retrieval from lexical memory: Evidence for facilitatory and inhibitory processes. *Memory and Cognition, 4,* 648–654.
Palermo, D. S., & Jenkins, J. J. (1964). *Word association norms: Grade school through college.* Minneapolis: University of Minnesota Press.
Posner, M. I., & Snyder, C. R. R. (1975). Attention and cognitive control. In R. L. Solso (Ed.), *Information processing and cognition: The Loyola symposium* (pp. 55–85). Hillsdale, NJ: Lawrence Erlbaum Associates.

Postman, L., & Keppel, G. (1970). *Norms of word association.* New York: Academic.
Schneider, W., & Shiffrin, R. M. (1977). Controlled and automatic human information processing: I. Detection, search, and attention. *Psychological Review, 84,* 1–66.
- Shaffer, W. O., & LaBerge, D. (1979). Automatic semantic processing of unattended words. *Journal of Verbal Learning and Verbal Behavior, 18,* 413–426.
Shaw, M. L. (1984). Division of attention among spatial locations: A fundamental difference between detection of letters and detection of luminance increments. In H. Bouma & D. G. Bouwhuis (Eds.), *Attention and performance X* (pp. 109–121). Hillsdale, NJ: Lawrence Erlbaum Associates.
Shiffrin, R. M., & Schneider, W. (1977). Controlled and automatic human information processing: II. Perceptual learning, automatic attending, and a general theory. *Psychological Review, 84,* 127–190.
Smith, M. C. (1979). Contextual facilitation in a letter search task depends on how the prime is processed. *Journal of Experimental Psychology: Human Perception and Performance, 5,* 239–251.
Smith, M. C., Theodor, L., & Franklin, P. E. (1983). The relationship between contextual facilitation and depth of processing. *Journal of Experimental Psychology: Learning, Memory, and Cognition, 9,* 697–712.
Sperling, G. (1984). A unified theory of attention and signal detection. In R. Parasuraman & D. R. Davies (Eds.), *Varieties of attention* (pp. 103–181). New York: Academic.
Titchener, E. B. (1908). *Lectures on the elementary psychology of feeling and attention.* New York: Macmillan.
Underwood, G., & Thwaites, S. (1982). Automatic phonological coding of unattended printed words. *Memory and Cognition, 10,* 434–442.
Zimba, L. D., & Blake, R. (1983). Binocular rivalry and semantic processing: Out of sight, out of mind. *Journal of Experimental Psychology: Human Perception and Performance, 9,* 807–815.

33 Necessary Conditions for Repeated-Letter Inferiority: The Role of Positional Uncertainty

Gideon Keren
Louis C. Boer
Institute for Perception TNO, The Netherlands

ABSTRACT

Bjork and Murray (1977) have presented an experimental paradigm in which interference between letters presented simultaneously was maximal when target and noise items consisted of an identical letter. This repeated-letter inferiority effect is in apparent contrast with results reported by Eriksen and Eriksen (1974, 1979). Two experiments are reported here that suggest that positional uncertainty, as employed in the Bjork and Murray paradigm, is a necessary condition for obtaining repeated-letter inferiority. Implications concerning the locus at which noise elements affect the detection of target letters (i.e., at the perceptual or feature-extraction level of processing, or at a final decision level) are briefly discussed.

INTRODUCTION

A continuous debate in the recent literature concerns the processes underlying letter perception and the exact role of unwanted noise elements. One class of models (Eriksen & Schultz, 1979; G. T. Gardner, 1973; Shiffrin & Geisler, 1973) assumes that different letters in a display are encoded and processed independently up to a response or decision level. Consequently, any effect of irrelevant noise items (interference or facilitation) should be located at a relatively late response or decision stage. Empirical support for the independence of processing channels is received from studies by Eriksen and Eriksen (1974, 1979), Eriksen and Spencer (1969), G. T. Gardner (1973), and Shiffrin and Geisler (1973). In contrast, results from other studies (e.g., Bjork & Murray, 1977; Egeth & Santee, 1981; Santee & Egeth, 1980) suggest that perceptual encoding of display elements is not independent, and that mutual interference (inhibition) may take place. The results of these studies were taken as evidence for another class of models, which assumes interactive, dependent channels (e.g., Bjork & Murray, 1977; Estes, 1972). According to these models, at least part of the effect due to unwanted noise items occurs at an early stage of perceptual encoding.

In the present chapter we investigate possible causes for the apparently conflicting experimental results just mentioned, and we compare the experimental paradigm used by Eriksen and Eriksen (1974, 1979) with that used by Bjork and Murray (1977). The implications for the controversy concerning the two types of models are briefly presented in the final discussion.

The Two Experimental Paradigms

Generally, the experimental paradigm employed by Bjork and Murray (1977) and Santee and Egeth (1980) consists of a partial-report cueing procedure in a forced-choice detection task. On each trial the subject is forced to respond with one of two target letters (e.g., A or E). A typical sequence consists of the presentation of a 3 × 4 (rows × columns) premask matrix, followed by a stimulus matrix of the same size, in which the middle two positions contain two letters and the remaining positions are filled with a single repeated background character like $ or #. Finally, the stimulus matrix is replaced by a postmask matrix that remains in view until the subject responds. Simultaneously with the presentation of the postmask, an upward-pointing arrow appears under one of the two center columns, and the subject's task is to report the letter (always one of the two targets) that appeared in the cued column. Four basic conditions are used in this procedure: *repeated letters,* in which the cued and uncued letters are identical (e.g., AA or EE); *conflicting letters,* in which cued and uncued position each contain a different target letter (e.g., AE); *neutral noise,* in which the uncued position contains a nontarget letter (e.g., AK); *single letter,* in which the noncued position is filled with the background character.

The dependent variable in this procedure is accuracy (percentage correct) and the major finding reported by both Bjork and Murray (1977) and Santee and Egeth (1980) is that accuracy for the conflicting condition was significantly higher than for the repeated condition. This finding, termed the repeated-letter inferiority effect (Egeth & Santee, 1981), has been used as evidence in favor of a feature-specific inhibitory channels model, and for the claim that at least part of the interference occurs at an early stage of processing.

Although these results have been replicated in several laboratories, they are nonetheless surprising, and appear to be in direct conflict with studies reported by Eriksen and Eriksen (1974, 1979). These investigators used a nonsearch task in which the target letter always appeared in a (prespecified) fixed location, flanked on either side by noise letters. The most important result in the present context is that RTs in the repeated-letter condition were always equal to or faster than those in the conflicting noise condition.

A major difference between the two experimental paradigms concerns the dependent variable: Whereas Eriksen and Eriksen (1974, 1979) measured RTs, Bjork and Murray (1977; Santee & Egeth, 1980, 1982a, 1982b) used accuracy as the main dependent variable. Santee and Egeth (1982a) proposed that RTs and accuracy may not measure the same aspects of letter recognition. In the first experiment in their article they failed to obtain the repeated-letter inferiority effect when using RT in the Bjork and Murray paradigm. However, as Santee and Egeth (1982a) already noted, RT and accuracy measures cannot be directly compared when using Bjork and Murray's paradigm. The reason is that in RT tasks the repeated-letter displays may have an advantage over conflict displays: In repeated-letter displays subjects do not have to wait for the postcue in order to determine which letter should be responded to, whereas in the conflict displays the processing of the postcue is essential. This temporal advantage may account for the failure to obtain the repeated-letter inferiority effect with RT as a dependent variable.

Another tentative explanation proposed by Santee and Egeth (1982a) concerns the effects of masking. These authors argued that accuracy studies employ brief exposure times combined with masking and thus produce data limitation (Norman & Bobrow, 1975) or state limitation (W. R. Garner, 1970). RT studies, in contrast, use long exposure times without masking, which would result in resource (Norman & Bobrow, 1975) or process limitation (W. R. Garner, 1970). To test their conjectures, Santee and Egeth (1982a, 1982b) ran several experiments using modified versions of Bjork and Murray's paradigm. Unfortunately, these studies yielded conflicting results: In one study (Santee & Egeth, 1982b, Experiment 2) they obtained the repeated-letter inferiority effect under masking conditions, but failed to obtain it without masking. In another experiment (Santee & Egeth, 1982a, Experiment 1), however, accuracy in the repeated-letter condition (67%) was much lower than in the corresponding conflicting condition (81%), even though no masking was used. Because these two studies employed somewhat different experimental paradigms, it is not implausible that confounding of other variables may account for the discrepancy. One tentative conclusion from these experiments, irrespective of the discrepancy in findings, is that masking by itself cannot account for the repeated-letter inferiority effect.

An important aspect in which the two studies by Santee and Egeth differ concerns the positional uncertainty of the target. In the experiment in which repeated-letter inferiority was obtained without mask (Santee & Egeth, 1982a) the position to be reported was cued only after the stimulus display was removed (as in Bjork & Murray, 1977) and thus positional uncertainty was maximal. In the experiment in which Santee and Egeth (1982b) failed to obtain repeated-letter inferiority, the subject had to detect whether a target was present or absent (a yes–no task). In this experiment, there is also positional uncertainty, albeit of a different nature. In fact, in this experiment, even when the repeated-letter inferiority effect was obtained (under the masking condition), its magnitude was only half that obtained when positional uncertainty was maximal (i.e., when cueing took place after the stimulus display had disappeared). Krueger and Shapiro (1980) have proposed that the repeated-letter inferiority effect may result from difficulties in discriminating the location to be reported. Some support for this hypothesis is provided by Estes, Allmeyer, and Reder (1976). They showed that errors reflecting loss of positional information are prominent in accounting for lateral interference effects, and termed this factor *positional uncertainty*.

Uncertainty about the letter to be reported can be obtained in different ways. In the present text we reserve the term positional uncertainty to mean uncertainty about the position of the target letter relative to the noise letter. In an identification task in which a cue is used, the timing of the cue can be varied to produce a range from no positional uncertainty, when the target position is fixed and known in advance (as in Eriksen & Eriksen, 1974, 1979), to maximal uncertainty, when the cue is given after the stimulus display has been terminated (as in Bjork & Murray, 1977). Different levels of uncertainty can be obtained by varying the temporal position of the cue, as is shown in Fig. 33.1. *Spatial uncertainty* (to be distinguished from what we defined here as positional uncertainty) can also be apparent in paradigms that do not use a cue. For instance, Estes (1982) presented his subjects with triads of letters to their right or left visual fields and asked them to report the middle letter. In this case there was no positional uncertainty, because the target position *relative* to the other two letters in the display was known, yet spatial uncertainty was present because the location of the displays varied from trial to trial.

The typical experimental paradigms, together with some modified versions reported in the literature, are described in Table 33.1 in terms of several dimensions relevant to the issue of positional uncertainty. From inspection of the Table it is apparent that the paradigms of Eriksen and Eriksen (1974, 1979) and Bjork and Murray (1977) differ on several important aspects of positional uncertainty.

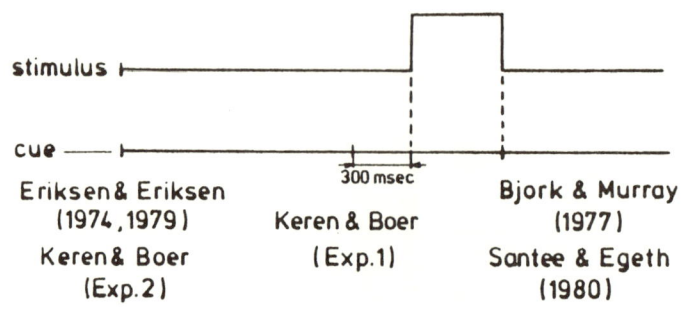

FIG. 33.1. Varying positional uncertainty as a function of the temporal position of the cue.

TABLE 33.1
Classification of Experimental Paradigms on Different Dimensions of Positional Uncertainty

	Eriksen & Eriksen (1974, 1979) Nonsearch Task	Bjork & Murray (1977) Santee & Egeth (1980, Exp. 1) Basic Paradigm	Santee & Egeth (1980, Exp. 3) Yes–No Detection Task	Keren & Boer (Exp. 1) Precueing	Keren & Boer (Exp. 2) Target-Fixed Position	Keren & Boer (Exp. 2) Noise-Fixed Position	Estes (1982) Varied Display Location
Display position	Fixed	Fixed	Fixed	Fixed	Variable	Variable	Variable
Target location							
Absolute	Fixed	Variable	Variable	Variable	Fixed	Variable	Variable
Within display	Fixed	Variable	Variable	Variable	Fixed	Variable	Fixed
Temporal position of cue	Pre-	Post-	None	Pre-	Pre-preinstructions	None	None[a]
Task judgment level	Single target identification	Single target identification	Display detection	Single target identification	Single target identification	Single target identification	Single target identification
Positional uncertainty resolved by	Fixed preinstructions	Postcue	Stimulus	300 msec precue	Fixed preinstructions	Stimulus	Stimulus
Transparency of transposition errors	Yes	Yes	No (not relevant)	Yes	Yes	Yes	Yes

NOTE: *Display position*: Does the stimulus array occupy a fixed position in the visual field?
Target location: absolute: Is target position fixed in the visual field?
within display: Is target position fixed relative to other elements in the display?
Temporal position of cue: Timing of cue relative to stimulus presentation as shown in Figure 34.1.
Task judgment level: Identification or detection (nature of task).
Positional uncertainty resolved by: How and when is positional uncertainty (of the target to be reported) resolved?
Transparency of transposition errors: Can (potential) transposition errors affect the response?
[a] There is only relative, but not absolute, precueing in this paradigm.

605

Of special interest is the comparison of the study by Santee and Egeth (1980, Experiment 3) with the paradigm used by Bjork and Murray (1977). Santee and Egeth's purpose was to test the hypothesis that positional uncertainty may account for the repeated-letter inferiority effect. They used a yes–no paradigm in which subjects indicated whether at least one target letter was present in the display. Because the repeated-letter inferiority effect was still obtained, they ruled out the positional uncertainty explanation.

The underlying assumption of Santee and Egeth in this study is that any effects of positional uncertainty have been eliminated in the yes–no paradigm. Inspection of Table 33.1, however, suggests that not only does the yes–no paradigm differ from Bjork and Murray's (1977) on several important dimensions, like the judgment task, but also that it contains positional uncertainty, albeit different in nature from that in the Bjork and Murray paradigm.

Moreover, as Santee and Egeth (1980) themselves pointed out, the pattern of their results (i.e., repeated-letter inferiority) could have been predicted on the assumption that the sensitivity of feature detectors varied independently and randomly from trial to trial. In that case, the conflicting trials,[1] which consist of both targets A and E, have a higher probability of being detected than repeated trials, which consist of a single letter. Estes (1982) provides similar arguments against the yes–no paradigm. The following Experiment 1 was designed to provide a more valid test of the role of positional uncertainty.

EXPERIMENT 1

Design

The design of Experiment 1 was similar to that used by Santee and Egeth (1980). The major difference was the use of two different cueing conditions: one before stimulus presentation (positional certainty) and one after (positional uncertainty).

Subjects

Eight students, with normal or corrected-to-normal vision, served as paid subjects in four experimental sessions of 45 minutes each. The first two sessions for all subjects were in the poststimulus cueing condition. Approximately 1 week later the subjects returned for the prestimulus-cueing-condition session.

Apparatus

All displays were presented in a three-channel Scientific Prototype tachistoscope, at a luminance of 16 cd/m^2. The testing room was kept dimly illuminated.

---

[1]Literally, under the yes–no paradigm, these are not any more conflicting stimuli.

Stimuli

Premask, stimulus, and postmask displays each contained a 3 × 4 (rows × columns) matrix of symbols presented in the center of the visual field. Each character subtended a visual angle of .18° and .24° for width and height, respectively. Horizontal and vertical spacings were correspondingly .18° and .24°.

The pre- and postmask matrix contained dollar signs ($) and the stimulus display matrix consisted of number signs (#) surrounding the middle two positions. The postmask also contained an upward-pointing arrow positioned below one of the middle two columns. The target letters A and E appeared equally often in each condition, and as the cued letter in each of the middle two positions.

The nontarget letters K and N appeared equally often with each target letter. There were four types of trials randomly mixed within each block: repeated letters (e.g., EE); conflicting letters (e.g., AE); neutral letters (e.g., EK); and single letters (e.g., A#).

Procedure

Each of the two cueing conditions started with a practice session during which exposure times were adjusted, individually for each subject, to yield approximately a 75% accuracy level. This session was followed by two experimental sessions (each containing three blocks of 72 trials).

In the postcueing condition, subjects were instructed to focus on the middle two positions of the premask matrix and then initiate a trial by pressing a push button. Three hundred ms later the premask was replaced by a stimulus display, which stayed on for the individual subjects' predetermined exposure times. It was then replaced by a postmask matrix containing the cueing arrow, which stayed on for 300 ms. Each subject had to report whether the cued location contained an A or an E and then had to initiate the following trial.

The order of events in the precueing condition was similar, except that the cueing arrow appeared during the last 300 ms preceding the stimulus display. Subjects responded verbally; no feedback was provided except during the practice session.

Results

The results of Experiment 1 are summarized in Table 33.2. As can be seen, the pattern of results for the postcueing condition was very similar to that reported by Bjork and Murray (1977) and Santee and Egeth (1980). In contrast, for the precueing condition there was no effect. The data were subjected to a three-way repeated-measures ANOVA. Factors were time of cueing (pre- or post-), display condition (single, neutral, conflicting, repeated), and target letter (A vs. E). The ANOVA revealed a significant main effect of cueing—$F(1,7) = 8.8; p < .05$—

TABLE 33.2
Mean Proportions of Correct Detections
for Each Target Letter in Each Display Condition,
for Pre- and Postcueing

	Postcueing			Precueing		
Condition	A	E	Mean	A	E	Mean
Repeated	61.7	64.7	63.2	79.8	84.4	82.1
Conflict	82.0	77.7	79.8	76.2	79.3	77.8
Neutral	73.2	73.9	73.5	78.6	81.7	80.1
Single	76.6	71.0	73.8	80.6	75.6	78.1

and a significant cueing × condition interaction—$F(3,21) = 14.2; p < .001$. None of the other effects were significant at the .05 level.

The average exposure time in the precueing condition (34.7 ms) was significantly lower than in the postcueing condition (60.6 ms)—$t(7) = 10.08, p < .001$.

Discussion

The manipulation of positional uncertainty produced clearcut results: Whereas the usual repeated-letter inferiority effect was obtained with postcueing, it disappeared in the precueing condition. In fact, in the precueing condition there was a slight advantage for the repeated-letter compared with the conflict condition, although this difference did not reach significance. The experiments of Eriksen and Eriksen (1974, 1979) have shown a clear advantage (shorter RTs) for identical noise as compared with conflicting noise. Why was this facilitation not observed in the present study? Several studies (e.g., Colegate, Hoffman, & Eriksen, 1973) have noted that processing the location indicator may require several hundred milliseconds. It is quite possible that in the present study the 300 ms precueing was sufficient to eliminate the repeated-letter inferiority effect, but was not long enough to produce any facilitation.

To test the positional-uncertainty effect further, we designed a second study. In one condition positional uncertainty was completely removed by instructing the subject in advance to attend to a fixed position (as in Eriksen & Eriksen, 1974). A prespecified, fixed target position does not only mean that the subject knows where to attend, but simultaneously implies which part of the display can be ignored or disregarded. In a second condition, the position of the irrelevant noise items was fixed (and known in advance), but not the position of the target. The purpose was to test the extent to which positional certainty of unwanted noise items is sufficient to eliminate the repeated-letter inferiority effect.

EXPERIMENT 2

Subjects

Eight students with normal or corrected-to-normal vision served as paid subjects in four experimental (and two practice) sessions of 45 minutes each.

Apparatus

Displays were generated (at 15 cd/m^2 intensity) on a cathode ray tube (CRT) with a fast-decay P4 phosphor. Stimulus letters were formed by thin, illuminated lines on a dark gray screen. Subjects sat in a dimly lit room, with their heads held steady in chin rests located 70 cm from the display screen.

Stimuli

Premask, stimulus, and postmask displays all contained a 3 × 5 (row × columns) matrix of symbols. Two (adjacent) positions out of the middle three in the stimulus display were occupied by letters. The capital letters (A and E as targets, N and K as nontargets) subtended a visual angle of .19° and .25° for width and height, respectively. The spacing between adjacent rows and columns subtended a visual angle of .27° and .20°, respectively.

Design and Procedure

The main variable in this experiment was the position of target and noise elements: In the target-center condition, subjects were instructed to report the letter in the center position (A or E) and to ignore the irrelevant noise letter flanking the center position randomly to the right or left. In the noise-center condition, they were instructed to ignore the center position and to report the letter beside it, occupying at random the right or left position. Thus, in the target-center condition there was positional certainty regarding the location of the target to be reported but not with regard to the noise letter; in the noise-center condition this was reversed. Half of the subjects had the target in center condition on the first day and the noise in center condition on the second day of experimentation; for the other half of the subjects the order was reversed. Within these two conditions, the four different display types (repeated, conflict, neutral, and single) were randomly and equally often presented.

Results and Discussion

The data were subjected to an ANOVA with three factors: display condition (repeated versus conflict), center instruction (target or noise in center), and letter identity (A or E). The analysis revealed a significant main effect of letter identi-

TABLE 33.3
Mean Proportions of Correct Detections
for Each Target Letter in Each Display Condition,
for Noise and Target in Center Conditions

| | Noise in Center ||| Target in Center |||
Condition	A	E	Mean	A	E	Mean
Repeated	83.1	73.1	78.1	84.4	83.9	84.1
Conflict	85.2	76.3	80.8	74.8	71.4	73.1
Neutral	84.3	76.4	80.4	80.4	79.1	79.8
Single	84.9	83.2	84.0	82.4	81.6	82.0

ty—$F(1,7) = 5.80$; $p < .05$—and a strong interaction between center instruction and display condition—$F(1,7) = 77.7$; $p < .0001$. No other effect reached significance.

Inspection of Table 33.3 reveals no effect of display condition when noise is in the center, and higher accuracy for repeated (compared to conflict) displays in the target in the center condition. This superiority for repeated-letter displays confirms the conjecture that the facilitation reported by Eriksen and Eriksen (1974, 1979) can also be obtained by using accuracy measures, provided that there is no positional uncertainty with regard to the target. Eliminating positional uncertainty of the noise elements is apparently not sufficient.

Finally, the mean exposure time for the target in the center condition ($X = 46.5$ ms) was significantly lower than for the noise in center condition ($X = 56.8$)—$t(7) = 2.91, p < .05$.

GENERAL DISCUSSION

Combined with the studies reported in the literature, the present two experiments support the claim that positional uncertainty may be a necessary condition for obtaining the repeated-letter inferiority effect. The question still remains as to why positional uncertainty is crucial for obtaining repeated-letter inferiority, and how the conflicting results reported by Bjork and Murray (1977) and Eriksen and Eriksen (1974, 1979) can be accounted for.

Unlike most authors referred to in the present chapter, we believe that both Bjork and Murray's (1977) results, as well as those reported by Eriksen and Eriksen (1974, 1979), can be treated in the same framework without a necessary contradiction. Two points to emphasize in this connection are: (a) that the interactive-channels hypothesis does not necessarily imply that channels will always interact, but rather that they may interact under certain conditions; (b) whether or not interference is possible at an early stage of processing (due to interactive channels), there may still be a possible effect of response competition in a late decision stage. The hypotheses are not mutually exclusive. Interference among channels (and, consequently, the repeated-letter inferiority effect) may be limited to situations in which subjects are uncertain about the exact position of the target. In that case, they are forced to divide attention between two locations, which in turn may lead to interference among channels as proposed by Bjork and Murray (1977). When, however, subjects know beforehand the exact position of the target, they may direct their attention to that particular location and consequently provide a preentry (or at least some priority) for the desired target, which may eliminate the interference at this stage of processing. But other neighboring letters may well be processed, too, and have an effect at a later decision stage (as has been demonstrated by Eriksen & Eriksen, 1974, 1979).

The paradigm employed by Eriksen and Eriksen (1974, 1979) eliminates any possible positional uncertainty. In contrast, the paradigm employed by Bjork and Murray introduces what may be termed maximum positional uncertainty. Other experiments have introduced different degrees of positional uncertainty that are difficult to measure because, as is apparent from Table 33.1, the concept of positional uncertainty is not unidimensional. What exact "type" of positional uncertainty is needed for producing the repeated-letter inferiority cannot be inferred from the present studies. One speculative proposal is that it may not be the positional uncertainty per se that leads to repeated-letter inferiority, but rather the means by which this uncertainty is resolved. In particular, when a cueing stimulus has to be processed in addition to the stimulus display, the cue requires resources and may therefore limit the effectiveness of processing the stimulus display, eventually promoting the inhibitory effects of interactive channels (see Santee & Egeth, 1982a). Obviously, such a conjecture needs to be tested further.

The experiments reported here are not intended to support or refute either the interactive-channels model (Bjork & Murray, 1977) or the response-competition model (Eriksen & Eriksen, 1979). The hybrid model proposed can be justified only on the grounds that it can account for the empirical findings reported in the literature and the two experiments reported here. The major point of the present chapter is that any future attempt to account for the repeated-letter inferiority effect will also have to take into consideration the role of positional uncertainty.

ACKNOWLEDGMENT

The authors wish to thank Anke Bouma of the Free University, Amsterdam, for providing us with the facilities to run Experiment 1, and Michiel Ruzius for his assistance through all stages of the project.

REFERENCES

Bjork, E. L., & Murray, J. T. (1977). On the nature of input channels in visual processing. *Psychological Review, 84,* 472–484.

Colegate, R., Hoffman, J. E., & Eriksen, C. W. (1973). Selective encoding from multielement visual displays. *Perception and Psychophysics, 14,* 217–224.

Egeth, H. E., & Santee, J. L. (1981). Conceptual and perceptual components of interletter inhibition. *Journal of Experimental Psychology: Human Perception and Performance, 7,* 506–517.

Eriksen, B. A., & Eriksen, C. W. (1974). Effects of noise letters upon the identification of a target letter in a nonsearch task. *Perception and Psychophysics, 16,* 143–149.

Eriksen, C. W., & Eriksen, B. A. (1979). Target redundancy in visual search: Do repetitions of the target within the display impair processing? *Perception and Psychophysics, 26,* 195–205.

Eriksen, C. W., & Schultz, D. W. (1979). Information processing in visual search: A continuous flow conception and experimental results. *Perception and Psychophysics, 25,* 249–263.

Eriksen, C. W., & Spencer, T. (1969). Rate of information processing in visual perception: Some results and methodological considerations. *Journal of Experimental Psychology Monograph, 79* (2, Pt. 2).

Estes, W. K. (1972). Interactions of signal and background variables in visual processing. *Perception and Psychophysics, 12,* 278–286.

Estes, W. K. (1982). Similarity-related channel interactions in visual processing. *Journal of Experimental Psychology: Human Perception and Performance, 8,* 353–382.

Estes, W. K., Allmeyer, D. H., & Reder, S. M. (1976). Serial position functions for letter identification at brief and extended exposure durations. *Perception and Psychophysics, 19,* 1–15.

Gardner, G. T. (1973). Evidence for independent parallel channels in tachistoscopic perception. *Cognitive Psychology, 4,* 130–155.

Garner, W. R. (1970). The stimulus in information processing. *American Psychologist, 25,* 350–358.

Krueger, L. E., & Shapiro, R. G. (1980). Repeating the target neither speeds nor slows its detection: Evidence for independent channels in letter processing. *Perception and Psychophysics, 28,* 68–76.

Norman, D. A., & Bobrow, D. G. (1975). On data-limited and resource-limited processes. *Cognitive Psychology, 7,* 44–65.

Santee, J. L., & Egeth, H. E. (1980). Interference in letter identification: A test of feature-specific inhibition. *Perception and Psychophysics, 27,* 321–330.

Santee, J. L., & Egeth, H. E. (1982a). Do reaction time and accuracy measure the same aspects of letter recognition? *Journal of Experimental Psychology: Human Perception and Performance, 8,* 489–501.

Santee, J. L., & Egeth, H. E. (1982b). Independence versus interference in the perceptual processing of letters. *Perception and Psychophysics, 31,* 101–116.

Shiffrin, R. M., & Geisler, W. S. (1973). Visual recognition in a theory of information processing. In R. L. Solso (Ed.), *Contemporary issues in cognitive psychology: The Loyola symposium* (pp. 53–102). Washington, DC: V. H. Winston & Sons.

34 Disruptive Effect of Precueing on the Identification of Letters in Masked Words: An Attentional Interpretation

Daniel Holender
Université libre de Bruxelles

ABSTRACT

A letter is better identified in a word than in a pseudoword or a nonword, or when presented alone. These different aspects of the word-superiority effect are obtained in new experiments using the probed task devised by Reicher (1969). The procedure consists of requiring a forced choice between two letters after a brief, patterned, masked presentation of a letter string. Precueing of the identities of the alternatives, but not of the position in which one of them will be presented, has a detrimental effect on word performance, and, less consistently so, on pseudoword performance as well. Performance for nonwords and single letters is unaffected by precueing. If, instead of typing the letter strings normally, extra spaces are introduced between letters, the word-superiority effect almost disappears, and precueing no longer exerts any detrimental effect on word performance. It has also been shown that the drop in performance for words is stronger with physically larger than smaller words, although not always strongly so. One firm conclusion of the study is that it is the mechanism of the word superiority that is affected by precueing. A tentative explanation of the detrimental effect of precueing is also proposed. It is assumed that precueing determines a spatial focusing of attention at the time of stimulus presentation, which implies delayed processing of the letters falling outside of focus, thereby hampering word perception.

INTRODUCTION

Literally, the *word-superiority effect* simply describes the observation of a better performance with word stimuli compared to other kinds of letter strings like nonwords, pseudowords, or even single letters. Both nonwords and pseudowords are nonsense letter strings that do not exist in the lexicon. Nonwords violate the orthographical rules of the language of the test, whereas pseudowords do not. It is, however, in a more restricted sense—the better identification of a letter in a word than in the other contexts—that the phenomenon has been judged most relevant to the understanding of perceptual aspects of word recognition in reading. Among the experimental situations leading to this particular observation, the forced-choice letter-probe task devised by Reicher (1969) is certainly the one that has given rise to the most extended empirical and theoretical work (e.g., Henderson, 1982; McClelland & Rumelhart, 1981; Rumelhart & McClelland, 1982). The aim of this chapter is to discuss a rather neglected aspect of the seminal finding of Reicher: the disruptive effect of precueing of the probed letter.

Reicher (1969) compared the performances of the subjects in two situations: one in which they were only postcued and one in which they were both precued and postcued about the probed letter. The "no-precue" procedure involved the brief presentation of either a word (ROSE), a nonword (EOSR), or a single letter (–– S–). Stimulus exposure was immediately followed by a patterned mask (superimposed Xs and Os) and by a forced choice between two letters (––S– or ––L–). These letters both constitute words (ROSE or ROLE) or nonwords (EOSR or EOLR) when embedded in the context of the three other letters comprising the stimulus. Hence, in the case in which the target letter is not identified, the probability of choosing the correct response by chance is .5 for each kind of stimulus. The position of the target letter varied randomly from trial to trial. The "precue" procedure was the same except in one important respect: Subjects were precued about the two alternative letters, which were named before stimulus exposure, but no information was provided about the position in which one of them would occur. Percentages of correct responses in the no-precue condition were 89, 76, and 78 for words, nonwords, and single letters, respectively. In the precue condition the corresponding percentages of correct responses were 80, 65, and 67. There was, therefore, a considerable advantage for a letter to be part of a word compared to being presented in isolation or embedded into a nonsense string. This word-superiority effect is not trivial, because it is obtained with a forced-choice procedure that controls for postperceptual guessing. A second aspect of the results, which was almost as startling as the first, is that precueing of the alternative letters impaired rather than improved performance.

The detrimental effect of precueing remained unexplained when it was first observed by Reicher (1969). During the decade following its discovery, this aspect of the results was almost forgotten and Reicher's use of a precue condition often was not even mentioned in many subsequent publications. Meanwhile, the issue of whether the word superiority would be maintained under precueing about alternative letters became central in the debate about guessing strategies. Almost everybody agreed that the forced choice presented after the masked stimulus should prevent postperceptual guessing. However, there is still the possibility for guessing strategies to take place at the time of presentation of the stimulus. The idea, as it was outlined by Thompson and Massaro (1973), is that when only partial visual information about the target is available, subjects could synthesize the best possible choice in relying on both sensory data and inferences based on their knowledge of the language. In the case in which the three contextual letters are identified, the probability of synthesizing the correct target would, of course, be greater with words than with nonwords. One of the predictions of this model is that the word-superiority effect should disappear if subjects were precued about the alternative letters. This actually happened in the first four studies that tested the prediction (Bjork & Estes, 1973; Estes, Bjork, & Skaar, 1974; Massaro, 1973; Thompson & Massaro, 1973).

Two points should be stressed. First, the contradiction between these results and the maintainance of a word superiority in the precued condition of Reicher's experiment was almost completely overlooked. Second, in order for the sophisticated guessing hypothesis to be supported, the way the word-superiority effect disappears is even more important than the disappearance itself. Compared with the no-precue condition, the hypothesis predicts an improvement in performance for each kind of stimulus under precueing of target identity. Moreover, the improvement should be greater for single letters or nonwords than for words, leading either to a suppression, or at least to a reduction, in the word-superiority effect. The reason for this is that precueing should be useful in every case when single letters or nonwords are presented. With words, precueing should be useful only in the case in which subjects are unable to take advantage of the contextual letters. Contrary to this prediction, Holender (1979) and Johnston (1981) showed that precueing about target identity led to a decrement in performance for words, whereas performance for single letters was either unaffected (Holender, 1979) or improved (Johnston, 1981). The net effect was a suppression of the word superiority in both cases. Notice that the decline in performance for words under precueing confirms the already-mentioned similar effect shown by Reicher (1969), whereas his drop in performance for single letters under precueing was not replicated. In analyzing the literature up to 1978 (Holender, 1979), I reached the following conclusions:

1. With single letters, precueing the identity can entail a full range of effects, from an increment in performance when no mask is presented to a decrement in performance when the features of the mask resemble the features of the stimulus letters.
2. With words, the effect of precueing is much less dependent on the physical characteristics of the stimulus-mask display and is mainly dependent on the strategy adopted by the subject to process the stimulus.

The change in strategy compared with the no-precue condition is supposed to disrupt the process that normally produces the word-superiority effect; hence, only decrements in performance can possibly be observed. As can be seen in Table 34.1, the detrimental effect of precueing on word performance occurs either under precueing of target identity alone (Holender, 1979; Johnston, 1981; Reicher, 1969), or under precueing of target position alone (Johnston & McClelland, 1974), or both (Johnston, 1981).

In the remainder of this chapter, I argue further for the specificity of the effect of precueing on word perception in Reicher's paradigm and I propose a tentative attentional interpretation of it. The new data described are taken from a series of five experiments in which performance for words, pseudowords, nonwords, and letters was studied as a function of stimulus physical size, letter spacing, and physical characteristics of the mask. Due to lack of space, only the last three experiments are presented in detail and only results relevant to the present issue are discussed.

The first two experiments contrasted small and large (1° vs. 3° of visual angle; see Fig. 34.1a and 34.1b) with a mask similar to that of Reicher, superimposed Os and Xs, instead of the curved intersecting lines I used before (Holender, 1979). In spite of this, there was no effect of precueing on letter or nonword performance. Aside from my new failure to replicate part of Reicher's initial observation, an interesting interaction between visual angle and precueing for words and pseudowords emerged. With small words and pseudowords, precueing determined small, nonsignificant drops in performance amounting to 2.3% and .9%, respectively. With large stimuli, the drops in performance were significant, amounting to 7.8% for words and 6.7% for nonwords.

It is worth comparing these results with another set of data in the literature. Instead of precueing of the alternatives with a different pair of target letters before each trial, many studies have used the same small subset of either two or four target letters throughout the experiment. A rather consistent pattern of results arises from these studies. With small stimuli subtending less than 2° of visual angle, an advantage of words over nonwords is almost always observed,

TABLE 34.1
Percentages of Correct Forced Choices
for Letters Embedded into Words as a Function
of Precueing Conditions[a]

Author	NP	IP	PP	IP & PP
Reicher, 1969	89	80		
Holender, 1979	70	63		
Johnston & McClelland, 1974	79		72	
Johnston, 1981: Exp. 1	77		68	64
Exp. 2	85		77	76

[a]NP = no precue; IP = identity precue; PP = position precue.

AUBE   ETAT   COIN   M U S E

a   b   c   d

FIG. 34.1. Examples of words used in Experiments 1 to 3. (a, b) 1° and 3° in Experiment 1; (c) 2° normal spacing in Experiment 2; (d) 2° large spacing in Experiment 3. The correct visual angle is obtained by holding the book at a distance of 56 cm from the eyes.

whether the position of the target letter is known in advance (Paap & Newsome, 1980, Experiment 1; Purcell & Stanovich, 1982, Experiments 3, 4, and 8; Purcell, Stanovich, & Spector, 1978, Experiments 1 and 2; Spector & Purcell, 1977, Experiment 2), or whether the position is unknown (Carr, Lehmkuhle, Kottas, Astor-Stetson, & Harnold, 1976). With stimuli subtending more than 2° of visual angle, there is no advantage of words over pseudowords whether the position of the target is known (Greenberg & Krueger, 1980; Massaro, 1973, Experiment 2) or not (Bjork & Estes, 1973, Experiments 1 and 2; Estes et al., 1974; Greenberg & Krueger, 1980). The only exception is the huge word advantage observed by Purcell and Stanovich (1982, Experiment 8) with position known.

The picture that emerges from these data is that precueing exerts a detrimental effect on word recognition, thereby suppressing the word-superiority effect, provided the stimuli are physically large but not if they are small. Precueing about the position alone is little documented but there seems to be no fundamental difference between the effect of precueing of the identity alone or precueing of both the identity and the position of the target letter. An attempt at interpreting these effects is presented after the results of three more experiments have been described.

Experiment 1 is a replication of the contrast between small (1°) and large (3°) visual angle. Instead of presenting the mask before and after the stimulus, as I did in 1979 and in the experiments alluded to earlier, I closely matched Reicher's conditions by presenting a white field, the stimulus, and then the mask, hoping this time to obtain a drop in performance for nonwords and single letters. Experiments 2 and 3 contrast normal spacing of the letters with large spacing, keeping the visual angle constant. After presenting the main results in the traditional way, the main focus of this analysis concerns the effect of precueing on performance for each kind of stimulus and each condition. There is a methodological problem associated with this analysis because the opportunity for performance to decrease or to improve under precueing is not the same at all levels of accuracy ranging from chance (50% correct forced choices) to 100% correct. Hence, we need an index of the precueing effect that is independent of the overall level of performance. This problem has been adequately dealt with in the framework of the study of laterality (Bryden & Sprott, 1981; Marshall, Caplan, & Holmes, 1975; Repp, 1977). I use the index proposed by Bryden and Sprott (1981).

EXPERIMENTS 1, 2, AND 3

Method

Stimuli. Sixty-four pairs of French common nouns were selected from a pool of four-letter words. Both members of a pair had the same orthographic structure and differed by only one critical letter (e.g., BOUE–ROUE, NOTE–NOCE). There were an equal number of pairs differing in each position. Pairs of pseudowords were obtained by changing one noncritical letter in the corresponding words (BOIE–ROIE, NUTE–NUCE). All pseudowords were pronounceable and orthographically legal in French. Pairs of nonwords were generated from pseudowords by making anagrams, keeping the critical letters in their original positions. Nonwords were orthographically illegal in French (BIEO–RIEO, UETN–UECN). Pairs of single letters were simply the critical letters kept in their original positions, with empty positions filled with small equal signs (B===–R===, ==T=–==C=).

One set of four blocks of 64 trials was constructed by taking one member of each pair as the stimulus and the other member as the associated distractor in the forced choice task. A second set of four blocks yoked to the first was obtained by inverting the roles of stimulus and distractor in each trial. A block consisted of four series of 16 trials each, one for each type of letter string. Within each series, the four positions were tested randomly an equal number of times. Trials with and without precueing were alternated. Derived forms of the same basic stimulus (e.g., BOUE, BOIE, BIEO, B===) were never included in the same block. Each set of four blocks was presented in a different session.

Procedure. A blank fixation field with a centrally located fixation point was continuously visible except during stimulus and mask exposures. A no-precue trial started when the experimenter named out loud the number of the next trial. This was used as a warning signal for subjects to trigger the next stimulus exposure when they felt ready. A pressure on a hand-held switch determined the immediate disappearance of the fixation field and its replacement for an individually predetermined duration by the exposure of a stimulus. The stimulus was immediately followed by the mask, which remained present for 1 sec, before the fixation field came back. Immediately after exposure, subjects turned the page of a small booklet and found a forced choice between the actual stimulus and its associated distractor. They were asked to name their choices in the case of words, pseudowords, and isolated letters, and to spell them out in the case of nonwords. A precued trial differed from a no-precue trial in one respect: Instead of the number of the next trial, the experimenter named the two alternative critical letters, thereby precueing the subject about their identity but not about the position that would be occupied by one of them in the next stimulus exposure.

Sixteen French-speaking subjects were used in each experiment. No subjects participated in more than one experiment. They were given two sessions lasting about 1 hour, one per day on two consecutive days. Each session started by an individual adjustment of the exposure duration based on two series of 16 single letters and two series of 16 pseudowords, which were presented under the no-precue procedure just described. Starting at 50 msec, exposure durations were modified according to a staircase method yielding roughly 75% correct responses. The mean of these two durations minus 5 msec was used for the first block of trials and for the next blocks, as long as the performances for each series remained between 10 and 14 correct responses. Otherwise, 5 msec were added or deleted to provide the exposure duration for the next block of trials.

Experiment 1: Variation in Physical Size with Normal Spacing. Stimuli were typed normally, without extra spaces between letters, on an IBM typewriter using upper-case Courrier 10 type font with spacing set at 10 characters per inch. In this condition, the width of a four-letter string was approximately 1 cm, which corresponded to 1° of visual angle at the 56 cm viewing distance of the tachistoscope. Small stimuli were exactly those just described (Fig. 34.1a). Large stimuli were obtained by photographic enhancement. They were three times as large as the other ones, subtending nearly 3° horizontal visual angle (Fig. 34.1b). One session was devoted to each stimulus size. The mask consisted of three lines of six adjacent, superimposed Xs and Os of the same font, same case, and same size as the letters used in the stimuli. The four central superimposed Xs and Os occupied the same position as the stimulus in the visual field.

Experiments 2 and 3: Normal versus Large Character Spacing. These experiments were designed to contrast the effects of normal and large spacing of the characters composing the stimuli under equal horizontal stimulus extension. In Experiment 2, the four-letter items subtended 2° of visual angle and letters were normally spaced (Fig. 34.1c). For Experiment 3, the typewriter was set at a spacing of 12 characters per inch, and multiletter strings were typed with two spaces inserted between each letter, yielding items subtending a little more than 2°. A reduction to 93% of their size provided the actual stimuli of Experiment 3 (Fig. 34.1d). Subjects were given two sessions, one with a mask identical to that of Experiment 1 (superimposed Xs and Os), and one with a mask consisting of intersecting curved lines. For present purposes, the mask characteristics are disregarded. Results were, therefore, collapsed across both types of mask.

Results

The percentages of correct forced choices, averaged across subjects, are shown in Fig. 34.2. It is immediately apparent that the overall patterns of results are very similar in the three conditions using normal spacing of the letters, whereas spreading out the letters leads to a different pattern. With normal spacing, there is a trend toward a decrement in performance under precueing, the main effect of cueing being significant in each case—$F(1,15) = 4.59, p = .05$; $F(1,15) = 17.68, p < .01$; $F(1,15) = 9.94, p < .01$, for 1°, 3°, and 2°, respectively. There is also a strong effect of the type of stimulus—$F(3,45) = 12.99, p < .01$; $F(3,45) = 9.36, p < .01$; $F(3,45) = 12.79, p < .01$, for 1°, 3°, and 2°, respectively. The interaction between these effects was significant with normally spaced stimuli subtending 3°—$F(3,45) = 4.62, p < .01$—and 2°—$F(3,45) = 3.79, p < .05$—indicating a differential effect of precueing on the different types

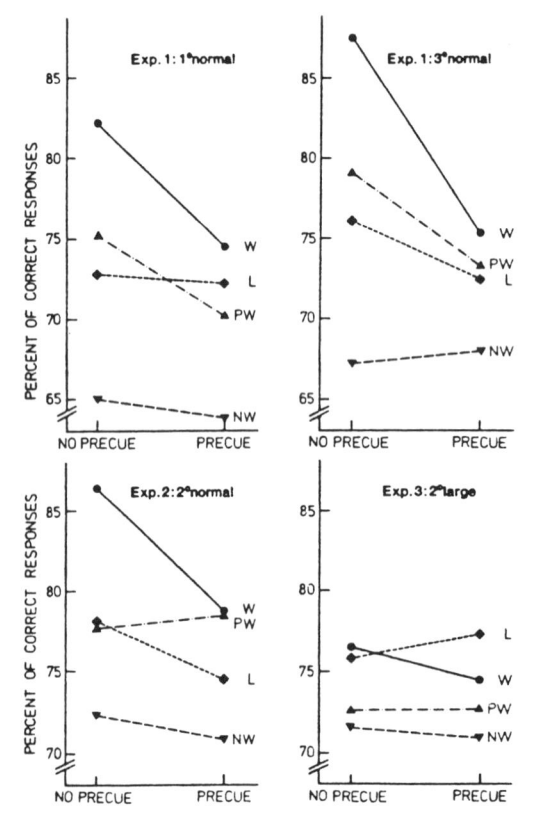

FIG. 34.2. Mean percent of correct forced choices as a function of cueing conditions with stimulus type as parameter (W = word; NW = nonword; PW = pseudoword; L = isolated letter) in Experiments 1 to 3.

of stimuli. Although nonsignificant, a similar trend was present with stimuli subtending 1°.

By contrast, with large spacing of the letters it is clear from Fig. 34.2 that precueing exerts no effect on performance, whatever the type of stimulus. In addition, although the effect of the type of stimulus is significant—$F(3,45) = 5.18, p < .01$—the differences in performance between different kinds of letter strings are much smaller than in the other conditions.

With respect to the type of stimuli, four among the six possible paired comparisons have been considered informative. Three types of letter strings—word, nonword, and pseudoword—are equivalent as visual configurations, differing only by the amount of linguistic and lexical information they convey. Paired comparisons between the performances associated with each of them provide information about the sources of the word-superiority effect. By contrast, a single letter flanked by small plus signs is less laterally masked than a corresponding letter in a string of four letters. In addition, the location in the visual field where relevant information has to be extracted is salient at the time of a single-letter presentation, whereas it is not in the case of the corresponding multiletter strings. The exact level of performance for a single letter relative to the other kinds of letter strings is, therefore, determined by a subtle interplay between several visual parameters of the situation, besides the linguistic properties. In spite of this, many studies have provided a comparison between words and single letters; the comparisons of single letters with nonwords or pseudowords are generally considered as irrelevant to the understanding of word recognition.

Table 34.2 provides the differences between the percentages of correct responses in the four relevant paired comparisons together with their associated levels of significance. Without precueing, the superiority of words over nonwords is significant in each condition. It is, however, much weaker with large than with normal spacing. This is confirmed by a significant interaction—$F(1,30) = 10.6, p < .01$—between typography (normal vs. large) and stimulus type (word vs. nonword) in the no-precue conditions of Experiments 2 and 3. Exactly the same pattern is observed for the weaker advantage of words over pseudowords. Here, too, a significant interaction between typography and stimulus type (word vs. pseudoword) is obtained in the no-precue condition of Experiments 2 and 3—$F(1,30) = 4.20, p < .05$. The advantages of pseudowords over nonwords and of words over single letters are confined to the normal spacing conditions, being nonsignificant in Experiment 3 (large spacing). It is clear from Table 34.2 that aside from weaker but still significant advantages of words over nonwords, most of the other effects disappear under precueing. This is caused by the differential effect of precueing on different type of stimuli, which is the standpoint from which I analyze the interaction.

The basic effect of precueing is a drop in performance. Simply looking for an interaction between the effect of precueing expressed as a difference in percent

TABLE 34.2
Word and Pseudoword Advantages Expressed by Various Differences between Percentages of Correct Forced Choices and Associated Levels of Significance (in Parentheses) as a Function of Typography and Precueing Conditions[a]

	No Precue				Precue			
	W − NW	W − PW	W − L	PW − NW	W − NW	W − PW	W − L	PW − NW
1° normal	17.0	6.9	9.7	10.2	10.6	4.3	2.4	6.3
(Exp. 1)	(.01)	(.05)	(.01)	(.01)	(.01)	(ns)	(ns)	(ns)
3° normal	20.3	8.5	11.5	11.8	7.2	1.8	2.8	5.2
(Exp. 1)	(.01)	(.01)	(.01)	(.01)	(.05)	(ns)	(ns)	(ns)
2° normal	14.1	8.7	8.0	5.3	7.9	0.3	4.3	6.3
(Exp. 2)	(.01)	(.01)	(.01)	(.01)	(.01)	(ns)	(.05)	(.01)
2° large	5.0	3.9	0.7	1.0	3.5	1.8	−2.9	1.8
(Exp. 3)	(.05)	(.05)	(ns)	(ns)	(.05)	(ns)	(ns)	(ns)

[a]ns = nonsignificant ($p > .05$); W = word; NW = nonword; PW = pseudoword; L = letter.

TABLE 34.3
Mean Values of the Precueing Indices (see Text and Footnote 1) as a Function of Stimulus Type and Typography[a]

	Word	Pseudoword	Nonword	Letter
1° normal (Exp. 1)	.53 (.01)	.22 (.07)	.07 (ns)[b]	.07 (ns)
3° normal (Exp. 1)	.95 (.01)	.33 (.05)	.02 (ns)	.15 (ns)
2° normal (Exp. 2)	.54 (.01)	−.04 (ns)	.12 (ns)	.18 (ns)
2° large (Exp. 3)	.15 (ns)	.05 (ns)	.09 (ns)	−.13 (ns)

[a]The levels of significance of the test of the null hypothesis of equality to zero are between parentheses.
[b]ns = nonsignificant.

correct for different types of stimuli is inappropriate because it implies that a difference of x% is considered as equivalent whatever the overall level of performance. It is clear, however, that the opportunity for performance to drop under precueing is not the same if the no-precue performance is near the maximum rather than near chance level. The problem is exactly the same as the one encountered in comparing side advantages at different absolute levels of performance in laterality studies. It has led to the development of laterality indices that are independent of the overall level of performance (Bryden & Sprott, 1981; Marshall et al., 1975; Repp, 1977).

For each subject, each condition, and each type of stimulus, I have calculated a precueing indice on the basis of equation (8a)[1] of Bryden and Sprott (1981). Table 34.3 shows the averages across subjects of these indices, together with the level of significance of the test of the null hypothesis that the mean value of the index is zero. Positive values indicate decrements in performance under precueing and negative values indicate increments in performance.

As can be seen in Table 34.3, the indices indicating a drop in performance for words with normal spacing are all significantly different from zero, whereas no drop is observed with large spacing. The intrasubject comparison of the indices for words of 1° and 3° was marginally significant—$t(15) = 1.71$, $p = .11$—as

---

[1]The precueing index is based on the natural logarithms of the ratios $P_{np}/(1 - P_{np})$ and $P_p/(1 - P_p)$ where P_{np} and P_p are the probabilities of correct forced choices in the no-precue and precue conditions, respectively. The index $\pi = \ln[P_{np}/(1 - P_{np})] - \ln[P_p/(1 - P_p)]$ varies between $-\infty$ and $+\infty$, with a mean value of 0 when $P_{np} = P_p$, whatever the overall level of performance. With n trials in each cueing condition and x_{np} and x_p correct responses in the no-precue and precue conditions, respectively, the value of the precueing index is estimated by: $\ln[x_{np}/(n - x_{np})] - \ln[x_p/(n - x_p)]$ (derived from Bryden & Sprott, 1981, equation (8a), p. 575).

was the intersubject comparison between words of 2° and 3°—$t(30) = 1.93$, $p = .07$. The only other indices significantly different from zero concern the pseudowords of 3° and the marginal effect for pseudowords of 1°. None of the indices concerning single letters or pseudowords reached significance, indicating that precueing exerts no effect on performance for these kinds of stimuli. Within each typography, a one-way analysis of variance involving type of stimulus as a factor led to a significant effect with normal spacing and a nonsignificant effect with large spacing. With normal spacing, post hoc paired comparisons between indices showed words to be significantly different from all the other types of stimuli except for a nonsignificant difference between words and pseudowords of 1°. No other comparison reached significance.

DISCUSSION

There are three aspects of the results that, although deserving of attention in their own right, are nevertheless tangential to the main purposes of this chapter. They are, therefore, mentioned only briefly.

1. As I suggested in the *Introduction,* there is evidence that the effect of precueing on single letters is strongly influenced by the relationship between the physical properties of the stimulus and the mask (see Holender, 1979). By inference, nonwords that provide no linguistic information should be affected by precueing in a way similar to letters, which was indeed the case in Reicher's experiment and in the present study. However, I repeatedly failed to replicate the drop in performance found by Reicher (1969) with nonwords and single letters, even by approximating his visual conditions closely (present experiments). More empirical work is needed to determine the factors influencing the precueing effect with letters and nonwords.

2. There is now a wide consensus that it is the existence of words as lexical units in memory, rather than their conformity to orthographical rules, that is responsible for the word-superiority effect (e.g., Henderson, 1980, 1982; McClelland & Rumelhart, 1981; Rumelhart & McClelland, 1982). Moreover, the advantage of pseudowords over nonwords can also be attributed to the fact that, on the average, pseudowords share more letters with lexical units than do nonwords (McClelland & Rumelhart, 1981; Rumelhart & McClelland, 1982). Hence, one should expect pseudowords to be affected by precueing in a way similar to words. Although the effect of precueing with pseudowords is less consistent across experiments than with other kinds of letter strings, there is an overall tendency for pseudowords to behave like words, as expected. The prominent exception is the absence of the precueing effect on pseudowords in Experiment 2.

3. There is also strong evidence that letters are functional in word identification and that the word-superiority effect is not mediated by the extraction of supraletter features or of the word shape (see Henderson, 1982, for an extended discussion). Models assuming the parallel extraction of the identity of each letter, with the possibility for the identity of the word to emerge before the processing of any of the component letters is completed (e.g., McClelland & Rumelhart, 1981) would not have predicted that spreading the letters would almost eliminate the word-superiority effect. It is, however, easy to account for that possibility by assuming that spacing the letters reduces the amount of lateral masking between them. This would entail a speeding up of the processing of the letters, which might become available before the activation of the corresponding lexical unit is sufficient to enhance their perception.

The most important aspect of the results is the dissociation between the detrimental effect of precueing on words and the absence of the precueing effect with letters and nonwords, provided the letters are normally spaced in multiletter strings. In the rest of the discussion, I provide a tentative attentional explanation of this phenomenon.

The word-superiority effect results from an automatic process. It does not depend on the subjects' adopting a set for words because it is obtained with mixed presentations of words and nonwords (e.g., Reicher's mixed presentations vs. blocked presentations in the present experiments). Furthermore, the overall word performance does not depend on the frequency of words in such mixtures or on the subjects' degree of expectancy for words (Carr, Davidson, & Hawkins, 1978). By automatic, I mean that the effect is not under voluntary control; more specifically, the word superiority is not generated by any strategic intervention of the subject. It does not imply, however, that the word advantage cannot be hampered by changes in processing strategies. This is exactly what happens under precueing of the identity of the alternative letters in the present experiments (see also Holender, 1979; Johnston, 1981; Reicher, 1969). When subjects try to find where in the word information compatible with the two precued letters could be found, there is a severe drop in performance. A similar change in strategy does not affect performance on nonwords and single letters. Moreover, when the visual conditions are such that the word superiority is almost suppressed, as with spacing of the letters (Experiment 3), further changes in strategy no longer exert any detrimental effect. There is, therefore, converging evidence to indicate that it is really the mechanism underlying the word superiority that is affected by precueing.

Is it plausible that the strategy induced by precueing of the identity of the alternatives, which I conceptualized as a search process, can exert a detrimental effect on the lexical activation responsible for the word-superiority effect? At first sight the answer should be negative because in a genuine search task, a target letter is detected faster in words than in nonwords (e.g., Krueger, 1970). The complete picture is more subtle, however. First, the advantage of words over nonwords is not suppressed by precueing in the present experiments, but only reduced (see Table 34.2); hence, there is no contradiction with the explicit search task. Second, it has been shown that, even if there is a word-superiority effect in a speeded letter detection, the search abolishes the semantic priming potential of a word (Henik, Friedrich, & Kellogg, 1983; Smith, 1979). Such an effect is compatible with the view that the availability of a word as a lexical unit can be dissociated from the availability of its meaning, a fact embodied, for example, in the logogen model of Morton (1969). This observation could provide a basis for future attempts to distinguish between a lexical and a semantic component of the word-superiority effect. If precueing induces a search in Reicher's paradigm as well, the reduced but still substantial advantage of words over nonwords could be accounted for by the same two-component model.

Assuming that a search process is indeed involved in the precueing effect, does it take the form of a serial scanning of the letter string or not? One way to answer the question is to look at the position effect. For each typographical condition, an analysis of variance involving type of stimulus (restricted to word and nonword), cueing condition, and position revealed a significant effect of position in each case except for stimuli subtending 3°, but none of the interactions involving position were significant. Basically, the position effect reflects a trend for performance to decline from left to right, which might imply that a scanning process is indeed involved. Unfortunately, even disregarding the outcome of the analysis of variance, which might not be powerful enough to reveal subtle interactions, a close examination of the data does not show any consistent difference between the position effect for words and nonwords or between the precue and no-precue conditions. The position analysis provides, therefore, no insight into the mechanism of the detrimental effect of precueing on word performance.

My initial finding of an interaction between visual angle and the amount of detrimental effect exerted by precueing on word performance is only slightly reproduced in Experiment 1. There is still a statistically unreliable trend in the same direction, the drop in performance being smaller with words subtending 1° than with those of 3°. However, this time, the drop in performance with 1° is much larger (7.6%) than in the other experiment 2.3%). Were it only for the present data, I would have left this trend undiscussed. However, as I mentioned in the *Introduction,* most of the studies using a small number of predesignated alternative letters have shown an advantage of words over pseudowords with small visual angles but not with large ones, whether the position of the target was known in advance or not. It is unfortunate that none of these experiments have provided a no-precue baseline against which the precueing effect could be evaluated. I am nevertheless inclined to assume, partly on the basis of my own results and partly for the reasons explained next, that the suppression of the word superiority with large, but not with small, words results from a stronger detrimental effect of precueing on the former than on the latter. On the other hand, I have no reason to suspect a differential effect of precueing on nonword performance as a function of their visual angle.

That visual angle should interact with precueing of position alone, or of both position and identity of the target, is rather straightforward. It is well known that there is a limit to the amount of focusing of attention that can be reached in the visual field (e.g., Eriksen & Eriksen, 1974). With small visual angles, subjects just cannot help benefiting from the contextual letters surrounding the fixated position because these letters still fall in an area of high visual acuity and high attentive resolution. This is progressively less the case when the physical size of the stimuli increases, which implies that the availability of the contextual letters is delayed. This should determine a decrease in the overall performance for words, as is actually the case when the contextual letters are effectively presented shortly after the target (Rumelhart & McClelland, 1982, Experiment 3).

At first sight, it is far from obvious that precueing of the identity of the target, but not of its position, should affect performance the same way position precueing does. On second thought, however, it is conceivable that subjects choose to test for the presence of one of the precued letter by focusing on one particular position at the time of presentation of the stimulus. Systematic focusing on the same position—for example, the leftmost letter of the stimulus—would probably entail a modification of the shape of the position function compared with the no-precue condition, but unsystematic focusing on different positions would not necessarily do so. Hence, the negative results of the analysis by position do not constitute an argument against the spatial-focusing hypothesis. Actually, even though present-day evidence is not completely conclusive, I still consider this hypothesis as highly plausible and deserving of further attention. It has the merit of accounting for the maintenance or the disappearance of the word-superiority effect as a function of visual angle, whether or not the position is precued. It accounts for my initial observation of a stronger detrimental effect of target identity precueing with large than with small words. That this effect barely shows up in the present Experiment 1 has perhaps more to do with an incomplete understanding of the underlying determinants of the effect than with the falsehood of the hypothesis of spatial focusing of attention under precueing about the identity of the target.

To conclude, taken together, the results of the present experiments offer a good example of the way automatic and strategic components of processing affect performance in Reicher's paradigm. With normal spacing of the letters the automatic, irrepressible, word-recognition process elicited by the foveal exposure of a word usually leads to a word-superiority effect. However, changes in strategy induced by new task requirements can profoundly modify the normal processing, eventually impairing performance. If, however, visual conditions are such that the automatic information uptake does not lead to a word-superiority effect, then changes in strategy are no longer exerting any detrimental effect on performance.

ACKNOWLEDGMENTS

I wish to thank Chantal Kempenaers, Regine Kolinsky, and Michel Symons for helping collect the data for Experiments 1 to 3. This work has been partially subsidized by the Belgian "Fonds de la Recherche Fondamentale Collective" (F.R.F.C.) under convention 2.4505.80, and by the Research Council of the University (Project: "Processus cognitifs dans la lecture"). Attendance to the meeting was partially supported by a NATO grant for scientific research. Requests for reprints should be sent to the author, Laboratoire de Psychologie Experimentale, 117 avenue Adolphe Buyl, B 1050 Brussels, Belgium.

REFERENCES

Bjork, E. L., & Estes, W. K. (1973). Letter identification in relation to linguistic context and masking conditions. *Memory and Cognition, 1*, 217–223.
Bryden, M. P., & Sprott, D. A. (1981). Statistical determination of degree of laterality. *Neuropsychologia, 19*, 571–581.
Carr, T. H., Davidson, B. J., & Hawkins, H. L. (1978). Perceptual flexibility in word recognition: Strategies affect orthographic computation but not lexical access. *Journal of Experimental Psychology: Human Perception and Performance, 4*, 674–690.
Carr, T. H., Lehmkuhle, S. W., Kottas, B., Astor-Stetson, E. C., & Harnold, D. (1976). Target position and practice in the identification of letters in varying contexts: A word superiority effect. *Perception and Psychophysics, 19*, 412–416.
Eriksen, B., & Eriksen, C. W. (1974). Effects of noise letters upon the identification of a target letter in a nonsearch task. *Perception and Psychophysics, 16*, 143–149.
Estes, W. K., Bjork, E. L., & Skaar, E. (1974). Detection of single letters and letters in words with changing vs unchanging mask characters. *Bulletin of the Psychonomic Society, 3*, 201–203.
Greenberg, S. W., & Krueger, L. E. (1980). Limitation of the word superiority effect with a fixed target set. *Bulletin of the Psychonomic Society, 15*, 25–28.
Henderson, L. (1980). Is there a lexicality component in the word superiority effect? *Perception and Psychophysics, 28*, 179–184.
Henderson, L. (1982). *Orthography and word recognition in reading*. New York: Academic.
Henik, A., Friedrich, F. J., & Kellogg, W. (1983). The dependence of semantic relatedness effects upon prime processing. *Memory and Cognition, 11*, 366–373.
Holender, D. (1979). Identification of letters in words and of single letters with pre- and postknowledge vs. postknowledge of the alternatives. *Perception and Psychophysics, 25*, 313–318.
Johnston, J. C. (1981). Effects of advance precueing of alternatives on the perception of letters alone and in words. *Journal of Experimental Psychology: Human Perception and Performance, 7*, 560–572.
Johnston, J. C., & McClelland, J. L. (1974). Perception of letters in words: Seek not and ye shall find. *Science, 184*, 1192–1193.
Krueger, L. E. (1970). Search time in a redundant visual display. *Journal of Experimental Psychology, 83*, 391–399.
Marshall, J. C., Caplan, D., & Holmes, J. M. (1975). The measure of laterality. *Neuropsychologia, 13*, 315–322.

Massaro, D. W. (1973). Perception of letters, words, and nonwords. *Journal of Experimental Psychology, 100,* 349–353.

McClelland, J. L., & Rumelhart, D. E. (1981). An interactive activation model of context effects in letter perception: Part 1. An account of basic findings. *Psychological Review, 88,* 375–406.

Morton, J. (1969). Interaction of information in word recognition. *Psychological Review, 76,* 165–178.

Paap, K. R., & Newsome, S. L. (1980). Do small visual angles produce a word superiority effect or differential lateral masking? *Memory and Cognition, 8,* 1–14.

Purcell, D. G., & Stanovich, K. E. (1982). Some boundary conditions for a word superiority effect. *Quarterly Journal of Experimental Psychology, 34A,* 117–134.

Purcell, D. G., Stanovich, K. E., & Spector, A. (1978). Visual angle and the word superiority effect. *Memory and Cognition, 6,* 3–8.

Reicher, G. M. (1969). Perceptual recognition as a function of meaningfulness of stimulus material. *Journal of Experimental Psychology, 81,* 275–280.

Repp, B. H. (1977). Measuring laterality effects in dichotic listening. *Journal of the Acoustical Society of America, 62,* 720–737.

Rumelhart, D. E., & McClelland, J. L. (1982). An interactive activation model of context effects in letter perception: Part 2. The contextual enhancement effect and some tests and extensions of the model. *Psychological Review, 89,* 60–94.

Smith, M. C. (1979). Contextual facilitation in a letter search task depends on how the prime is processed. *Journal of Experimental Psychology: Human Perception and Performance, 5,* 239–251.

Spector, A., & Purcell, D. G. (1977). The word-superiority effect: A comparison between restricted and unrestricted alternative sets. *Perception and Psychophysics, 21,* 323–328.

Thompson, M. C., & Massaro, D. W. (1973). Visual information and redundancy in reading. *Journal of Experimental Psychology, 98,* 49–54.

35 Visual Selection from Multielement Displays: A Model for Partial Report

Claus Bundesen
Copenhagen University, Denmark

Hitomi Shibuya
University of Tsukuba, Japan

Axel Larsen
Copenhagen University, Denmark

ABSTRACT

A model for partial report from briefly exposed visual displays (Bundesen, Pedersen, & Larsen, 1984) is further developed in this chapter. Performance is assumed to reflect the number of targets that enter a short-term memory store. Any target that enters the store is retained and reported with probability Θ. The total number of items (targets, distractors, or extraneous noise) entering the store (parameter K) is independent of the number of targets and distractors in the stimulus. Entrance is determined by selective sampling according to a Luce (1959) ratio rule: Parameter α is the impact per distractor with impact per target as the unit, and parameter ε is the total impact of extraneous noise. With ε kept constant near zero, the model gave fairly accurate fits to observed frequency distributions of the number of correctly reported items as functions of the number of targets (2, 4, or 12), the number of distractors (0, 2, 4, 6, 8, or 10), and the selection criterion (color or alphanumeric class). Estimates for parameters K and Θ were nearly constant across conditions. Variation in α accounted for difference in performance with selection by color versus selection by alphanumeric class.

INTRODUCTION

An important paradigm in the study of visual selection from multielement displays is based on the partial-report technique introduced by Sperling (1960). In this paradigm, a selection criterion partitions the stimulus ensemble (consisting of all the elements that might appear in a stimulus display) into a set of targets and a set of distractors. A naming rule maps the stimulus ensemble onto a set of permissible names. The subject is instructed to respond to each stimulus display by reporting as many targets as possible while ignoring the distractors, so the task is to apply the naming rule to those, and only those, elements in the display that satisfy the selection criterion.[1] Performance with different selection criteria may be compared while keeping constant the naming rule (cf. von Wright, 1968, 1970). Performance with displays without distractors provides a whole-report baseline.

Whole-report performance is limited and stable. With briefly exposed visual displays of letters or digits, Sperling (1960, 1963) found that the number of items correctly reported was close to the number of items in the display when displays contained four or fewer items, and averaged between four and five items for displays containing five or more items (whole-report limitation). The same result held for various spatial arrangements of the stimulus items and for exposure durations varying between 5 and 500 msec with dark or moderately light pre- and postexposure fields. If an appropriate mask is presented at display offset, the number of items reported increases rapidly from zero to about four as display duration is increased from zero up to some value between 50 and 100 msec; with further increase in display duration, the rate of increase in number of items reported is much smaller, about one item per 100 msec at most (see Coltheart, 1972, 1980; Sperling, 1963, 1967). To comprehend these findings, Sperling (1967) suggested that the whole-report limitation reflects the limited capacity of a short-term store (recognition buffer memory) with fast read-in and slow read-out.

Efficiency of selection by a given criterion is often expressed in terms of partial-report advantage (Sperling, 1960), a measure computed by subtracting the whole-report score (number of items correct in whole report) from the so-called partial-report score (number of items correct in partial report divided by the proportion of targets in the display). Numerous studies have shown clear advantage for partial report based on simple physical characteristics such as spatial position (e.g., Sperling, 1960), color (von Wright, 1968), brightness (von Wright, 1968), and certain aspects of shape (Bundesen et al., 1984; Turvey & Kravetz, 1970; von Wright, 1970). Early studies showed negligible advantage for partial report based on alphanumeric class (Sperling, 1960; von Wright,

---

[1]Broadbent (1970) proposed a distinction between stimulus-set and response-set conditions. Briefly, a combination of a selection criterion and a naming rule yields stimulus-set conditions if, and only if, there are elements x and y such that x is a target, y is a distractor, and the names of x and y are the same. Conversely, response-set conditions are obtained if, and only if, the partition of the stimulus ensemble defined by the naming rule (consisting of sets of same-named elements) is either identical to, or a refinement of, the partition defined by the selection criterion (consisting of the target set and the distractor set).

1970), suggesting a fundamental difference between selection by simple physical characteristics and selection "by category" (see Coltheart, 1972). Later results were different. When timing and uncertainty of cues were equated across partial- and whole-report conditions, partial-report advantage was also found for selection by alphanumeric class (see Bundesen et al., 1984; Duncan, 1983; Merikle, 1980).

Partial-report advantage demonstrates that selection occurs, but not how it occurs. It is a crude measure of selective efficiency, inversely related to the proportion of targets in the stimulus display (Bundesen et al., 1984). To interpret the data, a model is needed. In this chapter, a model for partial report proposed by Bundesen et al. (1984) is further developed. The model relates performance to the number of targets (T) and distractors (D) in the stimulus, providing a measure for efficiency of selection that is independent of T and D.

MODEL

The model assumes that, whether partial or whole report is required, performance on any trial reflects the number of targets that enter a limited-capacity short-term memory store. Any target that enters the store is correctly reported with probability Θ, regardless of the fate of other items.

Items that enter the store may be targets, distractors, or extraneous noise. The total number of items entering the store, K, is independent of the number of targets and distractors in the stimulus.[2]

Read-in to the store is conceived as selective sampling of items, one by one, without replacement. Selection among items occurs in accordance with a constant-ratio rule (Clarke, 1957; Luce, 1959; Luce, Bush, & Galanter, 1963). Specifically, for a given selection criterion, there is a ratio scale v such that, given that $k - 1$ items have been selected, the conditional probability that item i is the kth ($1 \leq k \leq K$) to be selected equals

$$\frac{\delta(i, k)v(i)}{\sum_{j} \delta(j, k)v(j)}, \qquad (35.1)$$

where the summation extends over all items; $\delta(j, k) = 0$, if item j is among the first $k - 1$ items selected; otherwise, $\delta(j, k) = 1$. In words, items are assigned *impacts* such that the probability that any not-yet-selected item is the next one to

---

[2]The formulation implies that if the number of items in the stimulus is smaller than K, then one or more extraneous noise items must enter the short-term store. Note that expectations concerning the number of targets sampled would be the same in case the model were modified by assuming that, say, if and when all items in the stimulus had been sampled, sampling terminated.

Four-Parameter Version

Assume that, to a first approximation, only those targets that enter the short-term store get correctly reported. If so, the model implies that in case n targets enter the short-term store, the conditional probability distribution for the number of targets correctly reported is the binomial distribution for n Bernoulli trials with probability Θ for success.[3]

Consider two further simplifications. First, if selection among targets is random, all targets have identical impacts. If selection among distractors is random, all distractors have identical impacts. If both conditions are met, no generality is lost in setting the impact of a target to 1 and the impact of a distractor to α, where α is a constant.

Second, let the number of extraneous noise items (in the experimental situation or in long-term memory) be large, and let each one have a small probability of entering the short-term memory store on a given trial. If K is small, then, the total impact of the not-yet-selected extraneous noise items changes little during a trial. Accordingly, the effect of extraneous noise items can be summarized by a single parameter ε representing the sum of their impacts.

The suggested simplifications leave four parameters: number of items entering the short-term store, K; impact per distractor with impact per target as the unit, α; total impact of extraneous noise with impact per target as the unit, ε; and the probability that a target that has entered the store gets reported, Θ. Parameter α is proposed as a measure for efficiency of selection. If α is zero, selection is perfect. If α equals 1, sampling is nonselective. If α is greater than 1, the subject selects distractors rather than targets.

To see how the model works, consider a subject trying to select as many targets as possible from a briefly exposed display containing T targets and D distractors. Let K equal four. Regardless of T and D, a total of four items is transferred to the short-term memory store. As an example, if both T and D are greater than 1, the probability that the first item selected is a distractor, the second a target, the third an extraneous noise item, and the fourth a target is given by the product of $\alpha D/(T + \alpha D + \varepsilon)$, $T/[T + \alpha(D - 1) + \varepsilon]$, $\varepsilon/[(T - 1) + \alpha(D - 1) + \varepsilon]$, and $(T - 1)/[(T - 1) + \alpha(D - 1) + \varepsilon]$. In case two targets enter the short-term store, the conditional probability distribution for the number of targets correctly reported is the binomial distribution for two Bernoulli trials with probability Θ for success.

---

[3]The model yields no precise predictions for the number of erroneously reported items.

Previous Work

Bundesen et al. (1984) investigated a three-parameter model for partial report identical to the present four-parameter model with parameter Θ kept constant at a value of 1 (perfect retention and report of targets that have entered the short-term store). The model was tested in a variety of conditions with partial reports based on brightness, color, shape, or alphanumeric class. In each condition, targets and distractors were positioned at random within a 5×5 matrix. Number of targets T and number of distractors D were varied orthogonally from 0 to 20 in steps of 5 with the constraint that $0 < (T + D) \leq 25$. The three-parameter model gave good fits to the mean number of items correctly reported as a function of T and D. Parameter K showed little variation with the selection criterion, estimates for parameter ε were rather small, and parameter α varied widely across conditions.

Consider the effect of introducing Θ as a free parameter. In the previous study, T and D were either zero or else larger than K, so predicted mean scores (number of targets sampled and reported) were close to those that would have been obtained if the model had assumed sampling with replacement, rather than sampling without replacement. Thus, the predicted mean score was approximately equal to K (i.e., the number of items sampled) times $T/(T + \alpha D + \varepsilon)$ (i.e., the probability that the first item sampled is a target). By the present four-parameter model, the predicted mean score (number of targets reported) approximately equals the same value multiplied by Θ. When Θ is treated as a free parameter, then, reliable separate estimates for K and Θ cannot be derived from patterns of mean scores like those collected by Bundesen et al. (1984). However, reliable estimates for the product of K and Θ can be obtained, and previous estimates for K by the three-parameter model may be regarded as estimates for $K\Theta$ in the four-parameter model.

EXPERIMENT

The four-parameter model for partial report was tested against observed frequency distributions of the number of items correctly reported as functions of number of targets (2, 4, or 12), number of distractors (0, 2, 4, 6, 8, or 10), and selection criterion (color or alphanumeric class). All analyses were based on individual data.

Method

Subjects

Two subjects participated. Subject HS was a Japanese female, aged 25, and among the authors. Subject MJ was a Danish male, aged 38, trained as an observer in psychophysical studies, but naive with respect to the purpose of the experiment. MJ was paid by the hour. Both subjects had corrected-to-normal visual acuity and normal color vision.

Conditions

There were two color and two alphanumeric conditions. In the color conditions, stimulus items were blue and green capital letters with approximate Munsell notations of 7.5B 8/4 and 5GY 8.5/10, respectively. In one condition, blue items were targets, and green ones were distractors; in the other, green items were targets, and blue ones were distractors. In the alphanumeric conditions, stimulus items were blue-green (7.5BG 8/4) capital letters and digits. In one condition, letters were targets, and digits were distractors; in the other, digits were targets, and letters were distractors.

Displays

Every stimulus display showed a number of characters positioned around the perimeter of an imaginary circle centered on fixation. Each of the characters was positioned at either 1 o'clock, 2 o'clock, ..., or 12 o'clock, such that no position was occupied by more than one character. Under the experimental viewing conditions, a single character subtended about .4° in width and .6° in height. Stroke width was about .09°. The distance from the center of the character to the fixation point was 2.23°, and the center-to-center distance between characters in adjacent positions was 1.16°.

Let T be the number of targets in a display and D the number of distractors. T was either 2, 4, or 12. When T was 2, D was either 0, 2, 4, 6, 8, or 10. When T was 4, D was 0, 2, 4, 6, or 8. When T was 12, D was 0. In each display, the spatial distribution of the $T + D$ items over the 12 positions was random. Identity of individual letters was determined by drawing at random, with replacement, from a set of 18 consonants (including *B, C, D, F, H, J, K, L, M, N, P, Q, R, T, V, W, X,* and *Z*). Identities of individual digits were drawn at random, with replacement, from a set of nine digits (excluding *0*).

Apparatus and Procedure

The displays were presented on a SONY CVM–2250E RGB monitor equipped with P–22 fast-decay phosphors. The monitor was controlled by a Digital Equipment Corporation PDP–11/40 computer with a DEC VT–125 graphics processor. Refresh rate (raster and image frequency) was 50 Hz. All displayed characters were selected from the standard character set supplied with the VT–125 processor.

The subject viewed the displays from a distance of 2 m in a semidarkened room. The luminance of the characters was about 300 cd/m² (blue and blue-green) or 500 cd/m² (green), and the background luminance of the screen was about 5 cd/m². Viewing was binocular, and a fixation mark (a small cross) was permanently visible at the center of the screen.

Each trial was initiated by the subject. When adequately fixated, he or she pressed a key to give an immediate exposure of the stimulus display. Exposure time was 60 msec. The task was to report as many targets as possible and to ignore the distractors. The instruction specified that a target should be reported if, and only if, the subject was "fairly certain" that it was correctly identified; the location of the target should be indicated as accurately as possible, if necessary by guessing. The subject wrote the report on a response sheet by filling in a number of cells in a printed circular representation of the possible positions from 1 o'clock up to 12 o'clock. On the average, a trial took about 15 sec. A 15 min break was required after each block of 144 experimental trials.

Design

All variables were manipulated within subjects, and all randomizations were independently done for the two subjects. Each subject served in 2304 experimental trials corresponding to 48 replications of each of the 12 combinations of T and D for each of the four conditions. The trials were distributed over four sessions and were blocked by condition within sessions such that a 4 × 4 matrix showing condition as a function of number of session (1, 2, 3, or 4) and order of block (1, 2, 3, or 4) formed a Latin square. Each block (one-fourth of one session) comprised 12 experimental subblocks, and each subblock consisted of 12 trials, one for each combination of T and D, ordered at random.

Every block was preceded by 24 trials for warming up with the selection criterion. The first experimental session was preceded by a practice session comprising about 200 trials in which similar stimulus material was employed to familiarize the subject with the apparatus and procedure.

Results

The two subjects by four conditions yielded eight data sets. Four additional data sets were made by pooling results for the two color conditions and pooling results for the two alphanumeric conditions within subjects. The analyses of the 12 data sets were parallel.

All analyses were based on item scores, rather than position scores.[4] The number of erroneously reported items was relatively low. For selection by color, the mean number of erroneously reported items averaged .43 (SD = .22) across the 12 combinations of T and D for subject HS and .16 (SD = .08) for subject MJ. For selection by alphanumeric class, the average was .39 (SD = .10) for HS and .17 (SD = .07) for MJ.

---

[4]In the terminology proposed by Sperling and Speelman (1970), the position score is the number of items written correctly and in their correct positions. The item score is the position score that would be obtained if, before scoring, the order of the items was permuted so as to maximize the position score.

TABLE 35.1
Observed and Theoretical Frequency Distributions of Number of Correctly Reported Items (Score) as Functions of Number of Targets and Number of Distractors for Subject HS and Selection by Color

		\multicolumn{10}{c}{Number of Distractors}
		0		2		4		6		8		10	
Number of Targets	Score	Obs.[a]	Th.[a]	Obs.	Th.	Obs.	Th.	Obs.	Th.	Obs.	Th.	Obs.	Th.
2	0	.00	.01	.02	.01	.02	.01	.02	.02	.05	.02	.05	.03
	1	.13	.17	.24	.17	.16	.19	.13	.21	.21	.24	.29	.27
	2	.88	.82	.74	.82	.82	.80	.85	.77	.74	.74	.66	.70
4	0	.00	.00	.01	.00	.00	.00	.00	.00	.00	.00		
	1	.01	.01	.01	.02	.03	.04	.06	.05	.04	.07		
	2	.14	.13	.21	.19	.28	.23	.24	.27	.36	.31		
	3	.46	.50	.44	.51	.42	.50	.53	.49	.42	.47		
	4	.40	.36	.33	.28	.27	.23	.17	.18	.18	.15		
12	0	.00	.00										
	1	.00	.01										
	2	.14	.13										
	3	.61	.50										
	4–12	.25[b]	.36										

[a]Observed (Obs.) frequencies are proportions based on 96 trials. Theoretical (Th.) frequencies are probabilities predicted by the partial-report model.

[b]Twenty-three trials with a score of 4 and one with a score of 6.

Maximum likelihood fits of the partial-report model to each of the data sets were computed by a program using an iterative method for searching the space of parameters. All parameters were treated as continuous; for nonintegral values of K, predicted values were calculated as weighted averages such that, for instance, a value of 3.53 for K was treated as a mixture of values of 3 and 4 with a probability of .53 for sampling four items on a trial. Initial explorations showed that little was gained by having ε as a free parameter. In the analyses to be reported, ε (total impact of extraneous noise with impact per target as the unit) was kept constant at 10^{-10}.

Color Conditions

Subject HS. Table 35.1 shows the observed and predicted frequency distributions for the item score of subject HS as functions of T and D for selection by color. Observations are pooled across target colors (blue vs. green), giving 96 trials for each combination of T and D. Out of the 48 observed frequencies, 43 were less than 2 standard deviations from the predicted values, and all were less than 3 standard deviations from predictions.[5] The fit was obtained with K

---

[5]The standard deviation associated with a predicted probability p equaled $\sqrt{p(1-p)/N}$, where $N = 96$.

35. MODEL FOR PARTIAL REPORT 639

(number of items entering short-term memory store) at about 3.5, α (impact per distractor with impact per target as the unit) at about .06, and Θ (probability that a target that has entered the store gets reported) at about .91. Observed and predicted mean item scores derived from the distributions in Table 35.1 are displayed in Fig. 35.1 as functions of D with T as a parameter. The fit accounts for 99.3% of the variance in the observed means.

Results for each of the two color conditions (blue vs. green targets) underlying the observed distributions in Table 35.1 were similar in pattern, and estimates for the parameters were similar in magnitude (see Table 35.2). For each data set, deviations from predictions were evaluated by: (a) subjecting the observed frequency distributions for the item score to exact multinomial tests against the predicted distributions, one test for each combination of T and D (with scores 4 to 12 combined for $T = 12$); (b) converting one-tailed probabilities to values of chi-square for two degrees of freedom (cf., e.g., Gordon, Loveland, & Cureton, 1952); and (c) summing over the 12 combinations of T and D to obtain a statistic distributed as chi-square for $12 \times 2 - 3 = 21$ degrees of freedom on the null hypothesis. As indicated in Table 35.2, deviations from fit reached significance at the .05 level for the pooled data (color total) in Table 35.1. Deviations from fit were significant at the .01 level for the results obtained

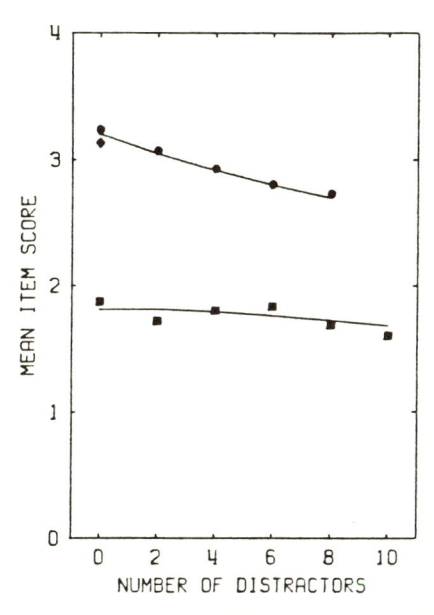

FIG. 35.1. Mean item score (number of correctly reported items) as a function of number of distractors with number of targets as a parameter for subject HS and selection by color. (Number of targets was 2 [squares], 4 [circles], or 12 [diamond]. Unmarked points connected with straight lines represent a theoretical fit to the data by the partial-report model.)

TABLE 35.2
Maximum Likelihood Estimates of Parameters
and Goodness of Fit Measures
for Partial-Report Model Applied to Data for Selection
by Color and Alphanumeric Class

Target Feature	K^a	α^a	θ^a	$\%V^b$	$RMSD^c$	$\chi^2(21)^d$
Subject HS						
Color						
Blue	3.51	.077	.897	97.9	.089	40.6**
Green	3.54	.044	.916	99.3	.055	17.3
Total	3.53	.061	.906	99.3	.052	36.0*
Class						
Letter	3.42	.396	.886	98.2	.092	31.0
Digit	3.64	.440	.878	95.6	.159	29.2
Total	3.52	.419	.883	98.5	.086	31.0
Subject MJ						
Color						
Blue	3.59	.033	.927	97.6	.100	41.8**
Green	3.63	.055	.958	98.0	.095	29.9
Total	3.61	.043	.942	98.3	.087	46.9***
Class						
Letter	3.65	.283	.959	97.9	.110	39.8**
Digit	3.41	.327	.970	97.8	.108	45.6**
Total	3.53	.304	.965	98.5	.090	58.3***

[a] K = number of items entering short-term memory store; α = impact per distractor with impact per target as the unit; θ = probability that a target that has entered the store gets reported. A fourth parameter, ϵ, representing the total impact of extraneous noise with impact per target as the unit, was kept constant at 10^{-10}.

[b] Percentage of variance (with number of targets and number of distractors) in observed mean score (number of items correctly reported) accounted for by the fit.

[c] Square root of the mean squared deviation between observed and theoretical mean scores.

[d] Based on exact multinomial tests (one for each combination of number of targets and number of distractors) for deviations between observed and theoretical frequency distributions of the number of correctly reported items.

*$p < .05$.
**$p < .01$.
***$p < .001$.

with blue targets, but deviations were not significant ($p = .69$) for the results with green targets.

Subject MJ. Results for subject MJ were similar. Fairly close correspondence was found between observed and predicted frequency distributions for the item score as functions of T and D. For data pooled across target colors, 39 out of 48 observed frequencies were less than 2 standard deviations from the predicted values, and all were less than three standard deviations from predictions. The fit was obtained with K at about 3.6, α at about .04, and Θ at about .94. Variation with T and D in the predicted mean item scores accounted for 98.3% of the variance in the observed means.

Results for the two color conditions (blue vs. green targets) were similar in pattern, and estimates for the parameters were comparable (cf. Table 35.2). For the pooled data, deviations from fit reached significance at the .001 level. Deviations from fit were significant at the .01 level for the results with blue targets, but insignificant ($p = .09$) for the results with green targets.

Alphanumeric Conditions

Subject HS. Close correspondence was found between observed and predicted frequency distributions for the item score as functions of T and D. For data pooled across target classes (letters vs. digits), 45 out of 48 observed frequencies were less than 2 standard deviations from the predicted values, and all were less than 3 standard deviations from predictions. The fit was obtained with K at about 3.5, α at about .42, and Θ at about .88. The observed and predicted mean item scores are displayed in Fig. 35.2 as functions of D with T as a parameter. The fit accounts for 98.5% of the variance in the observed means.

Results for the two alphanumeric conditions (letter vs. digit targets) were similar in pattern, and estimates for the parameters were comparable (cf. Table 35.2). Deviations from fit were insignificant for both the pooled data ($p = .07$), the data for letter targets ($p = .07$), and the data for digit targets ($p = .11$).

Subject MJ. Fairly close correspondence was found between observed and predicted frequency distributions for the item score as functions of T and D. For data pooled across target classes, 36 out of 48 observed frequencies were less than 2 standard deviations from the predicted values, one was at a distance of 3 standard deviations, and none were beyond. The fit was obtained with K at about 3.5, α at about .30, and Θ at about .96. Variation with T and D in the predicted mean item scores accounted for 98.5% of the variance in the observed means.

Results for the two alphanumeric conditions (letter vs. digit targets) were similar, as were estimates for the parameters (cf. Table 35.2). For the pooled data, deviations from fit were significant at the .001 level, and for both the results with letter targets and the results with digit targets, deviations from fit were significant at the .01 level.

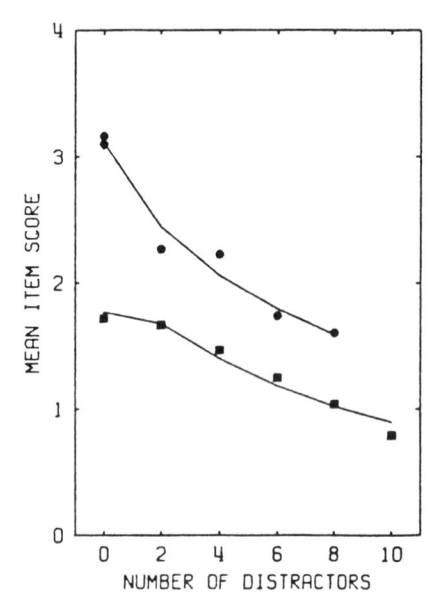

FIG. 35.2. Mean item score (number of correctly reported items) as a function of number of distractors with number of targets as a parameter for subject HS and selection by alphanumeric class. (Number of targets was 2 [squares], 4 [circles], or 12 [diamond]. Unmarked points connected with straight lines represent a theoretical fit to the data by the partial-report model.)

Summary Statistics

For both color and alphanumeric conditions, correspondence between observed and predicted frequency distributions for item scores as functions of T and D was fairly close. Out of 192 observed frequencies in the four pooled data sets, 163 were less than 2 standard deviations from the predicted values, and none were more than 3 standard deviations from predictions. For the observed mean item scores, the proportion of variance accounted for averaged 98.7%.

Some systematic deviations from predictions did appear. Combining the exact multinomial tests for the pooled data sets, $\chi^2(84) = 172$, which is highly significant. The largest contributions to chi-square came from $T{:}D$ combinations 4:0, 4:2, and 12:0, reflecting that, even though predictions for 12:0 and 4:0 were the same, observed scores for 12:0 were slightly lower than those for 4:0. Another systematic deviation appeared in the results for T equal to 12: On six out of 384 trials (1.6%), more than four items were correctly reported. As the model stands, scores above 4 should never be obtained with parameter K set below 4.

Estimates for parameters K and Θ varied little with the selection criterion. Across the two subjects, estimates for K averaged 3.57 for the color conditions and 3.52 for the alphanumeric conditions. Estimates for Θ averaged .924 for the color conditions and, again, .924 for the alphanumeric conditions. Estimates for parameter α varied widely with the selection criterion, averaging .052 for the color conditions and .361 for the alphanumeric conditions.

DISCUSSION

Our model for partial report provided fairly accurate accounts of the rather complex patterns of data observed in the current experiment and the experiments reported by Bundesen et al. (1984). Further speculations on the model seem warranted. Let us consider, first, the units among which selection is made; second, impacts of these units; and finally, order of processing.

Units

In our experiment, the units among which selection was made were individual letters and digits. Under whole-report conditions, Allport found the number of correctly reported items to be essentially the same function of onset–onset time between stimulus display and noise mask whether the individual items were letter strings forming familiar words or single letters (see Allport, 1977). We predict that, under partial-report conditions with selection among words instead of single letters and digits, performance would still conform to our model.

In the current experiment, selection could be based on the distinction between letters and digits. Using meaningful words as items and animal names as the target set, Allport (1977) showed some efficiency of selection on the basis of semantic class. The results suggest that semantic characteristics of items are retrieved before items enter the short-term store.

Impacts

The impact of an item measures the tendency to attend to that item. A comprehensive account of impacts might be as intricate as the theory of cathexis in psychoanalysis. We make do here with a few conjectures. First, as illustrated in the reported experiment, the impact of an item varies with the selection criterion. In our studies, the effect of changing the criterion by reversing the roles of targets and distractors has been particularly simple; to a first approximation, the impact of distractors relative to targets (parameter α) has been the same before and after a reversal.

Second, with a given selection criterion, we predict increase in impact of distractors with increasing similarity between distractors and targets. For example, if target color were kept constant, increasing the similarity in color between distractors and targets should increase the impact of distractors as measured by parameter α without affecting other parameters in the model.

Third, practice may be important. To account for effects of practice in visual search with initially unfamiliar groups of characters as target sets, Shiffrin, Dumais, and Schneider (1981) suggested that the "attention strength" (impact) of individual items is altered during training such that items gradually gain in strength when serving as targets and lose in strength when serving as distractors.

Processing Order

Read-in to the short-term store is modeled as sampling of items, one by one, without replacement. Before entrance to the store, targets and distractors are assumed to be processed in parallel. These assumptions should hold whether or not "automatic attending" has developed. On the hypothesis suggested by Shiffrin et al. (1981), development of automaticity may be viewed as follows:

Given a selection criterion that initially is unfamiliar, impact per distractor is initially about the same as impact per target. Accordingly, items are transferred to the short-term store, one by one, such that selection is random with respect to the distinction between targets and distractors. During training, items serving as targets acquire greater impact than items serving as distractors. As parameter α gets smaller, performance becomes indicative of the parallel organization of preattentive processes. For the limiting case in which α is zero, the number of distractors D should have no effect at all, and if number of targets T is kept constant at 1, the processing system may behave as a parallel one with unlimited capacity (cf. Duncan, 1980).

A note is in order that, when α is small, effects of D may be invisible in observed scores when T is small, but obvious when T is large. The point is illustrated by the data obtained in our color conditions. With parameter α at about .05, there was virtually no effect of D for T equal to 2, but obvious effects of D for T equal to 4. To see how the model predicted this pattern, consider an example with parameter K set at 4. For T equal to 2, up to two misses (cases in which a distractor is selected before a target) might occur without affecting the item score. But for T equal to 4, effects of distractors would appear in the score once a single miss occurred.

Concluding Discussion

Achievements

The model for partial report advanced in this chapter has provided accurate accounts for the joint effects of number of targets and number of distractors on the number of items correctly reported with a variety of selection criteria. In the present study, the model was found to do fairly well at describing not only mean scores, but also the frequency distributions of scores for individual subjects. Estimates for the parameters were psychologically plausible, and variation in a single parameter, α, accounted for the strong contrast in performance obtained with selection by color versus selection by alphanumeric class. The model seems generally consistent with the literature on visual search through briefly exposed displays, and it has clearly testable implications regarding which of its parameters ought to be influenced by variables such as practice and target–distractor discriminability.

Limitations

The present study showed some small, but significant, deviations between data and model. In particular, although predictions for T:D combinations 12:0 and 4:0 were the same, observed scores for 12:0 were slightly lower than those for 4:0. The effect might be due to difference in strength of lateral masking (cf. Wolford & Hollingsworth, 1974). Lateral interference effects are well documented (see, e.g., Bouma, 1978), but not treated by our model.

Perspectives

By extensions in scope and depth, the model for partial report might be developed into a general theory for visual selection from multielement displays. A possible extension in depth—a derivation of the constant-ratio rule expressed in Eq. 35.1 from a simple process model—is outlined in the Appendix.

ACKNOWLEDGMENTS

This research was conducted at Copenhagen University and was supported by a Danish State scholarship and traveling grant to Hitomi Shibuya. The authors are indebted to Søren Ellegaard and Jørgen Rathje for engineering assistance.

Appendix

Consider a selection process that is a parallel race between N items toward the state "selected." We outline a proof that, if processing times for individual items are independent exponentially distributed random variables with rate parameters $v(i)$ and $v(j)$ for arbitrary items i and j, then selection occurs in accordance with the constant-ratio rule. Specifically, the rate parameters form a Luce (1959) v scale such that, given that $k - 1$ items have been selected, the conditional probability that item i is the kth ($1 \leq k \leq N$) to be selected equals

$$\frac{\delta(i, k)v(i)}{\sum_j \delta(j, k)v(j)}, \qquad (35.1)$$

where the summation extends over all items; $\delta(j, k) = 0$, if item j is among the first $k - 1$ items selected; otherwise, $\delta(j, k) = 1$. (See Luce & Suppes, 1965, p. 338, for a related result.)

Proof

According to the assumptions, the processing time for any item i has probability density function $v(i)\exp[-v(i)t]$ and distribution function $1 - \exp[-v(i)t]$, for $t > 0$. For $t \leq 0$, both functions are 0.

For $t > 0$, let $n(t)$ be the number of items that get selected at or before time t. For $h > 0$, $n(t + h) - n(t)$ is the number of items that get selected in the interval from t to $t + h$. It is easy to show that, as h tends to 0, the conditional probability

35. MODEL FOR PARTIAL REPORT

that $n(t + h) - n(t) = 1$, given that $n(t + h) - n(t) \geq 1$, tends to 1. In this sense, items are selected one by one.

The probability that a given item i is the first to be selected equals

$$\int_0^\infty v(i)\exp[-v(i)t] \prod_{j \in S - \{i\}} \exp[-v(j)t]\,dt = \int_0^\infty v(i)\exp\left[-\sum_{j \in S} v(j)t\right] dt$$

$$= \frac{v(i)}{\sum_{j \in S} v(j)},$$

where S is the set of all items. The constant-ratio rule expressed in Eq. 35.1 thus holds for first choices.

Due to the Markovian character of the exponential distribution, the constant-ratio rule in Eq. 35.1 holds for succeeding choices as well. To see this, let T_{k-1}, where $1 < k \leq N$, be the time at which the $(k - 1)$th selection occurs. Note that, given that item i is among the first $k - 1$ items selected, the conditional probability that item i is the kth to be selected equals 0. Given that item i is not among the first $k - 1$ items selected, the conditional probability that item i is selected at or before time t equals 0 for $t \leq T_{k-1}$ and

$$\int_{T_{k-1}}^t v(i)\exp[-v(i)t]\,dt \bigg/ \int_{T_{k-1}}^\infty v(i)\exp[-v(i)t]\,dt$$

$$= 1 - \exp[-v(i)(t - T_{k-1})] \text{ for } t > T_{k-1}.$$

The corresponding conditional probability density function is 0 for $t \leq T_{k-1}$ and $v(i)\exp[-v(i)(t - T_{k-1})]$ for $t > T_{k-1}$. Hence, given that item i is not among the first $k - 1$ items selected, the conditional probability that item i is the kth to be selected equals

$$\int_{T_{k-1}}^\infty v(i)\exp[-v(i)(t - T_{k-1})] \prod_{j \in R - \{i\}} \exp[-v(j)(t - T_{k-1})]\,dt = \frac{v(i)}{\sum_{j \in R} v(j)},$$

where R is the set of all items remaining after selection of the first $k - 1$ items. Eq. 35.1 is thus established.

Remark

In our partial-report model, selection consists in entrance into a short-term store, and for some K such that $1 \leq K \leq N$, the first K items entering the store are the ones selected. Effectively, the race between items toward selection stops when K items have been selected, so k is restricted to the range from 1 to K.

REFERENCES

Allport, D. A. (1977). On knowing the meaning of words we are unable to report: The effects of visual masking. In S. Dornic (Ed.), *Attention and performance VI* (pp. 505-534). Hillsdale, NJ: Lawrence Erlbaum Associates.

Bouma, H. (1978). Visual search and reading: Eye movements and functional visual field: A tutorial review. In J. Requin (Ed.), *Attention and performance VII* (pp. 115-147). Hillsdale, NJ: Lawrence Erlbaum Associates.

Broadbent, D. E. (1970). Stimulus set and response set: Two kinds of selective attention. In D. I. Mostofsky (Ed.), *Attention: Contemporary theory and analysis* (pp. 51-60). New York: Appleton-Century-Crofts.

Bundesen, C., Pedersen, L. F., & Larsen, A. (1984). Measuring efficiency of selection from briefly exposed visual displays: A model for partial report. *Journal of Experimental Psychology: Human Perception and Performance, 10,* 329-339.

Clarke, F. R. (1957). Constant-ratio rule for confusion matrices in speech communication. *Journal of the Acoustical Society of America, 29,* 715-720.

Coltheart, M. (1972). Visual information-processing. In P. C. Dodwell (Ed.), *New horizons in psychology* (Vol. 2, pp. 62-85). Harmondsworth, England: Penguin Books.

Coltheart, M. (1980). Iconic memory and visible persistence. *Perception and Psychophysics, 27,* 183-228.

Duncan, J. (1980). The locus of interference in the perception of simultaneous stimuli. *Psychological Review, 87,* 272-300.

Duncan, J. (1983). Perceptual selection based on alphanumeric class: Evidence from partial reports. *Perception and Psychophysics, 33,* 533-547.

Gordon, M. H., Loveland, E. H., & Cureton, E. E. (1952). An extended table of chi-square for two degrees of freedom, for use in combining probabilities from independent samples. *Psychometrica, 17,* 311-316.

Luce, R. D. (1959). *Individual choice behavior.* New York: Wiley.

Luce, R. D., Bush, R. R., & Galanter, E. (Eds.) (1963). *Handbook of mathematical psychology* (Vol. 1). New York: Wiley.

Luce, R. D., & Suppes, P. (1965). Preference, utility, and subjective probability. In R. D. Luce, R. R. Bush, & E. Galanter (Eds.), *Handbook of mathematical psychology* (Vol. 3, pp. 249-410). New York: Wiley.

Merikle, P. M. (1980). Selection from visual persistence by perceptual groups and category membership. *Journal of Experimental Psychology: General, 109,* 279-295.

Shiffrin, R. M., Dumais, S. T., & Schneider, W. (1981). Characteristics of automatism. In J. Long & A. Baddeley (Eds.), *Attention and performance IX* (pp. 223-238). Hillsdale, NJ: Lawrence Erlbaum Associates.

Sperling, G. (1960). The information available in brief visual presentations. *Psychological Monographs, 74*(11, Whole No. 498).

Sperling, G. (1963). A model for visual memory tasks. *Human Factors, 5,* 19-31.

Sperling, G. (1967). Successive approximations to a model for short-term memory. *Acta Psychologica, 27,* 285-292.

Sperling, G., & Speelman, R. G. (1970). Acoustic similarity and auditory short-term memory: Experiments and a model. In D. A. Norman (Ed.), *Models of human memory* (pp. 151-202). New York: Academic.

Turvey, M. T., & Kravetz, S. (1970). Retrieval from iconic memory with shape as the selection criterion. *Perception and Psychophysics, 8,* 171–172.

Wolford, G., & Hollingsworth, S. (1974). Lateral masking in visual information processing. *Perception and Psychophysics, 16,* 315–320.

von Wright, J. M. (1968). Selection in visual immediate memory. *Quarterly Journal of Experimental Psychology, 20,* 62–68.

von Wright, J. M. (1970). On selection in visual immediate memory. *Acta Psychologica, 33,* 280–292.

Author Index

Italics denote pages with bibliographic information.

A

Abrol, S., *564*
Acosta, E., 468, *471*
Acuna, C., 262, *265*
Adams, J. A., 476, *491*
Adelson, E. H., *280*
Ahmar, H., *564*
Aine, C., 67, 72, 74, *82*
Albano, J. E., 446, *455*
Albright, T. D., 49, 51, *58, 59, 60,* 108, *131*
Alderson, G., 393, *405*
Aldrich, K., 484, 487, 488, *492*
Alexander, M. P., 315, *317*
Alford, J. A., 548, *563*
Alho, K., 358, 359, 360, 361, 362, 363, 364, 367, *371, 372, 373*
Allard, F., 551, *563*
Allman, J. M., 46, 50, *58*
Allmeyer, D. H., 604, *612*
Allport, D. A., 101, *103,* 109, 110, 128, *130,* 149, *165,* 530, *542,* 550, 551, *563,* 576, *582,* 643, *648*
Alluisi, E., 494, *510*
Alston, W., 408, *423*
Ambler, B., 64, *82,* 94, 95, 96, *103*
Andersen, R. A., 68, *83*
Andersen, V. O., 51, *58*
Anderson, J. A., 109, *130,* 478, 485, *491*
Anderson, J. R., 476, 479, 482, *491*
Andrews, D. P., 200, *204*
Angel, R. W., 408, 422, *423, 424*
Anliker, J., 286, *300*
Antonis, B., 530, *542*
Anzola, G. P., 457, 458, 459, 461, 463, 465, 468, *470*
Arai, Y., 412, 418, *424*
Armstrong, W., 408, *424*
Ashby, F. G., 94, *104*
Ashton, J., 339, *353*
Ashton, R., 530, *543*
Astor-Stetson, E. C., 617, *628*
Atkinson, R. C., 94, *103*

B

Bach, M., 444, *454*
Bacharach, V. R., 64, 80, *82,* 88, *103,* 172, *186,* 190, *203*
Baddeley, A. D., 7, 29, 32, *34, 37,* 246, *248,* 494, 505, *509*
Bahrick, H. P., 404, *405*
Baird, J. C., 279, 281, *284*

AUTHOR INDEX

Baizer, J. S., 51, *58*, 444, *454*
Bakan, P., 495, *508*
Baker, C. H., 494, 506, *508*
Baker, J. F., 46, 50, *58*
Ball, K., 272, *283*
Ballard, D. H., 108, *131*
Banich, M. T., *564*
Banks, W. P., 87, *103*
Baribeau-Braun, J., 368, *372*
Barlett, N. R., 411, *424*
Barlow, H. B., 46, *61*
Barnes, M. A., 9, *36*
Baron, J., 8, *34*, 208, *218*
Barresi, J., *565*
Barrett, J., 319, 320, *334*, 538, *542*
Bartz, A. E., 411, *423*
Bashinski, H. S., 64, 80, *82*, 88, *103*, 172, *186*, 190, *203*
Bashore, T. R., 465, *470*
Basili, A. G., 7, 30, 31, *34*
Basili, A. M., 31, *34*
Batchelder, W. H., 549, *563*
Baumgartner, G., 51, *61*
Baxter, D. M., 244, *248*
Beatty, J., 507, *508*, *509*
Beauvois, M.-F., 7, 10, 17, *34*
Beck, J., 64, *82*, 94, 95, 96, *103*, 308, *317*
Becklin, R., 114, *132*, 297, *300*
Bellugi, U., *564*
Bender, M. B., 426, *440*
Benevento, L. A., 45, *59*
Benton, A., 251, 262, *264*
Berger, C., 495, *509*
Berger, D. E., *564*
Berger, T. W., 359, *373*
Berlucchi, G., 465, *470*
Berndt, R. S., 7, 30, 31, *34*, 322, 325, 327, *334*
Bernstein, N., 157, *165*
Berry, S. D., 359, *373*
Bertelson, P., 222, *236*, 467, *470*
Bertoloni, G., 461, 465, 468, *470*
Besner, D., 15, *34*, 551, *563*
Bespalec, D., 555, *565*
Beverley, K. I., 398, *406*
Bielek, K. H., 339, *353*
Biguer, B., 408, 415, 416, 419, 420, 421, 423, *423*
Binford, J. R., 498, 504, 506, *509*, *510*
Bisiach, E., 240, 243, 244, *248*, *249*
Bixby, J. L., 51, *61*

Bizzi, E., 408, *423*
Bjork, E. L., 601, 602, 603, 604, 605, 606, 607, 610, 611, *612*, 615, 617, *628*
Black, S., 32, *34*
Blake, R., 597, *599*
Blauert, J., 345, *353*
Block, R. A., *563*
Bobrow, D. G., 93, *104*, 514, *528*, 580, *583*, 603, *612*
Bobrow, D. J., 134, 135, 143, *146*
Boch, R., 67, *82*, 444, *454*
Boles, D. B., 531, *542*
Bongartz, W., 206, *218*
Bonnet, M., 150, 152, 155, 157, 161, 164, *165*, *166*, *167*
Boothe, R. G., 44, *60*
Boroughs, J. M., 303, *317*
Botwinick, J., 540, *542*
Bouma, H., 88, *103*, 645, *648*
Bowers, D., 222, *236*, 465, 466, *470*, 531, *542*
Bowers, J. C., 502, 503, 504, *509*
Boycott, B. B., 42, 43, *59*
Brachman, M. L., 344, 348, *354*
Bradshaw, G., 539, *542*
Bradshaw, J. L., 222, 223, 224, 226, 227, 228, 230, 232, 234, 235, *236*, 237, 465, 466, 467, 468, *470*, *471*, 531, 537, 541, *542*
Brady, S. A., 222, *237*
Branski, D. M., 531, *542*
Bray, N. W., 549, *563*
Brebner, J., 461, *470*
Bregmann, A. S., 338, *353*
Breitmeyer, B. G., 68, 81, *82*, 302, *317*
Briand, K., 120, *131*, 548, *563*
Brickner, M., 144, *145*
Briggs, G. G., 530, *542*
Brindley, G. S., 46, *59*
Broadbent, D. E., 85, 87, 89, 102, *103*, 110, 121, *131*, *132*, 302, 306, *317*, 356, 363, 371, 403, 406, 506, 508, *509*, 514, 527, 568, *582*, 632, *648*
Broadbent, M. H. P., 110, *132*
Brodmann, K., 43, *59*
Brookhuis, K., 376, *388*
Brouchon, M., 422, *424*
Brown, H. L., 549, 553, *563*, *564*
Bruce, C. J., 51, *59*, 108, *131*, 451, *454*
Bruce, R. C., 531, 537, *542*, *543*
Brunn, J., 321, 323, 333, *334*

Bryan, W. L., 404, *406*
Bryden, M. P., 319, *334,* 618, 623, *628*
Bub, D., 13, 14, 16, 20, 22, 23, 32, *34,* 404, *406*
Buchtel, H. A., 439, *440,* 461, 465, 468, *470*
Buck, L., 496, 500, *509*
Budayr, B., 114, *131*
Buell, T. N., 348, *353*
Bulgarelli, C., 243, *248*
Bullier, J., 45, 48, 49, *59*
Bundesen, C., 97, *103,* 110, *131,* 631, 632, 633, 635, 643, *648*
Bunt, A. H., 48, *60*
Burden, V., 222, *237*
Burkell, J., 91, 97, 98, 100, *104,* 105, 106, 311, *318*
Burt, P. J., *280*
Bush, R. R., 633, *648*
Bushnell, M. C., 67, *82,* 262, *264,* 444, *454*
Butler, B. E., 218, *218*
Butler, R. A., 359, *371*
Butler, S., 53, *62*
Byng, S., 13, 16, 20, *34*

C

Caan, W., 108, *132*
Caharack, G., 404, *406*
Cairney, P., 461, *470*
Callaway, E. C., 497, 498, *509*
Camarda, R., 262, *265*
Campbell, A. J., 207, *218*
Campbell, F., 302, *317*
Campbell, K. B., 356, *372*
Campbell, R., 15, *34*
Canceliere, A., 13, 14, 16, 20, 22, 23, *34*
Canham, L., 303, *317*
Capitani, E., 243, 244, *248*
Caplan, D., 618, 623, *628*
Caramazza, A., 7, 30, 31, *34*
Carden, D., 53, *62*
Carey, R. G., 44, *59*
Carhart, R., 339, *354*
Carpenter, P., 286, *299*
Carr, T. H., 119, *131,* 617, 625, *628*
Carroll, J. F., *564*
Carson, R. E., 531, *543*
Carter, R. C., 88, *104*
Cattelani, R., 467, *470*
Cave, K. R., 321, 323, 333, *334*
Chaddha, N. N., *564*

Chajzyk, D., 122, *131*
Chambers, L., 88, *105*
Cheng, M., 287, *298*
Chernikoff, R., 422, *423*
Cherry, C., 337, *353*
Cherry, E. C., 493, *509*
Chesney, G., 507, *509*
Chillag, N., 143, *146*
Chipuer, H., 539, *542*
Choate, L., 65, 74, 79, 80, *83,* 150, *166,* 195, *203,* 508, *511*
Chu, F. C., 255, *264*
Ciuffreda, K. J., 179, *186*
Clark, L. F., 344, *353*
Clarke, F. R., 633, *648*
Clarke, R., *563*
Clayton, T., 393, *406*
Cohen, C., *565*
Cohen, J., 184, *186*
Cohen, L. A., 408, *424*
Cohen, M., 286, *300*
Cohen, P., 184, *186*
Cohen, Y. A., 7, *36,* 64, 65, 74, 79, 80, *83,* 148, 150, *166,* 189, 190, 191, 192, 194, 195, 197, 198, 199, 202, *203,* 206, *219,* 248, *249,* 508, *511*
Cohn, T. E., 271, *283*
Cole, M., 54, *59*
Cole, R. A., 551, *563*
Colegate, R. L., 64, *82,* 608, *612*
Coles, M. G., 158, *165*
Collewijn, H., 285, 287, 288, 289, 290, 291, 292, 296, 297, *298, 299, 300*
Collin, N. G., 52, *59*
Colquhoun, W. P., 494, 500, 505, *509*
Coltheart, M., 7, 8, 13, 14, 15, 16, 20, 24, 29, 30, *34, 36,* 110, 129, *131,* 551, *563,* 632, 633, *648*
Compos-Ortega, J. A., 44, *59*
Conrad, R., 516, *527*
Conway, J. L., 439, *440*
Cook, J., 531, *543*
Cooper, R., 368, *371*
Corcoran, D. W. J., 494, *509*
Cornacchia, L., 243, *248*
Cornsweet, J. C., 352, *354*
Cornsweet, T. N., 352, *354,* 428, *439*
Corteen, R. S., 101, *104*
Cortese, C., 548, *564*
Costa, L., 235, *237*
Covey, E., 46, 49, 50, *60*

Cowey, A., 42, 43, 46, 48, 52, 53, 56, 57, 59, 61, 108, 131, 172, 187, 206, 218, 257, 264, 439, 440
Cox, P. J., 531, 532, 537, 538, 539, 542
Craft, J. L., 458, 461, 468, 470, 471
Craig, A., 495, 509
Craig, J. C., 224, 237
Craik, F. I. M., 533, 542
Crane, H. D., 292, 299, 428, 439
Crea, F., 465, 470
Cristoffanini, P., 549, 563
Crossman, E. R. F. W., 403, 406
Crowder, R. G., 363, 371
Crowne, D. P., 223, 237, 257, 264
Cunitz, R. J., 286, 288, 300
Cureton, E. E., 639, 648
Curio, G., 287, 298
Curry, S. H., 368, 371
Cynader, M., 398, 406

D

Dafoe, C. G., 142, 145
Dalbokova, D., 368, 372
Dallas, M., 548, 563, 571, 572, 582
Dalrymple-Alford, E. C., 114, 131
Damasio, A. R., 54, 59
Damasio, H., 54, 59
Dannebring, G. L., 120, 131, 548, 563
Danta, G., 53, 59
Dark, V. J., 64, 83, 365, 371, 568, 569, 570, 575, 580, 582, 586, 587, 592, 596, 598
Daroff, R. B., 439, 440
Darwin, C. J., 222, 237, 337, 352, 353
Davelaar, E., 551, 563
Davidoff, J., 468, 470
Davidson, B. J., 64, 65, 74, 80, 83, 172, 173, 187, 190, 197, 199, 204, 625, 628
Davies, D. R., 494, 495, 500, 505, 509, 510
Davies-Jones, G. A. B., 54, 61
Davis, E. T., 271, 272, 278, 279, 283, 284
Day, J., 555, 564
Deck, M. D. F., 428, 440
Deese, J., 505, 509
DeLong, M. R., 445, 454
Dember, W. N., 494, 511
de Monasterio, F. M., 45, 51, 59, 61
De Renzi, E., 223, 237, 251, 252, 262, 263, 264
Derouesne, J., 7, 10, 17, 34
Derrick, W., 507, 509

Desimone, R., 49, 51, 58, 59, 60, 108, 131
Desmedt, J. E., 357, 367, 371
Deutsch, D., 356, 364, 371, 568, 582
Deutsch, G., 319, 334
Deutsch, J. A., 356, 371, 568, 582
Diamond, I. T., 44, 59
Dirks, S. J., 358, 371
Di Stefano, M., 465, 470
Dodge, R., 287, 299
Dodson, J. D., 541, 543
Donald, M. W., 74, 82, 357, 366, 371
Donchin, E., 158, 165, 375, 387, 507, 509
Dosher, B., 276, 284
Douglas, R. M., 439, 440
Dow, B. M., 48, 59, 444, 454
Dowling, J. E., 42, 43, 59
Doyle, T. J., 322, 325, 327, 334
Dreher, B., 43, 60
Dubois, M. F. W., 287, 299
Dumais, S. T., 644, 648
Duncan, J., 88, 90, 91, 93, 94, 95, 96, 97, 104, 206, 218, 568, 586, 582, 633, 644, 648
Dunn, D., 101, 104
Durso, F. T., 548, 563
Dursteler, M. R., 52, 60
Dye, R. H., Jr., 339, 342, 343, 344, 345, 346, 353

E

Eason, C., 411, 424
Eason, R. G., 65, 67, 82
Eerland, E., 64, 84
Egeth, H., 122, 131
Egeth, H. E., 112, 132, 217, 218, 601, 602, 603, 604, 605, 606, 607, 611, 612
Ehrlichman, M., 538, 542
Eich, E., 571, 582
Ellis, A. W., 7, 34
El Massioui, F., 368, 372
Eriksen, B. A., 87, 104, 601, 602, 603, 604, 605, 608, 610, 611, 612, 627, 628
Eriksen, C. W., 64, 82, 87, 95, 104, 112, 131, 172, 187, 207, 218, 513, 514, 517, 518, 527, 586, 588, 598, 601, 602, 603, 604, 605, 608, 610, 611, 612, 627, 628
Erlichman, H., 319, 320, 334
Echallier, J. F., 407, 408, 420, 424
Estes, W. K., 602, 604, 605, 606, 612, 615, 617, 628

AUTHOR INDEX

Evarts, E. V., 158, *165*
Evett, L., 119, *131*
Evinger, C., 297, *299*

F

Farah, M. J., 320, *334*, 570, 575, 580, *582*
Favreau, D., 93, *104*
Feigin, D. S., 539, *542*
Feldman, J. A., 108, *131*
Feldman, M. L., 56, *59*
Feustel, T. C., 571, 572, 575, *582*
Findlay, J. M., 192, *203*
Finney, D. J., 200, *203*
Fiori, N., 152, 153, *165*
Fischer, B., 51, *59, 61*, 67, *82*, 444, *454*
Fischer, M. H., 287, *299*
Fischer, S. D., *564*
Fischler, I., 569, *582*
Fisk, A. D., 476, 479, 480, 484, 486, 488, 489, *491, 492*, 506, 507, *509*, 569, 570, *582*
Fitter, M. J., 93, *104*, 501, *511*
Fitts, P. M., 458, *470*
Fitzgerald, P. G., 378, 384, 387, *387*
Fitzpatrick, P., 44, *59*
Fleishman, E. A., 494, *510*
Flood, W., 408, *424*
Flowers, L., 67, *82*
Floyd, R., 286, *300*
Fodor, J. A., 4, *34*, 292, 406, 597, *598*
Folkard, S., 501, *509*
Forbes, S. M., 507, *511*
Ford, J. M., 358, 359, *371*
Forster, K. I., 26, *37*
Foster, K. H., 51, *59*
Fowler, C. A., 569, *582*
Fox, J. C., 287, *299*
Francis, W. N., 575, *582*
Francolini, C. N., 122, *131*
Franklin, P. E., 569, 570, 579, *583, 594*, 595, *599*
Freund, T. F., 57, *61*
Friedland, R. P., 251, *264*
Friedman, A., 142, *145*
Friedman, H., 532, 538, 541, *542*
Friedman, R. B., 315, *317*
Friedrich, F. J., 262, *265*, 569, 579, *582*, 594, 595, *598*, 626, *628*
Fries, W., 45, *60*
Fruhstorfer, H., 359, *371*

Fuchs, A. F., 48, *60*, 255, *264*, 297, *299*, 412, *424*, 426, *440*
Funnell, E., 10, 12, 18, 20, *34*, 550, 551, *563*

G

Gaillard, A. W. K., 357, 358, 359, 360, 361, 362, 363, 366, *372*, 375, 377, 378, 383, 384, *387, 388*
Galambos, R., 79, 81, *82, 83*
Galanter, E., 633, *648*
Gale, A., 496, 505, *509*
Ganz, L., 68, 81, *82*, 302, *317*
Garbart, H., 217, *218*
Gardner, E. B., 531, *542*
Gardner, G. T., 95, *104*, 601, *612*
Garland, H., 408, *423*
Garner, W. R., 150, *165*, 515, *527*, 603, *612*
Garvin, E. A., 533, *543*
Gaska, J. P., 51, *59*
Gaskill, S. J., 142, *145*
Gates, J., 428, *440*
Gattass, R., 46, 49, 50, 51, *60*
Gazzaniga, M. S., 227, *237*, 320, *334*, 426, 427, 428, 438, 439, *439, 440*
Gebhard, P., 555, *565*
Geffen, G., 531, 537, *542*
Geisler, C. D., 347, *354*
Geisler, W. S., 601, *612*
Gelade, G., 73, 81, *83*, 86, 91, 94, 95, 96, 102, *104*, 110, *132*, 141, *146*, 205, 206, 207, 208, 217, 218, *219*, 307, 308, 311, *318*
Gentilucci, M., 253, 262, 263, *265*
Georgopoulos, A. P., 262, *265*, 445, *454*
Gerard, L., *564*
Gilbert, C. D., 44, *60*
Gillund, G., 560, *563*
Gleitman, H., 517, *527*
Glencross, D. J., 412, 422, *424*
Gloerich, A. B. M., 376, *388*
Glushko, R. J., 9, *35*
Goldberg, E., 235, *237*
Goldberg, M. E., 67, 68, *82, 84*, 149, *167*, 172, *187*, 206, *219*, 254, 262, *264, 265*, 442, 444, 448, 450, 451, 453, *454, 455*
Goodale, M. A., 423, *424*
Goodman, D., 155, *165*
Gopher, D., 134, 135, 136, 142, 143, 144, *145, 146*, 530, *542*
Gordon, M. M., 639, *648*

Gough, P. B., 548, *563*
Graham, N., 269, 271, 272, 274, 276, 278, 279, 283, *283, 284*
Gratton, G., 158, *165*
Green, J., 75, *83*
Greenberg, S. W., 617, *628*
Gregory, M., 508, *509*
Grice, G. R., 303, *317*
Gross, C. G., 49, 50, 51, *58, 59, 60,* 108, *131*
Gross, N. B., 347, *354*
Grusser, O. J., 287, *298*
Guido, W., 367, *371*
Guitton, D., 439, *440*
Guld, C., 51, *58*
Gurnsey, R., 207, *218*
Guttman, D., 114, 116, *132*

H

Haber, N., 274, 275, 282, *284*
Haddad, G. M., 286, 289, 290, *300*
Hafter, E. R., 339, 342, 343, 344, 345, 346, 347, 348, 349, *353, 354*
Hämäläinen, M., 362, *371*
Hamayan, E., *564*
Hansen, J. C., 74, *82,* 366, 368, *371,* 508, *509*
Hari, R., 362, *371*
Harnold, D., 617, *628*
Harris, C. S., 302, *318*
Harter, M., 65, *82*
Harter, M. F., *83*
Harter, M. R., 67, 72, 74, *82,* 367, *371*
Harter, N., 404, *406*
Harting, J. K., 44, *60*
Harvey, A. R., 44, 48, *60*
Harvey, N., 508, *509*
Harvey, R., *563*
Hasher, L., 555, 559, *563*
Hawkins, H. L., 206, *218,* 625, *628*
Hayes, C. C., 412, *424*
Hayhow, W. R., 44, *59*
Hedge, A., 458, 459, *470*
Heilman, K. M., 72, *82,* 172, 178, *187,* 222, 236, 240, 249, 251, *264,* 465, 466, 467, 468, *470,* 531, *542*
Heinz, S. P., 90, 97, *104*
Hellige, J. B., 531, 532, 537, 538, 539, *542*
Henderson, L., 9, 16, 26, 29, *35,* 614, 624, 625, *628*

Hendrickson, A. E., 48, *60*
Hendry, S. H. C., 56, *60*
Henik, A. M., 121, *131,* 569, 579, *582,* 594, 595, *598,* 626, *628*
Henning, G. B., 339, *353*
Henry, G. H., 44, 48, *60*
Hepp-Reymond, M. C., 408, *424*
Herman, M., 286, 288, *300*
Hernández-Peón, R., 356, *371*
Heron, W., 465, *470*
Heywood, C. H., 53, *59*
Hicks, R. E., 539, *542*
Hicks, R. F., 530, 538, *543*
Higgins, J. R., 422, *424*
Hikosaka, O., 442, 444, 446, 448, 453, *454*
Hillyard, S. A., 65, 66, 67, 68, 72, 73, 74, 79, 81, *82, 83, 84,* 357, 358, 359, 366, 368, *371, 373,* 508, *509*
Hilton, R. C., 53, *59*
Hind, J. E., 347, *354*
Hink, R. F., 366, 368, *371*
Hinrichs, J. V., 458, 461, *471*
Hinton, G. E., 109, *130, 131*
Hintzman, D. L., *563*
Hirsch, J., 274, 276, 283, *284*
Hirst, W., 404, *406*
Hiscock, M., 530, 539, *542, 543*
Hitch, G. J., 246, *248*
Hochberg, J., 121, *131*
Hockey, R., 65, 74, 79, 80, *83,* 150, *166,* 195, 202, *203,* 505, 508, *509, 511*
Hoffman, J. E., 64, *82, 83,* 94, 97, *104,* 142, 145, 172, *187,* 490, *491,* 513, 517, *527,* 586, 588, 597, *598,* 608, *612*
Holender, D., 615, 616, 624, 625, *628*
Hollenhorst, R. W., 507, *511*
Holley-Wilcox, P., 548, *563*
Hollingsworth, S., 648, *649*
Holmes, G., 54, *60*
Holmes, J. M., 618, 623, *628*
Holmgren, J. E., 94, *103*
Holtzman, J. D., 320, *334,* 427, 428, 429, 433, 434, 438, *440*
Hopkins, G. W., 402, *406*
Horton, J. C., 51, *60*
Houck, M. R., 490, *491,* 586, 597, *598*
Houtgast, T., 341, *353*
Howell, J., 32, *34*
Howell, P., 222, *237*
Hu, G. G., 94, *104*
Hubel, D. H., 48, 49, 51, *60*

Huerta, M. F., 44, *60*
Hughes, B. G., 148, *166*
Hughes, H. C., 279, 281, *284*
Humphreys, G. W., 119, *131*, 304, 305, 308, 315, *318*
Hylton, R., 274, 276, 283, *284*
Hyman, R., 465, *470*
Hyvarinen, J., 255, 262, *264*

I

Ilmoniemi, R., 362, *371*
Inskeep, N. R., *563*
Isreal, J. B., 507, *509*
Iwai, E., 45, *62*

J

Jackendoff, R. S., 26, *35*
Jackson, J. H., 319, *334*
Jacoby, L. L., 548, 561, *563*, 568, 571, 572, 575, *582*
Jain, M., 551, *564*
James, W., 134, *145*, 148, *165*, 355, *371*, 475, 476, *492*, 585, *598*
Jansen, T. C., 287, *299*
Jarvella, R. J., 29, *35*
Järvilehto, T., 360, *372*
Jasper, H. H., 496, *511*
Jeannerod, M., 407, 408, 411, 415, 416, 419, 420, 421, *423*, *424*
Jenkins, J. J., 589, *598*
Jerison, H. J., 494, 496, 508, *509*, *510*, *511*
Jiang, Q., 502, 503, 504, 506, *510*
Johanson, G. W., 297, *299*
Johnson, L. E., 438, *440*
Johnson, M. K., 548, *563*
Johnston, J. C., 615, 616, 625, *628*
Johnston, W. A., 64, *83*, 90, 97, *104*, 365, *371*, 568, 569, 570, 575, 580, *582*, 586, 587, 592, 596, *598*
Jones, E. G., 56, *60*
Jones, G. V., 109, *131*
Jones, R. S., 478, 485, *491*
Jonides, J., 63, 64, *83*, 190, *203*, 517, *527*, 532, *543*
Jouvet, M., 356, *371*
Judge, S. J., 255, *264*
Julesz, B., 281, *284*
Juola, J. F., 94, *103*
Jusczyk, A. W., 5, *35*
Just, M. A., 286, *299*

K

Kaas, J. H., 44, 48, *60*, *62*, 246, *249*
Kahneman, D., 91, 97, 98, 100, *104*, 105, 106, 110, 121, 122, *131*, 134, 137, *145*, 148, *165*, 190, *203*, 276, 277, 281, *284*, 311, *318*, 495, *510*, 530, *542*, 568, *582*, 586, 597, *598*
Kalil, R. E., 408, *423*
Karttunen, M., 555, *565*
Katz, A. N., 593, 597, *598*
Kaukoranta, E., 362, *371*
Kay, J., 9, 11, 12, 15, 16, *35*
Keele, S. W., 109, *131*
Kellogg, W. A., 569, 579, *582*, 594, 595, *598*, 626, *628*
Kelso, J. A. S., 155, *165*
Kennedy, H., 45, *59*
Kenyon, R. V., 179, *186*
Keppel, G., 589, *599*
Kerr, B., 134, *145*, 150, 152, *165*
Kertesz, A., 13, 14, 16, 20, 22, 23, 32, *34*
Khun, T. S., 134, *145*
Kiang, N. Y., 344, *353*
Kimura, D., 221, 227, 235, *237*
Kinchla, R. A., 142, *145*, 148, *165*, 305, *318*, 585, 586, *598*
King, M-L., 551, *564*
Kinsbourne, M., 142, *145*, 235, *237*, 243, *249*, 263, *264*, 315, *318*, 530, 531, 538, 539, 541, *542*, *543*
Kirsner, K., 548, 549, 550, 551, 552, 553, *564*, 571, *582*
Kleiman, G., 29, *35*
Klein, D., 531, *543*
Klein, R., 286, *299*, 302, *318*
Klein, R. M., 148, *165*
Knoll, R. J., 151, *167*
Knoll, R. L., 199, *204*
Kocher, E. C., 272, *284*
Kohonen, T., 485, *491*
Kolers, P. A., 403, *406*, 548, 560, *564*
Koller, J., 7, 30, 31, *34*
Komilis, E., 407, 408, 420, *424*
Kopell, B. S., 358, 359, *371*
Kornblum, S., 151, 155, *166*
Kornmuller, A. E., 287, *299*
Kosslyn, S. M., 246, *249*, 320, 321, 322, 323, 324, 327, 328, 329, 331, 333, *334*
Kottas, B., 617, *628*
Kowler, E., 285, 286, 287, 288, 289, 290, 291, 292, 296, 297, *299*

Kramer, P., 271, 272, 274, 275, 279, 282, 284
Krause, A. E., 539, *542*
Kravetz, S., 632, *649*
Krebs, M. J., 458, 468, *471*
Kristofferson, A. B., 402, *406*
Kroll, N. A., 363, *371*
Krueger, L. E., 604, *612*, 617, 626, *628*
Krulee, G. K., 551, *564*
Krulewitz, J. E., 499, *510*
Krumhansl, C. L., 201, *203*, 207, *218*
Kučera, H., 575, *582*
Kuhl, D. E., 531, *543*
Kuhn, G. F., 338, *353*
Kulikowski, J. J., 53, *62*
Kutas, M., 72, *82*

L

LaBerge, D., 8, *35*, 121, 124, *131*, *132*, 135, *145*, 404, *406*, 476, *491*, 567, *582*, 588, *599*
Ladavas, E., 461, 465, 466, *470*
Laddaga, R., 286, *300*
Lagasse, P. P., 412, *424*
Lanzetta, T. M., 494, 495, *510*, *511*
Larsen, A., 97, *103*, 110, *131*, 631, 632, 633, 635, 643, *648*
Larson, D. W., 87, *103*
Lasley, D. J., 271, *283*
Latto, R., 257, *264*, 439, *440*
Lawrence, D. H., 110, *131*
Lawson, D., 68, *83*
Lawson, E. A., 377, 378, 384, *387*, *388*
Layton, W. M., 279, 281, *284*
Leary, J. N., 495, 506, *511*
Lecas, J. C., 150, 157, 158, 161, 164, *166*
Le Doux, J. E., 227, *237*
Lee, B. C. P., 428, *440*
Lee, D. N., 392, 393, *406*
Lehman, E. B., 559, *564*
Lehmkuhle, S. W., 617, *628*
Leigh, R. J., 427, *440*
Leinonen, L., 255, 262, *264*
Lépine, D., 155, *166*
Lesser, R., 15, 16, *35*
Lester, L. S., 279, 281, *284*
Leventhal, A. G., 43, *60*
Levine, J. M., 494, *510*
Levinson, J. Z., 291, 297, *300*
Levy, J., 439, *440*

Levy, W. B., 477, *491*
Lewis, M., 29, *34*
Ley, R. G., 319, *334*
Lieberman, K., 246, *248*
Light, L. L., *564*
Lindemann, W., 345, *353*
Lindsay, P. M., 507, *511*
Linebarger, M., 25, *35*
Linnankoski, I. I., 262, *264*
Lisberger, S. G., 297, *299*
Litvac, L., 532, 537, 538, *542*
Livingstone, M. S., 48, 49, 51, *60*
Lockhart, R. S., 551, *564*
Loeb, M., 494, 498, 504, 506, *509*, *510*
Loemker, K. K., 408, *424*
Loftus, G., 286, *299*
Logan, G. D., 135, *145*, 151, *166*, 207, *218*, 476, 484, *491*, 518, *527*
Lorge, I., 533, *543*
Lough, S., 393, *406*
Loveland, E. H., 639, *648*
Loveless, N. E., 358, 359, *372*
Lowe, D. G., 126, 127, 128, *131*
Lucas, M., 404, *406*
Luce, R. D., 150, *166*, 631, 633, 646, *648*
Lund, J. S., 44, 48, *60*
Lund, R. D., 48, *60*
Lupker, S. J., 23, *35*, 593, 597, *598*
Luppino, G., 457, 458, 459, 561, 563, 468, *470*
Luria, A. R., 529, *543*
Luschei, E., 412, *424*
Luzzatti, C., 240, 244, *248*, *249*
Lynch, J. C., 262, *264*, 265

M

MacFarland, K., 530, *543*
Mach, E., 287, *299*
Macht, M., 385, 386, *388*
MacKay, D., 101, *104*
MacKay, D. G., 476, *491*
Mackworth, J. F., 494, 495, 496, 498, *510*
Macworth, N. H., 494, *510*
MacQueen, C. L., 44, 48, *60*
Madigan, S. A., 575, *583*
Mahneke, A., 495, *509*
Mai, N., 53, *62*
Malmo, R. B., 541, *543*
Mandler, G., 313, 314, *318*
Mandler, J. M., 555, *564*

AUTHOR INDEX 659

Mäntysalo, S., 357, 358, 360, 361, 362, 363, 366, *371, 372*
Marcel, A. J., 7, 9, 11, 12, *35, 36,* 110, 119, *132,* 560, *564,* 567, 568, 569, 570, 573, 576, 579, 581, *582,* 587, *598*
Marchetti, F. J., 207, *218*
Marin, O. S. M., 7, 19, 30, *36*
Marr, D., 55, *60,* 101, *104,* 110, *132,* 185, *187*
Marroco, R. T., 51, *61*
Marsh, N. W. A., 458, 459, *470*
Marshall, J., 45, *62*
Marshall, J. C., 6, 7, 8, 12, 13, 17, 24, 29, *34, 35, 36,* 618, 623, *628*
Marteniuk, R. G., 408, *424*
Martin, I., 409, *424*
Martin, K. A. C., 56, 57, *60*
Martin, M., 305, *318*
Martins, A. J., 286, *299*
Mason, D. A., *564*
Massaro, D. W., 615, 617, *629*
Masterson, J., 13, 16, 20, *34*
Matelli, M., 252, 253, 254, 256, 257, 262, 263, *265*
Maunsell, J. H. R., 46, 48, 50, 51, *61*
Mayer, D. E., 151, *166*
Maylor, E. A., 65, 74, 79, 80, *83,* 150, *166,* 192, 195, 197, 199, 202, *203,* 508, *511*
Mays, L. E., 413, *424*
Mazziotta, J. C., 531, *543*
Mazzucchi, A., 467, *470*
McAdams, S., 338, *353*
McCallum, W. C., 368, *371,* 375, *387*
McCarthy, R., 12, 15, 16, *36,* 37
McCauley, C., 119, *131*
McClelland, J. L., 141, *145,* 514, 515, *527,* 614, 616, 624, 625, 627, *629*
McConkie, G., 286, *299*
McFadden, D., 339, *354*
McGrath, J. J., 508, *510*
McKee, S. P., 291, 297, *299, 300*
McKillip, J., 555, *565*
McLean, J. P., 110, *132*
McLeod, P., 148, *166,* 507, *510*
Meadows, J. C., 53, *60*
Megaw, E. D., 408, *424*
Mehler, J., 5, *35*
Melchner, M. J., 64, *83,* 142, 144, *145*
Merikle, P. M., 633, *648*
Merzenich, M. M., 246, *249*
Mesulam, M.-M., 223, *237,* 251, 252, *265*

Metzler, J., 330, 332, *334*
Mewaldt, S. P., 468, *471*
Meyer, D. E., 8, *35,* 126, *132,* 150, *166,* 551, *564,* 589, *598*
Mewhort, D. J. K., 207, *218*
Michie, P. T., 359, 366, 368, *372*
Mikami, A., 52, *60*
Milech, D., 549, 550, 552, *563, 564*
Miller, B. D., 240, *249*
Miller, J. O., 150, 155, *166,* 515, 518, 522, 526, 527, *528*
Mishkin, M., 52, *61,* 68, 72, 81, *84*
Moffitt, C. M., 339, *354*
Mohler, C. W., 262, *265,* 444, 448, 451, *455*
Mollon, J. D., 53, *60*
Monsell, S., 151, *167, 564*
Moody, S., 25, 26, 27, 28, 29, *35*
Morais, J., 222, *237,* 465, *470*
Moray, N., 93, *104,* 134, *145,* 494, 495, *510,* 530, *543*
Morton, J., 5, 8, 9, 16, 26, *35, 36,* 548, 550, 551, *564,* 626, *629*
Moscovitch, M., 465, 466, *470,* 531, *543*
Motter, B. C., 49, *60,* 68, *83*
Mountcastle, V. B., 49, *60,* 68, *83,* 158, *166,* 206, *218,* 246, *249,* 262, *265*
Moyer, N. J., 507, *511*
Mulder, G., 376, *388*
Mulder, L. J. M., 376, *388*
Mulligan, R. M., 490, *492*
Munte, T. F., 65, 66, 67, 68, 72, 73, *82*
Murphy, B. J., 286, 287, 289, 291, 297, *299*
Murray, J. T., 601, 602, 603, 604, 605, 606, 607, 610, 611, *612*
Murrell, G., 26, *35*
Myles-Worsley, M. M., 570, 575, 580, *582*

N

Näätänen, R., 357, 358, 359, 360, 361, 362, 363, 364, 365, 366, 367, 368, *371, 372, 373,* 376, 378, 383, 384, *388,* 541, *543*
Nachmias, J., 271, 272, 274, 276, *284,* 286, *299, 300*
Nagler, M., 51, *59*
Nagy, V., 93, *104*
Nathan, G., 222, 223, 224, 226, 228, 230, 234, 235, *236, 237,* 465, 466, 467, *470*
Naveh-Benjamin, M., 532, *543*

Navon, D., 133, 134, 135, 136, 142, 143, 144, *145, 146,* 303, 305, 306, *318,* 507, *510,* 530, *542*
Neely, J. H., 587, *598*
Neill, W. T., 109, 114, 126, *131, 132*
Neiser, J. J., 26, *37*
Neisser, U., 4, 5, *35, 36,* 114, 121, *132,* 297, *300,* 302, *318,* 363, *372,* 404, *406*
Nelson, B., 64, *83,* 172, *187,* 586, 588, 597, *598*
Nettleton, N. C., 222, 223, 224, 226, 227, 228, 230, 234, 235, *236, 237,* 465, 466, 467, 468, *470, 471,* 531, 537, *542*
Neumann, O., 476, *491*
Neville, H. J., 68, *83*
Newcombe, F., 6, 8, 12, 17, *35, 36,* 53, *60*
Newell, A., 140, *146,* 403, *406*
Newman, E. B., 345, *354*
Newsome, S. L., 617, *629*
Newsome, W. T., 46, 50, 52, *58, 60, 61,* 444, *455*
Nicoletti, R., 457, 458, 459, 561, 563, 568, *470*
Nisbett, R. E., 568, *582*
Nishihara, H. K., 185, *187*
Nissen, M. J., 64, *83,* 88, *104,* 190, *203,218, 219*
Norman, D. A., 93, *104,* 134, 135, 143, *146,* 356, *372,* 476, *491,* 514, *528,* 580, *583,* 603, *612*
Nosofsky, R. M., 150, *166*
Noton, D., 286, *300*
Nuechterlein, K., 502, 503, 504, 506, *510*
Nuetzel, J. M., 339, *353, 354*
Nyman, G. H., II, 255, 262, *264*

O

Oakley, M., 67, *82*
O'Boyle, D. J., 53, *59*
Oehler, R., 42, 43, *61*
Ogden, W. C., 64, *83,* 88, *104,* 190, *203, 218, 219*
Öhman, A., 369, *372*
Okita, T., 368, *372*
Olzak, L., 274, 276, *284*
Osman, A., 150, 151, *166*
Ostry, D., 93, *104*
Outerbridge, J. S., 287, *298*

P

Paap, K. R., 617, *629*
Paavilainen, P., 359, 361, 367, *371, 373*
Paillard, J., 422, *424*
Painton, S., 26, *37*
Paivio, A., 575, *583*
Palermo, D. S., 589, *598*
Palmer, S. E., 245, 246, *249,* 302, *318*
Papakostopoulos, D., 368, *371*
Parasuraman, R., 494, 495, 498, 500, 501, 502, 503, 504, 505, 506, 508, *509, 510*
Park, D. C., *564*
Parkin, A. J., 9, *36,* 569, *583*
Parmelee, C. M., 119, *131*
Pasanen, E., 339, *354*
Pasik, P., 426, *440*
Pasik, T., 426, *440*
Pasko, S., 555, *565*
Paterson, R., 91, 102, *105,* 311, *318*
Patterson, K. E., 7, 8, 9, 10, 13, 16, 24, 27, 29, *34, 36*
Pavel, M., 286, *299*
Pavesi, G., 252, 253, 254, 256, 257, *265*
Pedersen, L. F., 97, *103,* 110, *131,* 631, 632, 633, 635, 643, *648*
Pelisson, D., 423, *424*
Pelli, D., 272, 281, *284*
Perani, D., 240, 244, *248, 249*
Perrett, D. I., 108, *132*
Perry, V. H., 42, 43, *61*
Peterhans, E., 51, *61*
Peters, A., 56, 57, *61*
Peterson, S. E., 46, 50, *58*
Pew, R. W., 476, *492*
Peynircioglu, Z. F., *565*
Phelps, M. E., 531, *543*
Phillips, C. G., 46, *61*
Pickett, R. M., 496, *510*
Picton, T. W., 79, *83,* 356, 359, 366, 368, *371, 372,* 378, 384, 387, *387*
Pierson, J. M., 222, 223, 224, 226, 228, 230, 234, 235, *236, 237,* 465, 466, 467, *470, 471*
Pinker, S., 185, *187,* 338, *353*
Plomp, R., 341, *353*
Pocock, P. V., 368, *371*
Podgorny, P., 324, *334*
Poggio, G. F., 51, *59, 61*
Polden, P. G., 53, *60*
Pollen, D. A., 51, *59*
Polson, M. C., 142, *145,* 532, 538, 541, *542*

Polyak, S. L., 43, *61*
Pomerantz, J. R., 304, 305, 306, *318*
Porta, E., 243, *248*
Posner, M. I., 7, *36*, 64, 65, 74, 79, 80, 81, *83*, 88, *104*, 109, *132*, 135, *146*, 148, 150, *166*, 172, 173, 175, 179, 180, 184, *187*, 189, 190, 191, 192, 194, 195, 197, 198, 199, 202, *203*, *204*, 206, 218, *219*, *248*, *249*, 261, 262, *265*, 442, *454*, 476, *492*, 494, 502, 503, 508, *510*, *511*, 515, *528*, 550, 551, *564*, 567, *583*, 587, *598*
Postman, L., 589, *599*
Poulton, E. C., 541, *543*
Prablanc, C., 407, 408, 411, 415, 416, 419, 420, 421, 423, *423*, *424*
Previc, F. H., 72, 74, *83*
Pribram, K., 530, *543*
Prinzmetal, W., 87, *103*
Prior, M., 13, 16, 20, *34*
Prohovnik, I., 368, *372*
Proulx, G. B., 359, *372*
Provost, D., 324, 327, *334*
Puckett, J. W., 288, 290, *300*
Purcell, D. G., 302, *318*, 617, *629*
Pylyshyn, Z. W., 244, 245, 246, *249*

Q

Quinlan, P. T., 308, *318*

R

Raab, D., 518, *528*
Rabbitt, P. M. A., 403, *406*
Rafal, R. D., 7, *36*, 64, 65, 79, *83*, 206, *219*, 248, *249*, 262, *265*
Rashbass, C., 297, *300*
Ratcliff, G., 53, 54, *60*, *61*
Ratliff, F., 352, *354*
Rayleigh, Lord, 339, *354*
Rayner, K., 286, *299*
Rayport, M., 427, *440*
Reaves, C., 404, *406*
Reddish, P., 393, *406*
Reder, S. M., 604, *612*
Reeves, A., 172, *187*, 286, *300*, 428, *440*
Regan, D., 206, *219*, 398, *406*
Regan, J., 142, 144, *146*
Reicher, G. M., 613, 614, 615, 616, 624, 625, *629*
Reinikainen, K., 362, *371*

Remington, R. W., 64, *83*, 172, *187*, 190, 191, 201, *204*
Renault, B., 368, *372*
Repp, B. H., 618, 623, *629*
Requin, J., 150, 152, 153, 155, 157, 158, 161, 164, *165*, *166*
Reynolds, P., 530, *542*
Richards, V. M., 349, *354*
Richmond, B. J., 255, *264*, 444, *454*, *455*
Riddoch, J., 13, 16, 20, *34*
Riddoch, M. J., 304, 305, 308, *318*
Riggs, L. A., 352, *354*
Rinaldi, P. C., 359, *373*
Risberg, J., 368, *372*
Ritter, W., 358, *373*, 375, 378, 383, 384, 385, 386, *387*, *388*
Ritz, S. A., 478, 485, *491*
Rizzolatti, G., 252, 253, 254, 256, 257, 262, 263, *265*, 457, 458, 459, 461, 463, 465, 468, *470*
Robertson, D., 357, 367, *371*
Robinson, D. A., 255, *264*, 412, *424*, 426, *440*
Robinson, D. L., 67, 68, *82*, *84*, 149, *167*, 172, *187*, 206, *219*, 262, *264*, *265*, 442, 444, 453, *454*, *455*
Robinson, R. A., 297, *300*
Robson, J. G., 271, *284*, 302, *317*
Rock, I., 114, 116, *132*
Rodieck, R. W., 43, *60*
Rohrbaugh, J., 207, *218*
Roland, P. E., 368, *372*, *373*
Rolls, E. T., 108, *132*
Romashko, T., 494, *510*
Rose, J. E., 347, *354*
Rose, R.-G., *564*
Rosenbaum, D. A., 150, 154, 155, *166*, 412, *424*
Rosenbloom, P. S., 403, *406*
Rosenzweig, M. R., 345, *354*
Roth, W. T., 358, 359, *371*
Rovamo, J., 184, *187*
Ruddy, M. E., 551, *564*
Ruddy, M. G., 8, *35*, 126, *132*
Rumelhart, D. E., 140, 141, *145*, *146*, 301, 303, *318*, 614, 624, 625, 627, *629*

S

Saegert, J., *564*
Saffran, E., 7, 19, 25, 30, *35*, *36*

Saga, T., 158, *167*
Sakata, H., 262, *265*
Salasoo, A., 571, 572, 575, *582*
Salminen, J., 362, *371*
Sams, M., 358, 359, 360, 361, 362, 363, 364, 367, *371, 372, 373*
Samuels, M., 539, *542*
Samuels, S. J., 404, *406*
Sanders, A. F., 514, *528*
Sanders, M. D., 45, *62*
Sansbury, R. V., 286, 297, *300*
Santee, J. L., 112, *132,* 601, 602, 603, 604, 605, 606, 607, 611, *612*
Saraga, E., 206, *219*
Sato, T., 444, *454*
Saunders, R. C., 52, *61*
Scandolara, C., 253, 262, 263, *265*
Scarborough, D. L., 548, *564*
Scarborough, H. S., 548, *564*
Schachter, D. L., 560, *565*
Schaffer, W. V., 124, *132*
Scheerer, E., 206, *218*
Schein, S. J., 51, *61*
Scherrer, H., 356, *371*
Schiller, P. H., 439, *440*
Schmidt, H., 129, 130, *132,* 206, 208, *219*
Schneider, W., 86, 95, *104,* 135, *146,* 190, 204, 365, *373,* 392, 404, *406,* 476, 477, 479, 480, 484, 486, 487, 488, 489, 490, *491, 492,* 506, 507, *509, 511,* 567, 568, 569, 570, *582, 583,* 586, *599,* 644, *648*
Schroeder, C., 67, 72, 74, *82*
Schultz, D. W., 514, 518, *527,* 601, *612*
Schultz, I., 112, *131*
Schutta, H. S., 54, *59*
Schvaneveldt, R. W., 8, *35,* 126, *132,* 589, *598*
Schwartz, E. L., 49, *60*
Schwartz, M., 7, 19, 25, *35, 36*
Schwent, V. L., 366, 368, *371*
Searleman, A., 538, *543*
Seegmiller, D., 555, *564*
Seibel, R., 403, *406*
Seidenberg, M. S., 9, *36*
Sekuler, R., 272, *283*
Selfridge, O., 302, *318*
Semjen, A., 152, 153, 164, *165, 166*
Shaffer, W. O., 588, *599*
Shallice, T., 6, 7, 10, 12, 15, 16, *36, 37,* 206, *219,* 476, *491*
Shapiro, R. G., 604, *612*
Sharma, N. K., 549, 553, *563, 564*

Sharpless, S., 496, *511*
Shaw, M. L., 95, *104,* 172, *187,* 271, 279, 284, 298, *300,* 490, *492,* 526, *528,* 586, *599*
Shebo, B. J., 313, 314, *318*
Shelley, C., 404, *405*
Shepard, M., 461, *470*
Shepard, R. N., 245, 246, *249,* 324, 330, 332, *334*
Sherrick, C. E., 224, *237*
Shiffrin, R. M., 86, 95, *104,* 135, *146,* 190, 204, 365, *373,* 392, 404, *406,* 476, 486, 488, *492,* 506, *511,* 560, *563,* 567, 568, 571, 572, 575, *582, 583,* 586, *599,* 601, *612,* 644, *648*
Shimazaki, C., 412, 418, *424*
Sidtis, J. J., 427, 438, *440*
Silverstein, J. W., 478, 485, *491*
Simon, J. R., 458, 461, 468, *470, 471*
Simons, R. F., 490, *491*
Simpson, A. J., 501, *511*
Simpson, G. V., 65, 66, 67, 68, *82*
Simpson, M., 358, 359, *372*
Simson, R., 358, *373,* 378, 383, 384, 385, 386, *388*
Singer, W., 67, *83*
Siple, P., 301, 303, *318, 564*
Sjo, O., 51, *58*
Skaar, E., 615, 617, *628*
Skavenski, A. A., 286, 289, 290, 297, *300*
Skinner, J. E., 67, *83*
Slade, R., 569, *582*
Sly, P. E., 458, *471*
Small, A. M., Jr., 458, 468, *471*
Smight, J. E. K., 150, *166*
Smith, A. P., 494, *511*
Smith, M. C., 548, 551, *564,* 569, 570, 571, 579, 582, *583,* 594, 595, 596, 597, *599,* 626, *629*
Smith, R. L., 344, 348, *354*
Snodgrass, J. G., 556, *564*
Snyder, C. R. R., 64, 65, 74, 80, *83,* 172, 173, *187,* 190, 197, 199, *203, 204,* 207, *219,* 476, *492,* 567, *583,* 587, *598*
Snyder, E., 358, 359, *373*
Soininen, K., 360, *372*
Solis-Macias, V., 142, *145*
Solomons, L. M., 404, *406,* 475, *492*
Somogyi, P., 56, 57, *61*
Sousa, A. P. B., 46, 49, 50, *60*
Sparks, D. L., 413, *424*
Spector, A., 617, *629*

Speelman, R. G., 637, *648*
Spehr, K., 224, *237*
Speidel, C. R., 468, *471*
Spelke, E., 404, *406*
Spencer, T., 95, *104*, 586, *598*, 601, *612*
Spencer, W. A., 496, 499, *511*
Sperber, R. D., 119, *131*
Sperling, G., 64, *83*, 142, 144, *146*, 172, *187*, 271, 276, *284*, 286, 297, *300*, 586, *599*, 631, 632, 637, *648*
Sperry, R. W., 438, 439, *440*
Spitz, G., 143, *146*
Springer, S. P., 319, *334*
Sprott, D. A., 618, 623, *628*
Squire, R., 75, *83*
Squires, K. C., 358, *373*
Squires, N. K., 358, *373*
Standen, P., 550, 552, *564*
Stanners, R. F., 26, *37*
Stanovich, K. E., 617, *629*
Stapells, D. R., 356, *372*
Stark, H. A., 560, *565*
Stark, L., 286, 287, *300*
Steele, C. S., 292, *299*
Steele Russel, I., 257, *264*
Stein, G., 404, *406*, 475, *492*
Steinman, R. M., 286, 287, 288, 289, 290, 291, 292, 296, 297, *299*, *300*
Stelmach, G. E., 148, 155, *165*, *166*
Sternberg, S., 150, 151, *167*, 199, *204*, 376, 378, *388*, 514, 515, *528*
Sterzi, R., 243, *248*
Steward, O., 477, *491*
Stone, J., 48, *61*
Stone, L. D., 490, *492*
Strawson, C., 8, *34*
Strick, P. L., 158, *167*
Stroop, J., 517, *528*
Sully, D., 393, *405*
Sully, H., 393, *405*
Suppes, P., 286, *300*, 646, *648*
Sutherland, N. S., 301, *318*
Sykes, M., 110, *132*, 141, *146*, 208, *219*, 307, 308, 311, *318*
Szentagothai, J., 477, *492*

T

Taft, M., 26, *37*
Tagliasco, V., 408, *423*
Tamminga, E. P., 285, 287, 288, 289, 290, 291, 292, 296, *299*, *300*
Tanenhaus, M. K., 9, *36*
Taniguchi, K., 158, *167*
Tanji, J., 158, *165*, *167*
Tassinari, G., 465, *470*
Tassinary, L., 569, *582*
Taylor, D. A., 514, 515, *528*
Taylor, F. V., 422, *423*
Taylor, M. M., 507, *511*
Teichner, W. H., 458, 468, *471*
Ter Braak, J. W. G., 287, *300*
Theodor, L., 569, 570, 579, *583*, 594, 595, *599*
Thomas, E. A. C., 207, *218*, 344, *353*
Thompson, M. C., 615, *629*
Thompson, R. F., 359, *373*, 496, 499, *511*
Thorndike, E. L., 533, *543*
Thwaites, S., 593, 597, *599*
Timberlake, G. T., 286, 288, *300*
Tipper, S. P., 114, 117, 128, *132*
Titchener, E. B., 252, *265*, 585, *599*
Toh, K. Y., 500, *509*
Tondo, D. K., 551, *564*
Townsend, J. T., 94, *104*
Townsend, V. M., 207, *219*
Treisman, A. M., 73, 75, 81, *83*, 86, 91, 94, 95, 96, 97, 98, 100, 101, 102, *104*, *105*, 105, 106, 110, 129, 130, *131*, *132*, 141, *146*, 148, *165*, 205, 206, 207, 208, 217, 218, *219*, 276, 277, 281, *284*, 307, 308, 311, *318*, 364, *373*, 508, *509*, 568, *582*, *583*, 586, 597, *598*
Trevarthen, C. B., 68, *83*, 438, 439, *440*
Troost, B. T., 439, *440*
True, S. D., 439, *440*
Tsuchitani, C., 348, *354*
Tulving, E., 560, *565*
Tune, G. S., 494, *509*
Turvey, M. T., 514, *528*, 632, *649*
Tyldesley, D. A., 403, *406*

U

Uemura, T., 412, 418, *424*
Ullman, S., 185, 187
Umiltà, C., 227, 230, 232, 234, 235, *237*, 457, 458, 459, 461, 463, 465, 467, 468, *470*
Underwood, G., 124, *132*, 593, 597, *599*
Ungerleider, L. G., 47, 52, *61*, 68, 72, 81, *84*

V

Valciukas, J. A., 426, *440*
Valenstein, E., 72, *82*, 468, *470*

Vallar, G., 32, *37*, 243, *248*
Van Arkel, A. E., 377, 378, 384, *388*
van Cramon, D., 53, *62*
Van Dellen, H. J., 376, *388*
Van den Abell, T., 465, 466, *470*
Van der Heijden, A. H. C., 64, *84*, 110, 129, *132*
vander Heydt, R., 51, *61*
van der Mark, F., 287, *299*
Van der Meulen, E. C., 477, *492*
Vanderplas, J. M., 533, *543*
van der Steen, J., 285, 287, 288, 289, 290, 291, 292, 296, 297, *299*, *300*
Vanderwart, M., 556, *564*
Van Essen, D. C., 46, 48, 50, 51, *61*
van Hoesen, G. W., 54, *59*
Van Voorhis, S. T., 65, 67, 68, *82*, *84*
Vaughan, H. G., Jr., 358, *373*, 378, 383, 384, 385, 386, *388*
Vaughan, J., 202, *204*
Venables, P. H., 409, *424*
Vickers, D., 495, 506, *511*
Vigna, C., 531, *543*
Vilapakkam, S., 458, *471*
Vince, M. A., 422, *424*
Virsu, V., 184, *187*
Virzi, R. A., 217, *218*
Vitton, N., 158, *166*
Volpe, B. T., 427, 438, *440*
Von Wright, J. M., 206, 208, 217, *219*, 555, 565, 632, *649*

W

Walker, J. A., 262, *265*
Wallace, R. J., 459, 461, 468, *471*
Wallach, H., 345, *354*
Wallach, R. W., 321, 323, 333, *334*
Warabi, T., 408, *424*
Ward, L. M., 281, *284*
Warm, J. S., 494, 499, *510*, *511*
Warrington, E. K., 6, 7, 10, 12, 15, 16, *36*, *37*, 45, 54, 59, *61*, *62*, 244, *248*, 315, *318*
Watanabe, T., 344, *353*
Waters, G., 9, *36*
Watkins, M. J., *565*
Watson, A. B., 276, *284*
Watson, R. T., 240, *249*, 251, *264*, 267, *270*
Watt, R. J., 200, *204*
Weber, J. T., 44, *60*

Weber, R. B., 439, *440*
Weinrich, M., 158, 160, 161, *167*
Weinstein, E. A., 251, *264*
Weiskrantz, L., 45, 52, *61*, *62*
Weisstein, N., 302, *318*
Welford, A. T., 496, *511*, 530, *543*
Weller, R. E., 48, *62*
Wenzel, E., 339, 346, 347, *353*
Westheimer, G., 291, 297, *300*
White, C. T., 65, *82*, 411, *424*
Whiting, H. T. A., 403, *406*
Whittington, D. A., 408, *424*
Wickelgren, W. A., 94, *105*, 274, *284*
Widmayer, M., 302, *318*
Wiesel, T. N., 44, 51, *60*
Wickens, C. D., 142, *146*, 507, *509*, *511*
Wightman, F. L., 551, *564*
Wild, H., 53, *62*
Williams, M. C., 302, *318*
Williges, R. C., 505, *511*
Wilson, D. H., 227, *237*, 427, 428, 438, *440*
Wilson, L. E., 222, 223, 224, 226, 228, 230, 234, 235, *236*, *237*, 465, 466, 467, *470*
Wilson, T. D., 568, *582*
Winograd, E., *565*
Winston, P. H., 321, *334*
Winterson, B. J., 288, *300*
Wise, S. P., 158, 160, 161, *167*
Witherspoon, D., 568, *582*
Wohl, T. H., 499, *510*
Wolfe, J. M., 305, *318*
Wolford, G., 88, *105*, 569, *582*, 645, *649*
Woods, D. L., 65, 66, 67, 68, *82*, 359, *372*
Woollacott, M., 164, *167*
Woolsey, C. N., 55, *62*
Wright, C. E., 151, *167*
Wurtz, R. H., 52, *60*, 67, 68, *84*, 149, *167*, 172, *187*, 206, *219*, 254, 262, *264*, *265*, 442, 444, 446, 448, 450, 451, 453, *454*, 455
Wyman, D., 286, 289, 290, *300*

Y, Z

Yabe, K., 164, *167*
Yager, D., 271, 279, *284*
Yantis, S., 150, *166*
Yeo, C. N., 257, *264*
Yerkes, R. M., 541, *543*
Yingling, C. D., 67, *83*
Yoshida, K., 45, *59*

Yoss, R. E., 507, *511*
Young, D., 393, *406*
Young, I. L., Jr., 339, *354*
Young, M. J., 74, *82*
Yuille, J. C., 575, *583*
Yukie, M., 45, *62*
Zacks, R. T., 555, 559, *563*
Zaidel, E., 531, 538, *543*
Zechmeister, E. B., 555, *565*

Zee, D. S., 427, *440*
Zeki, S. M., 46, 50, 51, 53, *61, 62*
Zelaznik, H., 155, *167*
Ziglar, R. A., 468, *471*
Zihl, J., 53, *62*
Zimba, L. D., 597, *599*
Zingerle, H., 244, *249*
Zurek, P. M., 345, *354*
Zwislocki, J. J., 344, *354*

Subject Index

A

Absent distractors, 124
Accessing features and objects, localization in, 205–219
  color and, 208–211
  color and shape and, 208, 211–217
Achromatopsia, 53
Aggregate nature, 135
Agnosia, 53, 301
  visual, 54
Algorithms, unilateral neglect of space and, 239
Aphasia, imagery and language processing and, 319, 322–323
Architecture of the reading system, 21–24
Arm, head, and eye movements during pointing at a visual target, 408–415
Arousal, level of vigilance and, 505
Arousal theory of vigilance decrement, 500–502
Associative learning, 477, 485–487
Asynchronous Discrete Coding (ADC) model, 515–517, 522–523, 524, 525–526
Attention and coding effects, 457–471
Attention and motor control
  attention and coding effects, 457–471
  eye movement control, 425–440
  information encapsulation and automaticity, 391–406

  role of position of gaze in movement accuracy, 407–424
  stimulus selection and response mechanisms, 441–455
Attention division, 133
Attention-explanatory hypothesis, 613–629
Attention sharing, 133–146
  alternative explanations for task interference, 137–145
  mind without resources and, 134–137
Attention to symbols and words
  automaticity and semantic priming, 585–599
  disruptive effect of precueing, 613–629
  dissociable domains of selective processing, 567–583
  model for partial report, 631–645
  perceptual record, 547–565
  role of positional uncertainty, 601–612
Attribute retention
  perceptual record and, 552–554
  repetition priming and, 547–565
Auditory cues, near-threshold visual patterns and, 272
Auditory ERP
  N1 component of, 497–499
  P300 component of, 507
Automaticity
  information encapsulation and, 391–406
  semantic priming and, 585–599
  visual orienting and, 190

667

668 SUBJECT INDEX

Automatic processing development, 475–492
  category-search procedure, 479–490
  model overview, 476–477
  structure of a model, 478–479
Axoaxonic cell, 56, 57

B

Basal ganglia, 444–445
Basket cell, 56
Binaural detection, 337
Binaural interaction, transients in auditory space and, 347–348
Binocular cues, 396, 397
Brain
  parallel pathways in vision from eye to, 42–45
  postcategorical filtering and, 108–111

C

Capacity for sustained attention, 502–505
Capacity limitations, vigilance decrement and, 506–508
Case, repetition priming and, 555
Categorically related distractors, unrelated distractors versus, 123–124
Categorical priming by task-irrelevant distractors, 124–126
Categorical similarity, divided attention and, 516–517
Central errors, 24
Central visual fields, visual-spatial attention and, 68–72
Cerebral achromatopsia, 53
Chandelier cell, 56, 57
Choice manual reaction time, 192, 193–194
"Cocktail party" effect, 337–338, 493–494
Coding effects and attention, 457–471
Cognition, modular modelling of, 5
Cognitive disorder, unilateral neglect as, 243–246
Cognitive neuropsychology and reading, 3–37
  architecture of the reading system, 21–24
  dual-route models of reading aloud, 8–14
    phonological dyslexia, 10–12
    surface dyslexia, 12–14
  morphological processing, 24–29
  nature of the lexical procedure, 19–20
  nature of the nonlexical procedure, 14–19
  syntax and sentence comprehension during reading, 29–33
Color, localization in accessing features and objects and, 208–211
Commissurotomy in humans, eye movement control following, 425–440
Comparisons across paradigms, 375–388
Complex visual stimuli, near-threshold visual patterns and, 279–281
Compound search, 86–87
  number of targets and, 88–90
Compound visual stimuli, near-threshold visual patterns and, 272
Concurrent presentations, 273–277
Conflicting letters, 602
Conscious rejection, 277–278
Consistent mapping, 479
Contact time, visual array and, 393–394
Continuous models of divided attention, 513–528
Contralateral space, 253
Contraversive saccades, 439
Controlled processing, 476, 484–487
  with memory preload, 480–484
  selective processing and, 573–574
  semantic processing and, 576–578
Coordinated eye and head movement in hand-pointing accuracy, 415–423
Corporeal left/right, vibrotactile reaction times and, 228–230
Cortex pyramidal cells, 56–57
Cortical basket cells, 56–57
Cortical damage, visual disorders following, 51–55
Cortical visual areas, 46–51
Cortical visual processing, 172–173
Cross-domain selective cueing, 110
Cross-talk interference, 139–140
Cues (cueing)
  binocular, 396, 397
  cross-domain selective, 110
  direct, 190
  symbolic, 190

D

Data limitation, 603
Defining attribute of targets, 86
Derivational error, 24
Deviations from predictions, near-threshold visual patterns and, 276

Direct cueing, 190
Discrete models of divided attention, 513–528
Disruptive effect of precueing, 613–629
Dissociable domains of selective processing, 567–583
Distractors, encoding of, 121–126
Distributability, 135
Dividing and sustaining attention
   automatic processing development, 475–492
   discrete and continuous models of divided attention, 513–528
   priming and interference effects, 529–543
   sustained attention, 493–511
Double-bouquet cell, 56
Duplex probes, simplex probes versus, 126–127
Duplex theory of sound localization, 339
Dyslexia
   phonological, 10–12
   surface, 12–14

E

Early negativity (EN), 375–382
Early selection, 111
Effectiveness, 135
Electrophysiological indices of spatial attention, 65–68
Episodic memory, repetition priming and, 555
Event-related brain potentials (ERPs)
   comparisons across paradigms and, 375–388
   unattended stimuli and, 356–358
   vigilance decrement and, 496–499
   visual-spatial attention and, 63–84
Exclusive usage of units, 135
Executive brain processes, permissive brain processes versus, 157–164
Expectancy, vigilance decrement and, 505–506
Externally controlled orienting, 190–191
Extrinsic-uncertainty effects, near-threshold visual patterns and, 270–272
Eye
   conceptions of eye-movement preparations, 149–152
   head, and arm movements during pointing at a visual target, 408–415
   and head movements, coordinated, in hand-pointing accuracy, 415–423
   movement control, 425–440

   parallel pathways in vision to brain from, 42–45

F

Facilitatory component of externally controlled orienting, 190–201
Faulty visual-categorization, 54
Filtering paradigm, 148
First-order isomorphism, principle of, 244–245
Fixed input, 138
Forced-choice letter-probe, 614
Four-parameter model for partial report, 634–635
Frontal eye fields (FEF), 446
Functional cerebral distance (FCD) principle, 530, 531

G

Gamma-aminobutyric acid (GABA), 56, 57, 446
Generator of mismatch negativity, 362
Global-local studies of complex visual stimuli, 279–281
Grapheme-phoneme correspondences (GPCs), 15–16
Graphemes, 15
Graphemic parsing, 17n
Gravitational left/right, vibrotactile reaction times and, 228–230

H

Habituation of ERPs, vigilance decrement and, 496–499
Hand asymmetries, vibrotactile reaction times and, 230–234
Hand-pointing accuracy, coordinated eye and head movements in, 415–423
Head, eye, and arm movements during pointing at a visual target, 408–415
Head and eye movements, coordinated, in hand-pointing accuracy, 415–423
Hearsay evidence, near-threshold visual patterns and, 277–278
Hemineglect syndrome, 252
Hemispace and vibrotactile reaction times, 221–237
   corporeal left/right and, 228–230

Hemispace and vibrotactile reaction times
    (cont.)
  gravitational left/right and, 228–230
  hand asymmetries and choice of tasks, 230–232
  hand asymmetries and unilateral responses, 232–234
  hands operated in right hemispace and, 223–228
High-frequency clicks, transients in auditory space and, 339–341
Horseradish peroxidase (HRP), 42–43
Hypokinesia, unilateral, 240

I

Identity priming, 572, 579
Imagery and language processing, 319–334
  image generation, 323–327
  image maintenance, 327–329
  image rotation, 330–332
  image scanning, 329–330
  image task battery, 321–323
Index of relative priming (RP), 548
Individual graphemes, 15
Individual phonemes, 15
Information encapsulation and automaticity, 391–406
Inhibitory component of externally controlled orienting, 191–194, 197–200, 201–203
Input errors, 24
Integration of sensory attributes, 109–110
Interaural Differences of Intensity (IDIs), 338
Interaural Differences of Time (IDTs), 338
Interaural variability, transients in auditory space and, 341–343
Interference, attention sharing and, 137–145
Internally controlled orienting, 190
Interpretation of mismatch negativity, 362–365
Intrinsic uncertainty, near-threshold visual patterns and, 271–272
Ipsilateral stimuli, 263
Ipsiversive saccades, 439

L

Language processing and imagery, 319–334
  image generation, 323–327
  image maintenance, 327–329
  image rotation, 330–332
  image scanning, 329–330
  image task battery, 321–323

Lateral masking, 88
Late selection, 111
Left-hemisphere priming effect, 538–539
Lexical procedure for reading aloud, 9, 19–20
  surface dyslexia and, 12–14
Limited-capacity system, 90
Local-global studies of complex visual stimuli, 279–281
Localization in accessing features and objects, 205–219
  color and, 208–211
  color and shape and, 208, 211–217
Locations, visual-spatial attention and, 72–74

M

Manual reaction time
  choice, 192, 193–194
  simple, 191–192, 192–193
Mapping, 479
Masking-Level Difference (MLD), 338
Masks, precueing and, 615, 616, 618, 619
Master center model, 262–263
Matching indeterminacy, 140–141
Maximum positional uncertainty, 611
Mechanisms of selective attention, 365–368
Memory
  perceptual record and, 554
  recognition, 576–578
  two forms of, 554
Memory load, 532, 534–536
  sustained attention and, 500–502
Mental resources, attention sharing and, 134–137
Mesencephalic reticular formation (MRF), 445
Minimal requirements, attention sharing and, 144
Mismatch negativity (MMN), 358–365, 375
  comparisons across paradigms and, 383–385
  generator of, 362
  interpretation of, 362–365
Modality, repetition priming and, 554
Models
  of attention, 475–492
    multicentric, 262
  of divided attention, 513–528
  master center, 262–263
  for partial report, 631–645
  of perceptual analysis, 550–552
  of reading aloud, 8–14
  of sustained attention, 505–508

Modularity, 4
  principle of, 55–57
Modular modelling of cognition, 5
Modulation conception of eye-movement preparations, 149–152
Monomorphemic words, 27
Morphological processing, 24–29
Motor control, 147–167
  permissive versus executive brain processes, 157–164
  selective preparation and motor programming, 152–157
  stage versus modulation conceptions of preparation, 149–152
  See also Attention and motor control
Movement accuracy, position of gaze role in, 407–424
Multicentric model of attention, 262
Multielement displays, visual selection from, 631–645
Multifactor model of sustained attention, 505–508
Multimorphemic words, 27
Multiple nontargets, 86
Multiple sensory representations, 55–57
Multiple targets, 86

N

Name similarity, divided attention and, 517
Near-threshold visual patterns, 269–284
  concurrent experiments, 273–277, 282–283
  extrinsic-uncertainty effects, 270–272
  hearsay evidence, 277–278
  perception of complex visual stimuli, 279–281
  primary-plus-probe experiments, 278–289
  receptive-field model, 269–270
Negative priming, 107–108, 112–114, 128–130
  across changes in visual form, 115
  in picture naming, 115–117
  by semantically related distractors, 117–121
Neural habituation, 495–496
Neuropsychology and reading, 3–37
  architecture of the reading system, 21–24
  dual-route models of reading aloud, 8–14
    phonological dyslexia, 10–12
    surface dyslexia, 12–14
  morphological processing, 24–29
  nature of the lexical procedure, 19–20

nature of the nonlexical procedure, 14–19
syntax and sentence comprehension during reading, 29–33
Neutral noise, 602
N1 component of the auditory ERP, 497–499
Nonhabitual transitions, difficulty in making, 140
Nonlexical procedure for reading aloud, 9, 14–19
  phonological dyslexia and, 10–12
"Nonsearch" tasks, 87–88
Nontargets, 86, 90
  visual search and, 94–100
Nonwords, 613–614
No-precue procedure, 614

O

Object agnosia, 53
Oculomotor centers, 262
Onsets, transients in auditory space and, 349–352
Optic nerve, horseradish peroxidase and, 42–43
Optimum-maximum method, attention sharing and, 143–145
Orienting in visual space, 189–204
  facilitatory component of externally controlled orienting, 190–201
  inhibitory component of externally controlled orienting, 191–194, 197–200, 201–203
Orienting of attention
  localization in accessing features and objects, 205–219
  orienting in visual space, 189–204
  selective spatial attention, 251–265
  spatial structure of attention, 171–187
  unilateral neglect of space, 239–249
  vibrotactile reaction-times and hemispace, 221–237
Orthographic segmentation, 11–12
Outcome conflict, 137
Output errors, 25

P

Paradigms, comparisons across, 375–388
Parallel pathways in vision from eye to brain, 42–45
Parietal lesions, 54

672 SUBJECT INDEX

Partial report, four-parameter model of, 634–635
Perceptual integration and postcategorical filtering, 107–132
 negative priming and, 112–114, 128–130
 negative priming across changes in visual form, 115
 negative priming in picture naming, 115–117
 negative priming by semantically related distractors, 117–121
 selection of action among spatially non-overlapping objects, 121–126
 simplex versus duplex probes, 126–127
Perceptual organization, 301–318
 emergent features, 302–303
 global advantage and global-to-local interference effects, 303
 object superiority and object-line effects, 302
 processing compound letters, 305–307
 subitization, 313–316
 visual search against homogeneous distractors, 307–312
Perceptual record, 547–565
 attribute retention and, 552–554
 model of perceptual analysis, 550–552
 two forms of memory, 554
Performance trade-off, attention sharing and, 144–145
Peripersonal space, 251, 253
Peripheral visual fields, visual-spatial attention and, 68–72
Permissive brain processes, executive brain processes versus, 157–164
Phasic orienting, visual-spatial attention and, 74–81
Phonemes, 14–15
Phonological assembly, 11–12
Phonological dyslexia, 10–12
Phonological segmentation, 11–12
Physical similarity, divided attention and, 516
Pontine reticular formation (PRF), 445
Positional uncertainty, 601–612
Position of gaze, movement accuracy and, 407–424
Postarcuate cortex, 251, 252–253
Postcategorical filtering and perceptual integration, 107–132
 negative priming, 112–114, 128–130

negative priming across changes in visual form, 115
negative priming in picture naming, 115–117
negative priming by semantically related distractors, 117–121
selection of action among spatially non-overlapping objects, 121–126
simplex versus duplex probes, 126–127
Post onset effects of transients in auditory space, 343–345
Preconscious selection, 278
Precueing, disruptive effect of, 613–629
Precueing index, 623n
Precue procedure, 614
Preselective integration, 111
Preselective integration hypothesis, 129
Preselective system, 90
Present distractors, 124
Priming
 identity, 572, 579
 and interference effects, 529–543
 repetition, 547–565
 by unattended stimuli, 107–108
 See also Negative priming; Semantic priming
Priming display, 115
Principle of first-order isomorphism, 244–245
Principle of functional cerebral distance (FCD), 530, 531
Priority learning, 477, 485–487
Probe display, 115–116
Prosopagnosia, 54
Pseudowords, 613–614
Psychoacoustics, 338–339
P300 component of auditory ERP, 507

R

Reading aloud, dual-route models of, 8–14
 phonological dyslexia, 10–12
 surface dyslexia, 12–14
Reading and neuropsychology, 3–37
 architecture of the reading system, 21–24
 dual-route models of reading aloud, 8–14
 phonological dyslexia, 10–12
 surface dyslexia, 12–14
 morphological processing, 24–29
 nature of the lexical procedure, 19–20
 nature of the nonlexical procedure, 14–19

syntax and sentence comprehension during reading, 29–33
Receptive-field model of near-threshold visual patterns, 269–270
Recognition memory, 576–578
Relative priming (RP) index, 548
Repeated-letter inferiority, positional uncertainty and, 601–612
Repetition priming and attribute retention, 547–565
Report accuracy, 576
Reported attributes of targets, 86
Resources, theory of, 135
Response mechanisms and stimulus selection, 441–455
    conditional response mechanisms, 449–453
    stimulus-selection mechanisms, 442–449
Retinotopic "maps," 108

S

Saccade latency, 191, 192, 193
Saccades, 286–287, 442
    contraversive, 439
    ipsiversive, 439
Saccadic eye movements, 437–439, 444–445, 446, 453
Scarcity, 135
Selective attention
    smooth eye movement and, 285–300
        effect of selective attention on smooth eye movements, 287–289
        effect of target selection for smooth eye movements on visual processing, 290–296
    stimulus processing and, 355–373
        mechanisms of selective attention, 365–368
        mismatch negativity and, 358–365
        processing of unattended stimuli and ERPs, 356–358
Selective cueing, cross-domain, 110
Selective integration, 111
Selective-integration hypothesis, 128–129
Selective processing
    controlled processing and, 573–574
    dissociable domains of, 567–583
    motor programming and, 152–157
Selective spatial attention, 251–265
    fixation and saccade tasks, 254–255

testing results, 255–261
visual neurological testing, 253–254
Semantically related distractors, negative priming by, 117–121
Semantic priming, 569, 572, 578–579
    automaticity and, 585–599
        influence of spatial attention, 587–596
Semantic processing, 574
    controlled processing and, 576–578
Sensory attributes
    integration of, 109–110
    visual-spatial attention and, 72–74
Sensory systems and selection
    audition
        comparisons across paradigms, 375–388
        selective attention and stimulus processing, 355–373
        transients in auditory space, 337–354
    vision
        imagery and language processing, 319–334
        near-threshold visual patterns, 269–284
        perceptual organization, 301–318
        smooth eye movements and selective attention, 285–300
Sentence comprehension during reading, 29–33
Shape and color, localization in accessing features and objects and, 208, 211–217
Simon effect, 458, 460–462, 466–469
Simple manual reaction time, 191–192, 192–193
Simple search, 86–87
    number of targets and, 90–94
Simplex probes, duplex probes versus, 126–127
Simultaneous discrimination, 495
Single letter, 602
Smooth eye movement and selection attention, 285–300
    effect of selective attention on smooth eye movements, 287–289
    effect of target selection for smooth eye movements on visual processing, 290–296
Sound localization
    duplex theory of, 339
    transients in auditory space and, 338–339
Spatial attention
    electrophysiological indices of, 65–68

Spatial attention (cont.)
  influence on semantic priming of, 587–596
  selective, 251–265
    fixation and saccade tasks, 254–255
    testing results, 255–261
    visual neurological testing, 253–254
  See also Visual-spatial attention
Spatial behavior and its control, cognitive structures underlying, 246–248
Spatial compatibility, 458
Spatial frequency
  of grating patches, 282–283
  near-threshold visual patterns and, 274
Spatial location, repetition priming and, 555
Spatially nonoverlapping objects, 121–126
Spatial position
  of grating patches, 282–283
  near-threshold visual patterns and, 274–276
Spatial structure of attention, 171–187
  attentional costs in detection time for locations in a three-dimension display, 173–179
  two-dimensional attention gradient in three-dimensional representational medium, 179–185
Stage conception of eye-movement preparations, 149–152
State limitation, 603
Stimulus-by-stimulus ERP analysis, 78–81
Stimulus information, identification and use of, 100–102
Stimulus locations, visual-spatial attention and, 72–74
Stimulus masks, precueing and, 615
Stimulus onset asynchrony (SOA), 116, 569
Stimulus processing and selective attention, 355–373
  mechanisms of selective attention, 365–368
  mismatch negativity and, 358–365
  processing of unattended stimuli and ERPs, 356–358
Stimulus relevancy, 579
Stimulus-response (S-R) compatibility, 457–471
Stimulus selection and response mechanisms, 441–455
  conditional response mechanisms, 449–453
  stimulus-selection mechanisms, 442–449
Structural interference, 137
Substantia nigra (SNr), 444–453
Successive discrimination, 495

Superior colliculus (SC), 444, 445
Suprathreshold selection, near-threshold visual patterns and, 281
Surface dyslexia, 12–14
Sustained attention, 493–511
  effects of memory load, 500–502
  habituation of ERPs and vigilance decrement, 496–499
  multifactor model of, 505–508
  phase orienting and, 74–81
  probing sustained attention capacity, 502–505
  tonic arousal, time of day, and vigilance, 500–502
  taxonomy of vigilance, 494–496
Symbolic cueing, 190
Syntax comprehension during reading, 29–33

T

Tachistoscopic presentation, 115–117
Targets, 86, 88–94
  compound search and, 88–90
  simple search and, 90–94
Task interference, attention sharing and, 137–145
Task-irrelevant distractors, categorical priming by, 124–126
Task-related processing, 365
Task-unrelated processing, 365
Taxonomy of vigilance, 494–496
Temporary disablement, 141
Theory of resources, 135
TIGH (time interval between end of gaze movement and hand movement), 416–418
TIHH (time interval between end of head movement and hand movement), 416
Time of day, vigilance decrement and, 500–502
Tonic arousal, vigilance decrement and, 500–502
Transients in auditory space, 337–354
  attempts to discover what constitutes an onset, 349–352
  aural site of saturation, 346–348
  consequences of binaural system that receives only transients, 348–349
  interaction with other parameters, 345–346
  interaural variability and, 341–343
  postonset effects, 343–344

SUBJECT INDEX 675

postonset saturation as primary limiting factor in localization, 345
sound localization and, 338–339
trains of high-frequency clicks and, 339–341
Two forms of memory, 554
Type N part-whole relationships, 304, 312, 317
Type P part-whole relationships, 304, 312

U

Unattended stimuli, ERPs and, 356–358
Unilateral hypokinesia, 240
Unilateral inattention, ipsilateral stimuli in, 263
Unilateral neglect of space, 239–249
  as a cognitive disorder, 243–246
  cognitive structures underlying spatial behavior and its control, 246–248
Unilateral neglect syndrome, 251–252
Units, exclusive usage of, 135
Unrelated distractors, categorically related distractors versus, 123–124

V

Variable mapping, 479
Vibrotactile reaction times and hemispace, 221–237
  corporeal left/right and, 228–230
  gravitational left/right and, 228–230
  hand asymmetries and choice of tasks, 230–232
  hand asymmetries and unilateral responses, 232–234
  hands operated in right hemispace and, 223–228
Vigilance
  arousal and, 505
  taxonomy of, 494–496
Vigilance decrement, 493, 494
  arousal and, 500–502
  capacity limitations and, 506–508
  expectancy and, 505–506
  habituation of ERPs and, 496–499
Visual agnosia, 54

Visual areas and visual perception, 41–62
  advantages of multiple sensory representations, 55–57
  cortical visual areas, 46–51
  parallel pathways in vision from eye to brain, 42–45
  visual disorders following cortical damage, 51–55
Visual array, contact time and, 393–394
Visual disorders following cortical damage, 51–55
Visual hemifield shape recognition, word load and, 529–543
Visual neurological testing, 253–254
Visual processing
  cortical, 172–173
  effect of target selection for smooth eye movement on, 290–296
Visual search, 85–106
  identification and use of stimulus information, 100–102
  "nonsearch" tasks, 87–88
  number of nontargets, 94–100
  number of targets, 88–94
    compound search, 88–90
    simple search, 90–94
  terminology, 86–87
Visual selection from multielement displays, 631–645
Visual-spatial attention, 63–84
  behavioral studies, 64–65
  control and peripheral visual locations, 68–72
  electrophysiological indices of spatial attention, 65–68
  features and locations, 72–74
  phasic orienting and sustained attention, 74–81
Voice, repetition priming and, 555
Voluntary control, selective attention on smooth eye movements and, 287–289

W

Word load, visual hemifield shape recognition and, 529–543
Word-superiority effect, 613–614, 625